INTRODUCING
THE ❖ BIBLE

INTRODUCING THE ❖ BIBLE

WITH CD-ROM

JOHN DRANE

FORTRESS PRESS
MINNEAPOLIS

INTRODUCING THE BIBLE

First Fortress Press edition 2005

Introducing the Old Testament copyright © 1987, 2000 John Drane. *Introducing the New Testament* copyright © 1986, 1999 John Drane.

ISBN 0-8006-3672-4

Picture acknowledgments
AKG London: 318, 356/Erich Lessing 683
ASAP/Richard Nowitz: 116, 201
British Library: 723
British Museum: 32, 59, 127, 154, 188, 258, 261, 262, 271, 274, 280, 296, 397, 405, 420, 501, 556, 695
Capitoline Museum, Rome/The Art Archive: 232
Dinu Mendrea: 112
Dover Publications: 425, 429, 443, 457
Hanan Isachar: 208, 322–3
Israel Museum, Jerusalem: 400
J. Catling Allen Picture Library: 83
Jon Arnold: 14, 52, 92, 124, 150, 198, 270, 316, 379, 410, 463, 689
Julie Baines: 373, 375, 380, 384, 389, 513, 514, 541, 558, 603, 605, 622, 654
Landesmuseum, Trier/H. Thornig: 552
Lion Publishing: 19, 43, 128, 152, 174, 346, 376, 413, 577, 580, 584, 586, 590, 595, 599, 600, 602, 609, 613, 618, 632, 643, 644, 646, 699, 721/Alan Millard 82/Cairo Museum 63/Collection British Museum 657/David Alexander 15, 24, 129, 133, 153, 359, 264/David Reddick 402/David Townsend 240, 414, 449, 459, 539, 547/Frank Dabba Smith 287/John Rylands Museum 722/Mark astle 438, 651/Pauline O'Bolye 648/Phil Manning 451/Simon Bull 406, 571, 685, 698
Mary Evans Picture Library: 342, 343, 388, 470, 523, 679, 714, 715, 717
Middle East Archive/Alisdair Duncan: 670
Museum of London: 382
Reproduced by courtesy of the Trustees of the National Gallery, London: 20
PhotoRMN/H. Lewandowski: 279
Popperfoto: 474, 476
Preußishcer Kulturbesitz/Agyptisches Museum: 205
Scala: 576
Sonia Halliday Photographs: 34, 48, 50, 138, 181, 254, 337, 371, 383, 391, 399, 540/Barry Searle 561/James Wellard 195, 218/Jane Taylor 223, 348, 374, 681, 687
Stockmarket: 302, 331, 572/W. Braun 394
V&A Picture Library, by courtesy of the trustees of the V&A: 510
Werner Braun: 329
Werner Forman Archive/British Museum: 593
Zav Radovan: 98, 164, 165, 313, 350, 357, 385, 526, 636, 637, 641, 700

Printed in Canada

09   08   07   06   05   1   2   3   4   5

Contents

INTRODUCING THE ❖ OLD TESTAMENT

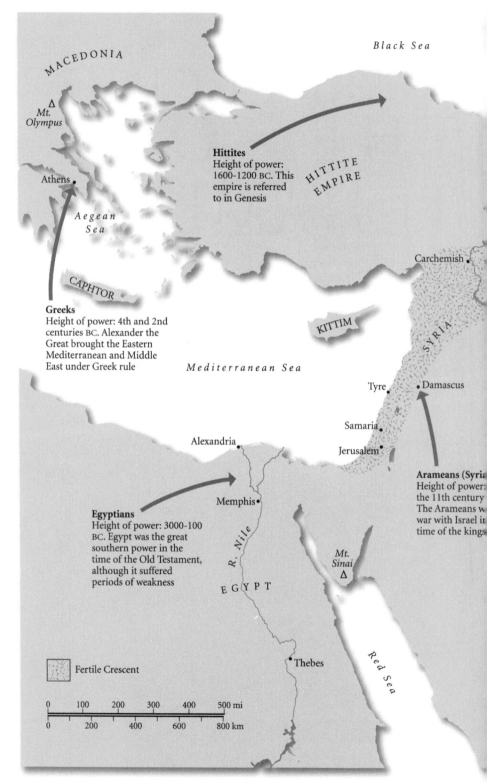

Hittites
Height of power:
1600-1200 BC. This
empire is referred
to in Genesis

HITTITE EMPIRE

Black Sea

MACEDONIA

Δ
Mt.
Olympus

Athens

Aegean Sea

CAPHTOR

Greeks
Height of power: 4th and 2nd
centuries BC. Alexander the
Great brought the Eastern
Mediterranean and Middle
East under Greek rule

KITTIM

Carchemish

SYRIA

Mediterranean Sea

Tyre

Damascus

Samaria

Alexandria

Jerusalem

Arameans (Syria
Height of power:
the 11th century
The Arameans w
war with Israel in
time of the kings

Memphis

Egyptians
Height of power: 3000-100
BC. Egypt was the great
southern power in the
time of the Old Testament,
although it suffered
periods of weakness

R. Nile

Mt.
Sinai
Δ

E G Y P T

Red Sea

Fertile Crescent

Thebes

| 0 | 100 | 200 | 300 | 400 | 500 mi |

| 0 | 200 | 400 | 600 | 800 km |

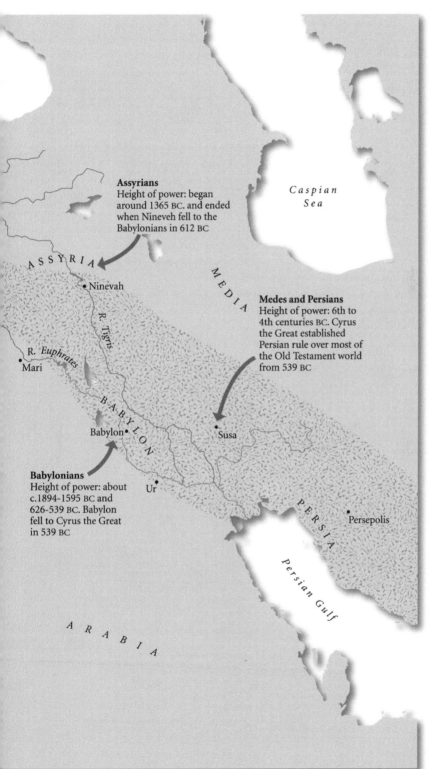

Assyrians
Height of power: began around 1365 BC. and ended when Nineveh fell to the Babylonians in 612 BC

Caspian Sea

ASSYRIA

• Nineveh

R. Tigris

MEDIA

Medes and Persians
Height of power: 6th to 4th centuries BC. Cyrus the Great established Persian rule over most of the Old Testament world from 539 BC

R. Euphrates
• Mari

BABYLON

Babylon •

• Susa

Babylonians
Height of power: about c.1894-1595 BC and 626-539 BC. Babylon fell to Cyrus the Great in 539 BC

Ur •

PERSIA

• Persepolis

Persian Gulf

ARABIA

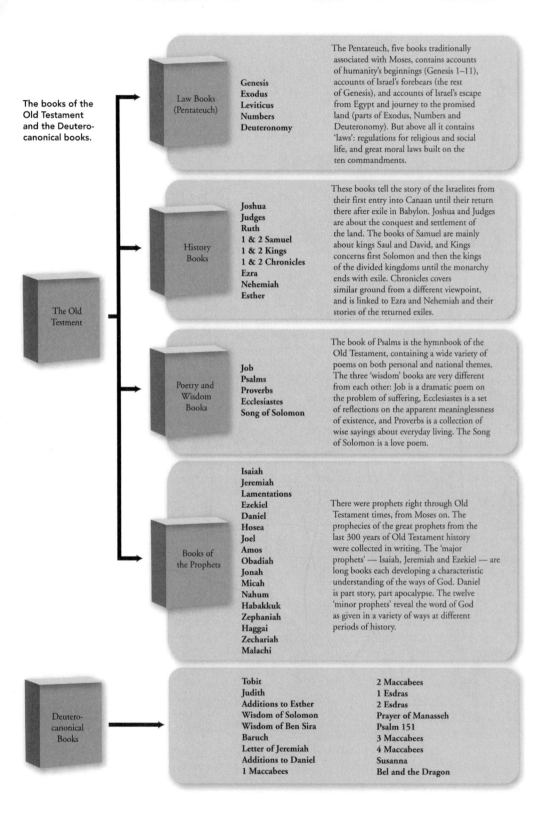

The books of the Old Testament and the Deutero-canonical books.

The Old Testament

Law Books (Pentateuch)

Genesis
Exodus
Leviticus
Numbers
Deuteronomy

The Pentateuch, five books traditionally associated with Moses, contains accounts of humanity's beginnings (Genesis 1–11), accounts of Israel's forebears (the rest of Genesis), and accounts of Israel's escape from Egypt and journey to the promised land (parts of Exodus, Numbers and Deuteronomy). But above all it contains 'laws': regulations for religious and social life, and great moral laws built on the ten commandments.

History Books

Joshua
Judges
Ruth
1 & 2 Samuel
1 & 2 Kings
1 & 2 Chronicles
Ezra
Nehemiah
Esther

These books tell the story of the Israelites from their first entry into Canaan until their return there after exile in Babylon. Joshua and Judges are about the conquest and settlement of the land. The books of Samuel are mainly about kings Saul and David, and Kings concerns first Solomon and then the kings of the divided kingdoms until the monarchy ends with exile. Chronicles covers similar ground from a different viewpoint, and is linked to Ezra and Nehemiah and their stories of the returned exiles.

Poetry and Wisdom Books

Job
Psalms
Proverbs
Ecclesiastes
Song of Solomon

The book of Psalms is the hymnbook of the Old Testament, containing a wide variety of poems on both personal and national themes. The three 'wisdom' books are very different from each other: Job is a dramatic poem on the problem of suffering, Ecclesiastes is a set of reflections on the apparent meaninglessness of existence, and Proverbs is a collection of wise sayings about everyday living. The Song of Solomon is a love poem.

Books of the Prophets

Isaiah
Jeremiah
Lamentations
Ezekiel
Daniel
Hosea
Joel
Amos
Obadiah
Jonah
Micah
Nahum
Habakkuk
Zephaniah
Haggai
Zechariah
Malachi

There were prophets right through Old Testament times, from Moses on. The prophecies of the great prophets from the last 300 years of Old Testament history were collected in writing. The 'major prophets' — Isaiah, Jeremiah and Ezekiel — are long books each developing a characteristic understanding of the ways of God. Daniel is part story, part apocalypse. The twelve 'minor prophets' reveal the word of God as given in a variety of ways at different periods of history.

Deutero-canonical Books

Tobit
Judith
Additions to Esther
Wisdom of Solomon
Wisdom of Ben Sira
Baruch
Letter of Jeremiah
Additions to Daniel
1 Maccabees

2 Maccabees
1 Esdras
2 Esdras
Prayer of Manasseh
Psalm 151
3 Maccabees
4 Maccabees
Susanna
Bel and the Dragon

1 Introducing the Old Testament

Of all the literature that has been handed down from the world's ancient civilizations, none is as compelling – or as provocative – as the Hebrew Bible. It is one of the great classics, highly esteemed as sacred scripture by three of the world's major faiths – Islam, Judaism and Christianity. That alone has ensured not only its survival, but also its widespread dissemination and continuing appeal to people far removed from either the cultural or the religious context in which it originated. Though its stories happened long ago and in unfamiliar places, they have an ongoing fascination for today's readers. Furthermore, in a postmodern society with a growing scepticism about what is modern and scientific, many of today's spiritual searchers are powerfully attracted by the possibility of discovering new directions for the future through uncovering spiritual truths that have been locked away for centuries in ancient and esoteric texts, which reflect other worlds and different ways of being. Whatever else may be said, the Hebrew Bible – or Old Testament – has plenty of mystery about it. Its pages contain the rich literary treasures of a whole nation – the ancient people of Israel – and its story embraces the formative period of world civilization as we know it today, beginning in the Stone Age and ending in the world of the Roman empire. That makes even the most recent parts more than 2,000 years old, while the origins of its earliest works are likely to remain for ever hidden in the mists of antiquity. Moreover, it is not a dull book, and its unique combination of epic stories, history, reflective philosophy, poetry and political commentary is woven together with all the elements of adventure, excitement and suspense that we might expect to find in a Hollywood thriller. Indeed, its traditional stories have themselves become the raw material for many movies on the grand scale, while at the same time they continue to provide personal inspiration for the millions of people all over the world who still read it regularly.

Even a quick glance through its pages soon shows that the Old Testament is, of course, not just one single book. In reality, it is a whole library of books, and it is the sheer diversity of its contents that partly helps to explain its perennial appeal. From the great epic stories of national heroes like Moses, Deborah, David or Esther, to the more reflective books such as Job or Ecclesiastes, there is something here for everyone's taste and for many different moods and emotions. Enchanting – and sometimes disturbing – stories of personal intrigue and passion stand side by side with philosophical enquiries into the meaning of human life. Trying to make sense of these apparently disparate books is, however, not a straightforward matter, and in the course of the last 200 years many theories have been put forward as scholars have sought to understand and explain their origins and relevance to the world in which their many authors lived and worked. Most hypotheses have not survived for long, and the last twenty years of the twentieth century saw the collapse of many opinions that previous generations would have regarded as the assured results of scholarship. But one conviction has survived: if we are to understand the books of the Hebrew Bible most fully, we must delve into the reality of the world in which they were written. Intepreting this literature is a complex and multi-layered enterprise, but a key element in this has always been the quest to uncover what these books meant when they were originally written. How did they relate to the needs and aspirations of their authors and their original readers? And what can an understanding of other cultures of the time tell us about the ancient nation of Israel? In order to address such questions, many different specialist disciplines need to be employed, including archaeology, sociological analysis, literary theory and historical investigation as well as more obviously religious and spiritual methodologies.

For much of the nineteenth and twentieth centuries, scholarship often emphasized the diversity of the materials contained within this collection, but for the community within which they originated the one thing that held them all together was the simple fact that they are part of a common story. Moreover, the heart of that common story focused on a set of spiritual perceptions, and without taking account of that it is virtually impossible to understand what the Old Testament writers were trying to articulate. Notwithstanding their diverse concerns and interests – and the centuries that separated them – they were all convinced that their books, and the experience of the nation which they reflected, came into being not just through social, economic or political pressures, but because of the activity of God running through it all. Beyond the obvious human interest of its individual stories, the Hebrew Bible is a deeply spiritual book, affirming that this world and all its affairs are not merely a haphazard sequence of coincidences, but are somehow the work of a divine being who is God of both creation and history. Moreover, this God is not depicted in terms of a remote, unknowable divine force, but is understood in essentially personal terms as one with whom human beings can – and do – have personal dealings. This message is set out in the opening pages of the first book (Genesis), and it is explained and emphasized many times in what follows. Today's readers will no doubt have many different reactions to such overtly religious claims, some of which will be examined in more detail in later chapters

here. But whatever response all this may evoke, any understanding
of the Old Testament which does not take serious account of its world-
view is likely to provide only a very partial insight into its meaning and
significance.

The story

One of the difficulties often encountered by the reader approaching
the Old Testament for the first time is trying to distinguish the main
storyline from the many individual stories which help to make it up.
This is partly related to the way in which these books evolved over
many centuries, and the fact that the collection as a whole went
through several different editing processes before reaching its present
form. As a consequence, it is not difficult to identify what look like
conflicting opinions within its pages. For example, the framework of the
entire collection clearly affirms that the God of whom it speaks has
universal jurisdiction over the whole world, whereas much of the story
seems to imply almost the opposite, for in the early stories God mostly
appears as a living reality only in the life of a particular ethnic group.
These apparent tensions within the narratives will receive a good deal of
attention in later chapters. But it will be worthwhile here surveying the
story as it stands. Scholars have often forgotten that, whatever else may
be said about their literary origins, the way these books were combined
to form the final edition of the Hebrew Bible was intended to present a
coherent message that would both sum up and take forward the stories
told by the individual writers. While it is certainly not illegitimate to
speculate on the various stages of development through which the
various books passed, the meaning of the collection as a whole is to be
judged on the basis of the end product. Just as the impact of a well-
cooked meal is more than the sum of its individual ingredients, so the
significance of the Old Testament transcends the insights contained
within its various components.

The stage is set on a grand, international scale in the opening pages,
and though the main focus is on the life of a specific group of people, the
earliest episodes span most of the ancient world. Before long, though, the
main interest centres on a childless couple – Abraham and Sarah – living
in the Mesopotamian city of Ur (Genesis 11:31 – 12:5). This unlikely
couple then become parents to a great nation who, by the end of the
introductory stories, have settled in a land so idyllic that it can be
described as 'flowing with milk and honey' (Deuteronomy 6:3). In
between these two points, the books from Genesis to Deuteronomy
recount many memorable stories about the children who were eventually born into this family, and of how their descendants unwittingly
ended up as slaves in Egypt. In the telling of the story of Israel's earliest
days, this time of enforced slavery became one of the pivotal points of
their experience, but under Moses, a dynamic leader trained in the royal

courts of Egypt, it was to become a central element in Israel's national consciousness. Generations of later writers had no doubt that even this was a part of God's plan for the people, and with great insight and sensitivity the eighth-century BC prophet Hosea pictured God at this time as a loving parent (probably a mother, given the form of the imagery) and Israel as God's child: 'When Israel was a child, I loved him and called him out of Egypt as my son... I was the one who taught Israel to walk. I took my people up in my arms... I drew them to me with affection and love. I picked them up and held them to my cheek; I bent down to them and fed them' (Hosea 11:1, 3–4). Almost 200 years later again, and after many more calamities, this conviction was still of central importance, as highlighted by Ezekiel's assurance to the people that 'When I chose Israel, I made them a promise. I revealed myself to them in Egypt and told them: I am Yahweh your God. It was then that I promised to take them out of Egypt and... lead them to a land I had chosen for them, a rich and fertile land, the finest land of all' (Ezekiel 20:5–6).

Escape from Egypt

The ancient and impressive civilization of Egypt must have intimidated the Hebrew slaves. This is the Temple of Karnak at Luxor.

With their dramatic escape from slavery in Egypt – the event subsequently referred to as the 'exodus' – Israel's destiny began to take shape. But between the exodus and their entry to the 'land flowing with milk and honey' (Canaan), there is the story of God's Law given to Moses at Mount Sinai. As the Old Testament writers reflected on the meaning of their nation's experience of God, they always gave this Law (Torah) a central place. The occasion when the Law was given is depicted as a

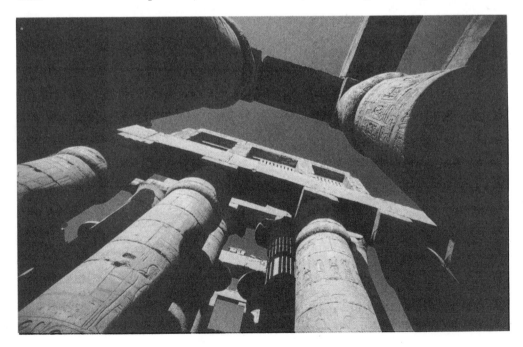

fearful and serious moment: 'The whole of Mount Sinai was covered with smoke, because Yahweh had come down on it in fire. The smoke went up like the smoke of a furnace, and all the people trembled violently... Moses spoke, and God answered him with thunder' (Exodus 19:18–19). To people nurtured on the values of Western democracy, the laws of the Hebrew Bible (contained mostly in the books of Exodus, Leviticus and Numbers) can seem harsh and unreasonable.

Surprisingly, perhaps, the people of Israel never regarded them in that way, and though God was to be honoured and respected, observing the requirements of the Law was never regarded as a heavy burden. On the contrary, it was something to be kept with great joy, for the people looked back beyond the smoke and fire of Sinai to the events that went before it – and in that context they could see that God's Law was very firmly based on God's love, and that their continued obedience was the free and loving devotion of those who are grateful for unexpected and undeserved benefits. It is no coincidence that the ten commandments begin not with an instruction, but with a reminder of God's love and goodness: 'I am Yahweh your God who brought you out of Egypt, where you were slaves' (Exodus 20:2).

God promised the Israelites that they would settle in a fertile land. The cultivation of olive trees became part of their agricultural life.

In due course, the nomadic way of life that could be traced right back to Abraham and Sarah gave way to a settled farming life in a new land. Here, Israel began to ask new questions about their faith in God. So far, they had known the God Yahweh whom Moses served as a God of the desert. But new questions began to bother them. Did this God know how to grow crops – or have any experience in rearing sheep to have many lambs? In a technological age, these can seem to be rather naïve questions, but for these people they were the most important questions of all. Life itself depended on the answers, and in one way or another the struggle to find those answers dominates the rest of the Old Testament story. For when Israel settled in their new land, other gods and goddesses were already well established there – and they had long and apparently successful experience in agricultural matters. So there began a long battle of loyalties between Yahweh, the God of the desert, and the gods and goddesses of the land of Canaan: Baal, Asherah, Anat and other members of their pantheon. The people of Israel were tempted to forsake their own God in preference for these others. The unfolding epic of the nation describes how, from the earliest times, there were local heroes like the so-called 'judges' who were prepared to resist such spiritual treason. But as time passed, things went from bad to worse, and the great prophets found themselves protesting over many generations that the people of Israel had left their own true God for the worship of false deities.

National decline

The story describes Israel's national fortunes reaching their high point in the days of David and Solomon (dated by some to about 1010–930 BC). But following them, it fell into serious decline as the great kingdom was partitioned, to be followed by the collapse first of the northern part (Israel), and then in due course by the southern part (Judah). Prophets, from the radical and outspoken Elijah to the introspective Jeremiah, spoke out in both north and south against the social and political corruption which they believed had led to the inevitable disintegration of the entire nation. Though the many prophets spoke in different circumstances, to the people of their own time, they were all united in their belief that the nation of Israel had come to ruination because of its neglect of the Law given at Mount Sinai, and an increasing fondness for the gods and goddesses of Palestine.

By 586 BC, the entire nation was finished. In that year the city of Jerusalem was captured by the Babylonian king Nebuchadnezzar II, and its Temple and most of the other significant buildings were destroyed. This was a disaster of immense proportions, whose impact on the national consciousness lasted for many centuries. But once more, out of the ashes of defeat new life was kindled by new leaders who, if anything, had an even more expansive vision than their predecessors. The sheer scale of the calamity forced a thoroughgoing reappraisal not only of national strategy, but more especially of the national faith, and as those who survived this dark time reflected on its meaning, they concluded that even this new disaster was all a part of God's plan for their people. As they set out to review the lessons of the past, they were quite sure that God would not forget the earlier promises. There would be a new creation and a new exodus on an even greater scale than before, for the whole world would now be the scene of God's renewed activity, and Israel's role in this new world would be to function as 'a light to the nations – so that all the world may be saved' (Isaiah 49:6).

With this, the story had come full circle. It began with Abraham and Sarah and the promise that through their family God would bless many nations (Genesis 12:1–3). In the intervening centuries, this promise had been repeatedly challenged from many different directions. Politically and economically, it was always under threat – whether from the Egyptians, the Canaanites, the Assyrians or the Babylonians. Religiously, it was undermined from within as the people of Israel were tempted to forget Yahweh, the God of their forebears, and turn instead to other forms of worship in religions which, the prophets complained, allowed their moral and spiritual responsibility to be left behind in the shrine instead of forming the basis of everyday life in home and market place.

This figure is a Cannanite Baal, or storm god. The struggle against idolatry recurs throughout the Old Testament. Was Israel's Lord just one god among many, or was this the only true God?

But God's intention for this world never deviated: 'the holy God of Israel remains faithful to the promises... I, Yahweh, was there at the beginning, and I, Yahweh, will be there at the end' (Isaiah 49:7; 41:4).

Understanding the story

It is not too difficult to gain a general impression of the Old Testament story. But once we begin to dig beneath the surface, this most fascinating of books also presents many puzzles. In later chapters, we will be looking at its complexities from different perspectives, but at the outset it is worth making just a few general comments on some of the most distinctive features of the Old Testament and its contents, which will identify some broad principles of interpretation that can then be applied to the exploration of specific questions.

■ Most readers today probably encounter the Old Testament as the first half of the Christian Bible. The fact that it is commonly called 'the Old Testament' only serves to emphasize this position, for in this context it is 'old' not because it is ancient, but by contrast to the records of the early church which are conventionally designated 'the New Testament'. Given that the Christian faith emerged from within Judaism, it is hardly surprising that Christians should have taken it for granted that these two quite separate collections of writings properly belong together. Within the Christian tradition, it has always been assumed that the events surrounding the origins of the Christian faith were yet a further stage in God's dealings with men and women that began through the ancient nation of Israel, recorded in the Old Testament. This of course is a particular interpretation of these books, for the Old Testament was not written by Christians, nor is its message intrinsically and necessarily a Christian message. Long before the emergence of Christianity, these books were the sacred writings of the Jewish faith (Judaism), and that is obviously their primary reference point. To understand them fully, they need to be read in their own original context, and in the light of their underlying spiritual orientation. Though Christians may legitimately feel that the Old Testament is incomplete without its Christian sequel, it can never be fully understood if it is viewed only through exclusively Christian spectacles. This is why many contemporary writers prefer not to speak of 'the Old Testament' at all, but rather of 'the Hebrew scriptures' or 'the Hebrew Bible'. Here, we have used both sets of terminology more or less interchangeably.

■ It is also important to remember that the Old Testament is quite different in character from a modern book. It is even different from the books that make up the New Testament, all of which had their origin in the same social and religious context as one another. Moreover, whereas we can, on the whole, be tolerably sure of the identity of the New Testament authors, and of the reasons why they wrote, the same cannot be said in the case of the Old Testament, and here there are very few books for which it is possible to give a positive identification of either a particular author or a specific date. The Old Testament is essentially an edited anthology – a collection of writings by different people, and from different ages. Nobody ever sat down to gather the New Testament into one unified collection: it just arose spontaneously from the reading habits of the early church. But somebody *did* set out to edit and organize the books of the Old Testament, to form a coherent account of the life of the nation of Israel. In fact, more than one person or group of people did so. The earliest editions of Old Testament materials were probably gathered together during the reigns of David and Solomon, who provided the stability and economic prosperity necessary for the flourishing of such an enterprise. It was natural that the people of Israel should begin at this time to take a keen interest in their past, revisiting the stories of their forebears as a way of identifying and celebrating their emerging national consciousness. Before this time, they no doubt had their own tribal histories which had been preserved and handed on by word of mouth from one generation to another, but they had not been written down. People whose life was a daily struggle for survival had neither time nor appetite for creating literary masterpieces: that was left to scribes working in the more leisurely atmosphere of the later royal courts of Israel.

Naturally, such researchers could only bring the story up to their own time, and the task of preserving and interpreting Israel's history was an ongoing and never-ending one, lasting through many generations. Much of the Old Testament is associated with the names of the prophets, and many of its books contain their words and actions dealing with various aspects of national life and policy. Parts of the history books were doubtless written by those whose outlook was deeply influenced by these prophets, though the final stage in the Old Testament story was reached only after the destruction of the state by Nebuchadnezzar of Babylon, which the prophets had so clearly foreseen and warned about. As new leaders emerged after that tragedy and began to reconstruct the broken pieces of a great heritage, they consciously set out to apply the lessons of the past to their own hopes for the future. To help do that, they began to collect the whole of Israel's national literature, as well as writing their own assessment of the nation's achievements, and it was out of this post-exilic reappraisal that the Hebrew Bible finally emerged in the form it has today.

■ A further distinguishing mark of the Old Testament is the enormous time span that it covers. Whereas the whole of the New Testament was written in the space of something like sixty or seventy years, the Old Testament story covers many centuries. There is a good deal of debate about where historical narrative in the proper sense begins, but even if (as many think) that was only in the time of David or Solomon, it still takes us back 1,000 years before the Christian era. In addition, though, the Old Testament contains accounts of things that appear to pre-date that, by a long way. The very earliest parts of its literature are located in a world where civilization itself was a relatively recent arrival. Its story begins in the region of what is now Iraq, in what the ancients called 'the Fertile Crescent', a part of the world that had witnessed many remarkable developments long before the story of Israel's history began. Great empires had come and gone, and as early as 3000 BC the Sumerian people of ancient Mesopotamia had written down their traditional stories and beliefs for the generations that would follow them. One of their most noteworthy successors was the Babylonian king Hammurabi, whose law code written on clay tablets some 1,700 years BC still survives as a lasting monument to the culture of those ancient times. Many other texts from this ancient world have come to light – from Nuzi in Iraq, from Ebla in northern Syria and from Ugarit further to the south. In addition, there are the many records and monuments of that other great and ancient civilization centred on the River Nile in Egypt.

By comparison with these empires, the people who wrote the Old Testament were undoubtedly latecomers on the world stage. The shape of their culture was already formed by other nations, and to understand their story fully it is necessary to know something of the story of these other peoples too. The fortunes of Israel were always inextricably bound up with the manoeuverings of the two superpowers of the day: the one based on the Nile, and the other based on the rivers Tigris and Euphrates. But then the Old Testament takes us beyond even the last of these great empires, for Israel survived longer than them all, and the latest books of their national literature reflect the concerns of the period that saw the rise and fall of Alexander the Great, and which was eventually to herald the arrival of the next great superpower of world history, the Roman empire.

The Old Testament is the Bible of the Jew as well as the Christian. It describes a grand vision for the transformation of the world. The difference lies in the two understandings of how these promises are being fulfilled.

It is hardly surprising if today's readers find the Old Testament slightly confusing at times, for its pages cover almost half the history of civilization as it has been documented in the West. In addition, the circumstances of the early parts of the story are quite different from the situation encountered in the later parts, while none of it bears much resemblance to the world as it is today.

■ Something of the Old Testament's distinctive character can also be observed when its books are viewed purely as literature. As has already been observed, it is above all a book infused with spiritual values. It does not set out to give what might be regarded as an impartial, independent account of the events it describes. The Old Testament story has been written for a purpose, and its different parts were used by men and women living at different times to speak to the people of their own

When Renaissance painters illustrated scenes from the life of Jesus, they portrayed people in the dress of their own day, rather than attempting to show them in biblical clothing. Similarly, the writers of the Old Testament were recording and reviewing life as they understood it from their perspective.

generation. Some have taken this to imply that the story it contains must be essentially fictional – a kind of moralizing tale, which is valuable for whatever lessons it teaches, but out of touch with what actually happened. In reality, things are much more complicated than this. For example, many events and people mentioned in the Old Testament also appear in the records of other nations of the time, which at least means that we need to explore the relationship between these various accounts. The truth is that there is probably no such thing as the 'bare facts' of history, whether biblical or otherwise – and if there was, they would be much less useful than people often imagine. To understand the past – or, for that matter, the present – events need to be interpreted, placed in a context and set alongside other aspects of human experience in order that their full significance might be discerned. A historian who merely reported past events in a disinterested way would not be a good historian. It is the judgments made by others on what things mean that actually enable us to form our own opinions

and understandings. In everyday life, we take all this for granted, and we know that when, for instance, we watch a television documentary, the overall perspective is going to reflect the world-view and opinions of the programme-maker, but we would not normally regard this as a barrier to understanding. We may wish to make a different judgment ourselves on this or that matter, but we simply take it for granted that to understand any situation fully we need to take account not only of the facts, but also of the outlook of our sources of information. It is the same with the Old Testament. The more clearly we can understand the intentions of those who wrote and handed on these books, the more likely we are to arrive at a useful appreciation of their significance and meaning.

In addition, we should remember that these writings are not just one person's assessment of the history of a nation: they are a national archive. The people who wrote and edited these books were themselves a part of that nation and its history. It is not easy for the detached observer to grasp exactly what this means. But we can find a useful analogy in the pictures that medieval artists painted of the life and times of Jesus. The crucifixion was a favourite theme, and there are many great works showing Jesus hanging on a cross between two thieves. But, on closer inspection, the people around the crosses often seem somewhat out of place, and instead of Roman soldiers, there are soldiers of sixteenth-century Europe. The people too belong to that age – and the city where the scene takes place is not Jerusalem in AD 33, but Venice or Rome in AD 1500. When today's art critics look at such pictures they do not usually feel that they cast doubt on the reality of the crucifixion of Jesus. Indeed, some may unconsciously follow the artist's example, and pencil in an image of themselves and today's social context. In a way, this is what the writers of the Old Testament story were doing as they depicted their national past. From generation to generation, they knew that the story of their national heroes and heroines was their own story. They were a part of it, because they saw in it the continuing story of God's dealings with their nation. It was this conviction that enabled them to recognize in the failures and triumphs of the past the realities and the potential of their own age, and gave them the freedom to reinterpret the traditional stories so as to equip new generations to address the challenges of the present.

The story and the faith

What of the distinctively religious aspects of the Old Testament books? It is, of course, possible to read the Old Testament and never discover its faith. Certainly, if definitions of spirituality or faith are restricted to collections of carefully articulated systematic beliefs or doctrines, then there is little in the Old Testament that would fit that description. The truth is that the story and the faith are so inextricably interwoven that it is both impossible and pointless to try to disentangle them from one another. But even accepting that and adopting a more open-ended approach, it is not easy to identify something that can plausibly be labelled 'the faith of the Old Testament', for several reasons:

■ It has already been observed that the Old Testament is not a single, unified book. It contains many different types of literature, and together they cover the greater part of 1,000 years in the history of ancient Israel. For this reason alone it is a good deal easier to identify the faith of various Old Testament authors than it is to discover a comprehensive system that might be described as 'Old Testament faith' in some definitive sense. Indeed, many scholars would argue that the best we can hope for is to find ways of speaking of 'the faith of the prophets', or 'the faith of the psalmists', and so on.

■ Was the Old Testament ever intended to be a guide to what people should believe, or is it rather a record of what people in ancient Israel did as a matter of fact believe? As a book of history, it contains elements of both these things, but depending on which one of the two is labelled 'Old Testament faith', quite different conclusions can be reached. For example, the prophets declared that true worship of God had to include the way a person behaved in everyday life, and could not just be restricted to ritual actions carried out at a shrine – but both prophets and historians make it perfectly clear that this understanding of worship was never shared by the majority of people in ancient Israel. Similar diversity of opinion can be found on many other issues, which means that from the outset we need to clarify what we are looking for when we talk of the Old Testament faith. Is it the sort

How many books are in the Old Testament?

There were thirty-nine books in the original Hebrew Bible. All Christian Bibles include these thirty-nine books as part of the Old Testament, but some contain additional works, which are variously referred to as the Apocrypha or deuterocanonical books. These were mostly written in Greek in the centuries immediately preceding the Christian era, and never formed a part of the Hebrew Bible. Different selections of them are contained in different versions of the Old Testament, though they typically include the following: Tobit, Judith, Wisdom of Solomon, Wisdom of Ben Sira, Baruch, 1–2 Esdras, The Letter of Jeremiah, 1–4 Maccabees, the Prayer of Manasseh, Psalm 151, and various additions to the books of Esther and Daniel.

After the time of the Persian empire, the world changed very rapidly, and it was not long before the ancient language of Hebrew was forgotten by all but a few, and Jewish people (the descendants of ancient Israel) were living in many different countries. In the time of Jesus, for example, there were more Jewish people in Alexandria in Egypt than there were in Jerusalem. The language most of these expatriates (or members of the Jewish Diaspora) spoke was Greek. By the time of the New Testament, the Hebrew scriptures were widely read in Greek translation, in a version known as the Septuagint (LXX). It was through this Greek version that these 'extra' books found their way into the Christian canon of the Old Testament, and their inclusion is related to the way the Septuagint evolved.

It is customary today to speak of 'the Septuagint' as if it were simply a Greek Old Testament. But the facts are not so simple.

of religious beliefs that were generally held in Israel, or are we trying to extract some system of normative beliefs out of the Old Testament records?

■ Just to complicate things a little more, we know for certain that both actual practice and the ideals of people such as the prophets did not remain static from one period of Israel's history to another, but were continually evolving to match new circumstances. The question of marriage and family provides a good example of this. By the time of Ezra (towards the end of the Old Testament period), it was assumed that one man would marry one woman, and both of them would be ethnically Israelite. In earlier times, though, it was the common practice for a man to have several wives, and not only is this practice never explicitly forbidden, but also almost all the leading male characters in the Old Testament stories had multiple regular sexual partners, who were not necessarily their wives. Nor were they all Israelites: the list of Solomon's wives and partners reads like a roll-call of all the nations of the ancient world! The same diversity can be found in the laws governing things such as food, keeping the sabbath day or circumcision, all of which were applied in a much more relaxed way before the time of exile in Babylon than they ever were after it.

In view of such complex problems, some doubt whether it will ever be possible to articulate anything remotely like a comprehensive account of the spiritual and religious teachings of the Hebrew Bible. On this

---

Modern translators would begin with a complete Bible in Hebrew and Greek, and produce its equivalent in their own language. But what is now called the Septuagint was never a complete Bible until the early centuries of the Christian era. Before that, no one knew the techniques necessary to bind such a large collection of literature into one single volume. Writing materials were painstakingly made by hand and individual sheets would then be glued or stitched together to make a strip long enough to contain a single book. This would then be rolled up for storage, and to possess a complete Hebrew Bible required a large number of different rolls. In addition to this, different people were busy making their own translations of the Old Testament books into Greek – and when the Christians eventually produced a single-volume Greek Old Testament, they simply made a selection from the translations that were available to them.

In the days before the Old Testament could literally become one book, bound together inside a single cover, the various rolls in which its writings were contained needed to be stored safely and were often kept in small boxes. These boxes were all of the same size, and were used as a classification system. If a particular box had unused space in it, it would be natural to fill it up by storing similar kinds of writings in the same boxes. This was probably how the deuterocanonical books came to be associated with the original writings of the Hebrew Bible. In content and style, they were not all that different from the books that had been translated from Hebrew, and it made good sense to keep them all together. In time, they came to be automatically accepted as constituent elements of the literature that collectively

The scrolls of the Law in a Jewish synagogue remind us of the high place the Old Testament writings have always held in Judaism. For Jews and Christians see these books as the record of how God's will was revealed to humanity.

How many books are in the Old Testament? continued

made up the Greek version of the Old Testament, and so when the early Christians came to bind them all into one volume, it was natural to include them, even though they had never been part of the Hebrew scriptures that evolved throughout the life of ancient Israel.

Like the original thirty-nine books, they represent different types of literature. Some are clearly history books (1 – 2 Maccabees), while others are books of philosophy and religious poetry (Wisdom of Solomon, Wisdom of Ben Sira), and yet others are moralistic novels (Tobit, Judith, and the additions to Esther and Daniel), or apocalyptic writings claiming to give a clairvoyant view of the future (2 Esdras). Though these books are known primarily from early Christian copies of the Greek Septuagint, it is highly unlikely that they all came from the same sources. Fragments of some of them have been discovered written in Hebrew, while others were certainly first composed in Greek, and yet others were probably first written in Hebrew, but have only survived in their Greek or Latin versions. It is unclear how the Jewish community in Egypt, among whom the Greek version was produced, regarded these books, though there is no evidence to suggest that it was a matter of great importance until after the emergence of Christianity, when Judaism found it necessary to define which books were to be considered authoritative – partly in response to the way Christians were then using sections of the Hebrew scriptures. The New Testament contains references to the deuterocanonical literature (compare, for instance, Hebrews 1:3 with Wisdom of Solomon 7:25; Hebrews 11:37 with 2 Maccabees 5–7; John 10:22 with 1 Maccabees 4:59 and 2 Maccabees 10:1–8), and second-century Christian

view, the best that might be achieved would be a carefully researched description of the history of Israelite religion, tracing the ways it developed and changed over many generations. This kind of historical understanding is certainly a vital part of any assessment of the message of the Old Testament, and much of this book is taken up with the discussion of questions that will help to identify how the Old Testament faith related to the world in which it developed. In the process of doing this, it needs to be compared with the religious beliefs and aspirations of other nations of the time, in order to highlight whatever it was that made its message distinctive. Many of the features that seem especially strange and unfamiliar to today's readers were just a natural part of everyday life in the ancient Middle East. Things like animal sacrifices, and much of the structure of Israelite worship, were common to many different cultural contexts in Old Testament times, so by understanding this context it is often possible to gain invaluable insights into religious themes in the Old Testament itself. Even the language used of Yahweh is at times very similar, if not identical, to terms used in other religions of the day, and this, too, can help to illustrate the full meaning of apparently obscure Old Testament passages.

But, of course, the Old Testament has another context than just the world of ancient Israel, and that is determined by the circumstances of the contemporary interpreter. A Jewish person will see something different in the Hebrew Bible from what a Christian sees, and a Muslim

---

writers regularly quote from or refer to these books. However, following the increasing circulation of all kinds of documents purporting to be Christian 'gospels', it became necessary for Christians to define exactly which books they could accept as authoritative – and that inevitably meant that some kind of decision had to be made about the shape of the Old Testament, as well as the New. Jerome (AD c. 345–419) regarded the books of the Hebrew Bible as specially authoritative, though he felt that the others could be useful for more general edification, and he accordingly included them all in his Latin version of the Bible (the Vulgate). However, at the same period Augustine (AD 354–430), one of the early church's greatest theologians, regarded the deuterocanonical books as fully authoritative. Subsequent generations of Christians perpetuated this ambivalence. The Protestant Reformer Martin Luther, for example, adopted Jerome's policy of commending the deuterocanonical literature as valuable but not authoritative, though the Westminster Confession of Faith in 1646 denounced them as completely unbiblical. A century earlier, though, the Roman Catholic Council of Trent had insisted that (with the exception of 1–2 Esdras and the Prayer of Manasseh) they were an integral part of the canon. The Orthodox Church, for its part, has always accepted an even larger collection of literature as an authentic part of the Christian Old Testament scriptures.

will discern its message differently again, while a secular atheist will have another perspective, and a New Ager will perceive it from yet another angle. While seeking to be aware of the various insights that can be gained from different standpoints and personal perspectives, it is not the intention of this book to present a comprehensive account of all the possibilities. As with the companion volume, *Introducing the New Testament*, this one is written from a self-consciously Christian position. When the Old Testament is approached from a Christian standpoint, it is not adequate to regard it solely as part of the religious history of the ancient world. Purely historical and literary matters are not unimportant, but they are not the whole story, and theological questions also need to be addressed. These include such matters as how the religious ideas of the Old Testament might be related to the Christian faith as it is explained in the teaching of Jesus and the rest of the New Testament, and whether it is possible to square the Old Testament's ideas with Christian beliefs. Even many Christians find it hard to think that what they understand of the descriptions of God in the Old Testament can be reconciled with the message of the New, while in some quarters it is taken for granted that there is an unbridgeable chasm between the ethical perspectives of the two parts of the Christian Bible. And what about things like sacrificial worship? To most Western Christians this has always been frankly offensive. But is it saying something fundamental about God's nature and about true religious belief and practice, or is it a peripheral part of the culture of the day that can easily be discarded?

These are all big questions, perhaps too big to be properly addressed in the scope of a book like this. But they are key questions for every Christian reader of the Old Testament, which is why it seems worth making the effort. Matters of faith are examined especially towards the end of the book, and the way they are dealt with there reflects the kind of questions that contemporary readers may wish to ask. But before coming to that, some considerable attention needs to be applied to setting the Old Testament faith in its proper social and historical context. Once we have understood it in its own world, we have a better chance of interpreting it sensibly in ours.

Ordering the books

Types of literature

The Old Testament is a complete library of literature, containing books of many different types. If they were taken separately to a modern library, it is certain that they would not all be placed on the same shelf, for they represent many different literary genres, each with its own distinctive style and requiring different methods of interpretation to appreciate their individual contributions to the overall picture.

HISTORY

Some books are easily recognizable as a kind of history: Genesis, Joshua, Judges, 1 and 2 Samuel, 1 and 2 Kings, 1 and 2 Chronicles, Ezra and Nehemiah. These tell the story of the nation's life, which is then continued in the deuterocanonical books of 1 and 2 Maccabees. But none of them merely records past events. They all report some things and not others, and always interpret what they include, explaining its significance in the light of the distinctive religious faith of their various writers. The nearest we come to historical archives in the generally accepted sense would be some sections of Chronicles.

LAW

Other books (Exodus, Leviticus, Numbers and Deuteronomy) are obviously law codes, though they are hardly the kind that today's Western lawyers might use, for they contain a mixture of civil and religious laws, as well as some stories that could just as readily be classified as a kind of history.

POETRY

There is a lot of poetry in the Old Testament, and some books consist of nothing else: religious poetry in Psalms and Lamentations, and love poems in the Song of Solomon. But many other books also contain poetry, including Job, Proverbs, and (from the deuterocanonical books) the Wisdom of Solomon and Wisdom of Ben Sira. The prophets also seem to have expressed many of their messages in poetic form, no doubt making it easier to remember and repeat.

STORIES

People have always loved good stories, and the Hebrews were no exception. Stories that were obviously carefully crafted, maybe by professional storytellers, include Job, Jonah and Esther, along with parts of Daniel and the stories about Joseph contained in Genesis. Among the deuterocanonical books, Tobit, Judith and the various additions to the stories of Daniel and Esther all fall into this category. They are all narratives that have obviously been skilfully designed, like a good novel, to engage the reader's attention and to get a message across at the same time. Some scholars believe they are novels, presenting a distinctive message by means of a fictional story, while others would rather classify them as history – though, nevertheless, history with a meaning. The stories of Job and Jonah have features which suggest they may originally have been meant to be performed as drama.

VISIONS

Visions are found scattered throughout the Hebrew Bible, but Daniel in particular is full of them, as also is the deuterocanonical 2 Esdras. These books were written in a distinctive apocalyptic style, and at a time when their writers and readers were suffering persecution and injustice. By looking at what was going on from God's angle in some other world, they were able to put such suffering in a wider perspective and assure their readers that it was only a temporary thing. They use symbolic images in a very precise way, which means they require quite specific interpretative skills.

LITURGICAL MATERIALS

The book of Psalms is, in effect, the liturgical handbook of the Jerusalem Temple. It is a specialized form of poetry, and includes prayers, litanies and songs, often with instructions for the musicians, and detailed directions for dancers and other worship leaders.

PHILOSOPHY AND ETHICS

Many books contain advice about how to live. Much of it, such as that found in Proverbs, is simple homespun wisdom of the sort found in every society across the world. Other books, however, wrestle with the great issues of life and death and the ultimate meaning of things – the existence of God, or the problem of undeserved suffering and the presence of evil in the world. These include Job and Ecclesiastes and (from the deuterocanonical collection) the Wisdom of Solomon and Wisdom of Ben Sira.

FAITH STORIES

Books of philosophy tend to address big questions in abstract ways, but people of all cultures have usually preferred to tell stories to one another, to explain things that just could not be explored in any other way. Many different terms have been used to describe such stories, 'myth' being one of the most popular – though in common speech, that can suggest they are somehow untrue or unreliable, which is why I have preferred the term 'faith stories' here because, far from being untrue, these stories express the most profound truths imaginable about some of life's most complex questions. The Old Testament begins with stories of this kind in the book of Genesis and, in doing so, sets the scene for all that then follows.

Sections of the Hebrew Bible

The order of the books in the Christian Old Testament is derived not from the manuscripts of the Hebrew Bible, but from a Greek version (the Septuagint) that seems to have originated in Egypt sometime before the beginning of the Christian era. The Hebrew Bible arranged its contents in a totally different way, with three separate sections: the Law, the Prophets and the Writings.

THE LAW

This consists of the first five books (Genesis, Exodus, Leviticus, Numbers and Deuteronomy), believed to be of special importance as they were traditionally regarded as the work of Moses himself. Genesis, of course, contains nothing at all that would nowadays be recognized as 'law'. It is a collection of stories, and at first sight it might more naturally be regarded as some sort of historical narrative. That reflects current understandings of 'law' as being a set of rules and regulations, a legal code that can be interpreted by lawyers and applied in a court by a judge. It would certainly be hard to imagine a modern person agreeing with one of the poets of ancient Israel who wrote that 'the law is my delight' (Psalm 119:77). But the biblical notion of 'law' was significantly more comprehensive and far-ranging than ours. The fundamental meaning of the Hebrew word conventionally translated 'law' (Torah) was 'guidance' or 'instruction', and the 'law' of the Hebrew Bible was the place where people could discover what to believe about God, and how they should live in order to reflect God's will. This is why the Torah and its development is so closely bound up with the stories of Israel's history. It is a basic assumption in the Old Testament that knowing and obeying God is not just a matter of blind obedience to a few religious and moral rules, but is rather a question of experiencing God's concern and love in a personal and social context. Though the Law might include principles of justice, it also needed to incorporate stories which could serve as everyday illustrations and case studies of how people were intended to live – and the likely consequences if they chose to follow other practices.

THE PROPHETS

This is the largest section of the Hebrew Bible, and takes its name from a number of religious and political activists who sought to influence the life of the nation over a period of several centuries. This collection of books itself falls into two distinct sections, 'the former prophets' and 'the latter prophets'. Since 'the latter prophets' are more obviously connected with the individuals whose names they bear, it will be most useful here to look at them first.

■ **The latter prophets** Prophets are mentioned throughout the history of the Israelite people. They were not primarily writers, but speakers and political activists. One of the central planks of the Old Testament faith in its final form was the conviction that spirituality is not so much concerned with the kind of rituals that go on in shrines and temples, but relates to everyday styles of life. As the people looked back to the traditional stories of how their forebears had lived, they came to the conclusion that God's values were essentially concerned with justice and freedom. Since their own ancestors had been enslaved in Egypt, and God had stood by them in their distress, before finally orchestrating their freedom through Moses, it was natural to conclude that God must be on the side of the poor and the oppressed – and this belief came to be enshrined in many of the nation's laws, particularly the book of Deuteronomy.

It is easy to hold such beliefs, but much more difficult to put them into practice. The prophets functioned as the conscience of the nation, always reminding the people of how much they themselves owed to God's generosity and love – and encouraging them to demonstrate these same values in their dealings with one another and with other nations. It was an uphill struggle, and many of the prophets were persecuted, imprisoned or even killed. But this message was at the heart of authentic Hebrew faith, and plays a large part in the books of the Old Testament.

Not all the prophets had books named after them. Of those who did, Isaiah, Jeremiah and Ezekiel (the so-called 'major prophets') have the longest, while twelve others (the 'minor prophets') are credited with much shorter books: Hosea, Joel, Amos, Obadiah, Jonah, Micah, Nahum, Habakkuk, Zephaniah, Haggai, Zechariah and Malachi. From what we know of them, it seems that the prophets themselves rarely made long speeches. They usually delivered short messages that could be easily remembered – many of them in poetry, though prophets were also on occasion mime artists and dramatists, acting out their messages in the market places and on street corners.

■ **The former prophets** These are the books of Joshua, Judges, 1–2 Samuel and 1–2 Kings, and in the Hebrew Bible they appear before 'the latter prophets'. At first sight, they look to be so different that it is not obvious why they too should have been included as part of the Prophets. They read more like history books, telling the story of the nation from the time when their ancestors escaped from slavery, through to the time in the sixth century BC when their national capital was destroyed by the Babylonian empire and its people were deported. In between, we read of how, under kings David and Solomon, Israel briefly enjoyed a period of political stability and influence. But most of the remainder of the story describes how their grand kingdom split into two parts (Israel and Judah), both of which struggled to maintain their independence in the face of growing pressures from larger states, notably Egypt, Assyria, Babylon and Syria.

The thing that makes these books also 'prophets' is that they do not merely relate the stories but – like all good history books – interpret them, informing their readers what the stories mean and showing how they were to be understood in relation to the sweep of wider world history of the time. In doing that, their writers looked at things from the perspectives they had learned from the prophets. As they reviewed their nation's history, they could see that whenever the people had commit-fted themselves to God's values and ways of doing things, they prospered – but when God's demands for justice and love were forgotten, then the nation suffered. As we have already observed, Israelite faith was not focused on philosophical abstractions, but began with the way God had dealt with people in the experiences of everyday life. History was therefore very important, and was one of the key places where God's activity could be seen. By a proper appreciation of its meaning and significance, as explained by the prophets, the people could discover how they were meant to live. All the prophetic works – former and latter – were regarded as accounts of how God had spoken to the people, sometimes through the events of history and at other times through the words of people. But in each case it was the same God, and the same message.

THE WRITINGS

This section includes all the remaining books of the Hebrew Bible. They are not all the same kind of works. Psalms, Proverbs and Job are very different from one another in content, for example, but they are all poetry. Then there are those books known as the 'Megilloth', or 'five scrolls': Ruth, Song of Solomon, Ecclesiastes, Lamentations and Esther. Again, these five are all different styles and genres, but they were grouped together because each of them had a particular association with significant religious festivals: Ruth was used at Pentecost, Song of Solomon at Passover, Ecclesiastes at Tabernacles, Lamentations to commemorate the destruction of Jerusalem and Esther at Purim. There are also the books of Ezra, Nehemiah and 1–2 Chronicles, all of which relate to the situation in which the remnants of the people of Judah found themselves after they were allowed to return to their homeland in the years following 538 BC, when the Persian emperor Cyrus the Great managed to overthrow the Babylonian empire. Last of all, there is the book of Daniel, containing visions and some stories, and relating to a later period still.

The reason for this unusual arrangement of the books was probably historical, and the three sections roughly represent the three stages in which the Old Testament was put together. The first part of it to be permanently recorded was the Law, followed by the Prophets, and then much later by the Writings. This is why the books of Ezra, Nehemiah and Chronicles were included in the final section, rather than being placed alongside the other history books in 'the former prophets', for they were written much later and from the perspective of the age that survived the destruction of Jerusalem in the sixth century BC. The books of Chronicles contain many of the same stories as the books of Samuel and Kings, but they are an analysis of the meaning of those stories and an application of their lessons to the people of a later generation. By then, both the Law and the Prophets were widely accepted as sacred and important collections of books, and it would not have been possible to make any further additions to their contents.

Archaeology and the Old Testament

Comparing books on the Old Testament written a century or more ago with one written today, the thing that is most obvious is the radical change that has taken place in our knowledge of the world of the Bible. In the nineteenth century, study of the Old Testament was largely a literary affair: the text itself was studied in minute detail, and dissected in much the same way as a pathologist might deal with a corpse. But today, Old Testament study is vibrant and living, and is dominated by social and cultural considerations that would have been quite foreign to earlier generations of scholars. One of the major concerns of contemporary scholarship is to understand how the Old Testament fits into the world of its day, and to analyse its contents not just ideologically, but historically

The Rosetta Stone, found by scholars who accompanied Napoleon's army when he occupied Egypt, is in Greek, in demotic and in ancient Egyptian hieroglyphs. It provided the first clues for understanding ancient Egyptian; the first hieroglyphs were deciphered through distinguishing the name 'Ptolemy' in all three scripts.

and sociologically. This has all been made possible through an enormous expansion of knowledge of the ancient world, and thanks to the consistent efforts of archaeologists we now have a better idea than ever before of what it was actually like to live in the world of ancient Israel. It is possible to appreciate the social and political realities of life in a new way that has shed untold light on many difficult passages of the Old Testament.

Explorers have always had an interest in the materials left over from earlier civilizations. In the seventeenth century many ancient objects of interest and beauty were randomly seized and taken by such people to their wealthy patrons all over Europe, but it was not until the eighteenth century that anyone took a systematic interest in the subject. The archaeological exploration of Bible lands began when Napoleon's armies invaded Egypt in 1798, taking with them a team of scholars to study the ancient monuments. They made many significant discoveries, one of the most useful being the Rosetta Stone which had an inscription in both Greek and Egyptian hieroglyphs, and enabled scholars to decipher ancient Egyptian for the first time. However, it was only at the end of the nineteenth century that rigorous procedures began to be applied to sites in the Bible lands on a widespread scale.

A typical site in Palestine will take the form of a large mound, or *tell*. Many of these sites look just like large hills, perhaps as high as thirty or forty metres, and covered with trees or grass, but under the surface is to be found the remains of an ancient city. Sometimes cities were built on a natural hill, for that was an easy site to defend. But many of these tells began at ground level, and have been raised to their present height by the normal processes of building over many years. In the ancient world most buildings were made of mud and wood, and when a settlement was either destroyed by an enemy or just fell into decay, the inhabitants would gather

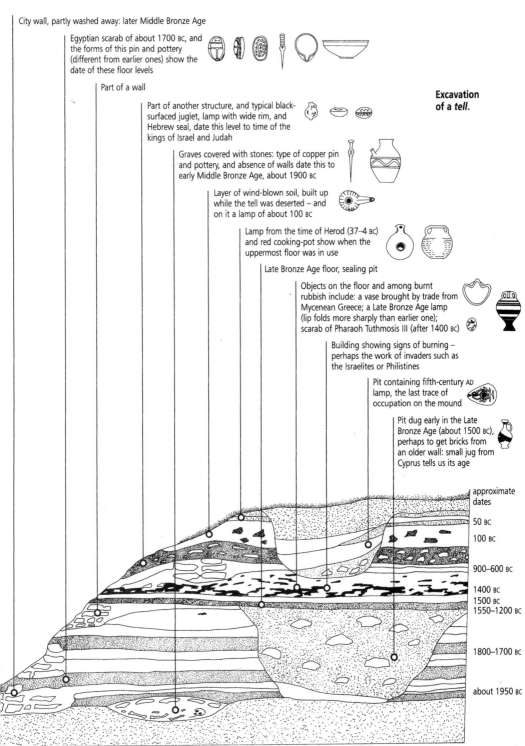

City wall, partly washed away: later Middle Bronze Age

Egyptian scarab of about 1700 BC, and the forms of this pin and pottery (different from earlier ones) show the date of these floor levels

Part of a wall

Excavation of a *tell*.

Part of another structure, and typical black-surfaced juglet, lamp with wide rim, and Hebrew seal, date this level to time of the kings of Israel and Judah

Graves covered with stones: type of copper pin and pottery, and absence of walls date this to early Middle Bronze Age, about 1900 BC

Layer of wind-blown soil, built up while the tell was deserted – and on it a lamp of about 100 BC

Lamp from the time of Herod (37–4 BC) and red cooking-pot show when the uppermost floor was in use

Late Bronze Age floor, sealing pit

Objects on the floor and among burnt rubbish include: a vase brought by trade from Mycenean Greece; a Late Bronze Age lamp (lip folds more sharply than earlier one); scarab of Pharaoh Tuthmosis III (after 1400 BC)

Building showing signs of burning – perhaps the work of invaders such as the Israelites or Philistines

Pit containing fifth-century AD lamp, the last trace of occupation on the mound

Pit dug early in the Late Bronze Age (about 1500 BC), perhaps to get bricks from an older wall: small jug from Cyprus tells us its age

approximate dates

50 BC

100 BC

900–600 BC

1400 BC
1500 BC
1550–1200 BC

1800–1700 BC

about 1950 BC

Archaeology and the
Old Testament
continued

together any available materials that could be reused, and set to work to build their own new town on the ruins of the old. The new level could be as much as two or three metres higher than the one that preceded it, which meant that over time the ground level was gradually raised, and the whole mound took on the structure of a giant gateau with many different layers superimposed one on top of the other.

Archaeologists have developed a number of basic procedures to guide their investigations at sites like this:

Great care is required as an archaeological dig progresses. Each fragment of pottery or other artefact has to be catalogued and the level at which it is found must be carefully noted.

● Digging is done in such a way as to keep separate and distinct the successive strata, or layers, of occupation. The ideal way to do this, of course, would be to start at the top and slice off each layer in turn. But this would be impractical, taking up too much time and for that reason being impossibly expensive. Instead, the archaeologist usually cuts into the mound in much the same way as a slice might be cut from a cake. This technique can provide access to a cross-section of the mound's contents in a process known as 'stratigraphic excavation'.   e one disadvantage is that the archaeologist can easily cut a slice at the wrong place in the mound and miss significant remains as a result. For instance, the site of the city of

Hazor in northern Israel was excavated in 1928 by archaeologist John Garstang, who concluded that the city was deserted between 1400 and 1200 BC. But thirty years later, the Israeli archaeologist Yigael Yadin dug a trench at a different point on the same mound, and found extensive evidence of people living there at just that period!

● If objects were to be removed and taken away indiscriminately, it would be impossible to assess their significance. To understand what they mean, they need to be studied in relation to the precise spot where they are uncovered and with respect to other items that are found alongside them. Making an accurate record of every level that is excavated and of every object that is found is therefore an essential part of the process. Plans must be drawn and photographs taken, because once a layer of a mound is removed, no one can put it back together again.

● Archaeologists must also compare what they find with what others have found in other places. Pottery provides a good example of the importance of this. For every basket of significant objects recovered, dozens of baskets of pottery are unearthed. This is because pottery was always in common use, and it was very easily broken – but it was virtually impossible to destroy completely. Fashions in pottery changed from time to time, and though some styles were in use for a long period, distinctive aspects of size, shape, texture and decoration were generally limited to a specific period. So when the same types are discovered at several different locations, it is reasonable to conclude that the layers in which they are found were occupied at about the same time. In fact, pottery is one of the most important clues to the dating of a particular find. Early in the twentieth century, English archaeologist Sir Flinders Petrie realized this, and by comparing pottery from different sites and noting the various distinctive styles, he developed what he called a 'Ceramic Index' – a catalogue of typical pottery types which could be accurately dated, and which has proved to be an invaluable aid to the work of all subsequent excavators.

In trying to apply information discovered in this way to the study of the Old Testament, there are some basic principles that should always be borne in mind:

● Though the records of the Assyrian and Babylonian kings contain a good number of accounts of events that are also mentioned and described in the Old Testament, this kind of direct correlation is unusual. It is only rarely that archaeologists have discovered things with a direct and specific reference to events and people mentioned in the Bible.

● More often, archaeology helps to place the Old Testament story in its true context. It is, for example, highly unlikely that any archaeologist will ever find a reference to the story of Abraham, but investigations have shown that migrations like those described in the Genesis stories were taking place all over the Fertile Crescent during the second millennium BC, and that some of the customs mentioned in Genesis were practised at the time.

● Occasionally, the findings of archaeologists can illuminate specific passages in the Old Testament. In 1 Samuel 4 there is the story of how the Philistines captured the ark of the covenant from Israel in a fierce battle near the town of Shiloh, where the ark was kept. Readers of the Bible had often surmised that Shiloh itself must have been destroyed at the same time, for when Israel recovered the ark it was not returned there. Excavation at the site has confirmed that Shiloh was indeed destroyed at the time of this incident in the eleventh century BC.

● Archaeology is also often a help in interpreting difficult parts of the Old Testament. For example, Ezekiel 14:14 mentions three people as examples of great goodness: Daniel, Noah and Job. But it is curious that the prophet should place Daniel, believed to be one of his own contemporaries, in the same class as two ancient figures. Archaeology has shown that he was probably not talking of the hero of the Old Testament book of Daniel at all, but of an ancient king of similar name renowned for his religion and justice, who is mentioned in religious poems from Assyria to Canaan, some of which are nearly 1,000 years older than Ezekiel.

● Sometimes the findings of archaeology seem as if they cannot be reconciled with what is found in the Old Testament. For example, according to Joshua 7:1 – 8:29 a great battle was fought at a place called Ai during the conquest of Canaan, whereas archaeological evidence shows the town was destroyed about 2400 BC and was not rebuilt, which means there cannot have been a town there in the days of Joshua. Of course, there could be many reasons for this apparent discrepancy. It may be that archaeologists have wrongly identified the site: it would certainly not be the first time such a mistake had been made, though it seems unlikely in this instance. It is also possible that other discoveries could be made in the future which would resolve the problem. Or it could be, as many think, that we should look for the meaning of the Old Testament story elsewhere – perhaps in the fact that the word *Ai* in Hebrew means simply 'the ruin'. Whatever the full explanation may be, it is important to take seriously both the Old Testament picture and the evidence that can be provided by archaeological investigation.

2 The Founding of the Nation

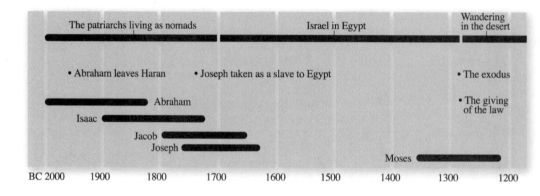

The patriarchs living as nomads			Israel in Egypt				Wandering in the desert

- Abraham leaves Haran   • Joseph taken as a slave to Egypt   • The exodus

Abraham
Isaac
Jacob
Joseph
Moses

• The giving of the law

BC 2000	1900	1800	1700	1600	1500	1400	1300	1200

Where does Old Testament history begin? At one time, it was taken for granted that there was a very simple answer to that question: 'real' history began on the very first page of Genesis, with an account of the origins of all things, and the remainder of the story just unfolded consecutively from there. That was the basis on which Archbishop James Ussher (1581–1656) was able to claim confidently that the creation of the world took place in 4004 BC, for by adding up all the chronological indications contained in the early books of the Old Testament, and working backwards from dates that seemed to be assured, that was the mathematical result that would inevitably be arrived at. No one would now expect to be able to make such a calculation in any sort of convincing way, for a variety of very good reasons.

■ As has already been indicated in the last chapter, it is obvious from the literary genre of the writings contained in the opening books of the Old Testament that they were not all intended to be historical writing. Nineteenth-century Bible students allowed themselves to be caught up in lengthy debates about how the creation stories of Genesis could be harmonized with the emerging scientific consensus about the origins of the world, and in the process not only found themselves unable to reach a conclusion, but also frequently brought biblical faith as a whole into disrepute, and allowed religious believers to be portrayed as cranks who were more interested in halting progress than in discovering the truth. With greater detachment from the heat of that particular battle, scholars of all persuasions can now see that, whatever the original purpose of these stories was intended to be, they were certainly not attempting to provide an account of human history that would satisfy the rationalistic science inspired by the European Enlightenment. They are immediately distanced from that by the fact that God is actually their central character, and while there can be different opinions of their claims about God, the methodology of scientific rationalism is not going to be the way to evaluate them. That is why discussion of these matters is left aside here until much later in the book, when we come to consider the spiritual dimensions of the Old Testament and its message.

■ While the stories found in Genesis 1–11 clearly belong to a different genre from that of history writing, there are others found in the remainder of Genesis, and extending forward through Joshua and Judges, that do have an appearance of perhaps being 'real' history, in the sense of being intended to document the actual events surrounding the origins of the Israelite nation. Notwithstanding the fact that several key sections of these narratives have clearly been carefully crafted so as to read like a good story, they do more obviously tell stories that appear to integrate with events in the real world, and while once again the appearance of God as a major player marks them out as distinctive, much of what they report is not at all hard to envisage actually taking place. For example, the stories of Abraham and Sarah, and the later members of their family, contain incidents that are true to family life, and could easily be paralleled in many families, even today in the twenty-first century. Indeed, the abuse and violence that is perpetuated from one generation to another in Bible families is all too familiar to modern people. But therein lies just the problem, when we try to discern where Old Testament history in the narrow sense actually starts. For all these stories are domestic episodes, a feature which at once renders them more interesting (for everyone likes to explore the dynamic of human relationships), as well as making it more complicated to try to estimate how – if at all – they might be intended to provide some definitive account of Israel's actual historical origins. As we shall see, many of their details are certainly historically plausible within the context of the kind of ancient nomadic lifestyle they depict. But that is not the same thing as being able to establish their literal accuracy, for a novel can be historically plausible without being an actual account of the experience of real people.

■ A historical novel, of course, finds its plausibility precisely in the fact that, while it may not be the actual story of particular individuals, it nevertheless reflects the kind of challenges and opportunities that most people continually face, and they recognize their own struggles within it. In that sense, it is absolutely 'true' despite not being a historical narrative – and certainly more relevant to the lives of later generations than a mere chronicle of events would be likely to be. In the case of these early Old Testament stories, we know for certain that they have been shaped over time so as to address such questions of life and its ultimate meaning with relevance to the experiences not of one, but of several generations of readers. The central conviction of the narratives remained unchanged – that God can be trusted to make, and keep, great promises – but in articulating that message in new ways, the goal of the community of faith was not to preserve its own history as some kind of antiquarian exercise, but rather to ensure that each new generation would receive adequate teaching about the ways of God.

Questions of this sort are a major concern in relation to all the early Old Testament stories – not only the accounts of Israel's earliest ancestors, but also the stories of the exodus and the subsequent settlement of the tribes in the land of Canaan. In different ways, we shall need to keep returning to them throughout our discussion of these narratives. For the moment, it will be sufficient to observe that they are among the most complex of all the questions we need to deal with, and there are no simple answers. Indeed, in the context of an introductory book like this perhaps the most we can aim for is a clear understanding of the nature of the questions, with some indication of possible ways of addressing them. In terms of procedure, I have decided to follow the course of events as they are outlined in the Old Testament narratives, while recognizing that different sections may be of different literary genres and therefore require us to adopt a variety of interpretative approaches. At the same time, I have aimed to keep a clear focus on the underlying spiritual concerns of the final editors of these stories, so as not to lose sight of the message that was the ultimate purpose for which the books were written in the first place.

National identity

The one thing that can be said without any fear of contradiction is that the people of ancient Israel had a well-developed sense of their own national identity. They were especially conscious of the fact that their own values and way of life were different from that of many of their neighbours. The main concern of the average Palestinian farmer was with agriculture, and much of the prevailing religious worship was designed to ensure that nothing would interrupt the cycle of the seasons from one year to another. By contrast, Israel believed that the key to understanding life's mysteries was not to be found primarily in the world of nature, but in the unique and unrepeatable facts of history, and God's hand could therefore be traced in the stories passed down from their forebears, for as far back as it was possible to go.

By the time these stories had been gathered together and written down, the people of ancient Israel were themselves farmers, and they too

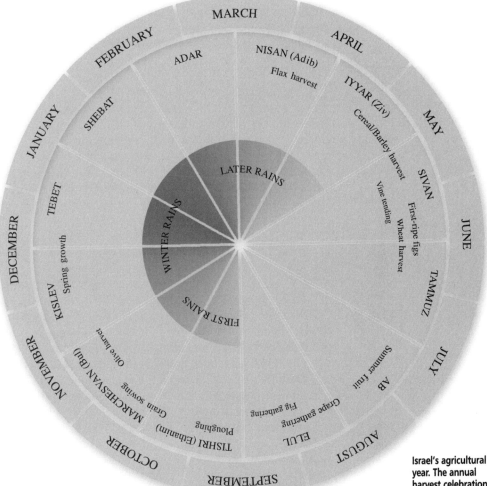

Israel's agricultural year. The annual harvest celebration was a time when the Israelites remembered their indebtedness to God. They gave the 'firstfruits' of the harvest as an offering to maintain the worship of Yahweh.

celebrated the annual gathering of the harvest in a religious ceremony. But as they did so, their thoughts centred not on the operations of ploughing, sowing and reaping, but on the past experience of their nation, in partnership with God. As they presented a part of the harvest to God in a religious ceremony, they affirmed their deepest convictions about life in words that have been central to the faith of Jewish people throughout the centuries:

My ancestor was a wandering Aramean, who took his family to Egypt to live. They were few in number when they went there, but they became a large and powerful nation. The Egyptians treated us harshly and forced us to work as slaves. Then we cried out for help to Yahweh, the God of our ancestors, who heard us and saw our

suffering, hardship, and misery. By God's great power and strength
we were rescued from Egypt, amidst miracles and wonders, and all
kinds of terrifying events. God brought us here and gave us this rich
and fertile land. So now I bring to Yahweh the first part of the
harvest (Deuteronomy 26:5–10).

No other statement sums up so eloquently what the Old Testament
is all about. In just a few words, this ancient creed recalls the most
important elements in the remembered story. It tells how God had
rescued a disorganized group of slaves from Egypt and made them
a nation in their own right; and how in response to this
undeserved goodness, the people had given to this God,
Yahweh, their worship and obedience.

The founders

The 'wandering Aramean' is occasionally given
the name 'Israel', someone who is more often
referred to in the Old Testament as Jacob
(Genesis 32:28). It is not clear why he should have
been referred to as an 'Aramean'. The Arameans
became prominent only after about the eleventh century
BC, when they established a small empire based in Syria.
But like the Israelites, who also emerged as a nation at
about the same time, their origins must go further back
than that. Throughout the third millennium BC (3000–
2000 BC) large numbers of wandering nomads were
constantly moving from the deserts of Arabia into the
territories controlled by the great civilization centred on
Mesopotamia. The reasons for these movements are
complex and uncertain. In about 2000 BC, groups of people
whom the Babylonians called 'Ammuru' ('westerners'), and
who are perhaps to be associated with the Amorites of the
Old Testament, moved in and established their own culture
in Babylon itself, at Mari, and elsewhere. Many scholars
believe that some of these people were the ancestors
not only of the Arameans and the Canaanites, but also
of Israel. The Old Testament certainly suggests there
was some close ethnic connection between all these
groups, and this is the context in which its earliest stories
of Jacob's ancestors are placed.

The story proper begins with Abraham and Sarah – or, rather, with
Abraham's father Terah – in the city of Ur, at the very heart of the
ancient Mesopotamian civilization (Genesis 11:27–30). For some
undisclosed reason, they left their home city and the whole family
moved some 560 miles (900 km) north-west to the city of Haran. Both
these towns had important shrines for the worship of the moon god Sin,

This figure
of a goat was
excavated from
the Royal Graves
at the site of Ur.
It has been dated
to approximately
2500 BC. The site
of this ancient
city, associated
with Abraham,
gives evidence
of a civilization
that reached
back to the fifth
millennium BC.

and if they were devoted to this deity the move could have been part of a journey of pilgrimage to different centres of worship. There is certainly plenty of evidence to show that Abraham and his family were not originally worshippers of Yahweh: in another account of the same events, a much later leader of Israel began his story of the nation's history with the words, 'Long ago your ancestors lived on the other side of the River Euphrates and worshipped other gods' (Joshua 24:2). Some have discerned traces of religious arguments which involved Abraham's family in physical danger, for in a rather obscure passage he is said to have been 'rescued' from Ur (Genesis 15:7; Isaiah 29:22) in just the same way as the escaping slaves were later 'rescued' (the same Hebrew word) from Egypt (Exodus 20:2; Deuteronomy 5:6).

On the other hand, it is only in the Hebrew manuscripts of Genesis 11 that the city of Ur is mentioned at all. The Greek (Septuagint) version places Abraham and Sarah's original home 'in the land of the Chaldeans', and this could have been a place much nearer to Haran in northern Syria than to Ur, which is on the Persian Gulf. Other stories certainly suggest that their roots were much stronger in Haran than in Ur, for when messengers were later sent to find a wife for their son Isaac, they were told to go to the country of Abraham's birth, a location which turns out to be not Ur, but the area around Haran (Genesis 24:4).

Haran, in modern Syria. From here Abraham, the 'wandering Aramean', with Sarah his wife, moved south into Canaan.

Despite this close connection with the town of Haran and its surrounding countryside, Abraham and Sarah did not make a permanent home there. Instead, they moved on to a different part of the Fertile Crescent – this time travelling another 450 miles (720 km) south-west, into the land of Palestine. There they lived a wandering life, moving about from place to place to find enough grazing for flocks and food for the family. This was the only way newcomers could settle, for the best parts of the land were already occupied by both farmers and city dwellers. This no doubt explains why their movements seem to have been mostly in the south of the country, just to the north and west of the Dead Sea. This was not the best land, but it had many areas suitable for grazing, and only a small resident population. When the grass was exhausted there, nomadic tribes could move either to an oasis like Beersheba or into the fields adjoining towns like Shechem and Hebron. No doubt this land was farmed by the Canaanites, but they probably allowed nomadic groups to put their animals onto it after the crops had been gathered. Even this source of supply was uncertain, though, and like many others of the period, Abraham and Sarah were forced to move as far afield as Egypt at times of particular hardship (Genesis 12:10–20).

Early expressions of faith

Though matters of historical accuracy have become of great concern to modern readers of the Old Testament, this is not where the central interest of the book of Genesis is to be located. In a very specific way, all its books are about God – in particular, about Israel's God, Yahweh – and the entire collection has been formulated in the light of what came to be recognized as the normative spirituality described by the later prophets. God is actually the central character of all these early stories. Abraham and Sarah's move from Haran was not determined by political and social issues, but by their experience of God. Nor was this

Were Abraham and Sarah and their family real people?

One of the major preoccupations of Old Testament scholars for the greater part of the twentieth century concerned the question of how these stories about Israel's ancestors might be understood in the light of what is known of wider events taking place at this time in the lands of which they speak. By the end of the nineteenth century, the stories had come to be commonly regarded either as fiction, or as the vaguely remembered exploits of tribes – even at times of ancient deities – personified to become the story of just a few individuals. On this view, people like the families of Abraham, Isaac and Jacob (conventionally referred to by scholars as 'the patriarchs', though of course many women were among them) could not be regarded as real people, but as representations of various social and religious movements in the millennium before Israel became a nation in the true sense.

As the twentieth century progressed, however, it became obvious that the matter was not quite as simple as that. Expanding knowledge of life in the region during the Middle Bronze Age (2000–1500 BC) has highlighted the fact that, whatever may be said of the details of the stories, the way of life attributed to these people and the kind of activities they are said to have been engaged in do seem to reflect an authentic perception of what was happening in these lands at this time. Ancient documents found at the sites of places like Mari and Nuzi have alerted us to the fact that this was a period of creative cultural innovation initiated by people with a long history of

civilization behind them. By the middle of the twentieth century, increasing numbers of scholars were concluding that these 'patriarchal' stories actually described the existence of real people. One of the leading Old Testament scholars of the day (John Bright) claimed: 'We can assert with full confidence that Abraham, Isaac, and Jacob were actual historical individuals... a part of that migration of seminomadic clans which brought a new population to Palestine in the early centuries of the second millennium BC.' In the light of further study, few people would now wish to express an opinion with quite the same degree of confidence, not least because we can now appreciate that the actual questions to be addressed are more complex than was once imagined. But the various pieces of evidence which were claimed to prove that the patriarchs were 'real people' still stand, and are worth reviewing here, even if they do need to be placed in a somewhat wider context.

Names

Names with linguistic forms similar to Abraham, Isaac, Jacob and others have been found in many ancient documents. This kind of name seems to have been especially popular among the Amorite peoples living in various parts of northern Mesopotamia about 2000 BC. Other names familiar from Genesis – Terah, Nahor, Serug, Benjamin, Levi, Ishmael – were also widely used, though not always as the names of people. Sometimes they appear as place names. Of course none of the occurrences of these names outside the Bible actually refers to the specific people mentioned in the Old Testament as the

something unique to them, for it was also the common experience of all their descendants, most notably their son Isaac and grandson Jacob.

The central thread of the Old Testament story shows how personal experience of God was to be a vital element in the very survival of the whole nation of Israel, over many generations. Yet there is a clear demarcation made here between 'Yahweh', the God on whom Israel's later

---

ancestors of Israel. But these coincidences do show that names of this type were commonly used during the second millennium BC.

Lifestyle

The Tale of Sinuhe describes a nomadic chief in about 1900 BC living in much the same way as is portrayed in the stories of Abraham's family. Like Abraham (Genesis 14:1–16), this clan leader also took part in a war with an alliance of kings. Here again, the names of the kings mentioned in the Old Testament story are typical of the kind of names people had at the time – though there is no way of connecting those with whom Abraham fought to actual named people in other sources. There is, however, plenty of evidence to show that the wandering style of existence portrayed in Genesis reflects many aspects of what is otherwise known of life in the early part of the second millennium BC. Evidence from Mari in particular shows that many tribes were moving about freely at this time, adopting both nomadic and sedentary lifestyles at different times depending on particular circumstances. Those who were wandering lived in a generally stable relationship with those who based themselves in towns and villages. Indeed, they each needed the other to provide goods and services, and the one thing that they both resisted was the attempt of larger city states to exercise a centralized political control over them. All these features are found in the Genesis narratives. The forebears of Israel generally camp near to smallish settlements (Genesis 12:6–9; 13:12–18; 33:18–20),

sometimes staying for long enough to become farmers (26:12), and at times of particular stringency they even become town-dwellers for a while (12:10–20; 20:1–18; 26:6–11). According to some, these narratives depict them operating in locations which would not have been places where wandering nomads could have found a temporary home in later times, a feature of the narratives which has therefore been claimed as further circumstantial support for the overall plausibility of the Genesis narratives.

Customs

The social and legal customs attributed to this period are often different from those which were advocated in later Israel. For example, the law of Leviticus 18:18 forbids a man to be married to two sisters at once, though Jacob certainly was (Genesis 29:15–30). Abraham himself married his half-sister Sarah (Genesis 20:12), though this was also

The nomadic existence described in Genesis fits in well with the picture built up by archaeologists of life in the region in the early part of the second millennium BC.

faith focused, and the religion of the ancestors. One later passage makes it quite clear that these people did not know 'Yahweh', but worshipped a deity they referred to as 'El Shaddai' (Exodus 6:2–3). This phrase has often been translated into English as 'God Almighty', which rather obscures the fact that El was actually a personal divine name, just like Yahweh. 'El Shaddai' meant 'El, the God of the mountain', and in addition the stories of Israel's forebears also mention 'El Elyon' ('El, the Exalted

---

Were Abraham and Sarah and their family real people?
continued

prohibited later (Leviticus 18:9, 11; 20:17; Deuteronomy 27:22). The fact that these anomalies have been preserved in the early stories seems to suggest that the people who wrote them down did not try to assimilate them to the practices of their own day, but handed on authentic traditions in the form they had received them.

This general impression may be confirmed by certain legal documents discovered at Nuzi, for some of the customs described there seem to explain and illuminate otherwise obscure parts of the Old Testament stories. For instance, there is the story of how Abraham's childless wife Sarah presented him with a slave girl by whom to have a child (Genesis 16:1–14). A text from Nuzi explains how in certain marriage contracts a childless wife could be required to provide her husband with just such a substitute. Furthermore, if a child was subsequently born to such a slave, Nuzi law prohibited the expulsion of the slave – a custom that could provide a cultural context to explain why Abraham was so reluctant to send away Hagar and Ishmael (Genesis 21:9–13). Another way in which childless couples at Nuzi could ensure the continuation of their family line was by adopting a slave who would take the place of a son. Such a slave would then inherit their property – though if a natural son was eventually born, the slave-son would lose his rights. When Abraham expressed a fear that his slave Eliezer would succeed him (Genesis 15:1–4), some such custom could be implied. Other social conventions that appear in the stories of Jacob have also been documented at Nuzi.

Considerations of this kind may seem to provide compelling reasons for thinking that these stories of Abraham and Sarah and their descendants make most sense when understood as straightforward narratives of people living in the early part of the second millennium BC. But there are some arguments on the other side.

Anachronisms
Some elements of the stories certainly do not fit into the historical circumstances of the Middle Bronze Age. For example, we know for certain that neither Philistines (Genesis 21:34; 26:6–22) nor Chaldeans (Genesis 11:31; 15:7) were around at that period. It is also the case that camels (Genesis 12:16; 24:35; 30:43; 32:7, 15) were not in widespread use before the twelfth century BC. It is of course not difficult to explain such features as incidental anachronisms that were introduced unconsciously when the stories were first written down, reflecting the knowledge and experience of those who preserved and edited the stories at a much later date. They could even have been introduced deliberately, as a way of hinting at how the old traditions might still be relevant to the concerns of a changing world. Whatever the explanation, they do highlight the fact that these stories have been passed on and reformulated over several generations, and the form in which we now have them is the end product of a fairly extensive process of reinterpretation. By definition, therefore, the reinterpretation needs to be taken into account when seeking to understand them. At the same time, we should remember that the fact that a story has come through a long

One', Genesis 14:18–20), 'El Olam' ('El, the eternal one', Genesis 21:33), as well as 'El-Elohe-Israel' ('El, the God of Israel', Genesis 33:20). El was the chief deity of the Canaanite pantheon, documented most extensively in the religion of ancient Ugarit (which we consider in more detail in a later chapter). By the time of the final editing of the Old Testament books, it tended to be taken for granted that, though they had apparently not realized it, the God who actually was working in the lives of these

---

period of transmission does not of itself determine its literary genre. A narrative about events that allegedly took place sometime between 2000 and 1200 BC could easily have been written down much later without intrinsically being worthless as history. This is especially the case with stories that have been handed on by word of mouth for many generations before being committed to writing, and there are many examples of this in world literature, particularly accounts preserved in a non-Western context. The existence of anachronisms does not undermine this general consideration.

Interpreting cultural parallels
The way that some scholars have used the evidence from Nuzi and Mari to argue in favour of the essentially historical character of these stories has come under critical scrutiny, particularly from a methodological point of view:
● For such parallels to be really relevant and illuminating, they need to come from a time and place with which the Hebrew ancestors could reasonably be associated. In this case, the place is no problem, for both Mari and Nuzi are located in areas that feature prominently in the Genesis stories. But the date is another question. It has usually been claimed that these parallels date the patriarchs somewhere between 2000 and 1800 BC. The Nuzi texts, however, only go back to about 1500–1400 BC. Against this, it can be argued that customs of the sort described do not come from nowhere. They most typically evolve over a long period of time, and must therefore have existed long before they were written down. That is

probably true, but it proves less than some interpreters imagine, for they also continued long after the date of the written evidence, and most of the practices to which attention has been drawn were probably carried on throughout the whole period from 2000 to 1200 BC.
● The Nuzi materials have sometimes been used quite selectively. For example, the childless wife who gave her husband a slave girl was not at all typical of Nuzi practice in general. The more normal practice would have been for the man to be allowed to find another wife. There are in excess of 300 known texts from Nuzi that deal with family affairs, but less than half a dozen of them have been used to reconstruct a possible cultural background for the Genesis stories.
● In the past, some Nuzi texts have been misinterpreted in the enthusiastic rush to find parallels to the Old Testament. It was at one time claimed that a Nuzi text could explain Rachel's theft of Laban's household gods (Genesis 31:17–21). It was supposed that the possession of them would give her certain rights of inheritance. But it is now clear that the text believed to provide a 'parallel' does not suggest this at all. Of course, one mistaken parallel does not discount the others, but it should alert us to the difficulties involved in making such comparisons accurately so many centuries later. Part of the difficulty is that the Nuzi texts are legal documents, whereas in Genesis social and legal practices are described only incidentally. In such circumstances, it is all too easy to try to fill in what we perceive as gaps by stretching the external evidence to fit – even when it could be quite irrelevant.

ancient figures was the God Yahweh, whose full character was only apparent from the time of Moses onwards. But the stories themselves clearly preserve reminiscences of a belief that Israel's ancestors had been fully a part of the religious culture of Canaan, and when the nation's allegiances were later transferred to Yahweh, that was the starting point for the emergence of a different outlook on life.

Another feature common to these narratives is the way in which

---

Were Abraham and Sarah and their family real people?
continued

Abraham and Sarah's journeys.

It is clear from all this that some scholars have in the past tried to claim too much, in particular on the question of precise dates for the patriarchs. But it is equally clear that the way of life depicted in these stories in Genesis is quite different from the practices of later Israel, and has some significant similarities to what can otherwise be known of life in the second millennium BC. Any understanding of the historical setting of the family stories of Abraham, Isaac and Jacob must account for these features, which is why many scholars continue to believe that, whatever questions remain unsolved, the way to understand them is by starting from the

assumption that they preserve a broadly accurate account of the activities of those characters whom they describe. Perhaps in reality, though, the most that can be claimed with certainty is that the experiences these stories describe correspond to what is known of population movements that were taking place in the Fertile Crescent throughout the Middle and Late Bronze Ages (roughly 2000–1200 BC). Desert tribes were constantly moving into the Fertile Crescent from outside, and within this rich area individual tribes were always moving from one place to another in search of food and water for themselves and their flocks.

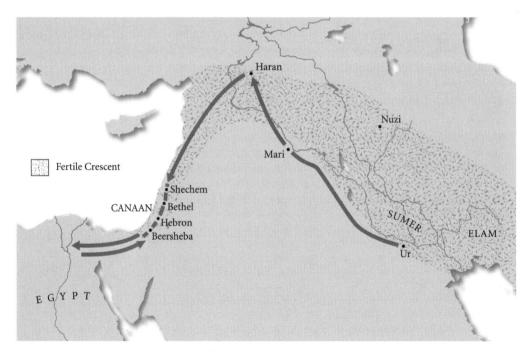

God is depicted not as a remote, impersonal force, but as a personal presence deeply connected to the concerns of everyday life. God helped them to find spouses and to have children, as well as meeting their deepest personal and emotional needs. This close involvement of God with the life of the family is repeatedly highlighted by the description of God as 'the God of my father' (Genesis 26:24; 31:5, 29, 42, 53; 32:9; 46:1, 3; 48:15; 49:25; 50:17). God was as close to them as their own family – indeed, in one sense could be thought of as a part of their family. God was the tribal leader. Though from today's perspective, we can no doubt appreciate the potential dangers in this way of thinking of God – for it was easily utilized in the establishment of a patriarchal culture in which men (tribal leaders) were placed in a unique relationship to God, ahead of that available to women and children – that should not prevent us from appreciating this insight into the personal nature of God as one of the most valuable spiritual legacies of this early generation not only to later Israel, but through them to Western culture more widely. There is a deep commitment here to the belief that faith can never be fully satisfied within the rituals of sacred spaces and times, but must be relevant and meaningful in the context of everyday life. Though Abraham's behaviour is frequently less than worthy, it is this aspect of the stories that caused later generations to bestow upon him the accolade of being a 'man of faith' (Hebrews 11:17–19), for he and Sarah found their new destiny through a wholehearted and open-ended commitment to what they knew of the God whom they worshipped.

The birth of the nation

A similar theme underlies the narrative that was to become the foundational story of the nation's self-consciousness: the deliverance of a group of their ancestors from slavery in Egypt in the event which came to be known as the exodus. We have now moved well beyond the story of Abraham and Sarah's first visit to Egypt, and into the family life of Jacob, their grandson. As a result of feuding and jealousy among Jacob's family, one of his sons found himself being sold into Egypt as a slave (Genesis 37:2–28). However, after many hardships and misadventures the unfortunate Joseph was unexpectedly elevated to an important position in Egyptian society. In the face of a great famine, the Egyptian king appointed this foreigner to supervise the rationing of food, and especially to control its distribution to those wandering pastoralists who would inevitably make their way over the Sinai peninsula from Canaan to the more prosperous land of Egypt (Genesis 41:14–57). It was while Joseph was engaged in this work that his brothers (who had sold him into slavery years before) came before him to ask for food, although he was unknown to them. After much suspense and heart-searching, Joseph revealed his true identity, and the brothers, along with their aged father, were reunited and went to live in Egypt (Genesis 42:1 – 45:28).

An Egyptian frieze depicts the harvesting of cereals. The Israelites were leaving the cultivated regions round the Nile for a wilderness where water was scarce and crops non-existent.

Their new-found prosperity was, however, only temporary. Jacob, Joseph, and the rest all died in old age, but their descendants were not to have a happy life. A new Egyptian ruler came to power, and he did not like what he saw: 'These Israelites are so numerous and strong that they are a threat to us' (Exodus 1:9). So the family of Jacob was gradually reduced to slavery, poverty and despair. It is tempting to set the story of Joseph in the times of the Hyksos empire in Egypt. These rulers were themselves non-Egyptians, and for that reason may have been more likely to appoint an outsider like Joseph to a position of some authority. Much of the detail of the Old Testament story seems to reflect what we know of the life of Egypt at this time – and the 'new king, who knew nothing about Joseph' (Exodus 1:8) would perhaps be an appropriate way to describe a native Egyptian king who came to power after the Hyksos had been removed from office.

Here again, this narrative displays the same tantalizing features as the earlier ancestral stories. While preserving just enough historical details to imply that all this could plausibly be related to what is otherwise known of Egyptian culture, the Old Testament takes no interest in such matters, preferring to concentrate on more intimate personal stories. For though this period of slavery was a real evil, it was also ultimately the source of great triumph, and this knowledge is what has determined the way in which the story was told to later generations. As the oppression of the slaves grew worse, so the need for deliverance grew stronger – deliverance that at first was an impossible dream, but which finally became a reality through the dynamic leadership of a man called Moses. Though he had an Egyptian name, and was brought up as an Egyptian, Moses had been born into an Israelite family (Exodus 2:1–10). Moses is depicted as a person with close familiarity with Egyptian

life and culture. Indeed, some have suggested there is enough evidence in the narrative to conclude that he was deeply influenced by the religion of Egypt, especially the worship of the sun god Aten. Akhen-aten, pharaoh of Egypt from 1369 to 1353 BC, had been a fanatical worshipper of this one god, and Moses also turned out to be devoted to the service of just one God, though not the same one. There are certainly some resemblances between Atenism and the worship of Yahweh introduced by Moses. Like Moses' God, Aten was described as 'the god beside whom there is none other'. The worshippers of Aten also laid heavy emphasis on teaching, just as the Torah later came to be associated with Moses. Parts of Psalm 104 praise the wonders of Yahweh's creation in language similar to an Egyptian hymn to the sun that was attributed to Akhen-aten. None of this proves anything specific about Moses and Egypt, for this use of similar language and imagery in worship was common throughout the ancient world. In any case many scholars think that the hymn of Akhen-aten was itself based on another piece of religious poetry that originated in Canaan.

What Moses taught the slaves from Egypt actually had many distinctive features that are not found in Egyptian religion. Like the early ancestors, Moses knew a God who was not just a manifestation of the world of nature, but the God who controlled the world and who could be known in a personal way. The origin of Moses' faith was found not in Egypt, but in the deserts of the Sinai Peninsula. After dropping out of Egyptian society, Moses had come to this region where he met Jethro, the leader of a nomadic tribe. He married Jethro's daughter, and looked after his flocks. It was while doing so that he met God, and standing by a bush that was on fire, yet seemed as if it would not burn away, Moses was commissioned by 'the God of Abraham, Isaac, and Jacob' to rescue the slaves from Egypt (Exodus 3:1–10). At that time, Moses had no interest in seeing either the Egyptians or the slaves, but he finally agreed to return to Egypt to try to persuade the king to release them. But he also had a message for the slaves themselves. In their affliction, they had not always remembered God. But now they would experience God for themselves in a new and dynamic way. For Moses took with him a fresh and deeper understanding of the nature of God: he was to tell the slaves in Egypt, 'The one who is called Yahweh has sent me to you' (Exodus 3:14). There are many unresolved questions about the precise meaning of this personal name of God, which are discussed more fully in a later chapter. It is not absolutely certain that the Hebrew letters YHWH should even be spelled or pronounced as 'Yahweh'. But in spite of that, the general significance of this personal name of God is clear. The meaning given in Exodus is 'I am who I am', that is, a declaration that Yahweh is the creator and sustainer of the whole world and its history. God's work began in the past, continues in the present, and will reach into the future.

The exodus

As with most of the earliest stories in the Hebrew Bible, there continues to be vigorous debate about the nature of the account of the exodus. But there has never been any doubt about its significance either for ancient Israelite faith, or for the Jewish religious tradition more widely. It is a central part of modern Judaism, celebrated in the annual Passover festival. At this, the Jewish child asks about its meaning, and is given the answer in the following traditional terminology:

> *We were Pharaoh's slaves in Egypt, and the Lord our God brought us forth with a mighty hand and an outstretched arm. And if the Holy One, Blessed be He, had not brought our forefathers forth from Egypt, then we, our children, and our children's children would still be slaves in Egypt. So, even though all of us were wise, all of us full of understanding... we should still be under the commandment to tell the story of the departure from Egypt. And the more one tells the story of the departure from Egypt, the more praiseworthy He is.*

Brick-making in Egypt has not changed all that much from the days of Israel's slavery. But they were reduced to making bricks without straw.

As far back as we can probe within the developing Old Testament library, it is impossible to find a single strand of the tradition which does

not, in some shape or form, have a place for the deeply held conviction that in these events God had been directly at work on the people's behalf. The conviction that in this event Israel had their true beginning is deeply embedded in the very oldest parts of the literature. As we shall see, there is much debate about the historical significance of it all, though it is hardly the sort of story that a proud nation would invent to explain its origin, if it had absolutely no basis in fact. Other Old Testament passages contain indications that suggest what later became the nation of Israel consisted of an amalgam of people drawn from various racial and cultural backgrounds, but it was to this event of the exodus, and to this particular group of ancestors, that Israel traced their unique relationship with God. They had not escaped by their own effort, for they had so internalized their oppression that the prospect of overcoming it had never occurred to them. Nor did they have a specially deserving cause, for the world of their day was full of dispossessed ethnic groups suffering at the hands of those who were more powerful.

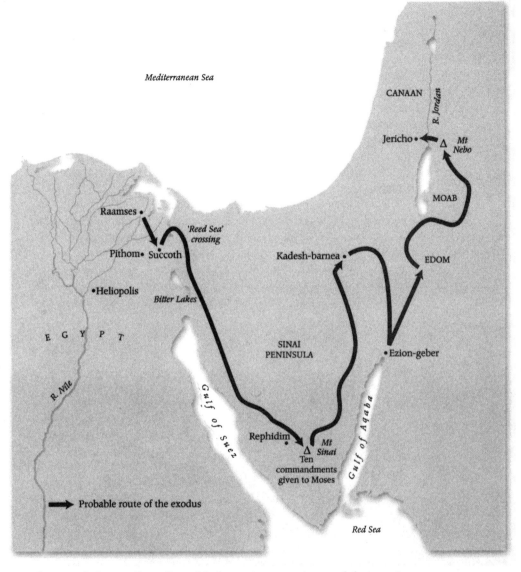

Mediterranean Sea

CANAAN

R. Jordan

Jericho • △ *Mt Nebo*

MOAB

Raamses •

'Reed Sea' crossing

Pithom • Succoth

Kadesh-barnea •

EDOM

• Heliopolis

Bitter Lakes

E G Y P T

SINAI PENINSULA

• Ezion-geber

R. Nile

Gulf of Suez

Gulf of Aqaba

Rephidim •

△ *Mt Sinai*
Ten commandments given to Moses

➤ Probable route of the exodus

Red Sea

The probable route of the exodus.

As the people later reflected on this formative experience of their nation, they could only conclude that it happened to them only because the God of whom Moses spoke had, for some inexplicable reason, chosen to deliver them.

The account of that momentous deliverance contains all the characteristic ingredients of a great epic story. The slaves leave secretly in the middle of the night, only to be pursued by the Egyptian armies. Then, just as they are about to be caught, trapped by a stretch of water, a way miraculously opens before them and the slaves get to the other side, while the pursuing army perishes beneath the waves (Exodus 12:1–51; 13:17–22; 14:1 – 15:27). Guided by Moses, they head out into the Sinai desert, and to their first and most important destination: Mount Sinai (Exodus 16:1 – 18:27). Much energy has been expended in trying to pinpoint an actual location for all these events. For example, the crossing of the water was traditionally located at some point on the Red Sea, though the Old Testament itself does not make this identification. The Hebrew text speaks of a 'sea of reeds', which would be an unlikely name for the Red Sea. In any case, the area of Goshen where the slaves had lived was much further north than the Red Sea, probably near the city of Avaris. It is therefore likely that, insofar as the writers of the story intended to point to a particular geographical location, the water that divided to allow the escaping slaves to cross was most probably somewhere in the region of what is now the Suez Canal.

The location of Mount Sinai is also a matter of some dispute. Traditionally, it has been located in the south of the Sinai Peninsula, at the site now called Jebel Musa. But since Moses' father-in-law Jethro, who was a Midianite, is clearly associated with this mountain, some have suggested that it should be located much further east, across the Gulf of Aqaba, which was the land of the Midianites (Exodus 3:1; 18:1–12). Others have suggested that Sinai should be located at Jebel Hilal, just to

The mountains of Sinai, where Israel's covenant relationship with Yahweh was formed.

the south of Palestine itself, since the escaping slaves had an encounter with Amalekites, who also lived much further north than the traditional site (Exodus 17:8–16). But it is difficult to locate the mountain by such considerations, for both these other ethnic groups were pastoral nomads themselves, and at any given moment could have been found almost anywhere in the region. It is certainly not unlikely that a group such as the Old Testament describes would have headed south on their escape from Egypt, rather than going directly east, for the main roads between Egypt and Canaan were patrolled by many Egyptian garrisons, whereas the only activity in the south centred around a number of isolated copper mines.

The covenant

The exodus itself was just the beginning of the story, and it was not until the escaping slaves reached Mount Sinai that the full impact and meaning of all this became clear to them. Just as the escape from Egypt formed the core of later Israel's national consciousness, so the events at Mount Sinai became the crucial factor in their religious outlook. For here in a solemn convocation, prompted by Moses, the escaping slaves recognized their debt to Yahweh

and pledged themselves to serve and worship this God alone (Exodus 19:1 – 24:18). Though the narrative contains both dramatic and terrifying descriptions of the presence of God on the holy mountain, the central feature of this awesome occasion was actually the commitment that God made to Israel, and the obligations that Israel accepted in return. God's care and concern for these enslaved people had been active even before they were aware of it. The escape from Egypt was the culmination of God's purposes for them, and the memory of that momentous event and the people's response to it came to dominate the national life of Israel. This is what the Old Testament means by 'the covenant': an agreement in which the freed slaves were reminded of what God had done for them, and they were called in return to promise to be loyal to the laws Moses now gave them in God's name. Somewhat surprisingly, these commands were essentially moral require- ments rather than being narrowly concerned with the observance of more obviously religious duties, such as worship. The tension between these two ways of understanding true spirituality was to extend throughout the subsequent history of the nation, but the central theme of the Old Testament is that honesty, truth and justice were far more important to Yahweh than the perfunctory performance of religious rites. These values are summarized in the ten commandments (Exodus 20:1–17) and, in important ways, can be said to have formed the basic foundation for the whole of later Israelite society.

At one time it was imagined that the high moral ideals recorded in the book of Exodus and elsewhere are too sophisticated to have originated in the primitive age of Moses, and therefore must have been read back into Israelite history at a relatively late stage in the editing of the stories, after the age of the great prophets. In the nineteenth century, there was much support for an evolutionary view of history, which imagined that the moral development of the human race must have

The ark of the covenant

The Old Testament depicts the spiritual realities of the covenant relationship being expressed in Israel's worship of God right from the very start, even in the desert. Worship there is described in a special tent-shrine, often called the 'tabernacle', at the centre of which was a wooden box called 'the ark of the covenant'. Like similar 'holy boxes' in Egypt, it was decorated with religious symbols, and overlaid with gold. Naturally, it needed to be portable, and was equipped with rings so it could be carried shoulder-high on poles. According to one of the most ancient pieces of poetry in the Old Testament, this portable ark represented in symbol the fact that God was with the escaping slaves (Numbers 10:35–36). Yahweh was not a God who could be depicted in a visual way, through a statue or some other artifact, but the ark served as a visible throne for the invisible Yahweh. It was a symbolic reminder of the central events of Mount Sinai, declaring that God was always with the people, and was to be their only guide. Indeed, the connection with the covenant-making events may have been quite a literal one, for at least one passage suggests that the ark itself contained the actual tablets on which the covenant agreement had been set out (1 Kings 8:9).

As time passed, the ark assumed even greater importance in the life of the people. The fates of Israel's earliest kings, Saul and David, hinged on their treatment of the ark. Saul despised it, and was rejected; David respected it, and was politically successful. It also came to play an important part in the worship of the Temple at Jerusalem. The liturgy contained within Psalm 132 suggests that in a covenant renewal ceremony the ark would be paraded through the streets of Jerusalem, before returning to the Temple as a sign of God's renewed and lasting presence with the nation. Other psalms also reflect its important position in the ritual of worship at the Temple, though they do not always mention it by name. Many scholars believe that when the Old Testament uses the title 'the Lord of hosts', this is a cryptic reference to God's presence as symbolized in the ark. Other terms, such as 'glory', also seem to be used regularly in reference to it (e.g. 1 Samuel 4:21–22). The Old Testament gives no hint of the ark's ultimate fate, though it is reasonable to suppose that it would be one of the religious objects that later kings of Judah moved in and out of the Temple as they changed their religious allegiances in the desperate effort to preserve political independence. Certainly, all trace of it disappears after the invasion of Nebuchadnezzar in 586 BC.

followed the principles of biological evolution, moving from primitive to more sophisticated moral attitudes. Since the prophets clearly had a highly developed moral sensitivity, then by definition previous generations must have operated with much cruder assumptions and expectations. Philosophically, this way of understanding human development was killed off early in the twentieth century by the manifest brutality of the First World War, and then later the Nazi holocaust, which showed that highly sophisticated people could easily behave in barbaric ways. In any case, growing knowledge of life in the ancient civilizations of the Akkadians, the Sumerians, the Egyptians and others has shown that their standards of morality were very highly developed, and much of the civil (case) law of the Old Testament bears a close resemblance to concepts of justice going back at least as far as the law code of King Hammurabi of Babylon (c. 1700 BC). Some scholars have argued that the distinctively religious and moral requirements of the Old Testament law (the apodictic law) can also be traced to a very early period. It seems that an important aspect of the religious life of Israel was a festival held every autumn, in which the covenant between God and the people was both celebrated and renewed. On this occasion, the people were reminded of what God had done for them, and of the responsibilities placed on them in return – to which they in turn would then reaffirm their allegiance. It is assumed

The form of the covenant

The general idea of a 'covenant' was not unique to ancient Israel. Covenants regulated all sorts of behaviour in the ancient world, notably international relations. Close scrutiny of the legal framework of the covenant drawn up between Israel and God at Mount Sinai reveals a number of similarities to other legal documents from the Late Bronze Age period (1550–1200 BC). One of the clearest examples of this legal form is to be found in a series of treaties relating to the Hittite empire, spelling out the duties of smaller states which had been annexed by the more powerful Hittites. Similar legal formulations were also used by other nations, and naturally their subject matter was generally of a political nature. But they are of interest to Old Testament scholars because of a number of formal elements that they have in common with the way the covenant made at Mount Sinai was expressed. The following similarities can be traced:

● **Introduction of the speaker** In a political treaty, the king would introduce himself by name, just as God does in the introduction to the ten commandments (Exodus 20:2).

● **Historical background** The king then reminded the other party of what he had done on their behalf – usually military intervention of some kind. In the Old Testament, God reminds the people of their unexpected deliverance from Egypt (Exodus 20:2).

● **Requirements** Then follow the obligations which are placed by the king on the other party. In a political treaty these would normally be military obligations, while in the Old Testament they consist of the requirements of the Law.

● **The document** Arrangements were then made for the treaty to be written down, and deposited in a suitable place to be read at specified times. There is no such provision directly linked to the ten commandments in the book of Exodus, but similar instructions are given in Deuteronomy 27:1–8.

that the ten commandments, and other laws associated with them in the book of Exodus, would be recited on these occasions. Since evidence for such a covenant renewal ceremony appears quite early in the narratives of Israel's story, there is every reason to suppose that the high ideals found there, and the covenant basis on which they exist, go back to the earliest period of Israel's experience of God.

To the promised land

Most of the material in the books of Exodus, Leviticus, Numbers and Deuteronomy is set in the context of an extended journey by the liberated slaves, as they crossed the desert from Egypt to the land of Canaan, where they would eventually settle. Like other aspects of the earliest stories of the nation, all this was eventually edited into its present form from the perspective of a quite different political and spiritual situation many centuries after the events it describes. Embedded within the narratives, however, are glimpses of the kind of challenges that people would have encountered at that historical period. Like many emerging nations, they began as a motley collection of refugees, who were joined by other people as they left the land of Egypt, and the events at Mount Sinai then became the first stage in the process by which this disparate bunch of people began to be moulded into the nucleus of a

---

The form of the covenant *continued*

● **Witnesses** were called to seal the covenant – usually the deities of both states. The Old Testament contains several examples of witnesses to the covenant. In Exodus 24, twelve pillars were set up, probably for this purpose, while a central part of the covenant ceremony recorded in Joshua 24 consisted of a large stone being put in a public place to serve as a witness to the promises that had been made (Joshua 24:25–28).

● **Curses and blessings** were then invoked, depending on whether the treaty was observed or disregarded. In the Old Testament, there is a long series of such curses and blessings in the book of Deuteronomy (Deuteronomy 27:11 – 28:68).

It is not suggested that a legal document of this kind was self-consciously used to form a basis for the way in which the covenant between Yahweh and Israel was set out. Indeed, it is not possible to make an exact correlation between the covenant made at Mount Sinai and these covenant forms used in the political sphere. For example, while it is not at all difficult to locate all the elements of the secular treaty form somewhere in the Old Testament, there is no one single context which contains them all. In addition, since the Israelites perceived themselves as being in covenant with God, rather than with a military ruler, that must presumably have added a distinctive element to how the covenant would be understood and expressed. However, there are indications that Israel was familiar with this form of political covenant, for they made one themselves with the Gibeonites (Joshua 9). In addition, the fact that the events at Mount Sinai were articulated and preserved in a form of words that had such a widespread use in the Late Bronze Age – which was certainly the time of Israel's emergence as a nation – can be taken to imply that, whatever other questions may remain outstanding, the origin of Israel's distinctive faith may quite plausibly be traced back to the earliest period of national consciousness.

single nation. As they pressed on towards their ultimate goal, the journey through the desert was to prove hazardous. Not only were the refugees forced to work out the full implications of their embryonic faith in terms of their everyday living, but they also found themselves in conflict with other groups of wandering nomads who, like them, were wanting to establish a permanent homeland for themselves. But these isolated political and military skirmishes are not the central concern of the story. The one thread that holds everything else together is Moses' faith and determination. Though he himself did not live to set foot in the land that was to become his people's national home, he had no doubt of the final outcome of their quest for self-determination. Like the members of Abraham and Sarah's family before him, he was convinced that the direction of his own life, and the future of the escaped slaves and their descendants, was not at the mercy of impersonal social and political forces, but would always be under the care and protection of a loving and all-powerful God: 'People of Israel, no god is like your God... There is no one like you, a nation saved by Yahweh [who is] your shield and your sword, to defend you and give you victory' (Deuteronomy 33:26, 29).

Flocks of migrating quails would appear in the wilderness, and they became a source of food for the Israelites as they journeyed through the desert. Quails were also eaten by the Egyptians, as depicted in this wall painting of men using nets to catch the birds.

Dating the exodus and conquest of Canaan

The question of Israel's emergence as a nation is one of the most hotly debated aspects of Old Testament scholarship today. There are many diverse and mutually exclusive views on the matter. Some have complete confidence in using the Bible stories of exodus and conquest as a basis for historical investigation, while others dismiss these narratives entirely as the creation of later generations, specifically the attempts of the royal house of David to establish a long historical pedigree for itself. In between, it is possible to find every imaginable shade of opinion on the matter. So asking how we might date these events is not a simple matter, and many scholars would say it is a waste of time to try to do so anyway. There are certainly many complex issues involved, and there is much confusion over basic issues, such as the nature of the 'conquest' itself. This debate is discussed in relation to the emergence of Israel as an identifiable nation in Canaan in the next chapter. Here we shall confine ourselves to a review of some of the evidence that has been deemed to relate to a possible date for the exodus.

Attempts to set a date for the exodus have ranged from the third millennium to the eleventh century BC, though three possibilities have received more support than others:
● Some place the exodus in the middle of the sixteenth century BC, at the time when the Hyksos were expelled from Egypt. This view goes back at least as far as the first-century AD Jewish historian Josephus, who equated the two events (*Against Apion* 1.16). This is certainly the only known large-scale population movement of ethnically Asiatic peoples from Egypt in roughly the direction of Canaan. In spite of its attractions, this view is hard to justify, if only because it would imply that a further 400 years elapsed before the formation of anything that can be identified as an Israelite state, under Saul and David.

● Others, beginning from what seems to be the chronology of the Bible itself, have placed the exodus in about 1440 BC. But this is problematical for a variety of reasons, especially the difficulty of correlating it with any possible interpretation of the archaeological evidence relating to early Israel, and again the excessively long time span that would need to be covered by the period of the Judges.
● The most widely accepted date would place the exodus somewhere between about 1280 and 1240 BC. This seems to accord with some of the archaeological evidence, and also matches what is otherwise known about population movements and the emergence of new settlements not only in Canaan itself, but in the region to the east of the River Jordan as well.

The chronological evidence which has been used to try to establish some plausible date for the exodus falls into three main categories: the biblical material, various textual remains ar.._ the discoveries of archaeologists in Canaan. They do not always all point in the same direction as one another, hence the diversity of opinions on the matter.

Old Testament dates

According to 1 Kings 6:1, Solomon began to build the Temple in Jerusalem in the fourth year of his reign, which is said to be 'Four hundred and eighty years after the people of Israel left Egypt'. Working back from Solomon's time, this would imply that the editor of Kings believed the exodus took place in about 1440 BC. However, even the evidence of the Old Testament itself does not consistently support that:
● The book of Judges contains a good many chronological indications, and adding together the successive periods of rule of the various judges gives a minimum time between the exodus and Solomon of 554 years. Of course, we do not know for certain that the judges followed one another in chronological succession. Since

they were mainly local leaders, there was probably a good deal of overlap between them, in which case the total time span indicated in Judges could in reality be much less than it first seems to be. In addition, the period of forty years often figures in these stories, and that was a conventional way of referring to the time from one generation to the next – so perhaps it was never intended to be a very precise measurement of time.

● At the end of the book of Ruth, the genealogy of Solomon separates him from Nahshon, his ancestor who lived at the time of the exodus (Numbers 1:7), by only six generations. That would normally be about 200 years – though here, as in other biblical ancestor lists, some generations may have been left out.

● According to Exodus 12:40, the Israelite tribes left Egypt after they had lived there for 430 years. That would seem to imply a possible date for the exodus in about 1250 BC, which in turn would mean that Joseph went to Egypt in the time of the Hyksos rulers, something that at least sounds plausible because as non-Egyptians themselves they would have been more likely than native rulers to favour a person like Joseph. This timescale would also appear to rule out the traditional view that the exodus took place around 1440 BC, because adding 430 years to that would arrive at a date for Joseph much earlier than any plausible dating of the generation represented by the stories of Abraham. Here again, though, even the biblical evidence is not straightforward for the Septuagint makes the 430 years include both the time the Israelites were in Egypt, and the time they were in Canaan prior to that.

The only reasonable conclusion is that the dates in the Old Testament are inconsistent, and in particular the indication contained in 1 Kings 6:1 is problematic. Of course, it may well be that it was never intended to be taken as a strictly chronological statement, for 480 years is twelve times forty, which could be

a way of indicating a dozen generations, or simply a very long time. Insofar as the other biblical dates can be harmonized with one another, they appear to imply a thirteenth-century date for the exodus.

Evidence from other texts

The Amarna Letters are one particular source of information used by scholars to elucidate aspects of this period. They consist of a series of pillar-shaped tablets written in cuneiform script, mostly in a form of Akkadian, which was the diplomatic language of the time. They date from the early fourteenth century, and were written by various rulers in Canaan

The Amarna Letters, tablets written in cuneiform script, give evidence of a period of instability in their relationships between Egypt and its neighbours in the years before Israel settled in Canaan.

and Syria to Pharaoh Akhen-aten (1369–1353 BC) and his predecessor Amenhotep III (1398–1361 BC). In particular, they complain of the activities of groups of people called 'apiru' (also

Dating the exodus and conquest of Canaan *continued*

variously spelled 'hapiru', 'habiru' and 'aperu'), whose warlike activities were creating tensions and disturbance throughout the area. The names 'apiru' and 'Hebrew' probably have some linguistic connection, though it is not possible to make a simple identification between these groups and the stories of Israel's early life in Canaan. At least one letter refers to them as former slaves, while the general picture is of a significant underclass on the fringes of Canaanite society who, if they succeeded in their aims, were regarded as likely to provide a rallying-point around which other disadvantaged people might gather and instigate some sort of social revolution. As we will see when we move on to the stories of Joshua and Judges, this seems to have been one aspect of the upheavals that took place as Israelite culture came to birth.

The 'shasu' are another group of nomadic people mentioned in various Egyptian texts compiled between about 1500 and 1150 BC. Their lifestyle is also described in terms reminiscent of the Old Testament depictions of early Israel, wandering in and out of Egyptian settlements, sometimes living peaceably, at other times engaged in military skirmishes, and again occasionally being captured as slaves.

While various scholars have claimed that either or both of the apiru and shasu peoples are to be identified with groups that later became part of Israel, the main value of these records is to show that the kind of population movements described in the accounts of the exodus do seem to reflect what was happening on the borders of Egypt and Canaan during the Late Bronze Age. Insofar as they may be relevant, these texts therefore seem to support a date for the exodus in the thirteenth century BC.

Archaeological evidence

Exodus 1:11 names two Egyptian cities and claims that 'The Israelites built the cities of Pithom and Rameses to serve as supply centres for the king [of Egypt].'

This relief, from the temple of Rameses II, depicts prisoners of different nationalities, and gives some indication of the extent of Egyptian military activity. From the left, a Libyan, a Syrian, a Hittite, a Philistine and another Syrian.

Pithom was actually an old town, but the finest structure in it was a temple built by Rameses II (1290–1224 BC), and there is no evidence for any earlier pharaoh building there. Rameses is certainly to be identified with the capital city of Rameses II, built by him on the site of the ancient capital Tanis. This may have been the capital of the Hyksos kings in the century preceding their expulsion in 1540 BC, but the pharaohs of the succeeding dynasty had their capital at Thebes (except for Akhen-aten, who moved even further from Tanis). All this would appear to support the notion that the exodus took place sometime after 1290 BC. Evidence from the reign of a later pharaoh, Merneptah, suggests that it could not have been later than about 1240 BC, for in 1220 BC he recorded an attack on various peoples in Canaan, in the course of which he mentions 'Israel' as a recognizable component of the Canaanite population.

The archaeological evidence from Canaan itself, however, is more uncertain and its interpretation continues to be the subject of changing fads and fashions among scholars. There is a more extensive account of this debate in the next chapter, but a number of points should be noted in relation to its possible relevance to dating the exodus:

● At one time, the strongest argument for dating the exodus towards the end of the fifteenth century BC was the conclusion of archaeologist John Garstang that Jericho had been taken by Joshua not later than 1400 BC. Indeed, he excavated the remains of walls and other buildings which he believed proved the literal truth of the Old Testament story even down to its details. However, it is now known for certain that his interpretation of the evidence does not square with the facts.

● Much the same is true for most other sites that have been excavated. For while there is much evidence of destruction throughout Canaan in the thirteenth century BC, there is nothing much that can positively be connected with the Old Testament story. Many sites do provide evidence of a destruction in which the sophisticated culture of the Canaanite city states was replaced by a much more primitive lifestyle, and some scholars have taken this as evidence of the Israelite invasion. But in reality, it is not quite so simple, for there is no real knowledge about the nature of a typically Israelite culture at this period, other than what might be deduced from the self-validating assumption that this less sophisticated style must have been Israelite. In any case, with only a few exceptions, the cities that have yielded most evidence for such a thirteenth-century destruction are not those that feature most prominently in the Old Testament record.

There are so many different possible conclusions to be drawn from all this conflicting data that almost the only safe thing to say is that we cannot certainly date the exodus, though a majority of scholars who engage with this discussion would tend to place it in the thirteenth century. However, there are so many uncertainties in this entire enterprise that a growing number of scholars are wondering whether this is the right kind of question to be asking. Should it be that, instead of searching for evidence of a once-for-all conquest of Canaan by the Israelite tribes, their arrival in the land ought rather to be understood from a completely different perspective – either by supposing that only one particular group of what later came to be Israel was involved in the exodus events, or by seeing the emergence of Israel as a nation more in terms of the internal development and change of Canaanite society itself? These possibilities cannot be considered in relation to the exodus without also taking account of the stories of the Israelite conquest of Canaan contained in the books of Joshua and Judges.

3 A Land Flowing with Milk and Honey

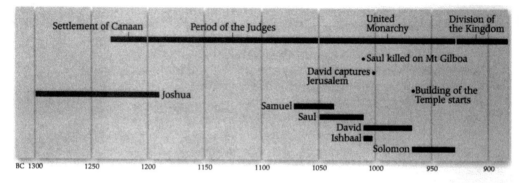

Settlement of Canaan	Period of the Judges	United Monarchy	Division of the Kingdom

• Saul killed on Mt Gilboa

David captures • Jerusalem

Joshua

•Building of the Temple starts

Samuel

Saul

David

Ishbaal

Solomon

BC 1300   1250   1200   1150   1100   1050   1000   950   900

Canaan and its history

The land of Canaan had a long and illustrious history. Documents discovered at Ebla in north Syria testify to the existence of many important towns there as early as 2300 BC, and the city of Jericho is believed to be the oldest inhabited settlement in the world, going back perhaps as far as 9000 BC. Throughout most of the second millennium BC this land was controlled by the Egyptians, who generally governed it through local rulers, of whom there were a great many. Both Egyptian records of the time and archaeological findings from different sites reveal a complex system of intensely populated city states, especially in the central, most fertile parts of the country. Each city was independent and self-sufficient, with its own land and its own rulers. The next city might be as little as 3 miles (5 km) away, but every local king was considered to be directly responsible to Egypt, rather than to other neighbouring rulers. This was an important part of Egyptian policy, and helped to minimize the possibility of local alliances emerging to challenge Egyptian rule. Throughout ancient times, the land of Canaan was always of strategic importance to whatever major power was dominant in the region. The great trade routes linking Egypt with Mesopotamia ran through this land, and the greatest concentration of small city states was to be found alongside the road from Egypt to Syria, ensuring that strategic sites were controlled by vassal rulers who could be trusted to maintain Egypt's own security. In the hill country, things

This stone monument (or 'stele') was erected by King Merneptah of Egypt after a military expedition into Canaan. Its text includes the earliest reference to 'Israel' outside the Bible.

were never quite so well organized. Fewer people wanted to live there anyway, and in addition, a city in the hills needed much more land to be self-sufficient. For this reason, it had always been easier for pastoralist nomads to move about in these more remote areas of the country.·

By the end of the Late Bronze Age, however, Egypt's power was diminishing, and towards the end of the thirteenth century BC we find the first reference outside the Bible to 'Israel' as the name of a nation. After a military expedition into Canaan, Pharaoh Merneptah of Egypt (1213–1203 BC) constructed a stone monument as a record of his exploits. In its inscription, he gives an account of various Canaanite people whom he had defeated: 'Ashkelon has been overcome; Gezer has been captured; Yanoam is made non-existent; Israel is laid waste and his seed is not.' The actual terminology used in this inscription is significant in understanding the nature of 'Israel' at this period. The fact that Israel is listed alongside other significant powers within Canaan suggests that it was a force to be reckoned with, and in military terms was their equal, if not an actual partner in some anti-Egyptian coalition. However, the phraseology of the inscription draws a subtle distinction between Ashkelon, Gezer and Yanoam as fortified city states, and Israel as a more loosely organized people group, which may not have had fixed territorial boundaries.

This inscription is complemented by a series of four battle reliefs in the temple at Karnak, which were once believed to have been commissioned by Rameses II, but are now considered to be the work of Merneptah, depicting the same three city states and the 'people' of Israel. This is the earliest-known visual representation of Israelites, and the

For centuries before the time of Israel's entry into Canaan, Egypt had raided other lands and taken captives. This relief from a temple at Abusir shows an Egyptian ocean-going vessel laden with Syrian prisoners. The masts of the boat have been lashed down, and the three rudders lifted out of the water.

interesting thing about it is that it shows them dressed in exactly the same way as the other Canaanites, and not like nomadic 'shasu', implying that these particular Israelites, at least, were not nomadic migrants, but indigenous Canaanites.

In the event, Merneptah's optimism about his military achievements turned out to be unjustified, for Egypt's power in the area soon collapsed, and the strong alliance of Egyptian-backed Canaanite city states began to lose its grip. Within a short time, the whole land had fallen into the hands of only four or five separate rulers, all of whom were newcomers. Israel was certainly one such group, while the Philistines were another. Egyptian records mention the arrival of at least two separate waves of 'Sea Peoples' during the thirteenth and twelfth centuries BC. They consisted of several groups of migrants, all of whom threatened Egyptian dominance of the region. Prominent in the second wave were the Philistines, though they were not the only group among these 'Sea Peoples', which also included the Tjeker, Shekelesh, Denyen and Weshnesh – none of whom feature in the narratives of the Old Testament. These related groups appear to have originated from Crete and the area around the Aegean Sea, to the east of Greece, and had been recruited as mercenaries to help fortify and defend the Canaanite city states. A temple inscription of Rameses III (1198–1167 BC) depicts these people, and shows not only soldiers, but also women and children, suggesting that they were not just armies, but entire populations, searching for a new place in which to live. The Philistines later appear in the Bible narratives as Israel's major competitors, struggling to gain control of the same land. They eventually settled mainly along the sea coast, adopting the same kind of political structure that the Egyptians had imposed, and establishing five city states of their own: Gaza, Ashkelon, Ashdod, Ekron and Gath. They also eventually gave their name to the whole country (Palestine). But at this earlier period, they were just one of several ethnic groups – Israel included – who were struggling to establish a foothold in Canaan, and given that what became Israel seems to have incorporated people of different origins, it is even conceivable that some of those who were originally the 'Sea Peoples' were included in what later became 'Israel'.

The one distinguishing feature of the state that eventually emerged as 'Israel' seems to have been its concept of statehood. Under the old regime in Canaan, political power had always gone hand in hand with the possession of a city, which in turn meant that real power always resided in the hands of just a few privileged people. But the kind of state that developed under the influence of the covenant from Mount Sinai was underwritten by a different understanding of human society, in which class structure had no part to play. For a nation whose corporate identity was forged out of the story of a group of people who had been slaves, it was difficult to justify any one individual claiming a position of personal superiority, for in the beginning they had all been nobodies, and the only thing that made them a nation was the undeserved generosity of God. Israelite national identity was always firmly based on their understanding of the nature of God, and this was to have far-reaching consequences not only during the formative period of their history, but also throughout their entire existence as a nation. It meant that all elements of their population were of equal importance, and their ultimate responsibility was not to some centralized power structure, but to God alone.

The emergence of Israel

These changes in Canaanite political life are all well documented from Egyptian records, as well as by archaeological evidence from various sites throughout the land itself. Between about 1400 and 1200 BC, there was radical transformation of many aspects of life in Canaan. The power of Egypt declined, and the relatively advanced culture of the Canaanite city states was mostly replaced by a different way of life, and shortly after the end of this period, Israel had emerged as a recognizable national entity of some kind. So much is clear. But beyond that there is no generally agreed understanding of the course of Israel's development at this period, and in trying to integrate all the many different strands of information relating to the changing culture of Late Bronze Age Canaan, perhaps the only certain conclusion is that the story of how the nation of Israel first took shape within this context is going to be very complex. Great political and social movements leading to the formation of a new nation can hardly be simple and straightforward, though there is always a strong temptation to search for neat solutions to questions about such matters. It is intrinsically probable that the people of Israel became a nation in their own land by adopting different tactics at different times and places. The Bible story itself describes a 'mixed multitude' of various ethnic origins attaching themselves to the Israelite slaves who left Egypt (Exodus 12:38), and other hints throughout the narratives of Joshua and Judges imply that the emergence of Israel did not happen in a simple linear fashion. The Old Testament itself incorporates diverse strands in its stories, and during the course of the twentieth century different scholars formed their own theories in the effort to explain exactly how these strands related to one another and how they can be understood in the light of known facts about changes taking place in Canaan during the Late Bronze Age and on into the beginning of the Iron Age. All of them can claim some support in the Old Testament itself, but none is entirely free from problems. Over the years, at least three main models have been used to try to give the best explanation of how the nation of Israel emerged from the changing social and political circumstances of Canaan at this period.

Armed struggle

A quick reading of the stories in the Old Testament book of Joshua can give the impression that the land of Canaan became the land of Israel almost overnight, as a result of a series of spectacular battles and conquests. In fact, the account in Joshua records the capture of only a few Canaanite city states, and makes it clear that even at the end of Joshua's successful military exploits much of the land remained unconquered (Joshua 13:1–7). Nevertheless, the successes of Joshua's armies form the core of the Old Testament story, and many scholars believe that the successful establishment of the Israelite tribes in Canaan owed more to this than to any other cause.

The evidence of archaeology has often been claimed to support this belief. In the 1930s, John Garstang carried out extensive excavations at the site of Jericho, and discovered what he took to be incontrovertible evidence of Joshua's capture of the city: walls that had literally fallen flat, and much evidence of destruction by fire (Joshua 6). On his calculations, this destruction had happened not long after 1400 BC, and since he gave a fifteenth-century date to the exodus, this therefore coincided almost exactly with the time when he believed the Israelite armies were invading the land. Investigations by later archaeologists, however, have shown this conclusion to be totally false. Following the usual procedure, Garstang dated his finds by reference to the layer of the mound at Jericho in which he found them, but what he did not know was that over the centuries much of the top of the mound had

Although the book of Joshua suggests that the Canaanites were easily defeated by Israel, this may only have been because the separate city states failed to unite. Their weaponry, from war chariots down to swords and daggers such as these, was fairly sophisticated.

been worn away at this point – and for that reason, the remains he found were actually from a much lower level than they appeared to be. In fact, they were from a city that had existed on the site a full 1,000 years earlier than the time of Joshua. Unless other finds come to light (and archaeologists have not yet worked over the whole mound of Jericho), it seems that nothing substantial is left of the city that stood there at the end of the Late Bronze Age.

Evidence from other sites is more specific, and shows signs of widespread violence and disruption in many cities during the thirteenth century BC. The fact that this destruction was apparently followed by the emergence of a more primitive culture than the one it replaced has been taken to prove that it was the work of the Israelite tribes, on the assumption that nomads coming in from the desert would have a less sophisticated way of life than that of the Canaanite city states. None of this can prove by itself that the destruction uncovered by archaeologists was the work of Israel's armies, or indeed that it happened as a result of any kind of invasion from outside: it is at least as plausible that this evident collapse of Canaanite culture came about because of internal feuding among the city states, which in turn was encouraged by the decline of the Egyptian power that had so successfully united the land. In addition, since the people who later emerged as 'Israel' were not the only ones trying to establish themselves at this time, much of this disruption could as easily be attributed to Philistines, Ammonites or others.

Facing page: the division of Canaan between the tribes of Israel.

While it is natural to speculate, the truth is that archaeology really has little useful information to offer on a possible Israelite conquest of the land. This has led some to doubt whether there ever was a 'conquest' in any significant sense. They point out that the military strength of the Canaanite city states would easily have repelled wandering tribes with no previous experience of warfare, especially since the Canaanites possessed relatively sophisticated equipment, such as chariots. This argument, however, can be turned on its head in light of the fact that the existing Canaanite culture was already declining at this time – not to mention the fact that, throughout history, minority groups inspired by a vision of what they believe to be right have often been able to overthrow highly organized and well-equipped armies that in theory should have quelled their opposition effortlessly. The whole picture of Israel's early history is so dominated by the stories of military success that it is hard to ignore it completely without dismissing the Old Testament account altogether. Equally, however, it is not the only element in the Old Testament story, even if it is the most prominent. The book of Joshua itself claims only that military campaigns secured a foothold in the central hill country which was to be the heart of Israelite territory, while the flatter and more fertile areas like the Plain of Jezreel were not taken over at this time – and in addition, many fortified towns such as Jerusalem and Gezer also stayed firmly in Canaanite hands.

Peaceful infiltration

The apparently incomplete nature of the initial conquest of the country has led other scholars to suggest that much – or even all – of the land was taken over in a different way as the Israelite tribes gradually infiltrated Canaanite society until eventually they became the dominant group. This understanding of the situation has been especially articulated by the German scholar Albrecht Alt. He began by analysing the social structure of the land both before and after the period when Israel was emerging as a nation, noting that the organization of Israelite society was quite different from the closely controlled hierarchies that had been established under the Canaanite city states. But he also drew attention to the fact that those invaders like the Philistines, who settled where the city states had been strongest, were forced by social and economic pressures to take over this form of government themselves. Since this did not happen in Israel, he argued that the Israelites must have established their rule first in those parts of the land where the power of the city states was minimal, that is in the hill country. Instead of a violent conquest, Alt believed that the Israelite tribes had settled in a gradual way. As pastoral nomads they had originally wandered about with their flocks from season to season, but as they began to stay for longer periods in particular places they were able to penetrate the structure of the few power centres that were to be found in the hill country, and eventually became the most significant element of the settled population.

This view clearly has some considerations in its favour:
■ It is consistent with the fact that the new settlements were in the poorer hill country rather than the central plains. Nomadic people attempting to settle permanently would be more likely to inhabit remote villages first, rather than taking on the military might of the strong city states.
■ It also fits with the archaeological evidence, which bears witness to occasional battles and destruction of cities rather than to a coherent and extensive military invasion.
■ The way of life of the 'shasu' described in Egyptian documents corresponds closely to Alt's hypothesis, and according to some interpreters, texts referring to them can be understood to imply that they worshipped a god with a name similar to Yahweh.
■ The Old Testament itself provides evidence that some cities came into Israelite hands by other means than conquest. Shechem is a good example, for there is no record of a military conquest there by Joshua, and yet even before his death it had become a major centre of Israelite activity, and seems to have served as a sort of capital town (Joshua 24). The evidence of archaeology is consistent with this, for Shechem did not share in the wave of destruction and decline that can be documented elsewhere in the thirteenth century BC. Others have drawn attention to an earlier story telling how Shechem was conquered by

Jacob and his sons, and try to integrate that into the armed struggle model by suggesting that when the invading tribes arrived several centuries later they found the city was occupied by people who were, literally, their relatives, and this is why they did not need to overthrow it (Genesis 34; 48:22). Either way, Shechem provides an example of a city that passed from being Canaanite to Israelite in a more or less peaceful way.

Overall, however, this understanding of the emergence of Israel has won few supporters. It is doubtful whether Israel's earliest nomadic life followed the kind of pattern that Alt suggested, and in addition it is very difficult on this understanding to explain why the story of the exodus should have come to occupy such a central place in the thinking of people who not only had not shared in the experience themselves, but who also, as outsiders entering a new land, would presumably have had their own traditions of their origins and forebears.

Social revolution

Yet another possibility that has been put forward is the idea that some inhabitants of Canaan could have been won over to Israel's side by a process of political and religious conversion. The family of the prostitute Rahab at Jericho may be an example of this (Joshua 6:22–25), as also may be another group associated with the city of Bethel (Judges 1:22–26). Then there is the rather odd position of the Gibeonites, who came and asked to be incorporated into the nation of Israel, and who were accepted by Joshua on the basis of a covenant treaty (Joshua 9).

Incidents like these have been taken as evidence that Israel's 'conquest' of Canaan was far more dependent on moral victories than on military might. Indeed some have asserted that there was no 'conquest' in any physical sense at all, but that what changed the population from 'Canaanites' into 'Israelites' was the result of some sort of social revolution, a 'peasants' revolt', inspired not by political considerations, but by moral and religious convictions. They point out that the understanding of God's character preserved in the stories of the covenant at Mount Sinai was quite different from other religious and political belief systems of the region. Moses had spoken of a God who was interested in people on a personal level, and was active in the events of everyday life for their benefit. From what is known of religion in Canaan, the gods were there to preserve the existing order both in the world of nature and in the world of politics. They were powerful supporters of the ruling classes, whereas the God of Israel was committed to supporting the oppressed and downtrodden – and had proved it in the events of the exodus. It is therefore not surprising that many Canaanite peasants should have been attracted by this new assessment of the human situation. Among scholars holding to this position, various explanations are given as to how this might have happened, whether as a result of a group who had been part of the exodus experience coming in and inspiring others to revolt through the sharing of their story, or as a more indigenous movement among the existing population of Canaan. On this understanding most, if not all, of the people who were later known as Israelites were originally Canaanites, and 'Israel' was not so much an ethnic group as a spiritual and political ideology.

This view has been criticized on the grounds that it owes more to a Marxist view of history than to any objective evidence. It also struggles to explain how, if the 'conquest' was an internal revolt, the characteristically 'Israelite' settlements were restricted to the relatively infertile hill country. If Canaan became Israel by overthrowing the original rulers, why did the victors not take over the best land, instead

'Canaanites' and 'Israelites'

The Old Testament narratives draw a simple demarcation between people they call 'Canaanites' and the nation of Israel. Understandably, the nature of these Canaanites is never clearly spelled out, if only because the Old Testament historians were most interested in the Israelites, and as a result 'Canaanite' is mostly used as a blanket term to describe whoever were the inhabitants of Palestine before the emergence of Israel as a separate entity. So far as we know, there was no one group of people during the period of which we are speaking (Late Bronze Age) who would have described themselves as 'Canaanites'. Indeed, there is very little evidence to suggest that Canaan would have been thought of as a definable territorial location. The Amarna Letters, for example, use the term but do not identify it. That may have been for the simple reason that both writers and readers already knew where it was anyway, though there is not absolute consistency in the way it is used, with some letters including a place like Ugarit within Canaan, while others exclude it. Most likely, 'Canaan' was at this time a general way of referring to the whole of Syria and northern Palestine.

If the land of Canaan itself is difficult to define with precision, then the nature of its population raises even more questions, and during the period when Israel was emerging as a nation it seems to have

of moving out to the margins? Supporters of this view also need to explain why, on the face of it, the Bible tells such a different story. Given the multifaceted nature of the Old Testament narratives, and the variable nature of the information they provide regarding early Israel, it might have been expected that if there was a successful internal Canaanite revolt of this kind, at least some indication of it would have remained embedded in the traditional stories. At the same time, it does address some facts that the other models find problematic:

■ There is evidence of a strong element of continuity between the culture of Canaan and what emerged as the culture of Israel. The Ugaritic texts, discussed below, show that early expressions of Israelite

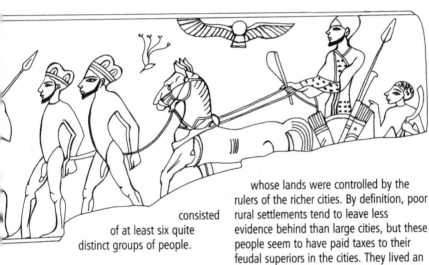

This ivory tablet, found at Megiddo, probably commemorates the victory of a Canaanite king. He is seated at the left on his throne, and before him is shown a queen or goddess and a musician with a lyre. The king appears again on the right in his chariot. Two prisoners are roped to his horse's bridle.

consisted of at least six quite distinct groups of people.

City states

Politically, the most obvious feature of this area was a large number of semi-autonomous city states. These were all heavily fortified, and must have had large armies. The different types of housing found in them also indicates a social structure in which the ruling classes lived off the production of the lower classes. Of course, the rulers were not independent, as they had to pay significant taxation to the Egyptians.

Rural dwellers

Not everyone lived in a city; in fact the majority of the total population did not, and many of them were peasant farmers whose lands were controlled by the rulers of the richer cities. By definition, poor rural settlements tend to leave less evidence behind than large cities, but these people seem to have paid taxes to their feudal superiors in the cities. They lived an insecure life, needing the protection of the armies from the cities, while resenting the control that their overlords imposed on them.

Apiru

These people have been mentioned in connection with the exodus stories. The Amarna Letters mention them raiding fields and rural settlements in Canaan. They seem to have been displaced people, maybe including criminal elements, who mostly found a niche for themselves around the cities, at some times working as mercenaries and at others raiding weaker communities on their own account.

faith had a lot in common with Canaanite religious language, and in addition the worship of Canaanite deities continued for centuries in later Israel. The other two models find it difficult to explain these similarities, and find themselves hard pressed to offer convincing explanations as to why people moving in from outside should so soon have adopted Canaanite ways of being. If the Israelites were originally Canaanites, that would not be a difficulty.

■ This explanation also correlates readily with the archaeological evidence from Canaanite cities. For whereas an invading force could be expected to have attacked buildings and fortifications, an internal revolt would be more likely to target rulers and their agents, leaving less evident destruction of their strongholds.

'Canaanites' and 'Israelites' continued

Pastoralists and nomads

There is evidence of people living in the more remote and hilly regions of the land, where the ground was less fertile but it was easier to survive without the interference of the city states. During the Late Bronze Age, this population was not as large as it had been previously, nor as it would become in the Early Iron Age with the development of recognizably Israelite settlements in this same region. At the time Israel was emerging, the people living here might have been nomadic pastoralists, or even groups of apiru – it is not possible to be more certain.

Shasu

The texts mentioning these people mostly place them around the fringes of Palestine, in Edom and generally to the south-east of Canaan. But they certainly seem to have had some connections with Canaan,

At about the time the Israelites were arriving in Canaan, the Philistines were settling along part of the coast. They came originally from Crete, and were known by the Egyptians as the 'Sea Peoples'. This relief, from the temple of the dead of Rameses III at Medinet Habu portrays a naval encounter between 'Sea People' and Egyptians. The Philistines can be recognized by their tall, feathered headgear.

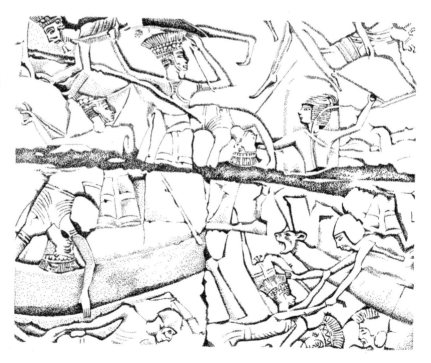

The judges

Though the book of Joshua contains some of the most memorable stories in the entire Hebrew Bible, with its stirring tales of military prowess and individual bravery, the real struggle to bring Israel to birth continued long after the death of Joshua. Those promoting this new style of life were fortunate in being able to avoid confrontation with the various great world powers of the time. The Egyptians and the Hittites were both in decline, while the new power of Assyria was not yet ready to expand into Canaan. The real challenge was in Canaan itself, where the Israelite tribes held control of only a few areas of the country. To make matters worse, the Israelite settlements were isolated from each

---

especially following the decline of the power of Egypt.

Incomers

This would include Philistines and other 'Sea Peoples'. Unlike the others, who all seem to be from roughly the same ethnic background, these people were from totally different stock, originating from the area around the Aegean Sea. Presumably some of the ancestors of Israel could also be classified under this heading.

Though these groups were all different, they shared a similar culture, both in terms of the material remains they left behind and in relation to their religious world-view. The one thing they did not share was a common political or national identity, though throughout this time Egyptian dominance was declining and there was considerable upheaval and social change. As the power centres shifted, new villages emerged in the highlands, the influence of the city states was fragmented, and new alliances between villages emerged, in such a way that by about 1050–1000 BC the kingdom of Israel began to take shape.

In the past, discussions of the origins of Israel have taken account of the existence of this population diversity, but scholars have generally preferred to trace historical Israel to only one strand or another, debating whether all the nation came from slavery in Egypt (and therefore none of

them were Canaanites to start with), or conversely proposing that 'Israelites' were originally 'Canaanites', and therefore the exodus stories could not be trusted. The truth is likely to be more complex than that, for there seems to be evidence that elements from all these different groups did in time align themselves with the vision of nationhood propounded by Israel, and which traced its origins back to the stories of exodus and covenant at Mount Sinai. Even those whose ancestors did not literally share in those events were attracted by the underlying political and spiritual ideology which they represented, and 'Israel' the nation was therefore more the product of a shared vision of the future than an ethnic entity. At this point, the likely historical course of events corresponds almost exactly with the message of the later interpreters of Israel's history, the prophets, who regularly found themselves having to insist on the universal scope of both their nation and their faith, in the light of others who would have interpreted things more narrowly.

other by two powerful groups of existing Canaanite city states: one group, just to the north of Shechem, was centred on towns like Megiddo, Dothan and Beth-Shan; and another, to the south of Shechem, extended westwards from the northern end of the Dead Sea right across to the Mediterranean coast. On top of that, the Israelite tribes were not always able to banish the Canaanite rulers even in those areas where they had achieved some sort of dominance. The tribes of Manasseh, Ephraim, Zebulun, Asher and Naphtali were all forced to reach some compromise agreement with other elements in the land, and when this is added to the fact that several other groups were also trying to carve out their own territories, it is hardly surprising that the situation was so volatile and unstable (Judges 1:27–36).

All this is described in the Old Testament book of Judges. The book takes its name from the fact that its heroes are called 'judges'. This terminology would most obviously suggest they were concerned with the administration of law, and the Hebrew word for 'judge' is in fact very similar to titles given to government officials elsewhere in the ancient world – at Mari, Ebla and Ugarit. Some of the people mentioned in Judges

Life in the days of the judges

What was life really like in those early years when the character and identity of the nation of Israel were being established? Like any other emerging nation, Israel certainly had their troubles. Looking back from the perspective of a more settled period, the editor of the book of Judges felt that at times it verged on anarchy: 'all the people did what was right in their own eyes' (Judges 21:25).

It is not hard to find evidence to support such an opinion. The gruesome story of how a woman traveller was sexually assaulted and murdered in the town of Gibeah is no doubt a typical example of what was going on (Judges 19:1–30). But what happened as a result of this incident is of great significance in understanding the nature of emerging Israelite society at this time. For after the woman's male companion sent a message to all the other tribes, telling them what had happened, they were so outraged that they formed a large army to punish the tribe of Benjamin for allowing such a thing to happen in their territory, and in the struggle that followed, the tribe of Benjamin was all but

exterminated (Judges 20:1–48). This seems to depict a situation where, under normal conditions, the different tribes of Israel were primarily concerned with their own affairs, but when the need arose they obviously had a strong sense of national solidarity, and could unite to confront a common threat – whether it came from outside enemies, or from internal subversion. But what was it that held them together like this? A clue may be found in the deep remorse that was felt after the Benjaminites had been subdued. For there was great concern that Benjamin should not be wiped out altogether: 'Israel must not lose one of its twelve tribes. We must find a way for the tribe of Benjamin to survive' (Judges 21:17). The alliance of twelve tribes – and no less – was clearly of some importance to them.

The sense of corporate identity implied by these stories can readily be understood by reference to the nature of tribalism as it can be traced more widely throughout the ancient world, and indeed in other cultures of more recent date. Groups of people conscious of belonging to one another tend to define that belonging by reference to different distinguishing marks at different times. The need for such

may well have had some administrative functions, though it can be misleading to compare the 'judges' of early Israel with figures in other cultures. Without exception, these other states all had a monarchy, and a much more sophisticated political apparatus than Israel had at this time. By contrast to the powerful kings who headed up the many city states of the land, the great judges of the Old Testament stories did not owe their position to a bureaucratic or hereditary appointment. It was, rather, something that stemmed naturally from their remarkable gifts of great wisdom, bravery and leadership – qualities that were demonstrated not in legal arguments about justice, but in the actual work of getting justice for their people. They were men and women of great political vision and religious devotion, and the stories about them show people who were determined that the promises of God and the commitment of the people, as expressed in the covenant made at Mount Sinai, should be enshrined in the very fabric of their new emerging society.

The Old Testament names twelve judges, but records details about only six of them. Of these, only one, Othniel, is linked with the tribes who eventually came to be associated with the southern part of the

definition typically only arises when the tribal identity appears to be threatened in some way, and the nature of the threat tends to determine how corporate uniqueness will then be described. It may be by reference to common ancestry, or different lifestyles, or religious taboos. In Israel, however, over and above individual tribal loyalties there was also a sense of commitment to being a part of the people of Yahweh, which could both incorporate and supersede such loyalties. During the twelfth and eleventh centuries BC, that was expressed in the form of a tribal league, then later from the tenth century onwards, in the form of the monarchy. The nature of the tribal league of this period can almost certainly be explained quite simply by reference to such fluid alignments among different elements of the population. However, other more complex models have been used to understand the nature of Israelite social organization at this time, and one of these in particular is worth noting here, if only because it has in the past exercised considerable influence over interpret-ations of Israel's early history.

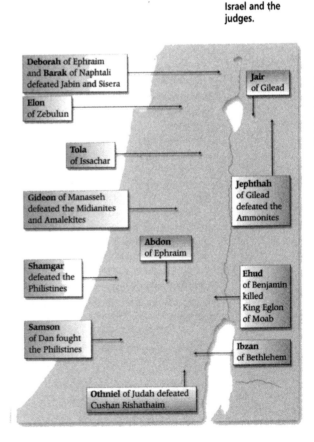

Israel and the judges.

Deborah of Ephraim and Barak of Naphtali defeated Jabin and Sisera

Jair of Gilead

Elon of Zebulun

Tola of Issachar

Jephthah of Gilead defeated the Ammonites

Gideon of Manasseh defeated the Midianites and Amalekites

Abdon of Ephraim

Shamgar defeated the Philistines

Ehud of Benjamin killed King Eglon of Moab

Samson of Dan fought the Philistines

Ibzan of Bethlehem

Othniel of Judah defeated Cushan Rishathaim

country (Judges 1:11–15; 3:7–11; Joshua 15:13–19). All the others are associated with northern tribes. This perhaps reflects the relative strength of Israel in different parts of the country at the time. But it could also suggest that the stories themselves were first handed on, and later written down, in the northern part of the country. The meaning that the editor of the book of Judges found in these stories is certainly similar to the message of the prophets who later flourished in that part of the land. The interpretative framework of the book of Judges implies that the real meaning of Israel's experience can only be understood from a religious viewpoint, and describes all the stories as following the same pattern, and teaching the same lessons (Judges 2:11–23):

■ When Israel was faithful to God, the nation prospered.

■ When Israel deserted their own God, Yahweh, and turned to other deities, they were unable to resist their enemies.

■ Finding themselves in great distress, the people of Israel turned again to God, who in turn provided a deliverer for them (a judge).

■ After the death of a judge, the same pattern of events was typically repeated all over again.

Life in the days of the judges *continued*

This is the work of the German scholar Martin Noth who in 1930 proposed a model derived from information about associations of tribes in ancient Greece and Italy, especially a group that was associated with the shrine of the god Apollo at Delphi. These groups came to be known as 'amphictyonies', from two Greek words which mean 'to live around'. They lived around a particular religious centre, and their common allegiance to the worship of their particular deities was the thing that bound them together and gave them mutual obligations to one another. Noth observed that many ancient communities were divided into a regular number of groups, or tribes, including in the Old Testament itself twelve Ishmaelite tribes (Genesis 25:13–16) and twelve Edomite tribes (Genesis 36:9–14), as well as those found in Israel. Unfortunately, nothing else is known about these near-neighbours of Israel, though Noth identified a number of distinctive features of the life of such an amphictyony, which he believed could also be found in the Old Testament.

A fixed membership
The Greek amphictyonies always had either six or twelve members. The reason for this

was perhaps a practical one, for with twelve months in a year it meant that each tribe could take it in turn to look after the central sanctuary on a regular basis. Whatever the origin of Israel's twelve tribes, it is certainly interesting that, though the actual names given to the tribes could vary, the number twelve is always preserved in the Old Testament.

A central shrine
The main focus of the Greek amphictyonies was the central shrine, and this also became a place for the administration of laws that were common to all the member states. By definition, an amphictyony must have such a central place of worship. But was there such a place in ancient Israel? The story in Joshua 24 seems to suggest that Shechem could have served as that kind of central sanctuary. But later, when the tribes united against Benjamin, they went not to Shechem but to Bethel (Judges 20:18) – and not long after, in the time of Samuel, Shiloh appears as the most important centre of worship (1 Samuel 1–4). The apparent absence of just one shrine could be due to the fact that, unlike other deities, the God of Israel could not be contained in just one

Every one of the stories about the judges is used to illustrate and give substance to this theological understanding of Israel's fortunes. For this reason, it has often been suggested that the narrative is less than accurate as history. Given the personal nature of much of the story, it is obviously impossible either to prove or disprove that, though the overall picture that emerges of life in Canaan at this period seems to match what is otherwise known of lifestyles at this time.

Deborah and Barak fight with 'Canaanites', a term generally used to denote the indigenous people of the land (Judges 4–5), while the others deal with various groups who were outsiders trying to gain access to the land for themselves: the Moabites (Ehud, Judges 3:12–30); the Midianites (Gideon, Judges 6:1 – 8:35); the Ammonites (Jephthah, Judges 10:6 – 12:7); and the Philistines (Samson, Judges 13:1 – 16:31). Most of these people were local heroes, fighting local battles. The story of Samson is almost a personal crusade against the Philistines, though the fact that he was able to marry a Philistine woman suggests that at this stage relationships between the two groups were reasonably friendly, and certainly not as hostile as they were later to become.

---

place, but was believed to be present everywhere, a presence that was more appropriately symbolized by the portable ark of the covenant. Perhaps, therefore, this sign of God's presence, which could be moved about from place to place, was itself the central focus for all the tribes. But if so, could it also have been a kind of administrative centre, served by its own officials? Martin Noth believed that it could, and he argued that the officials of the Israelite amphictyony were to be identified with the so-called 'minor judges' – that is, those of whom we know nothing more than their names (Judges 10:1–5; 12:8–15). He further suggested that the law which they administered is to be found in Exodus 20:22 – 23:33, the 'book of the covenant'.

An annual festival

In the Greek amphictyonies, each member state sent official delegates to an annual convention, which took place at the central shrine. This was partly a religious occasion, and partly an administrative council. The evidence for such an annual pilgrimage in the Old Testament is limited, though there is the story of how Joshua gathered the tribes together at Shechem, to remind them

of their obligations under the covenant (Joshua 24), and the later story of Samuel's parents describes them undertaking an annual pilgrimage to the sanctuary in Shiloh – though there is nothing to suggest they were any sort of official delegates (1 Samuel 1:1–8). It is in fact very difficult to find evidence of such delegates in early Israel, though Noth believed that passages like Numbers 1:1–16 could have been lists of these people.

A common purpose

The job of an alliance like this was to defend the central shrine and to uphold the common interests and laws of the constituent states. There are two striking illustrations of such a common concern in the book of Judges. On the one hand, we have the story of how six tribes united under Deborah to oppose a common threat from the Canaanites (Judges 4–5), and on the other is the story of how eleven tribes acted against a gross violation of covenant law by the tribe of Benjamin (Judges 19–20). According to Noth, these two incidents document the development of the amphictyony, with an alliance of twelve tribes arising out of the

The story of Deborah and Barak provides a good illustration of the nature of Israelite society at this period. Their exploits against the Canaanites, led by Sisera, the army commander of Jabin, king of the city of Hazor, are vividly described in the great poem which was almost certainly written by an eyewitness of the events it describes (Judges 5:1–31). It was certainly written sometime in the twelfth century BC, and that takes us right back to the time of the judges themselves. Deborah and Barak were probably trying to break through the line of Canaanite city states that isolated the northern area of Galilee from the Israelite settlements around Shechem. For though Jabin's city, Hazor, lay to the north of Galilee, the battle itself took place just to the south-west of the Plain of Jezreel, and involved a coalition of Canaanite city states. Possession of this great plain was of vital importance: all the significant trade routes had to go this way, and whoever controlled this area effectively controlled most of the land. The outcome of the battle was victory for Israel. The Canaanite kings were not entirely routed, but their power was broken, and it was only a matter of time before Israel was able to overthrow Jabin and his influence (Judges 4:23–24).

Life in the days of the judges *continued*

six-tribe group headed by Deborah. But other interpretations are possible, especially if one is prepared to imagine that the stories have been rewritten in the light of social conditions in later Israel.

Martin Noth's reconstruction of life in the time of the judges has many attractions, not least being the way that it offers an all-embracing ideological framework within which to understand the biblical stories about early Israel and its organization. But it was always going to be difficult to match every detail of the Old Testament with the evidence from Greece and Italy. Not only did these Greek amphictyonies flourish in a time and place far removed from Israel in the period of the judges, but they may also be too complex to be appropriate for understanding early Israel. The most useful model for our purposes is probably not that of a religious league, but of a segmentary tribal system, comprising autonomous tribal units of diverse origins, who were able to act together without the need for a central organizational structure.

At the same time, Noth's theory did serve to highlight some of the key aspects of Israel's emerging national consciousness.

For it is certain that a shared faith in God was a major element in the alliance between the Israelite tribes, even though it may not have been expressed in just one central place. The power of the spiritual vision was no less notable for that, and though different tribes had their own leaders (typified by the judges) there was the underlying consciousness that God was the only real 'judge' of the people (Judges 11:27), and the devotion given to human leaders was therefore secondary and derivative (Judges 8:23; 9:1–57). It would be surprising if such a devotion was not given some tangible expression in the way the social and political institutions of Israel's national life were structured.

The rulers of the Canaanite city states had many sophisticated weapons, including chariots, and the Israelites were successful in this instance only because they were able to form an effective alliance. Deborah managed to unite six of the Israelite tribes – Zebulun, Naphtali, Ephraim, Benjamin, Manasseh and Issachar – and the one thing that brought them together was their common religious faith. In this sense, it was not an exaggeration for the editor of the book of Judges to claim that obedience to God would lead to success, while disobedience would lead only to failure. When the tribes were united by their common heritage derived from the covenant at Mount Sinai, they were an effective coalition. But when they began to drift away from the worship of the God of whom Moses had spoken, purely sectional and selfish interests came to be all-important, and they were powerless to make much headway in establishing their new society.

Israel and the religion of Canaan

Politically, the Canaanite city states were eventually displaced by the people who came to be known as Israel. But ideologically, what had been traditional Canaanite culture exerted an enormous influence on Israel for many centuries. The editor of the book of Judges saw the religion of Canaan as a more formidable force than its armies, and when Israel was tempted to adopt its values, disaster was the inevitable outcome: 'Then the people of Israel sinned against Yahweh and began to serve the Baals. They stopped worshipping the Lord, the God of their ancestors, the God who had brought them out of Egypt, and they... served the Baals and the Astartes. And so Yahweh lost patience with Israel and allowed raiders to attack them and rob them... and the Israelites could no longer protect themselves... They were in great distress' (Judges 2:11–15). This message sums up the perspective from which almost all the historical narratives of the Hebrew Bible were written, and was applied as a means of understanding the ever-changing fortunes of the nation. Centuries after the time of the judges, all the great prophets, from Elijah to Jeremiah, were saying the same thing: that the people of Israel were going to ruin because of their love for the gods and goddesses of Palestine.

So who were these other deities, 'the Baals and the Astartes'? Some of the answers to that question have been unearthed by archaeologists at the tell of Ras esh-Shamra, on the coast of modern Syria, just opposite Cyprus. This was the site of the ancient Canaanite citadel of Ugarit. Its heyday was in the fifteenth and fourteenth centuries BC, something like 200 years before any likely date for the exodus, but there is every reason to believe that the religion practised in southern Palestine at the time of the emergence of early Israel was very similar to the religion of these people who lived further north. In an annex to the temple at Ugarit, archaeologists have made one of the most exciting discoveries of all

The Canaanite god Baal was regarded as a controller of the weather, and one on whom the fertility of the land depended. This claim conflicted with the Israelite belief that Yahweh was God of every aspect of life. This Baal mask dates from about 1300 BC.

Israel and the religion of Canaan *continued*

time, for in a large collection of clay tablets, we find the story of Baal and the other Canaanite gods and goddesses who are mentioned in the Old Testament. These tablets date from about the thirteenth century BC, and are written in a language that has come to be known as Ugaritic. It is one of the earliest-known scripts to have

On the coast of modern Syria, at the tell of Ras esh-Shamra, was once the Canaanite city of Ugarit. This picture is of an entrance to the great palace. Archaeologists have unearthed at Ugarit a great deal of evidence about Canaanite religion and civilization in the centuries leading up to the exodus.

used an alphabet, and though it is completely different from Hebrew in appearance, there are many underlying similarities in the two languages, in specific vocabulary and terminology as well as in general structure. These tablets contain much valuable and important information not only about the deities of ancient Ugarit, but also about religious practices of the time. In addition, the many religious objects also found here – altars, statues and so on – provide added insights into how these gods and goddesses were worshipped.

A number of key characters play a part in the various stories. There is El, the chief of the gods, and his female companion Asherah. But they take a back seat to Baal, the weather god, and his lover Anat, the goddess of love and war. One story tells how Baal was attacked by Mot, the god of barrenness and sterility. As in many ancient fertility myths, he overcomes Baal and destroys his powers of life and fertility, scattering his body to the four corners of the earth. While El, the father-god, leads the heavenly mourning for his lost son, Anat, the goddess of fertility, goes out to take her revenge:

She seizes Mot, the son of El,
with the knife she cuts him,
with the shovel she winnows him,
with fire she burns him,
with millstones she grinds him,
on the field she throws him.
The birds eat his remains,
the feathered ones make an end to what is left over.

Baal's power is then restored through the renewal of his sexual relationship with Anat – and that in turn ensures the fertility of the earth and its inhabitants for another season. The maintenance of the agricultural status quo appears to have been one of the main ideological purposes of this kind of religion. Without the rains that fall from October to April, agriculture would have been impossible, and so when the rains stopped in May it seemed as if Baal was dead, and needed to be revived. Some experts believe that the story of Baal's revival by Anat was the central feature of an annual New Year festival that was celebrated throughout Palestine, and perhaps more widely. On this occasion, held every autumn, the king and a temple prostitute would act out the story of Baal and Anat, to make sure that all would be well for another year. No doubt the same kind of rites were enacted in many local shrines: sexual acts with temple prostitutes feature prominently in Old Testament denunciations of Canaanite worship, and physical union with them was probably considered to be as much a part of the job of a farmer as were the actual operations of agriculture.

It is hardly surprising that there should be evidence of people within Israel adopting similar forms of worship. The Old Testament books in their final form were written with the benefit of hindsight, and later generations could look back and surmise that, if Israel had preserved the distinctive elements of faith in Yahweh, instead of going along with the indigenous religious practices of Canaan, things might have turned out differently. But in the earliest period, the issue was not quite so simple, even to those who wanted to be faithful to the values that could be traced back to Moses and the covenant. For though these stories depicted Yahweh as all-powerful in relation to life in the desert, that was no guarantee that such power would automatically extend to control of the weather and the fertility of fields and flocks. As a consequence, it is not difficult to find traces of a diversity of religious practices at this time. Some appear to have accepted the worship of Yahweh only with reluctance, if at all, and for all practical purposes continued the worship of traditional Canaanite deities. Others tried to hold both traditions alongside each other, while yet others worshipped mainly Yahweh, but played safe by using Canaanite shrines and Canaanite ritual in doing so. The extent to which this kind of thing happened can be seen in the way that even leading Israelite families, who were otherwise praised as faithful to the worship of Yahweh, could on occasion give their children names that would invoke the protection of these traditional deities. For example, one of the sons of Saul was named Jonathan ('Gift of Yahweh'), while another was Ish-Baal ('Man of Baal'), and the names of Baal and Anat were attached to many Israelite towns and villages.

Given the fluid cultural matrix out of which Israel emerged as a separate nation, it is not surprising that we should find evidence of such syncretistic ways in the Old Testament. The gods and goddesses of Canaan represented the inherited spirituality of at least some elements of the population that came to be called 'Israel', and in any case even incomers could hardly fail to have been impressed by the agricultural and economic success of the Canaanite city states – and if they claimed this was due to their religion, then at least such rituals would seem to be worth consideration. But those who created the Old Testament in its final shape could see that the worship of Yahweh and the worship of Baal could not be mixed, for there were fundamental differences between the two:

● Yahweh, the God of Israel, was a God who acted in history, and not a god of nature who was revealed only in the annual cycles of summer and winter. Though Yahweh's character could be disclosed in the context of relationships (as illustrated through the stories of the family of Abraham and Sarah and their successors), being a personal God did not necessarily imply that Yahweh had either gender or sexuality. Indeed, the claim that God is not so much asexual, as beyond sexuality, came to be one of the key distinguishing characteristics of Israelite faith.

● The rituals of traditional Canaanite religion were first and foremost magical rites. Though the behaviour of deities like Baal and Anat was in most ways regarded as unpredictable, there was also a belief that due to innate correspondences between human activity and the life of the gods and goddesses, it was to some extent possible for people to make the gods do their bidding. This was the reasoning behind the assumption that sexual intercourse between a farmer and the

Gezer was a well-defended city lying only a few miles from the main trade route between Egypt and Mesopotamia. Ten stone pillars, some more than three metres tall, formed the 'high place' which was of religious significance for the city.

deity's representative (usually in the shape of a temple prostitute) would produce more fruitful crops, by inducing the deities to have sex among themselves. By

Israel and the religion
of Canaan *continued*

contrast, however, the God of Israel could not be bullied by magic. Yahweh had not been forced to call Abraham and Sarah, or to deliver the slaves from Egypt: those and other things like them had all arisen out of God's own spontaneous love and care for the people.

● Any magical understanding of ritual runs the risk of encouraging its practitioners to assume that religion has nothing to do with behaviour in normal life, but only with the special actions that take place in shrines and temples. This notion runs completely contrary to the Hebrew Bible's understanding of the personality of Yahweh. The God of Israel was not most concerned with the empty performance of hollow rituals, but with the way people behaved in everyday life. This lesson was hammered home over and over again by the prophets, as they declared that Israel's religious duty was not something that took place in a shrine, but in the market place: 'to do what is just, to show constant love, and to live in humble fellowship with our God' (Micah 6:8).

● In view of this, it is not surprising that Israel's God demanded exclusive worship. The gods and goddesses of Canaan were always tolerant of other gods, who were, in a sense, their own relatives. But the formative stories that gave Israel their sense of national identity all showed Yahweh demanding the exclusive commitment and obedience of the people (Exodus 20:1–3).

The deuteronomic history

Mention has already been made of the fact that the stories of Israel's history as they are now presented in the Hebrew Bible are the result of a long process of collection and edition that took place over several centuries. The fact that history is presented from a particular perspective does not, in itself, question the authenticity of the narratives. But in order to understand the stories as thoroughly as possible it is necessary at this stage to have some understanding of the purposes for which they were put together in their final form.

Back in 1943, Martin Noth proposed that the books of Joshua, Judges, 1–2 Samuel and 1–2 Kings were gathered together to form an epic history of Israel not long after the state of Judah and its capital Jerusalem had been destroyed by the Babylonians under Nebuchadnezzar (586 BC), and that in this edition the book of Deuteronomy, which immediately precedes these historical books in the Old Testament, was incorporated almost as a kind of introductory section to explain the theological basis on which Israel's history was to be understood. Hence he called this extended story 'the deuteronomic history'. He believed that this great reassessment of Israel's history took place sometime after 561 BC (the year when Jehoiachin, former king of Judah, was released from prison in Babylon, 2 Kings 25:27–30), but before the Persians came to power and overthrew the Babylonian empire (539 BC), a change which enabled the subsequent rebuilding of the Temple in Jerusalem to take place in about 520 BC.

This is a bold hypothesis to explain the origin of these Old Testament books, and it has repercussions for how the compilation of other books took place – something that is explored in more detail in Chapter 7. But it is also an attractive one, and a number of facts seem to speak in its favour:

● It is not at all unlikely that those who survived the destruction of Jerusalem would begin to look at their past history as a way of making sense of their present predicament. The book of Jeremiah mentions inhabitants of Judah who were exiled in Egypt, and who engaged in this kind of reflection, and there is every reason to suppose that the same thing would have happened in Judah itself. Not only that, but in the immediate aftermath of the fall of Jerusalem there must have been an added incentive to gather together the traditions of the nation for their own sake, simply as a means of preserving the ancient records for posterity. All these books refer to other ancient sources of information from which their own stories have been extrapolated or summarized, and all these other records have subsequently disappeared with the passage of time.

● At the same time, these Old Testament history books are more than just an anthology of extracts from older historical materials. For they also present a clear and coherent view of the meaning of the events that are recorded. The nature of this interpretative framework is made quite explicit in the book of Judges, but it is clearly present in many other passages too. It has not been superimposed on every detail of the narratives, but at strategic points the lessons of history are made plain: Israel was committed in a covenant relationship to God, and this placed upon them certain responsibilities. Accordingly, if the people were willing to accept these responsibilities and obey the Law of the covenant, they could expect the blessing that God had promised. On the other hand, deliberate disobedience would lead to failure and destruction. This message is often conveyed in the form of speeches at strategic points in the story (Joshua 23; 1 Samuel 12; 2 Samuel 7; 1 Kings 8:22–53), a literary device that is common to much ancient history writing.

● The fact that the covenant forms the basic framework within which Israel's history is understood in these books also gives a certain plausibility to Noth's claim

that Deuteronomy was the preface for the whole work. For the literary structure of Deuteronomy is closely linked to the covenant pattern which has been traced in Hittite and Assyrian sources. In addition, the speech with which the book opens (Deuteronomy 1–4) is almost a classic exposition of the theological perspective of the so-called deuteronomists. What is more, it seems to contain an explicit appeal and reassurance to the people for whom the exile proved to be such a great crisis: 'Yahweh will scatter you among other nations, where only a few of you will survive... There you will look for Yahweh your God, and if you search... with all your heart, you will find... When you are in trouble and all those things happen to you, then you will finally turn to Yahweh in obedience. God is merciful, and will never abandon you or destroy you, nor forget the covenant made in person with your forebears' (Deuteronomy 4:27, 29–31).

This understanding of the nature of the deuteronomic history has not been universally accepted by scholars, though it has won a considerable measure of support and most would acknowledge its existence, while debating various aspects of the perspective it appears to represent. Three major issues may be highlighted:

● Noth regarded the deuteronomic history as simply an explanation of the tragedy that had befallen the people of Israel, and he therefore understood it as an essentially pessimistic work. But this is not the whole story. The main emphasis is certainly on Israel's past, but not simply from an antiquarian standpoint. Indeed, it is questionable whether anyone in ancient Israel ever would have been interested in the past in the way that today's Western people tend to be, merely out of curiosity to know what happened. For the biblical writers, the past was always seen as the theatre of God's activity, and therefore it inevitably became far more than merely a collection of things that had happened: it was a mirror of the future, and a challenge to the people to face up to that future, particularly in relation to its spiritual dimensions. The prophets came to think of the failures of the past as an invitation to renewed obedience, and these history writers were inspired by the same perspective. Perhaps that is why they ended with the story of Jehoiachin's release, for that in itself must have generated renewed hope in the hearts of the people.

● Some have questioned whether there is such a thoroughgoing, unified presentation of the meaning of Israel's history in all these books. They point out, for example, that some passages of Samuel and Kings (like the succession narrative contained in 2 Samuel 9–20 and 1 Kings 1–2) seem to show very little trace of the deuteronomic point of view. They also ask whether the simple viewpoint of Deuteronomy itself, related to the earliest stages of Israel's history, is truly compatible with the elevated position of the king and the significance of the Jerusalem Temple in the later books. But these observations have more bearing on the complex way in which the various stories were gathered together. It is quite likely that the long job of writing a continuous history of Israel had already been started long before the dark days of the exile. Many scholars think that even before the time of Josiah (640–609 BC), the outline for such a

narrative was already in existence, and even in the earliest parts of the history, it is universally agreed that some of the stories were first written down more or less as they happened. For the later editors were not so much concerned to rewrite the stories, but to present them in a way that would be most meaningful to the people of their own day.

● Scholars have often asked just who these so-called deuteronomists actually were. They have been identified in turn with groups of priests, prophets and wisdom teachers, though it can hardly be doubted that they had a good deal in common with the great prophets. Of these, Isaiah is the only one who is actually mentioned by name in the Old Testament histories (2 Kings 19–20), but the underlying message of these books is the same as theirs: the facts of Israel's history were taken as proof that the prophets were right. There are also a number of passages in the books of the prophets which are quite similar to parts of the deuteronomic history. Indeed, it is quite possible that these prophetic books were first gathered together by the same people who issued this great historical work. It is perhaps more than accidental that the Jews themselves came to regard the books from Joshua to Kings as 'the former prophets'.

4 'A King Like Other Nations'

'You have been our king from the beginning, O God; you have saved us many times' (Psalm 74:12). The words were written centuries later, but they sum up well enough the ideals of the early days of Israel's history, at least as seen through the spectacles of the final editors of the Hebrew Bible. Though the tribes may from time to time have their human leaders, in the end God was to be their only true sovereign. Even the great judges were not important in themselves, but were just men and women whom God had inspired to lead their people in times of special need.

The stories generally show the judges themselves recognizing this. When some of the tribes suggested to Gideon that his bravery and courage deserved the reward of a permanent position of power, he would have nothing to do with it. It was, he declared, impossible for his people to be ruled both by God and by a human king (Judges 8:22–23). His son Abimelech did not have the same scruples, and managed to persuade the people of the city of Shechem to make him their ruler, though in the event his success was short-lived (Judges 9). It was unthinkable that the monarchies of the Canaanite city states should have provided an acceptable model for the emerging Israelite culture: the belief that Yahweh was their ruler was not meant to be a pious fiction, but something that would be given practical application in the affairs of everyday life. The tribes were held together not by the institutions of a shared government, but by the experiences of a shared faith, symbolized by the ark of the covenant. Of course, there were already movements afoot that would both challenge and undermine the loosely knit tribal federation of this period, movements that were probably inevitable rather than necessarily being the outcome of conscious choice on the part of the people. Population growth and movement, and the consequent need to find more efficient ways of feeding larger numbers, not to mention climatic changes and the natural tendency of those in positions of leadership to want to better themselves, all contributed to the evolution of the Israelite state during the Early Iron Age (1200–1000 BC). The deuteronomic editors of these narratives in the Hebrew Bible had little to say about such matters, but chose instead to concentrate on stories that brought the Israelite tribes into conflict with other groups who were also trying to establish themselves in the land at this time. This was a way in which they could tell the old stories so as to address the circumstances of their own day all the more effectively. Their procedure in doing so does not in itself invalidate their narratives, though it does serve to underline the essentially selective nature of them. There is plenty of evidence to show that the Philistines in particular were making a powerful bid for exactly the same territory, and while relations between these two groups were somewhat fluid and flexible, and the Philistine threat was not the only factor that led to the emergence of an organized state with its own monarchy, there can be no doubt that this still acted as a powerful catalyst for social change at this period.

Samuel and the ark

There is a degree of uncertainty about the exact relationship between the Philistines and the Israelites at the earliest period of the tribal federation. It could even be that certain elements which eventually joined Israel may have originally been part of the 'Sea Peoples', just as the Philistines were. Samson, for example, is described as belonging to the tribe of Dan, though he married a Philistine woman and was involved with several others. There is no suggestion that by doing so he was stepping outside any accepted boundaries, and the squabbles with the Philistines that grew out of these relationships were essentially matters related to his own personal life rather than having any connection with larger tribal conflicts (Judges 13–16). Indeed, some evidence may point to the tribe of Dan having originally been connected to the 'Sea Peoples'. They seem to have used a similar type of pottery to the Philistines, and one later passage implies that they had a different god to the rest of Israel (Amos 8:14). Amos does not name this god, which means it is not possible to make a definite connection between Israel and the Philistines through this route. However, even David at a later stage had no hesitation in turning to the Philistines for support, which tends to suggest that he saw at least that group of them as not unsympathetic to his own ambitions (1 Samuel 21:10–15).

The relationship between the two groups might therefore be much more complex than was formerly supposed, though they did eventually emerge as competitors. As military opponents, the Philistines would certainly have been a strong and powerful force. They had adopted the political structures of the Canaanite city states to their own advantage, but they had one thing their Canaanite predecessors never had: a strong sense of national unity. Though they were independent, the Philistine cities could act in a concerted and unified way. This made them a formidable enemy, for in addition they were also technically more advanced than Israel, and knew how to use chariots and iron weapons in war.

Both politically and militarily, Israel was less well organized than

the Philistines, and could offer no effective resistance to a more
sophisticated military machine. After a devastating defeat near Aphek,
the leaders of the Israelite tribes realized that they were powerless
(1 Samuel 4:1–11). Not only were the rising generation of tribal leaders
unable to emulate the brave exploits of those whose reputations
survived from previous generations, but in the course of one battle in
particular the ark of the covenant was captured, its shrine at Shiloh
destroyed, and the Israelite army decimated (1 Samuel 5:1 – 7:1). This
kind of defeat was not difficult for the deuteronomic editors of the
traditions to explain, and was linked directly by them to religious
mistakes, not least the assumption that it would be possible to get God
on their side through such means as carrying the ark of the covenant
into battle. Following the lead of the sons of Eli the priest (who were
themselves killed in the battle), the people had forgotten the close
personal nature of Israel's relationship to God, preferring to replace the
dynamic understanding of the covenant with a more static spirituality
which imagined that God could not only be contained in a box, but
could also actually be manipulated by mere humans. With the box
gone, the people found themselves militarily powerless and socially
disenfranchised, as the Philistines took the leading place in the land. It
is unlikely that the Philistines wanted to possess the whole land for
themselves. More probably they were trying to take over the position
once occupied by the Egyptians: they would be the rulers, and the
Israelites and other groups living in Canaan would be their subjects.
That did not make it any less painful for Israel. But what could they do
to carve out a niche for themselves in this competitive situation?
Samuel seemed powerless, yet he was the only surviving representative
of the old order. And although the ark of the covenant took its own
revenge on the Philistines and was eventually returned to Israel, the old
fervour and enthusiasm did not return with it. It became clear that the
old forms of loose tribal alliances were no longer adequate to address
the challenges of changing circumstances. Moreover, the Philistines
were not the only challenge that the Israelite tribes had to face.

Saul

The man who put new life into the Israelites was Saul. He enters the
narrative through another chilling tale of gratuitous violence. Among
other groups trying to establish themselves in the land at this time were
the Ammonites, who were pressing in from the east side of the River
Jordan. They attacked the people of Jabesh Gilead, and made it a
condition of peace that the right eye of every citizen should be put out.
It was not long before this news had travelled far and wide, and Saul
heard it as he was on his way home from the fields. Like the judges
before him, he was moved to fury by 'the spirit of God', whereupon he
cut up the oxen he was driving and sent pieces of them throughout

the whole district, with the gruesome message: 'Whoever does not follow Saul and Samuel into battle will have this done to their oxen!' (1 Samuel 11:7). Under Saul's leadership, a powerful army was raised from among the tribes of Israel to deal with this new threat, and Jabesh Gilead was liberated.

Up to this point, the story is quite similar to the tales told about the judges. But a new element is introduced into the narrative after Saul's great victory, for the people gathered at the shrine in Gilgal, and acclaimed him as their king (1 Samuel 11:13–15). According to the stories in Samuel, this was not a spontaneous action, but the culmination of much debate among the Israelite leaders. For the appointment of a king was not something to be taken lightly. After all, if it had previously been wrong for Gideon to be king, how could it now be right for Saul? The deuteronomic history reports this argument in some detail. Indeed, the two sides were put with such vigour that scholars commonly

'Has even Saul become a prophet?'

The question arises out of an incident recorded in 1 Samuel 10:5–13. After being anointed by Samuel, Saul went up to worship at the sanctuary of Gibeah, and as he was on his way he encountered a group of prophets who were shouting and dancing to frenzied music, in some sort of religious ecstasy. Quite unexpectedly, Saul himself was caught up in the same excitement, and he too joined in their dancing and singing. This was such an unexpected turn of events that bystanders spoke of Saul becoming 'a different person' under the influence of this religious enthusiasm, and many expressed their surprise that a reputable person like him should have become mixed up with this kind of behaviour.

The fact that this could happen to Saul will surprise no one, for there are plenty of well-documented examples of religious groups whose fervour and excitement leads them into wild and uncontrollable behaviour of this sort, often stimulated by music, as was the case here.

Many readers, however, are surprised to see people like this described as 'prophets'. For the typical prophet of the Old Testament is not a person who indulges in religious excitement, but someone with a message from God to the people, who expresses that message in clear language, appealing not to the emotions of their hearers, but to their reason and sense of religious commitment.

A number of observations can be made on this issue:

● Some have drawn attention to the statement in 1 Samuel 9:9, that 'at that time a prophet was called a seer'. A seer would be someone who tried to discover God's will by psychic or semi-magical means. Perhaps then, it is argued, the confusion is just a matter of terminology, and the great classical prophets with their incisive comments on social and political affairs simply evolved over a period of time out of such unsophisticated practitioners. There are certainly some statements in the Hebrew Bible that could be taken to support this view. Amos, for example, seems to distinguish himself from a 'prophet' who would give messages for money (Amos 7:14), while Micah 3:5–7 appears to make reference to the same sort of people.

● At the same time, some passages do seem to refer to ecstatic experiences of this sort in the lives of the great prophets. Even Jeremiah was described as a 'madman' (admittedly, by his enemies,

reckon they can trace two distinctive accounts of Samuel's role in the affair, which have been combined by the later editors:

■ The first is contained in 1 Samuel 9:1 – 10:16 and 11:1–15, and here Samuel is introduced as a relatively unknown local figure, who appoints Saul as king under God's direct guidance. The monarchy will save Israel from their enemies, and for this reason is generally looked on with favour in these sections of the story.

■ In another account, though, Samuel seems to be already well known as a national figure, and a man who disapproves of the appointment of a king because this would mean a rejection of God as the only true ruler of Israel (1 Samuel 8:1–22; 10:17–27).

Given the conscious literary artistry with which these narratives have been constructed, it is likely that the editors of the book of Samuel incorporated these different perspectives with the specific intent to

---

Jeremiah 29:26–27). Hosea was accused in much the same way (Hosea 9:7) – and some of the experiences of these later prophets (especially people like Ezekiel) were certainly most unusual. We also know of at least one occasion when the prophet Elisha gave his message to the accompaniment of music (2 Kings 3:15–19), while the behaviour of one of his colleagues provoked a king of Israel to call him 'that crazy fellow' (2 Kings 9:11).

● There are parallels to all this in other cultures of the time. The Old Testament itself provides descriptions of typical behaviour of the prophets of Baal, who sought to invoke divine power by a self-induced religious ecstasy (1 Kings 18:20–29). Given the close parallels between the culture of Canaan and that of the Israelites, it would not be especially surprising to find such similarities. There is little external evidence about the practices of such people in Canaan itself, though there is some from Mari in the form of a series of letters dating from the eighteenth century BC. They concern a wide variety of prophetic functions, one of the most important of which was the encourage-ment of a king in times of particular difficulty, especially the giving of advice in times of war. This aspect of the work of a prophet certainly features regularly in the Old Testament,

though their advice (as at Mari) was not always what their rulers wanted to hear (2 Samuel 12:1–15; 1 Kings 22:1–28).

Ecstatic enthusiasts frequently assume a new importance, especially at times of social uncertainty and cultural upheaval. When the accepted norms look to be changing and ordinary people feel out of control of their own lives, the prospect of being able to tune in directly to spiritual forces beyond this world is bound to offer a welcome sense of safety and security. No doubt ancient Israel was no exception, and it is not difficult to understand how guidance received from such sources should have been welcomed as providing inspiration at a time of great difficulty. Certainly, no period was more difficult for the emerging nation of Israel than the time of Saul. This function of ecstatic spirituality may later have been continued and refined in those prophets who were attached to the royal courts of Israel and Judah. The precise relationship of this kind of religious devotee with the great preaching prophets of the Old Testament is still uncertain, though both types of prophet obviously thought of themselves as the communicators of a message from God to the people.

highlight the tensions inherent in them. For between them they represent the contradictions to which the deuteronomic historians traced the ultimate collapse of their nation many centuries later. On the one hand, a strong leader was needed to consolidate the position of Israel as a national entity; but on the other, the existence of such a leader would inevitably weaken the conviction that God was Israel's only true ruler. This tension is clearly reflected in the stories about Saul, and to a greater or lesser extent is represented in the stories about all those who succeeded him.

In some respects, Saul is presented less as a king than as a kind of perpetual judge. It was certainly important that he should be seen to have the same popular appeal and military prowess that the judges had possessed. In practical terms, however, Saul had his difficulties. Up to this point, the main military force in Israel had been the large army of

volunteers from the tribes. It was with such a spontaneously recruited force that Saul had been able to avenge the people of Jabesh Gilead. But this sort of arrangement was only appropriate for great emergencies. It was not the way for a king to operate, nor was it likely to be an effective way of securing the nation's territory militarily. Given the nature of population movements in Canaan at this period, guerrilla warfare would be a far more effective strategy than large-pitched battles – and for that, a small body of professional soldiers would be much more suitable than a large force of untrained volunteers. So, like the rulers of the Canaanite city states before him, Saul formed his own personal army (1 Samuel 13:2; 14:52).

At En Gedi by the Dead Sea, a stream flows down a gorge to the shore. The whole area abounds in caves, and this is the region where David hid from Saul and his soldiers during the years of his exile from court.

By all accounts it was a successful move, for he was able to keep the Philistines at least out of the hill country, which provided greater freedom of movement for the Israelites (1 Samuel 13–14). But this sense of security was bought at a price. For though Saul lacked most of the trappings of other kings of the time, and even his headquarters at Gibeah was by no means a palace, he was separating himself from his people. His professional army owed its allegiance not to the tribes in general, but to Saul himself as its commander-in-chief. Since Saul appears to have had no resources of his own, he must have needed someone else to pay for the army – and that meant the tribes. Though there is no direct evidence for it in the Old Testament, he was probably forced to raise some kind of taxation from the people. It could well have been financial stringency that forced Saul to disregard Samuel's instructions about the goods of the defeated Amalekites (1 Samuel 15:1–35), but whatever the reason, as a result of this episode Saul came to be regarded as a headstrong, selfish man who put his own will and wisdom before the will of God, and who was too ready to jettison the old religious ideals when they interfered with his own state-building strategy.

In the event, Saul's efforts to bring coherence to his people failed. No doubt there were many reasons for this. The stories show him as a king who ultimately lost the popular support that had brought him to power, largely as a result of doing things that any king could have been expected to engage in: establishing an army, and trying to impose some centralized government on the land. Transforming a loose federation of tribes into a coherent state is not an easy task, and Saul did not have the diplomatic skill necessary to carry it out effectively. His popularity was further undermined by the emergence of one of his young subjects, a shepherd called David, who had the personal charisma that Saul lacked (1 Samuel 16–31). Overtaken by jealousy and suspicion, Saul eventually fell into a deep depression and by the end of his life was mentally deranged. He died a lonely and forlorn figure, taking his own life on the battlefield after a crushing defeat at the hands of the Philistines on Mount Gilboa. The complexity of Saul's personality eludes us, though he emerges as a tragic figure. He had great potential as the recognized successor to the judges, but the nature of the task to which he was committed was too great for him; he

Israel becomes a state

The deuteronomic historians emphasize the need for military security as a key catalyst that led to the emergence of Israel as a state, rather than it remaining a loosely federated group of tribes. It is not difficult to see why they would do that, for much of the later history of their people was determined by power struggles in the region, and their lack of military prowess turned out to play a significant part in the ultimate collapse of both Israel and Judah. There need be no question that the ability to deal effectively with others who were also trying to carve out territory for themselves played an important part in the development of the early monarchy. The Philistines were only one group who needed to be kept in check, and nearby states such as Edom, Moab and Syria all had vested interests in the land (1 Samuel 14:47; 2 Samuel 8:1–14), along with other tribal peoples like the Ammonites (1 Samuel 11:1) or Amalekites (1 Samuel 30:1). But other factors clearly played a part as well, and help to explain why the development of the monarchy – whatever its shortcomings might eventually turn out to be – was inevitable. When the stories of Israel's kings are placed alongside what is known of life in Canaan during the

Early Iron Age (1200–1000 BC), at least three other significant factors can be identified:

● Population growth seems to have been quite rapid at this time, and is of course an easy way for an emerging national entity to expand its territory and influence. But growing populations require more resources, and if those resources are not easily obtainable, social tensions are the inevitable result. In some Middle Eastern states at the time, populations were kept in check by crude forms of birth control, generally by disposing of unwanted infants. There is no evidence of that at any period of Israelite history, which meant that population movement was the most obvious way of dealing with the growing numbers. There is ample evidence that this was indeed what was happening at this time, but given the generally inhospitable nature of the terrain outside the central plains, and the unpredictability of the annual rains, the highland communities that emerged never had much chance of being materially self-sufficient. The land they were trying to farm was simply inadequate to produce the food required for a balanced diet, and in order to sustain a satisfactory lifestyle in such circumstances some kind of centralized arrangements for

was incapable of incorporating the old tribal ideals of his people within the structures of an emerging state, and his downfall was inevitable. In addition, he made very little headway against the well-organized armies of other groups such as the Philistines, which left him as a king without a kingdom. The three major city states of Jerusalem, Aijalon and Gezer still separated the centre of the country from the south, and to the north the strategic Plain of Jezreel was still controlled by the Philistines.

David

David was made of different stuff from Saul. He was a charismatic figure in every sense of the word, and would overcome tribal suspicions and resistance to the idea of a king, to unite the whole of Israel into a remarkably powerful alliance. The deuteronomic historians looked back on David knowing that he had turned out to be Israel's greatest national hero. He was the traditional composer of Israel's best-loved songs (the

---

Israel becomes a state *continued*

the exchange and distribution of different foodstuffs was necessary.

● The evolution of more complex societies in a marginal environment inevitably requires more sophisticated structures to deal with the kind of disputes that arise in relation to the fair distribution of resources. Some matters cannot be decided by informal meetings of tribal leaders, particularly when external factors such as the nature of the land, or the location of water are involved, for they generally transcend the ways in which territory is divided on a tribal basis. Arguments about equitable access to such resources invariably requires the development of more sophisticated systems of justice, accountable to some centralized individual or structure capable of enforcing decisions about such matters. When the book of Judges characterizes the early period as a time when 'there was no king in Israel; all the people did what was right in their own eyes' (21:25), it could easily have been this kind of free-for-all struggle for essential commodities that was implied. It is certainly striking that one of David's achievements is said to have been that he 'administered justice and equity to all his people' (2 Samuel 8:15).

● The increasing use of iron at this period was another feature that called for the

structures of a more centralized state. For reasons that no one quite understands, what is now known as the Late Bronze Age ended in Palestine about 1200 BC because the raw materials for making bronze were no longer easily obtainable. The move to new agricultural sites in the highlands of Canaan from about this time onwards required tough materials for tools, as the land itself was difficult to work and generally stony. Iron was the obvious choice, but Palestine had little indigenous iron ore, and none of it was of very high quality. This was not an insuperable obstacle, for the extensive international trading partnerships that existed made it relatively easy to import supplies from elsewhere. But in order to do that efficiently, and ensure the fair distribution of such implements as could be crafted, required a centralized body that would not only be able to deal with international traders, but that could also organize the manufacture of tools in urban centres and their efficient supply to those living in more remote areas.

Psalms), and the man about whom many of the most popular stories were told. All this is obvious from the way in which the books of Samuel introduce him to the narrative. In contrast to the stories of Saul, the accounts of David's life have been composed with great artistry and literary skill. The stories of his friendship with Saul's son Jonathan (1 Samuel 19–20), and of his unexpected defeat of the Philistine giant Goliath (1 Samuel 17) have remained firm favourites with Bible readers through many centuries and in all cultures. The sheer quantity of material relating to David's exploits also underlines his importance to the final editors of the Hebrew Bible: between 1–2 Samuel and 1 Kings, almost 70 per cent of the stories are about David, compared with only 20 per cent about Solomon, and even less about Saul.

David's rise to power

David was obviously a striking character. Not many shepherds become kings, and he must have had some extraordinary talent to rise so quickly to a position of such eminence in Saul's court. The features that impressed Saul also caught the imagination of the people, and it was not long before they were singing David's praises in the streets: 'Saul has killed thousands, but David tens of thousands' (1 Samuel 18:7). This kind of popularity aroused Saul to intense jealousy, and so he dis- missed David from the court, giving him instead the command of 1,000 soldiers in his private army. But David could not be held back. His military exploits were amazing, and 'everyone in Israel and Judah loved David because he was such a successful leader' (1 Samuel 18:16). His admirers even included Saul's daughter Michal, who fell in love with David and married him (1 Samuel 18:17–27). But Saul became more and more envious, and set out deliberately to kill him. As a result, David was forced to go into exile, in the south of the country (1 Samuel 19–22).

There he was secure from Saul,

David extended the boundaries of Israel well beyond the kingdom ruled by Saul.

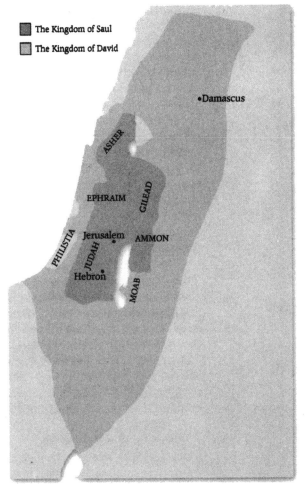

The Kingdom of Saul

The Kingdom of David

Damascus

ASHER

EPHRAIM

GILEAD

PHILISTIA

Jerusalem

JUDAH

AMMON

Hebron

MOAB

for between them lay a number of fortified Canaanite city states, including Jerusalem. In the south, David probably forged some sort of alliance with the Philistines (1 Samuel 22:1–2), for he was able to organize a court at Adullam and to protect himself and his troops by running a protection racket (1 Samuel 25). He also strengthened his position here by marriage alliances, and obviously became closely involved with Achish, the Philistine king of Gath (1 Samuel 27). Achish wanted to take David with him to the battle of Gilboa, where Saul met his death, but he was left behind when his loyalty was questioned by the other Philistine chiefs. They were right to do so, for David had been playing a double game with Achish (1 Samuel 29). But their suspicion of him turned out to David's advantage, for while the Philistines had been arguing about David, Amalekite raiders had attacked the town of Ziklag. On his return, David went out to avenge his own people. He took back all that the Amalekites had taken, and more besides, and then tactfully distributed it among the people of the towns where he was best known (1 Samuel 30).

Saul was finished and died in disgrace, having failed to win the allegiance and support of his people (1 Samuel 31). But David's position was assured. He had already established himself among the southern tribes, and he was now recognized as their leader. In effect, he became the king of Judah, reigning at Hebron. The southern tribes of Judah had always been isolated from the northern tribes and they had probably never been fully integrated into Saul's kingdom. So they had no qualms about accepting David: he had already shown his prowess in battle, and he continued to protect the people for a further seven and a half years (2 Samuel 2:10–11). But David was not satisfied with this. He knew that Israel would never be truly great until northern and southern tribes were fully united. In the north, Saul's son Ishbaal (Ishbosheth) had taken his father's place, but he had no popular support. In his fury against David, Saul had gone so far as to kill the priests who looked after the tribal sanctuary at Nob (1 Samuel 22), an action that was enough in itself to ensure that no son of his would ever be acclaimed by the tribes. Ishbaal's only real supporter was Abner, the commander of Saul's personal army, and when even he defected to David's side, Ishbaal was finished (2 Samuel 2:8 – 4:12). David agreed to become king of all the Israelite tribes, and the northern group pledged their allegiance to him (2 Samuel 5:1–5). The consolidation of a centralized state provided the infrastructure through which a new national identity could finally emerge, and David successfully established new conditions for internal social stability as well as the external security that was required to establish Israel as a dominant political force in the land.

A new king and new ways

A new kingdom needed a new capital. Hebron was too far south, and the north had no organization to speak of since the defeat at Gilboa and the murder of Ishbaal. So David found a new capital in Jerusalem. This was a particularly clever move, for the city had belonged to neither northern nor southern tribes, which meant that it had the potential to overcome any residual jealousies among the old tribal groupings. Strategically, the capture of this city by David's troops, who gained access to it by climbing up a water shaft (2 Samuel 5:6–10), also removed one of the last physical barriers to the unity of the kingdom, for Jerusalem had been one of the last remaining independent city states that had effectively isolated north from south during the time of Saul.

For all these reasons it could become 'the city of David' in a distinctive way. He constructed new fortifications, and built a palace for himself, and in the process established significant relationships with foreign powers, especially the Phoenicians, by employing craftworkers from all over the region (2 Samuel 5:11–12). Unfortunately, very little still remains of the Jerusalem of David's time, though there can be no doubt that he and his successor Solomon transformed it into a major administrative centre, probably aided by the considerable bureaucratic expertise of its original Jebusite inhabitants, who were now incorporated into the kingdom of Israel. This was just a small section of a fairly large foreign population that became a part of David's kingdom, for as he extended his influence in all directions he defeated Edomites, Moabites, Ammonites and Syrians, as well as Philistines, and their towns and people naturally pledged their allegiance to David.

The spoils captured in these military expeditions, and the taxes paid to him by conquered peoples, financed the construction of many fine buildings in Jerusalem. It also enabled David to increase the number of mercenaries in his personal army, and to establish a full royal court at his new palace. But he was always careful to preserve those all-important links with the looser tribal alliances that had preceded the emergence of the Israelite state. One of his earliest acts was to bring the ark of the covenant to Jerusalem. To the tribes, this had always been a central symbol of their commitment to one another, representing the story of the escape from Egypt, the covenant with God at Mount Sinai and the common worship of Yahweh that held them together (2 Samuel 6).

We need not doubt that David's religious commitment played an important part in all this. But the arrival of the ark of the covenant in Jerusalem also had social consequences, for it gave David's own position a special seal of approval. More than that, for in a sense, the ark installed in David's city now became David's personal possession. It certainly removed the power centre from the tribes themselves, and vested it in a state authority that could transcend the old tribal loyalties. In other words, David achieved what Saul had failed to do: he established his own position independently of the continued acclamation of the people. The nation was controlled by his own army, with his own city, and now he had his own national shrine at the centre of things.

David was undoubtedly a great leader. By combining military

prowess with inspirational leadership he secured for himself a significant place not just as a successful ruler, but also, through the royal ideology which evolved to underpin his dynasty, as a significant religious icon for future generations. Politically, David's rise to fame was facilitated by the relative weakness of Egypt and Assyria at the time, but his achievement was still remarkable nonetheless.

The old ways and new ideas

One of the most significant stories told about David in the Old Testament is of his adultery with Bathsheba and the murder of her

Jerusalem was captured by David, who moved his capital there from Hebron. Known ever since as 'the city of David', Jerusalem became and has remained the focus of devotion for the people of Israel. The original part of the city is in the foreground of the picture, on the spur of land leading up to the Temple Mount, and bordered on one side by the Kidron Valley.

husband Uriah (2 Samuel 11). This kind of behaviour has been typical of royal households from time immemorial, and continues to be so. But somewhat surprising is the bold denunciation of David's behaviour by the prophet Nathan, and the apparently deep sincerity of David's subsequent change of heart (2 Samuel 12:1–15). The inclusion of such a personal story relates to the concerns of the deuteronomic historians, who wanted to remind their readers that even David, the greatest of all kings, was still subordinate to a higher power than himself, namely the values of the covenant with Yahweh. But David's personal failings did not threaten his position, as is underlined by the inclusion of an oracle

previously delivered by the same prophet Nathan, declaring that God had established a specially close personal relationship with David's family, ensuring that David's sons would succeed him in perpetuity, and David himself could enjoy special privilege as God's 'son' (2 Samuel 7:1–17).

Throughout the ancient world, kings were described in this kind of lofty language, and though on occasion it could imply a claim to divinity (as with the pharaohs of Egypt), more often it was just a general part of the metaphorical language used to highlight the uniquely privileged position of a monarch. Of course, it could easily be used as a way of legitimizing anything that a king might want to do, and that certainly happened from time to time in Israel, just as it did elsewhere.

Trade in Solomon's time.

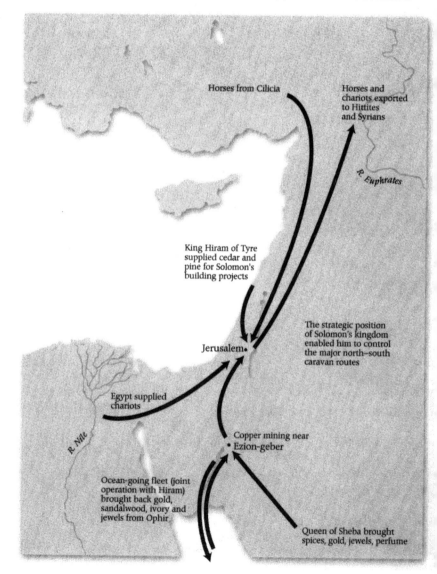

Horses from Cilicia

Horses and chariots exported to Hittites and Syrians

R. Euphrates

King Hiram of Tyre supplied cedar and pine for Solomon's building projects

The strategic position of Solomon's kingdom enabled him to control the major north–south caravan routes

Jerusalem

Egypt supplied chariots

R. Nile

Copper mining near Ezion-geber

Ocean-going fleet (joint operation with Hiram) brought back gold, sandalwood, ivory and jewels from Ophir

Queen of Sheba brought spices, gold, jewels, perfume

But the editors of these stories make it clear that continued divine approval of the royal family operated within a moral framework, whose values derived from the covenant relationship between God and people established at Mount Sinai. In effect, the kind of royal ideology represented by Nathan's oracle became a way of incorporating the king into the covenant, thereby investing him with special privileges. But by the same token, he was also faced with the moral requirements of the covenant, and his position as God's 'son' meant he could be punished by God, just as any other parent might punish their children for wrongdoing.

As the story unfolds, this lesson is reinforced in many different ways. The kings of David's dynasty did not live up to these high aspirations but, as Samuel had foreseen, became like the kings of other nations, more often concerned for themselves than for their covenant obligations to God and to their people (1 Samuel 8:10–18). However, this promise to David and his family was to assume great importance at a later stage in Israel's history, as frustrated political ambitions came to be transferred to a future hope for an ideal descendant of David, the Messiah.

Solomon

Towards the end of David's reign, the prospective heirs began to jockey for position. Revolts led by David's son Absalom (2 Samuel 13–19) and Sheba, a man from the tribe of Benjamin (2 Samuel 20:1–22), were crushed, and by the time of David's death his son Adonijah was the most obvious successor. He had the support of Abiathar the priest and of Joab, who was commander of the national army (1 Kings 1:5–10). But another son, Solomon, had more powerful friends. His mother Bathsheba had been David's favourite wife, and she was supported by Nathan, the priest Zadok and Benaiah, the commander of David's own private army. In the end, Solomon won, and with the exception of Abiathar the priest, who was sent off into exile, Adonijah and all his supporters were killed (1 Kings 1:11 – 2:46). Right from the start, Solomon's emergence as king was founded on court intrigues and military strength. Unlike his father David, and Saul before him, his position depended only on the fact that he was the head of state. He was indeed a king like the rulers of other nations, who did not need to seek the approval of his people because by now a ruling class had developed, in which Solomon was pre-eminent. This development was viewed ambivalently by the deuteronomic editors, who applauded the achievements which had led to the emergence of Israel as a powerful nation state, while at the same time raising serious questions about the kind of spirituality often invoked to strengthen the position of the kings.

The empire
Militarily, Israel's position had been secured before Solomon came to power, and though there is evidence to suggest that both the Edomites and the

Syrians recovered some territory during his reign (1 Kings 11:14–25), this was a period of consolidation rather than expansion. Solomon set about securing the position of the state and enhancing his own situation, and at this time poured vast resources into the development of the private army that his father had left to him. What had probably been in David's day little more than a personal bodyguard for the king now developed into a sophisticated fighting force, whose resources are listed as 1,400 chariots and 12,000 men and horses (1 Kings 4:26; 10:26). Chariots had once been the monopoly of the Canaanite city states, and it was this more than anything else that had prevented the tribes in the days of the judges from establishing their own settlements in the plains at the centre of the country. No doubt Solomon utilized the wider expertise of Canaanite culture in developing such weapons, for his own chariots were stationed exclusively in old Canaanite strongholds.

Alliances

Solomon adopted a policy of forging alliances with other neighbouring states as a means of consolidating his own position. Phoenicia, Arabia, Syria and Cilicia, and some states in north and east Africa, all became significant trading partners, while relationships with Egypt were cemented by Solomon's marriage to an Egyptian princess. This must have been an especially important alliance, for a special palace was built for this Egyptian wife. The pharaoh of the time also took it seriously, for he captured the city of Gezer and gave it to Solomon as a wedding gift (1 Kings 9:16–17), the archaeological evidence from Gezer showing both the destruction caused when the Egyptians destroyed it and Solomon's reconstruction of it in a distinctive style.

Another of Solomon's close allies was Hiram, king of Tyre. The Phoenicians had widespread trading links throughout the Mediterranean Sea, and they gave Solomon assistance to develop his own sea trade in the Red Sea and the Indian Ocean (1 Kings 9:26–28; 10:22). They also probably helped him with the expertise necessary to build and operate his own copper refineries on the Gulf of Aqabah. Solomon was also a horse dealer on a grand scale, trading with the Egyptians to the south and the Hittites in the north.

A ship from Solomon's merchant fleet.

The Temple

The profits from all this activity helped to finance the construction of many buildings in Jerusalem: Solomon's own palace, a palace for his Egyptian wife, a hall of audience for state occasions, a smaller judgment hall and, of course, the Temple.

David had originally wanted to build a permanent temple to house the ark of the covenant (2 Samuel 7:1–17). He had been unable to do so, but that did not stop him securing a site and gathering together items to

Solomon's Temple

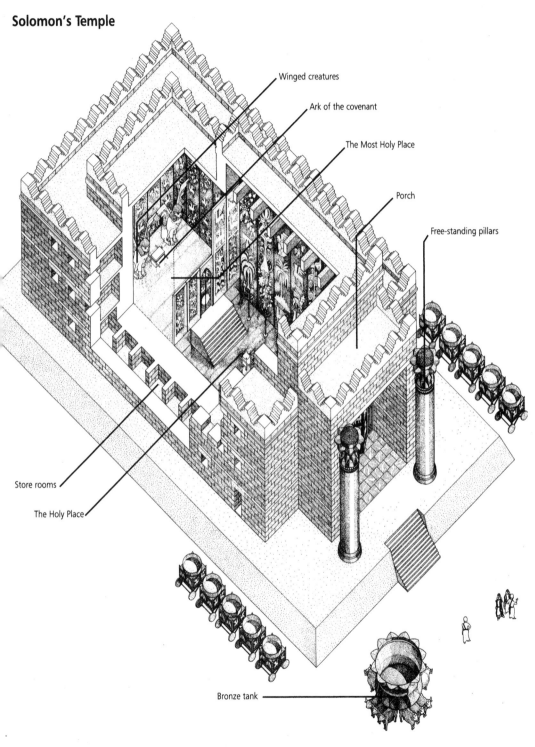

Winged creatures

Ark of the covenant

The Most Holy Place

Porch

Free-standing pillars

Store rooms

The Holy Place

Bronze tank

go into a temple (2 Samuel 24:18–25; 2 Chronicles 3:1). Solomon was remembered by later generations of Israelites largely because of his completion of this project. Like everything else that he attempted, the work was carried out on a lavish scale. The best materials were imported at great cost, and skilled craftworkers were brought in from Phoenicia. Throughout the region, the building of a temple was part of the process of establishing royal ideology and providing a religious legitimization for the existence of a state. The general design of the Temple Solomon had built in Jerusalem was typical of others throughout the region, and though it was to contain the ark of the covenant, which symbolized the presence of Israel's God Yahweh, the actual plan was identical to shrines in honour of Baal that have been discovered elsewhere in Palestine (1 Kings 5–7).

It is difficult to know exactly how Solomon viewed his Temple, though the similarities with temples honouring other deities certainly extend well beyond the architecture. For example, the Jerusalem Temple was consecrated at exactly the same time in the year as the Baal temple at Ugarit, just before the beginning of the all-important autumn rains (1 Kings 6:1, 37–38; 8:2), and Solomon assumed for himself some of the most important religious functions (1 Kings 3:15; 8:62–66), such as the offering of sacrifices and blessing the people (1 Kings 8:14–61). These were all functions that monarchs would naturally undertake, for they were a way of affirming their own position as head of state. But it is striking that, only a few pages before in the deuteronomic history, Saul and David had been expressly forbidden to do both these things, and Saul's attempt to do so had led directly to his downfall (1 Samuel 15:10–35), whereas in this narrative the editor makes no comment at all on these features of Solomon's kingship – presumably because of the

The stories about David and Solomon

The books of Samuel and Kings belong together, and are a compilation of different stories gathered by an editor or editors to make one great account of Israel's history, which probably included the books of Joshua and Judges as well. Quite often, the editors refer to their sources of information (e.g. 1 Kings 11:41). At other points, scholars have tried to uncover the origins of their stories. More often than not, this has proved to be an unprofitable exercise, but in the case of the stories of David and Solomon many people believe that such 'source analysis' can show that we are actually reading a kind of 'court

history' that was written down more or less at the same time as the events themselves happened.

The stories in 2 Samuel 9–20 and 1 Kings 1–2 are undoubtedly among the most vivid narratives in the entire Old Testament. They are well written and excitingly presented, with the kind of psychological appreciation of human relationships that gives an added plausibility and realism to what they say. In this respect they are quite different from what precedes or follows them – and even from the final chapters of 2 Samuel itself (21–24).

In 1926, the German scholar Leonhard Rost suggested that this section of Samuel and Kings was originally a self-contained

central importance later attached to Jerusalem and its Temple. Such criticism as there is was reserved for what many saw as Solomon's active promotion of the interests of 'foreign deities' (1 Kings 11:1–13). Looking back from a longer historical perspective, his careless disregard for the original values of the covenant could be seen to have been a major factor in his eventual downfall. Solomon may have been renowned for his wisdom, but it was not the kind of practical wisdom that led to a sympathetic understanding of his own people, or to an appreciation of the kind of king that Israel's faith would tolerate.

Arts and science

The 'wisdom' attributed to Solomon was in fact not just common sense and human insight. It was, rather, part and parcel of a great international intellectual movement of the day that is often simply referred to as the 'wisdom movement'. As such, Solomon's involvement with it was yet another indication of his royal status, not only within Israel, but also on the wider world stage. The writer of 1 Kings explicitly compares Solomon's 'wisdom' with that of other ancient rulers: 'Solomon's wisdom surpassed the wisdom of all the people of the east, and all the wisdom of Egypt. He was wiser than anyone else' (1 Kings 4:30–31). The nature of this intellectual endeavour becomes clearer when we learn that 'he composed 3,000 proverbs and more than a thousand songs. He spoke of trees and plants... he talked about animals, birds, reptiles, and fish' (1 Kings 4:32–33). This is comparable to the intellectual pursuits of kings and philosophers throughout the history of ancient Egypt and Mesopotamia, who compiled encyclopaedic descriptions of the world and all its affairs, covering subjects as diverse as astrology, mathematics, politics and zoology. The knowledge thus gained was sometimes distilled

---

story, compiled in order to prove that Solomon was the legitimate heir to David's throne. There is no doubt that the accession of Solomon is surprising, for he was a relatively minor son, and apart from a short notice of his birth in 2 Samuel 12:24–25 there is no mention of him before he became king. He also came to power through a court intrigue and by murdering his opponents, something which Rost suggested must have stirred many loyal Israelites to start asking awkward questions. In response, a supporter of Solomon set out to justify his position as legitimate heir to the throne – and, in the nature of things, he must have done so at an early date in Solomon's reign.

There was a well-established tradition of such political apologetic among other nations at the time, especially the Hittites. So, encouraged by international contacts, and the new opportunities for artistic endeavour provided by Solomon's court, Solomon's friend took the older traditional stories about David's reign, and showed how the elder sons Amnon, Absalom and Adonijah, had all disqualified themselves by their disregard for the covenant traditions (2 Samuel 13:8–14; 16:22; 1 Kings 2:13–17). This was why Solomon emerged as David's successor, and the brutal events which brought him to power were a regrettable but necessary evil.

Rost hailed this narrative as the beginning of real history writing in the ancient world, though recent scholars have

into pithy sayings, such as we find in the Old Testament book of Proverbs, parts of which are said to have been composed by Solomon himself (Proverbs 10:1; 25:1). In a later period, professional wisdom teachers could be found as religious advisers, occupying an official position comparable to that of a priest (Jeremiah 18:18), though at this stage the pursuit of 'wisdom' was probably a secular interest.

All this activity stimulated the development of other literary skills in Israel. We know that Solomon had his own official archivists who recorded the events of his reign (1 Kings 11:41), and it is also widely believed that the stories of Samuel, Saul and David were written down in a continuous narrative at this time (though not in their final form). It is certainly not unlikely that a successful king would want to record the events that led up to his accession to the throne. Many scholars have also postulated that as a reaction against all this self-centred artistic and intellectual endeavour, other writers during Solomon's reign wove the traditional stories handed down by the tribes into a great epic account of Israel's earliest history, which later was incorporated into the books of the Torah. The purpose of this was to emphasize again how Abraham, Moses and the early tribes had prospered not because of their own efforts, but because of their humble dependence on the love and goodness of God.

Balancing the books

For a variety of reasons, there was growing ill-feeling and resentment against the style of Solomon's rule. Some still regretted the replacement of voluntary tribal associations by the apparatus of a state, while the emerging underclass that was inevitably created saw no reason why they should actually pay for the king's extravagant lifestyle through

---

The stories about David and Solomon *continued*

been more hesitant. They point out, for example, that these stories contain much that is unfavourable to David and Solomon, and therefore perhaps what we now have is an expurgated version of a series of stories that originally disapproved of the Davidic dynasty. This argument carries less weight if the original intention was apologetic, for in such a situation, unfortunate facts have to be faced, and explained away in some way or another rather than ignored altogether. But it has also been suggested that much of the material is more like a novel than historical narrative. It certainly includes some surprising details, such as the conversation that Amnon had with Tamar as he raped her (2 Samuel 13:1–22), though features

like that do not necessarily call into question the general impression created by the narrative. It simply shows that it was written in the first instance by a journalist rather than an annalist, which in turn perhaps suggests that it was not really the official court record of David, but a popular account of Solomon's origins, designed to win the support of the average person in the street for their new king.

taxation. Taxation, however, is an inevitable part of the infrastructure required to support any state, and Solomon's trading activities could never have generated sufficient funds to finance what needed to be done. On occasion, he tried to pay off his creditors by giving them land or cities, as with Hiram of Tyre (an offer which was refused, 1 Kings 9:10–14).

The administrative framework for the collection of taxes already existed, for David had inaugurated a modest system whereby twelve different districts of his territory would support his court with provisions for one month each year. Solomon extended this to provide the means for collecting taxes, and each district was placed in the charge of a single officer (1 Kings 4:7–19). The idea had little appeal for the people, not so much because they were reluctant to pay their dues, but more because of resistance to the idea of a privileged elite being served and paid for by the ordinary citizens. But this is all part and parcel of how a state needs to operate, and though the deuteronomic editors might hint that it was a Canaanite way of doing things, and therefore an erosion of the traditions represented by the ancestral faith of Israel, it was an inescapable consequence of the kind of political entity that Israel had now become.

Worse was to come, however, for the taxation raised in the districts was still not enough to balance Solomon's books, and so he introduced what the Old Testament euphemistically calls 'forced labour' – in other words, slavery (1 Kings 5:13; 11:28). There has been debate as to whether Israelites were included in such schemes, but whoever the workers were, the whole idea turned out to be one of the key factors in precipitating a coup under the leadership of Jeroboam, one of the officers in charge of the taxation districts. This plot was uncovered, and he fled into exile in Egypt for a while (1 Kings 11:26–40), but the movement that he represented was too deeply rooted to be stopped. The tribes in the northern part of Solomon's kingdom – the original tribes who had chosen Saul as their leader – had had enough. Not only did they regard Solomon's demands as excessive, but they believed them to be unfair, for the southern tribes – who first made David their king – appear to have been excluded from the taxation districts altogether (1 Kings 4:7–19).

The seeds of Solomon's destruction germinated in the same soil as many revolutionary political movements: the exploitation of an underclass by the rulers. Later generations regarded that not only as incompetent government, but also as a gross violation of the standards of the covenant, by which all rulers would be judged – and by those standards Solomon was a miserable failure, no matter how successful he might otherwise have been.

After Solomon

When Solomon died he was succeeded by his son, Rehoboam. But by then an irreversible change of mood had come over the northern tribal grouping: they had had enough of dynastic kingship, and they were looking for a return to a simpler ideal of statehood in which the people, and not an elite ruling class, would decide their own fate. As we have seen, the exact details of the evolution of the Israelite state are among the most hotly debated subjects in Old Testament scholarship. But however it might be accounted for, it seems indisputable that there was by this period a deeply ingrained conviction among much of the population that the true calling of the nation was to form an egalitarian social community based on the understanding of God's own personality as revealed through the stories of the covenant forged at Mount Sinai.

So when Rehoboam went north from Jerusalem to Shechem to secure the allegiance of the northern tribes, their local leaders announced the terms on which they would be prepared to acknowledge him as their king (1 Kings 12:1–7). Rehoboam's oldest and most experienced advisers told him to listen sympathetically, but he rejected their advice and warned the northern leaders that worse was to come: 'My father placed heavy burdens on you; I will make them even heavier. He beat you with a whip; I'll flog you with a horsewhip!' (1 Kings 12:14). He regarded them as rebellious subjects, and got ready to force them back into line. But it was too late: Jeroboam had already returned from Egypt, and the people had acclaimed him as their king. It was an

---

The psalms and Israel's worship

The psalms were fundamental to Israelite worship, and in many respects can be understood as providing a detailed account of the religious activities at the Jerusalem Temple in the period before the exile to Babylon. Two points in particular have contributed much to our understanding of this subject:

● Many of the psalms can be understood not just as hymns, but as more comprehensive liturgies. Not only do they reflect the praise and penitence of the worshippers – they also contain God's response to that worship (e.g. Psalms 2; 12; 20; 21; 45; 50; 81; 89; 91; 95; 108; 110; 132). Moreover, these responses are often similar in both style and substance to the messages of the Old Testament prophets, and on this basis it has been suggested that in the Temple at Jerusalem there was a group of prophets who worked alongside the priests in leading the people in worship. When it was first made, this claim was a surprise to many Old Testament scholars. In the nineteenth century it had often been taken for granted that in Old Testament times the prophets and the priests were firmly opposed to each other, with the priests being concerned with the mechanical performance of rites of 'religion', while the prophets concerned themselves with a more dynamic spirituality, bringing a living word from God to their people. It is certainly true that most of the prophets had hard things to say about the meaningless performance of empty religious rituals. But this perception of a sharp division between priest and prophet often owed more to the intense anti-Catholic views of Protestant (especially German Lutheran) scholars than it did to the evidence of the Hebrew Bible itself. Even Amos, who is often thought to be one of those most fiercely opposed to religious rituals, apparently delivered his messages in the context of organized worship at Bethel, while the book of Jeremiah not only lists prophets and priests

irreversible change, and from this point onwards the northern tribes had their own king and their own kingdom (Israel) while the descendants of David in Jerusalem ruled over a much smaller kingdom in the south (Judah). Israel's golden age was past, and the future would witness gradual dissolution and decline until both kingdoms would eventually disappear.

Society and religion

The years between Saul and Solomon saw the establishment of a distinctively Israelite society for the first time. Despite the problems that it caused, the idea of a monarchy was accepted, and even when the ten tribes broke away under Jeroboam they did little to change the outward forms of the state established by Solomon; they simply explained them in a different way. So it is to be expected that the events of these years should have set the pattern for Israel's life for many years to come. In spite of the tensions that surfaced among different factions in the population, the reigns of David and Solomon were looked back upon with affection by all later generations. Though the deuteronomic editors of Israel's history books could see much to be ashamed of in the activities of them both, that did nothing to diminish the esteem in

together as leaders of the community (Jeremiah 18:18), but also gives other indications of the association of prophets with the Jerusalem Temple (e.g. Jeremiah 5:30–31; 23:11; 26:7, 16; 27:16; 29:26). Scholars have described these people as 'cult prophets' in an effort to distinguish them from figures such as Amos or Jeremiah. In Jeremiah's time, most of them were giving false reassurance to the people, and as a result their office disappeared after the Babylonian exile. But the book of Psalms gives some indication that at an earlier period they had a full and perfectly legitimate part to play in the worship of God at the Temple.

● A number of scholars have also claimed on the basis of the psalms that the king played a significant role in the worship at the Temple. This is intrinsically likely anyway, as involvement in public ritual was a key way in which rulers could establish and reinforce the legitimacy of their reign. There was a good deal of diversity in the ways that ancient people thought of their kings. Some of them were

Many different instruments were used in worship at the Jerusalem Temple, one of which was the harp. Here, a musician seated on a folding stool plays a harp.

which they were held, David being credited with the authorship of much of the Old Testament book of Psalms, while Solomon was thought of as the founder of the 'wisdom movement' in ancient Israel. Regardless of their weaknesses, these kings and their successors in Jerusalem exerted a considerable influence on the religious and cultural life of their people. The important religious message of the various books traditionally connected with David and Solomon will be considered in some detail in later chapters. But it is appropriate here to notice some aspects of the picture they provide of religious life and culture in ancient Israel.

The psalms

The Old Testament book of Psalms consists of 150 separate pieces of religious poetry or songs, arranged in five separate sections, or 'books'. The way in which the psalms are numbered is slightly different in the Hebrew Bible from in the Greek (Septuagint) version, and Christian Bibles all follow the Greek scheme. Psalms 1–8 are the same in both, but then Psalms 9–10 in the Hebrew Bible were combined into just one, Psalm 9, in the Septuagint. From that point on, the numbers do not correspond until the final section of the book, where they come together again at Psalm 147. The Greek Bible also included a Psalm 151, which

The psalms and Israel's worship
continued

regarded as divine or semi-divine beings, whose well-being was crucial to the continued prosperity of their people. The king's involvement in religious ritual might be connected with the cycle of the seasons, as appears to have been the case in Babylon, for example, where the king appeared in the annual New Year Festival acting out the part of a god, whose ritual death and resurrection then symbolized the death and renewed vitality of nature. Israel never thought of their kings as divine, though the royal ideology of the House of David did insist that they enjoyed a special position as a result of God's blessing upon them (Psalm 2:7). Whether there was an annual festival in Israel at which the king underwent a ritual humiliation and restoration along the lines of the Babylonian festival is more debatable, though it seems likely that the annual celebration of the New Year was a major religious event in Israel, albeit centred on the enthronement of God, and the celebration of Yahweh's continued sovereignty over the forces of chaos and

disorder that continually threatened Israel's precarious existence. Others, however, have denied this, preferring instead to see the New Year festival in Israel (the feast of Tabernacles) as an occasion for solemn renewal of the covenant made at Mount Sinai, or even as an annual celebration of the establishment of the royal family of David. Beyond inferences that can be drawn from some of the psalms, and cryptic passages elsewhere, there is little hard evidence to show just what religious functions the king might have carried out in ancient Israel, though he is unlikely to have been exclusively, or even mainly, a religious functionary. Religious imagery and ritual could be used to bolster the king's position, but the overall impression given by the Old Testament is of men whose activities had some interaction with religious worship, but whose main sphere of operation was elsewhere, in the judicial and diplomatic functions of the ancient monarch.

was never included either in the Hebrew Bible or in any version of the Christian Old Testament. This was ascribed to David, and consists of a reflection on the story of David's choice as king (1 Samuel 16:1–13). Though Psalm 151 is known from the Greek version, the Dead Sea Scrolls contain sections of two psalms in Hebrew which seem to have formed the basis for it, so presumably it was originally translated into Greek, rather than compiled in that language. Its date is impossible to determine.

As a collection, the book of Psalms was probably brought together for use in the worship of the restored Temple that was built in Jerusalem about 520 BC, after the Jewish exile in Babylon. Naturally, some of the psalms were written at that time (e.g. Psalm 137), though the majority were not, and it is widely agreed that they mostly originated in the worship of God by ancient Israel during the period from about 1000 BC to 586 BC. Many of the psalms have titles, but these were not a part of the original compositions, and are rightly relegated to footnotes in modern versions of the Bible. Some of these titles contain musical directions, indicating the tune to which particular compositions were to be sung, or the musical instruments that might be used to accompany them. Others indicate that a particular psalm was connected with David, the sons of Korah, sons of Asaph, and others. The precise meaning of such ascriptions is often unclear. Even the term 'a psalm of David' could just as easily mean 'a psalm for David', and may not necessarily have been intended as a claim that he was its author. Such a title could also indicate that the psalm in question originally belonged to a collection of songs issued by the Davidic royal house in Jerusalem, or that it was written for the king there, who was of course always David's descendant. There is no compelling reason for rejecting the possibility that some of these psalms could go back to David himself, though in the nature of such things it will never be possible to know for certain.

Life is always a kaleidoscope of conflicting experiences and emotions – and we find this variety reflected in the contents of the Old Testament psalms. Not all psalms are the same. Some of them are majestic hymns of praise to God, reflecting the joy of the jubilant worshipper who is at peace with God and with the world (Psalms 145–150). By contrast, others reflect the darker moments of human experience. Feelings of guilt feature in some of them (Psalms 51; 130), while others consist of songs of protest complaining about unjust suffering (Psalms 13; 71). Some psalms give a glimpse of how the whole nation might react in a time of national disaster or uncertainty (Psalms 44; 74; 80; 83), while others invite us to share in the great ceremonial events of national life, such as the coronation or wedding of a king (Psalm 45), and yet others contain intimate expressions of heartfelt gratitude to God by an individual worshipper who had been delivered from some personal trial (Psalms 30; 92; 116).

In the early years of the twentieth century, the psalms were classified along these lines by a German scholar, Hermann Gunkel, who proposed five main categories: hymns of praise, individual songs of lament, community laments, individual songs of thanks, and royal psalms. This classification has stood the test of time, though it is in some respects unsatisfactory. For example, Gunkel tended to make too sharp a distinction between individual and community psalms: a number of psalms that begin as the words of a single person go on to speak not just of an individual, but of the whole nation of Israel (Psalms 51; 102; 130). It might also be questioned how distinctive the category of 'royal psalms' actually is, for all the royal psalms could easily be fitted into other categories, the only thing that binds them together being their reference to the king.

A number of the psalms depict Jerusalem as a place of security, and encourage people to pray for the peace of the city.

Their diversity and versatility suggest that the psalms must have been used in a number of different ways. Gunkel, for example, assumed that they were mostly personal expressions of piety, the sort of poetry that any worshipper might use to express their deepest feelings about life and about God. Others have argued that the psalms do not reflect individual experiences, but the experience of the whole nation of Israel over a long period of time. It has even been suggested that they are a kind of spiritual temperature chart of Israel's history from the earliest days up to the time after the exile. Both these elements are no doubt present, but what is fundamental to the varied thoughts of the psalms is a deep religious experience that their authors knew to be relevant to the whole of life. For the sense of God's reality can come as readily from nature (Psalms 8; 104) as from Israel's history (Psalms 78; 105) or from the writer's own private experiences (Psalms 31; 130).

Wisdom

Just as David was traditionally associated with the types of religious poetry we find in the book of Psalms, so Jewish tradition has linked Solomon with the so-called 'Wisdom' books of the Hebrew Bible, and the deuterocanonical books of the Christian Old Testament actually contain one such book, called the Wisdom of Solomon.

Paradoxically, there is only one book in the Hebrew Bible that mentions Solomon in its title, the Song of Solomon – and that is not a wisdom book at all! Moreover, it probably has no direct connection with Solomon, other than the fact that his name occurs in it a number of times (Song of Solomon 1:1, 5; 3:7–11; 8:11–12). Indeed, the way he is mentioned in these passages rather suggests that he was not the author of it. Its exact origins are uncertain. It contains at least one Persian word (4:13) and one word that may be Greek (3:9), which would suggest it was written sometime after the rise of the Persian empire in 539 BC. But it also has features that suggest a much earlier origin, while there is some evidence of similar poetry in the nations surrounding Israel, dating from long before the time of Solomon. It is quite likely, therefore, that it is really an anthology of poetry, rather than a continuous composition written at one particular point in time. Its subject (sexual love) is certainly timeless, and it consists of a collection of erotic poems in which a woman and her lover exchange intimate details about their relationship. Many readers of the book, both Jewish and Christian, have been alarmed by its frankness, and have preferred to think of it as a symbolic writing, representing the relationship between God and the people of Israel, or between Christ and the church. But such ideas were certainly not in the minds of those who first included it in the Hebrew Bible. For them, God was the creator of all things, including sex and relationships, and a collection of love poems was therefore no more out of place than the story of God's dealings with Israel in the great events of their national history.

Solomon's name and influence has more often been connected with two other Old Testament books: Proverbs and Ecclesiastes. Along with the book of Job, and (from the deuterocanonical books) the Wisdom of Ben Sira and Wisdom of Solomon, these are usually classed together as 'wisdom' books. Their message is explored in detail in later chapters, but knowing a little of their origins will help us here in understanding the nature of Israelite culture.

What is wisdom?

There is no short, simple answer to this question. When Solomon is described as a 'wise man', the description seems to include many different characteristics. To be wise was 'to know the difference between good and evil' (1 Kings 3:9), but it also included political skills to deal with his own people and diplomacy in international relations (1 Kings 5:7, 12), as well as possession of the sort of knowledge we would associate with a botanist or zoologist (1 Kings 4:33). In addition to all that, Solomon's wisdom also included the ability to write poetry (1 Kings 4:32) and sensitivity in resolving legal disputes (1 Kings 3:16–28).

From this, it seems that when the ancients spoke of 'wisdom' they included all those elements in a person's character and upbringing that enable them to be a mature and successful member of society. In order to find a meaningful place in society, there are certain things we need to know. Nowadays, much emphasis tends to be placed on educational achievements, or proficiency in particular skills which will equip people to perform a specific job. No doubt vocational training had its place in the life of the ancient world, but being fully human involved much more than that – and this is what forms the substance of the wisdom literature of the Old Testament. These wisdom books reflect a broad cross-section of moral insights, intellectual thinking and social skills that would equip a person to live in an informed and mature way. The influence of several specific life situations can be traced in this literature.

THE FAMILY
In recent Western culture, it has often been assumed that the state should prepare children for life, both in terms of vocational training and in moral and religious teaching. But in most other cultures, it is in the context of the family that children can learn by both precept and example the distilled wisdom of previous generations. Here, they discover effective ways of relating to other people, and what to avoid if they want to have a happy and fulfilled existence. All of this is based on

---

The wisdom books

Like the Psalms and most of the messages of the prophets, the wisdom books are written in poetry. In Hebrew poetry the most important feature is not its metrical form, but a device known as 'parallelism', in which the ideas that are communicated are the most important thing. In the simplest form of poetry ('synonymous parallelism'), the second line of a typical couplet simply repeats in different words the thought of the first line:

> Who has the right to go up Yahweh's
>   hill?
> Who may enter God's holy Temple?
> (Psalm 24:3)

'Antithetic parallelism' can make the same point by placing one part of the couplet in a positive form, while expressing the other negatively:

> Good people will be remembered as a
>   blessing,
> but the wicked will soon be forgotten.
> (Proverbs 10:7)

There are a good many other more subtle and intricate forms of verse, and sometimes there is a parallelism just of form, and not of meaning.

Many other literary devices are used in the wisdom books, including riddles, parables and autobiographical advice, as well as dialogue (as in Job). The acrostic is also occasionally used, that is a poetic composition in which each couplet or section begins with a different letter of the alphabet, starting with the first letter and working through to the end. Psalm 119 is the most striking example of this in the Old Testament, but Proverbs 31:10–31 also uses the same device.

Proverbs
This book is a collection or anthology of practical wisdom. The title (1:1) attributes the book to Solomon, though it is only in two places (10:1 – 22:16; 25:1 – 29:27) that Solomon is explicitly connected with its teaching. Other sections are attributed to Agur (30:1–33) and Lemuel (31:1–9), both characters of whom nothing else is known. Yet other sections are presented as anonymous compositions, which is exactly what we would expect in view of the likely origins of the kind of practical advice that the book contains.

Many of the wisdom sayings in Proverbs go back a long way into Israel's history, and were obviously composed long before the book itself was edited in its present form. The earliest date that could possibly be

the experience of their parents, and before them of their grandparents, who in turn inherited much from their own forebears. The family was the place where children learned social skills in ancient Israel, and many of the sayings in the book of Proverbs originated in this context and have the form of advice given by a parent to a child (e.g. Proverbs 4:1, 3–4, 10, 20).

THE VILLAGE

In addition to being a part of a family, we all belong to a larger community in the place where we live, and much of the 'wisdom' that equips us for life is derived from relationships in that context. Again, this is something that has become increasingly alien to many Western people, who live in physical isolation from others, often relying on the television or the Internet to provide them with a sense of 'community'. Even in the West, though, there are still many places which have the

---

given to this final editing would be the sixth century BC, since Hezekiah (king of Judah from 715 to 687 BC) is mentioned in 25:1. But it is more likely that the final editing of Proverbs was not completed until around the third century BC.

The book is mostly concerned with advice about relationships in different areas of life. As such it contains the sort of guidance about good manners and sensible behaviour that could have originated in any society. But the editors have gone out of their way to emphasize that the true meaning of such wisdom could only be found in a living relationship with God: 'To have knowledge, you must first have reverence for Yahweh' (1:7).

Ecclesiastes

This is a very different kind of book from Proverbs. Whereas Proverbs takes an optimistic view of life, and makes a positive assessment of its potential, Ecclesiastes is essentially negative and sceptical. If the wisdom books are indeed based on the distilled experiences of real people, its negative cynicism need not come as a surprise. There can be few people who could not at some time identify with the questions posed by the author of Ecclesiastes, who in the opening words asks whether life has any real

meaning, or whether instead it is 'all useless' (1:2). The author vacillates between these two, and though there is an underlying belief in God, there is also the honest recognition that faith sometimes seems to give little meaning to the details of everyday activities. There is no mention of Israel's history here, nor of the nation's experiences in events like the exodus, which other authors of the Hebrew Bible would have referred to as some sort of answer to the writer's questions. Instead, the author concedes that, while the mere reiteration of traditional religious dogmas is sometimes powerless to solve life's most pressing problems, ultimately the meaning of it all is known to God, even if the human mind finds it impossible to comprehend. In practical terms, 'all we can do is to be happy and do the best we can while we are still alive. All of us should eat and drink and enjoy what we have worked for. It is God's gift' (3:12–13).

The apparent unbelief of Ecclesiastes has caused problems for both Jewish and Christian readers of the book. But it does bear witness to two facts that are of fundamental importance. It reminds readers that there is a dimension of human life which cannot be understood by the exercise of rational thought, and it testifies to the reality – and acceptability – of doubt and

In Israelite communities, the city or village gate was the place where the elders sat. There, judgments were passed, and business transacted.

sense of community that is widespread elsewhere in the world. In Israelite villages, everything happened at the city or village gate. Justice was dispensed there, and it was also the place where the great issues of life were debated. It was the place where people went to exchange views and ideas, and some of this kind of 'wisdom' is also contained in the wisdom books of the Hebrew Bible. In one of his speeches, the hero of the book of Job says that he had regularly taken his place at

The wisdom books *continued*

uncertainty about God's ways, even in the midst of a community of believing people.

Ecclesiastes identifies its author as 'David's son, who was king in Jerusalem' (1:1). This was probably meant to indicate Solomon, though there are compelling reasons against supposing that he had any connection with it:

● The author often writes from the point of view of an oppressed subject rather than that of an absolute monarch like Solomon (4:1).

● He also seems to have lived in a province of a great empire like that of the Persians, for the book contains a warning against the spies of the rulers (5:8).

● Political upheavals are mentioned, but of a kind that were not experienced in Solomon's time (4:13–16).

● The Hebrew language in which Ecclesiastes is written shows clear signs of the influence of Aramaic, which was the language of the Persian empire. This suggests a date in the third or second century BC.

Job

The book of Job falls into two parts, with a prologue and epilogue written in prose (1–2; 42:7–17) and the rest in poetry. The prologue and epilogue contain an old story about an otherwise unknown individual

called Job, who was an upright and God-fearing person and also 'the richest man in the east' (1:3). But then in a series of inexplicable calamities he lost all that he had and was himself afflicted with a painful and disfiguring disease. This part of the story depicts God as the president of a heavenly court, and explains Job's sufferings by reference to an accusation brought against him by the prosecutor, who is named as Satan. The charge was that Job's spiritual commitment was not genuine, and so his sincerity was put to the test as a means of verifying his faith, and at the end of the story (42:7–17) Job's proverbial patience was rewarded by renewed prosperity and happiness. Some features of this story (such as the part played by Satan) suggest a fairly late date in Jewish history, though other features seem to set it in a very early historical context. Perhaps it was an ancient story that was adapted by a later wisdom writer, to provide an opportunity for the exploration of the place of suffering and evil, which is the theme of the major part of the book.

Job is clearly not a wisdom book in the same sense as Proverbs. Whereas much of the homespun advice of Proverbs implies that doing good will automatically lead to success and prosperity, Job puts a series of question marks against that kind of

the city gate with those who went to debate and ponder on life's great mysteries (Job 29:7), thereby perhaps hinting that much of the argument contained in that book had been well rehearsed in such a setting in many an Israelite settlement. Proverbs also refers to the discussions at the city gate (24:7; 31:23, 31), and no doubt much of the advice contained in that book had its origins in the same context.

THE ROYAL COURT

The sort of advice that was given in the family and at the city gate would not have been unique to Israel. People of all cultures have their equivalents, and the ancient world was no different from the modern one in that respect. One of the results of Solomon's great expansion of trade and international diplomacy was that the people of Israel became familiar with the 'wisdom' traditions of the surrounding nations. Just as the Queen of Sheba came to Jerusalem to find out about Israelite

---

easygoing optimism. In Job's case, doing good had evidently led to exactly the opposite outcome, and the conventional view connecting goodness with prosperity was so deeply entrenched in the culture that the only way his friends could think of to try to help him was by suggesting that maybe he was not as good as he thought he was – otherwise why would he have suffered at all? Job knew this to be untrue, and rejected their diagnosis out of hand. But this was not the only problem with which he had to contend, for in the midst of it all he found himself wrestling with the same problems as the writer of Ecclesiastes. Far from finding God in these adversities, Job felt abandoned by the very God whom he had so diligently served. Where was God, he asked – indeed, what sort of a God would leave someone as upright as Job to suffer the unpredictable fate determined by a meaningless and evil universe?

Job's friends had no answer to that question, nor is any answer given to it in the book. When the writer eventually records God's answer to Job's questions, it does not include an explanation either of Job's suffering or of the apparent meaninglessness of life itself. Instead, in an impressively majestic poem it draws attention to the grandeur and greatness of both God and the world, and in doing so

redirects Job's thoughts away from himself and towards the glory of God and the created world (38–41). In the face of this self-revelation of God's character and personality, Job recognizes that the only response to make is one of trust and worship. The 'why' of human suffering was not answered as an intellectual question; indeed it is never answered in that way anywhere in the Bible. Job's friends might have been looking for an easy explanation of the presence of so much evil and undeserved suffering in the world, but the writer of the book of Job rejects all simple understandings. Here, the presence of evil in God's world remains an inexplicable enigma, but there is a message for those who struggle with it. As Job realized that he could never resolve his own predicament, and was forced to rely on God alone, he found his broken heart was healed as God burst into his life and surrounded him once more with constant care and love. In the end, renewed and consistent trust in God is the only way to deal with the vicissitudes of human life.

Other wisdom passages in the Hebrew Bible
In addition to those works that can readily be identified as belonging to this genre, scholars have often claimed that materials

wisdom (1 Kings 10:1–13), Israelites themselves were no doubt busy discovering the wisdom of other races. There was a good deal of such wisdom literature available elsewhere, especially in Egypt. One Egyptian text has many striking similarities to parts of the Old Testament book of Proverbs, and it was probably in such international circles that the knowledge of 'trees and plants… animals, birds, reptiles, and fish' (1 Kings 4:33) was handed on. Solomon specialized in such 'wisdom', and in this form it was probably a more intellectual pursuit than the moral advice that was handed on from generation to generation in the family and the village community. The more intellectual nature of such knowledge has led to the suggestion that from the time of Solomon onwards there may have been in Israel a group of professional wisdom teachers, whose job it was to study and teach such subjects in specialized schools. The much later book, the Wisdom of Ben Sira, certainly originated in such a context, though by then (c. 180 BC) the

---

The wisdom books continued

originating from wisdom schools can be traced elsewhere in the Old Testament. They point to some of the oracles of the prophets, especially in Amos and Isaiah, which seem to propound similar views to those found in the wisdom literature. We have already noted the theory that the 'succession narrative' (2 Samuel 9–20; 1 Kings 1–2) could have been moralistic 'wisdom' writing, and the same is possibly true of the stories of Joseph (Genesis 37; 39–50), which portray him as an ideal example of a person who lived his life according to the kinds of rules found in the book of Proverbs. It has also been suggested that the portrayal of the heroine of the book of Esther may owe something to such motives. There is nothing to prove any of these specu-lations, and it is unlikely that any of these stories came into existence purely as a means of demonstrating the value of practical wisdom. However, at the same time, the book of Job does provide a specific example of how an older story could be taken up and reinterpreted in this way, and if the concerns of the wisdom books were deeply embedded in the fabric of Israelite society, then it would be surprising if the same lessons were not articulated in other types of Old Testament literature.

Wisdom in the deuterocanonical books
Two books in the deuterocanonical collection deriving from the Greek Old Testament also fall into the category of wisdom writings. These are the Wisdom of Solomon and the Wisdom of Ben Sira (sometimes known as Ecclesiasticus). Wisdom 9:7–18 seems to imply that Solomon was its author, though without actually naming him, but few in the ancient world regarded it as his composition, and in addition the general cultural and historical circumstances reflected in it, not to mention the style and substance of its teachings, all indicate a much later date. There is no significant evidence to suggest it was ever compiled in any language other than Greek, and indeed it contains many technical terms that were typical of Greek philosophical speculation in the centuries immediately preceding the Christian era. The most obvious place to locate it would be among the Jewish community at Alexandria in Egypt and, since it seems to be unacquainted with the work of Philo of Alexandria, perhaps sometime in the first century BC. The teachings of the Wisdom of Solomon indicate familiarity with concepts drawn from Plato (7:22–24; 11:17; 14:3; 16:21; 17:2; 19:2) as well as the ideas of the Stoics (8:20; 17:11), though the author does not always use them in a technical philosophical

main subject of study would have been the Hebrew scriptures themselves. But at an earlier date, Jeremiah 18:18 mentions 'the wise' alongside priests and prophets as leaders of the nation, and of course from the time of Solomon onwards there were many professional diplomats, who must have been taught reading, writing and other intellectual skills by someone. There may well have been schools in ancient Israel in which knowledge was pursued for its own sake, though in the absence of specific evidence it is not possible to be certain.

---

way. Its aim appears to have been to encourage Jewish believers to continue in their faith, knowing that even in a culture dominated by a different and apparently more sophisticated world-view, their ancient stories and traditions still made sense. In the process, its message also appealed to those who were not themselves descended from the Israelite people, but who may have been attracted by the ideals of biblical faith, inviting them to abandon the worship of false gods and commit themselves to the covenant faith of Yahweh.

The prologue to the Wisdom of Ben Sira (Sirach) says that it was originally written in Hebrew and then translated into Greek by the author's grandson, and there is no reason to doubt this as copies of sections of the original Hebrew text are known. It is less clear to what extent the two versions were identical, as the translator himself says he made some substantial alterations. The translation itself is precisely dated, to 'the thirty-eighth year of the reign of Euergetes', that is Ptolemy VIII Euergetes Physcon (170–116 BC), which would make the date of the original composition perhaps about 180 BC. All of this seems plausible, and fits the contents of the book, which means this is the only writing of the entire Old Testament which can be precisely dated and attributed to a specific author, whose full name was Jesus ben Sira (50:27) and who lived in Jerusalem. The work itself is a striking example of the international character of the wisdom movement, for it combines elements of Greek philosophical thinking with traditional concepts from the Hebrew scriptures in a new and creative synthesis. As is often the case with this sort of literature, it is hard to trace a single line of argument running through from start to finish, though the general theme of it is clear: that true wisdom is found in the Torah, and exercised through trust in God. The way in which Ben Sira personified the figure of Wisdom, connecting it with concepts found in the wider culture of the day, provided an important framework within which Christians could later explain their beliefs about Jesus of Nazareth as both human and divine. As with the earlier wisdom books of the Hebrew Bible, however, the main emphasis is on practical morality and acceptable forms of behaviour in the context of everyday life.

5 The Two Kingdoms

A kingdom divided

What happened after Solomon's death is often referred to as 'the division of the kingdom'. As a statement of fact, that is what happened: the extensive empire ruled over by Solomon was split into two. To a large extent, however, this split seems to have been the natural culmination of an ideological division that had existed for much longer. The northern tribes, led by Ephraim, and the southern tribes, led by Judah, had only ever been truly united by their common allegiance to David. Both groups looked on him as a leader following in the footsteps of the judges, whose position was therefore assured only because God had chosen and equipped him. His continued rule was valid only insofar as he lived up to the responsibility that was involved in such a lofty calling. Solomon had come to power in different circumstances altogether, and became king for no other reason than that David was his father. He was part of an established dynasty, and that factor in itself raised new questions about his relationship to the national self-understanding. The fact that Solomon had violated so many of the values associated with the Sinai covenant, together with the fact that he was not a northerner, helped considerably to revive deeply ingrained rivalries and suspicions between the two groups of tribes.

Back to the old ways

When the tribes in the north saw their chance to opt out of the vast bureaucratic state centred on Jerusalem, they lost no time in choosing to do so. They were not motivated purely by political expediency, nor even primarily by a feeling of outrage at the injustices that Rehoboam promised to impose on them, though both of those considerations no doubt played a part. But over and above all this, the narratives reflect a deeply rooted desire to get back to the old ways, to retrace their national footsteps and go back to their traditional roots. As we have already seen, there is considerable debate about the extent to which different elements of the population had been a part of the actual events of the exodus from Egypt. But it is clear that, by now, significant numbers of people had adopted that story as their own, and wanted to see the values embedded in it being worked out in the realities of political life. Though there were many good economic and social reasons why Israel had become a state with a king, looking back it seemed as if the days of the judges had represented some kind of golden age when the tribes had at least made the effort to live with the spontaneous belief and action that had been enshrined within the covenant, even if they had not always carried it through to perfection. Of course, the changing political realities made it impossible just to turn the clock back and return to the way things had been in those early days. Then, the judges had been leaders of their own tribes, and it was exceptional for them to unite all the tribes. In the new climate, that was impractical, and whatever new leader might emerge needed to be a national figure. Equally, though, he must never succeed to the throne just because his father had been king before him. Every king must demonstrate that he had been called and equipped by God for the job at hand – and he would stay as king only for as long as he was seen to be carrying out God's will among the people.

This view was accepted in theory by the people of the southern state of Judah: they too believed that God should be the ultimate ruler of the nation. But the political context in which they found themselves had led to the emergence of a permanent royal family, and they were firmly convinced that God's rule would now be exercised only through the royal house of David. The old ideals represented by the stories of the judges had found their fulfilment in the promise to David and his successors, and therefore it was both pointless and unnecessary to try to ascertain God's direct will in each different generation. This view doubtless owed a great deal to the political – even geographical – situation of the southern kingdom, especially the position of its capital Jerusalem. For it is striking that once Omri, king of Israel, had founded his own royal capital in Samaria, the northern state too came to accept the concept of a royal family – first Omri's own family, and later that of Jehu and his successors.

The divided kingdom.

Political changes

A casual reading of the books of Kings may suggest that Judah was by far the more important of the two kingdoms – and, in its lasting religious influence, it has certainly proved to be. But this reflects the choice of material made by the editors of the deuteronomic history, who were writing to encourage and challenge the remnants of the people of Judah in the aftermath of Babylonian domination, and for that purpose the history of their own nation was obviously more relevant than events in the rival kingdom of Israel. But in the two centuries following the death of Solomon, there is no question that the northern kingdom of Israel had more territory, a larger population, and was in every way the more wealthy, more civilized, and even at times the more religious of the two. Israel was therefore a greater force in the international politics of the time. Its strategic location within Palestine ensured that the superpowers of the day would always be interested in what was going on there, and while this ensured its citizens a prosperous lifestyle, it also made it more vulnerable to invasion. Life in Israel was a good deal less secure than it was in Judah, whose capital, Jerusalem, was well away from all the main trade routes, and therefore of less interest to the rulers of surrounding states. As a result, the kingdom of Israel had a shorter and more turbulent history than the kingdom of Judah,

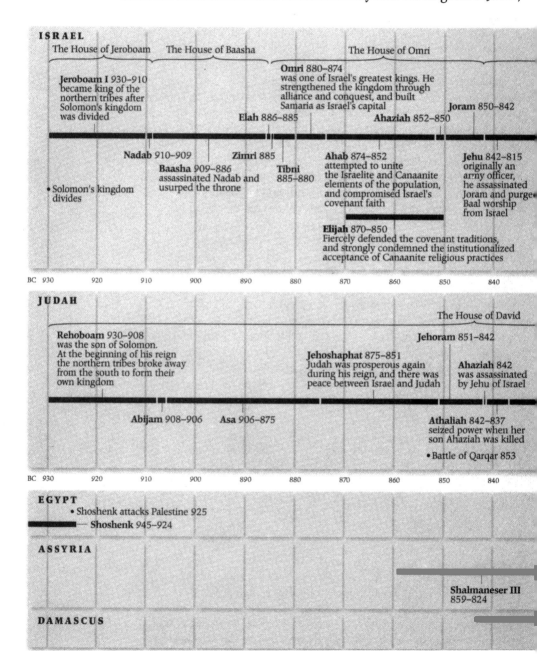

ISRAEL

The House of Jeroboam   The House of Baasha   The House of Omri

Omri 880–874
was one of Israel's greatest kings. He strengthened the kingdom through alliance and conquest, and built Samaria as Israel's capital

Jeroboam I 930–910
became king of the northern tribes after Solomon's kingdom was divided

Elah 886–885

Joram 850–842

Ahaziah 852–850

Nadab 910–909

Zimri 885

Ahab 874–852
attempted to unite the Israelite and Canaanite elements of the population, and compromised Israel's covenant faith

Jehu 842–815
originally an army officer, he assassinated Joram and purged Baal worship from Israel

Baasha 909–886
assassinated Nadab and usurped the throne

Tibni 885–880

• Solomon's kingdom divides

Elijah 870–850
Fiercely defended the covenant traditions, and strongly condemned the institutionalized acceptance of Canaanite religious practices

BC 930   920   910   900   890   880   870   860   850   840

JUDAH

The House of David

Rehoboam 930–908
was the son of Solomon. At the beginning of his reign the northern tribes broke away from the south to form their own kingdom

Jehoram 851–842

Jehoshaphat 875–851
Judah was prosperous again during his reign, and there was peace between Israel and Judah

Ahaziah 842
was assassinated by Jehu of Israel

Abijam 908–906   **Asa 906–875**

Athaliah 842–837
seized power when her son Ahaziah was killed

• Battle of Qarqar 853

BC 930   920   910   900   890   880   870   860   850   840

EGYPT
• Shoshenk attacks Palestine 925
── Shoshenk 945–924

ASSYRIA

Shalmaneser III
859–824

DAMASCUS

and almost 200 years after Jeroboam was first acclaimed as king of Israel, the whole of his kingdom was wiped out, and its subjects taken away to Assyria to become the so-called 'ten lost tribes'.

In the shorter term, too, the decision of the northern tribes to go their own way led to considerable social and economic changes in the life of the people of the two kingdoms.

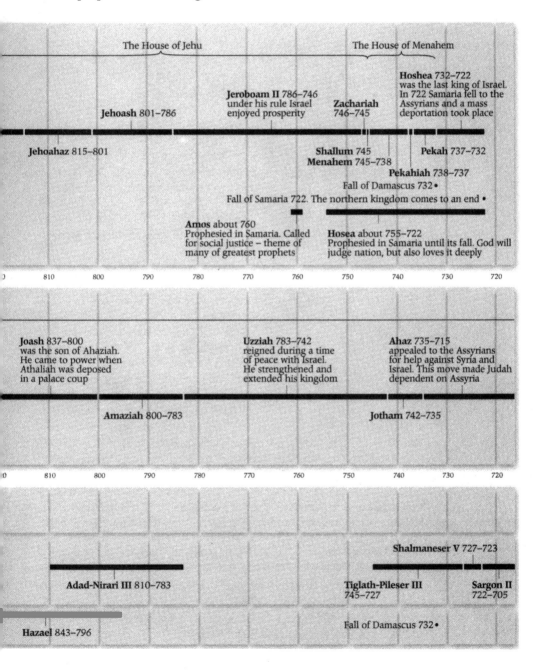

The House of Jehu

The House of Menahem

Hoshea 732–722
was the last king of Israel.
In 722 Samaria fell to the
Assyrians and a mass
deportation took place

Jeroboam II 786–746
under his rule Israel
enjoyed prosperity

Zachariah
746–745

Jehoash 801–786

Jehoahaz 815–801

Shallum 745
Menahem 745–738

Pekah 737–732

Pekahiah 738–737

Fall of Damascus 732 •

Fall of Samaria 722. The northern kingdom comes to an end •

Amos about 760
Prophesied in Samaria. Called
for social justice – theme of
many of greatest prophets

Hosea about 755–722
Prophesied in Samaria until its fall. God will
judge nation, but also loves it deeply

810   800   790   780   770   760   750   740   730   720

Joash 837–800
was the son of Ahaziah.
He came to power when
Athaliah was deposed
in a palace coup

Uzziah 783–742
reigned during a time
of peace with Israel.
He strengthened and
extended his kingdom

Ahaz 735–715
appealed to the Assyrians
for help against Syria and
Israel. This move made Judah
dependent on Assyria

Amaziah 800–783

Jotham 742–735

810   800   790   780   770   760   750   740   730   720

Shalmaneser V 727–723

Adad-Nirari III 810–783

Tiglath-Pileser III
745–727

Sargon II
722–705

Hazael 843–796

Fall of Damascus 732 •

LOST TERRITORY

The people of Israel and Judah were no longer able to hold separately the large empire that they had held together under David and Solomon. The province of Aram (Syria) in north-east Palestine had already been lost in part during the reign of Solomon, and it soon became a powerful nation in its own right, based on the city state of Damascus. It was a serious rival to both Israel and Judah, and frequently invaded the Israelite territory to the east of the River Jordan. All but one of the Philistine city states regained their freedom from Judah in the south, though by this time they were no longer a military threat. The Ammonites also took this chance to free themselves from Israelite rule, and the Moabites probably did the same. Judah fared slightly better than Israel, and still retained some kind of control over the trade routes through the Gulf of Aqaba in the south, and Rehoboam built new fortifications in many of his cities (2 Chronicles 11:5–12).

King Shoshenk I of Egypt invaded Judah about five years after the division of the kingdom. His conquests in Palestine are listed here at the temple of Karnak (modern name for Thebes). King Rehoboam gave him treasures from the Temple to persuade him not to attack Jerusalem.

But the loss of all this territory left both Israel and Judah as very second-rate powers. In the time of David and Solomon, the united kingdom had been the major power centre in the whole area, whereas from now on the two kingdoms were little more than pawns in the political games of the superpowers based in Egypt and Mesopotamia. The strength of both kingdoms was considerably weakened by the invasion of Shoshenk I, pharaoh of Egypt (945–924 BC), who moved in about five years after the separation of the two states, eager to re-establish the authority that Egypt had enjoyed in Canaan before the emergence of Israel as a nation. The Old Testament only mentions this campaign in relation to Judah, and relates how Rehoboam was forced to give him treasure from both the Temple and palace, to stop Shoshenk (called Shishak in 1 Kings 14:25–28) from actually attacking Jerusalem. This seems to have worked, for in an inscription in the temple of Amun at Thebes, Shoshenk makes no mention of towns in Judah being taken. He does, however, mention a number of towns in Israel, and an Egyptian inscription found at Megiddo suggests that he must have overrun most of Palestine. In an interesting detail of his temple list, he mentions a place called 'the Field of Abram', which is the only reference outside the Bible to connect a person of that name with Palestine. Of course, Shoshenk did not

want to occupy the country, though no doubt he left troops at strategic
places. A later king of Judah, Asa, faced an attack from the same quarter
led by a man called Zerah, who is described as a Sudanese but was
probably an Egyptian officer left in charge of troops in south Palestine
at the time of Shoshenk's invasion (2 Chronicles 14:9–15).

PETTY SQUABBLES

The fact that the two kingdoms were also fighting each other further
reduced their chances of being able to retain all their original territory.
They were at war for something like fifty years, fighting over the border
territory that was just to the north of Jerusalem (1 Kings 14:30; 15:16–
22). This was perhaps inevitable, for Jerusalem's original appeal to David
had been its unique position midway between the two groups of tribes.
But now what had been a tactical advantage became a strategic liability,
as Judah's capital was too near the border with the northern kingdom,
and that made it especially vulnerable to attack. Rehoboam, Abijam and
Asa (kings of Judah), and Jeroboam, Nadab and Baasha (kings of Israel)
were squabbling over the land in this area for a considerable time.
Baasha of Israel managed to move in as close as five miles from the city
of Jerusalem, and when it looked as if he would advance further, Asa of
Judah appealed for help to Benhadad, king of Damascus. This king
already had a treaty with Baasha, but Asa must have made him a very
attractive proposition, for he sent an army to attack the towns in the
north of Israel, thereby forcing Baasha to withdraw his army from the
frontier with Judah. It was not the last time that Judah adopted such
tactics, but they eventually discovered to their cost that it was a very
short-sighted policy.

SOCIAL UNREST

The northern kingdom of Israel also turned out to be politically
unstable. In theory, they thought it was right to try to reinvent the
pattern of a loose tribal federation in which every leader of the people
should be individually chosen as a result of their personal charisma and
religious commitment. But, as a political and social institution, this was
simply unworkable. At best, it meant that Israel became what Albrecht
Alt called 'a kingdom based on revolution by the will of God'. In practice,
what this more often meant was that the nation was torn apart over the
issue of the kingship. For one thing, it was open to any military
adventurer to try to seize the throne, whether or not he had any
religious support, or indeed any leadership skills. In addition, it was only
natural that those kings whose reigns had been properly accredited
should in due course want their own sons to succeed them, especially if
they had built up personal fortunes. As a result, Israel was in constant
turmoil and in the course of the first fifty years, the throne was seized
three times by a usurper who assassinated his predecessor. Jeroboam
reigned for twenty-one years, but only one of the six kings who followed

him reigned for more than ten years (Baasha), and some lasted only a matter of months.

Religious problems

It was all very well for Jeroboam to come to power in the north on a wave of popular enthusiasm, but he soon needed to get down to the business of running the kingdom. In doing so, he faced many formidable obstacles, not least of which was that there was no obvious capital city that might form the administrative centre of his government. The Old Testament mentions three capitals where he operated in turn: Shechem, Penuel and Tirzah (1 Kings 12:25; 14:17). There may have been a simple military reason for this, as he was forced to retreat from one to the other in the face of Shoshenk's invading armies. But it is more likely that there was a popular resistance to the very idea of having a capital city, on ideological grounds. For it had been through the possession of his own personal city that Solomon had been able to behave with such disregard for the sensitivities of the people and their inherited traditions. At least if Jeroboam had no fixed capital, there was less chance that he would build up a state apparatus to work for his own personal benefit.

But it was essential that at least one of the functions of the city of Jerusalem should be located at a permanent site in the north. The Temple built at Jerusalem to house the ark of the covenant was part of the trappings of statehood that reinforced the power and prestige of the monarchy. But it had also provided a significant and important link with the spiritual heritage of the people, and it was only to be expected that the tribes in the north, motivated and inspired by a fierce devotion to the covenant which the ark symbolized, should want to go on pilgrimage there. Yet, politically, it was essential that Jeroboam should stop them from doing so, for to allow this would have been tantamount to an acknowledgment that Jerusalem still had a hold over the loyalty of the northern tribes, and the free passage of pilgrims from one state to the other would only increase the risk of subversive action to undermine Jeroboam's position as king.

On top of that, a significant proportion of Jeroboam's territory was rural and remote. That had worked to his advantage in seceding from the south, for the support base of the Jerusalem kings had to a large extent been among urban city dwellers. In addition, however, these rural communities also seem to have been the places where traditional forms of Canaanite religious practices had flourished, independently of what went on in Jerusalem. Yahweh was certainly worshipped, but often through rituals and belief systems that reflected not the underlying rationale of the covenant traditions, but the inherited spiritual ideology of traditional Canaanite practice. It was important for Jeroboam somehow to unite these two different religious traditions, and he came up with an idea that he believed would solve several problems at once.

He would displace the old loyalties to the Temple in Jerusalem by building his own new religious centres. The sites he chose were at Dan in the extreme north, and Bethel in the south near to the border with Judah. These had a long history connected to traditional Canaanite spirituality, yet both of them also had important connections with events in the earlier history of the people of Israel (Genesis 12:8; 28:19; Judges 18:30; 20:18–28; 1 Samuel 7:16).

However, Jeroboam's actions in establishing these places of worship were to earn him the lasting condemnation of the deuteronomic historians. For at these two shrines, Jeroboam placed golden bulls (1 Kings 12:28–33). This was a bold effort to bind the different elements of the population together, and to reconcile Canaanite beliefs with the distinctive faith of Israel. It would not be too difficult to associate these bulls with the traditional worship, because Baal himself had often been represented as a bull. At the same time, however, it was possible to think of these bulls as thrones for the invisible God of the covenant, Yahweh, just as the ark of the covenant also represented God's invisible presence in the Temple at Jerusalem. From one perspective, this could be seen as a stroke of genius, but as the editors of the books of Kings looked back on it all they regarded it as an incredibly foolish move. When judged from the perspective of the deuteronomic history as outlined, for example, in the first chapter of Judges, this represented a dilution of the worship of Yahweh with alien practices, and Jeroboam's best efforts were therefore doomed to failure for, like Saul before him, he had overstepped his authority. He had conspired to undermine the very convictions that had brought him to power in the first place, and the prophet who announced his accession now pronounced his doom. Though he had been God's choice, Jeroboam had lost God's approval, and he would have to go, to be replaced by a king who would be more sensitive to the requirements of the covenant faith (1 Kings 14:1–16).

A bronze bull calf from about the 12th century BC. Jeroboam placed golden bulls at the shrines of Dan and Bethel as a counter-attraction to the Temple at Jerusalem.

New alliances

Jeroboam's immediate successor was his son Nadab, though he was not accepted by the people, and had the approval of no religious leaders. He lasted for little more than a year before Baasha came to power (1 Kings 15:25–32). The people recognized him as the right man, and he had a relatively long reign of twenty-four years, though the judgment of the historians was that he too followed in Jeroboam's footsteps and 'led

Israel into sin' (1 Kings 15:34). Like Jeroboam, he was also rejected by a prophet speaking in the name of Yahweh (1 Kings 16:1–7), and when he died his son Elah tried to succeed him. He in turn reigned for less than two years, but lacked any popular support, and Zimri assassinated him in a military coup, seizing the throne for himself (1 Kings 16:8–14). He was not the right man either, and survived for only seven days (1 Kings 16:15–20). This kind of instability naturally weakened the position of the nation of Israel. But the man who got rid of Zimri was to be one of Israel's greatest kings. Not only did he re-establish much of the nation's prestige, but also he did it so successfully that when he died his son was recognized as the most appropriate person to follow him. The father was Omri and the son was Ahab.

Prosperity again

The Moabite Stone, put up by King Mesha of Moab in Omri's day. Its inscription includes information not included in the Old Testament account.

The Hebrew Bible says very little about Omri for, in the view of the editors of 1 Kings, he was even more wicked and irreligious than any of his predecessors (1 Kings 16:21–28). As with so many of Israel's rulers, his social and political achievements are mentioned only briefly, and those who are interested to learn more about them are told that 'Everything else that Omri did and all his accomplishments are recorded in *The History of the Kings of Israel*.' Statements like this remind us that the deuteronomic historians were basing their narratives on sources that were much older than their own day, but are of little help in uncovering details that we might now be interested in, for none of these other ancient sources still survive. By contrast, Omri's son Ahab features very prominently in the Old Testament story, though here again we are told far more about his religious outlook than about political affairs during his reign (1 Kings 16:29 – 22:40). Despite the relative lack of information about them, however, there can be no doubt regarding the greatness of Omri and his son. For under their rule, Israel once again became a force to be reckoned with.

INTERNATIONALLY

Omri and Ahab strengthened the kingdom's position with a number of new alliances and fresh conquests. They put an end to the long-standing but pointless warfare with Judah, and this led to a new period of prosperity and peace in the southern state also. Jehoshaphat, king of Judah, took control of many trading routes in the south, and the new friendship between the two states was eventually sealed by the marriage of Ahab's daughter, Athaliah, to Jehoshaphat's son, Jehoram

(1 Kings 22:41–50; 2 Kings 8:18). Israel made peace in the same way with the Phoenicians of Tyre. This alliance was also sealed with a marriage: this time, Ahab himself married a Phoenician princess called Jezebel (1 Kings 16:31). Omri also managed to regain control over Moab. The Old Testament says nothing of this, but it is documented on a large black stone inscription erected by king Mesha of Moab after he had finally managed to release his kingdom from Israel's grasp again, following the death of Ahab (2 Kings 3). Naturally, much of this inscription dwells on Mesha's victory rather than on his previous submission to Omri. But it says quite plainly that 'Omri, king of Israel, humbled Moab for many years.'

INTERNALLY

Omri secured his own position by building a new capital. This is what David had done by capturing Jerusalem, but Omri went one better and chose an entirely new site, with no previous settlement on it. It is almost certain that he was trying to imitate David's success, for just as Jerusalem had been chosen because of its central position between the northern and southern tribes, so Samaria was roughly midway between the mainly Canaanite cities nearer the coast, and the predominantly Israelite towns further inland. This was to be Omri's own city, just as Jerusalem had been David's own city, and under Omri and Ahab it was built up into a fine place, well fortified and with many elegant buildings. Like Jerusalem, it also had a temple, and this came to be regarded as Ahab's greatest mistake: 'He sinned against Yahweh more than any of his predecessors. It was not enough for him to sin like King Jeroboam; he went further... and worshipped Baal' (1 Kings 16:30–31). Viewed from a less hostile angle, Ahab's religious observance was probably more concerned with politics than with spirituality as such. Like Jeroboam before him he had the problem of uniting the Canaanite and Israelite elements of his population. What went on in Samaria was mainly, if not exclusively, for the benefit of the Canaanites, and it was even organized like a traditional city state. But the city of Jezreel was still of great importance, and it could well be that Ahab had in effect two capitals: Samaria for the Canaanites, with a temple dedicated to traditional Canaanite deities, and Jezreel for the Israelites, with a temple for their God, Yahweh. It is certainly significant that both Ahab's sons had distinctively Israelite names (Ahaziah and Joram), something that could not have been said even for a great hero like David.

The ruins of Ahab's palace look down from the hill on which once stood the city of Samaria, capital of the northern kingdom of Israel.

Decay and collapse

The tensions that Omri and Ahab created between their state and the inherited covenant faith of their people soon became overpowering, and the stories about them highlight better than any other section of the deuteronomic history the kind of internal conflicts between different ideologies of statehood that were never successfully reconciled throughout Israelite history. The divergence between the inherited assumptions of Canaanite culture and the radical views reflected in the covenant from Mount Sinai are highlighted especially by the stories featuring Ahab's wife Jezebel. Her role in Ahab's monarchy can be interpreted in several ways, all of which probably reflect different aspects of her aspirations. Their marriage was a political alliance as much as anything else, and Jezebel's enthusiasm for promoting Canaanite religious practices may easily have had political overtones: if Israel's official religion was the same as that of her own kingdom of Tyre, that would not only have cemented relations between the two, but might even have emphasized the superiority of her own people over the Israelites. In addition, though, she emerges as a woman deeply committed to her husband, and with high ambitions for him – and some of the stories certainly illustrate the different philosophies of kingship that prevailed depending on whether the pattern of the Canaanite city states was adopted, or whether the covenant principles of Yahweh formed the basis of political power. The king would always have enjoyed more personal power and prestige under the traditional Canaanite structures than in the Israelite view. The idea that a peasants' revolt was one of the key elements leading to the emergence of Israel as a nation may well have been overstated, but the theme was certainly one that recurred repeatedly in later years, and nowhere is this more clearly illustrated than in the stories of Ahab and Elijah. Elijah was a fierce defender of the covenant traditions, and he realized that the kind of institutionalized acceptance of Canaanite practices that was now being proposed was something quite different from the casual adoption of traditional religious practices that still went on in village shrines throughout the land. This time, it was a direct threat to the very fabric of the nation because, if successful, Jezebel's plan would undermine all that the nation was supposed to stand for.

Ahab managed to survive, and was succeeded in turn by his two sons Ahaziah and Joram (1 Kings 22:51–53; 2 Kings 3:1–27). But there was nothing they could do to prevent the disintegration and eventual collapse of the royal house of Omri. It was not long before a revolution was instigated by devotees of the covenant faith of Israel. They had chosen an army officer by the name of Jehu to be the next king of Israel, and he was anointed in the aftermath of a great battle between Israel and Syria at Ramoth-Gilead (2 Kings 9:1–13). Joram had been wounded in the battle and had returned to Jezreel to recuperate. Jehu therefore left the battlefield, and with a band of his own men headed straight for

Jezreel. When he got there he found that by a stroke of luck Ahaziah, the king of Judah (not to be confused with King Ahaziah of Israel, Ahab's son), was also there visiting Joram. Since he too was a relative of Ahab, Jehu had no hesitation in assassinating both of them, along with Jezebel the queen mother (2 Kings 9:14–37). He followed up this bloodbath with an appeal to the city rulers of Samaria to come over to his side, which they did, and signify their allegiance to him by presenting him with the heads of seventy members of Ahab's family who were left there (2 Kings 10:1–11). Not content with that, Jehu managed to trick all the priests of Baal into entering the temple in

Elijah and the religion of Baal

Elijah is a significant character in the Old Testament. The stories about him are reminiscent of the account of Saul's encounter with a group of ecstatic prophets (1 Kings 18:4, 13), and he certainly had that mystical quality about him which instilled in people a mixture of fear and admiration in equal amounts. His movements could at times be unpredictable and beyond human comprehension (1 Kings 18:12), though these things are not the most distinctive marks of his personality. For he was first and foremost a man with a message, driven by the conviction that the God whom he knew and worshipped was not just a God who had lived and worked in the past, but one who was present with the people here and now, and who had a distinctive understanding of the important issues in their national life. In this respect, Elijah was the forerunner of the great prophets whose messages are presented in the books of the Old Testament that bear their names.

The precise nature of the conflict between Canaanite values (represented by Baal worship) and the ancestral faith of Israel is made clear in three stories from the life of Elijah:

● Elijah came from Gilead, from the very edge of the desert in the east of the country (1 Kings 17:1–7). His lifestyle was spartan, his clothes were rough, and he was immediately recognizable as an enthusiast for the style of life described in the stories about Moses and the tribes in the desert in the period following the exodus. He was a miracle worker (1 Kings 17:8–24), and significantly perhaps, his miracles were mostly concerned with the fertility of the land, especially the holding back or sending of rain. This was supposed to be the special function of the Canaanite Baal, but Elijah was determined to prove that it was really his own God, Yahweh, who controlled the rain. So he challenged 450 prophets of Baal and 400 prophets of Asherah to a contest on Mount Carmel. This was a high ridge near the territory of the Phoenicians, which had belonged to Israel during the days of David and Solomon. The altar to Yahweh built there then had by now reverted to the honouring of Baal, and Elijah was determined to sort out once and for all the religious priorities of his people. He challenged the prophets of Baal and Asherah to bring fire from heaven, presumably the lightning that would normally come before a rain storm. After much religious ecstasy, they were both exhausted and unsuccessful, but where they failed Elijah succeeded, not by following their practices, but by a simple prayer to his own God. As a result, the long period of drought ended with deluges of rain (1 Kings 18:1–46); it was Yahweh, and not Baal, who controlled the weather.

● In spite of that, Jezebel still held the power, and she was all the more determined to track down the elusive Elijah. He felt (mistakenly) that he alone was left as a faithful representative for the

Samaria, and there had them all butchered on the spot (2 Kings 10:18–31). Though the editors of Kings depict Jehu as a fanatical worshipper of Yahweh, his purge was obviously based more on political expediency, for the same tensions between different religious ideologies persisted throughout his reign and also that of his son Jehoahaz (2 Kings 13:6). Jehu's lack of commitment to serious change alienated his religious backers, who withdrew their support – and 100 years later the prophet Hosea denounced the violence that accompanied his rise to power as being incompatible with the authentic covenant faith of Israel (Hosea 1:4–5).

Elijah and the religion of Baal *continued*

God of Israel. In fear of his life he ran away from Jezebel right to the south of Judah, then south again from Beersheba to Mount Sinai. This was the place where Moses had taken the escaping slaves, and was the very centre of his people's faith. This was where the covenant had been made, and where God's people could still gain fresh inspiration. In an experience infused with much emotion and mystery, Elijah was reminded that though Yahweh did indeed have power over the forces of nature, that was not the centre of Israel's faith, but God's supreme activity was to be seen in the events of everyday life, not only through the deliverance of the slaves from Egypt, but also in the ongoing concerns of Elijah's contemporaries. Elijah was sent back to stir up a political ferment in both Syria and Israel, which would lead to the overthrow of the house of Omri and its allies (1 Kings 19:1–18). Commitment to the covenant faith did not make him a mere reactionary: it transformed him into a political activist reminding his people by his social involvement that the God of Mount Sinai was still their only true leader.
● The story of Naboth's vineyard brings out the meaning of all this in social terms (1 Kings 21:1–29). When Ahab wanted to have this piece of land to extend his own garden, he knew it was impossible. For in Israel, land belonged not to individuals, but to God – and particular people only held it in trust because God had given it to them. This was quite different from the traditional Canaanite norm, as Ahab well knew. After all, his father Omri had been

able to buy the site of Samaria outright from a Canaanite. But Ahab was still too committed to the Israelite ideals to accept that land could be seized by the king just to suit his own inclinations, and so he sulked for what he knew he could never rightly possess. His wife Jezebel, on the other hand, took a different view. She regarded the life and property of every subject as belonging to the king, and so she had no hesitation in having Naboth killed, and confiscating his property for her husband's use. It was Elijah who boldly denounced the queen's action – just as Nathan had done when David acted on the same principles of self-interest (2 Samuel 12:1–15). For Elijah, religious belief was concerned with common life and politics, and even the queen was not above the Law of the covenant from Mount Sinai. For in the covenant community, every man and woman stood equal. This meant that economic and social justice had to be a concern of God's representatives just as much as more apparently 'religious' matters connected with ritual and worship. This theme was taken up by all the great prophets of the Hebrew Bible, but it first emerges in the testimony of Elijah, who pronounced the death sentence on Jezebel and the whole house of Omri, and declared that God would ultimately intervene to restore justice and freedom to the people.

Whatever its weaknesses, it is not difficult to see why Jehu's revolution succeeded. Though Omri's dynasty had been remarkably successful, it was suffering from so many tensions that its collapse was inevitable:

■ The strongest opposition had been evoked by the Baal worship at Samaria, instigated by Jezebel and encouraged by Ahab. The fact that Jehu joined forces with a fanatical religious movement led by Jehonadab, son of Rechab, shows just how strong the reaction was (2 Kings 10:23–24), for these Rechabites were trying to opt out of civilized, settled life altogether. They neither built houses, nor cultivated the soil, nor drank wine (Jeremiah 35:6–10). All these things were regarded as part of a typical Canaanite lifestyle, but they wanted to get back to the kind of life the escaping slaves had with Moses in the desert. They were convinced that the settled life of farming could never be reconciled with Israel's ancestral faith, and so it must be abandoned.

■ There was also a certain amount of social unrest and injustice in the land, much as there had been towards the end of Solomon's reign. This time it had been caused partly by a great famine during the time of Ahab, which had increased the number of poor people and led to a radical division in society between the rich merchants and the poor

The hills of Samaria, which formed part of the northern kingdom of Israel.

peasants. The story of how Ahab took over Naboth's vineyard was by no means unique, and many small farmers found themselves being displaced by rich and powerful princes at this time.

■ Externally, too, Israel was under pressure. New enemies were making their presence felt, especially Assyria (based in Mesopotamia) and Syria (based in Damascus). The Assyrians had pressed as far west as the Mediterranean Sea during Ahab's reign, and at that time a casual alliance against them was formed by the king of Damascus, in partnership with Ahab and the king of Hamath. They all met Assyria at the Battle of Qarqar, just north of Hamath, in 853 BC, and managed to repel the Assyrians. Ahab's military strength at this time can be judged from the fact that though he could provide only half as many troops as Syria (but the same as Hamath), he had 2,000 chariots, which was more than Syria and Hamath put together. Israel obviously had fewer people than Damascus, but far greater material resources. But Benhadad, the king of Damascus, was not interested in a lasting peace with Ahab, and, though there is some debate about it, the Old Testament appears to suggest that Ahab was killed in battle against the Syrians at Ramoth-Gilead (1 Kings 20:1–34; 22:29–40). His sons were powerless to regain this lost territory, and no doubt lost the support of the army for that reason – which goes a long way towards explaining why the swashbuckling Jehu, fast driving and ready for desperate action, was so readily accepted as the new king of Israel.

The Assyrian obelisk, the famous 'Black Obelisk' of Emperor Shalmaneser, depicts Jehu of Israel paying tribute as leader of a vassal state. It is the only known portrait of an Old Testament figure.

Growing insecurity

As things turned out, Jehu himself was relatively powerless in political terms. He naturally lost the support of the powerful alliance with Phoenicia, and since he had also murdered the king of Judah, Ahaziah, any residual backing he might have expected from Jerusalem also vanished. Power was seized in Judah by Athaliah, the mother of Ahaziah of Judah and daughter of Ahab. She murdered all the other possible claimants to the throne, except for one child, Joash, who was rescued by the priest Jehoiada. Athaliah reigned in Jerusalem for six years, and is dismissed by the editors of Kings for the same reasons as Ahab: she, too, was compromised in relation to Canaanite ways of doing things, including religious practices. In due course, she was deposed in a palace coup led by Jehoiada, and Joash was installed as king (2 Kings 11:1–21).

During this period of

uncertainty and weakness, Israel was under pressure from the Syrians of Damascus, as illustrated by a broken basalt monument recovered from the city of Dan. This seems to describe the same battle as 2 Kings 8:28–29, and appears to imply that the Aramean Hazael killed both Ahaziah of Judah and Joram of Israel. 2 Kings 9:15–29 suggests that Jehu murdered them, although 2 Kings 8:29 does mention that Joram was already suffering from wounds received in battle with Hazael. Whatever the full story, the fact that Hazael was able to place his inscription in Dan itself makes it obvious that Israel could easily have been overcome at this time by the Syrians, had they not also been faced with the armies of the Assyrian king Shalmaneser III (859–824 BC). This was the king who had been successfully repelled by the coalition of which Ahab had been a part, but shortly after Jehu came to power, he was back with a vengeance. He had a carefully calculated plan for extending his own empire, and made annual military expeditions. Some territories he conquered altogether, but from most he simply collected tribute. In 841 BC he moved systematically through the whole area: Damascus was besieged, and much of the Syrian kingdom was invaded, while Phoenicia and Israel

Countries in conflict.

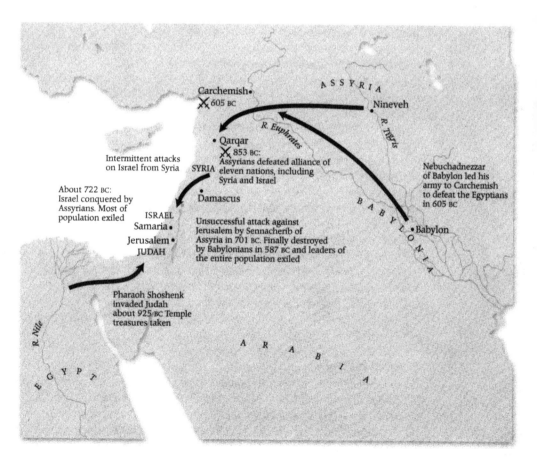

both had to pay tribute to keep the Assyrians at bay. Shalmaneser kept meticulous records, in which he describes all this in great detail. Not only does he mention that he took tribute from Jehu of Israel, he also lists what he was given, and depicts Jehu himself bowing down low to present these gifts. This is a most interesting record for the picture of Jehu preserved on Shalmaneser's Black Obelisk is the only surviving contemporary portrait of any Israelite named in the Hebrew Bible.

Before the end of Shalmaneser's reign, a revolt back in Nineveh weakened Assyrian power. But this was of no advantage to Israel, for it simply gave Hazael yet another chance to get even, and under Jehu's son Jehoahaz, Israel became almost a province of Syria (2 Kings 13:1–9, 22–23). The whole of Israel east of the River Jordan was occupied, and the Syrians pressed into Judah in the south. Joash, the king in Jerusalem, prevented Hazael from attacking the city only by offering him a part of the treasure from the Temple (2 Kings 12:17–18). In little more than 100 years, the states of Israel and Judah had been reduced from the great empire that Solomon held to satellites of the city state of Damascus.

New prosperity and false security

International relations were in such turmoil at this period that by the time Jehu's grandson, Jehoash, came to the throne in Israel things were quite different. The power of Assyria was building up again under Shalmaneser's grandson, Adad-Nirari III (810–783 BC), and his renewed interest in Palestine was to enable both Israel and Judah to regain some of their former glory. According to the Assyrian annals, Israel was again forced to pay tribute, along with the Edomites and Philistines – but not, apparently, Judah. Damascus was worst hit by this renewed Assyrian advance. The Old Testament describes how 'Yahweh gave Israel a saviour, so that they escaped from the hand of the Syrians' (2 Kings 13:5), and this might well be a reference to the Assyrian king Adad-Nirari III. In any event, the Assyrian attack on Damascus gave Jehoash the chance he was looking for, and he soon began to recover Israel's lost territory to the east of the River Jordan. Amaziah, the king of Judah, also recovered land from Edom at this time, but then foolishly declared war on Israel, and as a result Judah was so decisively defeated that Jehoash of Israel actually raided Jerusalem itself (2 Kings 14:1–16). With this, Amaziah lost the confidence of his own people and was soon assassinated (2 Kings 14:17–22). But, as had always been the case in Judah, his place was taken by his son Uzziah.

National revival

There followed then two of the longest and most prosperous reigns in all Israelite history: Jeroboam II of Israel (786–746 BC) and Uzziah of Judah (783–742 BC). They reigned for over forty years each, and though the Old Testament gives no specific details of their military activities, the two kings between them extended their borders almost to the original reach of Solomon's united kingdom (2 Kings 14:23 – 15:7).

Uzziah repaired the fortifications of Jerusalem, reorganized his army and equipped it with new types of weaponry. He introduced new agricultural practices to the land, and was even able to reopen part of Solomon's copper refineries on the Gulf of Aqaba (2 Chronicles 26:1–15). This led to a revival of trade through the Red Sea, and since the two kings of Judah and Israel were at peace with one another, between them they must have controlled all the major trade routes of the area.

The splendid buildings constructed by Jeroboam II in Samaria demonstrate well enough the prosperity of the northern state. Many people became very rich as a result of the increased opportunities for international trade, and they also became very religious, for they concluded that their new-found wealth must be a sign of God's favour upon them. In this optimistic atmosphere they came to believe that their position was assured, and their kingdom was impregnable, and began to

---

The book of Amos

A prophet is commonly thought of as a person who predicts the future. But this was not the way the great Hebrew prophets saw themselves. They were essentially God's messengers, sent to remind their people of the covenant made at Sinai, and to apply it to the everyday life of their towns and villages. They were not fortune-tellers or psychics, but politicians and preachers.

They did occasionally write some parts of their message down (e.g. Jeremiah 30:2; 36:1–2), but it is unlikely that any prophet actually wrote the books now found in the Old Testament. Indeed, these writings are not really 'books' in the sense of having a connected argument from start to finish, but are much more like an anthology of ideas, linked together by editorial sections typically containing historical and biographical notes or stories highlighting selected incidents from the prophet's life. The book of Amos contains all these types of material.

The person and the message
Though Amos himself came from the town of Tekoa, which was just south of Jerusalem in Judah (1:1), his message was for the people of the northern kingdom and he delivered it in one of the religious sanctuaries set up by the first Jeroboam, at Bethel (7:10–17), and possibly also in Samaria itself (3:9 – 4:3). While he was in Bethel, Amaziah, the priest of the sanctuary, tried to send him back to Judah, telling him that his own people should pay for his services. He obviously thought Amos was some kind of professional prophet, who was looking for a full-time job attached to a permanent place of worship. We know that there were such full-time prophets in both Israel and Judah, some of whom seem to have had an official position alongside the priests (Jeremiah 35:4–5), while others were court officials who would say anything that the king wanted to hear (1 Kings 22:1–28). But Amos was not this kind of person. He is described as a simple shepherd, who was not delivering his challenging messages to tickle the ears of his political masters, but because God had shown him the rotten state of Israelite society, and he felt impelled to do something about it (3:3–8; 7:10–17). Amos saw a complete breakdown of morality and covenant faith not only in Israel, but also in the nations with whom it was most closely associated: Syria, Philistia, Tyre, Edom, Ammon, Moab and Judah. (1:3 – 2:5). Of course, all but Judah had never pledged themselves to

look forward with eager anticipation to the coming of a great 'day of Yahweh', when Israel would finally be victorious over all enemies. But not everyone thought like that, for during the reign of Jeroboam II many people once again began to question whether all this high living was compatible with the covenant faith of Israel. Some scholars believe that in reaction against it, a new edition of Israel's early history was written, this time reflecting the memories that had been handed down in the northern tribes (unlike the similar early history of Solomon's day, which essentially drew on the collective memory of the southern tribes). If so, this narrative (which emphasized the work of Moses) would later be incorporated into the books of Genesis and Exodus (often referred to as 'E' because of the constant use of the divine name 'El' or 'Elohim', in distinction from the Solomonic collection – 'J' – where the term 'Yahweh' predominated). Whether or not that hypothesis is correct, there can be no doubt that there was strong disapproval of Israel's style of life at this time, for it was towards the end of Jeroboam II's reign that the prophet

The book of Amos
continued

observing the values and standards of the covenant faith, but Amos still condemned them in God's name for they had refused to treat each other with the kind of dignity that befits human beings. The things Amos complains about are what today would be described as violations of human rights: acting with great cruelty, taking whole communities into slavery, breaking treaties and exacting merciless revenge on neighbouring states.

All this was just a prelude to God's judgment of Israel. Israel might not have done any of these things, but they had still broken the covenant relationship with Yahweh in very fundamental ways. Though the northern state had ostensibly been founded on a conviction that all members of the community were of equal worth and value, this had never become a social reality. Instead, some had become rich on the back of others, and continued to increase their wealth at the expense of the rest. People were selling themselves into

The prophet Amos, the earliest whose words are systematically recorded in the Old Testament, was a shepherd. His message to Israel was an uncompromising warning that God's judgment would come unless they brought back justice into their society.

Amos delivered his strident messages, in which he declared that Israelite society was rotten to the core. Though many were rich and prosperous, others were penniless and oppressed (Amos 8:4–6). The great shrines like Bethel were full of worshippers, but it was all just empty ritual – and for people like that 'the day of Yahweh', when it came, would not be a time of triumph but a day of doom (Amos 5:18–27).

Assyria on the move

It was not long before Amos's dire predictions were to become a painful reality. The moral disintegration that began in Jeroboam II's reign led to social and political disintegration in the years after his death, with a rapid succession of weak kings, assassinations and revolts. At the same time, the power of Assyria was increasing again with the accession to the throne of Tiglath-pileser III (745–727 BC). He had a new expansionist policy, which he hoped would avoid the failures of his predecessors, whereby instead of merely taking tribute from defeated nations, he would incorporate

---

slavery because they could not repay trivial debts (2:6–8). The rich were feasting themselves and playing in idle luxury, while others were homeless (3:9 – 4:1; 5:10–13). These features are all well documented as regular characteristics of life in an advanced agrarian society, as an economic elite come to possess most of the land, thereby rendering others homeless, while an increasingly powerful merchant class prospers by trading in the necessities of life, as well as in luxury

goods. Whether this social structure had permeated the entire nation is unclear, and there is some evidence that in more rural parts life was more egalitarian. But in the urban centres, where power was based, there is plenty of evidence to support Amos's picture.

Judgment and hope

Paradoxically, in the middle of all this there was a great religious fervour. The shrines were full of worshippers, all carrying out their ritual observances with meticulous care. They would make sure they did not violate the weekly day of rest – but as soon as it was over, they could hardly wait to get back to what Amos regarded as the legalized robbery that went on in every market place. It was this false confidence in religion that incensed Amos more than anything. The rich believed they were prospering because they were very religious – but, if only they had had the eyes to see it, they would have realized they were wealthy because they had disregarded the basic requirements of their covenant faith. This is the context in which Amos declared God's total lack of interest in such empty ritual: 'go to the holy place in Bethel and sin, if you must! Go to Gilgal and sin with all your might! Go ahead and

conquered states into the Assyrian empire. To ensure that they did not then revolt again, the leading elements of the population would be moved away to other parts of the empire, and replaced with settlers similarly displaced from elsewhere. The first mention of an Assyrian invasion of Israel occurs in the account of Menahem's reign (2 Kings 15:17–22). He tried to keep the kingship within his own family by paying tribute to Tiglath-pileser, but his son Pekahiah reigned for only two years before he was removed by an anti-Assyrian revolt led by Pekah. He in turn went on to form a new alliance against the Assyrians with Rezin, king of Syria. They tried to persuade Jotham, king of Judah, to join them, but he refused, and when a new king came to power in Jerusalem, they declared war on Judah (Isaiah 7:1–9). This move struck terror into the people of Jerusalem, and brought into prominence one of the Old Testament's greatest prophets: Isaiah. He advised the new king, Ahaz, that this threat to his security would come to nothing, and promised that before the newly born child Immanuel could tell the difference between good and bad, both

The use of ivory in decorations and furnishing was a typical feature of the self-confidently affluent society of Israel in its final years.

bring animals to be sacrificed… offer your bread in thanksgiving to God… This is the kind of thing you love to do' (4:4–5). But God had other ideas: 'Yahweh says, "I hate your religious festivals; I cannot stand them!… I will not accept the animals you have fattened to bring me as offerings"' (5:21–22). These had not been the things that characterized Israel's experience of

God in the desert.

The covenant relationship forged at Sinai was concerned not with religious ritual, but with a personal relationship between God and the people, a relationship of love and concern that should have created a new society marked by the same qualities. So Amos pleaded in God's name, 'Stop your noisy songs; I do

Syria and Israel would collapse (Isaiah 7:10–25). As it turned out, Isaiah was right, but Ahaz did not believe him. It was perhaps on this occasion that in desperation he offered his son as a sacrifice to try to change what looked like the inevitable course of events (2 Kings 16:3–4). He certainly made strenuous efforts to win Assyrian backing, and in response to his appeal they attacked Damascus, killed Rezin and took away his people (2 Kings 16:5–9). This turned out to be a short-sighted move, for Ahaz had bought short-term security at the expense of his own continued independence. He went to Damascus to pay homage to Tiglath-pileser, and brought back from there the plan for an altar that was erected in the Temple at Jerusalem, as a sign of submission to the Assyrian empire and its gods (2 Kings 16:10–18). As Isaiah had warned, it was a foolish idea to go to the Assyrians for help.

Meanwhile in Israel, things were going from bad to worse. Pekah's position was weakened because the Assyrians took over yet more of his territory, and he was assassinated by Hoshea (2 Kings 15:29–30). Hoshea

---

not want to listen to your harps. Instead, let justice flow like a stream, and righteousness like a river that never goes dry' (5:23–24).

Not that Amos expected to be heard, for in his opinion the real trouble was that the worship at Bethel and Gilgal was not the worship of Israel's covenant God at all. Yahweh's name might be invoked, but what was going on was the worship of Canaanite deities, with their rather different view of society (2:7–8; 5:26–27; 8:14). Evidence of this kind of syncretism has been found in a series of drawings on storage jars of this same period, from Kuntillet Ajrud in the northern Sinai, and an inscription which mentions a blessing 'by Yahweh of Samaria and his Asherah'. In Amos's view, this was a step too far. Israel's leaders were no longer able to tell the difference between truth and lies. But it would all come to an end – and soon. Just as God had intervened in Israel's history before, so the same thing would happen again, only this time it would be Israel that would be totally destroyed, with the people taken away into exile, and their cities devastated (5:1 – 9:10). The prosperity of the day of Jeroboam would indeed culminate in 'the day of Yahweh'. But instead of a day of great blessing, it

would be a day of judgment and despair (5:18–20).

The last paragraph of Amos (9:11–15) gives just a slight ray of hope, and because of this some scholars believe it was added later by the book's editor, to alleviate the blackness of Amos's message. That may well be, though it is worth noting that this final section does not really contradict what he says. Amos knew that the nation was heading for a great disaster, but he also knew that events were in God's control: 'I will give the command and shake the people of Israel like corn in a sieve. I will shake them among the nations to remove all who are worthless' (9:9). It was precisely because of this that Amos felt an element of mercy and love would always be found even in judgment. For this was the same God who had rescued the people from Egypt, and who had shown overpowering love for them in so many ways throughout their history. It was inevitable, therefore, that though the present looked bleak, beyond the storm clouds of God's anger Amos could still dimly see the clear rays of God's love.

The book of Amos
continued

The Assyrian ruler Sargon II, who completed the siege of Samaria and deported much of the population of Israel to other parts of his empire.

for his part realized that the kingdom was in grave danger of disappearing entirely, and so he surrendered – unwillingly – to the Assyrians, but then, as soon as the immediate danger was past, he began plotting against them. He saw his chance to break free when Shalmaneser V replaced Tiglath-pileser III, and he appealed for support to the pharaoh of Egypt (2 Kings 17:1–4). Egypt, however, was powerless to help, and when Shalmaneser moved his armies against Israel, no one was in a position to stop him. Samaria fell after a siege lasting two years (2 Kings 17:5–6), and in his annals Sargon II (Shalmaneser's successor) reports that he removed 27,290 people from Israel and replaced them with others from elsewhere in his empire. An Assyrian officer was put in charge of the land, and Israel was finished.

The Assyrians

The Assyrian empire was based in northern Mesopotamia, chiefly around the cities of Nineveh, Asshur and Kalah. The people of this area had exerted a strong influence in that region for a long time, and their existence can be traced back to a time well before Israel emerged as a nation. But it was not until the early days of the Hebrew monarchy that the Assyrians began to take an interest in the lands that lay to the west of their home.

Tiglath-pileser I (1115–1077 BC) was the first king to try to move westwards. But he had not thought out his strategy with sufficient care, and though he got as far as the northern part of Syria he was unable to establish a firm power base in that region. In the next few centuries, the Assyrians concentrated on setting up a strong administrative structure, into which conquered territories could easily be incorporated. They also developed a well-

trained and highly disciplined army, ready to move at a moment's notice. The description of them in Isaiah 5:26–29 vividly reflects the impression that these troops made on those who saw them: 'here they come, swiftly, quickly! None of them grows tired; none of them stumbles. They never doze or sleep. Not a belt is loose; not a sandal strap is broken. Their arrows are sharp, and their bows are ready to shoot. Their horses' hooves are as hard as flint, and their chariot-wheels turn like a whirlwind. The soldiers roar like lions that have killed an animal and are carrying it off where no one can take it away from them.'

Ashurnasirpal II (883–859 BC) rebuilt the Assyrian capital at Kalah, and established a firm control over his Mesopotamian territories, and this new security gave his son Shalmaneser III (859–824 BC) the chance to expand his empire to the west. He was the emperor whose forces met Ahab and his Syrian allies at the battle of Qarqar in 853 BC. But it was almost another century before the toughest emperor of them all came to the throne: Tiglath-pileser III (745–727 BC). He was also acclaimed as king of Babylon in southern Mesopotamia, and turned out to be an expert military strategist. He saw that the key to imperial expansion was the establishment of a clearly defined policy. Though many of the records from his reign are confused and uncertain, he obviously had a clear strategy for annexing other states, which was carefully followed in the case of Israel (though there was some flexibility, for neither Judah nor the Philistine city states were ever dealt with in precisely the same way):

● First, he would try to make a treaty with other rulers, persuading them to acknowledge his sovereignty in exchange for certain limited privileges.

● Any hint of revolt by such vassals would be dealt with at once – usually by direct invasion, followed by the annexation of a good deal of their territory, and the installation of a new king to rule over what was left in accordance with Assyrian instructions.

● Any further resistance would lead to the whole state being taken over and turned into an Assyrian province, with its native leaders being deported to other parts of the empire.

Tiglath-pileser III represented the zenith of Assyrian power. Some of his successors still had expansionist ideas, and Esarhaddon (681–669 BC) even annexed Egypt. But by the end of Esarhaddon's reign, Assyria's imperial power was spent and though the reign of his successor, Ashurbanipal (669–627 BC) saw the establishment of a remarkable library of cuneiform texts at Nineveh, it also witnessed an extended civil war in Babylon, and revolts in other parts of the empire. By the end of his reign, the empire was beginning to disintegrate and its collapse was inevitable.

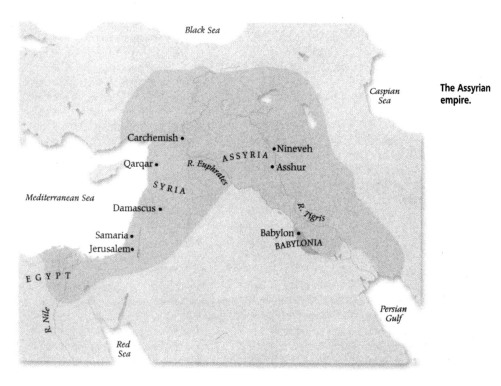

The Assyrian empire.

Hosea and the fall of Samaria

The indecision and opportunism of the last few kings of Israel are both reflected in the book of Hosea. Hosea began his work as a prophet after Amos, but probably before the end of Jeroboam II's reign, and he continued until after the Assyrians had captured Samaria. The disorders and constant revolts of the people against their kings are all vividly described here: 'In the heat of their anger they murdered their rulers. Their kings have been assassinated one after another, but no one prays to me for help' (7:7). The people thought they could do without God, and so Israel 'flits about like a silly pigeon; first they call on Egypt for help, and then they run to Assyria! But I will spread out a net and catch them like birds as they go by. I will punish them for the evil they have done' (7:11–12). Yet, in spite of the impending doom, Israel seemed to be quite unaware of what was happening: 'Yahweh says, "The people of Israel are like a half-baked loaf of bread. They rely on the nations around them and do not realize that this reliance on foreigners has robbed them of their strength. Their days are numbered, but they don't even know it"' (7:8–9).

Hosea's life and message

Very little is known about Hosea himself, though like Amos he was probably a member of the emerging upper classes, who unlike some of the others was greatly concerned about the social consequences of economic change. He was obviously a country person who could refer with the knowledge of experience to the morning mist and the dew (13:3), to the fragrance of the cedar trees of Lebanon (14:6), to corn and wine and olive oil (2:8), and to the work of ploughing and harvesting (10:11–13). Along with all this, Hosea displays a strong nostalgia for the life of the desert, for he loved not only his own countryside, but also its history, and he could look back with excitement to the old stories of Jacob and Moses and the exodus

(11–13). Whereas Amos was logical and impartial, Hosea was too deeply attached to his own homeland to imagine that God did not have a special affection for this place and its people. He loved the land, he loved the people and he was sure that God loved them too.

Hosea's message is inextricably interwoven with his own personal story, which starts with his marriage to a woman called Gomer. Some interpreters believe that this woman was a temple prostitute whom Hosea tried to win over to his own understanding of God's way of relating to people, though it is just as likely that she was his wife and her unfaithfulness was quite unexpected. In any event, Hosea and Gomer had three children, each of whom were given symbolic names that would convey a message about the fate of the nation. The first was called Jezreel, as a statement that God would still avenge Jehu's massacre there; the second was called Unloved, to declare that Israel seemed to have gone beyond God's love and forgiveness; and the other was called Not-my-People. Gomer subsequently left Hosea to live with another man (1:2 – 2:5), and in the next recorded event from Hosea's life, he goes to the market place and sees a prostitute who has fallen into some sort of slavery from which she can be released for a small payment. Moved by her plight, the prophet buys her and takes her to live with him (3:1–5). Some interpreters believe this was a different woman altogether from Gomer, though if the details of the story are compared to Hosea's subsequent message about God's relationship with Israel, it makes more sense to assume that this prostitute was in fact Gomer, who had presumably therefore been abandoned by the man she was living with.

Certainly this personal tragedy was the key to Hosea's message for the nation. Just as his love for Gomer had been rejected and despised, so had God's love for Israel. If an ordinary mortal like Hosea could feel so deeply grieved when his partner left him, how must God then feel over the unfaithfulness of Israel? Because of his personal involvement in this way, Hosea was able to see deeper into the nature of Israel's wrongdoing than Amos. Amos denounced the great public evils of the people, but Hosea saw behind them the breakdown of commitment to the covenant ideal in the everyday relationships found in homes throughout the land.

God and Israel

The people of Israel believed they would gain prosperity and good harvests by observing the traditional fertility rites of Baal worship. But from Hosea's standpoint, these rituals involved the very same sexual indulgence that had ruined his own home life. Just like Gomer, Israel was saying, 'I will go to my lovers – they give me food and water, wool and linen, olive oil and wine' (2:5). This, said Hosea, was the typical thinking of the Canaanite mentality, worshipping Baal for what they could get out of him, like prostitutes who would have sex for money. But in fact, Hosea knew that it was Israel's own God, Yahweh, who provided all these things: 'She would never acknowledge that I am the one who gave her the corn, the wine, the olive oil, and all the silver and gold that she used in the worship of Baal' (2:8). This was not what religious devotion in Israel should have been like. The worship of Yahweh was to grow out of gratitude for the undeserved love that had already been showered upon the nation. So Hosea returns over and over again to what God had done for Israel. Sometimes he uses imagery drawn from his own relationship with Gomer. At other times, he thinks in terms of God as the parent (mother) of the people and Israel as a recalcitrant son: 'the more I called to him, the more he turned away from me. My people sacrificed to Baal; they burnt incense to idols. Yet I was the one who taught Israel to walk. I took my people up in my arms, but they did not acknowledge that I took care of them. I drew them to me with affection and love.

I picked them up and held them to my cheek; I bent down to them and fed them' (11:2–4).

There was little sign of hope in Amos's message, and for him, the 'day of Yahweh' was almost entirely a day of punishment. But Hosea speaks of God making 'Trouble Valley' into 'a door of hope' (2:15). God still loved these people, and in due course Israel would return: 'She will respond to me… as she did when she was young, when she came from Egypt. Then once again she will call me her husband – she will no longer call me her Baal' (presumably a reference to the use of Canaanite practices in the worship of Yahweh, 2:15–16). To be sure, Gomer had suffered the consequences of her action, and so would Israel: 'Samaria must be punished for rebelling against me. Her people will die in war; babies will be dashed to the ground, and pregnant women will be ripped open' (13:16). Still, God would never give up Israel, any more than Hosea could give up his own wife: 'How can I give you up, Israel? How can I abandon you?… My heart will not let me do it! My love for you is too strong' (11:8).

In return, God was looking only for the unreserved commitment of the people. Unlike Baal, Yahweh was not primarily interested in religious rituals, but instead was seeking a renewed style of personal relationship: 'What I want from you is plain and clear: I want your constant love, not your animal sacrifices. I would rather have my people know me than burn offerings to me' (6:5–6). What was required was a return to the old simplicity that had characterized the life of the slaves who escaped from Egypt. They knew how much God had done for them, and because of that faithfulness and love they knew they could unreservedly commit themselves to God's care. Israel had come a long way since those days, but God's love was unchanging – and that message was to become increasingly important to the Bible writers as time went by.

Dating the Old Testament story

At first glance, it might seem easy to give dates to the events recorded in the Old Testament. There are certainly many lists of ancestors and descendants of prominent people, as well as complicated comparative datings at a number of points in the narratives. But it is extraordinarily difficult to condense all this material into one consistent chronological system. There are a number of significant problems:

● Different ancient versions of the Old Testament actually have different figures at many points. The Hebrew Bible is not always the same as the Greek version (the Septuagint).

● We do not wholly understand the basis on which the Old Testament's dating system operates. For instance, it usually refers to numbers of years within a given king's reign. But do these years include the year in which he became king, or is 'the first year' of a reign actually the first full year after the king's accession? Lack of certainty on this point can lead to considerable differences in dating, even over a short period of time.

● In the earlier Old Testament books, people are often credited with amazingly long lifespans, regularly running into hundreds of years. There are similarly extravagant claims in many records from ancient Mesopotamia, but we do not know precisely how to understand them in relation to our own calendar. It seems likely that such calculations were based on a shorter year than our twelve-month period, but in the absence of more certain knowledge we can deduce very little from them.

● Many scholars feel that the figures given in the Old Testament are stylized, and perhaps even symbolic. For example, when viewed as a whole the time scheme looks to have been designed so as to give special prominence to four important events in Israel's history: the exodus, Solomon's building of the Temple, the end of the Babylonian exile and the Maccabean reconsecration of the Temple. We also find the frequent use of the number forty, which perhaps suggests that it stands for something – maybe just indicating a long time, or a generation (though a literal generation would be much shorter than that). This figure occurs frequently in the stories of the judges, and if we add together all the time indications found there, we have a period in excess of 300 years. Yet we know from other evidence that, whatever understanding of the emergence of early Israel is adopted, the time between Moses and Samuel can hardly have been more than half that length.

There are obviously many uncertainties in trying to assign accurate dates to events in this literature. But from the time of the great empires founded by the Assyrians and the Babylonians, we have detailed records written by their own annalists, and these often mention people and events also described in the books of the Hebrew Bible. Moreover, the Assyrian and Babylonian records can easily be dated in absolute terms. This means that it has been possible to work out a general chronological framework for the Old Testament, by using these other materials and combining them with the dating methods found in the Bible story. Naturally, different scholars make their own judgments on such complex issues, though the dates used in this book are widely recognized as being accurate to within about ten years or less for the stories of the early monarchy, while the dates given for events and people during the Assyrian and Babylonian periods (and later) are much more accurate than that.

6 Judah and Jerusalem

Danger and uncertainty

With Israel gone, and Samaria reduced to a heap of ashes, life in Judah changed dramatically. Jerusalem was no longer protected from Assyria by its remote location. The border of the Assyrian empire was now less than twenty miles away, and Judah's security was threatened. Ahaz had only made things worse by actually offering to subject himself to the Assyrians, in exchange for protection against the kings of Damascus and Israel. Isaiah had been unable to prevent this, but he had no doubt of the likely outcome of such political madness, and in a characteristically picturesque message he declares that the people of Jerusalem 'have rejected the quiet waters from the brook of Shiloah' (near Jerusalem), in exchange for 'the flood waters of the River Euphrates, overflowing all its banks. They will sweep through Judah in a flood, rising shoulder high and covering everything' (Isaiah 8:6–8). Instead of trusting in God, Ahaz and his people had deliberately courted disaster in their cowardly submission to the Assyrians.

Ahaz himself was too cautious to allow that to happen during his reign. But he was sowing the seeds of eventual collapse.

POLITICALLY

Ahaz's acceptance of Assyrian rule was inept, but it also had immediate and serious social repercussions for his people. The halcyon days of Uzziah were gone for ever: much of Judah's territory had been lost, and along with it, a large slice of the royal income. That in itself would have been bad enough to lead to a major economic recession for Ahaz, but his problems were increased by considerable numbers of refugees trying to escape from the northern kingdom of Israel. He was forced to extend Jerusalem, building new houses and defences to settle these people. In such a situation it was perhaps inevitable that people should be tempted to get whatever they could for themselves with no thought of the wider social and moral consequences.

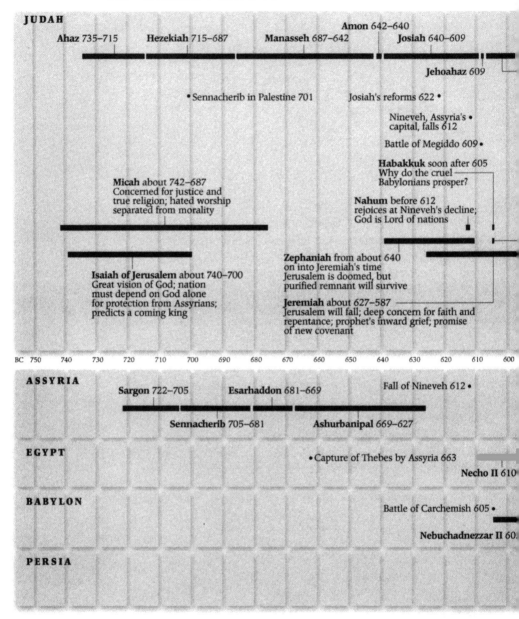

JUDAH

Amon 642–640
Ahaz 735–715   Hezekiah 715–687   Manasseh 687–642   Josiah 640–609

Jehoahaz 609

• Sennacherib in Palestine 701   Josiah's reforms 622 •

Nineveh, Assyria's •
capital, falls 612

Battle of Megiddo 609 •

Habakkuk soon after 605
Why do the cruel
Babylonians prosper?

Micah about 742–687
Concerned for justice and
true religion; hated worship
separated from morality

Nahum before 612
rejoices at Nineveh's decline;
God is Lord of nations

Zephaniah from about 640
on into Jeremiah's time
Jerusalem is doomed, but
purified remnant will survive

Isaiah of Jerusalem about 740–700
Great vision of God; nation
must depend on God alone
for protection from Assyrians;
predicts a coming king

Jeremiah about 627–587
Jerusalem will fall; deep concern for faith and
repentance; prophet's inward grief; promise
of new covenant

BC 750   740   730   720   710   700   690   680   670   660   650   640   630   620   610   600

ASSYRIA

Sargon 722–705   Esarhaddon 681–669   Fall of Nineveh 612 •

Sennacherib 705–681   Ashurbanipal 669–627

EGYPT

• Capture of Thebes by Assyria 663

Necho II 610

BABYLON

Battle of Carchemish 605 •

Nebuchadnezzar II 60[.]

PERSIA

RELIGIOUSLY

Ahaz was encouraging this. Not only was he officially promoting the
worship of Assyrian deities, even in the Temple itself, but he also
allowed many other forms of traditional Canaanite spirituality to
prosper. The arrival of northern refugees probably just added to the
pressure for more such syncretistic diversity, but all these things added
together meant that the distinctive message of Israel's own faith was
once again in danger of being lost. Isaiah was deeply concerned about

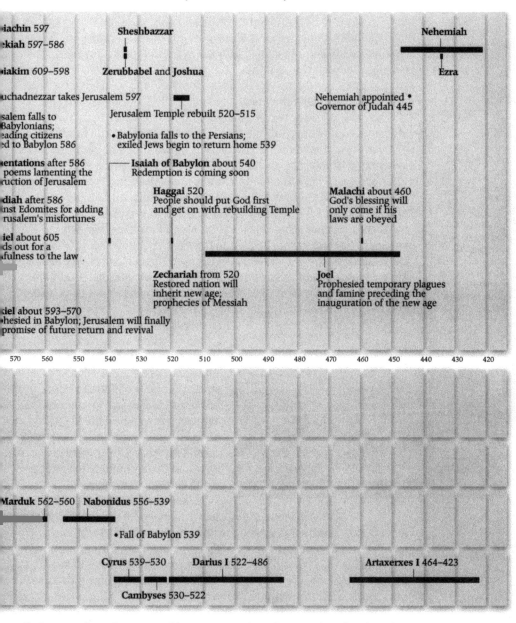

iachin 597

kiah 597–586

iakim 609–598

Sheshbazzar

Zerubbabel and Joshua

Nehemiah

Ezra

uchadnezzar takes Jerusalem 597

salem falls to
Babylonians;
eading citizens
d to Babylon 586

ientations after 586
poems lamenting the
ruction of Jerusalem

diah after 586
inst Edomites for adding
rusalem's misfortunes

iel about 605
ds out for a
fulness to the law

ciel about 593–570
hesied in Babylon; Jerusalem will finally
promise of future return and revival

Jerusalem Temple rebuilt 520–515

• Babylonia falls to the Persians;
exiled Jews begin to return home 539

—— Isaiah of Babylon about 540
Redemption is coming soon

Haggai 520
People should put God first
and get on with rebuilding Temple

Zechariah from 520
Restored nation will
inherit new age;
prophecies of Messiah

Nehemiah appointed •
Governor of Judah 445

Malachi about 460
God's blessing will
only come if his
laws are obeyed

Joel
Prophesied temporary plagues
and famine preceding the
inauguration of the new age

| 570 | 560 | 550 | 540 | 530 | 520 | 510 | 500 | 490 | 480 | 470 | 460 | 450 | 440 | 430 | 420 |

Marduk 562–560 Nabonidus 556–539

• Fall of Babylon 539

Cyrus 539–530   Darius I 522–486

Cambyses 530–522

Artaxerxes I 464–423

all this, not least because of his opinion that the social and political
collapse of the northern kingdom had been caused by its failure to pay
due attention to the demands of the Law from Mount Sinai. He could
see the same things happening in Judah, where there was plenty of
religious activity, but little evidence of its impact in everyday life.
Isaiah's messages at this period bear a remarkable resemblance to the
dire warnings that Amos had given: 'Listen to what Yahweh is saying
to you... "Do you think I want all these sacrifices you keep offering to

me?... I am tired of the blood of bulls and sheep and goats... I am disgusted with the smell of the incense you burn... I hate your New Moon Festivals and holy days; they are a burden that I am tired of bearing... Stop all this evil that I see you doing... and learn to do right. See that justice is done – help those who are oppressed, give orphans their rights, and defend widows"' (Isaiah 1:10–11, 13–14, 16, 17).

The same message was emphasized by the prophet Micah. But whereas Isaiah belonged to the upper classes, Micah was a farm worker who saw even more clearly what was wrong with society, because he had experienced its injustice for himself. Judah, he said, was rotten from top to bottom, and even the national leaders 'hate justice and turn right into wrong... building God's city, Jerusalem, on a foundation of murder and injustice' (Micah 3:9–10). They might manage to persuade their own prophets to promise that 'wine and liquor will flow' for them, but messages like that were just 'lies and deceit' (2:11). By imagining that God's approval and support could be secured by religious observances alone, people had got their standards mixed up. For Micah, though, the real basis of the covenant society was not empty ritual, but justice and equality: 'What shall I bring to Yahweh, the God of heaven, when I come

Isaiah described Judah as God's vineyard. He expected a good harvest, but the grapes it produced were sour.

to worship...? Shall I bring the best calves to burn as offerings...? Will Yahweh be pleased if I bring... thousands of sheep or endless streams of olive oil? Shall I offer... my firstborn child to pay for my sins? No, Yahweh has told us what is good, and this is what is required: that we should do what is just, show constant love, and live in humble fellowship with our God' (Micah 6:6–8).

Like Amos before him, Micah saw little hope for people whose view of God's nature was so alien to the covenant faith: 'Twist and groan, people of Jerusalem, like a woman giving birth, for now you will have to leave the city and live in the open country. You will have to go to Babylon... Zion will be ploughed like a field, Jerusalem will become a pile of ruins, and the Temple hill will become a forest' (Micah 4:10; 3:12).

There were times when even Isaiah felt the same. In a dramatic picture, he describes Judah and Jerusalem as God's vineyard which had great potential, though only ever produced sour grapes. So the vineyard must be destroyed: 'I will take away the hedge round it, break down the wall that protects it, and let wild animals eat it and trample it down' (Isaiah 5:5). Ahaz was not disposed to listen to this kind of message. He believed he had already secured a measure of prosperity for his people, though in reality he was undermining the foundations of society. Instead of trusting in God, he was terrified of the Assyrians, and insisted on relying on his own political judgment. Judah had lost its independence to Assyria, and Isaiah could see no hope as long as Ahaz was king. So he withdrew from public life, and until the death of Ahaz he gave his teaching only to a small group of his own personal friends.

False confidence

Ahaz was succeeded by his son, Hezekiah. By the time he came to power, the Assyrian emperor Sargon II had become preoccupied with other problems in the east and north of his empire. This meant the states in Palestine had a little more freedom, and they lost no time in trying to turn that freedom to real political advantage. Egypt's power was also increasing at this time, and the Philistine city states were soon plotting with the Egyptians to get rid of Assyrian domination once and for all. Naturally, they tried to get the support of Judah, and no sooner was Hezekiah enthroned in Jerusalem than Philistine ambassadors came to ask for his help. But Isaiah warned them that Assyria's power was far from broken: 'Howl and cry for help, all you Philistine cities! Be terrified, all of you! A cloud of dust is coming from the north – it is an army with no cowards in its ranks' (Isaiah 14:31). Undaunted, the Egyptians tried to persuade Hezekiah to join their revolt, and Isaiah repeated his message. In a dramatic anticipation of what would happen to the rebels, the prophet took off all his clothes and walked naked round the streets of Jerusalem. This, he said, was 'a sign of what will happen to Egypt and Sudan. The emperor of Assyria will lead away naked the prisoners he captures from those two countries. Young and old, they will walk barefoot and naked, with their buttocks exposed, bringing shame on Egypt' (Isaiah 20:3–4). Hezekiah had more sense than his father, and listened carefully to Isaiah's advice. It was just as well he did, for in a short time the Assyrian army had moved in strength against both the Philistines and the Egyptians, who proved incapable of defending themselves, let alone Judah, and their power collapsed just as Isaiah had predicted it would.

Reform in Jerusalem

Hezekiah was still tempted to make his own bid for freedom, but he now realized that he would need to move carefully. So he began in a low-key way by reforming the religious practices of his people (2 Kings 18:1–8). Isaiah and Micah had both complained that the worship of their own God Yahweh was being mixed up with the worship of other deities. Some of this was certainly the continuation of traditional Canaanite practices of the kind that had long been popular, especially in the northern kingdom of Israel. But, in addition, Ahaz had created an altar to the Assyrian gods in Jerusalem. There is some debate about Ahaz's motivation, for as a general rule the Assyrians did not insist on this as a sign of political subservience, and it may be that this kind of thing is to be understood more generally as an indication of Judah's openness to the wider culture of the region. Hezekiah soon saw that by getting rid of these things, he could not only please religious fanatics like Isaiah, but it would also be a way of re-establishing a distinctively Judahite culture. A number of features of Hezekiah's reforms seem to indicate there was some political intention behind them:

■ As well as clearing the Jerusalem Temple of all the paraphernalia of alien worship, he also tried to close down even legitimate places of worship elsewhere in the country. That would ensure the Temple in Jerusalem would be the only place where the people could worship Yahweh. Of course, this Temple had always been Judah's national shrine, but when Solomon first built it, it also became an instant symbol of the king's own power. Hezekiah knew that if he could persuade his people to worship only in his own Temple, that was bound to strengthen their loyalty to him and to his successors.

■ Hezekiah's own people were not the only ones who were invited to worship in Jerusalem. He also sent a message to those who were left in what had been the territory of northern Israel (2 Chronicles 30:1–12). This state was now part of the Assyrian empire, and therefore had no official ties with Israel's national faith. But Hezekiah knew that many of its inhabitants still held to the loyalties of the old Israelite tribes, and if they could be tempted to travel south to worship in Jerusalem, that may begin to undermine the Assyrian power on his doorstep. Hezekiah certainly made strenuous efforts to link his reign with the corporate memory of the old kingdom in the north, even calling his son Manasseh, which was the original name of one of the ten northern tribes.

■ As well as reorganizing religious worship, Hezekiah also made military preparations for the inevitable Assyrian backlash. He built new defences in Jerusalem and many other cities (2 Chronicles 32:5;

Isaiah 22:9–11), reorganized the army, built new store cities, and rationalized his civil service (2 Chronicles 32:5–6, 27–29). In Jerusalem itself he built the Siloam Tunnel, to make sure the city would have plenty of water in the event of a siege (2 Kings 20:20; 2 Chronicles 32:30; Isaiah 22:9–11). Hezekiah was determined that, when the right opportunity presented itself, he would have a good chance of seizing a real and lasting independence from the Assyrians.

His chance came with the death of Sargon II. Soon after that, both the king of Babylon and a new Egyptian pharaoh sent a message asking Hezekiah to help overthrow the Assyrians. Isaiah warned against this, but his words fell on deaf ears (Isaiah 30:1–7; 31:1–3). The only ruler in Palestine who was opposed to this plan was the Philistine king of Ekron, but Hezekiah soon overcame his opposition by giving his support to some sort of revolt among his own officials. The Assyrian king Sennacherib describes how 'the officials, the

Below:
'Sennacherib's prism', an Assyrian document inscribed on stone, describes the siege of Jerusalem from the invader's point of view. Sennacherib speaks of shutting Hezekiah in Jerusalem 'like a bird in a cage'.

politicians, and the people of Ekron, had thrown Padi, their king, into fetters... and handed him over to Hezekiah the Jew'. After this, all the Philistine city states seem to have fallen in with this new anti-Assyrian alliance.

The Assyrians move in

It was entirely predictable that Sennacherib would not tolerate this kind of revolt, even on the edge of his empire. He marched south through Palestine, and Egypt and the Philistines collapsed at once. Then he moved against Judah, using the same tactics that his predecessor Shalmaneser V had adopted against the northern kingdom of Israel. First, he would weaken Hezekiah's position by taking over much of his territory. In this instance, instead of making the towns and villages of Judah a part of his own empire, he handed them over to various Philistine kings, but the end result was the same: Hezekiah had no supporters to whom he could appeal for help. By the time the Assyrians moved in the direction of Jerusalem, Hezekiah was, in Sennacherib's own vivid imagery, 'like a bird in a cage'. Hezekiah could see there was no chance of escape. The best he could hope for was to

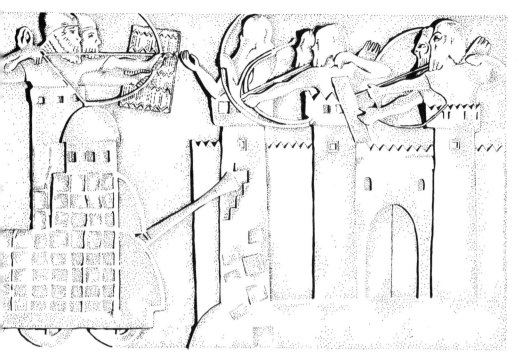

save the city itself by paying Sennacherib a huge tribute. The Assyrian king was prepared to accept this, and so Hezekiah sent large quantities of gold and silver treasures to the town of Lachish, where Sennacherib was encamped with his army.

It is not altogether clear what happened next. The Old Testament continues with the story of a siege of Jerusalem which ended in complete failure (2 Kings 18:17 – 19:37). The Assyrian army apparently camped outside the city in force, in the hope that the people would depose Hezekiah and so save themselves from the hardship of a long siege. Then, just as the fall of the city seemed imminent, the Assyrian army suddenly withdrew, after many of its soldiers had died in some mysterious way. The Assyrian records have a detailed account of Sennacherib's activities in Judah, but make no mention of this event. That in itself is not too surprising, for their official annals regularly ignored defeats. Most scholars believe that the Old Testament story is authentic enough, but they differ about when it actually happened. Though it seems unlikely that he would have besieged Jerusalem just after receiving a large payment of tribute, some think this must have been a part of Sennacherib's campaign in 701 BC. Others have noted that the story mentions 'King Tirhakah of Sudan', and since a king of that name ruled in Egypt from about 689 BC, it is therefore possible that this incident took place later, perhaps as a result of another attempted revolt by Hezekiah. On the other hand, Assyrian sources provide no evidence for such a second expedition by Sennacherib into Palestine.

The irresistible weight of Assyrian military might is directed towards a walled city in this relief from the palace of Ashurnasirpal II at Calah. Archers on the ramparts attempt to defend the city against others in a siege tower.

Assyria's final fling

Comparatively little is known of what was going on in Judah in the years immediately following Sennacharib's invasion. Sennacherib himself was soon murdered, and his successor was Esarhaddon, who was to be one of Assyria's most powerful rulers (2 Kings 19:37; Isaiah 37:37–38). When he died, his empire was divided between his two sons. Ashurbanipal (669–627 BC) reigned at Nineveh, and Shamash-Shanakin at Babylon. During this period, the Assyrians eventually achieved their greatest ambition. Ashurbanipal finally managed to crush Egypt, and capture its capital city, Thebes, which meant that Assyria now dominated the whole of the Fertile Crescent, including the rival super-power of Egypt. But Ashurbanipal was not primarily a great warrior. He had no need to be: his predecessors had already established the empire on a firm foundation. He was able to turn his attention instead to the enrichment of Assyrian culture, and his palace at Nineveh became a great centre of both the literary and the visual arts. His artists produced some of the most striking work anywhere in the ancient world, and his scribes gathered an amazing library of literature. Not only did they catalogue the events of recent history with great precision, but they also gathered together the ancient traditions of Mesopotamia, which went back right to the very dawn of civilization. Their writing methods may seem primitive to us today, for they used the material that lay ready to hand: river mud. First they formed the mud into conveniently sized blocks, then they wrote on them with wedge-shaped sticks while the mud was still wet. Once this 'cuneiform' writing was complete, the blocks could be baked solid in the heat of the sun. This meant their books were bulky, but it also ensured they would be virtually indestruc-tible, and even today it is still possible to piece together mud blocks that have been broken for centuries. It is due to this royal library at Nineveh that we have so much detailed knowledge of the ancient civilizations of the area and of their national traditions.

There was little to say about life in Jerusalem and Judah at such a time as this. Hezekiah's successor, Manasseh, had no room to flex his nationalistic muscles. He was no match for Assyria's power, and was in complete subjection to it. The Assyrian records mention him only as a source of building materials and troops, and confirm that he continued to pay regular taxes. The Hebrew Bible makes no direct mention of Assyrian power during Manasseh's long reign, but the reality of it is reflected quite clearly in the description of affairs in the Jerusalem Temple (2 Kings 21:1–18). Judah's own national faith was once more neglected, and all sorts of alien ceremonies were promoted, including star worship. Like Ahaz before him, Manasseh was forced to express his subservience to the Assyrians by worshipping their deities, but this time he made sure there would be no protests from people like Isaiah: those who disagreed with his policies were put to death (2 Kings 21:16). Because of this, the editors of the deuteronomic history eventually came to regard him as the most incorrigibly wicked of all the kings. His son Amon continued the same unhappy policies (2 Kings 21:19–26).

Reform and renewal

Then came an unexpected opportunity for change. Things suddenly began to move on the fringes of the Assyrian empire. The Egyptians regained their independence, while the kingdom of Lydia in the north-west, and the Medes in the east, began to harass the Assyrians, and at the same time, hordes of Asian raiders (Scythians) swept down from the north. The internal stability of the empire had already been shaken by feuding between Ashurbanipal and his brother and this, combined with all the external factors, had an unsettling effect. Within a few years of Ashurbanipal's death, the Assyrians found themselves fighting for survival against the Babylonians and the Medes.

As before, the weakening of Assyrian power led to the revival of national hopes in Judah. This time, they centred around Amon's son, Josiah, who became king in Judah while he was still only a boy (2 Kings 22:1–2). As soon as he grew up, Josiah set about reasserting his country's independence. Assyria's problems now looked serious, and he saw a real chance of restoring the kingdom to something like the glory of the days of David and Solomon. His achievements fell short of that, but nevertheless Josiah had considerable success in extending his territory. Archaeological evidence shows that he controlled land as far north as Galilee, and his influence extended east of the River Jordan into Gilead. He also had some power over the Philistine states in the west, and all of this was consolidated with at least two marriages. This territorial expansion went hand in hand with a thoroughgoing religious reformation. This was now following a predictable pattern, for Hezekiah's earlier move for independence had also started with the removal of non-Israelite religious symbols. In the event, Josiah was far more successful than Hezekiah and even managed to remove altars and images related to Assyrian beliefs from the territories of the former northern kingdom of Israel. At this time, the sanctuary established at Bethel by Jeroboam I was destroyed, along with many local shrines and their priests.

But the central feature of Josiah's reform was the recovery of a book of the Law in the Temple at Jerusalem. The account in 2 Kings does not suggest this book was the cause of the reform, for it only came to light after workers had moved in to renovate the Temple. But once discovered, it played a significant part in the subsequent course of events (2 Kings 22:3–20). The Old Testament narrative does not directly identify this book, but from what is said, three main ideas seem to have dominated it:

■ Israel could only ever be one united people, and therefore the political division between Judah and Israel was meaningless.

■ The central plank of Israel's faith must be belief in only one God, Yahweh.

■ Israel's one God must be worshipped in only one place.

A lost book

Up to this point, Josiah's reforms had probably been more concerned with getting rid of Assyrian objects than with promoting the worship of Israel's God Yahweh. But this book provided a new, positive impetus. At times of political crisis and uncertainty, people often try to go back to the old ways, even today. In Josiah's time, many nations in the ancient world were taking a fresh look at their own national heritage, and for the same reasons. So when an ancient book was discovered in Jerusalem, it was naturally treated with special reverence. As it happened, this book also played right into Josiah's hands, for its main ideas seemed to give a religious backing to the political moves he was already making. He was trying to restore Judah's control over the former territory of the whole of the united nation of Israel; he was getting rid of Assyrian gods; and he needed to strengthen his personal position by insisting that the religious allegiance of the people should be given to his own royal Temple in Jerusalem.

There can be no doubt that this law book was the book of Deuteronomy. Some scholars have occasionally suggested that, far from being an ancient book, Josiah had actually arranged to have it written for precisely the reasons just mentioned. But this is highly unlikely. It is not intrinsically improbable that such documents would be stored in the Temple, for temples in the ancient world often served as repositories for significant national archives. Moreover, if Deuteronomy had been newly written in Josiah's time, it would have reflected his own situation much more clearly than it does. In particular, it would surely have identified the one place where God should be worshipped as the Temple in Jerusalem. But in fact, Deuteronomy does not do this – and in any case, it was not a new idea, as Hezekiah himself had tried to strengthen his own position by a similar stratagem long before the time of Josiah.

Deuteronomy does not in itself support the centralization of worship in Jerusalem, and it actually has many close links with the dynamic view of kingship that had been followed more self-consciously in the northern kingdom of Israel. For this reason, many scholars believe that the 'one sanctuary' mentioned in Deuteronomy was not Jerusalem, but the place where the ark of the covenant had been kept during the earliest period of Israel's emergence as a nation (Deuteronomy 12:5). The whole book clearly emphasizes the lessons that had been forcefully presented by northern prophets like Amos and Hosea: that the nation's prosperity could only be assured if they were willing to return to the old ways, and recognize the demands for justice and equality that had been such an important part of the covenant made at Mount Sinai. This is something that the people of Judah had forgotten, preferring to emphasize the promises given to David and to his successors. Instead of asking what they had done to deserve the punishment that was being handed out to them by Assyria, they reassured themselves with the belief that Jerusalem was God's chosen city – Zion – and so nothing could ever happen to it. It was impregnable, and would always be that way. Even Isaiah had agreed with this point of view, and though he regarded Assyria's iron hand as the agent of God's punishment, he still could not believe that Judah's day was finished (Isaiah 1:10–20; 2:6–21; 5:26–30; 9:1–7; 11:1–16; 14:1–2). But now, as Josiah and his people read this old book, they could see very clearly that unless they changed their ways, Judah and its people were indeed at an end. So, in a solemn ceremony, itself reminiscent of the events of Mount Sinai, the people of Judah pledged their allegiance once again to the long-forgotten ideals of their ancient faith (2 Kings 23:1–3).

The Babylonians

While all this was going on in Judah, the Assyrians were fighting desperately to hang on to the fragmented remnants of their once-great empire. The Babylonians were now more powerful than ever, and it was only a matter of time before they had captured all the main Assyrian cities. The defeated Assyrians tried to re-establish themselves at Haran, but they were soon ejected from there as well. Some thirteen years after Josiah's reformation in Judah, the Assyrians made a last-ditch effort to regain this town. This time, their old enemies the Egyptians came to help them. Necho II, now pharaoh of Egypt, could see that his real rival was no longer the king of Assyria but Nabopolasser, king of Babylon. There was absolutely no reason at all why Judah should have become involved in all this, but for some inexplicable reason Josiah decided that he would try to stop the Egyptians from reaching the beleaguered Assyrian army. He was unable to do so, and died in the attempt at Megiddo. The sense of loss that swept the nation can be judged from the fact that, centuries later, a poem mourning his death was still being repeated as part of the regular liturgy for worship (2 Chronicles 35:25). Indeed, there is some evidence that it was at this time that the books of Kings were first compiled, as a tribute to the achievements of Josiah. It is certainly striking that in these books he is the only king who manages to pass the test of loyalty to Yahweh, and all the others are judged by their failure to achieve what he did.

Politically, Judah came under Egyptian domination for a while at this time, but nothing could stop the advance of the Babylonians. Four years after the final collapse of Assyria, the Babylonian army met the Egyptians in battle at Carchemish, and decisively defeated them. At this Jehoiakim, a king of Judah who had been put in power by the Egyptians, was forced to transfer his allegiance to the Babylonian Nebuchadnezzar (2 Kings 24:1). Like his predecessors, he continued to keep his eyes open for a suitable opportunity to reassert his own independence, and when Babylon was defeated by the Egyptians some four years later, he decided to take his chance. But he had seriously misjudged the situation. Nebuchadnezzar moved in strength through the whole of Palestine, and besieged Jerusalem with his army, determined to replace Jehoiakim with a king who could be trusted. As it happened, the job was done for him, for Jehoiakim died during the course of the siege, and was replaced by his son Jehoiachin. He realized that resistance was futile, and surrendered to Nebuchadnezzar. Not surprisingly, the Babylonian did not trust him and took him off into exile in Babylon, along with many of the leading citizens and a large quantity of the treasures from both palace and Temple.

Three prophets

Three of the shorter prophetic books seem to have originated during the reigns of Josiah and Jehoiakim: Zephaniah, Nahum and Habakkuk. Virtually nothing of a personal nature is known of the prophets whose messages they contain, but they were all concerned with one subject: the way that God was using nations like Assyria and Babylon to punish Judah and encourage the people to be true to their own faith.

Zephaniah

Zephaniah is identified as a descendant of Hezekiah (1:1), and he probably delivered his messages in the earliest days of the reign of Josiah. Judah and Jerusalem, he declared, were being brought to ruination by the worship of traditional Canaanite gods like Baal, as well as the astral deities of the Assyrians (1:4–6). But Zephaniah did not blame Josiah himself for this state of affairs. Instead, he singled out his court officials (1:8–9), which suggests that Josiah was still a boy and his great religious reforms were a thing of the future. Probably, therefore, Zephaniah delivered his messages sometime between 640 and 622 BC, and this date would also fit in well with the theme of the poem which ends the book (3:14–20). For this is a celebration hymn, following the deliverance of Judah and Jerusalem from some particular enemy – possibly the Scythians, who were advancing south towards Egypt at about this period. However, the jubilation with which the book closes is not reflected in the rest of the prophet's messages.

Zephaniah warned his people against a false confidence in the security of Jerusalem just because of God's promises to David. The 'day of Yahweh' would be coming soon enough – and it would not be a day of rejoicing for the people of Judah, any more than it had been for the people of Samaria (1:7–18). They would experience God's anger, along with the other nations. Even Assyria, which God had used to punish the people of Israel, would in turn be destroyed because of their pride and self-satisfaction (2:13–15). But like Isaiah before him, Zephaniah saw that God could both punish the people, and yet still show love for them. Though Jerusalem was doomed, 'a humble and lowly people' would survive (3:12), and through them God's promises would come true.

Nahum

This book belongs to a period nearer the end of Josiah's reign, either just before or just after the collapse of the Assyrian capital Nineveh in 612 BC. Nahum too saw that, though Assyria had been the instrument of God's punishment for the people of Judah, they had over-reached themselves – and they would be punished in their turn. The collapse of Nineveh (Nahum 2–3) is described in such vivid language that some scholars have argued the prophet must actually have witnessed the scene. But others believe that his apparent realism is a purely imaginary – though remarkably accurate – description of the city's fall, and was probably composed even before the Babylonians finally moved in. Either way, the message of the book centres around the conviction that Yahweh, and not the Assyrians, is the one who determines the course of history and can use the nations at will. The knowledge that God was in control was an important lesson for the people of Judah to learn, for they had suffered so much at the hands of Assyria, which otherwise might have seemed very unfair.

Jeremiah and the fall of Jerusalem

Even before Josiah's reformation in 622 BC, another young prophet by the name of Jeremiah had already begun his work. He belonged to a family of priests from Anathoth, a village located about four miles northeast of Jerusalem. Like the other prophets, he was convinced that God

Because of the poetic form of the book, and its dramatic content, some have suggested that Nahum's messages were compiled in this way so as to be used liturgically in the Temple at Jerusalem, to celebrate Nineveh's downfall, and to remind the worshippers of God's great power.

Habakkuk

This book tackles a similar set of questions, though from a more reflective perspective. Habakkuk lived slightly later than Nahum, in the reign of Jehoiakim. By the time he delivered his messages, Egypt had been defeated at the battle of Carchemish (605 BC), and Habakkuk now had a chance to reflect on the Babylonian style of government. He was not impressed with what he saw. Things in Judah were bad enough, and society was collapsing in moral and political anarchy (1:2–4). God was rightly using superpowers like Babylon to discipline the people of Judah. But were the Babylonians any better? They 'catch people with hooks, as though they were fish. They drag them off in nets and shout for joy over their catch! They even worship their nets and offer sacrifices to them, because their nets provide them with the best of everything' (1:15–16). So, asked Habakkuk, how could God tolerate this kind of inhumane wickedness, while dealing so sternly with the lesser evil that was going on in Jerusalem?

He found the answer to that in the conviction that the Babylonians would themselves be punished by God. Like Nahum, Habakkuk had no difficulty in believing that God was personally in charge of history, and could therefore use even evil nations to accomplish good. But such people would never be allowed to get away with their wrongdoing: 'You are doomed!

You founded a city on crime and built it up by murder. The nations you conquered wore themselves out in useless labour, and all they have built goes up in flames. The Lord Almighty has done this. But the earth will be as full of the knowledge of God's glory as the seas are full of water... Yahweh will make you drink your own cup of punishment, and your honour will be turned to disgrace' (2:12–14, 16). Of course, Habakkuk realized that this kind of answer to the problem of evil in the world is not much direct use to those who are actually suffering. But he also included some practical advice for his people: 'Those who are evil will not survive, but those who are righteous will live because they are faithful to God' (2:4). There is some debate as to the precise meaning of these words, but almost certainly the Hebrew expression used in this passage should be understood as referring to God's own faithfulness, first experienced in the events of the exodus and repeated many times in the nation's history since then. It was in these words that St Paul and Martin Luther later found the heart of biblical faith, and of course the commitment of which they spoke is essentially a human response to the personal faithfulness of God. This confidence in God was eloquently expressed by Habakkuk in the closing verses of his book – and it was to be needed in the dark days that lay ahead for Judah: 'Even though the fig trees have no fruit and no grapes grow on the vines, even though the olive crop fails and the fields produce no corn, even though the sheep all die and the cattle stalls are empty, I will still be joyful and glad, because the Lord God is my saviour. The Sovereign Lord gives me strength, and makes me sure-footed as a deer, and keeps me safe on the mountains' (3:17–19).

had spoken personally to him, and entrusted him with a message for the people. He was to be 'a prophet to the nations', communicating the will of God in the midst of much international turmoil (Jeremiah 1:5). This was certainly an appropriate time for the emergence of such a person, for by the year of his call (627 BC) Assyria's power was crumbling and independence for Judah once more seemed a real possibility. But Jeremiah could not share in the mood of national optimism. He saw many things wrong in his nation: the people had chosen to ignore the covenant laws of God, and would have to face the inevitable consequences of such disobedience. One day he saw an almond tree in blossom. The Hebrew word for 'almond' had a similar sound to another Hebrew word that meant 'watching', and Jeremiah saw this tree as a sign that God was watching over the people, looking for the appropriate time to carry out the sentence of destruction (Jeremiah 1:11–12). When he saw a pot of boiling water on a fire that was fanned by a wind from the north, he realized that this, too, had a message in it. God's anger was about to boil over against Judah: 'Destruction will boil over from the north on all who live in this land, because I am calling all the nations in the north to come. Their kings will set up their thrones at the gates of Jerusalem and round its walls, and also round the other cities of Judah. I will punish my people' (Jeremiah 1:14–16).

Misplaced trust

Things soon began to change with the religious reforms instituted by Josiah. Jeremiah no doubt was in favour of all this: he certainly wanted to get rid of foreign religious influences, and some of his messages may well have been delivered in support of Josiah, for they angered his relatives in Anathoth, who decided to try to kill him (Jeremiah 11:18–23). Their reaction would have made sense if Jeremiah was supporting Josiah's closure of all the sanctuaries except the Temple in Jerusalem, for as priests they would presumably be in danger of losing their jobs. Jeremiah soon realized that Josiah's reforms were not going to have much lasting effect on the way of life of the people, and by the time of Jehoiakim things were as bad as they had ever been. But Jeremiah also came to think that Josiah's emphasis on the Jerusalem Temple had actually undermined the faith that was emphasized in the ancient law book uncovered there, for instead of facing up to their responsibilities under the covenant Law, the people developed a pathetic and misguided confidence in their religious institutions. They came to imagine that as long as they performed the prescribed rituals in the Temple, God would actually preserve them from their enemies and all would be well.

In the end, events proved Jeremiah was right. But in the short term, he was disappointed and depressed. The people refused to listen to his message, and he was puzzled himself, because it appeared not to be coming true. Instead of the doom that Jeremiah had predicted, Judah was enjoying a period of great prosperity. Under Josiah the nation's territory was enlarged and there seemed to be no shortage of money for grand new building projects. Under the circumstances, people like Jeremiah were unlikely to be taken seriously, and then when Nineveh was destroyed in 612 BC his message seemed to be quite discredited.

The end is coming

However, within a very short period of time the picture had changed quite radically. Three years later, Josiah was dead and the Egyptians had taken over the land of Judah. The prosperity that had gone before had been attributed to the fact that things had been set right in the Temple at Jerusalem. So what had gone wrong now? Why had God not saved these apparently faithful people from the power of Egypt? In this situation, Jeremiah's messages began to look less unrealistic, and when under Jehoiakim the reforms of Josiah virtually disappeared, the stage looked set for the scenario of disaster that Jeremiah had so vividly described. Even Jehoiakim himself could see that, and he made a concerted effort to get rid of opponents like Jeremiah. At least one prophet, Uriah, was killed, and Jeremiah himself was brought to trial (Jeremiah 26:7–24). He escaped death, but still continued to deliver his messages of doom and destruction, and was beaten up and put into the stocks for a night. Even that did not stop him. God had spoken, and he could not refuse to communicate the message: 'When I say, "I will forget Yahweh and no longer speak in God's name," then your message is like a fire burning deep within me. I try my best to hold it in, but can no longer keep it back' (20:9). But he was still banned from delivering his messages in public at the Temple, and so he withdrew from public life for the rest of Jehoiakim's reign, and distributed his messages by getting his friend Baruch to write them down and then take them into the streets to read them aloud. At this time, Jeremiah's messages were no longer general declarations of disaster, but definite predictions of the impending end of Jerusalem, and especially of the destruction of its Temple. Jeremiah had no doubt that the idea that God was bound to protect the Temple and city was false.

But Jeremiah was not only struggling against opposition from his enemies. He also had his own problems with the message God had given him. If it was correct, why did no one else accept it? After all, Jeremiah had not refused God's call, even though he wanted to do so. He had laid himself open to disbelief and ridicule, and had become involved in endless arguments (15:10–21). He had given up the ordinary human joys of home and family to speak on God's behalf, and he was tempted to feel that God had somehow deceived him (20:7–18). This was a hard time, and some of the most striking passages of the book of Jeremiah are concerned with this kind of self-examination. But it was also a significant period of spiritual learning for this most open-hearted of all the prophets, and the record of his personal journey of faith and self-discovery at this time has become one of the most inspirational sections of the entire Bible for more than one generation of spiritual searchers. The story of Jeremiah provides one of the most outstanding models of what it means to trust God in a personal and living way.

Dark days in Jerusalem

When Nebuchadnezzar captured Jerusalem in 597 BC, he placed a new king, Zedekiah, on the throne there. But things did not change. Instead

of learning their lesson, the people of Jerusalem concluded that they were specially favoured by God, because they had escaped the ultimate fate of being carried off into exile. Jeremiah had no time for this easy optimism: he knew that what had happened was a just punishment for the people's wrongdoing, and that worse was to come. He pointed to two baskets of figs in the market, one containing good figs and the other full of rotten figs. The good ones, said Jeremiah, were the exiles in Babylon. The bad ones were the people left in Judah – and everyone knew what happened to figs that were too bad to eat (Jeremiah 24).

The people of Jerusalem were deported to Babylon in stages. At first only the leaders were taken in the days of King Jehoiachin, while Zedekiah was put on the throne as a puppet ruler. Only after his revolt was the city finally destroyed. Jeremiah characterized this intervening time as being like a basket of figs, of which the good ones stood for those already in exile, and the bad ones for the leaders who remained.

Zedekiah hardly knew which way to turn. Jeremiah advised him that the only sensible thing to do was to accept Babylonian domination. He wanted to listen, but he was a weak man and when the Egyptians tried to persuade him to join a revolt against Babylon there was no shortage of other prophets who advised Zedekiah to do so. Jeremiah, however, refused to change his mind. In a dramatic presentation of his message, he appeared wearing a wooden yoke on his shoulders, as a mime to show what would happen to the nation (Jeremiah 27). He was confronted in the Temple by a prophet called Hananiah, who ridiculed Jeremiah's message, and to prove his point he proceeded to smash Jeremiah's yoke. Determined not to allow his message to be subverted in this way, Jeremiah quickly replaced the wooden yoke with an iron one (Jeremiah 28). In the event, Jeremiah was right. The Babylonian army moved up to crush the rebellion masterminded by Egypt, and Judah was finished. After a siege of eighteen months the city of Jerusalem fell to Nebuchadnezzar. Zedekiah tried to escape, but he was captured. His family was killed before his eyes, and then he was blinded and carried off to Babylon along with most of the leading people of the land. This time the Babylonians made sure of their victory by systematically destroying all the main buildings in Jerusalem, including the Temple. A palace official named Gedaliah was made governor of Judah, and from this point on there would never be a king again (2 Kings 25:1–26).

Jeremiah's dreadful predictions had come true, and even the Temple lay in ruins, its treasures plundered. Still, Jeremiah was confident that

God's promises could not be overthrown so easily and, like Habakkuk before him, he knew that there would be a future for his people. Even while Jerusalem was under attack, Jeremiah had purchased a piece of land in his native village, as an expression of his confidence for the future (Jeremiah 32:1–15). The action nearly cost him his life, for as he was leaving the city to go and view the property he was arrested on suspicion of being a traitor (Jeremiah 37:11 – 38:13). Yet his trust in God was not founded on a crudely materialistic expectation. He had already made it plain that his people's future and the real meaning of the faith from Mount Sinai was not to be found in the Temple. All the institutions connected with that were only of limited value. God was not most truly to be found in the ritual of sacrifice, but in a personal and living relationship of trust and commitment. The exiles in Babylon were to learn that soon enough, but it was an insight that had already been given to Jeremiah. For he saw beyond and through the disaster and destruction, to a new relationship that God would establish with humankind. God had remained faithful to the covenant made at Mount

Other traditions related to Jeremiah

In addition to the book of Jeremiah contained in the Hebrew Bible, the deuterocanonical books with their origins in the Greek Bible (Septuagint) also include two writings connected to Jeremiah: Baruch and the Letter of Jeremiah.

Baruch

A person named Baruch is mentioned in the book of Jeremiah, where he is the prophet's friend and secretary, responsible for writing down his messages and distributing them when Jehoiakim had silenced Jeremiah himself (Jeremiah 36:4–8). The book of Baruch is presented as a compilation of such teachings, the first section (1:1 – 3:8) in prose and the rest (3:9 – 5:9) in poetry. The opening sentence dates these messages to 'the fifth year' of the exile, written in Babylon and delivered to the exiles in that city. Since Jehoiachin is mentioned and Temple worship still appears to be continuing (2:26), the natural implication seems to be that the exile in question was the first deportation of 597 BC, which would place this book in 593 BC. However, none of this can be reconciled with what is otherwise known of Baruch from the book of Jeremiah. There, he was still with the prophet even after the fall of Jerusalem in 586 BC (Jeremiah 43:5), and the natural implication of that passage is that he was taken to Egypt, along with Jeremiah. Other historical references are confused and contradictory, and some scholars have concluded that the book is not even a single piece of writing, but combines two or three originally separate pieces. Some passages appear to reflect a later stage again, around the time when the Babylonian empire was collapsing and there was a real prospect that the exiles might be able to return home (4:5 – 5:9). The book of Baruch is known only in Greek, though the terminology used in some sections seems to indicate that it may have been translated from a Hebrew or Aramaic original. There are many connections with the books of Jeremiah, Lamentations and Isaiah 40–55, which suggests it was written later than them, while some passages have links with Daniel, which was not written until the second century BC. Possibly it was written about the same time as Daniel, at another time of great persecution for the Jewish people,

This seal may have belonged to Baruch, friend and secretary of the prophet Jeremiah.

Sinai, but the people had been unable to respond to this freely shared love. They had not managed to live up to the high ideals of the past, and what they needed now was a 'new covenant' that would both fulfil and supersede the original one. This time it would be a covenant that not only asked them to be obedient to God, but also actually gave them the moral power to do so: 'The new covenant that I will make with the people of Israel will be this: I will put my law within them and write it on their hearts. I will be their God, and they will be my people... all will know me, from the least to the greatest. I will forgive their sins and I will no longer remember their wrongs. I, the Lord, have spoken' (Jeremiah 31:33–34).

Other traditions related to Jeremiah *continued*

encouraging them to remain faithful to their heritage, and maybe also, like Daniel, it incorporated materials that had been originally written earlier, but edited and applied to the new situation.

The Letter of Jeremiah

This is neither a letter, nor does it have any direct connection with Jeremiah. It consists of a polemic against the worship of idols, in the context of a time when the Jewish people were still trying to work out how and why God's judgment on them should have lasted for so long even after the exile. It may originally have been written in Hebrew, because a play on words in verse 72 would only have made sense in that language, though it is most likely that it originated among the people of the Babylonian exile, for whom it must have seemed as if the deities of other nations, with their grand visual representations and statues, were more powerful than Yahweh. Since the book is mentioned in 2 Maccabees 2:2, it cannot have been compiled later than about 100 BC, and the best guess as to its date would place its composition sometime in the second half of the second century BC.

The Lachish Letters

The last days of Judah are depicted vividly in the book of Jeremiah, where the prophet's message reflects the disarray and confusion of the people as they could see the Babylonians coming, and yet were powerless to do anything about it. Unlike the edited accounts of history we get in the books of Samuel and Kings, this is the kind of first-hand evidence that helps to bring past events to life. The situation described by Jeremiah is also documented in one of the most remarkable finds ever made by archaeologists in a Bible city: the Lachish Letters.

The city of Lachish lay to the south-west of Jerusalem, and its history began long before Israel ever emerged as a nation. It was an important city from the earliest period, and has been more thoroughly excavated than most Israelite towns. The material found there has been of great importance in helping to understand the development of the Hebrew language, while the discovery of traditional altars and other religious objects using Canaanite designs has added to our knowledge of the kind of practices so often denounced by the prophets. The city was destroyed by Sennacherib in 701 BC, and then later Nebuchadnezzar captured it in about 587 BC, just before the final collapse of Zedekiah's Jerusalem. The Lachish Letters relate to this sequence of events.

The letters themselves are actually what archaeologists call 'ostraca', that is, scraps of broken pottery with messages written

The Assyrian king Sennacherib receives the surrender and booty from the Judahite town of Lachish. The siege of the town was graphically documented by the Assyrians in a series of reliefs in Sennacherib's palace at Nineveh.

The Lachish Letters
continued

on them. A total of twenty-one of these ostraca were found, mostly in what appears to have been the guardroom of the city gate. Not all of them are now legible, but the majority of those that are were addressed to a man named Yaush, who was probably the military commander of Lachish at the time. Many of the messages were written by someone called Hoshayahu, who seems to have been

Fragments of a letter, written on pottery by a military commander at an outpost near Lachish, bear witness to a desperate state of affairs as the Assyrian army advanced.

the officer in charge of a military outpost to the north of Lachish. The same name is found in Jeremiah (42:1; 43:2), though there is no way of knowing whether they were the same person. Still, the letters do provide a fascinating insight into the same situations as were described by Jeremiah:

● Jeremiah 34:1–7 reports a message given by Jeremiah to Zedekiah while Nebuchadnezzar's army was moving against Jerusalem. At the same time, 'The army was also attacking Lachish and Azekah, the only other fortified cities left in Judah' (Jeremiah 34:7). Azekah was almost halfway between Lachish and Jerusalem, and in one of the Lachish ostraca Hoshayahu writes, 'We are watching for the signals from Lachish… for we cannot see Azekah.' Azekah was perhaps midway between Hoshayahu's post and Lachish, and was therefore used as a signalling station. But at the time of writing, it had apparently fallen to the Babylonians.

● The name Jeremiah is found in two of the letters, though there is no reason to identify this person with the Old Testament prophet in either case. There is, however, a clear reference to 'the prophet' in at least two of these letters, and the same term may also be found in a further two. Someone who could be referred to as 'the prophet' without further explanation must have been a high-profile public figure, and it has been proposed that the person indicated here must have been Jeremiah himself. Of course, that is impossible to prove one way or the other, and it has also been suggested that 'the prophet' could be Uriah, since the same letter also refers to 'Coniah, son of Elnathan' going to Egypt, and according to Jeremiah 26:22 Jehoiakim sent a man called Elnathan to bring Uriah from Egypt to face death in Jerusalem. This identification is more problematic, for the letters did not originate in Jehoiakim's reign, but later in the time of Zedekiah. Nevertheless, even though the exact identity of 'the prophet' remains uncertain, references like this do indicate that such prophets as Jeremiah were playing an important part in national affairs at this period in Judah's history.

Other more fanciful efforts have been made to link these texts more closely to the prophetic movement, its supporters and detractors, in Jerusalem. But their greatest value is the insight that they give us into the people of Jeremiah's day, and their reactions as they faced the inevitable end of their nation at the hands of the Babylonian army.

The prophets

People who are described as 'prophets' clearly played a crucial role in the history of the two nations, Israel and Judah, and in addition their messages dominate the Old Testament as we have it today. They are among the greatest religious teachers of all time, and have had a profound impact not only on the life of those who knew them, but also, through their writings, on the life of every subsequent generation of Bible readers.

In the nineteenth century, it was fashionable to suppose that it was through the activity of the prophets that an originally primitive and superstitious faith was transformed into the high ideals of morality that are now found in the Hebrew Bible. But it is obvious that approaches of this kind said more about the religious perspectives of those who proposed them than about the prophets themselves, and biblical prophecy is a much more complex and diverse phenomenon than that kind of simplistic explanation might suggest.

Four different Hebrew expressions are conventionally translated as 'prophet'. Some passages seem to suggest that the terminology changed with the passage of time (1 Samuel 9:11), but in reality we cannot now tell the technical difference between these terms. The fact that the terminology is so diverse, however, clearly suggests that prophets differed from each other, and that prophecy was not just a single social and religious phenomenon. People who could be called prophets operated in many different social contexts: as diviners (1 Samuel 9:1–25); as ecstatics, often in groups who were distinguished by special marks and clothing (1 Samuel 10:5–8; 19:18–24; 1 Kings 20:35–43; 2 Kings 1:8; 2:23–24; 4:38; 6:12); as royal court prophets (1 Samuel 22:5; 2 Samuel 12:1–15; 24:11; 1 Kings 20:35–43); as war prophets (Judges 4:4–9; 1 Kings 20; 22:1–28); as cultic prophets (1 Samuel 10:5–8; 2 Kings 4:18–25); as 'false' prophets (1 Kings 22; Isaiah 9:15; Jeremiah 6:14; Ezekiel 13:2; Micah 3:5–6).

Some prophets seem to have operated in more than one way. For instance, when Samuel tells Saul about his lost asses he is a seer with psychic powers (1 Samuel 9:11, 19–20), but he then goes on to give specific messages about the kingship in a more spontaneous kind of prophetic utterance (1 Samuel 10:1–8). Yet others, like Amos, claim not to have been real 'professional' prophets at all (Amos 7:12–15).

Several models have been used by scholars to try to explain the form and function of Hebrew prophecy. Here we shall notice just four of the more significant approaches.

A history of religions approach

In view of our ever-increasing knowledge of social and religious situations throughout the ancient world it is natural to compare Old Testament prophets to similar characters elsewhere. One of the earliest exponents of this view was the Scandinavian scholar Alfred Haldar. According to him, prophecy was a phenomenon found in the context of organized religion (the cult). A close analysis of texts from Babylon (Old Babylon, 1894–1595 BC) showed that they distinguished between two types of prophet. On the one hand were the *Mahhu*, priests or prophets who specialized in wild, ecstatic, trance-induced behaviour. But alongside them were the *Baru*, who specialized in divination, that is, they would be asked a specific question, the answer to which they would discover by throwing dice, or by astrological speculations, or by offering sacrifices and examining the entrails of the dead animals in order to discover the will of the gods.

Haldar claimed to find Old Testament evidence for this pattern, mainly in the dual functions of Samuel. He believed that other isolated passages provide evidence for the work of 'divination corporations'

The prophets
continued

(Isaiah 21:6–10) or sacrificial inspection (Psalm 5:3). But this view of the nature of prophecy is difficult to substantiate from the Old Testament:

● Although the Old Testament does provide evidence for wild behaviour on occasion (1 Samuel 10:9–13), and of prophets giving specific answers to questions (1 Samuel 9:3–20), it is not the most obvious or common form of Old Testament prophecy. There is a good deal more evidence for a more 'rational' kind of prophecy. Indeed, when Jeremiah finds a message in a potter's workshop (Jeremiah 18:1–12), or in a basket of figs (Jeremiah 24), it is at least arguable that his message is essentially the result of rational deliberation on the everyday happenings of life, and has nothing at all to do with special emotional or religious experiences.

● Even when prophets do answer specific questions ('divination'), the Old Testament provides no evidence that they manipulated special objects such as dice or sacrifices in order to arrive at an answer (1 Samuel 9:17–20; 1 Kings 22).

● To use such technical means of divination required special training and a lot of practice. Again, there is no Old Testament evidence of the prophets being trained at all, and a fair amount to the contrary (e.g. Amos 7:12–15).

Others have looked to Egypt and Syria as sources of possible models for Old Testament prophecy. Mari is another society in which there was evidently a kind of 'prophecy'. Texts from there speak of 'prophets' who were religious func-tionaries, of trance prophets, and of yet others who brought messages to the attention of the king and who were therefore a specialized kind of bureaucrat. At one time or another, all this material has been regarded as a possible 'source' of Old Testament prophecy, and there is no doubt that much of it can help us to a better understanding of the Old Testament. But there is unlikely to be any direct line of connection between them:

● The social functions performed by diviners, ecstatics and so on can arise in any society, ancient or modern, quite independently of external direct contact.

● There is in the Hebrew Bible a much wider diversity than in any of the comparative materials so far identified. There tends to be less emphasis on divination here than elsewhere, and Samuel's example is quoted so frequently only because there are no other biblical examples of this kind of thing.

● In general, the Hebrew prophets were concerned more about the great sweep of history and the meaning of human life in the grand sense, than about the trivialities of everyday life.

A psychological approach

Julius Wellhausen (1844–1918) argued that the prophets were essentially inspired individuals, who changed the form of Israelite religious belief. The presence of apparently irrational prophetic behaviour in certain Old Testament stories seemed to suggest that a useful perspective on the prophets would be gained by asking what it was that made them such exceptional people. This line of enquiry was especially associated with the work of Hermann Gunkel (1862–1932), who concluded that the key to understanding the prophets was 'ecstasy'. By this he meant the kind of irrational, over-emotional behaviour that is familiar from many contexts the world over. There are many contemporary examples of such things, not only in the Judeo-Christian religious tradition, but also in Sufism and many aspects of the New Age.

Gunkel described the prophetic experience in the following way: 'When such an ecstasy seizes him, the prophet… loses command of his limbs; he staggers and stutters like a drunken man; his ordinary sense of what is decent deserts him; he feels an impulse to do all kinds of strange actions… strange ideas and emotions come over him… he is seized by that sensation of hovering which we know from our own dreams.' Scholars of this earlier generation often referred to what they knew of Canaanite prophecy to back up their theories, though in reality they knew next to nothing about that apart from what is reported in 1 Kings 18. But like many things connected to the emergence of Israel as a nation, this kind of simple explanation does not match all the facts. Of course, a passage like that shows the prophets of Baal producing ecstatic hysteria by a series of self-inflicted moves – music, shouting, dancing, drink, drugs and so on. But then there are other narratives which show Israelite prophets doing exactly the same things (1 Samuel 10; 2 Kings 2). Because of the apparent difficulty of reconciling such descriptions with the kinds of messages delivered by the great prophets of the Old Testament, Gunkel concluded that prophecy must have evolved from this kind of ecstatic mass hysteria to become an altogether more rational phenomenon. But it is possible to assess the evidence differently. Some, for example, have tried to identify the ecstatics with 'false prophets', contrasting them with the 'real' prophets who were rational speakers, though this is very difficult to do as there are many indications that the great prophets could also have unusual psychical experiences (Jeremiah 4:19; 23:9; Ezekiel 1:1 – 3:15). Others have tried to distinguish the experiences of the great prophets from the content of their messages, surmising that the messages were delivered in a rational way after the experiences, but with no particular reference to what had gone before. But all such rationalizing explanations are unsatisfactory. The Old Testament itself makes none of these distinctions, and all the prophets mentioned there have unusual experiences of one sort or another. The way in which the experiences are related to life situations seems to depend on the circumstances of the moment, and although analysis of ecstasy and other related emotional states can shed some light on prophetic experience, it is clear that a full understanding of the prophets is not to be found there.

A literary approach

It was the search for a meaningful life situation that led Claus Westermann to begin to analyse the literary form of the prophetic messages in the Old Testament. In the ancient world, the way a person spoke was determined by their context to a much greater extent than it is today. By analysing the forms of prophetic speech it is therefore possible to locate it in various contexts, such as the law court (Amos 7:16–17; Micah 2:1–4), the wisdom school (Jeremiah 17:5–8), the context of worship (Habakkuk; Isaiah 40–55), or the royal court ('Thus says...' is a royal messenger speech-form). That being the case, it can be argued that the prophets must have been essentially ordinary people, whose background lay in the official functions of these different life situations. It has even been suggested that the descriptions of 'visions' and other 'ecstatic' experiences could perhaps be stylistic devices, rather than literal descriptions of things that happened.

This way of looking at the prophets and their messages has added enormously to our understanding of them. But by itself, it can lead to a one-sided view of their functions:

● It is to some extent a reaction against the extreme 'ecstatic' view: instead of prophets being seen as innovators, they are here viewed as conventional persons operating within the normal structures of society. But the fact is that the element of 'ecstasy' is still there in the Old Testament, and cannot be disposed of quite so simply.
● Then there is the question of a jump from literary form to life situation. A person who uses a legal form is not necessarily a lawyer, but may be just a good communicator, using language that will be especially evocative and challenging to those who hear.

The prophets
continued

A theological/cultic approach

A century ago, Wellhausen was arguing that the prophets had broken completely with cultic worship in ancient Israel, and were attempting to introduce morality into what had hitherto been a barren and empty form of ritualism. Today, many scholars would argue the exact opposite, suggesting that the religious life of Israel had started with a covenant based on a distinctly moral view of God, and that the prophets were closely associated with this covenant ideal and with its celebration in the context of worship. There can be no doubt that the idea of a 'covenant' is at the heart of the Old Testament faith. All these books centre on the unmistakable conviction that God had burst into the lives of the people of Israel as an act of unmerited love ('grace'), and that as a result of this the people were called upon to respond by loving obedience in return. When we talk of 'the covenant', this is all we mean: the responsive obedience of the people, consequent upon their experience of God's grace. In historical terms, that experience had been demonstrated most dramatically in the events of the exodus and what followed, and this is a major theme in the messages of many of the greatest prophets. It was also celebrated regularly in the great worship festivals that marked the progress of Israel's religious life. Some scholars in the past have no doubt exaggerated the role of the prophets in this religious worship. But it certainly makes sense to see them as guardians of the covenant faith. It explains why they spoke in full expectation that people would listen, for they were calling them back to their spiritual roots.

No one of these models by itself can fully explain Old Testament prophecy. The whole phenomenon is so diverse that perhaps we need to speak individually of particular prophets rather than trying to speak of them all in one breath. But they were all conscious of having been in the presence of God in some mystical sense, and then of speaking or acting in God's name as interpreters of the covenant faith in relation to the events of their own day and to the lives of their contemporaries.

7 Dashed Hopes and New Horizons

The period following the Babylonian invasion of Judah was one of the most important in the entire history of the Israelite nation and faith. The previous millennium had seen many striking changes, as Israel first emerged as a nation, soon to become a significant political entity, and then to sink into economic and spiritual decay, so that in the years immediately prior to the fall of Jerusalem, the state of Judah had become a relatively unimportant middle-eastern kingdom. Politically, the nation was finished. Yet by the Christian era the religious beliefs based on the life of this ancient people had achieved a worldwide influence, and large groups of their descendants were making a significant contribution to the life and culture of major cities throughout the known world.

This amazing transformation, in which Judaism arose phoenix-like out of the ashes of the old kingdom of Judah, can only be explained after a careful analysis of the new currents of thought that swept through this faith community in the centuries immediately following the Babylonian exile. These centuries were an incredibly creative time, as the lessons of the past were assessed. and their spiritual power was harnessed to a new cause. Unfortunately, less is known about this period in Israel's history than the one that immediately preceded it, and there are many decades in the exilic age about which virtually nothing at all is known. Even such scraps of information as can be gathered from the Old Testament and other sources are often confused and incomplete. Interpreting them is sometimes a matter of pure guesswork, and always a process of painstaking deduction from partial and incomplete evidence.

Facing up to disaster

The nature of the problem can easily be identified by enquiring about life in Judah itself in the days immediately following Nebuchadnezzar's invasion. The general outline of events is reasonably clear: the royal family was deported to Babylon, along with most of the leading citizens, after which a palace official called Gedaliah was made governor of Judah, with his capital at Mizpah (2 Kings 25:18–24; Jeremiah 40:7–12). This fact suggests that neither the destruction nor the deportation was as extensive as has often been imagined: there would have been little purpose in appointing Gedaliah if there were no territory and no population over which he could rule. But at the same time, it is not at all clear what his status actually was. Was he, for example, regarded as a Babylonian official, and Judah a Babylonian province? Or was the social structure much less rigid than that? We simply do not know.

What we do know is that his existence soon provoked opposition and it was not long before he was assassinated by a man called Ishmael, who was a member of the former royal family (2 Kings 25:25–26; Jeremiah 40:13 – 41:3). As a member of the Jerusalem aristocracy Ishmael had managed to escape the Babylonians by fleeing to the neighbouring state of Ammon. He was not the only one, and once the Babylonian armies had left the scene other such people came out of hiding and allied themselves with Gedaliah. They imagined that they would be able to continue the grand lifestyle which they had enjoyed previously, but that dream was never realized. For though Ishmael

himself was put to flight after his murder of Gedaliah (Jeremiah 41:11–15), those who were left at his head-quarters now feared a Babylonian reprisal, and so they decided to go and live in Egypt, where they would be able to obtain employment as mercenary soldiers (2 Kings 25:26; Jeremiah 41:16–18). Jeremiah did not want to go with them. When he had been offered a choice earlier, he had decided to stay in Judah rather than go to Babylon, and nothing had happened to change his mind (Jeremiah 42–43). He felt that his people had suffered enough, and God would soon restore their fortunes. But to be sure of that they must stay in their own land. By going abroad they would forget the God of their ancestors. Jerusalem was the place where they had lost their true faith, and it was where they must try to regain it. In spite of this firm conviction, however, Jeremiah was forced against his will to join the exiles in Egypt, and he spent the rest of his life there. No doubt those who took him to Egypt felt they had done the right thing, for it seems that the Babylonians did indeed return to Judah, and a further deportation in 582 BC may well have been a reprisal for the chaos that followed the murder of Gedaliah (Jeremiah 52:30).

We know virtually nothing of life in Judah for at least the next forty years, though what little we do know suggests that its people

At the time of Nebuchadnezzar II, the main entrance into Babylon via the Processional Way was through the Ishtar Gate. The brick surface of the gate was decorated with reliefs of animals which were coloured with bright glazes. This head of a serpent-dragon represents the city god Marduk.

were profoundly disillusioned by what had taken place. Considering the high expectations they had held, this is hardly surprising. They had convinced themselves that there was no possibility that Jerusalem could fall to an alien army, because it was God's city whose safety was guaranteed because of the divine covenant with David's family. As they faced up to the realities of their predicament, it must have seemed to these people as if very little was left of Judah's great national heritage.

Not everyone, however, accepted that Israel's national faith could explain the tragedy. Some people gave up their faith altogether. One way of coming to terms with it all was to think of these sad events as a battle between Israel's God and the Babylonian gods, and on that reckoning the gods of Babylon had apparently won. Others felt they had been misled all along by the very prophets who claimed to speak in the name of their own God, Yahweh. Those who took Jeremiah to Egypt believed

The book of Lamentations

The depth of feeling about this national tragedy is reflected with great pathos in the book of Lamentations. The book consists of five poems, the first four of which are arranged in an acrostic pattern based on the letters of the Hebrew alphabet. This is an unusual literary device in the Old Testament, and though it may have been used here simply as an aid to the memory, it is more likely to be connected to the deeply felt message of these poems. They are essentially an adaptation of the mourning songs that were conventionally sung at every funeral, and their literary form (covering all the letters of the alphabet) may well be intended to reflect the all-embracing character of the tragedy which left the people emotionally and morally distraught.

The people were forced to accept the truth of what prophets like Jeremiah had been saying all along: that the havoc now wrought upon Jerusalem was the work of God, and it had been brought about by the disobedience and unfaithfulness of their own people. Though 'No one has ever had pain like mine, pain that Yahweh brought on me in the time of God's anger' (1:12), nevertheless 'Yahweh is just, for I have been disobedient' (1:18). This first poem could well refer to the situation in Jerusalem after 597 BC, but before the final destruction some ten years later. But the whole book offers a striking insight into the despair that now engulfed those whose arrogance and vanity have been depicted so graphically in the book of Jeremiah. His message of doom had been opposed by false prophets, and their teaching now lay exposed for what it really was: 'Your prophets had nothing to tell you but lies; their preaching deceived you by never exposing your sin. They made you think you did not need to repent' (2:14).

The pitiful trust of the people in the sanctity of their capital city and its institutions is clearly reflected here too: 'No one anywhere, not even rulers of foreign nations, believed that any invader could enter Jerusalem's gates. But it happened because her prophets sinned and her priests were guilty of causing the death of innocent people. Her leaders wandered through the streets like the blind, so stained with blood that no one would touch them' (4:12–14). Jeremiah had seen all this coming long before the final tragedy, and now those who opposed him had been forced to agree. As they realized what they had done, and what it all meant, their unbridled despair and grief knew no boundaries.

that the Babylonian invasion had been the fault of people like him, who had encouraged them to abandon the worship of the traditional deities of Canaan. If the land had belonged to these other gods and goddesses for centuries, they reasoned, then why should anybody be surprised if the land met with such disaster once they were no longer honoured? For people who thought this way, the path to renewed prosperity could only be found in an enthusiastic return to the old ways of the Baal religion: 'We will offer sacrifices to our goddess, the Queen of Heaven, and we will pour out wine offerings to her, just as we and our ancestors, our king and our leaders, used to do in the towns of Judah and in the streets of Jerusalem. Then we had plenty of food, we were prosperous, and had no troubles. But ever since we stopped sacrificing to the Queen of Heaven... we have had nothing, and our people have died in war and of starvation' (Jeremiah 44:17–18).

Jeremiah, of course, strongly resisted such an opinion, and argued once

---

The book of Lamentations *continued*

Yet, even in the midst of such shattered dreams, the broken remnants of a once-proud nation could still see cause for hope: 'The thought of my pain, my homeless-ness, is bitter poison; I think of it constantly and my spirit is depressed. Yet hope returns when I remember this one thing: God's unfailing love and mercy still continue, fresh as the morning, as sure as the sunrise. Yahweh is all I have, and that is where I put my hope... good to everyone who trusts the promises, so it is best for us to wait in patience – to wait for God to save us' (3:19–26). That in itself could never relieve the anguish that these people felt, but it did give them the confidence to pray for restoration, and that prayer is the theme of the fifth and final poem in the book: 'Bring us back to you, Lord! Bring us back! Restore our ancient glory' (5:21).

Author and date

In the Hebrew Bible, Lamentations appears as an anonymous work. But other traditions, mostly within Christian circles, have attributed it to Jeremiah himself. The main reason for this seems to be found in 2 Chronicles 35:25, where it is stated that 'Jeremiah composed a lament for King Josiah... The song is found in the collection of laments.' But Lamentations has no connection at all with this early period of Jeremiah's life, and it in fact makes much better sense when understood as the composition of those very elements of Jerusalem society that had been originally opposed to all that Jeremiah stood for. Various aspects of the political outlook reflected in Lamentations seem to suit Jeremiah's opponents rather than the prophet himself. For example, it is strongly anti-Babylonian (1:21–22; 3:59–66), and suggests its authors had relied on Egypt for help (4:17), something that Jeremiah consistently opposed (Jeremiah 37:5–10). It is also difficult to imagine Jeremiah referring to Zedekiah as 'the source of our life, the king whom Yahweh had chosen, the one we had trusted to protect us from every invader' (4:20). To the prophet, he had been one of the 'bad figs' (Jeremiah 24:8–10).

Nevertheless, the book certainly stands as a vindication of Jeremiah's message, as it reveals how even those who had been implacably opposed to him were forced to admit their guilt in the face of God's judgment. These five poems probably reflect the ways they did this in Judah itself, in the period immediately following 586 BC, and before the collapse of the Babylonian empire in 539 BC.

again that it was the other way round: this was precisely the kind of worship that had led to the disaster in the first place and doing more of what had caused the problem would never solve anything (Jeremiah 44:23). But who could the people believe? This was a crucial question for the restructuring of Jewish society. Eventually, it was Jeremiah's argument that won the day, for his interpretation of Israel's history was embodied in the stories of the Old Testament itself. The idea that obedience and loyalty to Israel's own God led to success and prosperity is the organizing principle of the books of the deuteronomic history, which almost certainly were issued in a new revised edition in Judah during these years immediately following the Babylonian invasion. In previous times of rapid cultural change, the people had regularly looked to their past to help them redefine the nature of their nation, and that seems to be the context in which the historical narratives of the Hebrew Bible were first compiled. As they began to rebuild their shattered lives at this time, it was only to be expected that they would review the past once more, in an effort to see where they had gone wrong and thereby identify things to be avoided in the future.

By the rivers of Babylon

Far more is known about the life of the exiles who were taken off to Babylon than about those who were left behind in Judah. They seem to have been settled mostly in the border regions between Babylonia and Assyria, perhaps as part of some official policy to reclaim derelict sites that had been devastated during the many wars between these two powers. The names of some of the Jewish settlements certainly seem to imply that: places like Tel Abib ('mound of the flood', Ezekiel 3:15), Tel Harsha and Tel Melah (meaning 'mound of broken pottery' and 'mound of salt' respectively, Ezra 2:59). Unlike the Assyrians, who forced the exiles from Samaria to mingle with other races, the Babylonians generally allowed exiles to maintain their own ethnic identity, and organize their own communal life together. The Judean deportees therefore enjoyed considerable freedom to continue their traditional customs, both social and religious. The fact that Jehoiachin was there no doubt helped to develop this community spirit. He was one of those taken from Jerusalem in the first deportation of 597 BC, but since he was also the last true member of the royal family of David, it was to be expected that the exiles would focus their national allegiance on him. His exact position is not absolutely clear. According to 2 Kings 25:27–30, Nebuchadnezzar's successor, Amel-Marduk, released Jehoiachin from prison and gave him a distinctive position at the Babylonian court. That was in 561 BC, though even before that the Babylonian annals describe Jehoiachin as 'king of Judah'. Perhaps, therefore, his imprisonment was little more than a nominal house arrest. His presence in Babylon was certainly important for the exiles: they counted the years of their exile in relation to him, and his sons and grandsons continued to play an important part in Jewish affairs for a considerable time (1 Chronicles 3:17–24; Ezra 1:8; 2:2; Ezekiel 1:2). But he seems to have been a figurehead rather than a ruler in any sense and the Jewish community itself was organized by groups of elders (Ezekiel 14:1–11; 20:1).

On the whole, life in Babylon was probably quite comfortable – even prosperous – for the exiles from Judah. Jeremiah's advice to some who were clamouring to get back to Judah captures it well: 'Build houses and live in them; plant gardens and eat what they produce. Take wives and have sons and daughters; take wives for your sons, and give your daughters in marriage... seek the welfare of the city where I have sent you into exile, and pray to the Lord on its behalf' (Jeremiah 29:5–7). From a slightly later period than this, we have detailed business records relating to the activities of a Jewish firm run by the Murashu family in Nippur, and the Old Testament itself suggests that within a relatively short space of time many of the exiles had become economically well-off (Ezra 1:6; 2:68–69). They adopted Babylonian language (Aramaic), and were soon giving their children names reflecting Babylonian customs. Yet though they were secure, they were not always happy. No matter how comfortable life in Babylon might be, it was not the same as the homeland they had left behind. The despair and dereliction felt by these people made such an impression on them that, like the story of their slavery in Egypt centuries before, it achieved a permanent place in their national consciousness:

> *By the rivers of Babylon we sat down;*
> *there we wept when we remembered Zion.*
> *On the willows nearby we hung up our harps.*
> *Those who captured us told us to sing;*
> *they told us to entertain them:*
> *'Sing us a song about Zion.'*
> *How can we sing a song to the Lord in a foreign land?*
> *May I never be able to play the harp again*
> *if I forget you, Jerusalem!*
> *May I never be able to sing again if I do not remember you,*
> *if I do not think of you as my greatest joy! (Psalm 137:1–6)*

By the standards of international justice of their day, the Babylonians had been relatively benevolent. But the exiles still hated them, and the same poem which contains such a moving expression of Jewish anguish ends on a note of hatred that is unparalleled anywhere else in the Bible: 'Babylon, you will be destroyed. Happy are those who pay you back for what you have done to us – who take your babies and smash them against a rock' (Psalm 137:8–9). The messages of the prophet Ezekiel paint a similarly bleak picture. He himself was one of the exiles, and he knew that this dreadful experience had sapped all spiritual

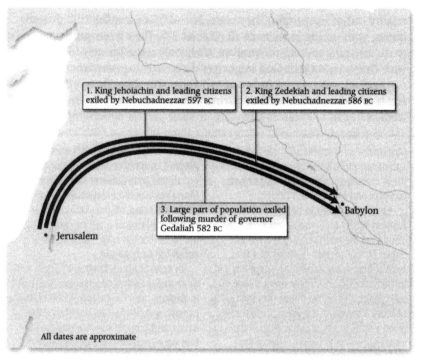

1. King Jehoiachin and leading citizens exiled by Nebuchadnezzar 597 BC

2. King Zedekiah and leading citizens exiled by Nebuchadnezzar 586 BC

3. Large part of population exiled following murder of governor Gedaliah 582 BC

Babylon

Jerusalem

All dates are approximate

The exile from Judah.

Ezekiel

Ezekiel's career was roughly contemporary with that of Jeremiah. Both of them came from priestly families, but Ezekiel was far more conscious of his background, and he maintained a much closer interest in the Jerusalem Temple than Jeremiah ever had. Ezekiel was one of those who were taken to Babylon in the first deportation of 597 BC, and his carefully dated messages were given between 593 and 571 BC.

The book of Ezekiel falls neatly into four sections:
● Messages concerning the people of Jerusalem before the city was destroyed in 586 BC (1:1 – 24:27)
● Oracles against foreign nations (25:1 – 32:32)
● Messages given in Babylon, mostly relating to the return of the exiles to Judah (33:1 – 39:29)
● A priestly blueprint for a future reconstructed Jewish state (40:1 – 48:35)

The book and its message are nothing like as straightforward as this neat literary structure might suggest. Indeed, the book's contents are so diverse that it is not difficult to imagine many different people having been involved in its composition. At one time the prophet is a person who has strange visions of winged animals and of wheels with eyes (Ezekiel 1:4–28), while at another he seems much more like Jeremiah, pronouncing doom on a wicked Jerusalem and laying a new emphasis on a personal relationship between God and the people (15:1–8; 20:1–49). Then there is a prophet whose messages to other nations reflect an extensive grasp of the intricacies of international politics (25:1 – 32:32), and in addition there is a priest who plans with great detail for the operation of a new temple with even stricter ritual than it had before (40:1 – 48:35). Because of this, some scholars have regarded the book as a compilation of the work of several different people. As long ago as the first century AD, the Jewish historian Josephus mentioned 'two books' of Ezekiel

vitality out of his people. They were, he said, like a valley full of dead bones, with no life in them at all (Ezekiel 37). They were quite powerless to do anything to help themselves: their only hope for new life now lay with the prospect that God might yet do something new among them.

Ezekiel was not the only one who saw the situation in these terms. For it is widely believed that during the exile in Babylon, the Jewish leaders began to reassess the state of their people by looking back into

---

Ezekiel *continued*

(*Antiquities of the Jews* 10.5.1). The balance of probability, however, is that all these messages originated with just one complex and multifaceted person.

Ezekiel was called to be a prophet in Babylon in 593 BC. He had a vision of a fiery cloud from the north containing a chariot drawn by four winged creatures of a kind familiar from many Babylonian sculptures and inscriptions (1:4–28). There was a throne on this chariot, and on the throne was the God of Israel, Yahweh. In the vision, Ezekiel was given a scroll to eat, which contained the message he was to deliver: 'cries of grief... and wails and groans' (2:10).

These messages are contained in the first section of the book, and were addressed to the people of Jerusalem in the dark days of the reign of Zedekiah. Ezekiel depicts the moral and spiritual decline of Jerusalem society with such realism that it is hard to believe he was not there, but in Babylon. Indeed, some scholars think Ezekiel must have paid visits to Judah at this time, though it is more likely that he had some kind of psychic experience, the most obvious possibility being a form of astral projection or out-of-body experience. Ezekiel's experiences as a prophet are much closer than those of the other great prophets to the behaviour of those bands of ecstatics who are mentioned in the early period of Israel's history. He obviously had a psychic personality, for after receiving his initial vision, he lay in a trance for a full week (3:15). In view of all this, his extraordinary accuracy in portraying life in Judah could well have been due to such experiences rather than being drawn from actual observations made on the spot. At the

same time, Ezekiel was not an irrational prophet, and his essential message was not significantly different from Jeremiah's: Jerusalem would be destroyed shortly, and its people taken off into exile. He saw no immediate hope of a return, though there are hints that the exile might be limited to about forty years (4:6).

In spite of his declaration of doom and destruction, Ezekiel's message to the exiles in Babylon after the events of 586 BC was a positive one. He had no doubt that the nation had brought ruin on itself, but he was equally convinced that the nation's fate was not in their own hands. It was God's loving actions that had made them a nation in the first place, and it was this same power that would restore them, even giving them the ability to repent and start afresh: 'I will give you a new heart and a new mind. I will take away your stubborn heart of stone and give you an obedient heart. I will put my spirit in you and I will see to it that you follow my laws and keep all the commands I have given you. Then you will live in the land I gave your ancestors. You will be my people, and I will be your God' (36:26–28). God was personally concerned for the people, just like a good shepherd caring for their sheep. No matter how far they might be scattered, God would retrieve them and lead them to new life: 'I will take them out of foreign countries, gather them together, and bring them back to their own land... I myself will be the shepherd of my sheep, and I will find them a place to rest' (34:13, 15).

Two distinctive features of Ezekiel's messages are worth special notice:
● When he looks forward to the restoration of a kingdom of Israel under a

their past. We have already seen how the deuteronomic history emerged in Judah itself at this time, for precisely the same reasons. But the emphasis of that history on a close connection between the people's obedience and the blessing of God could easily lead to the false conclusion that the exiles themselves were responsible for their own destiny. The message of prophets like Amos and Hosea, and even Jeremiah, could be misunderstood to suggest that good behaviour was

prince of the royal family of David, he often describes it in terms that clearly go beyond a literal nationalism. The earlier prophets had often hoped for better things to come, but they generally believed that it was at least theoretically possible that the new and better age would come through a restored monarchy in Jerusalem, and a new king who would actually obey God's will, unlike his predecessors who had found that so difficult. Ezekiel, however, implies that the inauguration of a golden age, when God and the people would live in complete harmony, could not be achieved by any ordinary king. It would have to be the direct work of God acting in person. This kind of thinking led eventually to the development of a new type of Jewish religious literature, the so-called apocalyptic books, and we can see traces of its beginning in passages like Ezekiel 38–39. Here the prophet describes how the enemies of Judah under a mysterious leader called Gog would attack Palestine, only to be annihilated with torrents of fire and brimstone raining down from the sky. After this the exiled Jews would be restored to their own land, and the spirit of God would be poured out on them. The same kind of extravagant language is used when Ezekiel describes a wonderful life-giving stream flowing from the restored Temple in Jerusalem out to the Dead Sea, and changing the Judean desert into a land of great fertility (47:1–12).

● Ezekiel's messages also contain a detailed plan for a renewed Temple in Jerusalem (40:1 – 48:35). Not only does he describe the building itself, but he also lays down the rules that should regulate its worship. Some scholars have seen this as

the symptom of an arid legalism which they believe to have been rampant in the exilic age. The same influences are said to be found in other prophets of the period, and this interest in religious ritual is often contrasted with the convictions of the truly 'great' prophets like Amos and Hosea, who declared that God's will was not fulfilled through cultic practices, but as part of ordinary everyday behaviour. But this sharp differentiation between worship and life misrepresents Ezekiel's message. It owes more to modern Protestantism than anything else, and as a result the significant features of Israel's worship have often been misunderstood. Ezekiel was not emphasizing the performance of religious ritual for its own sake, but he knew that the renewal of the spiritual life of the nation was not something the exiles could accomplish for themselves. Even in the days immediately following the exodus from Egypt, obedience to God's covenant Law had not been easy. Failure and disobedience were an inescapable reality, and it had not been the innate goodness of the tribes that had made them a great nation, but the unchanging presence of God. Right from the start, that presence had been represented by the formal institutions of worship, from the simple tent of worship in the desert to the elaborate Temple in Jerusalem. Far from being an aberration, these things were a permanent symbol of the centralities of Israel's faith, representing not only God's own faithfulness and power, but also the path to forgiveness for those who had lost their way. It was for this reason that the same symbols must be an essential part of the restored community.

Nothing can live in the salt waters of the Dead Sea. But the prophet Ezekiel saw a vision of a new temple in Jerusalem with a river flowing from it towards the Dead Sea. As the water reached the sea, it turned the salt water to fresh, and the sea produced an abundance of life.

a way of blackmailing God into blessing Israel. But at the earliest period of Israel's history, that kind of moral quid pro quo had been only one side of the story. The prophets' demand for obedience to God's Law had itself been based on the unsought goodness of God's love in events like the calling of Abraham and Sarah, or the exodus from Egypt. The prophets had rightly declared that the roots of the nation's religious problems were to be found in the culture of Canaan.

The Pentateuch

It is widely believed that the historical reassessment which took place among the exiles in Babylon had strong connections with the compilation of the first five books of the Hebrew Bible, the Torah or Pentateuch – though if the book of Deuteronomy was indeed originally a preface to the deuteronomic history, it would be more accurate to speak here of a 'Tetrateuch', consisting of Genesis, Exodus, Leviticus and Numbers.

In Jewish thinking, the Pentateuch was always traditionally regarded as the work of Moses, though no one today would argue for that. At least five reasons can be given for believing that the writing of these books was a much more complex process that took place over many centuries.

Anachronisms

Deuteronomy 34 tells the story of Moses' death, which at least makes it unlikely that he wrote this section, though Philo (*On the Life of Moses* II.291) and Josephus (*Antiquities of the Jews* 5.8.48) both claimed that he did. More significantly, however, a number of other incidental features of some of the stories in these books reflect the perspective of a later age. For instance, Genesis 36:31–39 lists the kings of Edom who ruled 'Before there were any kings in Israel'. Or again, a couple of incidents in Abraham's life are said to have taken place when 'the Canaanites were still living in the land' (Genesis 12:6; 13:7). In another place, part of the land of Canaan itself is given the name 'Philistia', though it was never called that until after the arrival of the Philistines (Genesis 21:34; Exodus 13:17).

Duplicate stories

The same story has sometimes been recorded in two different versions. For example, Beersheba is given its name twice (Genesis 21:31; 26:33), as is Bethel – once when Jacob was running away to Haran (Genesis 28:19), and again when he was coming back (Genesis 35:15). Similarly, in the story of the covenant-making at Mount Sinai, Moses is said to have gone up the mountain three times, though there is no mention of him ever coming down (Exodus 24:9–18).

Inconsistencies

For example, in the story of creation, Genesis 1:26–31 suggests that people were created after all the animals, whereas in Genesis 2:7–20 a person is created first, and the animals are later created to be companions for the human. Or in the story of the great flood, the number of animals to be saved in the ark is either one pair of each species (Genesis 6:19–20), or seven pairs (Genesis 7:2). Joseph appears to have been taken off to Egypt by both Ishmaelites (Genesis 37:25) and Midianites (Genesis 37:28) – and, in the same story, was it Reuben (Genesis 37:22) or Judah (Genesis 37:26) who was the good brother who tried to rescue him?

Legal differences

The laws set out in Deuteronomy are sometimes different from laws about the same things contained in other books of the Pentateuch. For example, in Exodus 20:24 sacrifices can be offered to God 'In every place that I set aside for you to worship me'; but in Deuteronomy 12:14, 'you must offer them only in the one place that

But as the stories of an even earlier period were revisited, it became apparent that the time before that had hardly been perfect. Perhaps, then, there was a lesson here for the exiles as they struggled to come to terms with their national disaster.

Inspired by such thoughts, it seems likely that religious leaders in Babylon set out at this time to write a history of the very earliest experiences of their nation, beginning from creation itself. They did

---

Yahweh will choose in the territory of one of your tribes'. Exodus 28:1 suggests that only Aaron's family had the necessary priestly qualifications to offer sacrifices, while Deuteronomy 18:6–7 allows any Levite to do so. The actual methods to be adopted also vary: in Exodus 12:8–9 the Passover lamb must be roasted, while in Deuteronomy 16:7 it is to be boiled.

God's name

According to Exodus 6:2–3, Moses was the first person to know God's personal name 'Yahweh', though Genesis 4:26 states that from the very earliest times people had used this name in their worship. Alongside this, there are many other passages which call God by the name 'El' or 'Elohim', and it has been proposed that these different names indicate different ideas about God's character: in the stories that use the name Yahweh, God can be represented almost as a kind of superhuman person who speaks and meets with people in everyday circumstances, while in those where the name Elohim predominates, God appears more remotely through intermediaries such as dreams or messengers.

These five features are not all that important when considered separately, but taken together they have generally been regarded as a conclusive demonstration that the Pentateuch was certainly not the product of just one author, whether that might have been Moses or indeed anyone else. According to the most widely accepted view, the Pentateuch in its final edited form was compiled from four separate documentary sources,

conventionally labelled J, E, D and P: J being the source using the name Yahweh, E using the name Elohim, D being Deuteronomy and P a priestly source, dealing mainly with religious matters connected with worship, sacrifice and so on. This theory was put forward in its classical form by the nineteenth-century German scholars, K.H. Graf and J. Wellhausen, and for that reason is often referred to as the Graf–Wellhausen theory. Wellhausen also believed that these source documents represented an evolutionary development from primitive to more sophisticated views and therefore could be used as a way of understanding the whole course of Israel's national history, beginning with J (950–850 BC), which was followed in turn by E (850–750 BC), D (621 BC) and P (c. 450 BC).

In the early decades of the twentieth century, scholars set out with great enthusiasm to 'recover' and 'reconstruct' these four apparently lost documents. They concluded that J had originated among the southern tribes in the time of Solomon, and E among the northern tribes in the time of Elijah, and the two had been joined together sometime after the fall of Samaria in 722 BC. D was generally identified with the law book recovered in the time of Josiah, though possibly of a northern origin. It was certainly quite a different kind of 'source' from the others, for whereas J and E could apparently be traced more or less extensively throughout the Pentateuch, D appeared to be restricted to just the book of Deuteronomy. Finally, P was regarded as an exclusively priestly collection, containing mainly the details of organized cultic ritual, and anything

not compile this narrative from nothing, any more than the deutero-nomic historians did with theirs. On the contrary, they had at their disposal the full riches of their nation's heritage, going back over many centuries. As they retold these familiar stories, they could see that the problem of human disobedience was nothing new, but was actually an intrinsic part of human life itself. Yet, in spite of that, God's living presence had been with their people. From the very

---

The Pentateuch
continued

connected with it – though also including certain other materials of a narrative type. This understanding of the matter prevailed in one form or another for most of the twentieth century. There were always those who pointed out the limitations of this or that detail in Wellhausen's analysis, but scholars who rejected it entirely were isolated individuals, usually regarded as eccentrics. The situation today, however, is quite different, and probably no significant scholar would now accept the theory as Wellhausen proposed it. It is still worth understanding, though, as his presentation of these hypothetical sources has provided the frame of reference within which other approaches have been explored. It will only be a matter of time before his theory is formally declared to be finished, but in the meantime scholars are generally preferring to explore other methods of understanding these pivotal books within the Hebrew Bible. There are a number of reasons for such a radical rejection of what at one time would have been regarded as the unassailable conclusion of scientific scholarship:

● Wellhausen's view was firmly based on a particular philosophical understanding of history and its development. Along with other thinkers of his day, he believed that human society had gradually evolved from primitive beginnings to the sophisticated thinking of his own time. Wellhausen therefore took it for granted that Israel's religious experience must have started off as a simple nature worship (animism), which later evolved into the high moral standards of the Old Testament prophets, based on belief in only one universal God (monotheism), having passed through the

intermediary stage of henotheism (commitment to only one God, though in a context of belief in the existence of many). This evolutionary theory has since been totally discredited, and it is arguable that the literary analysis which Wellhausen built upon it has, therefore, been left with no credible ideological foundation.

● Since Wellhausen's day, knowledge of life in the ancient world in general, and of Canaan and Israel in particular, has changed almost beyond recognition. Wellhausen and his contemporaries were writing before the development of the techniques of systematic archaeology. It was not difficult for them to look at the Old Testament as a kind of theological source book, rather than as a body of literature to be understood with reference to the social circumstances within which it was compiled. Viewed in this way, it seemed plausible to think that Israel's religion could have evolved from a primitive animism to an elevated monotheism in the course of just a few hundred years. But the more that becomes known about the world in which Israel became a nation, the more implausible it is to imagine that Israel's faith should be thought of in these terms. According to Wellhausen's theory, for example, almost all the details of Israel's ritual worship were the invention of the P writer, late in the period of Babylonian exile. But the discoveries at the site of ancient Ugarit, for example, have shown that even quite technical terms used in the Hebrew Bible were in common use in Canaan long before Israel became a nation, let alone the time of the exile. Far from reflecting later stages in the development of religious thought, much of

earliest days in the desert, God had been there, even at times of disobedience. The thing that brought the tribes from Egypt to their own land was not their own goodness, but the love of God. So a new hope and concern began to emerge from the lessons of history. As they looked at their own meagre resources, they could see no hope, but when they reminded themselves of God's resources, anything seemed possible.

---

the Pentateuchal material reflects precisely the circumstances of the period of which it purports to tell. Of course, this does not prove that it was all written down at an earlier period, but it certainly demonstrates that the assumptions on which Wellhausen based his argument were simply mistaken.

● Criticisms of this sort have not prevented Old Testament scholars continuing to refine and articulate more fully the theory that Wellhausen put forward. Even today some are still arguing about the dates of the various so-called source documents. But their conclusions vary widely, with even the J source being dated in periods as far apart as the ninth century and the post-exilic age. Others have suggested there was no such thing as an E source, while yet others argue that the four-source theory is inadequate, and the Pentateuch in fact contains many more sources than that. Some have further claimed to be able to trace J, E and P not only in the Pentateuch, but also in Joshua, Judges, Samuel, and even Kings. Much of this debate has been engendered by the surprising fact that the so-called sources are not actually consistent in their use of the different names for God, even though this was supposed to be one of their most characteristic features. Considering that scholars have been trying to define the nature and contents of these source documents for more than a century now, it is not unreasonable to expect them to have come to some sort of conclusion on the matter. The fact that they have so strikingly failed to do so raises serious questions about their very existence.

A number of scholars have noted the strength of this particular criticism, and have accordingly directed their energies elsewhere. Gerhard von Rad, for instance, argued that this section of the Old Testament (which for him extended into Joshua/Judges – what he called the 'Hexateuch') was centred around two major themes. One was the exodus/entry into the land; the other was the covenant ceremony at Mount Sinai. Both of these were originally related to religious celebrations in the life of early Israel, and he suggested that the continuous narrative we now have grew out of the confessions and creeds that were so often repeated in worship. This process took place, he argued, in the time of Solomon. Martin Noth also proposed his own rather different thematic origin for the same materials. But all such attempts have still been firmly based on a Wellhausen-type source analysis, and they have not successfully avoided the general criticisms noted above.

● Recent discussion of this issue has emphasized the importance of treating the Pentateuch as real literature. Wellhausen and his followers worked with a very restricted view of how ancient literature was actually written. Their understanding has often been colourfully described as a 'scissors and paste' approach, which tended to assume that the final editors of the books sat down with four documents in front of them, and chopped bits and pieces from here and there, which were then glued together to make a 'new' book. Moreover, they were not joined seamlessly, but in such an incoherent fashion that we can still unpick them and identify the original source documents. That sort of idea could appear to make sense to the

A new beginning

The stories of Israel's past reminded the exiles of what God had done for their nation. Even at times of great despair, Yahweh's love had never failed them, and they could be sure that God would not abandon them now. It was not long before things began to stir in Babylonian politics that were regarded as the personal actions of God.

The Pentateuch *continued*

scholars of a previous generation, but more sophisticated understanding of how literature comes into existence – especially a national archive like the Hebrew Bible – shows that it is quite inadequate. Traditional ways of handing on ancient stories, frequently by word of mouth, simply do not operate like this. In addition, if these books are the inspirational masterpieces that most scholars believe them to be, then it is unlikely that editors capable of producing such works would not themselves have noticed the apparent discontinuities in their narratives. Could it therefore be that the features once presumed to betray the presence of ill-fitting source materials were from the very start consciously intended to perform some kind of literary or stylistic function in the presentation of the story? For instance, some believe that the use of different names for God can be explained in this way, by supposing that the term Yahweh was used when the writer was talking of Israel's own national God, with the term Elohim being reserved for contexts in which a more abstract, cosmic picture of God was in view. Even the existence of duplicate stories is not necessarily an indication of badly assimilated source materials, for the texts from Ugarit display a very similar phenomenon, and in that case the frequent repetition of the same material has been indispensable to scholars trying to guess what might have been originally there in texts that are now broken.

The obsession with uncovering hidden sources behind biblical documents dominated scholarship for many generations, not only in relation to the Pentateuch, but also other parts of the Hebrew Bible. The outcome of all this can be clearly seen in any of the traditional books of introduction to both Old and New Testaments, which tend to be preoccupied with questions of origin, date and authorship, often to the exclusion of anything else. But this way of looking at things was a product of the time of the European Enlightenment, when 'scientific' method was applied to everything in the mistaken belief that science was somehow neutral and objective, and therefore gave greater access to the truth than other forms of investigation. The science of the day was dominated by the theories of people like René Descartes (1596–1650) and Francis Bacon (1561–1626), and the starting point was generally based on the assumption that to understand anything it had to be dismantled, and split into its component parts which could then be studied in isolation under the microscope. That approach has long since been discredited in scientific enquiry, for it is now recognized that the sum of the parts is often more than that of the individual elements, and true understanding needs to begin by investigating things within the holistic context from which they gain their meaning, and to which they in turn contribute. The same thing is true of literature. The meaning of a book must begin with the text as it stands, because no matter how much a work of literature may have been edited or rewritten, its ultimate meaning is to be found in the form it now has. The search for possible sources may help to illustrate the perspectives of different editors who have worked on it, but the Pentateuch is a

When Nebuchadnezzar died in 562 BC he was succeeded by a number of very weak and inept rulers. Only Nabonidus had a reign of any length (556–539 BC), but he made himself very unpopular by neglecting the worship of Marduk, the traditional god of Babylon, and choosing to live in a self-imposed exile at Teima in the Arabian desert, leaving his son Bel-shar-usur (the Belshazzar of the book of Daniel) to look after things in the capital. This was a very unsettled period in

connected story with its own message, and the real significance of that message is going to be found not by taking it to pieces, but by careful study of its nuances and themes as they have been presented to the reader by those who compiled it in its final form.

The outcome of all this is that in the final decades of the twentieth century there was a comprehensive re-examination of almost all the basic issues in Pentateuchal scholarship. This was motivated partly by dissatisfaction with the traditional Graf–Wellhausen theory, but more especially by the realization that in the literary world at large there are other, more promising methods of analysis than source criticism. Some would like to think that the collapse of what was once the scholarly orthodoxy justifies a return to belief in a Mosaic authorship for the Pentateuch. But that would be going well beyond the evidence now available. The narrative itself gives no reason at all to link his name with all these books, and such scattered references as do connect Moses with them all relate to clearly defined parts of the narrative, rather than to the Pentateuch as a whole (Exodus 24:4–8; Numbers 33:2; Deuteronomy 31:19–29). Writing was widely used in the ancient world long before the emergence of Israel as a nation, so there is no intrinsic reason why some elements now incorporated in the Pentateuch should not have been written down in the earliest period. Indeed, some scholars confidently trace features such as the ten commandments back to the age of Moses. But later, even those things connected with Moses himself needed to be reinterpreted and applied to new situations. In addition, as new elements joined the population of Israel, their own stories handed on over many centuries would also be incorporated into what became Israel's national heritage. The inauguration of the monarchy and the transformation of the tribal confederation into a state must also have necessitated a considerable reinterpretation of Israel's traditional values and ideals, in order to suit the new circumstances.

It now seems quite likely that, instead of passing through several written stages, all this took place in a more or less haphazard fashion until the Pentateuch itself was written in its present form. It certainly makes good sense to think that this epic story of Israel's earliest days was reissued during the period of the early exile, as a means of explaining the failures of the past and to help chart a new course for the future. But the stories and laws were not freshly created at that time. The new element was the perspective that the experience of the exile had given, and with that hindsight the story of God and the people of Israel could become a source of renewal for the nation's life and an inspiration for the rediscovery of that ancient faith whose origins could be traced back to the covenant at Mount Sinai.

During the exile, the Babylonian empire went through a period of decline. Emperor Nabonidus, seen in this relief worshipping the sun-god, rejected the national religion and spent much of his time in retreat in the desert.

The Cyrus
Cylinder gives
details of the
reforms this
Persian ruler
undertook in
Babylon after he
had overthrown
the Babylonians
in a bloodless
take-over. In
Isaiah's prophecy,
Cyrus is seen as
the unwitting
agent of Yahweh
in establishing
the conditions for
the exiles' return
to Jerusalem.

Babylonian history, and life for the exiles may well have become more difficult. There is a strong tradition in Jewish literature of how the exiles were subjected to harsh treatment, almost amounting to official persecution. In the Hebrew Bible, the stories contained in Daniel 1–6 tell how Daniel and his friends were subjected to the most harrowing treatment during this time, and a similar picture is painted in various additions to the books of Esther and Daniel which were contained in the Greek Old Testament, as well as in books like Judith and Tobit. If this was a time of discomfort for the Jews in Babylon, it was short-lived. For by now, the power of the Babylonian empire was spent, and when a little-known king from southern Persia emerged as a new leader, it was only a matter of time before he was able to take over the whole of the country. His name was Cyrus, and in 539 BC the people of Babylon actually welcomed him as their king, and he took control of the city without the use of force.

Cyrus set about the restoration of Babylonian society. The temples which Nabonidus had neglected were restored to their former glory, and Cyrus himself shared publicly in the worship of the god Marduk. But he had a different outlook from his predecessors, and of all the ancient rulers with whom the Jews had to deal, Cyrus was the most liberal and humane. He did not see politics in terms of armed conflict between various national religions, but instead recognized the right of all nations to worship whatever deities they wished. Not only that, but he also gave his citizens the right to live wherever they chose. This was a massive reversal of the policies that had dominated Mesopotamian society for many centuries, but he was determined to make it work. He inherited a population with many ethnic groups who had been uprooted from their own lands and settled in Babylon against their will, and not only did he encourage these displaced people to go back home, but he also made available financial resources to enable them to do so. The Cyrus Cylinder contains details of all this, while the book of Ezra preserves the text of an official document issued by Cyrus that dealt specifically with the plight of the Jewish exiles.

Back to Jerusalem

Though Cyrus had issued an edict allowing the Temple in Jerusalem to be rebuilt at the beginning of his reign, there was no great rush by the exiles in Babylon to return to Judah. Indeed, Josephus (who, of course, was writing centuries later) reports that when they were given the

---

Isaiah of Babylon

The advance of Cyrus was seen by a Jewish prophet in Babylon, whose inspirational messages are to be found in Isaiah 40–55. As they stand, of course, these messages are part of the book which reports the life and teaching of another prophet named Isaiah, who lived in Jerusalem some 150 years earlier during the days of Ahaz and Hezekiah. But there are some compelling reasons for regarding these later sections of the book as coming from this later period:

● Isaiah 40–55 contains no mention at all of any personal details about the prophet Isaiah. This is in strong contrast to Isaiah 1–39 which relates a number of stories about the prophet himself, especially his dealings with king and people in Jerusalem.

● The style and language of Isaiah 40–55 is also quite different. These chapters use what is possibly the most sophisticated Hebrew in the entire Old Testament. In addition, these messages do not have the form of the short, pointed sayings that were typical of most of the prophets, but consist instead of sustained lyrical passages, celebrating God's sovereignty in creation and history. Because of their distinctive poetic structure, it has been thought that these messages may have originated in the context of worship. Perhaps they reflect the way that God's kingship was celebrated in the Temple at Jerusalem during the heyday of the kingdom of Judah. But they are not just hymns, for they also contain many specific historical references, directly related to the message of the prophet himself.

● The fact that these specific references are based on the experiences of the exiles in Babylon is one of the strongest reasons for assuming they are the work of a prophet who lived at this time. The fall of Jerusalem is clearly stated to be a past event (51:17–23) and the fall of Babylon is imminent (43:14–15; 47:1–15). The people are encouraged to think they will soon be set free (48:20), and Cyrus himself is mentioned by name as the person who would bring this about (44:28 – 45:4). Other passages clearly envisage Cyrus's triumph, without actually naming him (41:2–4; 48:1–16).

It seems likely, therefore, that the messages of Isaiah 40–55 were given to the exiles in Babylon just before 539 BC, when Cyrus's triumph was assured and it looked as if his policies were about to provide new opportunities for the renewal of the old state of Judah.

For the sake of convenience, the prophet who delivered these messages is generally referred to as Isaiah of Babylon, Second or Deutero-Isaiah. Of course, his personal name would not necessarily have been Isaiah, though there is a continuity between these messages and those of his illustrious predecessor. Indeed, Isaiah himself had gathered a group of disciples around him, so that the messages he gave could be

chance to go back home, they did not want to leave the comfortable life they had established in exile (*Antiquities of the Jews* 11.1.3). But it was important to the Persians that their repatriation policy should be set in motion. While they undoubtedly had humanitarian reasons for introducing it, the benefits of having loyal and grateful subjects at strategic parts of their empire can hardly have escaped their notice, and since Palestine was near to the border with Egypt it was important for them to re-establish a friendly state there.

Sheshbazzar was appointed governor of Judah. His name was thoroughly Babylonian, though that does not mean he was not a Jew. Apart from the fact that he made a start on rebuilding the foundations of the Temple, nothing is known of him (Ezra 5:16). We are better

---

Isaiah of Babylon
continued

safeguarded for later generations (Isaiah 8:16), and it is quite possible that these later messages could have come from the same circle of disciples. What they were saying was a fresh application of old truths to new circumstances, which would be why they had no hesitation in including them all in the same book as the messages delivered previously by Isaiah in Jerusalem. If this individual was indeed one of the great prophetic figures of the Old Testament story, it has often been thought strange that we evidently possess no explicit information about him (though, in the context of the day, we can at least be sure that it would almost certainly have been a male). But in reality we know almost nothing about most of the prophets, apart from the messages that are recorded in their books. In any case, the relative anonymity of this prophet in Babylon is consistent with the whole outlook of these messages, for he was concerned first and foremost with the might and power of God, rather than with himself. The change that he believed was about to take place would not be initiated by exiles: it could only be the work of God, a 'new exodus' to be compared with that under Moses, in which the escaping slaves (like the exiles) had been powerless, but were miraculously delivered by their all-powerful God (Isaiah 43:14–21).

A powerful God
Cyrus is seen as the instrument of this deliverance that was to come, but the people are warned against placing their trust in him. The real power that would restore the Jewish people could only come from God. The glorious return to their homeland was envisaged as a worldwide movement, to include also those who had fled to Egypt (49:12). God's power would not be restricted by geography or national boundaries, as had sometimes been thought by Israel in the past. This prophet was convinced that his God was not one among many, but the only true God: 'Yahweh is the everlasting God who created all the world, and never grows tired or weary' (40:28). It was important for him to emphasize this, for some of the exiles had come to regard their plight as a direct result of the weakness of Israel's God when faced with the apparent 'power' of the gods of Babylon. Those who clung to the old covenant faith may even have been in the minority (Ezekiel 20:3; Daniel 1–6), but Isaiah of Babylon knew they were right.

His contempt for the gods of Babylon was unbounded. In satirical vein, he points out how their own worshippers actually made them from the very same wood as they used to burn on the fire. To him, such an attitude was just blind ignorance: 'Such people are too stupid to know what they are doing. They close their eyes and their minds to the truth. The maker of idols hasn't the wit or the sense to say, "Some of the wood I burnt up. I baked some bread on the embers and I roasted meat and ate

informed about a further group of exiles who returned a little later under the leadership of Zerubbabel (another Babylonian name, this time certainly a Jew) and Joshua. Joshua was a priest, but Zerubbabel was the grandson of Jehoiachin, the last truly legitimate king of the royal family of David. He also held an official Persian appointment, and he could have been Sheshbazzar's successor as governor. The appointment of a member of the old Judahite royal family may have been a conscious effort by the Persians to persuade more Jews to return. Zerubbabel certainly appreciated that, with Persian help, a new Jewish state could emerge from the ashes of the past. With the disappearance of most of the familiar features of the earlier kingdom, however, there was just one thing that united the new settlers with

it. And the rest of the wood I made into an idol. Here I am bowing down to a block of wood!"' (44:18–19). That is not the kind of God who had been revealed in the formative events of Israel's history. Their God had been, and still was, a God of real power, the God of all creation: 'I am... the Creator of all things. I alone stretched out the heavens; when I made the earth, no one helped me' (44:24).

God's people and their land

With this emphasis on God's universal sovereignty, we might have expected God's special relationship with Israel to have been forgotten, or at least pushed into the background. But it was not. The fact that God's power extended over the whole world meant that the exiles could go back to their homeland without worrying whether God would have the power to take care of them. Many of them probably needed this kind of encouragement, for even after Cyrus gave them permission to return there was a natural temptation to prefer the safety and security of the life they knew over the hazards and unknown perils of a long journey and a strange land. But to those who would trust God, it was all a great spiritual adventure: 'From the distant east and the farthest west, I will bring your people home. I will tell the north to let them go and the south not to hold them back. Let my people return from distant lands, from every part of the world' (43:5–6). God had done it long centuries

before in the exodus from Egypt, and would do it again for no other reason than a continuing and great love for these people: 'Watch for the new thing I am going to do. It is happening already – you can see it now! I will make a road through the wilderness and give you streams of water there' (43:19). Jerusalem may be a ruined wasteland, but it would soon be restored to its former glory: 'I will show compassion to Jerusalem, to all who live in her ruins. Though her land is a desert, I will make it a garden, like the garden I planted in Eden. Joy and gladness will be there, and songs of praise and thanks to me' (51:3).

God's servant and God's world

Despite this renewed emphasis on God's concern for the people, this Babylonian prophet was convinced that God's love was not restricted to Israel alone. Just as the whole world was the arena of God's activity, so all the people of the world would now be the object of God's love. This is the message of one of those passages that have been called 'the servant songs': 'Yahweh said to me, "I have a greater task for you, my servant. Not only will you restore to greatness the people of Israel who have survived, but I will also make you a light to the nations – so that all the world may be saved"' (49:6).

There are four of these servant songs, and they seem to be separate and self-

their forebears, and that was their faith in God. In exile, that faith had been centred on customs like circumcision, and keeping the sabbath day, as well as prayer and the reading of the Torah. But now the Temple could be rebuilt, and its repair and renovation were to be Zerubbabel's main tasks.

The Temple ruins had probably continued to be a place of worship throughout the period since Nebuchadnezzar's destruction. Even in the aftermath of the invasion, Jeremiah 41:4–5 mentions worshippers who had come from the territory of the former northern kingdom of Israel on pilgrimage to the site. No doubt people from that quarter, as well as the Jewish population left behind in Judah itself, had continued to worship there all along. There is some evidence to suggest that the Babylonians

---

Isaiah of Babylon
continued

contained poems, though no doubt still the work of the prophet himself, and certainly an integral part of his message (42:1–4; 49:1–6; 50:4–11; 52:13 – 53:12). In these songs, the prophet talks of a specific individual, 'the servant', through whom God's plans for a great and glorious future will come to fruition. But who was this servant? Elsewhere the prophet talks of the nation of Israel as the servant of God, and the person mentioned in the servant songs is often described in the same language as is used of Israel. Israel is 'my servant... the people that I have chosen' (41:8), and so is the servant of the songs (42:1). Both of them were specifically created by God's personal action (Israel, 43:1, 7, 15, 21; 44:2, 21, 24; the servant, 49:5), and were endowed with God's own spirit (Israel, 44:3; the servant, 42:1). This has led many scholars to conclude that when Isaiah talks of the suffering servant it is simply another way of referring to God's people, Israel. But, at the same time, things are said about the servant which are explicitly denied about Israel. The servant 'will not lose hope or courage' (42:4), nor has he 'rebelled or turned away' from God (50:5), as the nation so often did. In addition, he suffers patiently – not for his own wrongdoing like the nation, but for the wrongs of others (53:3–5). Most significant of all is the fact that, while the nation needed restoration, the servant is sent to restore and renew Israel (49:5–6; 53:4–6). It is therefore difficult to see how

the prophet could have identified this servant of God with the nation itself.

Who then was this enigmatic servant? Some people think the prophet had a particular living individual in mind, possibly Jehoiachin or someone like Jeremiah, or conceivably even himself. But it is more likely that he was thinking of some future person in whose life the ideals of Israel's ancient faith would become a reality, and through whom God's intentions for the people of Israel and the wider world could be brought to pass. He is never actually called the Messiah in the Old Testament, nor did the Jewish people ever think to equate the two. But these passages exerted a powerful influence on the Christian understanding of Jesus as the Messiah of Old Testament expectation. In particular, the account of the servant's suffering in the last song (52:13 – 53:12) has some extraordinary correspondences with the death of Jesus himself. In theological terms, the understanding that salvation can be found through suffering, service, weakness and vulnerability is undoubtedly the most profound legacy from this prophet in Babylon.

had actually given some formal control over the territory of Judah to people from what had formerly been the northern kingdom of Israel. For whatever reason, these people naturally offered their assistance to Zerubbabel. But he would have none of it, for to him these people were not real Jews. They may have thought they were worshipping the covenant God of Israel, but they had not shared in the experience of the exiles in Babylon, and therefore were not regarded as true descendants of the ancient tribes. These other people were of uncertain (and partly non-Jewish) racial origins, and their worship of Yahweh was therefore suspect.

The people of Samaria and their friends in Judah realized that the newcomers from Babylon were bent on forming their own Jewish state, in which the people who already lived in the land would have no place. So, having had their offer of cooperation turned down, these people felt they had no option but to oppose the plans of the returned exiles. They succeeded in delaying work on the Temple for something like ten years or more, by persuading the Persian officials responsible for the western empire that something illegal was afoot. By this time, Darius I was the emperor, but Cyrus's original permission still stood, and the work was allowed to proceed (Ezra 5). The new Temple was much poorer than Solomon's had been, but its completion was a milestone in the life of this beleaguered community (Ezra 3:12).

The return of the exiles.

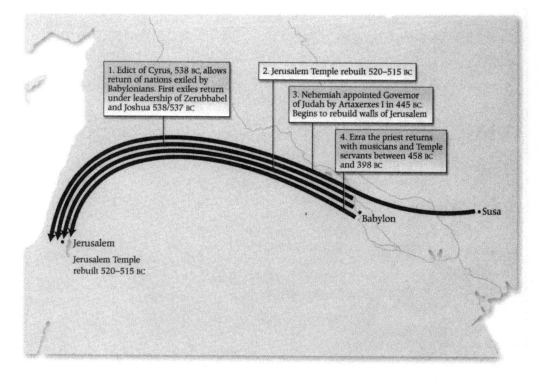

1. Edict of Cyrus, 538 BC, allows return of nations exiled by Babylonians. First exiles return under leadership of Zerubbabel and Joshua 538/537 BC

2. Jerusalem Temple rebuilt 520–515 BC

3. Nehemiah appointed Governor of Judah by Artaxerxes I in 445 BC. Begins to rebuild walls of Jerusalem

4. Ezra the priest returns with musicians and Temple servants between 458 BC and 398 BC

Susa

Babylon

Jerusalem
Jerusalem Temple
rebuilt 520–515 BC

Confusion and despair

The new Temple was completed in about 515 BC. Now at last the people had a new hope, and no doubt they went about their worship with joy and expectation, believing that the new age which they had been promised must surely be at hand. In the event, however, the reality was to be quite different. We have no absolutely certain knowledge of life in Judah from 515 BC until 444 BC, though there is no reason to suppose that conditions improved, either religiously or economically. A number of prophetic messages reflect life at this time. The book of Obadiah is a short poem deploring the advantage that the Edomites had gained out of Judah's national disaster – and also assuring the Jewish people that better times were on the way. The book of Joel also probably relates to this period. Its immediate occasion is a plague of locusts, which led to a great famine – something which Joel assured his hearers would be just a temporary setback, and they could soon look forward to the

---

Haggai and Zechariah

Zerubbabel and Joshua were encouraged in their work by the prophets Haggai and Zechariah, and their messages provide a vivid insight into the mood of despair and apathy that prevailed among the people at this time. The wave of euphoria that accompanied Cyrus's rise to power subsided soon after his death, for his son Cambyses (530–522 BC) did not share his father's ideals. He was more interested in military conquest, and during his campaign against Egypt in 525 BC it is likely that he plundered Judah for food supplies. This would have been bad enough in good

The Persian empire.

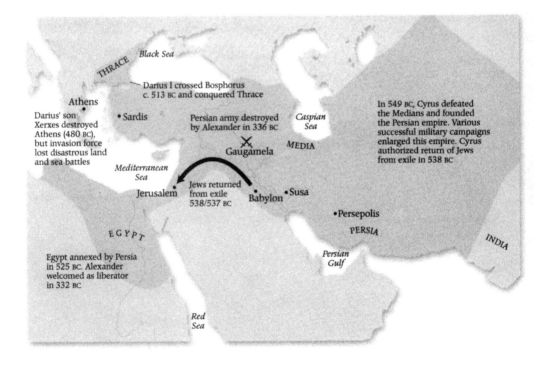

inauguration of the new age for which they were all longing. The same picture of despondency seems to be reflected in the final section of the book of Isaiah (Isaiah 56–66), which some therefore see as the work of yet another prophet (Third or Trito-Isaiah). These messages may well have been the work of followers of Isaiah of Babylon, for their general outlook is similar to his idealism, yet they seem to reflect the despair of this later age.

The only certain source of information from this period is the book of Malachi, and this shows that, though the Temple was standing again, the spiritual realities that it was supposed to represent were still not being taken seriously. The priests themselves were neglecting their proper duties, and the true covenant religion of Yahweh had become mixed up with magical practices (Malachi 3:5). The prophet regarded popular religion as little more than a form of practical atheism: "'You have said terrible things about me," says Yahweh... "You have said, 'It's

Emperor Darius I, from Media, continued Cyrus's policy of supporting the exiles' return. In his time the Temple was rebuilt at Jerusalem.

times, but Haggai's messages show that the returned exiles were living at poverty level, and their crops were blighted by drought and disease. This in itself made it hard to establish a stable society, but in addition, there was a military coup back in Persia while Cambyses was on his way home from Egypt. He committed suicide and Darius, one of his generals, seized control of the army. He returned to Persia and in due course emerged as one of the most powerful Persian emperors of all time. But while all this was happening, the whole situation must have seemed very confused and uncertain to the Jewish community in and around Jerusalem. Were these upheavals signs of the beginning of the new age that they had spoken of back in Babylon? Or was it an indication of worse yet to come?

Haggai began speaking to the people in 520 BC, early in the reign of Darius. He urged them to make the rebuilding of the Temple a real priority. They had built houses for themselves, so why should they neglect God? If God was not worshipped adequately, they could hardly expect prosperity. But if they were prepared to put God first, then literally anything could happen. Zerubbabel was already there as God's chosen representative, and the symbol of God's own presence – the

useless to serve God. What's the use of doing what God says or of trying to show the Lord Almighty that we are sorry for what we have done?''' (Malachi 3:13—14). As in the past, this neglect of Israel's covenant faith was leading to great social evils, and Malachi declared that God would step in to judge this rotten community, especially 'those who give false testimony, those who cheat employees out of their wages, and those who take advantage of widows, orphans, and foreigners' (Malachi 3:5). In addition to all that, the community of returned exiles was losing its true identity as some of the men were leaving their Jewish wives for more attractive younger women who belonged to the racially mixed population that had tried to stop the rebuilding of the Temple. This was regarded as a very serious matter, for it threatened the very existence of the fragile Jewish settlement as a distinctive ethnic entity, and for that reason Malachi was convinced that it would only be a matter of time before God would have to deal with these evils (Malachi 4).

Haggai and Zechariah
continued

Temple — should also be reinstated as the centre of national life. When that happened, the scene would be set for the new age that the exiles had hoped for: 'On that day I will take you, Zerubbabel my servant, and I will appoint you to rule in my name. You are the one I have chosen' (Haggai 2:23).

Zechariah was a contemporary of Haggai, and his messages are essentially similar in tone and content. He encouraged the completion of the rebuilt Temple, and in a series of visions he depicted the new age that God would soon bring about. He too saw a special place for Zerubbabel in all this (4:6—10; 6:9—15), but he also emphasized that Zerubbabel's success depended not so much on the fact that he was descended from King David, but on the fact that God was with him in a special way: 'You will succeed, not by military might or by your own strength, but by my spirit. Obstacles as great as mountains will disappear before you. You will rebuild the Temple, and as you put the last stone in place, the people will shout, "Beautiful, beautiful!"' (4:6—7).

The precise meaning of these statements made about Zerubbabel is unclear. The language used is undoubtedly similar to what would later be called 'messianic', though at the same time it can hardly have

been understood in that way for Zerubbabel seems to have retained the confidence of the Persians. There are also hints that the high priest Joshua came to occupy an even more important place than Zerubbabel in the new community. In the days of the old kingdom of Judah, the Temple in Jerusalem had been under the personal direction of the king, but with the disappearance of the kingly office, functions previously associated with the kings were now carried out by the priests. Indeed, in preparation for his new responsibilities, Joshua was actually crowned in what looks like a coronation ceremony (Zechariah 6:9—15). This was probably a significant development in Jewish thinking, for some 400 years later the Dead Sea Scrolls anticipated the coming of a priest who would be the Messiah, and who was at least as important as the 'secular' Messiah who would be descended from David. The same idea is also found in the letter to the Hebrews in the New Testament. Unfortunately, we have so little definite knowledge of the time of Haggai and Zechariah that it is no longer possible to trace the possible connections of this idea in any greater detail.

Renewing the covenant

It was not too long before moves were afoot to reform and re-establish the life of the Jewish community in Jerusalem. This took place through the work of Nehemiah and Ezra. There is some debate as to which of these two came first, and for the sake of clarity the arguments about that are dealt with separately below. One thing there is no doubt about is that Nehemiah was responsible for political reorganization, while Ezra's concern was more directly related to matters of religious practice.

Building the walls

Though he had risen to a position of some eminence in the Persian royal court, Nehemiah was himself a Jew, and when he learned about the deprivation of his people in Judah and Jerusalem, he asked the Persian king, by now Artaxerxes I, to let him go there and help to rebuild the community. So he was appointed governor of Judah in 445 BC (Nehemiah 1–2). There had probably been a succession of such governors ever since the days of Sheshbazzar about 100 years before, and though we know nothing of them or their work, the brief report of their activities included in the book of Nehemiah suggests they had been more concerned with their own comfort than with the well-being of their people (Nehemiah 5:15). The reaction of both upper-class Jews and the people of Samaria to Nehemiah's appointment certainly suggests that his predecessors did not share the commitment and religious idealism that were to be a hallmark of Nehemiah's work.

Nehemiah had a specific commission from the Persian emperor to rebuild the city of Jerusalem itself. But when he got there, he found that most of the Jews were satisfied with things as they were. From a social perspective, they had turned out to be model immigrants, for they had integrated almost entirely with the rest of Palestinian society. They had established strong trading links with the people of Samaria, to the mutual benefit of both groups, and this had led to cooperation over a wide range of other issues. Of course, the people of Samaria were not total foreigners, for they too could trace their ancestry back to the original Israelite tribes. The only difference was that whereas the Jews from Babylon regarded themselves as ethnically pure, these other people had, over many generations, married people of other races. Even so, they still worshipped the same God as the exiles from Babylon, and the two men from Samaria who turned out to be Nehemiah's most vociferous opponents – Sanballat and Tobiah – both felt that they had the same religious faith as their Jewish neighbours.

Nehemiah refused to condone all this; to him, integration between Jews and other people could only mean one thing: the loss of their distinctive Jewish identity. He believed that these people had abandoned the idealism that originally motivated their return from Babylon, and the fact that he also saw the rich sections of the community exploiting the poor only made him all the more determined to change things. He therefore challenged the moral standards of the Jewish business community, though he could see that as long as there was easy access from Samaria to Jerusalem, nothing was likely to change. If there was ever to be an ethnically pure Jewish community then it would need to have its own political identity centred in the city of Jerusalem itself. Among other things, that meant Jerusalem would need to be properly fortified, with its own city walls, not only to remind people like Sanballat and Tobiah that it did not belong to them, but also to give the Jewish population a city they could be proud of. Not surprisingly, Sanballat and Tobiah were deeply opposed to all this. Quite possibly they themselves had exercised some sort of jurisdiction over Jerusalem before Nehemiah's arrival, but in addition they enjoyed friendly relations with the leaders of

The rebuilding of the walls and gates of Jerusalem provided not only security, but a sense of identity.

the emerging community and felt it was quite unjust for them to be excluded in this way by an outsider. Still, Nehemiah managed to gather together a group of workers from the area surrounding the city and they got down to the task, with half of them doing the construction work while the other half guarded the unfinished wall. In the amazingly short time of fifty-two days, the wall was built (Nehemiah 6). It was not as extensive as the wall that had surrounded the city before 586 BC, but its completion gave a great boost to the morale of the inhabitants. For the first time since Nebuchadnezzar had destroyed their city, Jerusalem and its people had their own self-contained society, and a new opportunity to establish their distinctive national and religious identity.

Some twelve years after his arrival, Nehemiah went back briefly to the Persian capital Susa to report back to Artaxerxes (Nehemiah 13:6). He must have felt that he had made some progress, but on his return he discovered that things had not changed as much as he thought. In his absence, people who were not considered ethnically pure had come to live in Jerusalem, and the sabbath day was not being properly observed. On top of that, the worship at the Temple was not as strict as Nehemiah would have liked it to be, and some of the priests were so poor they had been forced to leave their posts to go to work on the farms, just to make a living. At the same time, Eliashib the high priest had given a suite of rooms in the Temple to Tobiah, the Samaritan whom Nehemiah hated the most! But that was not the worst thing, in his view, for many Jewish people were again marrying foreigners, including even the high priest's own grandson who had married the daughter of Sanballat (Nehemiah 13:4–31).

Handing on the Law

Nehemiah was determined to change all this. But it was a Jewish priest by the name of Ezra who issued the most far-reaching challenge to the people of Jerusalem. He too was a Persian state official, who came to Jerusalem with royal authority to reorganize religious affairs. He was accompanied by a further group of returning exiles from Babylon, who also brought with them a considerable financial endowment for the Temple in Jerusalem (Ezra 7:1–26). But they brought more than that, for Ezra was a 'scholar in the Law of the God of Heaven' (Ezra 7:12), and his interpretation of this law was to have a profound and lasting influence on the whole way of life and national identity of the community.

It is not absolutely clear from the Old Testament just what this law was, but it is reasonable to suppose that it would be substantially identical to the Torah as we know it today. The exiles in Babylon had never been able to construct their own temple, because they believed such a thing was prohibited. This meant that most of their traditional worship had been discontinued, but in order to carry on distinguishing themselves from other ethnic groups they had laid great emphasis on things like keeping the sabbath day, observing their own special food regulations and circumcision – all of which were laid down in the Law. The exiles clearly knew a good deal more about this than the people living in Judah itself. It is no cause for surprise to be told that they were unable to read it for themselves, because the Law itself was written in Hebrew, whereas the people now spoke Aramaic, which was the official language of the Persian empire. As Ezra read it aloud to them, a group of priests (Levites) then 'gave an oral translation of God's Law and explained it so that the people could understand it' (Nehemiah 8:8). The rough translation made by these Levites was the forerunner of many such translations, known as Targums. At first, a Targum was only an oral translation, but in due course the wording of these translations became more fixed, and the term Targum came to mean just the Aramaic version of the Old Testament. But the ignorance of the people in Judah went deeper than that, for they were apparently not at all familiar with the requirements of the Law. When they heard it for themselves, they were deeply moved and decided they must do something to reinstate the religious festivals which it mentioned (Nehemiah 8:9–18). Ezra, however, was determined to tackle other matters which he regarded as problematical, especially the question of Jews who were married to people of different ethnic origins. He was more diplomatic than Nehemiah, but also more ruthless, and he forced the Jews to agree to divorce all such partners. From the perspective of today's readers, Ezra's attitude can easily seem intolerant and bigoted, and given the way in which these and other sections of the Bible have subsequently been used to justify ethnic cleansing, there is certainly a broader issue here that needs to be explored – something that we will return to in a later chapter. But in the historical context of his own day, Ezra's view on such matters was not as unreasonable as it can be made to seem. In many of the marriage laws of ancient Greece and Rome, for instance, a man was not even allowed to marry a person outside his own class, let alone someone from a different race.

Whatever verdict history may eventually deliver regarding Ezra's attitudes, it is probably true that the community in Judah would not have survived as a distinctive entity without his efforts. But it is equally certain that the people paid a high price for their survival. For this new emphasis on ethnic purity and the accompanying insistence that a detailed observance of rules and regulations was somehow central to true spirituality was easily transformed into the kind of self-righteous legalism and hypocrisy that was roundly condemned by Jesus (Matthew 23:1–36), and which the Christian writer Paul later felt to be so contrary to the original intention of the covenant relationship between God and the ancient people of Israel.

Two dissidents

Not everyone was happy to accept this new emphasis on racial purity, the Law and the Temple. When Stephen, one of the leaders of the earliest Christian church, argued that the building of the Temple had been a mistake because 'the Most High God does not live in houses built by human hands' (Acts 7:48–50, quoting Isaiah 66:1–2), he had a long line of Jewish protest behind him. But at this earlier period, more criticism was focused on the policy of rigid separation from other races.

The book of Ruth may have been published at this time, as a protest against Ezra's actions. The fact that the Jews placed it in the third section of the Hebrew Bible (the Writings) certainly suggests that it was among the later books to be written, though in the Christian Old Testament it is placed after Judges, because its story is set in that age. It tells how Elimelech, a native of Bethlehem, emigrated to Moab at a time of famine, accompanied by his wife Naomi and his two sons, both of whom married Moabite women. The father and

the two sons all died in Moab, and Naomi returned to Bethlehem along with her daughter-in-law Ruth. There, Ruth met Boaz, who was a relative of her husband's family, and they got married. As a result, Ruth, a Moabite woman, became the great-grandmother of King David.

Like other parts of the Old Testament, this story may have originated in earlier times, though the opening phrase of the book, 'Long ago, in the days before Israel had a king', shows that it was written down much later. Though there is no positive evidence to prove it, it is plausible to think that it could have been written as a protest against the legislation of Ezra and Nehemiah: if a Moabite woman married to an Israelite could have been the ancestor of King David himself, then surely there was nothing wrong with mixed marriages!

The book of Jonah may also have originated in the same context. A prophet called Jonah is mentioned briefly in the time of Amos (2 Kings 14:25), but the book contains none of his messages. It tells the story of how Jonah was sent by God to go to Nineveh, the capital city of the Assyrian empire. Jonah, however, did not want to go, and boarded a ship going in the opposite direction. When a great storm blew up, the crew decided he must be the cause of it and at his own suggestion they threw him overboard, whereupon he was swallowed by a large fish which later deposited him on dry land. Jonah was once more sent to Nineveh to announce the destruction of the city, and this time he did so. His message resulted in such a dramatic and thoroughgoing change of heart on the part of Nineveh's people that God withdrew the threat of judgment.

Jonah was dispirited at this, and went to sit alone outside the city. A plant grew up to give him much-needed shade from the sun, only to disappear as quickly – much to Jonah's annoyance. But his frustration at this then becomes the occasion for the book's message to be emphasized: 'God said to him, "This plant grew up in one night and disappeared the next; you didn't do anything for it and you didn't make it grow – yet you feel sorry for it! How much more, then, should I have pity on Nineveh, that great city. After all, it has more than 120,000 innocent children in it, as well as many animals!"' (Jonah 4:10–11).

There are some indications that this book was written after the city of Nineveh had fallen (in 612 BC), and a few Aramaic expressions seem to date it in the Persian period. Its message would certainly be a corrective to the narrow exclusiveness of many Jews at that time. Like Jonah, they were often prepared to go to any lengths to avoid sharing their faith with others, preferring that non-Jews should be destroyed rather than change their ways and become the recipients of God's blessing.

Ruth, a Moabite woman, caught the attention of Boaz as she gleaned in his field near Bethlehem, and they were married. This mixed marriage resulted, three generations later, in the birth of King David. Was the account of their marriage written down centuries later as a protest against the racial reforms of Ezra and Nehemiah?

The history of the Chronicler

The books of 1 and 2 Chronicles were also written during this post-exilic period. In them, we have yet another interpretation of the story of ancient Israel, this time starting with Adam, the first man (1 Chronicles 1:1) and ending with Cyrus the Persian (2 Chronicles 36:22–23). The first nine chapters of 1 Chronicles consist entirely of various family and tribal lists and genealogies, and the story proper begins with the death of Saul, the first king of Israel (1 Chronicles 10). But he is mentioned only as a prelude to the story of David, and the main interest of the author of these books (generally referred to as 'the Chronicler') centres on the history of the southern kingdom of Judah from the time of David onwards.

Inevitably, therefore, the stories of the books of Chronicles parallel those of the deuteronomic history. Indeed, at many points the Chronicler shows that he has actually used the books of Samuel and Kings in the writing of his own story. This fact should make it easy to uncover his own special reasons for telling the story yet again, simply by comparing the Chronicler's accounts of events with the same ones described in the earlier books. Unfortunately, it seems likely that he was using a slightly different version of Samuel and Kings from the one that is now part of the Old Testament. We know of the existence of such a version from the Dead Sea Scrolls, a collection of scriptural and other writings preserved by a Jewish sect in the century immediately preceding the Christian era. But because of the doubt concerning the edition of Samuel and Kings used by the Chronicler, reconstructing his own historical method is not a straightforward business. Chronicles also contains other historical information not found in Samuel and Kings, much of which is of independent value in helping us to understand the events of Israel's earlier history.

On the whole, however, the Chronicler sets out not so much to record the facts about the past, as to comment on their meaning and significance, and though there may be doubt about some of the details, his main concerns are not difficult to discern. He looks back to the reigns of David and Solomon as a golden age in Judah's history. The kings who followed them were all disobedient to God's Law, and the northern kingdom of Israel is scarcely mentioned at all, for it was believed to be incorrigibly corrupt right from its inception. The deuteronomic picture of Solomon and David certainly provides a more realistic and balanced account of their reigns than we have in Chronicles. There is no extensive evidence to suggest that the Chronicler necessarily invented his facts: he simply omitted significant elements from the story, and emphasized other aspects that to him were more important. So, for instance, there is no mention here of David's struggle for the kingdom against Ishbaal, Saul's son, nor of David's adultery with Bathsheba, or indeed anything else that might show David in a bad light. The same is true of the narratives about Solomon. The court intrigues that brought him to power are not mentioned, nor are his extensive marriage alliances with other states, or his promotion of many aspects of traditional Canaanite spirituality. The Chronicler does not actually deny that any of these things took place, but simply chooses not to mention them. Instead, David and Solomon are both praised especially because they built the Temple, and David's preparations for doing so, as well as Solomon's execution of his father's plans, are described in far greater detail than in the earlier history books. Then, against this background, the later kings of Judah could all be depicted as men who led their country to ruin because they neglected this all-important feature of Judah's national life.

The fact that Cyrus's edict is mentioned in the last paragraph of 2 Chronicles has led some to suggest that the two books may have been written to provide support for the work of Zerubbabel in rebuilding the Temple after the exile. The fact that the issue of ethnic purity, which was so important later, does not feature in Chronicles may also support such a date. On the other hand, this may be too early, for the list of Jehoiachin's descendants in 1 Chronicles 3:17–24 goes well beyond the time of Zerubbabel, and possibly takes us to about 400 BC. In that case, the two books could have been written in support of Ezra's reforms. They certainly stress some of the same things, and of course in that political climate the total ignoring of the life of the northern kingdom of Israel could be seen as an encouragement to the people of Jerusalem to have no dealings with their descendants who now lived in Samaria. On the other hand, some scholars have argued that we should not try to link Chronicles up to specific events and situations in this way, but simply see it as the product of a number of different political and theological currents in the post-exilic Jewish community.

Ezra and Nehemiah

The date of 1 and 2 Chronicles is closely bound up with their relationship to the books of Ezra and Nehemiah. Many scholars believe that all four of them together were originally intended to be a history of the Jewish people from creation itself right up to the Chronicler's own day. If that is the case, then we would need to think of all four books as having been written about 400 BC, or possibly even later. The only substantial reason for seeing a connection between 1–2 Chronicles and Ezra/Nehemiah is the fact that the closing words of 2 Chronicles are identical to the opening paragraph of Ezra, but in other ways their concerns are rather different. In particular, the deep interest of 1 and 2 Chronicles in David's family is not reflected in Ezra or Nehemiah.

The style and general organization of material is also strikingly different. Whereas 1 and 2 Chronicles contain a coherent, well-organized account, Ezra and Nehemiah contain a very disjointed collection of stories and other materials. Temple records are quoted (Nehemiah 7:5–73; 12:22–23), as is the decree of Cyrus, both in Hebrew (Ezra 1:2–4) and in Aramaic (Ezra 6:3–5). Various other Aramaic letters are also included (Ezra 4:9–22; 5:7–17; 6:3–12; 7:12–26), while the actual story of Ezra's exploits is partly contained in the book of Ezra (7–10) and partly in Nehemiah (8:1 – 10:39). Some of this material has the appearance of being extracts from Ezra's own diary (Ezra 7:27 – 8:34; 9:1–15), and likewise much of Nehemiah's story appears in the form of extracts from his own personal diary (Nehemiah 1:1 – 7:73, and sections of 11–13).

Then, as the stories stand, there are complex issues involved in understanding the relationship between these two men. According to Ezra 7:7, Ezra went to Jerusalem in the seventh year of Artaxerxes' reign, and Nehemiah in his twentieth year (Nehemiah 1:1). That would place Ezra's arrival in 458 BC, and Nehemiah's in 445 BC. But this seems to imply that Ezra's reforms were a miserable failure, for when Nehemiah arrived he certainly found all the same abuses that Ezra fought so strenuously to overcome. There are other facts which further complicate matters. For instance, when Nehemiah arrived he set to work building a wall round Jerusalem, though Ezra 9:9 implies that there was already a wall there when Ezra arrived. There is also the fact that in Nehemiah's time, the high priest was Eliashib (Nehemiah 3:1), whereas in Ezra's time it appears to have been his son, Jehohanan (Ezra 10:6; Nehemiah 12:11, 22). Various attempts have been made to overcome this problem. Some suggest that Ezra perhaps came in the reign of Artaxerxes II, which would place his arrival in 398 BC, and therefore long after the time of Nehemiah. Others emphasize the fact that their careers do seem to have overlapped at some points (Nehemiah 8:9; 12:26, 36), and on

The history of the Chronicler *continued*

that basis it has been suggested that the correct date for Ezra was not the seventh year of Artaxerxes I, but the thirty-seventh, which would make it 428 BC. All three possible dates for Ezra – 458, 428 and 398 BC – have supporters today, and it is difficult to decide which is likely to be correct. In our account of the work of these two men, we have assumed that Nehemiah did precede Ezra, but probably not by a long period of time.

Perhaps the reason for this confusion can be found in the disjointed nature of the narratives of these two books. For, as we read them carefully, they seem to be not so much a continuous story of Ezra and Nehemiah, as the sort of preliminary collection of information that a historian might make before writing the final polished account. The first six chapters of Ezra are more or less continuous, but between them and chapter seven there is a time gap of at least sixty years, and possibly more. The further fact that some parts of Ezra are written in Aramaic, while other parts are in Hebrew, also reinforces this impression of a collection of notes rather than a carefully crafted story. If this is a correct understanding of the nature of Ezra and Nehemiah, it would then be possible that 1 and 2 Chronicles were written early during the period of the exile, and that these other materials were gathered together by some later author – perhaps a follower of the original Chronicler – as a means of bringing the story up to his own day. We have so little knowledge of this period that it is difficult to be certain. But this does not detract from the usefulness of these books, for all scholars are convinced that Nehemiah and Ezra contain important and valuable historical materials from the period which they describe.

Exiles in Egypt

The Jewish community in Jerusalem was not the only context in which the God of Israel was being worshipped at this time. We have already noticed that the inhabitants of Samaria felt themselves to be a part of the faith community of Israel, and a series of Aramaic documents discovered at the island of Elephantine, near Aswan on the River Nile, provide a fascinating glimpse of life in another Jewish community at roughly the time of Nehemiah and Ezra.

At the time of these documents, Egypt was a part of the Persian empire and the Jews who lived here were a military settlement, perhaps guarding the southern frontier of Egypt and the trading post of Syene where traders from further south met the ships of Egyptian traders on the Nile. These Jews may well have been in this area long before Cambyses the Persian conquered Egypt in 525 BC, but they certainly had a military function rather than being (as some have supposed) the descendants either of a group of religious dissidents who left Jerusalem in protest at Josiah's reforms (621 BC), or of those Jews who took Jeremiah to Egypt after the fall of Jerusalem in 586 BC.

There are many different kinds of documents in this collection, including deeds for property, marriage contracts, and other legal transactions, but the most interesting ones are those which describe the religious observances of this group. For it is clear from them that the kind of Judaism being practised in this Egyptian garrison was very different indeed from the Judaism that was being taught at the same time in Jerusalem by Nehemiah and Ezra.
● In spite of the deuteronomic law stipulating that sacrifices were to be offered only in Jerusalem, there was a Jewish temple in Elephantine at which sacrifices were offered. The priests who officiated there are not said to have belonged to the tribe of Levi, nor is there any evidence that they knew the Torah.

After their temple had been destroyed in 410 BC, the governors of Judah and Samaria advised them to limit their sacrifices to meal offerings and incense. This could have been a gesture intended to show that the Elephantine temple was inferior in status to that in Jerusalem, though it could just as easily have been because animal sacrifices were particularly offensive to the Egyptians. Various explanations have been offered to account for the existence of this temple. Perhaps the deuteronomic law of a single sanctuary applied only in Palestine – or possibly the Jews of Elephantine had left Palestine before the reforms of Hezekiah and Josiah had really taken a grip. We simply do not know, though some scholars have suggested that there may be a veiled reference to this Egyptian temple in Isaiah 19:19, which reads, 'When that time comes, there will be an altar to Yahweh in the land of Egypt and a stone pillar dedicated to God at the Egyptian border.' Very little is known about this temple, except that it had pillars of stone, five gateways made of carved stone and a roof of cedar wood. But there is not the slightest suggestion that the Jews of Elephantine thought there was anything wrong in having such a temple outside Jerusalem. Indeed, when it was destroyed they appealed for help in its rebuilding both to the Jewish leaders in Jerusalem, and to the people in Samaria who were so hostile to Nehemiah.

● Though this temple was definitely dedicated to Yahweh (or Yaho, as God is called here), other deities had some part in it. Some believe there were five gods and goddesses worshipped here, represented by the five gates of the temple, others that

This papyrus letter was written by Jews who were living in Elephantine in southern Egypt near Aswan. It mentions Sanballat, governor of Samaria in the time of Nehemiah. Documents found at Elephantine show that Jews who lived there at that time continued to worship Yahweh.

Exiles in Egypt
continued

there were only two or three, of whom Yaho was certainly one. Most of the others mentioned in the texts are clearly of Canaanite origin. Throughout the history of both kingdoms, traditional Canaanite religious practices had survived in Israel and Judah, in spite of the prophets' denunciations of such things. The extent of syncretism is highlighted by those exiles with whom Jeremiah met in Egypt, who justified their worship of 'the Queen of Heaven' by reminding him that this was 'just as we and our ancestors, our king and our leaders, used to do in the towns of Judah and in the streets of Jerusalem' (Jeremiah 44:17).

● One of the most interesting texts is the so-called 'Passover Papyrus'. This dates from 419 BC, and contains a decree said to have been issued by Darius, laying down regulations for the celebration of the festival of Passover. This suggests that the annual observance of Passover was not as regular in early times as it came to be in later Judaism. But the very existence of this text is itself unusual, though it is of the same type as other edicts contained in the books of Ezra and Nehemiah, which also give directions for the establishment of Jewish religious practices.

It is naturally tempting to try to establish clear links between these documents and the Old Testament narratives. There is, for example, mention of a person by the name of Hanani, as well as a Jehohanan and a Sanballat, all of whom feature in the stories of Nehemiah and Ezra. But there is no way of being certain that they indicate the same people. One of the things that is quite clear from these texts is that there were some people who believed it was possible to be a good Jew without necessarily following the rigid lines that had been drawn in Jerusalem. In the next few centuries, this strand of Judaism was to be increasingly important in many parts of the Mediterranean world, not least in Egypt itself.

8 The Challenge of a New Age

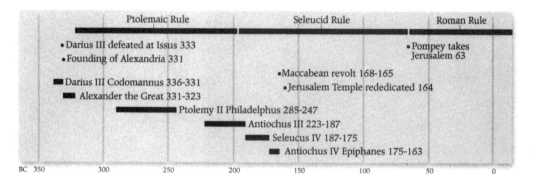

| Ptolemaic Rule | Seleucid Rule | Roman Rule |

• Darius III defeated at Issus 333
• Founding of Alexandria 331

• Pompey takes Jerusalem 63

• Maccabean revolt 168-165
• Jerusalem Temple rededicated 164

■ Darius III Codomannus 336-331
■ Alexander the Great 331-323
■■■ Ptolemy II Philadelphus 285-247
■■ Antiochus III 223-187
■■ Seleucus IV 187-175
■ Antiochus IV Epiphanes 175-163

BC 350   300   250   200   150   100   50   0

The history books of the Hebrew Bible only take their story as far as the times of Nehemiah and Ezra, and relate nothing of later events. But the period covered by the Old Testament does not end there, for life in Judah continued and the changing attitudes and experiences of this period are reflected in some of the later books. Though we have very little specific knowledge regarding what life was really like in Judah in the seventy or eighty years following the work of Ezra, the community that he founded on the twin principles of religious and racial exclusivism probably continued along much the same lines. Judah was still a Persian province, but it was allowed to mint its own coins, and enjoyed other privileges that the community based in Samaria never had. During this period the differences between Jerusalem and Samaria eventually forced the two populations of Palestine to go their own separate ways.

As they read the ancient stories of Abraham and Sarah, and their successors, the people of Samaria recognized them as their own story, and the God of whom they spoke was worshipped with as much fervour in Samaria as by the settlers in Jerusalem. Yet, in spite of the fact that they still felt themselves to be a legitimate part of the great national and spiritual movement that could be traced back through the traditional stories of the Israelite nation, the reality was that they would never again be allowed to worship at the Temple in Jerusalem. It is one of the great ironies of Old Testament history that, at the very earliest period of the

emergence of Israel as a nation, anyone who could embrace the vision of an egalitarian society based on the worship of Yahweh was welcomed as a legitimate participant, whereas by the end of the story the narrow ethnic definitions promulgated by Ezra were used to exclude even those who, on any reckoning, were undoubtedly the close relatives of those returning exiles who were now resettling the land of Judah. It was therefore inevitable that, as they reassessed their own national life in the light of changing circumstances, the people of Samaria would need to develop their own distinctive beliefs and culture. It is unclear whether the people who are called 'Samaritans' in the New Testament were the ethnic

A high priest from the small community of Samaritans still living in Israel today. Their origins reach back at least to Sanballat and Tobiah in Nehemiah's time and possibly even to the racially mixed community who survived the fall of Samaria and the northern kingdom to the Assyrians. Though kept at a distance by mainline Judaism, the Samaritans have always looked on themselves as heirs to the Old Testament traditions.

descendants of the people led by Tobiah and Sanballat, or whether they were in fact a completely new sect that emerged in the days just before the beginning of the Christian era.

Either way, the people of Samaria got their chance to establish their own national identity in 333 BC. This was the year when the Persian king Darius III Codomannus was defeated in battle at Issus in north-west Syria. The victor was a young, enthusiastic warrior from Macedonia, Alexander the Great. Having overcome the main Persian army, he moved south towards Egypt, and the Samarians saw this as an opportunity to enhance their own national security by cooperating with the Greeks. As a result, they were given permission to build a temple for themselves on Mount Gerizim, though their emerging independence soon disappeared when, for some unknown reason, they revolted against Greek rule and their city was then made into a Greek military colony.

A new empire

Alexander's progress was spectacular. Egypt offered no resistance to him, and in 331 BC he was able to found a new city on the Nile delta. This was the city of Alexandria, and it was to have a considerable influence not only on Egypt, but also on the Jewish people living in various parts of the Mediterranean world. It later became an important centre of early

Christianity. The establishment of such new cities played a key part in Alexander's strategy. For he was not just out for political power: he also had an almost fanatical fervour about spreading Greek culture and the Greek language. He was remarkably successful in doing so, and although his empire did not last long as a united political entity, the cultural world that he created, based on all things Greek (generally referred to as 'Hellenism') lasted for nearly 1,000 years. Though Alexander himself died young as a result of some kind of disease in 323 BC, by then his empire stretched from Greece in the west to the borders of India in the east. But it did not survive intact, and after much feuding among Alexander's generals, Judah – or Judea as it was now to be called – came under the control of Ptolemy, who established himself and his successors as a new ruling dynasty in Egypt. From about 320 BC until 198 BC, the Jews came under the jurisdiction of these Greek rulers of Egypt (collectively known as the Ptolemies). Their policy with regard to conquered peoples was not much different from that of the Persians before them, and was based on an essentially pragmatic approach that sought to promote anything that would be mutually advantageous to both the rulers and their subjects, though there is evidence that Ptolemy I forced many Jews to emigrate to the city of Alexandria, which was at the time underpopulated. Many others went voluntarily, however, and there was soon a thriving Jewish community in this new Egyptian city. During this time, priestly families in Jerusalem collaborated closely with the Ptolemies and, in effect, became their agents in collecting taxes and ensuring public order.

In cultural terms, this was a period of considerable change, as Jewish people encountered a way of life that was quite different from anything they had met before. On the whole, it seems that Greek ways of doing things were combined with traditional Hebrew culture on a purely pragmatic basis. The Greek language, for example, was now the essential medium for both commerce and diplomacy, and was widely adopted within Palestine itself as well as by Jewish people living elsewhere. Though Aramaic continued to be spoken in Judea in particular, this was not to the exclusion of Greek, though the use of Hebrew as a living language disappeared for good. Of course, Hebrew was the language in which the Jewish scriptures were written (with just one or two very short passages in the latest books in Aramaic). It was this significant change that led to a demand that the books of the Hebrew Bible be translated into Greek, and it was during this period that the Septuagint was produced. The *Letter of Aristeas* tells how this was accomplished, and claims that the Jews of Egypt managed to persuade the Egyptian king, Ptolemy II Philadelphus, to sponsor the project. Though details of how the translation was produced are no doubt embellished, it is not at all unlikely that such a project would have received official support, for Ptolemy II had a policy of promoting traditional culture, and facilitated the establishment of a considerable library in Alexandria. The story tells of how he sent to

The empire created by Alexander the Great's fourth-century conquests included Judea. For the next centuries the dominant influence in the whole Eastern Mediterranean was 'Hellenism' – a culture based on Greek language.

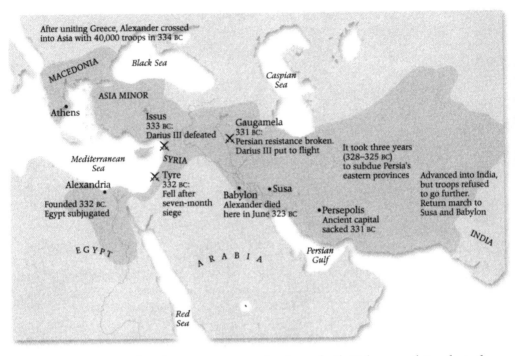

After uniting Greece, Alexander crossed into Asia with 40,000 troops in 334 BC

MACEDONIA

Black Sea

Caspian Sea

ASIA MINOR

Athens

Issus
333 BC:
Darius III defeated

Gaugamela
331 BC:
Persian resistance broken.
Darius III put to flight

It took three years (328–325 BC) to subdue Persia's eastern provinces

Mediterranean Sea

SYRIA

Advanced into India, but troops refused to go further. Return march to Susa and Babylon

Alexandria

Tyre
332 BC:
Fell after seven-month siege

Babylon
Alexander died here in June 323 BC

Susa

Founded 332 BC.
Egypt subjugated

Persepolis
Ancient capital sacked 331 BC

INDIA

EGYPT

ARABIA

Persian Gulf

Red Sea

The Greek empire.

Jerusalem for seventy men who knew both Hebrew and Greek, and locked them up in seventy cells while each one produced their own translation. When the work was finished, to everyone's amazement the seventy men not only expressed the same ideas, but also used the very same Greek words to do so – whereupon Ptolemy was so impressed that he was immediately convinced of the divine origins of both the Hebrew originals and their Greek translation. In reality, the process of translating the traditional scriptures into Greek was more humdrum than that, though the importance of the Septuagint can hardly be exaggerated, and its existence had far-reaching consequences not only for the spread of Judaism in the Mediterranean world, but also for the earliest Christian believers, who adopted it as their own Bible.

Jews and Greeks

At the time Alexander died, Ptolemy had not been the only one of his generals to have designs on Judea. Seleucus, who ruled from Antioch in north Syria, was not too happy that Judea and Lebanon should belong to the Ptolemies of Egypt, and throughout the third century their respective successors were constantly at loggerheads over possession of this territory. For the most part, this manifested itself in diplomatic efforts to out-manoeuvre one another, though there were several military skirmishes as well. The matter was finally decided in 198 BC, when the

Seleucid Antiochus III defeated Scopus, the general of Ptolemy V, at the battle of Paneon.

Antiochus was welcomed by the leaders in Jerusalem, some of whom (most notably the high priest Simon and members of the Tobiad family) had given him active support in his opposition to the Ptolemies. In return, the Seleucids adopted a tolerant policy towards the Jews, and Antiochus not only reduced their taxes, but also made a generous grant for the restoration of the Temple in Jerusalem, and formally affirmed their right to live according to their traditional laws and customs. All this ensured the continuation of the generally happy coexistence of Jewish values alongside Hellenistic culture, with mutual advantage to both sides. Unfortunately, Antiochus did not show the same wisdom in dealing with the rising power of Rome. Having extended his influence from Syria into the territory to the south, he tried to expand his empire westwards, something which the Romans took far more seriously. In 190 BC he was defeated in a land and sea battle at Magnesia, near Ephesus, and the peace treaty that he was subsequently forced to sign represented a considerable loss of face, for it required him to abandon completely his territory in Asia Minor. The humiliation of this was bad enough, but it also had financial repercussions, for this territory had always been the wealthiest part of the Seleucid empire and its loss pushed him to the brink of bankruptcy. He was soon desperate for money and just a year after signing the treaty with the Romans, Antiochus himself was killed in Elam while in the act of robbing a temple. Temples in the ancient world often served as banks where people could leave cash or jewellery in safe keeping, and the Temple in Jerusalem was no exception. Antiochus himself never sought access to its wealth, and in the early part of the reign of his son and successor Seleucus IV nothing changed. However, it was not long before the rise of dissenting factions among the ruling families in Jerusalem necessitated military intervention, in the course of which Seleucus dispatched his chancellor, Heliodorus, to plunder the Temple there. His attempt was evidently unsuccessful (2 Maccabees 3), but it alerted the Seleucids to the existence of substantial treasures in Jerusalem, while the knowledge of growing internal tension within the Jewish hierarchy encouraged them to keep a much closer eye on what was going on in this southern part of their domain.

Emerging tensions

There had been underlying tension in Jewish society long before the Seleucids had first gained control of Judea. Two leading families – the Tobiads and the Oniads – were behind all this, the one representing a more traditional Jewish orthodoxy and the other being eager to accept, as well as promote, the new Hellenistic culture. The climax of this power struggle happened to coincide with the murder of Seleucus IV and the accession of a new king, Antiochus IV Epiphanes. A member of the Oniad family called Jason bribed Antiochus to make him high priest in Jerusalem in place of his brother Onias. This suited Antiochus, for Jason was committed to the same policies of Hellenization as he was himself, and so with Jason's appointment, a thoroughgoing plan was set in motion to establish Jerusalem as a Greek city. Even the priests in the Temple were soon hurrying through their work in order to have time to go to the wrestling arena (2 Maccabees 4:13–15). The Greeks wore no clothes on such occasions, and to avoid possible embarrassment when they took part, the Jewish men even went so far as to try to disguise the fact that they had been circumcised (1 Maccabees 1:10–15; 2 Maccabees 4:7–17). All this was too much for those who wanted to remain true to the traditions of their people, and it was not long before Jason was deposed and replaced by Menelaus, a member of the Tobiad family, who was appointed by Antiochus for no other reason than the fact that he had offered a bigger bribe than Jason – something that could only inflame passions among the religious groups in Jerusalem (2 Maccabees 4:23–50).

Meanwhile, Antiochus had set his sights on Egypt. The ruler of Egypt, Ptolemy VI, was only a boy, and Antiochus defeated his army without difficulty (1 Maccabees 1:16–19). Desperate for money, he went to Jerusalem and robbed the Temple before returning home to Syria. But he was soon travelling south again, and in the spring of 168 BC he returned to Egypt. This time, he found the Romans had already arrived there, and they soon sent him packing. In the meantime, a rumour had spread in Jerusalem that Antiochus was dead, whereupon Jason seized the opportunity to try to get rid of Menelaus. Antiochus was in no mood for compromise. He had already been humiliated by the Romans, and he was determined to keep his grip on Judea. So he moved to Jerusalem again, and took what treasure was left in the Temple, assisted this time by Menelaus himself (2 Maccabees 5:1–20). Antiochus's visit to Jerusalem on this occasion was accompanied by great slaughter and destruction, and some of the inhabitants were forcibly removed and taken into slavery (2 Maccabees 5:11–14). But things went much further than that, and Antiochus also introduced stringent measures to restrict and control traditional expressions of Jewish spirituality. Circumcision, sabbath-keeping, and the reading of the Law were all banned, and in a very short time Antiochus was insisting that worship of the Greek god Zeus should be included in the rituals of the Temple. To add insult to injury, he opened the Temple to the whole population of the land, including those who were not ethnically Jews (1 Maccabees 1:41–50; 2 Maccabees 6:1–6). With this, Antiochus embarked on a comprehensive policy of enforced Hellenization, insisting that all elements of the population must be united by their acceptance of the Greek religion and Greek way of life.

National pride and religious zeal

The reasons for Antiochus's determination to stamp out all things distinctively Jewish are not altogether clear. The nearest comparable effort was 1,000 years earlier, in Pharaoh Akhenaten's attempt to eliminate from Egypt the worship of every god except Aten and himself. But this kind of attempt to annihilate an entire religion was not at all typical of ancient empires. People who believed in many deities did not usually think it was either worthwhile or necessary to try to get rid of any particular ones. Antiochus may to some extent have been motivated by an elevated sense of his own importance, perhaps regarding himself as an incarnation of Zeus. His epithet 'Epiphanes' literally means 'a manifestation of God', though some writers deliberately corrupted it to 'Epimanes', meaning 'madman'. Either or both possibilities could go some way towards explaining his actions, though he does not seem to have been the kind of person who would have had the capacity for sustaining the grand ideological vision implied by claims to divinity. Far from having any all-embracing strategy, he was the sort of ruler who reacted to events spontaneously, motivated by short-term pragmatism more than anything else. At this time, he was virtually bankrupt, his kingdom was in a shaky condition, and in addition it may well have been that Jewish leaders such as Menelaus and Jason were themselves supporting, if not actually proposing, these policies of extreme Hellenization.

No doubt Antiochus's actions had no one single explanation, but can be traced to all these factors in the social circumstances of the day. In and of itself, the influence of Hellenism had proved to be fairly neutral in relation to traditional Jewish values, and for more than a century the people of Judea had lived happily within this cultural matrix, as indeed their compatriots in other cities around the Mediterranean Sea continued to do. But the way in which Antiochus went about things in Palestine stirred up more resistance than anyone could possibly have bargained for. Jewish resistance was fanatical, and was only strengthened when Antiochus insisted that pigs (unclean animals to the Jews) should be offered in honour of Zeus. On 25 Kislev 167 BC, Antiochus inflicted the greatest indignity possible by having the altar of daily sacrifice in the Temple itself replaced by an altar to Zeus, on which pigs were sacrificed. At the same time, he issued orders that throughout the land people should be forced to offer similar sacrifices in their own communities. Though there was some support for this, the majority of the people were completely unprepared to take part in such ceremonies (2 Maccabees 6:7–31). The strength of their resolution was matched only by the cruelty of Antiochus's soldiers, who on one occasion skinned and fried alive an entire family who refused to submit to this compulsory Hellenization (2 Maccabees 7).

Such passive resistance may have been morally worthy, but it was hardly effective, and an armed resistance movement soon sprang to life. It began at the village of Modein, near Lydda, when a priest by the name of Mattathias was ordered to offer a sacrifice on a Greek altar. As he refused to do so, another man stepped forward in his place, whereupon Mattathias killed both him and the Seleucid officer who had given the

Antiochus IV Epiphanes, ruler of the Seleucid empire that controlled Judea, attempted to eliminate the distinctives of Jewish life and religion, but met with fierce resistance. The Seleucids wanted to make Jerusalem a purely Greek city, but the Jews fought strongly to retain the right to keep their Law.

order (1 Maccabees 2:1–26). That action marked the beginning of one of the most remarkable resistance movements in Jewish history. Mattathias and his family fled to the hills and began a sustained guerrilla war under the leadership of Judas, one of his five sons. Judas was nicknamed 'The Hammer' (*Maccabi*), and from that the whole movement came to be called 'the Maccabean revolt'. There was one particularly despicable act by Seleucid soldiers which ensured support from other groups. Jews generally had no interest in becoming involved in an armed struggle, and among them was a large ultra-religious group (the Hasideans) who had tried to isolate themselves from the conflict by retreating into the Judean desert. The Seleucid army pursued them, and challenged them to battle on the sabbath day. Naturally, they refused, for they would not work on the sabbath (1 Maccabees 2:29–38). When Antiochus's forces systematically murdered them, it became obvious that passive resistance was going to be useless – and equally obvious that if all Jews continued to observe the Law with that degree of strictness, there would soon be none of them left. So the Maccabees decided that they would sometimes need to be prepared to break the Law, and fight even on the sabbath (1 Maccabees 2:39–41).

This realistic policy attracted many new supporters, including the Hasideans themselves. Under the daring leadership of Judas, the rebels enjoyed some amazing successes, and it was not long before the weary Antiochus was forced to reverse his policies (2 Maccabees 11:27–33). The Jewish Law was reinstated as the foundation of Jewish society, and the Temple itself was cleansed and rededicated on 25 Kislev 164 BC, exactly three years to the day from its first violation (1 Maccabees 4:36–59; 2 Maccabees 10:5–8). The annual feast of Hanukkah (still observed today) was inaugurated to celebrate the occasion. The Hasideans were happy, for they had won the freedom to practise their own religion and keep their own laws. But Judas's family (the Hasmoneans) wanted more than that. This limited victory had given them the taste for power, and it was not long before they had more or less thrown off Seleucid rule and established themselves as a ruling dynasty in Judea. Under their leadership, Judea enjoyed a period of relative political independence until the Roman general Pompey took the city of Jerusalem in 63 BC. This period saw a continuation of the many complex internal struggles among different factions within the Jewish leadership, with some Hasmoneans seeming to favour the very things that Judas and his generation had fought so hard to overthrow. As a result, they soon lost the support of the Hasideans, who in turn disappeared as a single identifiable religious grouping. Some of them found the corruption and Hellenizing policies of the Hasmonean kings intolerable, and withdrew into the Judean desert, just as they had done in the days of Antiochus, and it was probably a movement of this kind that led to the foundation of the Essene community at Qumran by the shores of the Dead Sea. Other Hasideans did not go that far, but regrouped as a protest movement operating within mainstream Jewish society. Many scholars believe that they were connected with the rise of the Pharisees in the centuries before the birth of Jesus. The Hasmoneans, for their part, often seem to have favoured the Sadducees – another religious grouping which features in the New Testament stories of Jesus – though they themselves were perhaps the precursors of the intensely anti-Roman zealot movement that emerged in Palestine during the first century AD.

Keeping the faith

Throughout this period – and even more so in the centuries that followed – it became a major preoccupation to work out how the people of Judah could remain faithful to their ancestral beliefs while playing their full part in the rapidly changing world of their day. At the time of Ezra, it had seemed as if it might be possible for a renewed Jewish state to forge its own identity under the relatively benevolent oversight of Persia. The arrival of the Greeks did not bring any significant change of policy, though the realities of the much enlarged world-view that was now open to them meant that many Jewish people were happily experimenting to discover how their traditional practices might be adapted so as to be thoroughly at home in the new Hellenistic culture, while not losing touch with their roots in the past. This was bound to be a risky business, and three books in particular seem to have originated in this period as warnings against the possible dangers involved: Esther, Judith and Tobit.

The book of Esther was part of the Hebrew Bible, while Judith and Tobit were among those included in the Septuagint, which also included various additional passages in the text of Esther itself, not found in the Hebrew Bible. From a literary perspective, they all clearly belong to the same genre, and are what today might be called historical novels. That is, while they reflect an authentic perception of life at the time to which they relate, they were not intended to be historical narratives as such.

Esther

The story of Esther is set in Susa, the royal residence of the Persian empire, during the years when many Jews were returning from exile in Babylon. Esther herself was a Jewish woman who became queen to the Persian king Xerxes (486–465 BC), and then discovered that Haman, one of the king's leading advisers, was plotting to annihilate all the Jews. By a mixture of charm and cunning, Esther (whose husband knew nothing of her Jewish ancestry) managed to turn the tables on Haman, and he was executed while Mordecai (one of her own Jewish relatives) was promoted to high office in his place. This book was certainly one of the latest to be written, for it is found in the final section of the Hebrew Bible (the Writings). Its message seems to match the circumstances of either the later period of the Persian empire, or the early period of Greek rule, both of which raised similar questions, namely the importance of preserving Jewish distinctiveness even in the face of a relatively benevolent overlord. As later history would demonstrate, it was much easier to be fervent in devotion to traditional spiritual practices when such things were under threat. Esther's experience was meant to show that even those who were apparently well disposed to the Jewish cause could not always be trusted, and things might change literally overnight. It was always necessary to be vigilant, while at the same time recognizing that it

---

The book of Daniel and the Maccabean crisis

The story of these stirring and difficult times for the Jewish people is recounted in 1–2 Maccabees, which was not part of the Hebrew Bible but came into the Christian Old Testament textual tradition through the Septuagint. There is, however, one book of the Hebrew Bible which appears to reflect and comment on it: the book of Daniel. This is an obscure and complex book. Indeed, it is more like two books, for the first section contains a number of stories about a young Jew named Daniel who, along with his friends, faced opposition to his religion and way of life during the exile in Babylon (Daniel 1–6). But then the character of the book suddenly changes, and instead of telling stories about real people in plausible real-life situations it presents a series of grotesque visions. These depict the exploits of various mythological animals, and contain complicated speculations about the chronology of other Old Testament passages as they relate to the reigns of various unspecified kings (Daniel 7–12). In addition to this division in the book's contents, Daniel also has a linguistic division, for it is written in two languages, neither of which corresponds exactly to the two major sections of the book's message: Hebrew is used in 1:1 – 2:4 and 8:1 – 12:13, with Aramaic in 2:4 – 7:28. In addition to this, the vocabulary of Daniel is sprinkled with Persian, and even Greek, loanwords.

What, then, does this book mean, and why was it written? The answers to these two questions are very closely connected, for our understanding of the book's message will determine when we think it was written. We must therefore examine the two aspects of this book in some detail.

Stories about Daniel and his friends
This section of the book of Daniel is probably one of the best-known parts of the entire Bible. It recounts the adventures of a young Jew called Daniel who was taken off to exile in Babylon by Nebuchadnezzar in the course of an otherwise unknown attack on Jerusalem in 605 BC (1:1). He stayed there until at least after the triumph of Cyrus in 539 BC (6:28), and during this time Daniel and his friends were given the unexpected privilege of being educated in the king's own court. This, however, presented them with problems right from the start. For one thing, they were expected to eat food that was forbidden in Jewish tradition (1:3–17), and they were also required to worship a great statue that Nebuchadnezzar set up. They felt unable to do that and still remain faithful to their own religion, so as a punishment Daniel's three friends – Shadrach, Meshach and Abednego – were thrown into a furnace to be roasted alive. When they were miraculously saved from destruction, even Nebuchadnezzar himself was forced to admit the great power of their God (3:1–30). Daniel later found himself in a comparable situation during the reign of King Darius, thrown into a den of lions because he insisted on

was God alone who could ensure the nation's continuing safety. Paradoxically, the name of God is not actually mentioned in the Hebrew text of Esther, though the underlying logic of the story depends on the assumption that it was as a result of God's continuing care for the people that they were saved. The various additions to the story found in the Greek version include specific references to God, as well as other passages highlighting the role of dreams and visions, and also emphasizing how Mordecai's and Esther's prayers contributed to their final deliverance.

worshipping his own God – but again, he was unexpectedly delivered and Darius was forced to accept the supremacy of the God of Israel (6:1–28).

Many other stories about Daniel are found in other Jewish literature, including three significant additions to this book which are contained in the Greek version, but not in the Hebrew. The Prayer of Azariah (otherwise known as the Song of the Three Jews) consists of a poetic celebration of the experience of Daniel's three friends in the furnace, and includes extensive accounts of their prayers on that occasion. Another is the story of Bel and the Dragon, which shows Daniel exposing the deception of the priests by an idol called Bel, during the reign of Cyrus, and then causing a sacred serpent to burst – an action for which he is again thrown into a den of lions. Fed by the prophet Habakkuk, who is dispatched by God to keep him safe in such circumstances, Daniel eventually escapes what seems like certain death and the king is forced to accept the supremacy of Israel's God. The third addition, the story of Susanna and the Elders, comes at the end of the Greek text, though it seems to belong more naturally at the beginning of the story as it introduces Daniel as a child, showing him as one endowed with special wisdom and spiritual insight, whose timely intervention prevents the wrongful execution of Susanna, who has been falsely accused of seducing two elders of the community.

Apart from the stories of this book, nothing at all is known about Daniel. Some have suggested he may have been an ancient legendary figure, perhaps to be identified with the Daniel mentioned in Ezekiel 14:14, whose exploits are also recorded in the texts from Ugarit. But these stories are not told as part of a historical narrative. They are all intended to be moralistic presentations of the kind of experiences that were probably typical of Jewish life not only during the time of the Babylonian exile and the Persian empire, but also through into the Hellenistic period. They mostly emphasize that faithfulness to Israel's ancestral traditions would, in the end, lead to salvation, and the tables would be turned on Israel's opponents as they suffered the fate they had planned for others. There is also, however, an underlying emphasis on the horrific nature of the persecution that might need to be endured before deliverance would come, and it is this feature that, when combined with the historical allusions of the second section of the book, suggests that what may have been traditional stories of an earlier generation were brought together around the time of Antiochus IV's policy of enforced Hellenization, as a way of encouraging continued commitment to the faithful observance of Jewish Law and customs.

Visions of the future

The two sections are linked together by visions of four great empires. There is a story of how Nebuchadnezzar had a dream that he could not understand and, in the way of ancient Oriental rulers, he sent for his advisers to explain it to him (2:1–13). Where they failed, Daniel succeeded, and

Judith

The book of Judith is set in Judea after the return from the Babylonian exile, and concerns the resistance of the inhabitants of the town of Bethulia to a foreign general named Holofernes. Details of the story are taken variously to refer to Assyrians, Persians and Babylonians, but the core of it lies in Bethulia's resistance, inspired and led by Judith, a courageous widow who distracts Holofernes by her beauty and then, when he is drunk, decapitates him and takes his head back to the elders of the town.

In the preface to Judith in his 1534 translation of the Bible into

---

The book of Daniel and the Maccabean crisis *continued*

told Nebuchadnezzar that the dream was about four great empires, represented by a statue made of four different metals: gold, silver, bronze and iron. Nebuchadnezzar's own empire was the first of them (the golden one) and the others were to be empires that would follow on in turn (2:24–45). The fourth one would be the most terrifying of all, for 'it will shatter and

A Persian and a Median nobleman depicted on a frieze among the ruins of Persepolis. The second and third of the four empires in the apocalyptic vision in Daniel 7 have been identified with the Medes and Persians.

crush all the earlier empires' (2:40). But it will also have a weakness, for 'it will be a divided empire... part of the empire will be strong and part of it weak' (2:41–42).

The first of the visions in the second half of the book is very similar to that. This time, the four empires are depicted as four animals: a lion, a bear, a leopard and a fourth animal modelled on a goat. Again, the fourth one is to be even more terrifying than the others: not only did it have teeth

of iron with which to crush its victims, it also had a number of horns, capable of inflicting much terror. Indeed, the horns contended among themselves, until finally 'a little horn' with 'human eyes and a mouth that was boasting proudly' sprang up and 'tore out three of the horns that were already there' (7:1–8).

The precise identity of these kingdoms has been one of the most hotly disputed issues in the whole of Old Testament interpretation. But the book itself states clearly enough that the first empire was Nebuchadnezzar's (2:37–38), and if we start there the identity of the others becomes plain. The story of Belshazzar is probably meant to be a part of the first empire, for he is described as Nebuchadnezzar's son (5:2), but then comes a ruler of a different race, 'Darius the Mede' (5:31), and it therefore seems reasonable to suppose that he was the representative of the second empire. We certainly know that the power of the Medes was increasing in the years after Nebuchadnezzar's death, and they eventually joined with Cyrus the Persian in 550 BC, and thereafter were able to take over the Babylonian empire. Cyrus's Persian empire is the next one to feature in Daniel (6:8), and can therefore reasonably be identified with the third empire of the visions, which would make the fourth one the empire of the Greeks, founded by Alexander and subsequently divided among his successors. The symbolic language used of the fourth beast seems to allude clearly enough to the events following Alexander's death. One vision tells how 'at the height of his power his horn was broken. In its

German, Martin Luther suggested it was to be understood as an allegorical presentation of 'the victory of the Jewish people over all their enemies, which God at all times wonderfully guarantees... Judith is the Jewish people represented as a chaste and holy widow, which is always the character of God's people, while Holofernes is the godless or unchristian Lord of all ages.' Though to call it an allegory is an over-statement, that is still a fairly appropriate way of summarizing its message. Judith reflects and represents all that is most to be admired in the heroes and heroines of the books of the Hebrew Bible, and the way

In one of his visions, Daniel sees a raging goat moving so fast that its feet do not touch the ground, while hitting its enemy with great force. The description is of Alexander the Great, whose initial conquests were made with such lightning speed that they stunned the Persian opposition. The illustration is of Greek cavalry from Alexander's sarcophagus.

place four prominent horns came up, each pointing in a different direction. Out of one of these four horns grew a little horn, whose power extended towards the south and the east and towards the Promised Land... It even defied the Prince of the heavenly army, stopped the daily sacrifices offered to him, and desecrated the Temple. People sinned there instead of offering the proper daily sacrifices, and true religion was thrown to the ground' (8:8–9, 11–12). This corresponds so exactly to the events surrounding Alexander's death, the subsequent division of his empire among four of his generals, and the way in which one of those kingdoms later inflicted great persecution on the Jewish people under Antiochus IV Epiphanes, that it is impossible to imagine it could refer to anything else.

This impression is reinforced by later visions which describe the precise events leading up to Antiochus's arrival in Jerusalem, including the story of his visits to Egypt, his humiliation at the hands of the Romans, and his construction of 'The Awful Horror' in the Temple itself (11:21–31) – presumably the statue of Zeus he set up there. The Maccabean revolt which followed is also implied here: 'those who follow God will fight back... God's people will receive a little help, even though many who join them will do so for selfish reasons. Some of those wise leaders will be killed, but as a result of this the people will be purified' (1:32, 34–35). The fact that the hope of purification is in the future may well indicate that the book itself was written while the war was still in progress. It is perhaps slightly odd to find the brave efforts of Judas and his band of guerrillas described as only 'a little help',

in which she disposes of Holofernes has striking similarities to the stories of the exodus and of David and Goliath (1 Samuel 17), while her own personal disposition can be favourably compared to the stories about Sarah in Genesis 12–17.

The date of this book's composition could be more or less any time from about the fifth century BC onwards, though various political and religious allusions can be understood as referring to events and attitudes otherwise known from the second century BC, and that is where most scholars would place it.

The book of Daniel and the Maccabean crisis *continued*

Although Median influence grew after the reign of Nebuchadnezzar, it would have required the combined efforts of Medes and Persians to have toppled the Babylonian regime. Here a Median attendant leads two horses.

but some have concluded from this that the book of Daniel may have been the work of a Hasidean, who was still a bit uneasy about the Maccabean approach.

Despite the fact that this identification of the kingdoms of the book of Daniel makes the best sense out of other aspects of its message, some have argued otherwise. They point out that there never was a separate Median and Persian empire – and therefore the fourth empire would not be Alexander's Greek empire, but Rome. Others have wished to identify Alexander with the fourth empire, but used the same argument to suggest that

Daniel's historical sense is inadequate, and that he simply got it wrong when he seemed to infer that the Medes and the Persians were two separate kingdoms. But neither of these inferences is necessary:
● The Medes did develop their power even before the end of the Babylonian empire. Indeed, their position began to strengthen just after the death of Nebuchadnezzar in 562 BC. They subsequently united with the Persians under Cyrus in 550 BC, after which the two combined were able to achieve their imperial ambitions. They would probably

Tobit

The story of Tobit is set in Nineveh during the reign of the Assyrian king Shalmaneser IV (782–772 BC), and consists of two interwoven stories. The first shows Tobit as a man who is faithful to the traditional customs of Jewish spirituality, even when such things were unpopular. After ensuring that another Jew had been buried with proper concern for the regulations of the Torah, he found himself ritually impure and therefore needing to remain in the open air overnight. While sleeping, some bird droppings fell into his eyes, inflicting him with a blindness

---

not have been able to succeed separately, and in some places Daniel seems to reflect this quite clearly (5:28; 6:8; 8:20).

● We must also recognize that Daniel was using here a traditional literary scheme to describe these four kingdoms. It was quite common at the time to depict the activity of great nations by using the symbolism of the four metals gold, silver, bronze and iron. This literary device in effect required Daniel to have four kingdoms rather than three – whatever the facts might actually be. So he accommodated them by giving the Medes a semi-autonomous position which, had he been writing in a more historical style, he would probably not have done.

The book and its message

Interpreters of the book of Daniel are virtually unanimous in regarding it as a message of encouragement to those people who were suffering for their faith under the oppression of Antiochus IV Epiphanes. The visions of the second part of the book assure readers that, though things might seem to be out of control, their future – indeed, the whole of history – is in the control of a loving and all-powerful God. For the final terrifying beast is not overcome by their own efforts, but by God's personal intervention (8:25; 12:1–3), just as the great statue mentioned earlier in the book had been destroyed by a stone without any human assistance (2:31–35). That stone did not disappear, but 'grew to be a mountain that covered the whole earth' (2:35), and after these great empires have done their worst,

God 'will establish a kingdom that will never end. It will never be conquered, but will completely destroy all those empires, and then last for ever' (2:44).

This assurance that the world was not out of control must have meant a great deal to the beleaguered Jews in the early second century BC. But the book contains even more specific encouragement than that. For the stories about Daniel and his friends in the first section of the book have also obviously been selected with an eye to the circumstances that faithful Jews now had to contend with. Indeed, the prominence of Nebuchadnezzar in these stories may be intended as a conscious reference to Antiochus himself:

● The form of Nebuchadnezzar's name here is not the same as that found elsewhere in the Old Testament. But the word used in Daniel may have been intended to symbolize Antiochus. In Hebrew, as in many other ancient languages, names and words often had a numerical value, for each letter of the alphabet was also a number. It is unlikely to be a coincidence that when the numbers represented by 'Nebuchadnezzar' are added up they come to exactly the same figure (423) as the numbers of the name 'Antiochus Epiphanes'.

● The issue of food, which features so largely in the opening story of Daniel (1:3–16), was one of the crucial points in the whole argument about Hellenism. Much of the opposition that sparked off the Maccabean revolt was concerned with the unwillingness of faithful Jews to eat pork and other unclean foods.

from which no one could cure him, and which soon reduced him to poverty. Tobit sent his son Tobias off to Media to recover some money which he had left there. On the way, he met the angel Raphael, who accompanied him on the journey, in the course of which he also encountered a magic fish whose entrails then hold the key to the story's resolution. For on his arrival in the city of Ecbatana, Tobias met up with a Jewish woman named Sarah, who was a distant relative of his family. Married seven times, none of her marriages had ever been consummated because her husbands had all been attacked and killed first by a

---

The book of Daniel and the Maccabean crisis *continued*

● The worship of the great statue set up by Nebuchadnezzar (3:1–18), and the story of Bel found in the Greek text, also highlighted the same issues as Antiochus's action in setting up an image of Zeus in the Temple at Jerusalem. Indeed, in both cases it may be implied that the images were actually statues of the kings themselves. Even the story of Nebuchadnezzar's subsequent madness (4:19–33) may have been intended to be reminiscent of the commonly held belief that Antiochus was mad, because he thought of himself as an incarnation ('Epiphanes') of Zeus.

● Other details of the stories in the early chapters of Daniel are also similar to the conditions prevailing in the early Hellenistic age. Belshazzar, for example, falls from power because he defiled the sacred objects taken from the Temple in Jerusalem (5:1–4), in much the same way as Antiochus repeatedly robbed the Temple. The people of a later age would also recognize those Jews who collaborated with the unbelieving Seleucids in the duplicitous figures of the spies and informers who plotted against Daniel and ensured that he was shut up in the den of lions (6:1–14).

The book in its context

The book of Daniel is unlike any other Old Testament book. Its detailed descriptions of visionary experiences are found nowhere else in such proliferation. But books written in this style were to become increasingly popular in the two centuries before the start of the Christian era, and in the New Testament the book of Revelation is of a

similar type. These books have come to be known collectively as 'apocalypses', from a Greek word which means 'a revealing of secret things'. A number of special features make them readily recognizable and distinguish them from other literary genres:

● They are essentially literary works. In this respect they are quite different from the messages of the earlier prophets, who always used plain language that could be readily understood by anyone. The prophets also frequently used pithy poetic sayings that could easily be remembered, whereas the apocalyptic books are complex prose compositions. They contain long connected discourses, with many quotations and obscure allusions, and everyday events are invariably described in a symbolic way, often with many references to real or imaginary animals and monsters.

● They also often portray God as a transcendent, remote figure. Indeed, their whole emphasis is on the life of heaven rather than the everyday world of human experience. Events in this world are mentioned, but usually they are important only insofar as they are thought to reveal something about what is happening in some other, spiritual world. Because of this, the apocalyptic writings often emphasize dreams, visions and communications given to people by angels. God's plan for the nations is fixed and unchanging. The Old Testament prophets often gave the impression that the future course of history in some way would depend on how people responded to their messages. But for the apocalyptic writers,

demon called Asmodeus. Everyone thought Sarah must be responsible for what was happening, and when Tobias arrived she had been contemplating suicide. Raphael arranged a marriage between the two, and Tobias was able to banish the demon through the use of the fish's magic entrails. Raphael recovered Tobit's money, and the three of them then returned to Tobit's house in Nineveh, where his sight was restored using the gall from the same fish, after which Raphael returned to heaven – and the story ends with Tobit living into a long old age.

Almost certainly, this book was written in the early second century,

nothing could ever change the predetermined course of history as it moved to a final climax.

● This final climax is also to be revealed in a distinctive way. The new age is never thought of as part of the ongoing life of this world, but is either something that exists only in a different, heavenly world, or something that breaks into this world from outside by the direct personal intervention of God. This, too, is significantly different from the future hopes of most of the Old Testament prophets. For they generally expected a new age to dawn as a result of God's actions in the course of ordinary history, and insofar as an intermediary might be involved, it would be a human prince of the royal family of David rather than the kind of supernatural figures who appear in some apocalyptic books.

The apparent differences between apocalyptic and what seems to be the mainstream of Old Testament thinking have led many people today to regard all this as a rather eccentric and unprofitable sideline of later Jewish religious thought. It has often been dismissed as the result of alien influences being incorporated into the Jewish faith as a result of the exile. But there is more to it than that:

● The growth of apocalyptic must be understood within its own historical context. It is easy for readers who are detached from the hard realities facing the people of Judea at this time to dismiss their ideas as bizarre or irrelevant. The rise of apocalyptic was, however, directly related to changing

cultural circumstances and the corresponding need for theological redefinition. The prophets had suggested clearly enough that obedience to God would lead to prosperity, and disobedience would lead to hard times, and in a general sense the course of Israel's history up to the time of the Babylonian exile could be understood in a way that seemed to confirm this perspective. But in the days following the collapse of the Persian empire, things were quite different. With the arrival of an aggressive Hellenism under Antiochus IV, new questions began to present themselves, and the longer people agonized over the emerging situation the more obvious it seemed that the way to

prosperity must lie more in collaboration with people like Antiochus than in continued faithfulness to the old values of the Jewish faith. Those who tried to keep the traditional practices alive found themselves more and more in a minority, and those who prospered often did so not

The influence of Greek civilization throughout the eastern Mediterranean was enormous. Tadmor was a thriving city as early as the nineteenth century BC. However, its most dominant features today are remains of the endless rows of colonnades dating from Greek and Roman times.

probably in Hebrew though the only traces of it in that language are all fragmentary. The theme is a familiar one from this period, showing how the people could live in faithfulness to God's Law even in a hostile cultural context. Concern for the activities of angels and demons only emerged with the development of apocalyptic literature, and in later writings the book of Tobit became an important source for a Christian theology of angels. Tobit himself is presented as an example of holy living, faithfully observing the Law, then suffering in patience as a direct result of misfortunes stemming from his

---

The book of Daniel and the Maccabean crisis continued

by keeping the faith, but by ignoring it, or even abandoning it altogether. There were urgent questions to be answered: Why did faithfulness not lead to prosperity? Why were the righteous suffering? Why did God not put an end to the power of evil forces? And to add more weight to such questions, there seemed little sign of God's activity on the political and military front. God may well have raised up Cyrus in a previous generation, but in the period between Alexander the Great and Antiochus IV Epiphanes, Jerusalem had been captured at least ten times, while scores of major battles had been fought all over the country – and God was apparently nowhere to be seen. In facing up to facts like these, the apocalyptists asserted that all the present difficulties were only relative. They needed to be set in the broader context of God's overall control of the world and its destiny, and in that timescale, the righteous would eventually triumph and the oppressive domination of evil would soon be relaxed.

● There is an increasing body of opinion today that would regard apocalyptic not as an alien intrusion into the religion of the Old Testament, but as a legitimate – indeed, inevitable – development of the work of the great prophets themselves. Even in the earliest of the literary prophets (Amos) we find the expectation of a great day of crisis, 'the day of Yahweh', when God would step into history and inaugurate a new age of justice for the people (Amos 5:18–20). The same idea was developed by others, and passages in both Isaiah (e.g. 2:1–4; 9:1–7; 11:1–9) and Micah (e.g. 4:1–5) are couched in

such idealistic terms that they almost demand the apocalyptic perspective to give them some meaning. With the passage of time, these themes took on a greater importance, and when viewed from the perspective of Jewish experience during the exile and later it is not difficult to see how these earlier expectations were transformed into an altogether grander and more all-embracing vision. Some scholars have tried to link apocalyptic with the wisdom books of the Old Testament, through their common use of encyclopaedic lists, and interest in astronomy and chronology. If this could be sustained, it would again anchor it firmly in the centre of Old Testament thinking. But it is unlikely that its roots lie there, and it is more significant that the messages of Daniel are presented as in some sense a reinterpretation and new application of the messages of the earlier prophets (Daniel 9:1–2).

● From a Christian perspective, it is relevant to note that some of the most distinctive Christian beliefs seem to have originated among people who thought like this. It is unlikely that Jesus himself had too much sympathy for the apocalyptists of his day, but there can be no denying that the Christian understanding of life as a struggle against evil forces, together with the hope of future resurrection – not to mention the belief that history is moving towards a definite and meaningful goal – are clear developments of ideas that were first articulated in the writings of Jewish apocalyptists.

faithfulness, and engaging in traditional acts of piety such as alms-giving and prayer.

The end of the story

From the time of the Maccabees through to the Christian era, Jewish history was dominated by the issues that emerged in the course of these early struggles with Hellenism. The twin issues of politics and religion were to become inextricably interwoven as the Jewish people tried to reconcile their aspirations for a society in which God would be all-important with the plain fact that their world was dominated by rulers with a different world-view and spirituality. Within Jewish society itself, one political intrigue followed hard on the heels of another, until eventually the Romans stepped in and destroyed the Temple at Jerusalem in AD 70, and by the early part of the second century AD, Jerusalem itself had become a city just like any other in the Roman empire. A more comprehensive treatment of the social and religious history of this period is presented in the companion volume to this one, *Introducing the New Testament.*

It is clear that in the midst of this constant turmoil many ordinary people no doubt wondered what had happened to the ideals of the Old Testament stories. At the beginning of their shared history stood their ancestors Abraham and Sarah, a couple in whose lives God was a living reality, portrayed in personal terms as a friend to be known and loved, as well as a God to be worshipped. The same themes of God's love and the people's response had been repeated in the messages delivered by the great prophets, and was reflected in the compilation of Israel's historical narratives by both deuteronomic historians and the Chronicler, not to mention the codification of the Torah. But now, by common consent, the time of direct communication between God and the people seemed to have ended. In the closing decades of the first century BC, many groups in Jewish society were desperately searching for the word from God that would speak to them again in their own situation. Some sought for meaning in the solitary silence of the desert. Others looked in vain to the lurid speculations of the apocalyptists. And yet others concluded that their ancestral faith had lost its relevance, and sought fulfilment in political opportunism.

At the end of the Old Testament story we have a striking picture of God's people in turmoil, alongside a memorable reminder of God's continuing love even for people like this, for out of their failure of nerve the author of the book of Daniel fashioned a picture of a kingdom in which God alone would be the supreme sovereign. For Christian readers, of course, the whole of the Old Testament story needs to be viewed in the light of Jesus of Nazareth. The earliest Christians certainly viewed his life, death and resurrection as the climax without which this ancient story would be incomplete. They saw him as the one person in whose life God was most truly sovereign, describing him as the ideal descendant of David, the Messiah, of whom some of the prophets had dimly spoken. They identified him with 'the Son of man' to whom the authority of God's kingdom had been given in the visions of Daniel, and also as the true descendant of Abraham and Sarah. Not every reader of the Old Testament will wish to understand it from the perspective of Christian faith, and it is important to remember that this collection of literature also – and primarily – constitutes the scriptures of the Jewish faith. Either way, in addition to the Old Testament's value for its insights into the life of ancient Israel, it also highlights significant theological beliefs that go well beyond the times of which it speaks. In order to understand its message more fully, we need to give more detailed attention to this, and these are the themes which will occupy the remaining chapters of this book.

The books of the Maccabees

The books of 1–2 Maccabees are of special importance for understanding the history of the period immediately following the accession of Antiochus IV Epiphanes. The narrative of 1 Maccabees begins in the year of his coronation (175 BC) and ends with the death of Simon Maccabee in 135 BC, and 2 Maccabees documents events in the period from 176 to 161 BC.

1 Maccabees
While the various statistics and indications of dating contained in 1 Maccabees are not easy to integrate into a coherent picture, it is generally agreed that 1 Maccabees is closer to being a historical narrative than 2 Maccabees. It is a translation of a work that was almost certainly originally written in either Hebrew or Aramaic, and stylistically it bears some resemblance to the work of the Chronicler, incorporating official lists, genealogies and formal documents, along with carefully crafted speeches and prayers which are included at crucial points of the narrative, and which frequently serve as a means of

highlighting the important lessons to be drawn from this painful period of Jewish history. The author is nowhere named, though must certainly have been a Palestinian Jew in view of his ability to write in a Semitic language, and must have been writing before the capture of Jerusalem by the Roman general Pompey in 63 BC. Most scholars date the work to the final decades of the second century BC, perhaps during the reign of John Hyrcanus (134–104 BC). Whoever wrote it clearly held a view not unlike that promulgated in Ezra and Nehemiah, in which ethnicity and spirituality were combined as hallmarks of true Jewishness. However, while the Maccabees are praised as the deliverers of their people, their mistakes are not overlooked, and what emerges has the feel of an authentic portrayal of this family.

2 Maccabees
Apart from the fact that they cover roughly the same events, the book known as 2 Maccabees has no obvious intrinsic connection with 1 Maccabees, and is so called merely because the two appear alongside one another in the various ancient

manuscripts through which they are known. Indeed, whereas 1 Maccabees is clearly of Palestinian origin, 2 Maccabees itself claims to be some kind of summary of what were originally five volumes written by Jason of Cyrene, who is otherwise unknown. Since the book is introduced by two letters written to the Jewish community of Alexandria it is natural to assume this was the context in which it was written, quite probably at about the same time as 1 Maccabees, though there is no evidence that Jason had seen that book. Both the summary in 2 Maccabees, and the original sources from which it was taken, were originally written in Greek. The narratives contained in 2 Maccabees focus on the Temple in Jerusalem, its violation and rededication, interspersed with involved explanations of various aspects of Jewish law, which suggests that its readers were not as well informed about such things as they might have been. There is extensive praise for the martyrs of the Maccabean period, and in the New Testament 2 Maccabees 7:1–42 is referred to in this connection in Hebrews 11:35. Moreover, it also has a number of distinctive theological features, including an extensive angelology (e.g. 3:24–28; 5:2–4; 11:8), a clear belief in resurrection (7:11; 14:46), God's creation of the world from nothing (7:28), and a concept of eternal life and death (7:9, 14) which includes the notion of the living praying to God on behalf of the dead (12:43). The term 'Judaism', a designation for Jewish lifestyle and culture definition in opposition to 'Hellenism', appears here for the first time (8:1; 14:38).

3 Maccabees

This book has no connection at all with the Maccabees. Though it is found in the Greek Bible, it has never been included in the official lists of deuterocanonical books, and in literary style it is a similar work to Judith or Tobit, showing faithful Jews risking their lives for the sake of their beliefs, and being rewarded by God. It was probably written in Greek sometime during the first century BC.

4 Maccabees

This is a different kind of book again, and appears in an appendix to the Greek Bible. Its only possible connection to the Maccabees lies in the fact that events of that period are used as illustrations in some passages. It is essentially a philosophical reflection on certain aspects of Israel's history, which shows considerable signs of the influence of Stoic thought, especially in its insistence that the exercise of reason can control passion and help with resisting temptation. Since its allusions to events of the Maccabean period appear to be drawn from 2 Maccabees, it cannot have been written earlier than the first century BC, and possibly even later.

9 The Living God

Who is God?

The question, 'Who is God?' is as old as the human race itself. Philosophers and theologians, as well as countless multitudes of ordinary people down through the ages, have debated and discussed all the possible answers. To some, God is a kind of invisible 'force' who keeps things ticking over smoothly, maybe even to be identified with something comparable to 'the laws of nature'. To others, God is more specifically associated with the various features of the natural world, such as the sun or moon, trees or rocks, while yet others suggest that since the most significant aspect of existence is the human personality itself, then whoever or whatever 'God' might be will primarily be found in the depths of human experience. Surprisingly, perhaps, all these possibilities are actively pursued in contemporary Western culture. In spite of all the self-confident claims of philosophers during the past two or three centuries, inviting scepticism about the very possibility of religious belief, relatively small numbers of people would call themselves atheists. One of the more surprising facts about changing world-views in the twentieth century was that the number of atheists remained fairly constant at under 5 per cent of the population, while the popularity of spiritual world-views of all kinds increased exponentially, especially in the period from the 1970s onwards. At the start of the third millennium there is a great explosion of interest not only in traditional faiths such as Judaism and Christianity, or the great world faiths of other cultures, but also in the construction of 'designer spiritualities' which will be tailor-made to meet the personal needs of today's people.

Today's spiritual pilgrims tend to be orientated towards philosophical and theological abstractions as being the way to understand the complexities of the world and its workings. That is part of the legacy we have inherited from the time of the European Enlightenment, particularly the assumption that rationality is the only thing that matters. Because of this, any faith or world-view wanting to be taken seriously has been forced to express itself in analytical categories. This is not, however, where the Old Testament begins, and in order to comprehend its message it is important to try to understand the frame of reference within which its writers were operating. Of course, all readers will then want to go on to form value judgments on what it is saying. But in order for our opinions to be as well informed as possible, it is important to try to hear it first from within its own context. Far from arguing about God's existence, the Hebrew Bible simply takes it for granted, and we will look in vain to find any real discussion of the kind of case that might be put forward by the secular atheist. That is not to say that the Old Testament never expresses any searching questions about God's reality and activity; it contains at least one book which (in its original Hebrew form) never mentions the name of God at all (Esther), and another that puts a serious question mark against the idea that God really has a concern for the world and its inhabitants (Ecclesiastes). But even these books assume that God is there, and their questionings and probing are carried out in the context of a community which was well aware of the reality of the God whom it worshipped.

The actual statements made about God vary from one Old Testament book to another. New opportunities and fresh experiences of life pose new questions about many aspects of God's being and activity. 'The Song of Moses', an ancient poem celebrating God's greatness and goodness to the people of Israel, asks this rhetorical question: 'who among the gods is like you? Who is like you, wonderful in holiness? Who can work miracles and mighty acts like yours?' (Exodus 15:11). The implied answer, of course, is, 'No one,' and the poem ends with a commitment that 'You... will be king for ever and ever' (Exodus 15:18). Even at this early period in Israel's experience, they were certain that their God was more powerful than any other, and so must be given their undivided allegiance. They did not stop to ask whether other so-called 'gods' really existed. That was hardly necessary, for they knew in their own lives the reality and power of their own God.

The changing fortunes of the nation over the next 700 years, however, brought that question into clearer focus. In the face of great national disaster, some wanted to suggest that Israel's exclusive worship of just one God had been a major reason for their decline, and if they had paid more attention to the deities of other nations things might not have turned out as they did. But, taking their inspiration from the great prophets who had preceded them, the editors of the deuteronomic history, and also the Chronicler, were convinced that this was quite wrong. Far from allowing the events of Israel's history to turn them away from the exclusive worship of their own God, they felt even more confidence in trusting Yahweh, and went on to deny categorically that any other gods really could exist. The God of Israel was not one God among others – not even the most powerful of them – but, in the words of a later Old Testament prophet, could be described and celebrated as 'the first, the last, the only God; there is no other god but me' (Isaiah 44:6).

Given the immense timescale covered by the Old Testament books, it is to be expected that there will be evidence of how beliefs about God were redrawn from time to time. Nonetheless, the overall picture is consistent and quite clear in its main outlines: the God of whom it speaks is an all-powerful God, whose concern extends not only to the world of creation, but also to the events of history and to the lives of individual people. The changing contours of Israelite belief could be traced in a number of ways, but a good starting point will be to notice those things that particularly distinguish Old Testament beliefs about God from other ideas current in the world of its day.

God is invisible

Every nation with which Israel came into contact depicted its gods and goddesses in the shape of visible representations, such as statues. Animals were a favourite way to portray deities: the Egyptians used many such images drawn from the natural world, while the Canaanite culture represented at Ugarit used the image of a young bull, the symbol of life and sexual power, to portray Baal. There was nothing exceptional about this, and no matter where the origins of Israel as a nation can be placed, the cultural expectation would be that gods should have some form of tangible existence like this. It is not surprising that Israel should have taken it for granted that the same would be true of Yahweh also, and much of the Old Testament narrative history is concerned with the perceived tension between the cultural norms and the faith of Israel. While Moses was on Mount Sinai receiving the Law, his people were down below melting their gold jewellery to make a calf which could represent God, and become a focus for devotion (Exodus 32:1–35; Deuteronomy 9:7–21), but that was a relatively trivial matter when compared with the way this issue presented itself after the once-proud empire of David and Solomon had disintegrated to become the two states of Israel and Judah. At that time, the creation of two national shrines became a political as well as a religious necessity. King Jeroboam of Israel gave religious backing to his political stance by having golden bulls installed at the northern sanctuaries of Bethel and Dan (1 Kings 12:28–33). Both politically and theologically it is not difficult to appreciate his reasons for doing so. The population of his kingdom was ethnically disparate and religiously diverse, with some of his subjects looking to the stories of the exodus and the Sinai covenant as the inspiration for their faith, while others were giving their allegiance to the traditional deities of Canaanite culture. So what better way could there be of gaining the support of the more self-consciously Canaanite elements of the people than by making religious images that could be understood to represent their favourite god, Baal, while at the same time providing a substitute for the ark of the covenant which was now no longer accessible to worshippers in the northern kingdom, since it was still kept in the Temple at Jerusalem? Moreover, the ark itself had often been thought of as an empty throne that could give some visible form to the invisible presence of God – so could these bulls not now be regarded in the same way, as a mount for the invisible Yahweh to ride upon? Whatever Jeroboam's reasoning, and despite its obvious sophistication, he received the unreserved condemnation of the Old Testament history writers for his actions. Whether he had intended it or not, many people honoured these bulls as if they were themselves God, rather than symbols or icons, and as a result Jeroboam went down in history as the king who had 'led the people of Israel into sin' (1 Kings 14:16). It was a serious mistake to create any kind of statue that could be reverenced as divine. The belief that God is invisible is firmly embedded in every strand of the Old Testament. Visual representations are prohibited in the second of the ten commandments (Exodus 20:4–5; Deuteronomy 5:8–9), and the book of Isaiah contains one of the most sophisticated condemnations of idolatry to be found in any literature anywhere (Isaiah 44:9–20).

Canaanite religion centred on worship of Baal, god of fertility, sometimes portrayed as a young bull.

God and the forces of nature

Most of the religions in the world of ancient Israel were means of understanding and coming to terms with the power of nature as it affected the lives of men and women. In Egypt, the annual flooding of the River Nile was essential to the well-being of its people, and much Egyptian religion was therefore concerned with ensuring this would continue. Elsewhere in the region, the fertility of fields and flocks was bound up with the appearance of the rains at the right time of year. This was the case in Canaan, the land in which the people of Israel emerged as an independent nation during the Late Bronze and Early Iron Ages. Though many features of the sagas of traditional Canaanite gods and goddesses – El, Anat, Baal and others – are unclear, it is obvious that the activities of the gods personify the cycle of the seasons. For instance, the story of how Baal dies and is then restored to life by the sexual attentions of his lover, Anat, has close connections with the apparent death and rebirth of the life of nature that took place year by year as one season succeeded another. The historical narratives of the Old Testament show how there was continual tension between the way the people of Israel actually worshipped – using rituals and practices taken from the worship of Baal – and the kind of worship that was understood to be an authentic reflection of the nature of their own God, Yahweh. In the view of the prophets and the history writers, doing this was an indication that they were misunderstanding the character of God in some quite fundamental ways. For Yahweh was above nature, and not a part of it – and though God can on occasion be described in imagery derived from natural phenomena such as light or fire, it is never

acceptable to identify God with the forces of the natural world
(Exodus 19:18; Deuteronomy 4:33, 36; Psalm 104:2; Ezekiel 1:27–28).

God and the philosophers

The Old Testament never tries to define God. In one sense this is hardly
surprising, for in order to be greater than the sum of human intelligence
God must be beyond description. But that has not generally prevented
people from making the effort, and in the early centuries of the
Christian era readers of the Bible spent much time and energy trying to
decide how to describe God. The process still occasionally continues in
books of systematic theology, which can appear to be trying to define
God's being in abstract terms – almost as if there is some chemical or
mathematical formula that, if only it can be uncovered, will provide
access to the innermost depths of God's existence. This approach has a
long and venerable history, and owes a good deal to the work of the
great Greek philosophers who generally attempted to explain their idea
of 'God' in an abstract, or metaphysical, way. To answer the question,
'Who is God?' it therefore became necessary to ask a further question,
such as, 'What is God made of?' The ready acceptance of the validity of
such questions has had far-reaching repercussions for the ways in
which Christians in particular have articulated their beliefs. But this is
not the way in which the Old Testament thinks about God. Its writers
do not try to analyse God like a specimen under a microscope; indeed
the whole world of abstract ideas is generally quite foreign to their way
of thinking. Instead of defining belief metaphysically, by asking
what God is made of, they take a much more functional approach,
by exploring God's relevance to human life and experience.

A simple example will perhaps help to explain the difference
between these two approaches. If someone asked me to describe
my lover I could give two rather different answers. I might, for example,
describe her appearance – height, weight, colour of hair, colour of eyes
and so on. This would certainly answer the question, and it would allow
the questioner to form a mental picture of her appearance. But it would
also leave many things unanswered, and if the questioner really wanted
to get to know and understand my partner, it would be an altogether
unsatisfactory sort of answer. A more useful answer would include some
description of the kind of person that she is, illustrated with personal
anecdotes to show how she has reacted to life in particular circumstances. To give that sort of answer I need never mention things like the
colour of her hair, and I might well refer to vague and undefinable
notions such as 'love' as the key to her personality. I would certainly tell
stories rather than talking in abstract propositions, and for that very
reason this rather emotive description of my partner would quite likely
be more useful to most people than a more dispassionate one. From the
perspective of today's culture in the West, the storytelling approach
would correspond to what is generally called a 'postmodern' way of

Greek philosophers, such as Plato, speculated about God's being. The Hebrews were interested in how to relate to God.

dealing with life, whereas the more analytical one would be dependent on the philosophical assumptions of the European Enlightenment, many of which have now been seriously questioned, if not rejected altogether. In that sense, the Old Testament's way of addressing matters of truth is probably more accessible to today's spiritual searchers, for it takes what is, in effect, a 'postmodern' approach which answers the question, 'Who is God?' by laying all the emphasis on the way in which God relates to the world and its people, rather than attempting to analyse God's being in an abstract, 'scientific' kind of way.

What is God like?

In one sense, the entire Old Testament is the answer to this question. As we read its books we can see how they are all concerned to describe the different ways in which God has been made known through the experiences of the nation of Israel. At the very beginning of Genesis there is a series of ancient stories that tell how God relates to the world of creation. These are then followed by the long and complex accounts of God's dealings with the people from the time of Abraham and Sarah in the Middle Bronze Age (2000–1500 BC) right through to the time of the Persian empire and beyond, just a century or two before the start of the Christian era. Then, in addition to God's revelation through nature and history, the Old Testament contains many books showing how God relates to the more mundane circumstances of everyday life, either the corporate life of society or the personal spiritual experience of individuals. With such variety in its literature the Old Testament contains many different perspectives on the involvement of God in people's lives. But some themes are so common that they are obviously fundamental to the total picture of God that is presented here.

An active God

The Old Testament is distinguished from most other religious books by its great emphasis on historical stories. The messages of the prophets, as well as the history books themselves, all declare that God is most characteristically to be encountered in the varied events of Israel's national life. Other nations in the world of ancient Israel sometimes thought of their gods as being involved in political life, but what distinguishes the Old Testament is that God's activity is seen not in isolated incidents, but throughout the whole story. Indeed, it is only because God is at work there that the history has a coherent meaning at all.

Scholars of a previous generation often saw this as the main key to understanding the Old Testament, and laid all the emphasis on the notion of a 'God who acts'. This is perhaps too simplistic a way of describing the Old Testament faith, for some of its books scarcely mention God's actions in Israel's history at all. But there can be no doubt that this is one of its more distinctive features. Life is not just a meaningless cycle of empty existence, but has a beginning and an end, and events happen not in a haphazard sequence, but as part of a great design that in turn is based on the personal character of God. Moreover, this God is encountered by people in the ordinary events of everyday life, and not through tortuous intellectual debate. This confident assertion dominates the entire story, and from the early accounts of the call of Abraham and Sarah, right through to the apocalyptic visions of the book of Daniel, God is the one who is in control of history. In bad times as well as good, all that happens is dependent on God. Because of this overriding conviction, the way the Old Testament writers tell the story of their people is quite different from the approach of the modern historian. A modern reader may look for historical explanations of a particular event, assuming that if history makes sense at all it is a sense that comes from within itself rather than depending on the external influence of God. It is, of course, possible to read the Old Testament in this way, and to some extent this is what we have been doing in the chapters up to this point. But if we restrict our thinking to historical cause and effect we will miss an important dimension of what the Old Testament writers were saying.

GOD CHOOSES PEOPLE

The story of the people of Israel begins with Abraham, a typical merchant of the day who leaves his homeland in Mesopotamia and heads west and south to make a new life for himself and his family. Abraham's journey was, in fact, typical of many such journeys that were being made in the Middle Bronze Age (2000–1500 BC). People were moving in all directions through the Fertile Crescent, and Abraham was certainly not alone in making the journey from east to west in search of a new way of life. But this was not important to those who preserved the stories. For them, Abraham's migration was not just a symptom of demographic changes: it was an integral part of God's plan for his life. Not only was he to have a new lifestyle: he and his wife Sarah were to become the founders of a great nation. Through them God would 'bless all the nations' (Genesis 12:3). The driving force in Abraham's life – as in that of his successors – was the intention of a caring and all-powerful God whose love was to be shared with the whole world and its people.

This belief found its classical expression in the story of how a group of Abraham's descendants were released from slavery in Egypt (the exodus). Just as this story came to be the foundational epic from which the people took their national identity, so it is also at the very heart of Old Testament spirituality. For centuries afterwards, the people of

Israel looked back to this event to remind them of God's goodness and their responsibilities. Here again, it may well be that various details of the exodus story can be explained by reference to features of the geography or natural history of the area. But for Israel, it was more than just a story. The dramatic escape from slavery and their establishment as a nation in the land of Canaan was due not to social or geographical factors, but was the outcome of the personal action of God. Without that, the exodus could never have taken place, and Israel would never have become a nation. This is why, when later generations wanted to remind themselves of the character of their God, they turned especially to the exodus story. This event was celebrated in poetry and in song, and reported in family groups at every opportunity. It became the central focus of their faith, for not only did it remind them that God was active in history, it also gave a unique insight into the nature of that activity – and therefore into the innermost character of God.

GOD'S LOVE

This is a major theme running through the whole story. The slaves were powerless and weak. Even their leaders were uncertain of the future, and had the nation depended for its survival on human ingenuity and courage, then it would have failed. When later generations celebrated this great event, God's generous actions towards the people ('grace') were always in the centre of their thoughts. An ancient creed, recited as the first-fruits of later harvests were offered, put it like this: 'we cried out for help to Yahweh, the God of our ancestors, who heard us and saw our suffering, hardship and misery. By God's great power and strength we were rescued from Egypt' (Deuteronomy 26:7–8). The prophets took this story and put a powerful spin on it, to remind the people that God had shown a particular care for those who were victims of unjust oppression. For them, the exodus was not just a demonstration of God's powerful

Soldiers from Abraham's original homeland as depicted on the Royal Standard of Ur.

actions in history: it was also an experience of God's love, which found its truest fulfilment when it centred on those who were past helping themselves.

GOD'S POWER

God's power over the whole of life is another dominant theme in the exodus story. God acts in the lives of the people to bring about their salvation, and is also able to control the powers of nature itself. Yahweh meets Moses in the burning bush (Exodus 3:1–10), sends plagues on the Egyptians (Exodus 7:14 – 11:9) and parts the Sea of Reeds – and subsequently the River Jordan – to allow the escaping slaves to cross on dry land (Exodus 14:1–31; Joshua 3:1–17). Later again, God provides food and water in the course of the long desert journey, even sending flocks of birds to feed those who were hungry (Exodus 15:22 – 17:7). Nations are also under divine control, and God's purposes can be accomplished through both Egyptians and Canaanites. On some occasions they become instruments of judgment, at other times, of blessing – but always as part of God's loving purpose for the people.

GOD'S JUSTICE

At the heart of the exodus story is embedded the Old Testament Law, the *Torah*. It is significant that this is an integral part of the story of God's actions on behalf of the people. The Old Testament repeatedly emphasizes that God acts in accordance with clearly defined standards of justice, and never in an arbitrary or unpredictable fashion. The core of God's relationship with humankind is morality, and when a person encounters God it is always in the context of moral challenge. When Isaiah had a vision of God in the Temple, it was not the otherworldly, mystical or supernatural aspects of the experience that impressed him most. They undoubtedly played a part – that should not be under-estimated – but his first response was to confess his own inadequacy in the face of the great moral purity of God (Isaiah 6:1–5). When people encounter God, whether in temple or in exodus, they must first face up to the demands of God's justice.

Finding God in later history

It was in the process of trying to relate God's love, power and justice to the events of their national history that the prophets hammered out some of the most distinctive elements of the Old Testament faith. As time went on, it became increasingly clear that Israel's fortunes were closely connected to the international power politics of the day. Israel and Judah were just pawns in the strategic manoeuvres of the two superpowers based in Egypt and Mesopotamia who constantly vied with each other for domination of the Fertile Crescent. It often seemed as if these powers were in control of things, not God. What, then, was the value of God's promises – not only the promise to Abraham and Sarah, and the great deliverance of the exodus, but also the bold assurance to David that 'I will make you as famous as the greatest leaders in the world... You will always have descendants, and I will make your kingdom last for ever. Your dynasty will never end' (2 Samuel 7:9, 16)?

Viewed in this light, the facts of history raised many awkward questions. If Israel had been chosen by God, should they not be triumphant in all their battles? And if God was in control of things, how was it that other nations were so easily able to get the upper hand? The prophets had a clear answer to these questions. The fact that God had been personally revealed to Israel, demonstrating love and care in so many ways, imposed great responsibilities. As Israel were faithful to their calling, so they would prosper. But when they were unfaithful, then they would need to return and ask God's forgiveness. The misfortunes they suffered were all highlighted as evidence of that. This is how the editors of the book of Judges assessed Israel's early history, and it was a lesson that the prophets repeated in many a crisis of the nation's later life.

The people often misunderstood the nature of God's involvement in their history, and imagined this was a sign that they were God's favourites. But the prophets knew that God's purposes were never so restricted, and had always been motivated by a wider intention: the salvation of all peoples, as promised to Abraham. Though Israel had been the special recipient of God's love, and had witnessed such great acts of power, both love and power could only operate within the framework of God's justice. This conviction often brought the prophets into direct conflict with the politicians of their day. In political terms, they did not always take the same side. Isaiah, for example, could advise the king in Jerusalem that God would protect the city and all would be well in the face of an Assyrian invasion (Isaiah 31:4–5). But a few generations later, Jeremiah said exactly the opposite (Jeremiah 7:1–15). What united them was the knowledge that history was in God's control, and that things were being ordered in accordance with God's own absolute standards. Those who arrogantly set themselves up in opposition – whether Assyrians or Judahites – would be judged. And when the Babylonians took the king of Judah off into exile and later destroyed the city of Jerusalem, that was as much the work of God as the exodus itself had been (Jeremiah 24).

Many people found that kind of thing hard to understand. After all, their entire history seemed to suggest that God was on their side – and if so, how could a catastrophe such as the exile possibly befall them? It was at this time that Israel's historians compiled the story of their nation as we now have it in the Old Testament. The deuteronomic history, stretching from Deuteronomy to 2 Kings, retold the familiar stories in an effort to explain why God had apparently deserted these special people. Following the lead given by the prophets, it declares that Israel had been disobedient. They had failed in their God-given responsibilities, and had suffered the inevitable consequences. Others compiled the story of

Israel's earlier experiences, from creation to the exodus, and they too had a message for their people: disobedience had been a part of human life from the very beginning, but it was always balanced by God's grace and forgiveness. God's justice and God's love could not be separated. However, while the deuteronomic history had a sad and depressing tale to tell, the message from Genesis to Numbers was more encouraging, assuring those in exile that God's love would ultimately triumph.

But what about God's power? Had not the final days of Judah been, in effect, a battle not between two armies but between two sets of deities – and had not the gods of Babylon won? Where did the God of Israel stand in relation to the apparent power of other gods? This question had been faced in a practical way right from the earliest days, when the tribes had decided to worship only one God (Joshua 24:1–28). But they had not denied that other gods might exist – indeed, the enthusiasm with which they continued the worship of Baal suggests that some of them were not at all convinced that their own God really was all-powerful. Some of the earlier psalms (e.g. Psalm 47), as well as prophetic messages such as those found in Amos 1:3 – 2:5, had hinted that God was in control of the lives of people everywhere, and not only of Israel's destiny. But with the exile the question had become even more urgent, and it was given a very clear answer in some of the most remarkable passages anywhere in the Hebrew scriptures. In a series of prophetic messages, the God of Israel is declared to be the God of the whole world. Yahweh is all-powerful, and those who worship other gods are misguided as well as stupid (Isaiah 44:1–20). Far from being a sign of God's defeat, the exile had itself been God's punishment for the people. The Babylonians had indeed been used to accomplish God's purposes, but they in turn had been punished for their excessive violence (Isaiah 47:1–15). God's power was in no way diminished, and there was every expectation that a new deliverer would be raised up for the dispossessed people – this time, not a Moses from among their own ranks, but Cyrus, the emperor of Persia (Isaiah 45:1–4). The future would be even greater than the past had been, as God would move in a new way to fulfil the original intention of the promise given to Abraham and Sarah. God's servant, through whom this would be accomplished, would bring blessing to Israel, but would also be 'a light to the nations – so that all the world may be saved' (Isaiah 49:6).

A personal God

The fact that there is so much emphasis here on God's character being revealed in the great events of history may lead us to wonder if Israel's deity was not perhaps just a personification of 'fate', or even of 'history' itself. Many gods and goddesses of the ancient world were personifications of various aspects of the world of nature; could it be that the God of the Old Testament was just an embodiment of Israel's history?

The question is not quite as simple as that, however. In traditional

Canaanite culture, for example, the world of nature seemed to go its own way regardless of human interest, and there was very little that anyone could do to change things. The best one could hope for was to escape the most vindictive aspects of nature by avoiding too much personal involvement with the deities who were in control of it. The Old Testament accepts that God is to be given due respect and honour, and recognizes that God's ways are often beyond human understanding – but it also emphasizes that relationships between people and God do not operate in a purely mechanical way. Indeed, it often goes out of its way to claim quite the opposite, affirming that God is intimately interested in both the world and its inhabitants, and is not at all remote from people and their needs. All the great events of the Old Testament stress that God does not act in a capricious, unpredictable way, but is only concerned for people and their good. Even more striking is the way in which God's love is expressed, for it is not the patronizing care of a moralist who knows what is best, and is prepared to ride roughshod over human need in order to achieve their own ends. Some of the most striking, and unexpected, stories in the Old Testament depict God entering into discussion with people, and even having a change of mind as a result (Genesis 18:16–33; Amos 7:1–6). All this may be a little difficult for people today to understand, with our emphasis on justice as an abstract quality operating in predictable ways. But it explains why morality and justice are so fundamental to the Old Testament view of God, for it is in the context of personal relationships that such qualities are most important.

The Hebrews saw God as one who acted out of love and justice, and never in a capricious or vindictive manner. This would have contrasted with the beliefs of other ancient peoples who spent much time appeasing potentially violent deities. Here the god Ningirsu is seen smiting with a club victims who are caught in his net.

How then does God relate to people? There is no doubt that the Old Testament lays much emphasis on the corporate experience of Israel as a nation. Although it was only Moses who went up the mountain to receive God's Laws, making it a personal experience in that sense, what happened there was not something private and individual, but a representative experience in which all the people were included. The idea that one person could represent a whole nation in this way was widely held in the ancient world, where rulers were regularly regarded as the very embodiment of their nation. The term 'corporate personality' is sometimes used to describe this sense of national solidarity, though it is not a phrase found in the Bible itself and its importance has often been exaggerated. But it does draw attention to an aspect of Old Testament thinking that is sometimes difficult for modern Western people to grasp. The heritage of the Enlightenment has ensured that most of us are accustomed to thinking in terms of the work of an individual, and 'society' is often taken to be just the sum total of individuals living in a particular time and place. This kind of introverted individualism would have been a totally alien idea for the writers of the Old Testament, just as it has been to all cultures through-out the world, apart from the Europeans who first thought of it. The family, the village, the tribe and the nation were all of crucial importance in Israel, and a person could expect to find fulfilment in life only when she or he was in a proper relationship with others. Both happiness and misery were shared with other people, and a sense of social solidarity runs deep in the Old Testament, as it still does in many traditional cultures today. We find this most strikingly in the story of Achan, whose entire tribe was implicated in the wrongdoing of just one person (Joshua 7:1–26). There were clearly risks involved in being closely identified with others, but compared to the fear of being alone, such risks were very small. To have no friends, and to be an outcast, was the final indignity that an Israelite could suffer, for life only found its fullest meaning when a person was part of a broader community (Jeremiah 15:17; Psalm 102:6–7).

At the same time, it would be an exaggeration to suppose that people of the Old Testament period could see no meaning or purpose in life except in relation to their position as part of a large social unit. That

would be to press the idea of corporate personality to a logical conclusion that is never drawn in the Old Testament itself. The book of Psalms, for instance, contains many examples of prayers and hymns which show just how much worshippers in ancient Israel felt that God was personally interested in the details of their own everyday life, and the prophets also stressed the importance of individual commitment to the God who

Modern Western thinking tends to emphasize the individual over the needs of the community as a whole. Such an attitude is alien to the Old Testament, where a sense of social solidarity is deeply ingrained.

was revealed through the events of their national heritage. We would be quite mistaken to imagine that God only deals with people in large numbers. The same theme of God's personal care and concern is prominent in many of the Old Testament's best-known stories, for Abraham and Sarah and their children in a hostile land (Genesis 12:10–20), or for Joseph as he is sold into slavery (Genesis 37:12–36). Moreover, this kind of personal interest in people extends even to those who might be considered of no consequence, such as the boy Ishmael who, with his mother Hagar, was expelled from Abraham's family circle (Genesis 21:9–21). This sort of principle was enshrined in the legislation of the Torah, and in Jonah 4:11 God's pity includes not only the innocent children of the great city of Nineveh, but even the suffering animals in it.

Words for describing God

The importance of recognizing God as a person comes out clearly in much of the imagery used in the Hebrew Bible. The messages of the prophet Hosea apply the terminology of personal relationships to God and people in a particularly sensitive way. God is a loving mother to the people of Israel, who protected them and directed their footsteps from the very beginning of their national history, not only guiding them, but also caring for them: 'I drew them to me with affection and love. I picked them up and held them to my cheek; I bent down to them and fed them' (Hosea 11:4). According to Exodus 4:22–23, this was the message that Moses had given to the pharaoh of Egypt when he reminded him that Israel was God's 'firstborn son. I told you to let my son go, so that he might worship me.' And centuries later, Isaiah depicted God as a broken-hearted father whose children had rejected his guidance (Isaiah 1:2).

At other times God can be depicted as the husband of the people (Jeremiah 31:32; Hosea 2:14–23). After the fall of Jerusalem, God became for Ezekiel a generous stepfather who had rescued the city and its people from certain death (Ezekiel 16:1–7). The application of imagery drawn from family relationships to describe God came naturally to people who experienced God as an essentially personal being, encountered primarily in everyday relationships. It is fashionable in some circles to dismiss the Bible's metaphors for God as hopelessly patriarchal and masculine, but this is far from an accurate appraisal of the facts. God could be described as a father not because God was supposed to be male, but because the divine–human relationship can be as close and life-giving as the best of human family ties. The fact that God can also be described as a mother merely serves to underline the reality that the Bible does not present God in a gender-specific way. What is more, this can be traced throughout all periods of the evolution of the Old Testament as we now have it. 'The Song of Moses', for instance, is widely acknowledged to have originated in a very early historical period, and it contains this statement: 'You deserted the Rock who fathered you; you forgot the God who gave you birth' (Deuteronomy 32:18). God is here represented as the divine parent, both male and female. Elsewhere, God cries out 'like a woman in labour' (Isaiah 42:14), and showers the people with the affection of a mother (Isaiah 49:15; 66:13) – while Psalm 131:2 compares God's love with quiet rest in the arms of a divine mother. When you remember that all this was written in an ancient male-dominated culture, and that the major challenge to Israel's faith came from a traditional Canaanite religion which gave a high profile to sexual worship of the female form, then the acceptance of female imagery with which to describe God is all the more striking. The same inclusive quality of God's being even features on the very first page of the Hebrew Bible, where both women and men are described as made 'in the image of God', a statement that would most naturally imply that there is some aspect of God's own being that corresponds to both femininity and masculinity as those characteristics can be identified within human experience (Genesis 1:27–28).

The Old Testament has often been unfairly criticized for offering a very narrow understanding of the nature of God. The reality, however, is quite different, and the sheer variety of images invoked to explain God's person and purposes shows all the signs of a creative and imaginative people, no doubt struggling as they tried to explain the inexplicable, but certainly not falling back on safe and predictable language. It is this buoyant and lively imagery that has ensured the message of the Hebrew scriptures still speaks relevantly to people of many later times and places.

This is not to say that the Old Testament does not also include more strident imagery to describe God from time to time. God does indeed appear as ruler and sovereign of the people, sometimes in a very literal way. In some early narratives, God is depicted leading the people into battle as their army commander ('Yahweh, God of hosts'), something that was apparently symbolized by the ark of the covenant (1 Samuel 4:1–4; Psalm 24), and though from the time of Saul onwards a human king played a leading role in the affairs of the people, there was still a considerable emphasis on the fact that in reality God was Israel's only true king. Indeed, the Old Testament historians pass their verdict on the various kings of Israel and Judah mainly in relation to whether they have been prepared to recognize that greater kingship of God. This was clearly an important concept, for even when the idea of kingship is not explicitly mentioned, much of the imagery used in speaking of God comes from such a background. The well-known Psalm 23 refers to God as the people's 'shepherd', imagery which to us may suggest a different background altogether, but in the ancient world kings were often referred to as the 'shepherds' of their people, and this is almost certainly what the psalmist had in mind.

It is easy to see why the kingship imagery should have seemed appropriate for describing God, for the rescue of the slaves from Egypt was exactly the kind of thing that any good king would have done for his people. An earlier chapter has already drawn attention to some striking similarities between the covenant formulations of the Old Testament and the way in which a subject nation might define its relationship to a greater power that had delivered it from an enemy. Israel's allegiance to God as king was the grateful obedience of those who had been set free, not the fear of those who had been defeated. This is the context in which statements enjoining the people to 'serve' or even to 'fear' God are to be understood (Psalms 113:1; 123:2). Sometimes the expression 'the fear of Yahweh' is just a term to describe religious worship (Psalm 19:9), but more often it indicates an attitude of mind which recognizes the appropriate differences between God and people. In terms of contemporary usage, words like 'reverence' or 'honour' capture more of the original meaning than 'fear', and this is how many modern versions of the Old Testament translate it. To fear God in this sense has little connection with popular pictures of an angry God before whom men and women can only cower in insignificance. It is rather a matter of giving God an appropriate place in the scheme of things, and the importance of recognizing that God is so much greater than humankind is a common Old Testament theme. Even the prophets, who

God's name

The fact that God is to be understood in personal terms is highlighted by the emphasis the Old Testament places on God's name. In the ancient world a person's name was much more than just a label:

● A person's name established a person's identity, and revealed their character. So, for example, in the early stories of the book of Genesis, Eve (3:20), Cain (4:1) and Noah (5:29) are all given names that indicate something about their personalities. Later, all twelve ancestors of the Israelite tribes have names that reflect either the nature of the recipients or the experiences of their parents (Genesis 29:31 – 30:24).

● Knowing a person's name, or giving a name to someone, was often a way of gaining authority over that person. As the creator, God gives the stars their names (Psalm 147:4), and in naming Israel God asserts some sense of ownership of the nation (Isaiah 43:1). Similarly, when Jacob wrestles with an unknown deity, he first wants to discover that god's name so that he may establish a proper relationship with whoever or whatever it is (Genesis 32:29–30). To know the name of a god could therefore be very important, for a god's name gave the worshipper access to power. By invoking a god's name, the presence of that particular deity could be assured. Calling on God's name in this semi-magical way is expressly forbidden in the ten commandments (Exodus 20:7). For the Old Testament writers, God's name was not to be discovered and manipulated by mortals, but was something only God could reveal in the context of a loving relationship with the people.

What is God's name?

Because of this, there is an extraordinary reverence for God's personal name throughout the Old Testament. The reticence to mention the name of God is so widespread that we do not even know for certain how it was pronounced. Hebrew has no vowels, and this name was written down as YHWH. Vowel sounds are needed to pronounce it, of course, but we do not know precisely which sounds were used. By the time the Hebrew Bible emerged in its final form, Jewish religious teachers regarded the personal name of God as too sacred to say and whenever they came across it in reading the scriptures they would substitute the Hebrew word 'Adonai', which means 'my lord'. In this way, the vowels of 'Adonai' came to be pronounced with the consonants of God's name YHWH, to produce something like the English term 'Jehovah'. Nowadays it is customary to write this name as 'Yahweh', and this is the form we have used here.

It is often supposed that this avoidance of God's personal name was a relatively late development within Judaism, though traces of the same reticence can be found throughout the Old Testament. For example, in the stories of Joseph, God's name Yahweh is never found on the lips of non-Israelites (Genesis 37–50), and there is a whole section of the book of Psalms which avoids using it (Psalms 4–83). Other parts of the Old Testament use the expression 'the Name', instead of speaking directly of God (for example Psalms 5:11; 7:17; 9:2, 10; 18:49), and in Deuteronomy it is God's 'Name' that is bestowed on the Temple in Jerusalem to signify God's presence and blessing there (Deuteronomy 12:11; 14:23, and so on). By saying that it was 'the

regularly claimed to have access to God's innermost secrets and to be on close personal terms with God, nevertheless display a strong sense of awe and reverence as they describe how they have been in God's presence and heard the messages they were to deliver.

It is essential to realize that all these images are attempts to describe a phenomenon that is essentially indescribable. They help to portray

---

God's name
continued

Name' and not Yahweh in person that was dwelling in the Temple, the Old Testament was able to avoid the notion that God was restricted to just one locality, and yet still assure the people that the worship in the Temple had special power to put them in touch with the reality of God's presence.

What does Yahweh mean?
From a purely linguistic point of view, a number of suggestions can be made. The word Yahweh could, for example, be related to an Arabic word meaning 'blow'. Some scholars have argued from this that Yahweh was therefore originally the name of a storm god. Others have suggested that the clue to its meaning is to be found in a shortened form of the name Ya'u, which is known in Babylon and other parts of the ancient world. Or perhaps it was originally just a shout of excitement used in the context of religious worship which was subsequently taken and used as a proper name. Of course, explaining where a name comes from is not the same thing as understanding what it means, and the Old Testament gives a quite distinctive meaning to it. When Moses asks on whose authority he is to go and demand the release of the slaves from Egypt, he is told: 'I am who I am. This is what you must say to them: "The one who is called I AM has sent me to you"' (Exodus 3:14). Even this explanation is not without ambiguity. Several centuries later, when the Old Testament was translated into Greek (Septuagint), this phrase was taken as an indication of God's eternal existence, along the lines of Greek philosophical speculation of that period. But in the original context of Moses' encounter at the burning bush it is obvious that, although the name

Yahweh is related to the Hebrew verb 'to be', the emphasis is not on God's existence as such, but on God's activity. It is, like the rest of the Old Testament story, a declaration that God is characterized by actions, the name is intrinsically connected with the nature of the one who bears it, and knowledge of the name provided the assurance to the slaves in Egypt that God was active on their behalf. This God was the one who controlled time itself, and could be trusted for the future because of what had taken place in the past, and was going on in the present.

Other names for God
According to Exodus 6:3, Abraham and the others of that generation did not know God by the personal name Yahweh, but instead worshipped a God called 'El Shaddai' (Genesis 17:1). However, the name Yahweh is actually used in the narratives right from the beginning of the story, and is expressly said to have been given to Abraham and Sarah as the name of the God who led them out of Mesopotamia (Genesis 15:7). In addition, Israel's early ancestors are often said to have worshipped a deity who is simply called 'the God of the ancestors'.

These differences can be explained by reference to the theory that the first five books of the Old Testament were compiled from a number of different sources, one of which used the name Yahweh from the very beginning and another not introducing it until the time of Moses. But others have suggested that the matter is not quite as straightforward. They draw attention to four features in particular:
● The research of Albrecht Alt has shown that the worship of gods identified as 'the

some of God's characteristics insofar as they can be illustrated by reference to what we know and experience in human relationships. Emphasizing some aspects of the picture at the expense of others will inevitably lead to grotesque distortions. By concentrating on any one of them to the exclusion of the others, it is easily possible to misrepresent what is being said here. The sense of reverence and wonder expressed

---

god of the ancestors' was widespread among many tribes in the ancient world.

● We also know that the name 'El' was widely used as a name for local gods. The Ugaritic texts depict El as the father of the gods and head of the pantheon, though there were many local manifestations of this same deity.

● Moses apparently knew nothing of the worship of Yahweh until his meeting with Jethro in the desert of Midian. It was certainly in that area that Moses had his experience at the burning bush (Exodus 3:1–6), and it is notable that after the exodus from Egypt, Jethro reappears in the story and offers a sacrifice to Yahweh (Exodus 18:10–12).

● When Joshua and his people enter into a solemn agreement to worship only Yahweh, it is stated that both in Mesopotamia and in Egypt their ancestors had worshipped other gods (Joshua 24:14–15).

These apparently diverse facts can be explained in a variety of ways. Some have proposed that the worship of El and worship of Yahweh were originally quite distinct and separate. El was identified by the patriarchs with the high god of Canaan, of whom we know from other sources, and Yahweh was originally the mountain god of the Kenites, whose worship was adopted and reformed by Moses on the basis of the exodus experience. Then, eventually, either in the days of the judges or during the later monarchy, the worship of Yahweh became dominant and took over its more primitive predecessor. Others, however, take a different line, arguing that all these names (and others) used for God by the patriarchs referred to the one deity who was later

called Yahweh. To speak of 'the god of the ancestors' would then be just another way of referring to 'El', and 'Yahweh' was the way to address this one God in the context of worship.

This second view has more to commend it, not only because it is closer to the overall theological stance of the Old Testament itself, but also because it recognizes the reality of the fact that early Israel emerged from a religious context that was essentially diverse and syncretistic. There is plenty of evidence to show that the Old Testament was never averse to taking over both imagery and ideas from other religious contexts, just as long as it could be useful in giving authentic expression to Yahweh's known personality and behaviour. In suggesting that the earliest ancestors used traditional ideas from their cultural environment when thinking and speaking about their own experiences of God, the Old Testament's editors were not meaning to diminish Yahweh's power, but to enhance it, by demonstrating that Yahweh was able to do all that the Canaanite El was supposed to do, and much more besides. Whether the people knew it or not, it was none other than the God of the exodus – Yahweh – who had been the guiding force in the life of their nation from the very beginning.

by people in the presence of God will always seem to be in tension with passages that describe God in terms of intimate family relationships. But it is a creative tension, because the gap between God's perfect being and the imperfect world of humanity, which it apparently implies, is bridged by God's loving actions in saving and blessing. In order to make sense of that, it is essential to understand God not as an unseen force or an abstract will, but in personal terms, with all the ambiguities that that involves.

When God is absent

The Old Testament is dominated by the conviction that God's character is revealed most fully in dealings with people, both in history and in personal experience. It is in the common round of everyday life that people meet God. The fact that God is related to the world in which we all live, rather than being relegated to some esoteric, 'heavenly' world, is one of the great strengths of the Old Testament faith, though it can also look like one of its greatest weaknesses. For the plain fact is that we do not normally see events such as the exodus taking place all around us – nor do many of us have experiences similar to that of Isaiah when he stood in awe before God's glory in the Temple (Isaiah 6:1–7). So how realistic and relevant is the Old Testament's picture of God?

As with other aspects of its message, the Old Testament is more subtle and sophisticated than it can be made to seem. The triumphalist view of God's activity in history and personal experience is by no means the only element in its picture of God. God's hiddenness was no less a problem to people in the Old Testament world than it can be today. At the very time when they needed God's assistance to make sense of life, people often found it most difficult to find any traces of divine activity. The facts of history did not always portray the inevitable progress of an all-powerful God, nor did the facts of everyday life always give Israel the assurance that a living and personal God stood alongside them. There were times when life seemed to be quite the opposite, with evil and suffering as the dominating influences of human existence. How then did God relate to this darker side of life? Was Yahweh a God for bad days as well as for good?

The Old Testament takes full account of the fact that there are times when it seems that God, far from being powerful and active, is lost in the depths of human pessimism and despair. This honest recognition of God's apparent absence from the scene is most striking in the book of Psalms, which provide a series of fascinating glimpses into the life of a nation at prayer. Many psalms are great celebrations of joy and optimism, telling the people of God's mighty works and great love for them, and these psalms would no doubt be the ones that were used with enthusiasm at the great religious festivals, as Israel looked back on the major events of their history and traced God's goodness in them. But for every jubilant psalm there are two or three others in which the worshippers express not joy, but sorrow and dismay. Even those with a quiet confidence in God often recognize that spiritual meaning has to be sought in times of 'deepest darkness' (Psalm 23:4), while others complain that life's realities seem inconsistent with the reports of God's mighty deeds in the past (Psalm 44).

Hermann Gunkel's classification of the psalms into five main types has already been highlighted in a previous chapter, and it is significant that only two of these five categories celebrate the triumphs of God in an unreserved way. The other three are all concerned to varying degrees with the fact that God's activity and presence were not always obvious. Indeed, when the psalms are categorized using Gunkel's system, there turn out to be far more of the individual songs of lament than of any other type. Other poems included in this collection express the feelings of the whole nation, as it tried to come to terms with the difference between the great promises that God had made and the less thrilling realities of ordinary life. There is a strong thread of moral and religious realism running through the whole fabric of the Old Testament; God's apparent absence from the world and from human experience is one of its major themes.

When disaster struck, did it indicate that God was impotent or not interested in intervening?

Personal alienation

This is prominent even in the most striking Old Testament stories. Although Abraham, for example, is indeed depicted as someone of great faith who 'put his trust in the Lord' (Genesis 15:6), he also found God's intentions so puzzling and so difficult to reconcile with what he believed about God's character that he was even found arguing with God about it all (Genesis 18:16–33). Moses' experience is quite similar. He is described as having a closer and more direct experience of God than any other Old Testament character, for 'Yahweh used to speak with Moses face to face, as one speaks to a friend' (Exodus 33:11) – but at the same time, Moses' life was full of questions and complaints, as he tried to reconcile God's promises with what he saw going on around him (Exodus 5:22–23).

Nor are the prophets exempt from feelings of doubt and uncertainty about God's intentions. Elijah, for example, won a great and famous victory in the name of God, as the prophets of Baal were put to flight and their specious beliefs were repudiated (1 Kings 18:1–40). But almost immediately after that, it seemed as if God had deserted him, and Elijah suffered an extraordinary attack of uncertainty and doubt about the reality of God's power (1 Kings 19:1–18). For Jeremiah, doubt and uncertainty were a major influence in his life. On the one hand, God had explicitly told him, 'I chose you before I gave you life, and before you were born I selected you to be a prophet to the nations' (Jeremiah 1:4), and he had on many occasions been assured of God's continuing love and protection. Yet, on the other hand, God seemed singularly reluctant to back him up, and a quarter of a century after Jeremiah had first announced the doom of Jerusalem, nothing had happened except that a new mood of national optimism and self-confidence had swept over the city. In the light of that, Jeremiah had to question God's ways: 'Why are wicked people so prosperous? Why do those who are dishonest succeed?' (Jeremiah 12:1). At another time he even wondered why God allowed him to be born at all: 'Was it only to have trouble and sorrow, to end my life in disgrace?' (Jeremiah 20:18). Of course, the prophet knew that God had indeed spoken to him, but that did not make it any easier to come to terms with God's apparent remoteness. The passages in which Jeremiah addresses his complaints to God (the 'confessions', Jeremiah 11:18–23; 12:1–6; 15:10–21; 17:14–18; 18:18–23; 20:7–18) are remarkable for their frankness, and show the depths of despair and questioning to which even those with a personal knowledge of God in their lives can be driven.

National despair

It was not only individuals who often had to look hard to find God at work in their lives. The whole Jewish nation found itself in a similar crisis after the fall of Jerusalem to the Babylonian king Nebuchadnezzar in 586 BC. A once-proud nation had been brought to its knees by events that shattered all their expectations of God. Looking to the past, they could recall God's gracious actions through previous leaders of their nation, as they reminded themselves of God's unfailing promises to earlier generations. But what value could be placed on such a glorious past in the light of the harsh realities of exile in a strange land? The promises had apparently failed, and evidence of God's involvement with the people was now hard to find.

Much of the Old Testament story was hammered into shape on the anvil of this experience. Its pages often reflect the deeply felt anguish of those who survived this great tragedy, as they asked the inevitable question, Why should this have happened in a world controlled by God? In response to that the deuteronomic history asserted quite plainly that national disgrace was the outcome of national wrongdoing. But in looking to the past it did not give a simplistic explanation of the present. For although it emphasized God's great goodness in events such as the exodus, or the establishment of David's throne in Jerusalem, it also reminded them that there had been many a crisis in the past too. The exodus itself had been God's answer to a critical situation faced by the enslaved tribes in Egypt. God can hardly have seemed very real to them in Egypt – but one of the lessons of history was that God's mighty power had often burst in to change the lives of those who were least expecting it.

There could be no doubt that the exiles were suffering as a result of their nation's disobedience. A God whose character was defined in terms of justice and moral standards could not easily turn a blind eye to the rotten state of Jewish society. But though it might seem as if the stringency of

God's justice was greater than the power of God's love, nevertheless the promises could still be trusted and in the end would bring blessing upon the people. This was the view that finally triumphed and transformed the dead husks of exile into the seed corn of new life. Just as in the experience of the prophets and of people such as Job, so here there is no real effort to explain why God seemed to be hidden from the people at their time of dire need. But there is a clear practical message for those who found it difficult to see God at work in their lives. As men and women contemplated the suffering and injustice of their present existence, they were forced to confess that God really is different from humankind, dealing in apparently inscrutable ways. Yet alongside this they could place the evidence of God's

Wrestling with a hidden God

The apparent hiddenness of God is a major theme of one of the great masterpieces of the Old Testament: the book of Job. The book itself begins with an idyllic description of the life of its hero who was a successful man in every respect, surrounded by the material trappings of prosperity, as well as by an affectionate family group. He was also exceedingly upright and religious, and his lifestyle and disposition both show him as a paradigm of virtue. But then things change. God, depicted here as the president of a heavenly court, receives a formal request from the prosecutor (Satan) who suggests that Job is righteous only because he finds that it pays handsome dividends. So the prosecutor is given permission to put him to the test in order to ascertain the value of his faith. One calamity after another comes upon Job and his family, until he is reduced to misery and poverty – the exact opposite of his circumstances at the beginning (Job 1:1 – 2:10).

This ancient story serves the purpose of setting the scene for what is the main theme of the book, namely an extended discussion among Job and his friends about the nature of evil. The book of Job belongs to the wisdom literature of the Old Testament, and its main concern was to answer the questions that were raised by the story: If God rules the world, why do good people suffer so much? Wisdom teachers from Babylon to Egypt and

beyond had wrestled with this problem long before the author of Job, but two things gave it special urgency in Israel: Israel believed that God was active in controlling the life of this world, and Israel also believed that God acted in accordance with strict concepts of morality. The standard answer to the problem was easy, and is in fact represented in some other wisdom books, notably Proverbs: those who were prosperous must be good, and those who suffered must be evil. But it is often difficult to reconcile that with the facts, especially in the case of a person like Job. Of course, his friends were incapable of understanding that, and though they sympathized with Job in his suffering they were quite sure that – regardless of what he thought – he must have sinned against God and brought his suffering on himself. Job knew that he had not done so, and was convinced that the simplistic theology of his friends was quite misguided, even though that in itself did not make it any easier for him to see God at work in his own life: 'I have searched in the east, but God is not there, nor have I found any trace when I searched in the west' (23:8). But he never abandoned his certainty that, though it may be hard to discern, 'God has been at work in the north and the south' (23:9). Indeed, it was worse than just being blind to God's purpose, for it was God's very hiddenness that concerned Job most of all: 'It is God, not the dark, that makes me afraid' (23:17).

The meaningless cycle of Job's

mighty acts in history and in personal experience, both of which gave the assurance that though God may be hidden by the gloom of present experience, that did not mean the world had been abandoned to its fate, for to those who kept the faith the future would offer something even more glorious than what had been lost.

How can God be known?

Finally, we must turn briefly to consider some of the assumptions behind the Old Testament's view of God's relationship to people. Two themes are especially important here.

Wrestling with a hidden God
continued

existence is eventually broken when, after more conventional wisdom from his friends, God personally confronts the sufferer in a great storm (38:1 – 40:2; 40:6 – 41:34), something which reminds Job of God's greatness and might by drawing his attention to the complexity of the world and its workings. In the face of this, Job can place his own questions in their proper perspective: 'I know... that you are all-powerful; that you can do everything you want' (42:2). But what is the answer to the main question? Certainly there is no intellectual discussion here of the presence and power of evil in the world. But it is typical of the Old Testament that even a topic such as this should not be dealt with in an abstract, philosophical way. God is known to humankind not in flights of fancy, but in the reality of divine encounter. Job had appealed to God to answer him, and that is what happened – not in a way that he might have expected, but in a way that ultimately reminded him that, however difficult it might be to understand life's bitterest experiences, and however hard it might be to perceive God at work, nevertheless God was there, and to those who were prepared to seek diligently (unlike the friends who looked for easy answers) God would ultimately be revealed.

Another Old Testament book which tackles similar questions is Ecclesiastes, though its answer is very different from Job's. Indeed, it lays so much emphasis on God's apparent absence from the world

that the Jewish rabbis were reluctant to accept it as a part of scripture. Like Job, this book contains no mention of the great events of Israel's history in which God's hand had so clearly been seen. But unlike Job, it has no clear conviction that God's workings can be seen anywhere in the world at all. Job never actually loses sight of God, even if only in the negative sense that he blames God for his misfortune. The writer of Ecclesiastes does not actually deny that God exists (2:24–26; 3:13; 8:15), though the whole book seems to suppose that God's existence is fundamentally irrelevant, for the author is unable to see much evidence of it in the practical issues of everyday living. For Ecclesiastes, life is essentially meaningless in itself, and the most anyone can do is to try to enjoy what they have while they are here to enjoy it. This might seem a very negative attitude to take towards God. But it is more faithful to human experience than the fanciful and unsatisfying theology of Job's friends. The fact is that human life cannot be reduced to simple formulas – nor can faith in God. Not only Ecclesiastes, but also the whole of the Old Testament, bears witness to the fact that a faith which comes too easily has a certain lack of reality. The experience of honest and searching doubt is often the prelude not to a loss of faith, but to a deeper and more satisfying understanding of God's ways.

God's grace

It was not unusual in the ancient world for the gods to be portrayed almost as if they were a race of superhumans. It is of course inevitable that when people talk about God they should use human analogies to do so, and the Old Testament is no exception. It describes God in very bold figures of speech, describing God's hands or eyes, and imagining God crying and laughing, and sharing in other emotions that can be compared to human feelings. But for all that, there is a clear consciousness that in terms of essential being God is quite different from people, and the way God behaves is not simply to be deduced through a rationalization of the way men and women behave. Moreover, God cannot be bullied and cajoled by magic, or blackmailed in any way, and if God becomes known in the lives of men and women it is not because of discoveries made by people, but through initiatives taken by God.

This affirmation is central to the Old Testament faith: all relationships with God are based on God's own actions in grace and love. It is God's intention to be committed to the whole human race, and it is as a means to that end that Abraham and Sarah are chosen (Genesis 12:1–3). In behaving this way, God acts freely, with the only motive being to shower love on the people who live in this world. At every significant point of the story thereafter, the Old Testament emphasizes that God's own gracious actions are the starting point for any kind of meaningful spirituality. The exodus itself happens because God sees the plight of the slaves and takes pity on them – not because the enslaved tribes ask for it – and individuals can enjoy renewed relationships with God simply as a result of God's own love for them and not because of any inherent claim they might have on God. No one can work up a sense of God's presence for themselves.

Many ancient peoples portrayed their gods as having human characteristics, as if they were a race of super-humans. By contrast, the God of the Old Testament is presented as quite different from human beings. Representations of God were not approved of.

God's word

How then does God communicate? A simple answer would be: through the kinds of mighty acts demonstrated in the history of Israel. There is much truth in this, and the Old Testament often claims that God has been revealed through these things. Indeed, much of the Old Testament's moral law is based on the assumption that the way God acts displays important aspects of God's character. But this answer is not entirely satisfactory by itself. For the escaping slaves, and later generations who shared their perspective, the exodus was the greatest revelation of God's character and will, the crucial event in which God was made known. But what did it mean to the Egyptians? We do not know, of course, for Egyptian annals nowhere mention such an event. But it is quite certain that the exodus was not for them a means of divine encounter in which the God Yahweh met them and changed their national history. Something else was needed to transform the bare happenings of history into a message from God. This is always the way, of course. The 'bare facts' of history only gain significance when they are placed in an appropriate context. A historian does not simply record isolated incidents from the past, but tries to explain them in relation to other incidents, in order to make sense out of what has taken place. The Old Testament does the same, and what makes its story so distinctive is the interpretation that is given to the events it describes. As historians and prophets looked back to the nation's past they did not view it as just a historical chain of cause and effect, but saw in it the evidence that God had been at work in person.

If that was the end of the story, we might conclude that the Old Testament faith was little more than a historian's theory – a neat way of giving coherence and meaning to a rather amorphous collection of events that had happened at different times and places over many generations. But there is more to it than that. For the prophets did not interpret the history of their people in retrospect: they claimed to announce it before it took place. When Amos issued his scathing denunciations of Samarian society, and declared that it would soon come to an end, there was no sign of such an end. Indeed, the nation was enjoying a period of prosperity unparalleled at any other time in its history, either before or after. When Jeremiah announced the doom of Jerusalem, the mood of self-satisfaction that was sweeping the city led people to regard him as a madman. But they – and the other prophets – persisted with their message because they were convinced that what they were saying was the word of God to their people. The earlier story of the exodus was no different, for Moses himself is portrayed as a prophet – indeed, the greatest of all prophets according to Deuteronomy 34:10–12 – announcing the exodus while the people were yet in slavery. It is difficult for today's people to grasp this, and still more difficult to understand it, but it is an essential part of the Old Testament's picture of God. The Old Testament never claims to be able to fathom all the depths of God's personality, and there are many aspects of God's work that can never be fully understood. But this one conviction runs throughout all its writings: that the living God is not a static being, remote and irrelevant to the lives of ordinary people, but a God who acts and a God who speaks in order that men and women might have a full and meaningful relationship with God's own person and also with one another.

10 God and the World

Discovering God in nature and history

In the last chapter, we saw that God's most characteristic method of communication in the Old Testament was through the events of history: the exodus from Egypt, the establishment of David's royal city in Jerusalem – even the exile. When correctly understood and explained, all these things told the people of ancient Israel what God was really like. It would be misleading, however, to think that the spirituality of the Hebrew Bible is concerned exclusively with the events of Israel's history. While the heart of its message is certainly to be found in the stories that begin with the nation's forebears, Abraham and Sarah, and end with Judah's exile in Babylon, this by no means exhausts all that it has to say. The stories contained in the first eleven chapters of the book of Genesis, most of the psalms and all the wisdom books are only loosely related to the great themes of Israel's salvation history. Far from being narrowly concerned only with the experiences of Israel, these books in particular deal with the universal experience of men and women everywhere as they try to come to grips with the world in which they live. Moreover, these particular parts of the Old Testament have many close connections with the religious literature of other nations of the time. Their central concern is not with the unique and unrepeatable experience of Israel. Instead, they place God's activities in an international perspective, and suggest that Israel's spirituality is of such a character that Yahweh's claim over people's lives extends well beyond any single ethnic or racial grouping. Significant evidence of the God of whom the Bible speaks can be discerned in the very stuff of which the world is made, which means that the call to faith issued by the prophets and others is of correspondingly universal application.

It has often been supposed that an interest in this kind of creation-centred spirituality developed only at a relatively late date in the evolution of the Hebrew scriptures. It is certainly true that many aspects of Old Testament faith were worked out in their final detail only during the years following the Babylonian exile (which began in 597 BC). The majestic poetry of Isaiah 40–55 certainly reflects that period, and one of its most striking features is of course the imagery with which it celebrates God's power over the world of nature. Some of this language, together with that found in the creation story of Genesis 1:1 – 2:4, seems to have connections with traditional Mesopotamian stories of how the world was made, and for that reason scholars have suggested that during this period the originally narrow basis of Israel's faith was expanded, and the emphasis moved away from God's acts in history at a time when God seemed to be doing very little for this particular people. This view has been widely accepted and frequently repeated, but it is far too simplistic. Without doubting that some of the Old Testament's most sophisticated thinking about God and creation may well have been more fully articulated during the exile, there are a number of factors which clearly suggest that an understanding of God's relationship to the natural world was an important part of Israel's life long before that:

■ Most of the psalms reflect the worship and liturgy of pre-exilic Israel. They show quite clearly that Yahweh was worshipped as the creator of the world long before Israel had any first-hand dealings with Babylon. There is no creation story as such in the psalms, but creation imagery (often drawn from the common literary heritage of Canaan and Mesopotamia) is used so often that belief in God as creator was obviously a fundamental theme of worship in the Temple at Jerusalem.

■ We also know that the role of deities in relation to the natural world was a recurring theme throughout the spiritual environment in which

The Israelites began to discover the character of God in their time as nomads in the wilderness. But the discovery continued as they settled in the fertile land of Canaan and began to live an agricultural life.

Israel emerged as a nation. The texts from Ugarit may not contain a fully developed Canaanite creation story comparable with those found in ancient Babylon, but all the activities of the Canaanite gods and goddesses were related to the workings of the natural world. One of the key questions debated throughout the history of both Israel and Judah was whether Baal or Yahweh was in control of the natural world. It is inconceivable that those who were responsible for formulating Israel's world-view should have waited for half a millennium before giving an answer to that question. As the Old Testament story unfolds, one of its major concerns is to understand how Yahweh, the God of the exodus, could relate to the demands of life in a settled agricultural community. The prevailing popular view was that the world of nature and the world of the gods were one and the same, which is why the actions of gods such as El or Baal could be understood as a way of giving meaning to the mysterious workings of the world of nature in which Palestinian farmers had to eke out a precarious living. Was Yahweh only a God of history – and did that mean the natural world was controlled by deities such as Baal and Anat? The story of Elijah shows that this was a pressing issue as early as the ninth century BC (1 Kings 17:1 – 19:18). A hundred years later the prophet Amos denounced the behaviour of non-Israelite people in a way that would only have made sense on the basis of a coherent set of beliefs about God's relationship as creator to the whole of the natural world (Amos 1:3 – 2:3).

■ Similar questions must also have presented themselves on a personal level. After all, only one relatively small group of people had witnessed the amazing events of the exodus and the conquest of the land. Not many had any direct contact with the great promises made to David. And, mercifully, few had been left in Jerusalem to witness its final humiliation at the hands of Nebuchadnezzar. If these were the key events in which God was most clearly revealed to the people, then what chance was there that others might hear God's voice? Though the great events of the past could be celebrated in regular religious festivals, the fact was that the everyday experience of ordinary people was more closely tied to the world of nature than to the world of great and unrepeatable historical events. That in itself must have required the development of some coherent belief about the relationship between Israel's God and the natural world.

■ From as far back as the call of Abraham and Sarah, the Old Testament suggests that God's intervention in Israel's history was to be a means to the salvation of all nations (Genesis 12:1–3). This insight was clearly central to Hebrew faith, and is underlined by all the great prophets. It was frequently misunderstood, of course, and the easygoing national optimism that often dominated popular thinking in both Israel and Judah all too readily led people to conclude that other nations were of no concern at all to God. But to overcome such misunderstanding, it must have been necessary to know precisely how Israel was related to other nations. The stories of creation are the only parts of the Old Testament to answer that question.

■ Significant parts of the Genesis stories were certainly composed long before the exile in Babylon, for their imagery, and the assumptions made about the countryside and the moods of the weather, clearly point to a Palestinian background (Genesis 2:4–25).

In the light of all these considerations, it makes sense to conclude that belief in God as the creator was a significant and integral part of Israelite faith from relatively early times. Like other aspects of that faith, it developed and matured as time passed. But one of its underlying assumptions was that 'The world and all that is in it belong to Yahweh' (Psalm 24:1). Its importance is further emphasized by the fact that this subject is introduced in the opening page of Genesis, the first book of the Hebrew scriptures. It is reasonable to suppose that the writers and editors of the Old Testament would begin by outlining some of the most fundamental aspects of their faith.

Thinking about the world

The first eleven chapters of the book of Genesis in fact comprise one of the most important sections of the entire Old Testament. In the stories of creation, the fall, Cain and Abel, the flood and the tower of Babel, we have a concise summary of the underlying infrastructure of biblical spirituality. Such basic themes as the character of God, the nature of the world and the meaning of human existence are presented here with an imaginative subtlety that has given these chapters a place among the great classics of world literature. Yet we need be neither theologians nor literary critics to grasp their message, for like the parables of Jesus, these stories have a universal appeal to people in all times and places. They speak to the deepest needs of men and women, and give an honest answer to questions that have perplexed the world's greatest thinkers.

Understanding the Genesis stories

It is all the more surprising, then, that these early chapters of Genesis should have become a subject of such great controversy. Yet it can hardly be denied that in the last 200 years or so they have been the focus of so many complex debates that ordinary Bible readers are often at a loss to know what to do with them. Extensive studies have been written in the effort to find an appropriate way to understand them, and anything that we can say here must inevitably be brief and incomplete. But two things may be taken as basic for a satisfactory understanding:

■ Ever since Charles Darwin published his *Origin of Species* in 1859, the Genesis creation story has been used by the protagonists in many debates about science and religion. Scientists imbued with a materialistic world-view have sometimes claimed that these chapters demonstrate the naïvety of religious belief, while fervent believers have just as often replied that the creation stories prove the inadequacy of modern scientific endeavour. In some Christian circles, it has been taken for granted that Christian doctrine requires these chapters to be understood as a scientific account of the origins of the universe. This position in turn inevitably sets the Old Testament at variance with the findings of science, and identifies a biblical faith with what most people would regard as an outmoded view of how the world works. In dealing with this, it is important to realize that all this is a fairly recent development, and earlier generations of Bible scholars were much less inclined to try to force the book of Genesis into the straitjacket of a scientific textbook. Even to scientists as long ago as the sixteenth century, it seemed unlikely that there could be waters above the sky in the way that seemed to be implied by a literal understanding of the statement that the dome of the sky ('firmament') was separating 'the water under it from the water above it' (Genesis 1:6–7). John Calvin was no liberal, but in his *Commentary on Genesis* he agreed with this opinion, describing such a notion as 'opposed to common sense, and quite incredible', and going on to dismiss the idea that the Genesis story was supposed to be any kind of scientific account: 'to my mind, this is a certain principle, that nothing is here treated of but the visible form of the world. He who would learn astronomy, and other recondite arts, let him go elsewhere.' Calvin was quite clear that reading the Old Testament as if it was a book of science could only confuse and distort its essential message. The Old Testament writers, he argued, simply took for granted the sort of world-view that was widely held in their day. This assumed that the world was like a flat disc, set upon pillars below, with the sky arching over it like a dome. They never discussed whether this was scientifically correct or not: it was unnecessary for them to do so, for that was not why they were writing. Calvin described details such as this as only props on the main stage – background detail to reinforce the fact that the Old Testament's message was relevant to the world in which ordinary people lived.

■ The message, here as elsewhere in the Old Testament, is about God. We have already seen this same phenomenon in considering the meaning of the great events of Israel's history. The story of the exodus, for instance, was recorded not primarily because it happened, but because it demonstrated God's active and loving concern for the people of Israel. Even in the history books, the main emphasis is on theological explanation rather than historical analysis, and the deuteronomic history certainly explains and applies the lessons that were to be drawn from what it records, as do the books of the Chronicler. Genesis itself was a part of this enterprise. Moreover, the Old Testament uses a variety of literary genres to convey its essential message. Historical story is only one of them. The hymns and prayers of the psalms, the sermons of the prophets and the writings of Israel's wisdom teachers all explain important aspects of God's dealings with the world and its people. As the prophets loved to point out, the message ('the word of Yahweh') was the really important thing, not the medium through which it was communicated. Of course, those who do not share the prophets' faith could read the Old Testament histories and see nothing more than a diffuse account of a small and second-rate ancient Palestinian state. It is possible to do the same with the creation stories, and see nothing but an apparently factual account of the doings of two people in a garden full of plants and animals. At a more sophisticated level, we might join those scholars who have thought of these stories as a collection of folk tales designed to answer such everyday questions as why snakes have no legs, why weeds grow in fields, or why in ancient Israel it was better to be a shepherd than a farmer. But if these are the only things we see as we read the book of Genesis, then we have missed the most crucial points that its authors and editors were intending to make. For they were not concerned with the needs of ancient farmers, nor even with

Genesis in its context

The Assyrian emperor Ashurbanipal is shown on this relief hunting lions. The library that he created at Nineveh is one of our major sources of information about the ancient world.

Towards the end of the nineteenth century, archaeologists uncovered the library of the seventh-century BC Assyrian emperor Ashurbanipal. Politically, he was a failure, but his library survived and is one of our major sources of knowledge of the world in which Israel and Judah struggled for survival. It was written on cuneiform tablets, which are virtually indestructible: flat bricks of river mud inscribed with a wedge-shaped stick

while still soft, and then baked hard in the heat of the sun. The contents of these stories were ancient even in Ashurbanipal's day, and go back almost to the dawn of civilization.

As these tablets were deciphered, it soon became apparent that stories of creation and a great flood had circulated in ancient Babylon long before the Old Testament was written. In a wave of enthusiasm for new discoveries, the scholars who first studied these texts concluded that the Old Testament stories were derived from them, and were therefore of relatively little independent value. Things have changed a lot since then, and modern experts are now far less confident that a direct line of descent can be traced from the Babylonian documents to the stories in Genesis. One of the main reasons for this has been the more recent discovery of other religious texts from the Canaanite stronghold of Ugarit, which tell the stories of Baal and other Canaanite deities, and have shown that in many crucial respects Canaanite religion was rather different from its Babylonian counterpart. Though the precise connection between Ugarit and Israel is itself uncertain, it stands to reason that the religious context in which the Hebrew Bible developed must have had more in

some kind of primitive sociology, but with God. Just as Jesus often explained important aspects of his message by using the familiar experiences of everyday life, so the book of Genesis starts from the common experiences of human life, and goes on to show how God can relate to both the joys and the miseries of the world and its people.

The stories as literature

The Old Testament is a library of many different kinds of literature. In its pages we find not only history, but also law, drama, poetry, sermons, political tracts and much more. They are all held together by their common conviction that God is at the centre of all human life and activity. But before the significance of any particular passage can be fully appreciated, we must obviously decide what sort of literature we are dealing with. We would not read a political tract in the same way as we might read legal documents, while the kind of analytical judgment

---

common with such Canaanite beliefs than with the developed religious traditions of ancient Babylon. As a result, scholars now find it far more productive to compare the Old Testament with what we know of the religion of Ugarit.

Imagery from other religions

Many ordinary readers of the Bible may feel uneasy with the idea that it contains materials connected with the documents of other religions, but in fact this kind of religious borrowing is found not only in the stories of creation and the flood, but in many other parts of the Old Testament as well. The wisdom books contain teachings that are often very similar to ideas found in the wisdom literature of Egypt and elsewhere, and much of Israel's case law resembles the precepts of other nations. Parallels like that are perhaps to be expected, for they concern matters of morality and social organization that are common to people all over the world. It is perhaps more surprising to discover that the Old Testament's religious imagery is also quite similar to the language used of other deities. The Old Testament's language of sacrifice was essentially the same as that used in Ugarit, while the psalms in particular utilized many concepts that were by no means exclusive to Israel:

● For instance the statement that the temple hill in Jerusalem is 'in the far north' (Psalm 48:2) has puzzled many people, for Jerusalem was not in the north, but right in the middle of the country. But the Hebrew word for 'north' is virtually identical to the Ugaritic word 'Zaphon', and in the stories of Baal Mount Zaphon is frequently mentioned as the traditional home of the gods. So, when the psalmist penned these words, it is almost certain the intention was not that this should be understood as a (false) geographical statement about the location of the Temple, but rather as a claim that whatever was supposed to happen at Mount Zaphon was actually taking place on Mount Zion. There are other references to this home of the gods in Isaiah 14:13, and perhaps also in Psalm 89:12.

● Psalm 46:4 speaks of 'a river that brings joy to the city of God'. Again, there is no actual river in Jerusalem, but this statement makes perfectly good sense in light of the fact that the same imagery was used throughout the ancient world to illustrate the life-giving powers of divine beings. In a scene from the palace at Mari, for example, the king is shown being invested by a god, and in one corner two figures stand holding a vase containing the tree of life, from which

required to understand history would be quite out of place in the more aesthetic world of poetry and drama. So how can we classify these early stories in Genesis?

GENRE

Many books on the Old Testament refer to these passages as 'myths'. Though it has a long and venerable heritage in literary criticism, the way in which this term is used in ordinary speech today means that it is not a particularly helpful word to apply in this context. Most people think of a myth as something that is untrue. Literary scholars, of course, do not normally use it in this sense, but even they have no agreed definition of it and it is commonly used to mean at least three different things:

■ A myth can be simply a story about gods and goddesses and their doings, described as if they were human beings. There are many examples of this in Greek and Hindu mythology.

Genesis in its context
continued

comes a stream, dividing into smaller streams, and so dispensing the blessing of the gods among the people. The same theme is taken up and developed further in Ezekiel 47:1–12, where the stream that flows from the Temple in Jerusalem transforms the life of everything that comes in contact with it.

● In many passages celebrating God's triumphant power, Yahweh is depicted as winning battles over the sea and various monsters which lived in it. Some of these passages depict unruly waters which are threatening to bring chaos into the world that God has made (Psalms 18:15; 29:3–4, 10–11; 77:16–18; 93:3–4; Habakkuk 3:8), while others speak of monsters emerging from the unruly depths to challenge God's power (Job 7:12; Psalms 74:12–14; 89:10; Isaiah 27:1). These are obviously allusions to incidents that must have been well known to the people of ancient Israel, though the Old Testament nowhere contains a simple descriptive account of them. For that we need to look elsewhere, for these references to a battle between God and the powers of the sea are drawn from the general religious ideas of the time, rather than belonging uniquely to the Old Testament faith. Some of the closest parallels can be found in the texts from Ugarit. For example, when Isaiah speaks of Yahweh using a 'powerful and deadly sword to punish Leviathan, that wriggling, twisting dragon, and to kill the monster that lives in the sea' (Isaiah 27:1), the wording is virtually identical to a text that speaks of Baal: 'You have killed Lotan the primeval dragon, you have seen off that twisting snake, the powerful one with the seven heads.' Other Old Testament passages attest the belief that such monsters had multiple heads (Psalm 74:13–14), and that they could be called Rahab as well as Leviathan (Psalm 89:10; Isaiah 51:9).

After the outspoken prophetic condemnation of Canaanite religion, it might seem surprising that the Old Testament itself would use such language. Some have taken this to imply that Israelite spirituality was nothing like as distinctive as the prophets wanted to make it, and that this imagery is actually evidence that ancient Israel had a highly developed nature mythology in which Yahweh played much the same role as the Canaanite Baal. There is, however, no real evidence for that, either historical or religious, and the way these materials have been adapted for Israelite use is actually far more subtle. In

■ Myth can also be a technical term for what takes place during a religious rite. In ancient Babylon, for instance, the annual New Year Festival was the most important religious event of the year. Here, the Babylonian story of creation would be recited, while the king acted out the story as it was told. The recitation was a 'myth', to accompany the 'ritual' carried out by the king.

■ Yet others use the term 'myth' to describe a story which expresses a truth about human life that cannot adequately be described in terms of science or history. In this sense, myth is as valid and respectable a way of thinking about life's deepest meaning as science, art, or philosophy. This is the type of 'myth' scholars usually have in mind when they use this term in relation to the Genesis creation narratives.

The trouble is that, with so many possible meanings, 'myth' has become a very slippery term, and for that reason alone is unlikely to be of much

---

ancient thinking, the waters of chaos were essentially personifications of the natural forces that seemed to bring productive life to a standstill at the end of each season, though in the Hebrew scriptures this imagery is either set very clearly in the context of God's firm control over the powers of nature (Psalms 74:12–17; 95:5; 135:5–7; Isaiah 51:15–16), or else is given a completely different reference altogether by being used to describe and celebrate the great events of Israel's history. In particular, the waters of chaos are often transformed into the waters of the Reed Sea, controlled by Yahweh to allow the people to escape from Egypt (Psalm 77:16–20; Isaiah 51:9–11), and the monsters become symbols of the more tangible enemies with whom Israel had to deal throughout their troubled existence (as in Isaiah 27:1). In other words, the imagery seems to have been separated altogether from its original context, and in its new setting is given a fresh emphasis which is then used to highlight some of the most distinctive aspects of the Old Testament faith.

A 'Babylonian Genesis'?

The same thing has happened in the early chapters of Genesis, with the stories of creation and the flood. It is natural that here the Old Testament should have many

Kings in ancient times were often portrayed as being anointed by gods or other mythical beings, and so given a special status. Here, a magical figure, possibly a priest dressed in the head and wings of an eagle, is seen anointing the Assyrian king Ashurnasirpal II.

elements in common with other texts of its day, for though the events of history were the unique possession of just one nation, stories of creation were part of the common heritage of all humankind. When the Old Testament describes the world, it does so in conventional terms, but in the process it reinterprets these traditional ideas in such a way that they become a means of articulating its own distinctive beliefs about God.

● **The creation story** (Genesis 1:1 – 2:4)
This has often been compared with an old Akkadian tale called *Enuma Elish*. This was recited in the temple at Babylon on the occasion of the annual New Year Festival, and was a hymn in praise of the

help to us here. In addition, not all the stories in the early chapters of Genesis can easily be accommodated even within these three commonly used definitions of 'myth'. For although many people would be happy to think of the stories of creation and the fall as a kind of 'theology in pictures', the stories of the flood and the tower of Babel seem to have some connection with historical events. Archaeologists have found mud deposits from a number of great floods which swept over the ancient world from 4000 BC onwards, and the description of the tower of Babel recalls towers (ziggurats) that have been unearthed in the same areas of Mesopotamia.

HOW MANY STORIES?

The conventional way of explaining these stories has been to suggest that Genesis is actually a composite document, and what we now have has been put together out of a number of sources. Scholars have

---

Genesis in its context
continued

This Babylonian account of creation tells of a time when nothing existed except the gods and the great Deep. Then a movement took place in the waters and the god Marduk formed first the earth and then the living world.

god Marduk. It tells how at the beginning nothing existed except the dark waters of primeval chaos, personified as Apsu and Tiamat. In their turn they produced a series of other deities representing the various elements of the universe. Later, a revolt against these forces of chaos led by the younger and more active gods brought into existence the ordered world. Apsu was killed by magic, and Tiamat was cut in two, and Marduk used one half of her body to make the solid sky (firmament), and the other to make the flat earth. The gods were then divided between heaven and earth, and people were made to perform menial tasks for the gods. It is unlikely that there was any direct connection between this and the Old Testament account, though there are some superficial similarities. In both, light emerges from a watery chaos, followed by the sky, dry land, sun, moon and stars, and finally people, and after all this the creator or creators rested. There are, of course, many differences, but one of the most significant features is that, even at those points where there is the closest

resemblance, the Genesis account reads as if it is a deliberate undermining of the assumptions of the Babylonian story.

Scholars of an earlier generation often linked the 'raging ocean' of Genesis 1:2 (Hebrew *tehom*) with the Babylonian goddess Tiamat. This is linguistically unlikely, and in addition the Old Testament idea of the raging sea is quite different, with not the least suggestion of a conflict between God and the watery chaos. Instead, 'the power of God' was 'moving over the water' from the very beginning, and the 'great sea monsters' are explicitly said to have been only a part of what God created. The Hebrew word used to describe their creation is carefully chosen, to indicate that God's control over these creatures was quite effortless and in no way the outcome of some cosmic battle. Underlying the Babylonian story is the expectation that this 'raging ocean' would somehow again get the upper hand and plunge things back into chaos. The way to ensure this did not happen, or that order was soon restored, was through the ritual of the Babylonian New Year Festival, acted out annually by king and people. In Genesis, people are empowered to share in God's ongoing creativity, but the Bible story makes it clear that creation itself

often claimed to be able to distinguish not one, but two (or even more) accounts of creation and the flood. The reasons for this have already been fully explored in our earlier discussion about the writing and editing of the Pentateuch. But even supposing that this understanding is correct, it is difficult to see how it can help us to understand what Genesis is trying to say. To explain where an author's materials came from is not the same as explaining the message which the final narrative intends to convey. Unless we read these stories as they are, we are unlikely to make much headway in discovering their meaning.

WHAT KINDS OF STORIES?

If we take the stories of creation and the fall, it is easy to see that the beginning of the story (Genesis 1:1 – 2:4) is quite different in character from its sequel (Genesis 2:4 – 3:24). This is not because they are variant

---

happened once and for all, and the days of creation themselves could not be repeated.

Other aspects of the Babylonian worldview are also questioned here. Astrologers have always believed that the sun, moon and stars have power over people, but that idea is quite specifically undermined in this story by the description of the heavenly bodies as nothing more than 'lights' (Genesis 1:14–18) – and certainly not gods themselves. The understanding of people is also quite different. In many ancient stories, they were created as an afterthought to serve the deities, so that gods would not have to gather their own food. But in the Old Testament women and men are not only central to God's purposes: they are the pinnacle of the whole of creation. Far from being made for God's selfish benefit, God provides other things for theirs – and so the plants and grains are available for food (Genesis 1:29). As in the rest of the Old Testament, the destiny of people is in the hands of a loving and powerful personal God, and not in the control of either nature or superstition.

● **The flood story** (Genesis 6:9 – 9:17) This displays essentially the same characteristics. Neither Egyptian nor Ugaritic literature contains an account of a great flood, but again several such stories have been found in Babylon. The most complete of these is in a poem known as *The Epic of Gilgamesh*. This tells how Gilgamesh, king of Uruk (Erech in Genesis 10:10), shattered by the death of his friend Enkidu, realizes that he himself must soon die and decides to try to find the secret of eternal life. He seeks out his own ancestor Ut-napishtim, who had himself gained immortality, and asks him about it. He is told that first he must get a plant from the bottom of the ocean which will renew his youth. But at this point in the story, the dialogue is interrupted as Ut-napishtim goes on to tell Gilgamesh how he himself had escaped from a great flood. He had been warned by Ea, the god of magic wisdom, that the other gods, especially Enlil, had decided to send the flood. Ut-napishtim was advised to build a boat, which he did. This 'boat' was in fact a large cube, and in important respects was therefore rather different from Noah's 'ark'. After coating this cube inside and out with bitumen, he stocked it with food and brought all his family and belongings into it, together with animals and skilled craftworkers. The storm raged for seven days, at the end of which nothing but water was visible. Twelve days later, Ut-napishtim's 'boat' ran

accounts of the same thing (as some think), but because they are different literary forms. The first section has many close similarities to lyrical expressions that are also found in the psalms, and in certain passages in the book of Isaiah. It is written in an obviously poetic style, with a repetitive refrain, and from a literary standpoint it is a hymn in praise of creation, celebrating God's goodness and concern for every living thing. It takes the observable features of the world, and asserts that God is in control of them all. It is the sort of confession of faith that may well have been formulated and used in the context of worship in ancient Israel, and when we come to consider its message these are the terms in which we need to try to understand it.

What follows is quite different, and the dramatic action takes place in a different setting altogether. No longer is it reported in the measured language of lofty poetry, but with the directness of an expert storyteller. In a straightforward account, we read of how the man and

The Babylonian myths had a story of a Great Flood, parallel in some ways to the story of Noah. It forms part of the Epic of Gilgamesh, and tells of a man whom the gods instructed to make a boat and survive the flood.

woman who enjoyed a perfect relationship with God rejected that relationship, and chose instead to be the controllers of their own destiny. Their choice was simple, but its consequences incalculable, for as the story unfolds the reader soon becomes aware that this is no ordinary story. The garden, the trees and the creatures are all described in superlatives, as befits the momentous implications that stem from the action. For the effects of the human behaviour described here were not restricted to the earliest age of human existence, but were to have repercussions for people at all times and in all places. It is no coincidence that the author names the central actors Adam (meaning 'humankind') and Eve (meaning something like 'humanity'), for the experience of all subsequent generations was enshrined in their act of disobedience. This is why in the first chapter of this book I suggested that these stories could most usefully be categorized as 'faith stories', for they represent theological writing at its

---

Genesis in its context *continued*

aground on a mountain, whereupon he sent out a dove and a swallow in turn, both of which came back. Then he sent out a raven, which did not return as the waters had subsided. When he left the 'boat', he made a sacrifice to the gods, who crowded round like flies to smell it and promised that never again would they send a flood. They then bestowed immortality upon Ut-napishtim and his wife.

Here again, there is no compelling evidence to suggest that the Genesis story is in any way based on the Babylonian account, though once more there are sufficient resemblances to make it likely that both depend on the same general stock of ideas. Where they differ, they do so because the Hebrew story is based on a different understanding of the nature of God. In the Gilgamesh story, no explanation is given for the flood, though in another Akkadian source (the *Atrahasis Epic*), the gods decide to destroy men and women because they are making too much noise! In Genesis, however, God sends the flood as a judgment on human disobedience. Throughout this story the recurring theme is that there is only one God, who (unlike the Babylonian deities) is not afraid of the flood but is in complete control of it. Nor are people

dealt with in an arbitrary way, for the deliverance of Noah is the outcome of his own good behaviour just as the destruction of everyone else is traced to their own misbehaviour. In the Genesis story, morality is at the heart of the character of God, whose dealings with men and women therefore depend solely on verifiable standards of justice and love, rather than on capricious and unpredictable self-interest.

best and most imaginative, simple yet profound. No reader with even a glimmer of aesthetic appreciation can fail to grasp the message that the author is meaning to convey here.

The message of the stories

What then is the message of these chapters? We shall return to some specific aspects later, but the overall theme is well summed up in the refrain repeated throughout the creation hymn: 'God was pleased.' It is not surprising that the composer of the hymn should have repeated this statement so many times, for its implications seem to cut across some of the intuitive spiritual instincts of conventionally religious people. The idea that any kind of embodied existence is incompatible with spiritual enlightenment is a basic assumption of most eastern world-views, and has often been a dominant theme in Christian thinking as well, encouraging people to opt out of the world in the hope that by so doing they would somehow get closer to God. Within the Christian tradition, this understanding owes more to the influence of Greek philosophy than to the teachings of the Bible. Unlike the Greeks, who could regard the body as only a temporary 'prison' for the immortal soul, the Israelites thought of the body, and the whole physical world, as the most natural home for people, and took it for granted that God would most truly be found not beyond the created world, but in it. One of the basic affirmations of the Hebrew scriptures is encapsulated in the opening words of Psalm 24, with its confident declaration that 'The world and all that is in it belong to Yahweh; the earth and all who live on it are God's.' Moreover, the creation stories emphasize that God is directly involved with the life of this world. There is, of course, a tension here, for God is the all-powerful creator whose word alone is sufficient to bring order out of chaos (Genesis 1:3, 6, 9, 11, 14, 20, 24). But in describing the place of men and women within this wonderful creation, God's own personal involvement is always emphasized. God is like a potter, who takes soil from the ground and lovingly forms a human being out of it (Genesis 2:7). Yahweh can never be identified with nature, but is beyond it and above it – yet, at the same time, God is directly involved in the work of creation, thus demonstrating a close concern not only for Israel, but also for people and animals in general, and even for the very stuff out of which the universe is made.

Men, women and God

'What are human beings that you are mindful of them, mortals that you care for them?' (Psalm 8:4). As people compare their own meagre existence with the greatness of the natural world around them, this question often seems to sum up the basic problem of human existence. Why are we here? Some parts of the Old Testament emphasize the apparent insignificance of men and women, referring to life as 'a puff of wind... a passing shadow' (Psalm 144:4), or 'like grass. We grow and flourish like a wild flower; then the wind blows on it, and it is gone' (Psalm 103:15–16). Others reflect a more positive mood, declaring that people are only a little lower than God, 'crowned... with glory and honour' (Psalm 8:5). Yet all would agree that the life of men and women finds its true fulfilment when they are living in personal openness with God. This is why we were made, and no matter how insignificant or powerless a person may feel, they can be sure that God is still interested in their life and experience: 'for those who honour Yahweh, God's love lasts for ever, and God's goodness endures for all generations' (Psalm 103:17). In the Babylonian creation stories people were made last of all, almost as an afterthought on the part of the gods, and always for menial duties. But the Old Testament will have none of this: women and men are the pinnacle and crowning glory of the world and all its affairs. The heart of the Genesis creation stories is to be found in the simple statement that human beings were made 'in the image of God' (Genesis 1:27). When we recall that the Hebrew Bible consistently and expressly forbids making images of God, this may come as a rather unexpected sentiment. But we have previously noticed that the imagery of the Old Testament is always specific and positive, never abstract and philosophical. God's character and personality are described in relation to what God does, and not by reference to some metaphysical speculation about what God might be made of. This is precisely the emphasis that is intended here, and when men and women are described as being 'in God's image' that does not mean that they look like God, or that they are made of the same stuff. It is, rather, a way of saying they are intended to be extensions of God's own personality, and to play a central role in God's own ongoing activity in the world. They are God's representatives. In this claim at least three important ideas are put forward about the relationship between people, the world and God.

In relation to the earth

Men and women are given God's blessing and told: 'Have many children, so that your descendants will live all over the earth and bring it under their control. I am putting you in charge of the fish, the birds, and all the wild animals' (Genesis 1:28). This statement has often been misunderstood, especially by modern Christians who have taken it as a licence to exploit the natural world in any way that is to their benefit. Older Bible translations may have encouraged this, by articulating God's instructions in terms of 'subduing' the earth, and 'having dominion' over its creatures. But the Genesis story implies nothing of this kind – indeed, quite the opposite. The whole point of the story is that God has made a world of order and balance out of a state of chaos, and people are here called upon to maintain and preserve the world as God intends it to be. God has not wound the world up like a mechanical toy, but continues to be actively involved in its workings, changing night to day (Isaiah 45:12; Amos 4:13; 5:8), controlling the sun, moon and stars, the rivers, and giving life to crops and animals (Isaiah 40:26; 48:13). Any human activity which disrupts the life of nature is contrary to the will of God, for God intended there to be a mutual respect and service between people and the world in which they live (Psalm 104:10, 14–15, 27–30). This is strikingly emphasized when Genesis depicts God as a divine potter forming a person out of the ground. There is a subtle play on words here, for the Hebrew word for humankind (*adam*) is very similar to that for ground (*adamah*), and this similarity is used to emphasize that people are a fundamental part of the natural ecosystem in which they live. Men and women are not above nature: they are a part of it, and are responsible to God for the way they care for their world and the other creatures with whom they share it.

In relation to God

Humanity has been given a responsibility by God to maintain and preserve the order of creation and not merely to exploit it. This detail from the Royal Standard of Ur, made about 2500 BC shows farmers and fishing people.

Men and women are distinctive because God can and does speak to them. Though they are intrinsically connected to the world in which they live, that is not the only dimension in which life finds meaning. Indeed, a materialist view which tries to make sense of human existence by only analysing the world of our senses and reason is, in biblical terms, meaningless. Being made 'in God's image' means that people are incomplete without God. They are intended to be in partnership with God, and it is this which gives meaning and direction to life. Communication with God is of vital importance to human satisfaction. It is important to notice that by partnership, the Old

Testament does not mean a kind of conventional religiosity. One of the most striking features of these early stories in Genesis is the way God comes and talks with people, arriving in the evening to discuss with Adam and Eve the affairs of the day (Genesis 3:8). This statement is not to be regarded with embarrassment as either hyperbole or exaggerated anthropomorphism. It is a moving affirmation of the fact that communication between God and people was intended to be delightful and personal, not formal and rigid. In ancient Israel, 'the word of Yahweh' would come to people through many different channels: the priest would interpret the Law (Torah); the wisdom teachers would give advice on everyday affairs; and the prophets characteristically brought either a spoken or acted message from God as a comment on particular situations in the nation's life. But underlying all these modes of communication was the conviction that God and the people related to each other on a personal level. Like the characters in the Garden of Eden, each individual has been made for direct and personal encounter with God.

In relation to each other

There are important lessons here about human relationships to the world and to God, but some of the most striking points of these stories concern relationships between human beings themselves at different levels:

■ *Social relationships* The fact that all human beings are made 'in God's image' implies that all are of equal value and importance. The Bible solves the problems of ethnicity and race by declaring that we all belong to the same race. Israel often found it difficult to grasp that, but the prophets

were adamant that no one race was better than another, and no one group in society was of more importance than another. As far as God is concerned, all men and women are equal. Even though Israel was specially privileged to receive God's Law (Torah), this did not mean that others had

no access to God's will: however imperfectly they might have perceived it, every person knew the difference between basic issues of right and wrong, simply because they were made 'in God's image'.

■ *Sexual relationships* The Old Testament takes a pragmatic view here. There is no hint of the narrow asceticism that has often characterized Christian attitudes to sex. The idea that sexual knowledge only emerged in the context of broken relationships after the fall is clearly contradicted in Genesis.

The life of the market place was never intended to be distinct from the life of worship. Repeatedly the prophets condemned a religiosity which made no difference to everyday behaviour.

Human sexuality is an essential part of God's design for humankind right from the beginning. It is also worth noting that procreation is not the only reason given for this, for while men and women are encouraged to 'Have many children' (Genesis 1:28), considerable emphasis is also laid on the fact that an appropriate sexual partner is also to be 'a suitable companion' (Genesis 2:18). Nor is there any suggestion here that in such a relationship one partner is intrinsically more important than the other: a man is incomplete without a woman, and it is only the two of them together who can work out the full potential of human existence. Sex is a part of God's gift to men and women, something to be enjoyed and developed for its own sake – a point that is made most forcibly by the inclusion in the Old Testament of a book of erotic love poems, the Song of Solomon.

■ *Family relationships* Here, there is again an emphasis on the mutual sharing of one person with another. In the Old Testament world, the patriarchal family was the norm, and in that context men as well as women were often seen as chattels to be disposed of to suit the head of the family. The historical narratives themselves provide many examples of family heads doing just that, but it is striking that in this fundamental exposition of God's intentions for humankind there should be a rather different emphasis. There is nothing here that would give grounds for the exploitation of one sex by the other. On the contrary, there is a very strong emphasis on the mutual commitment of men and women to each other in the context of a committed sexual relationship. Moreover, this relationship takes precedence over all other traditional family commitments, and the book of Genesis issues a stronger challenge to traditional patriarchy than we realize, with its injunction that 'a man leaves his father and mother and is united with his wife, and they become one' (Genesis 2:24).

Broken relationships and new beginnings

The book of Genesis paints an idyllic picture of life in this world, with nature, people and God all working together in perfect harmony and mutual understanding and support. But, of course, life is not like that. Though most people have on occasion glimpsed the idealistic possibilities that are reflected here, human experience is more often marred by exploitation, disharmony and suspicion. The real world is a place of dysfunctional relationships.

The root of the problem

So what has gone wrong? Two stories here answer that question: the story of the fall (Genesis 3:1–24) and the story of the tower of Babel (Genesis 11:1–9). Both of them declare that the reason for human misery is that the delicate balance between people, nature and God has been disturbed. Instead of being content to accept God's values, men and women have tried to set themselves up as controllers of their own destiny. They are not content to accept even the benign guidance of a power greater than themselves. Instead, their chief concern has been to 'make a name for ourselves' (Genesis 11:4) or, as the story of the fall puts it, to 'be like God' (Genesis 3:5). One story expresses this as seeking after the fruit of 'the tree that gives knowledge of what is good and what is bad' (Genesis 2:17; 3:5). The fact that God bans the human pair from

The story of humanity's fall into sin speaks of a breakdown of relationships at every level. There is evidence of this breakdown throughout history, particularly in the cruelty and waste of wars.

eating this fruit has suggested to some that there was all along a built-in unfairness in God's original design. After all, why should God want people to be kept in ignorance like this? But a comment like that misses the point, for elsewhere in the Old Testament, knowing the difference between right and wrong is a phrase that is used with a distinctive connotation. It indicates that a person is yet a child, depending for guidance and direction on their parents (Deuteronomy 1:39; Isaiah 7:14–15). The picture of a child and a parent is often used as an appropriate way of depicting the relationship between people and God. Like a good parent, God has laid down limits within which life can prosper, and when human selfishness tries to overstep these limits, disaster will soon follow. One of the most moving aspects of these stories is the contrast between the world as God intended it to be and the world of broken relationships so familiar to us all. The Bible's understanding of the nature of sin at this point is, of course, quite different from the view taken by many people today. It has often been imagined that the history of the human race is one long story of continuous improvement, as people moved from primitive and savage beginnings to the so-called sophistication of our own day. Probably fewer people today believe that than would have been the case 100 years ago, for the experience of the twentieth century seems to have shown fairly conclusively that people are certainly not improving, and may even be getting worse. Genesis explains it by saying that human life has moved from a position of partnership with God to a position of rebellion – and it traces it all back to the disobedience of the man and woman in Eden who knew God so well.

The results of their disobedience and selfishness are simple.

DISHARMONY IN NATURE
Mutual service and interdependence between people and the natural world is replaced by hostility and mutual distrust (Genesis 3:14–21).

ALIENATION FROM GOD
Instead of meeting God in a close personal relationship, the man and woman do all they can to get out of God's way, and are ultimately sent out of the garden (Genesis 3:8–10, 22–24).

BROKEN SOCIETY
With broken relationships between people, the world and God, even family members can become enemies – and so Cain goes out and kills his brother Abel (Genesis 4:1–16).

Searching for the answer

The people of Israel knew well enough what all this meant in the ordinary details of everyday life, for by the time these stories were finally written down, they were already looking back on a long history which amply illustrated the tragedy of human disobedience. But they had also learned that even when God's judgment was well deserved, God's love could never leave people to languish in the results of their own wrongdoing. These early stories contain a vivid portrayal of broken relationships, but they also have an underlying emphasis on the ever-present possibility of a new beginning. Wrongdoing and disobedience are a tragedy, judgment is inevitable – and well deserved – but God's love and forgiveness for the world and its people will never be defeated. Even in the earliest stories there are hints that God cannot just abandon people. When Adam and Eve feel the need for clothing, God provides it for them (Genesis 3:21). When Cain kills his brother Abel, God condemns him – but then forgives him and takes steps to keep him

Looking to the future

The Old Testament clearly asserts that human existence finds its true fulfilment only in a close personal relationship with God. But where are the boundaries of that relationship to be drawn? Does it end with death – or does it extend further, into an afterlife? To people today this is a natural question to ask. For one thing, we tend to think of people as individuals rather than as a part of some much larger group, and the fate of each person is therefore of considerable importance to us. In addition, we have been nurtured in an environment where popular ideas about death often incorporate the ancient Greek view that a person is composed of two parts: a body, which is mortal and comes to an end, and a soul (or spirit) which is immortal and can last for ever quite independently of the body. Much contemporary New Age spirituality operates on the assumption that the essence of the human personality survives death in some transformed dimension on another plane of existence.

   None of these ideas would have meant very much in the Old Testament context. Although we should not overemphasize the corporate aspect of ancient Hebrew thinking, it is certainly true that Israel generally thought far less in terms of the individual than we do. At the same time, the Old Testament contains not a trace of the bipartite view of human nature that leads to the conclusion that people are souls imprisoned in bodies. For the Old Testament writers, all aspects of human

existence were just different facets of the same reality. Though it might be possible to speak of a person's 'heart', or even their 'spirit', terms of this sort did not refer to independent entities, but were only a graphic way of describing a person's emotions and general motivation. A person's bodily existence could in no way be distinguished from other aspects of the human experience. Within this kind of world-view, death was taken for granted as part of the whole business of human life. It may be regrettable, but was still a perfectly natural thing (2 Samuel 14:14), and there was nothing that anyone either could or should do about it (Job 7:9; Psalm 89:48). Two of the great heroes of the Old Testament story – Joshua and David – express this general view in their final speeches: 'I am about to go the way of all the earth' (Joshua 23:14; 1 Kings 2:2). The author of Psalm 90 defines the human lifespan as 'seventy years... eighty, if we are strong' (Psalm 90:10), while with characteristic coolness the author of Ecclesiastes states that 'For everything there is a season, and a time for every matter under heaven: a time to be born, and a time to die' (3:1–2). When the time comes, 'No one can keep from dying or put off the day of their death. That is a battle we cannot escape' (Ecclesiastes 8:8). Even if we try to understand it, 'no one can tell us what will happen after we die'

Old Testament people accepted death as a natural part of life. But are there some hints of belief in the life hereafter? This Philistine sarcophagus has echoes of a Mycenean death mask.

safe from the vengeance of others (Genesis 4:15). This theme comes to full expression in the story of the great flood. At a time when men and women were so determined to go their own way and disturb the delicate balance of relationships between God and this world, judgment was the only possible answer (Genesis 6:5–8). Yet, even here, God's purpose is not ultimately destructive, and Noah is saved, spared because of God's love, grace and forgiveness – all of which are encapsulated in the promise freely given by God to all humanity and symbolized by the rainbow, which is presented as a sign of God's continuing love even through the worst excesses of human wrongdoing (Genesis 9:8–17).

Looking to the future
continued

The Egyptians certainly believed in life after death. In this papyrus a man's heart is being weighed against a feather, as he prepares for his final journey.

(Ecclesiastes 10:14; 3:22). Of course, Ecclesiastes has its own cynical viewpoint, and we need to make allowances for that in reading these passages. But when they are compared to the rest of the Old Testament, comments of this sort are not altogether unrepresentative. For although many passages seem to allude to the continued survival of dead people, there is no consistent picture. We can trace a number of different emphases in the Old Testament:

● At a popular level, it seems likely that most people just shared much of the superstition of their cultural context in the ancient world. Egyptians and Babylonians, as well as the people of Ugarit in Canaan,

all believed that there was another life after death. The Egyptians made the most elaborate preparations for the comfort of the deceased in this new environment, and it was widely believed that the dead should be given sufficient provisions to ensure a comfortable existence in the hereafter. Just as the pyramids often contained supplies to be used in the afterlife, so tombs discovered at Ugarit were equipped with channels through which living worshippers could continue to pour food and drink to their dead ancestors. Such offerings were often motivated by the view that the dead could influence the lives of the living, and if they were kept well fed then their influence

It is little wonder then that these stories came to form the opening pages of the Hebrew Bible, and thence the Christian Old Testament. In them we have a profound and picturesque summary of all the essential features of the Old Testament faith. Here we meet a God who is both totally different from men and women, and yet deeply involved with them. We are given a glimpse of a world in which people and nature can relate meaningfully to each other, because both of them relate to God. And we see the tragic results that follow when that relationship breaks down. The tragedy is familiar enough to everyone. But the Old Testament has its own diagnosis of the problem. The world is out of

would be good rather than evil. There is evidence of much the same thing in Israel, as for example in Saul's belief that the dead Samuel could somehow affect the course of his own life (1 Samuel 28:3–19). Saul was roundly criticized for this – and other passages also condemn similar reverence for the dead as alien to the true Old Testament faith – though the fact that the prophets needed to keep returning to this theme only serves to emphasize how widespread such a belief must have been (Deuteronomy 26:14; Isaiah 8:19–20; 65:1–5; Ezekiel 43:7–9).

● A more orthodox view suggested that a person could in some way survive through the continuation of their family line. This assumption seems to lie behind the story of the book of Ruth, and is hinted at in many passages which suggest that a person who dies without children to preserve the family name is at a particular disadvantage.

● The most common description of the dead is that they live a shadowy indeterminate existence in a place called Sheol. Sheol is not to be confused with later Christian ideas of heaven and hell, but was a morally neutral term. What actually went on in Sheol was never spelled out in any detail. Sometimes, existence there could be spoken of as an imprisonment, where people would be isolated from God and completely unaware of anything (Job 14:20–22; Psalms 30:9; 88:10–12; 115:17; Ecclesiastes 9:5–6). At other times, God's power might be said to extend even to Sheol (Psalm 139:8; Amos 9:2) – though sentiments of that sort were essentially poetic and rhetorical, more intended to encourage the living to keep trusting God than to make definitive statements about the state of the dead.

● Yet other Old Testament passages have been taken to refer to the idea of resurrection from the dead. The Hebrew Bible contains only one absolutely clear statement of belief in a resurrection, and that is Daniel 12:2. Because of this it is often supposed that the idea of resurrection was a relative latecomer in the Old Testament faith, articulated at a time when the deaths of good people were especially hard to accept – as they were at the time Daniel was written. But this is difficult to

joint because men and women are in revolt against their creator. Human wrongdoing affects both human life and the life of nature; disobedience is a tragedy and wilful neglect of God's values will inevitably lead to judgment. The course of human history has demonstrated all this often enough, but the Old Testament does not leave it there. For it also affirms that God wishes to bring order out of this chaos, to replace alienation with healing, and to ensure that forgiveness and love are always available to those who in childlike simplicity acknowledge their dependence on the creator.

Looking to the future
continued

sustain, and it is more likely that the idea of resurrection emerged naturally from a much earlier period. Some of the oldest poetry in the Old Testament seems to imply resurrection (Deuteronomy 32:39; 1 Samuel 2:6), and there are three stories of resurrections from the dead told in the deuteronomic history (1 Kings 17:17–24; 2 Kings 4:18–37; 13:20–21). Though these stories present other questions, the way they are told suggests that their readers would be familiar with the possibility of resurrection from the dead. The same can also be said about other passages, for instance, Job 19:25–27; Isaiah 53:12; Ezekiel 37:1–14 and Hosea 6:1–3. Some scholars have also argued that the references to Sheol could at least imply resurrection, for existence there is characterized as a sleep in silence and darkness – and in Daniel, resurrection is referred to as an awakening from the sleep of death.

It certainly seems likely that this later articulation of a resurrection belief emerged from the earlier faith of Israel, rather than coming in from some other source, as was once believed. We know that it was the subject of continual argument for a very long time. The deuterocanonical books provide plenty of evidence for an increasing interest in the topic of life after death during the centuries immediately preceding the Christian era, though much later the Sadducees still could not bring themselves to accept that resurrection of the dead was an authentic part of the Old Testament faith, while the Pharisees, and

probably most ordinary people, took a different view. There can be no doubt that the period at the very end of the process of compilation of the Old Testament saw a massive increase in speculation about the subject, mostly connected with the issue of rewards and punishments and no doubt motivated by the knowledge that, following the purge of Antiochus IV, many upright people had suffered in horrendous ways and had apparently not been vindicated. If they had not received the rewards for their faithfulness in this life, then obviously they must be expected to find them somewhere else, presumably therefore in a life to come after the grave. In this context, where resurrection is mentioned it is essentially understood as involving the reversal of physical death, and typically consists of the restoration of the life in this world that was there before, most dramatically illustrated by the story of Razis who, as he was dying, took his entrails in his own hands and dramatically flung them down 'calling upon the Lord of life and spirit to give them back to him again' (2 Maccabees 14:46). This is all quite different from later Christian belief that resurrection life would have a distinctive and different quality from this life, or that resurrection in some way signified the defeat of death, both of which only arose out of the conviction of the earliest Christians that Jesus himself had risen from the dead.

11 Living as God's People

The world-view reflected in the pages of the Old Testament emerged from the corporate history of Israel's people, and this fact alone ensures that the kind of social morality it promotes has a different feel from more speculative systems of spirituality. Though Israel's theologians were constantly questioning and refining their understanding of God, their faith was never merely an intellectual process focused on abstractions about belief and behaviour. At the centre of it all was a strong sense that the people were in relationship with God, and that faith and lifestyle could not, therefore, be separated. Faith was something that could be tested in the affairs of everyday life, and was always expected to make sense in that context. So it is especially important that we reflect on how, in practical terms, Israel was expected to live as God's people.

Belief and behaviour

In traditional societies all over the world, organized religion has provided an almost universal language for people to express their deepest convictions about life. Ancient Israel was no exception to this, and the Hebrew scriptures provide plenty of evidence for carefully structured worship which took place at both local and national sanctuaries and included a wide variety of activities such as prayer, praise and sacrifice. When Israelite people met for organized worship, they were celebrating all that God had done for them not only corporately, but also individually. What the people actually did on such occasions is considered in some detail in the next chapter. But in order to understand the place of ritual in Old Testament spirituality, we need first to paint a much wider picture, for the leading religious activists in both Israel and Judah were constantly emphasizing that what went on in the shrine must never be separated from the way people lived day by day in the market place, on the farm or at home. Indeed some, such as the prophet Micah, could be outspoken in their condemnation of the empty performance of religious rituals, and emphasized instead that true worship of God was quite different and far more demanding: 'Yahweh has told us what is good. What God requires of us is this: to do what is just, to show constant love, and to live in humble fellowship with our God' (Micah 6:8). Most of the prophets made similar statements. So, too, did the history writers, as well as the poets and the wisdom teachers (1 Samuel 15:22; Psalm 51:16–17; Proverbs 21:3). Just as God's actions in history and nature had shown a love and concern that extended to every area of human life, so too every aspect of Israel's experience was to be affected by their commitment to God's values as highlighted and articulated in the covenant. The relationship between God and humankind was to have a moral, as well as a cultic basis. For Israel, that meant the nation's response to God must be shown in the way they behaved, and not just in what they believed.

This conviction runs deeply throughout the Old Testament, and even those books which relate to the formalities of organized worship lay considerable emphasis on moral and spiritual values. At the heart of the book of Deuteronomy is the instruction to 'Love the Lord your God with all your heart, with all your soul, and with all your strength' (Deuteronomy 6:5). Love for neighbours is also advocated in another section of Old Testament Law (Leviticus 19:18), while it is notable that the ten commandments sum up Israel's duty to God predominantly in terms of social and personal morality (Exodus 20:1–17; Deuteronomy 5:6–22). At one time, scholars imagined that this emphasis on behaviour was a late development within the faith of Israel. Many nineteenth-century thinkers believed that the sort of biological evolution popularized by Charles Darwin had been paralleled by moral and spiritual evolution, as human attitudes had developed and matured. Theories such as this encouraged people to take it for granted that Israel's religious experience must have begun as a simple nature worship, which only evolved into high moral standards under the influence of great thinkers such as the prophets, who tried to persuade their people to move from superstition to a more sophisticated understanding of God's person and ways. Although this sort of view continues to be promoted in some popular books on the Old Testament, it is simplistic and superficial:

■ The whole concept of evolutionary philosophy has been completely discredited. The idea that people began in primitive savagery and are getting better all the time simply does not square with the facts. The violence and brutality of our own generation makes it perfectly obvious that people are not improving, and the ferocity of the ethnic cleansing that marred the final years of the twentieth century suggested to many people that things might even be getting worse.

■ Throughout the twentieth century, there was a continual expansion of knowledge of the ancient world in general, and of Israel's cultural context in particular. Because earlier generations of scholars did not have the benefit of these insights, it was correspondingly difficult for them to understand the Old Testament in its own true life setting. We now know that some aspects of Israelite morality were familiar to people throughout the ancient world.

Much of Israel's civil law, in particular, bears a close resemblance to concepts of justice going back at least as far as the law code of King Hammurabi of Babylon (c. 1700 BC).

■ Literary analysis of the Old Testament stories has shown that a concern for good behaviour is central to many of the oldest traditions. The story of the destruction of Sodom and Gomorrah is certainly much older than the time of the prophets, and yet it condemns unacceptable behaviour in no uncertain terms (Genesis 18:16–33). The stories about Moses also go back to ancient sources, and show his anger at moral injustices as they affected both himself and his people (Exodus 2:11–13).

■ The Old Testament law codes themselves contain instructions about the conduct of religious ceremonies alongside clear guidelines for maintaining a just society. Such references were once dismissed as later additions to bring the laws into line with the message of the prophets, but further study has shown that even the very earliest strands of the Old Testament's legal material emphasize the importance of everyday behaviour as a way of serving God (Exodus 23:1–9; Leviticus 19:15–18; Deuteronomy 16:18–20).

The law-code of King Hammurabi of Babylon is inscribed on this column (or *stele*). This ancient code bears a considerable likeness to some Old Testament laws.

Religious people are always faced with the temptation of reducing faith to the perfunctory performance of familiar rituals, and Israel was no different. When the great prophets reminded them that faith in God should affect the whole of life, this was no new revelation: it was the recalling of the people back to the ideals of their ancient covenant faith. There are two main sections of Old Testament literature where these ideals are spelled out and their relevance to everyday life is explained: the wisdom books and the books of Law (Genesis to Deuteronomy), supplemented by the messages of the prophets. The literary and historical contexts of these various writings have already been dealt with extensively in previous chapters, and the discussion here will therefore focus more narrowly on their message as it related to the discovery of God's will, and the doing of it.

Discovering God's will through wisdom

When the Jewish historian Josephus (first century AD) described the wisdom books as 'precepts for the conduct of human life' (*Against Apion* 1.8), he was probably thinking especially of the book of Proverbs, which contains many easily memorized observations on how people should behave in order to enjoy a satisfying life. Here we find advice of the sort that parents throughout the world might give to their children, and for that reason many of the instructions of the book of Proverbs would not have been out of place in quite different cultural contexts. Indeed, Proverbs 22:17 – 23:11 is at many points identical to an Egyptian document of about the twelfth century BC, the *Teaching of Amenemope*.

Understanding 'wisdom'

In the ancient world, the pursuit of 'wisdom' seems to have involved many different skills. Sometimes a 'wise' person was a good diplomat; at other times, a person with specialist knowledge about the world and its workings – perhaps a botanist or zoologist (1 Kings 4:33). When Solomon prayed for 'wisdom', he asked to be given the ability 'to rule... with justice and to know the difference between good and evil' (1 Kings 3:9). But he could also be called 'wise' because of his literary and artistic interests (1 Kings 4:32). 'Wisdom' was obviously a very wide-ranging series of skills. Perhaps it was a term used simply to denote the possession of whatever abilities were necessary for a particular individual to be successful in their own sphere of life. For some, that meant technical training in the art of international relations, and Israel no doubt had schools attached to the royal courts where this kind of formal education would be given. For others, it meant the study of science and philosophy, the ancient equivalent of a 'liberal arts' education. But for most, it meant the cultivation of those personal qualities that would result in happy and meaningful relationships in the everyday life of home and workplace.

The Jewish historian Josephus described the wisdom books as 'precepts for the conduct of human life'.

Nowadays, most people would expect to learn these social skills in school, and there is some evidence that the Canaanite city states had a formal education system. But in Israel, the family was always the main influence in the life of a growing child: young people would learn most of what they needed to know from their parents, grandparents and the village elders. The practice recommended in the book of Deuteronomy almost certainly continued through most of the Old Testament period: 'Never forget these commands that I am giving you today. Teach them to your children. Repeat them when you are at home and when you are away, when you are resting and when you are working' (Deuteronomy 6:6–7).

Wisdom in practice

The Old Testament wisdom books contain examples of all these different kinds of 'wisdom'. Job and Ecclesiastes are the product of a well-developed intellectual approach to the great imponderables of human existence: the problem of evil, and the apparent meaninglessness of so much of life. As such, they have little to say about everyday behaviour in ancient Israel, though they do, of course, take certain moral standards for granted. The book of Proverbs lays much greater emphasis on 'practical wisdom', yet even here there seems to be a good deal of interest in scientific study, for moral lessons are often reinforced and illustrated by reference to the life of the animals and the phenomena of the natural world.

The book of Proverbs is itself an anthology of materials emanating from various wisdom teachers, though its contents are remarkably consistent, and deal with personal relationships in a number of different contexts.

THE FAMILY

It is not surprising that this should be a basic concern in Proverbs, since many of its precepts almost certainly originated in the context of advice handed on from one generation to another. As elsewhere in the Old Testament, a stable sexual relationship between husband and wife is seen as the key to family stability. Adultery is singled out as a particularly destructive evil whose repercussions affect more than the two individuals involved: 'A man can hire a prostitute for the price of a loaf of bread, but adultery will cost him all he has' (Proverbs 6:26). As we might expect in view of what we have already seen in the Old Testament creation stories, wisdom teachers in Israel spoke frankly and freely about both the attractions and perils of sexual unfaithfulness: 'The lips of another man's wife may be as sweet as honey and her kisses

There were 'wisdom' traditions in some of Israel's neighbouring cultures. The *Teaching of Amenemope*, an Egyptian document, is quoted almost verbatim in a section of Proverbs.

as smooth as olive oil, but when it is all over, she leaves you nothing but bitterness and pain' (Proverbs 5:3–4). The advice is always clear, but never narrow-minded or prudish. The love poems in the Song of Solomon have a number of connections with the wisdom books, and the frankness with which they depict a developing sexual relationship has often alarmed Christian readers. But the same open and joyful acknowledgment of human sexuality as part of God's creation is found also in the everyday advice of the book of Proverbs. For at the same time as its readers are warned against the dangers of adultery, they are also encouraged to develop and renew relationships within the marriage context: 'be happy with your wife and find your joy with the woman you married... Let her charms keep you happy; let her surround you with her love' (5:18–19).

Within a happy home there will be space for happy children to flourish, and the responsibility for bringing them up is one that should be shared between husband and wife (Proverbs 1:8–9; 6:20–23). Indeed, the provision of guidance to growing children is one of the major themes of Proverbs. Such instruction should be positive, by both example and precept: 'Train children in the right way, and when old, they will not stray' (Proverbs 22:6). Even when parents need to correct their children, that should always be done from a concern to promote moral maturity in the family: 'Those who never chastise their children do them no favours, but those who love them will be diligent to discipline them' (13:24). If the right course is followed in all these matters, then the whole family will be able to share in the mutual joy of a developing relationship in which 'Grandchildren are the crown of the aged, and the glory of children is their parents' (17:6).

FRIENDS

Next to a good family, a person needs good friends and neighbours. In practice, a friend can often be more valuable than members of the family: 'Do not forget your friends or your parents' friends. If you are in trouble, don't travel to go and ask your relatives for help; a neighbour near by can help you more than a family member who is far away' (27:10). Of course, in order to acquire friends we need to show ourselves to be friendly: 'Never tell your neighbours to wait until tomorrow if you can help them now' (3:28). We also need tact: 'Don't visit your neighbours too often; they may get tired of you and come to hate you' (25:17). Above all, a relationship between friends needs to be based on honesty: 'A hypocrite hides hatred behind flattering words... Like a maniac who shoots deadly firebrands and arrows, so is one who deceives a neighbour and says, "I am only joking!"' (26:24, 18–19). Gossip, then as now, was one of the commonest threats to wholesome friendship (18:8; 26:22). Indeed, the way people speak to each other is one of the major themes of the wisdom literature. A slogan in one of the early chapters of Proverbs sums up 'seven things that Yahweh hates' and most of them are related to the way people speak: 'a proud look, a lying tongue, hands that kill innocent people, a mind that thinks up wicked plans, feet that hurry off to do evil, a witness who tells one lie after another, and someone who stirs up trouble among friends' (6:16–19).

Those who behave like this are the opposite of 'wise': they are fools, and there is only one way to deal with them: 'Give a silly answer to a silly question, and the one who asked it will realize that they're not as clever as they think' (26:5). The wise person, on the other hand, is characterized by prudent thought and speech: 'Be careful how you think; your life is shaped by your thoughts. Never say anything that isn't true' (4:23–24).

SOCIETY

Wisdom teachers were not only concerned with the behaviour of people in small groups: they also gave much teaching on how society as a whole should operate. At the very beginning of the book of Proverbs, we learn that its advice 'can teach you how to live intelligently and how to be honest, just, and fair' (1:3). Honesty, justice and fairness in society were among the key themes in the preaching of the prophets – and they are just as important here. We may find this somewhat surprising, for most scholars are agreed that the wisdom books must have originated in fairly well-to-do circles. The fact that the wisdom teachers of Israel had international connections supports that assumption, for wealth is required to make and sustain worldwide contacts of this kind. We certainly know that later Jewish wisdom teachers must have been quite rich. Writing about 180 BC, Ben Sira tells of his wide travels (Wisdom of Ben Sira 34:9–12), and gives advice on such things as behaviour at banquets (31:12 – 32:13) and how to treat slaves (33:24–31). He also mentions the school that he operated in Jerusalem, and invites others to join him there so that they too might 'acquire wisdom for yourselves without money' (51:23–28). In the Hebrew Bible, the description of Job certainly suggests that the authors of that book moved in high-class circles (Job 1:1–3), and even in Proverbs, some pieces of advice suggest a context of relative affluence (e.g. Proverbs 21:14). In the light of all this, it is surprising to find here a morality which recognizes the limitations of wealth. 'Wisdom' itself is more important than riches (Proverbs 3:13–15), and so is 'peace of mind' (17:1) and 'a good reputation' (22:1) – all of which suggests that it is 'Better to be poor and fear the Lord than to be rich and in trouble. Better to eat vegetables with people you love than to eat the finest meat where there is hate' (15:16–17). The other Old Testament wisdom books make exactly the same points, and even the pessimistic author of Ecclesiastes declares that amassing money is pointless: 'It was like chasing the wind – of no use at all' (Ecclesiastes 2:11). The book of Job asserts quite bluntly that trust in money is incompatible with a living

relationship to God: 'I have never trusted in riches or taken pride in my wealth... Such a sin should be punished by death; it denies Almighty God' (Job 31:24–25, 28).

The imagery of the wisdom books may be less picturesque and dramatic than the words of the prophets, but their social perspectives are remarkably similar. Many of the abuses condemned by the wisdom teachers were the same as those that caused so much concern to the prophets: unjust business practices (Proverbs 11:1), bribery (15:27) and taking advantage of people by charging interest on loans (28:8). All of this could be summed up in the slogan that it is 'Better to be poor and honest than rich and dishonest' (28:6). On a positive note, the wisdom literature is full of injunctions to those who are rich to share what they have with the poor – whether it be allowing access to their land and crops (Proverbs 13:23), or giving them clothes (Job 31:19–20), or just general exhortations to be generous to others (Proverbs 14:21, 31). As elsewhere in the Old Testament, this generosity is to apply especially to those with no other visible means of support – which in ancient Israel meant especially widows and orphans (Job 31:16–18; Proverbs 23:10–11). Animals could also be specifically singled out as needing to be treated with due concern for their welfare (Proverbs 14:4). Alongside charity, the wisdom books also advocate justice. It is one thing to give freely to those who are poor, but social justice is a more fundamental human need. The wisdom writers are conscious that it is usually rich people who create divisions within society (Proverbs 30:13–14), and so they advocate taking positive steps to correct social injustices: 'Speak up for people who cannot speak for themselves. Protect the rights of all who are helpless. Speak for them and be a righteous judge. Protect the rights of the poor and needy' (Proverbs 31:8–9)

Here, in the wisdom books, we have much clear guidance on how God's people should behave. Morality, like charity, was to begin at home, but its effects went wider than the individual person: they were as broad as society itself.

Discovering God's will in the Law

The wisdom books reflect the standards of decent behaviour that most people might take for granted. But in any organized society, this kind of moral consensus needs to be clearly defined, and this is what we find in the Old Testament law books. The first five books of the Old Testament, from Genesis to Deuteronomy, were often referred to simply as 'the Law', though much of the material in these books is not at all like the kind of law most people would be familiar with today. Genesis in particular is a collection of stories, which at first sight we might expect to be regarded as some sort of history. But the Old Testament notion of 'law' was much more comprehensive and wide-ranging than ours. When we talk of 'the law' we generally have in mind sets of rules that can be interpreted by lawyers with special professional training, and applied in a court of justice by a judge. It would certainly be unusual for a modern person to agree with one of the Old Testament poets who wrote, 'I take pleasure in your law' (Psalm 119:77). But the Hebrew word for law (*Torah*) meant far more than just rules and regulations, and included everything that God had revealed to the people, especially the 'guidance' or 'instruction' that would enable them to live life to the full. The Torah was the place to discover what people should believe about God, and what might be required of them in return. This explains why the Torah was always closely bound up with the stories of Israel's early history, for knowing and obeying God was not just a matter of blind obedience to religious and moral rules, but a matter of experiencing God's concern and love in a personal and social context. God's undeserved love to the people – shown in events such as the exodus –

Wisdom and faith

People have often thought that the wisdom books present a different message from the prophets or the Old Testament laws. The main strands of Old Testament theology emphasize God's actions in the life of the people, whereas the wisdom books are said to be more 'secular', based not on God's personal revelation, but on human reason. In addition, it is often asserted that whereas the prophets and lawgivers of ancient Israel were concerned with the shape of society, the wisdom books are concerned more with personal morality. We can certainly agree that some features of these books seem to justify such observations:

● They are part of an international way of thinking, and as such have a number of similarities with literature from both Babylon and Egypt. They are not, therefore, unique to Israel, and in that sense cannot be said to be exclusively based on the distinctive characteristics of Israelite spirituality.

● They rarely, if ever, refer directly to the great events of the Old Testament story. Instead, their teaching tends to be based on common sense and on observation of the world of nature.

Some scholars have thought of the wisdom books and their moral teaching as a secular, humanistic intrusion into the Old Testament faith. They regard them as the religious side of those social and political changes that accompanied the institutionalization of the monarchy in ancient Israel, and the adoption of a lifestyle suited to the world of international politics. But this is too simple an analysis.

Is wisdom secular?

To say that the wisdom books are 'secular' is to impose a modern way of thinking on the ancient world. Certainly, the wisdom writers take their starting point from human experience of life, but in the ancient world in general this was never 'humanistic' in the narrow sense of being purely secular and non-religious. Throughout the ancient world, 'wisdom' was always based on an understanding of how the world works – but it was everywhere taken for granted that the world only worked at all because of the intentions of the deities or, in the case of the Hebrew Bible, of one all-powerful God. To refuse to take account of this was something that only a 'fool' would do. A really wise person would never forget that the ordinary world of everyday experience was directly sustained by God. Even a pessimist like the author of Ecclesiastes, who frankly confesses that he sometimes finds it hard to discover God at work in the

is basic to the Old Testament laws. Israel did not keep the Law in order to become God's people, but because they were already living in a close personal relationship to God.

The German scholar Albrecht Alt believed that some of the Old Testament's most distinctive laws emerged in this way out of Israel's experience of God. Many Old Testament laws are similar to the legislation of other ancient societies, for they concern the everyday happenings of rural life. Alt designated these 'casuistic' or case laws – laws in which very specific situations were envisaged, and guidance given as to how disputes may be resolved. A typical law of this kind might deal with violent assault (e.g. Exodus 21:20), or with the processes of responsible farming (e.g. Exodus 22:6). But there are also other, more absolute regulations, such as the ten commandments, in which worship of other deities, murder, adultery, theft and lying are all prohibited

---

Wisdom and faith
continued

world, nevertheless takes God's existence for granted as a fundamental part of his view of life. Other writers were more positive: 'To be wise you must first obey the Lord. If you know the Holy One, you have understanding' (Proverbs 9:10).

Wisdom and natural law

In view of the importance the Old Testament attaches to the relationship of God with this world, it is not surprising that contemplation of the way the world is should lead to personal encounter with God. If, as the writer of the first few chapters of Genesis suggests, God can be found in the realities of the natural world, then it is hardly surprising that the discerning moralist can discover there traces of God's way of doing things. This kind of 'natural law' is a widespread phenomenon, and in some respects is the basis for the modern definition of human rights, understood as being inalienable expectations based on some notion of 'natural justice' rather than on standards handed down from God or anyone else. The Old Testament wisdom books often appeal to precisely this sort of argument. Job, for example, asks for justice for himself because he has been just to his servants, and 'The same God who created me created my servants also' (Job 31:15). Moreover, this sort of appeal to 'natural

justice' is by no means restricted to the wisdom books, but can be found throughout the Old Testament. When the prophet Amos denounced the war crimes of the nations of his day, he did so on the basis of natural justice (Amos 1:1 – 2:3), and when the writer of Genesis condemned murder, it was because people were made 'in God's image' (Genesis 9:6). Likewise, when Isaiah complained about the disobedience of his people, he concluded that their behaviour was unnatural and irrational because it was so different from the way that things work in the world of nature (Isaiah 1:2–3). Apart from specific examples such as these, much of the imagery of the messages of the Old Testament prophets is also drawn from the world of nature, just as is the imagery in books like Proverbs. It is not necessary to speculate as to whether the prophets 'borrowed' such ideas from the wisdom teachers, for it is much more likely that both of them were independently basing their teaching on the kind of creation-centred spirituality that is a central element within the Old Testament faith.

Wisdom and social ethics

It has also been claimed that a 'wisdom' morality is inconsistent with an emphasis on social justice. It is certainly true that teaching on the shape of society is

The Israelites were instructed to teach each generation the laws God had given.

presented more forcibly by the prophets and lawgivers in relation to the great themes of Israel's salvation history, but we do an injustice to wisdom teachers in ancient Israel to suppose that they were interested only in themselves. Indeed, in the wider wisdom literature of the ancient world social justice was a major concern. Protecting the poor and disadvantaged members of society was a major theme in Babylonian and Egyptian literature as well as in the texts from Ugarit which tell of Canaanite kings showing the same sort of consideration. At the very beginning of Proverbs, the book's aims are summed up as teaching people 'how to live intelligently and how to be honest, just, and fair' (1:3), while the hero of the book of Job provides a perfect example of a person who always did the right thing by those less fortunate than himself (Job 31:13–23). No doubt the wisdom books generally offer different reasons for promoting equality and justice than did the prophets and history writers, but their ethical stance is none the less 'religious' for that.

Wisdom and the covenant
In point of fact, the actual ethical advice of the wisdom writers is often identical to the lessons drawn from Israel's past by the writers of the deuteronomic history. Caring for the poor, consideration for animals, justice in society and concern for orphans as well as the prohibition of false witness, adultery, bribery and vengeance – all these things are as common in the wisdom literature as they are in the Old Testament laws. Indeed, the wisdom writers often express these ideas more concretely by showing how they relate to specific situations in the life of the family or the community. Time and time again, the wisdom writers apply the same lessons as the prophets and others who stood in the 'covenant' tradition, for they were all consciously serving the same God, whose will could be made known to the people in both the created world and the great unrepeatable events of history.

without any further qualification or explanation (Exodus 20:1–17; Deuteronomy 5:6–22). Moreover, such prohibitions seem to be based on a simple statement about God's nature as Israel had experienced this in the course of their history. In a previous chapter, we have reviewed the evidence suggesting that in giving the commandments this precise form, the Old Testament writers may have had in mind the kind of covenant treaties that small struggling nations often made with more powerful states, in exchange for protection and security. Such covenant agreements would be reaffirmed at regular intervals, and Alt believed that 'apodictic' laws of this kind formed the centre of Israel's renewal of their faith in God every seven years at the festival of shelters, or Tabernacles (Deuteronomy 31:9–13). It was this form of absolute law that was most characteristic of the Old Testament, for it was nothing less than an explanation of the everyday ramifications of Israel's covenant faith. Insofar as it underlines the most distinctive aspects of the Torah, this understanding has certain attractions, though there are also a number of difficulties with it:

■ Casuistic law is a specific literary form, but this so-called 'apodictic' law is not strictly a literary form at all and these absolute laws are expressed in a variety of literary formulations. The two categories are not, therefore, directly comparable to one another.

■ Alt believed that these absolute rules were unique to Israel, though subsequent discoveries have shown that similar terminology could also be used in legal contexts elsewhere, especially among the Hittites, but also in Egypt and Babylon. It was not always the same actions that were prohibited there, of course, but the form itself was certainly found outside the confines of the Old Testament.

■ There is no real evidence that these 'apodictic' laws either originated in, or were regularly repeated at, the great religious festivals in Israel.

■ These statements are not really 'law' in the technical sense at all. They are more a general listing of accepted standards of behaviour, and in this respect the 'apodictic' law is not all that different from the teaching of the wisdom books. It is at least arguable that they could be based on Israel's understanding of the 'natural law' revealed in the work of creation, and not on the covenant at Mount Sinai.

The books of the Torah, like all modern collections of law (and many other parts of the Old Testament), are an anthology of laws relating to different situations and different periods during the whole span of the history of ancient Israel. They are not meant to be read from start to finish as a consistent account of Israel's legal system, and it is obvious that within the books of the Law there are at least four quite separate collections of material: the ten commandments, the book of the covenant, Deuteronomy and a number of priestly laws. The precise way in which these separate law codes might be related to one another will be determined by the view that is taken on the compilation of the first five books of the Old Testament, and the discussion of them here takes account of what has already been said on that subject in a previous chapter.

The ten commandments

Most people who know anything at all about the Bible will recognize this collection of moral rules (Exodus 20:1–17) as a basic part of the Old Testament's view of human behaviour. Its principles have been enshrined in many national law codes since Old Testament days, and in some respects form a charter of fundamental human rights. It was obviously intended to be learned by heart, and often repeated. The fact that there are ten commandments is certainly not accidental, but is a learning device so that they could be counted off on the fingers of both hands as they were repeated. This was a popular way of remembering things.

There are other groups of laws which may originally have been organized in the same way, though they are mostly concerned with the conduct of organized worship (Exodus 34:12–26; Leviticus 20:2–5; 18:6–18). The book of Psalms also contains at least one such list of ten things that summarize good behaviour (Psalm 15:2–5). This is the main subject of the ten commandments themselves. In that sense, they are not technically laws at all, for they contain no mention of penalties for those who break them. Rather, they are a kind of policy statement – a bill of rights – showing how relationships between God and humankind were to be viewed within the Old Testament faith community. It is widely agreed by scholars that this list must have originated at a very early period in Israel's history, and some claim it can be traced back to Moses himself.

The book of the covenant

Many parts of the book of the covenant (Exodus 20:22 – 23:33) are similar to other ancient law codes, especially the codes of Ur-Nammu of Ur (2050 BC) and of Hammurabi, king of Babylon (1700 BC). Though there are many differences of detail between the book of the covenant and these other laws, their general outlook is the same and simply reflects widespread customs in the ancient world. So this is much more like a code of law in the modern sense. It is, however, widely believed to be very ancient, going back to the time of Israel's earliest leaders, Moses and Joshua. The essential concern of these laws is with the life of the community, and they are mostly a 'casuistic' type of legislation, though some sections also deal with the conduct of organized worship.

Deuteronomy

The word 'Deuteronomy' means 'a second law', and here we find an amplification and interpretation of earlier law codes, showing how they could apply to the changing circumstances of Israel's national life. As such, this book is obviously based on ancient materials, and some believe that it found its present form as a liturgy for a covenant renewal

There are many similarities between the Old Testament covenant and the law code of King Ur-Nammu of Ur. In this relief, the king is seen on the left pouring out a libation in front of a seated god.

festival at which the worshippers in ancient Israel would regularly 'relive' the events of their national past, and commit themselves afresh to their God Yahweh. Chapters 5–11 certainly read like sermons, preached as a prelude to the presentation of the actual Law itself in chapters 12–26, and followed by the people's commitment to it in chapters 27–28. The book of Deuteronomy was a major influence in the reform of Temple worship carried out by King Josiah of Judah, though its actual origins were certainly earlier than his day (2 Kings 22:3–20).

Priestly laws

These are found in Exodus, Leviticus and Numbers and, in effect, include all the rest of the Old Testament laws, among which are large sections dealing with the tabernacle and its contents (Exodus 25–30), and various regulations related to priests and sacrificial worship (Exodus 35–40; Leviticus 1–10). There are also detailed regulations governing the preparation and eating of food as well as matters of domestic and personal hygiene (Leviticus 11–16). It was once believed that these rules concerning worship were relatively late developments in the story of Israel, partly because the message of the sixth-century prophet Ezekiel (Ezekiel 40–48) contains some similar notions, but closer investigation has shown that many of the practices referred to here are very similar to practices known elsewhere in the ancient world at a much earlier date. One section of the book of Leviticus (chapters 17–26) is generally regarded as another separate law code, the 'holiness code'. There are several reasons for this:

■ These chapters begin with rules about organized worship, but then make no reference at all to the very full legislation on the matter found in the preceding chapters.

■ The statement that 'All these are the laws and commands that Yahweh gave to Moses on Mount Sinai for the people of Israel' (Leviticus 26:46) seems to be a formal ending, which does not relate to what follows in the next chapter.

■ The theme of 'holiness' runs everywhere through these chapters, but is not a prominent theme at all in the rest of Leviticus.

From theory to practice

Life in the ancient world was significantly different from life today, and most readers now find all these laws dull and tedious. But they can still provide a number of insights into important aspects of the Old Testament faith. There seem to be so many collections of laws that it comes as a bit of a surprise to discover that they are far from comprehensive, and many situations are not mentioned at all. Other ancient law codes were the same, perhaps because the laws that were written down were only intended as samples of how justice should be administered. Or it could be that the written laws were to give guidance in cases of particular difficulty, and alongside them other more straightforward procedures were simply taken for granted. There are many ways of classifying these laws. One area of life controlled by the Torah was what we today would call religion, and those that fall into this category, describing how worship is to be conducted, are considered more fully in the next chapter. Of course, it is important to remember that religion and everyday behaviour cannot easily be separated in the Old Testament, and therefore this division is certainly artificial, if not arbitrary. But in addition to those dealing specifically with ritual matters, four other types of law may be traced within the Old Testament codes: criminal law, civil law, family law and social law.

Criminal law

Whereas civil law deals with arguments between individuals, about which there can be room for different judgments in different

circumstances, criminal law concerns principles of right and wrong that
are taken as self-evident. Every society has certain actions that are so
thoroughly and universally disapproved of that the community itself
feels it necessary to punish those who do them. This does not mean
that the criminal law of one nation will always be the same as the
criminal law of another. Indeed, there are often striking differences,
and activities that are branded as criminal in one state may well be
regarded as fundamental human rights in another. So by examining
those actions which a particular state regards as criminal, we can soon
understand the basic attitudes and fundamental values of its people. As
far as we can see, the only penalty imposed by the state itself in ancient
Israel was the death penalty. Fines were unknown, and though a person
could be put under arrest while a case was decided, imprisonment as
such was not introduced until after the exile in Babylon. Monetary
sanctions could be imposed, but they were regarded as restitution by
the wrongdoer to the victim, and therefore came within the jurisdiction
of the civil law. Even crimes such as personal assault or theft were dealt
with in this way. It is probably significant that every crime punishable
by death was related in some way or another to the ten commandments, which is why these commandments have often been described
as ancient Israel's criminal law. Of course, the ten commandments are
not strictly 'law' at all in the technical sense, but this way of looking at
them is still useful, for all those actions punishable by the community
as a whole were closely related to Israel's understanding of their
position as the people of God. In that context to commit a crime was,
quite simply, to deny the reality of the covenant faith. Such crimes
included the following.

OFFENCES AGAINST GOD

Examples of these offences would be the worship of other deities
(Exodus 22:20; Leviticus 20:1–5), blasphemy (Leviticus 24:10–16) and
magic (Deuteronomy 13:1–18; Exodus 22:18; Leviticus 20:27), all of
which in one way or another deny the very basis of the relationship
between God and the community. Other offences, such as a priest's
daughter working as a prostitute (Leviticus 21:9) or not keeping the
sabbath day (Exodus 31:14–15) might seem less serious to us, though
the Torah views them in the same light because both priesthood and
sabbath are 'a sign of the covenant' (Exodus 31:16).

OFFENCES AGAINST HUMAN LIFE

Intentional murder was a particularly serious crime, though accidental
killing was subject to other penalties (Exodus 21:12; Leviticus 24:17;
Numbers 35:16–21, 22–29). Kidnapping was an equally serious offence
(Exodus 21:16; Deuteronomy 24:7). In Israel, human liberty as well
as human life was of great value, and many scholars believe that
the eighth commandment refers not to stealing in general, but to

kidnapping more specifically (Exodus 20:15; Deuteronomy 5:19). The theme of personal freedom is certainly important in other sections of Old Testament law.

OFFENCES AGAINST THE FAMILY

If the unnatural termination of life was a criminal offence, so was interference with the natural context in which life is created, namely the sexual relationship between husband and wife. Other kinds of sexual activity, whether incest, buggery or even adultery, were all regarded as serious criminal offences (Leviticus 20:10–21), along with disdain for parents (Exodus 21:15; Deuteronomy 21:18–21).

Civil law

Old Testament civil law has many similarities to other laws found in the ancient world. It deals with everyday matters such as the treatment of employees, violence of various sorts and the duties of owners to protect third parties from injury caused by either animals or property. The book of the covenant consists entirely of this sort of law, and it may be significant that in this law code God is usually referred to as 'Elohim', meaning 'God' in general, rather than by the personal name 'Yahweh'. This may be an indication that Israel simply took over this legal form from the general stock of commonly accepted norms without making too many detailed changes or additions to it.

Punishment under this category was generally understood as compensation for the wrong done, and many penalties are similar to those prescribed in other codes such as the laws of Hammurabi. But there are some differences. Bodily mutilation, for example, was quite a common punishment in the ancient world, but there is only one specific example of it in the Old Testament (Deuteronomy 25:11–12). There is certainly provision for punishments to be exacted 'life for life, eye for eye, tooth for tooth, hand for hand, foot for foot, burn for burn, wound for wound, bruise for bruise' (Exodus 21:23–24; Leviticus 24:19–20; Deuteronomy 19:21), though this seems to be almost a symbolic statement, emphasizing that the punishment should always be in proportion to the wrong that has been suffered. In the ancient world, however, even this apparently ruthless retribution could be a means of limiting what might otherwise be excessive vengeance. In the light of Lamech's boast that 'I have killed a young man because he struck me' (Genesis 4:23), even a basic law of equal retribution could be regarded as an improvement. In the event, though the principle is stated in the book of the covenant, it is both preceded and followed there by laws which show that, in general, forms other than physical punishment could and should be preferred: generally, financial compensation. The payment of compensation to the victim in place of physical punishment was probably quite a widespread practice.

Family law

The whole of Israelite society was family and clan based, and the importance of the family unit is reflected in many Old Testament laws. Relationships between family members had a far-reaching effect on the overall shape of Israelite society. A stable relationship between husband and wife was basic to the Old Testament view of family life. Marriage itself was generally of one man to one woman (monogamy), though kings and other leading figures often seem to have had more than one wife (polygamy), and this practice is never actually prohibited anywhere. Marriages were generally arranged by parents, though love marriages are not altogether unknown (e.g. 1 Samuel 18:20). But alongside a legal wife, a man could also have any number of 'concubines'. They were slave wives, and had a correspondingly lower status than the main wife. Divorce was taken for granted, though in practice it could often leave a woman destitute and was probably not very frequent for that reason. But all these matters were entirely a family affair in which the Law as such would not be involved at all, except that the civil law contains a number of guidelines relating to circumstances that might arise with a breakdown of normal relationships, and the criminal law of course forbids adultery. Detailed regulations are given for the proper treatment of concubines (Exodus 21:7–11; Deuteronomy 21:10–14) and guidance is also given on what should happen after a divorce (Deuteronomy 24:1–4).

Wilful disregard for parents was in certain circumstances dealt with by the criminal law, but usually the authority of the father or patriarch of the family was absolute, and in the earliest period a father could even condemn members of his own family to death (Genesis 38:24). Later legislation provided for such cases to be referred to the village elders (Deuteronomy 21:18–21) and some passages suggest there was an ultimate right of appeal to the king (2 Samuel 14:4–11).

On the positive side, members of a family also had obligations to each other. If family members were forced to sell themselves into slavery to pay off a debt, then it was the duty of their close relatives to buy them back (Leviticus 25:47–49), circumstances which are well illustrated in the story of Ruth. Family life in Old Testament times was generally tough for all but the patriarchal leader of a clan, and though there was a measure of security on offer, that was accompanied by the demand of awesome responsibilities.

Social law

The Canaanite city states among which Israel emerged as a nation were essentially feudal societies, with a powerful and wealthy ruling class. This was in strong contrast to the tribal structure that is always held up as the ideal in the Old Testament. At its best, this emphasis was to ensure that Israelite society would not be dominated by a powerful hierarchy, but was a self-consciously egalitarian society in which all citizens enjoyed the same fundamental rights and privileges.

The conflict between these two models of society runs deep in the Old Testament. In the earliest Israelite settlements, local elders were the leaders of their own communities, but the need for a king was obvious and irresistible. That does not mean there was no opposition, and even once Israel had become a state the power of the king was stringently regulated by the Law (Deuteronomy 17:14–20). When the great kingdom split in two after Solomon's death, it was largely as the result of tensions between the Canaanite, bureaucratic ideal and the Israelite ideal in which every individual was equal, their freedom restricted only by the mutual obligations imposed by the family group.

In practical terms, the central issue was the possession of land. In the Canaanite city states all land was ultimately owned by the king (1 Samuel 8:11–17), whereas in Israel all land was regarded as belonging to God. It was given in trust to the family group as something that could be neither bought nor sold, but must be handed on from one generation to the next (Leviticus 25:23). In this way Israel hoped to avoid the emergence of a land-owning class, and to preserve the relative equality of all the people. Those who tried to amass land for themselves were tirelessly condemned by the prophets (Isaiah 5:8; Micah 2:1–2), and even the king was not exempt from such criticism (1 Kings 21). This emphasis explains why apparently tedious lists of people and land play such an important part in the Old Testament (Numbers 26; 34; Joshua 13–19). Many laws set out to preserve the freedom of the individual to live unmolested on the land which God had given to the family. The Law banned actions such as moving boundary stones (Deuteronomy 19:14), and many other prohibitions relating to loans and debts also find their real significance in this context (Exodus 22:25; Leviticus 25:35–38). Charging interest on loans was forbidden (Deuteronomy 23:19–20), though what often happened was that a person would give either clothes or property as security for a loan. Then, if the loan could not be repaid, the borrower would soon become virtually a slave of the lender, and while technically living on their own family land, would be reduced to a state of destitution. This is why the Law tried to regulate what could be used as security for loans (Exodus 22:26–27; Deuteronomy 24:6). It also provided for debts to be written off every seven years

Boundary stones marked the limits of a person's land; this one comes from Babylon in the time of Nebuchadnezzar I. Some Old Testament laws were aimed at preventing the absorption of smallholdings into great estates.

(the sabbatical year, Deuteronomy 15:1–11), or every fifty years (the Jubilee, Leviticus 25:8–17).

The Old Testament social ethic displays great concern for many disadvantaged groups – foreigners, the poor, the oppressed, widows, orphans and even personal enemies (Exodus 22:21–27; 23:1–9). This emphasis has been a significant reason why some scholars have argued that early Israel originated as a proletarian protest movement against the elitist structures of traditional Canaanite power. As has been pointed out in a previous chapter, there is a good deal to be said in favour of this view, though it is important not to exaggerate its uniqueness. Concern for despised people was not exclusively Israelite, and in the laws of Ur-

These slaves in Assyria at the time of Sennacherib were far worse off than slaves in Israel, where the laws protected them at many points.

Nammu, for example, the following list is given of the king's achievements:

The orphan was not delivered up to the rich man, the widow was not delivered up to the mighty man, the man of one shekel was not delivered up to the man of one mina.

The Old Testament is most distinctive in its treatment of slaves, who were clearly regarded as persons in their own right. Not only could they expect to be set free (Exodus 21:1–6), but they also had rights even if they ran away from their master (Deuteronomy 23:15–16). The master must give slaves a regular day off, and must recognize that there are limits to the power that can reasonably be wielded over another person's life (Exodus 23:12; Deuteronomy 5:12–15). The master who injured a slave could be forced to compensate by allowing the slave to go free (Exodus 21:26–27). If an owner killed a slave, that was regarded as a particularly serious offence, and was to be avenged by the community acting on behalf of the slave, presumably because slaves had no family of their own to defend them (Exodus 21:20). Some scholars believe that the death penalty was prescribed for this, and if they are right such concern for the welfare of slaves would have been absolutely without parallel in the ancient world. It would also suggest that the killing of a slave represented a spiritual as well as a social challenge to the community. The religious background to the slavery laws is certainly made clear in at least one law code, where special treatment of slaves is justified by the statement, 'you were slaves in Egypt and Yahweh your God set you free; that is why I am now giving you this command' (Deuteronomy 15:15). The distinctive nature of Israelite society emerged not out of purely humanitarian motives: it was part and parcel of Israel's experience of their God in the formative events of the nation's history.

Explaining God's will

The impact of Israel's history on the sort of society envisaged by the Old Testament can be seen quite clearly. Indeed, in one way or another, all the most distinctive features of Old Testament morality have been determined by Israel's encounter with God on the stage of human history. The great events which helped formulate Israel's understanding of God's character also gave a special insight into what God required of the people. Events such as the escape from Egypt and the entry into the promised land had their effect on God's people and their behaviour. In the Old Testament, correct behaviour, like many other things, was based on history. But how can the facts of history provide instruction in morality? As we read the messages of the great prophets and explore the teaching of the books of Law, the answer to that question soon emerges, for the Old Testament ethic is not only historical: it also has other characteristics that can be identified by an appreciation of God's involvement in the lives of the people of Israel.

The Old Testament ethic is theological

It is 'theological' in the strict meaning of that word, for the Old Testament code of behaviour always refers back to God's own personality. Correct human behaviour is closely related to the kind of God who was revealed in the events of Israel's history. It is, of course, always true that the kind of God people believe in affects the way they behave. The Hebrew Bible stresses that God is a personal and active being who can be known both by individuals and societies in the context of their everyday experience of life. It takes these characteristics of God and applies them directly to the life of ordinary people. Here, human goodness finds its authority, example and inspiration in the person of God, and nowhere is this summed up more eloquently than in Leviticus 19:2: 'Be holy, because I, the Lord your God, am holy.' God's people are to behave the same way as God behaves, something that has been well expressed by Emil Brunner's characterization of Old Testament morality as being 'the science of human conduct as it is determined by divine conduct'.

The Old Testament ethic is dynamic

How is God's own personality expressed? We have already observed that the Old Testament never tries to analyse or define God in an abstract way. God is not described 'metaphysically', but 'functionally', with the major emphasis being on what God does. Obviously, the two are closely related, because the way people are will be reflected in the way that they work. But Yahweh is not so much a 'God who is', but a 'God who acts' – a dynamic God rather than a static one. What then can be learned about human behaviour by looking at the characteristic actions of God? Three terms are often used in the Old Testament to describe God's moral disposition.

JUSTICE

This might seem to be a very abstract idea, for 'justice' is the kind of thing that lawyers and judges argue about in law courts. In the Old Testament, 'justice' includes this concern for fair play, but more characteristically justice is less something to talk about, and more something to be done. The leaders of early Israel were not 'judges' in the modern legal sense: they were leaders of their people who saw something wrong, and took action to put it right. Indeed, the Hebrew word that is normally translated 'justice' in English versions of the Bible really has a much wider meaning than that, and refers to everything that a ruler might do to ensure that people would enjoy a stable and satisfying way of life. God, therefore, is like a 'just' ruler, and is concerned to improve the quality of life for the people (Deuteronomy 32:4; Isaiah 5:16; 61:8).

MERCY

When this word is used to describe God, it is emphasizing that God deals with people in a loving and personal way. God's justice is not determined by the stringent requirements of some detached legal system, but always operates in a context of personal love and trust. The entire Old Testament story shows how, against all expectations, God has initiated a relationship with people who by nature are weak and often morally and spiritually powerless. God never abandons them, but stands alongside them to help in their weakness, and will never reject them despite all their inadequacy and imperfection. 'How can I give you up, Israel? How can I abandon you?... My heart will not let me do it! My love for you is too strong... For I am God and not a human being. I, the Holy One, am with you. I will not come to you in anger' (Hosea 11:8–9).

TRUTH

This is also something that we tend to think of in abstract terms, but again in Hebrew thinking 'truth' was most often regarded not as a characteristic of propositions, but of people. When the disguised Joseph put his brothers in prison, he did so to find out 'whether there is truth in you' – in other words, whether they could be trusted or not (Genesis 42:16). In the world of the Old Testament the deities were notoriously unreliable. They did whatever they wished, and all too often their human worshippers had to pay the price. But the God of the Old Testament is quite different, and is depicted as being wholly trustworthy. People can therefore trust God without any fear of failure: 'I have complete confidence, O God!... Your constant love reaches above the heavens; your faithfulness touches the skies' (Psalm 108:1, 4).

God is shown as being completely trustworthy, and it is a trait that should be reflected in dealings between people. The inscription on this clay tablet suggests that it was a receipt for a delivery of gold.

The Old Testament ethic is social

In what context is God's will most truly done? Is God concerned with the moral goodness of individuals, or with the shape of society? Inevitably, these two concerns are not mutually exclusive. Individual people are called upon to respond for themselves to the will of God. When Isaiah was confronted with the moral grandeur of God in the Temple, he confessed to his own shortcomings and became intensely aware of his own personal inadequacy to do the work to which God was calling him (Isaiah 6:5).

The story of Abraham pleading for the deliverance of two evil cities makes a similar point: God cares about the behaviour of individuals (Genesis 18:16–33). Yet throughout the Old Testament, there is also a major emphasis on the whole of God's people: God's will is to be shown not just in the lives of committed individuals, but in the structures of national life as well. We have already noticed this strong emphasis on social justice in both wisdom books and law codes, and it was born out of the formative events of Israel's history. On a social level, the exodus had demonstrated God's concern for those who were unjustly oppressed by the forces of imperialism. Yahweh saw that things were bad in Egypt, and stepped in to change the situation. This is why the ideal Old Testament society always had a special place for the dispossessed, the oppressed and the disadvantaged. Moreover, the very fabric of society should reflect this concern. The prophets loved to remind their people that in Israel all men and women must be equal: they had all started out as equals (as slaves) and therefore economic and social exploitation of one class by another was not only deplorable, but was also a fundamental denial of the very heart of the Old Testament faith.

The Old Testament ethic is personal

This brings us to the crux of the whole matter. Behaviour in the Old Testament is always seen in the context of the covenant that Israel had entered into with God. God was deeply involved in every aspect of the life of this world, not at all aloof from the human predicament, and this involvement was expressed in the notion of the covenant. For as Israel looked back to the foundation events of their national life, they saw the exodus and what followed as the culmination of God's purpose for this people. In the memory of that momentous event, Israel found the meaning of their national life. As the freed slaves had stood before Mount Sinai they had been reminded of God's great and loving actions on their behalf. In return, they were called upon to fulfil God's commands. Israelite society was based on this mutual relationship of love and responsibility, and as the people came together for celebration and worship in the annual cycle of religious festivals, each generation was able to commit itself afresh to this personal relationship between God and the people. That was where life found its deepest meaning. God had called them in love when they were neither expecting nor deserving it, and succeeding generations would respond to that love by following the example set by God in person.

When the Old Testament demands justice, mercy and truth in human relationships, it does not appeal to some abstract notion of morality. Instead, it goes back to the roots of the covenant faith in the justice, mercy and truth of God. When the prophets call for righteousness in society, they look back to the actions of God in caring for outcasts and strangers. It is no surprise, therefore, that one of the most eloquent expressions of God's values and ways of doing things – the ten commandments – begins not with a command, but with a statement: 'I am Yahweh your God who brought you out of Egypt, where you were slaves' (Exodus 20:2). Right behaviour should stem naturally from the response of a grateful people to what God has done for them. Morality and theology are inextricably interwoven with each other, for it is within the context of a personal relationship between God and people that the ethical principles of the Old Testament can most fully be understood.

The administration of justice

We have examined the content of the Old Testament law codes in some detail. But how were these laws put into practice? What sort of legal structures existed in ancient Israel? There is no single answer to that question, for Israelite society underwent a number of profound changes in the course of the events documented in the Old Testament. The life of the tribes in the days of the judges was socially and politically quite different from life in the kingdom of David and Solomon. Things changed again after their kingdom divided, and then following the demise of the northern kingdom of Israel. Changing circumstances inevitably led to changes in national institutions, and the admini-stration of law varied from one century to another in the course of the nation's story. But a number of individuals are mentioned in relation to the administration of justice, and consideration of their functions will provide an insight into some aspects of this complex subject.

The elders
Israelite society was always regarded as an extended family group. The head of each family had jurisdiction over his own relatives and household, and the town or village elders were just the leading members of the various families. The deuteronomic code mentions them quite specifically as acting as a regular court where disputes about the Law could be settled (Deuteronomy 19:12; 21:1–9, 18–21; 22:13–21; 25:5–10), and all the evidence suggests that this was the main law court throughout the entire history of Israel. The elders would gather at the gates of the town, which was a regular meeting place for serious discussion of the affairs of the community (Genesis 23:10–18; Job 29:7–10). There was no official prosecutor, and the complainant would present the case against the accused in person. Some passages suggest there would be an official 'defender' of the accused person (Psalm 109:31). Certainly, both prosecution and defence would call witnesses and produce material evidence (Exodus 22:13; Deuteronomy 22:13–17). Accusations and evidence would normally be presented verbally, though written statements could also be accepted (Job 31:35–36). The elders would be seated during the trial, rising to pronounce their verdict. If a penalty was involved, then the elders would impose it and would usually carry it out on the spot (Deuteronomy 22:13–21). The whole of this procedure reflects the view that most cases were essentially civil disputes. The job of the town elders was to adjudicate between the various parties, and thereby

The administration of justice *continued*

ensure that justice was done. The story of the book of Ruth provides a good example of how it worked in practice (Ruth 4:1–12).

The corruption of such local courts is a major theme in the prophets (Amos 5:10–15). It was all too easy for elders to be swayed by their own prejudices, or even to accede to the wishes of a king who wanted to act unconstitutionally. The story of Naboth's trial and subsequent execution is a striking illustration of how the whole system could be abused by the powerful for their own advantage (1 Kings 21:1–16). Though false witnesses were liable to severe penalties (Deuteronomy 19:15–20), this does not seem to have deterred perjury, and there is plenty of evidence to show that justice at the city gate was sometimes rough and ready.

The Law was held in great honour by the people of Israel, as it has been by orthodox Jews throughout the generations.

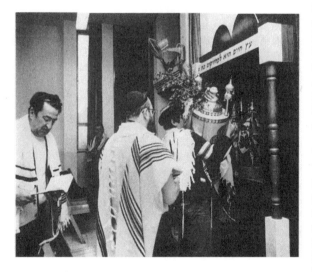

The judges

As well as the courts of elders, the Old Testament also mentions professional judges (Deuteronomy 16:18–20; 19:16–18). The laws of Deuteronomy seem to envisage a system of local judges, with a final court of appeal in Jerusalem itself (Deuteronomy 17:8–13). Albrecht Alt believed that professional judges were important even in the earliest days of Israelite society, and he equated them with

the 'minor judges' (Judges 10:1–5; 12:8–15), suggesting that the law they administered was the casuistic law contained in the book of the covenant. Martin Noth incorporated this insight into his theory that early Israel was organized along the lines of a tribal amphictyony, and these 'minor judges' thereby became the guardians of the covenant theology which held the various tribes together. This view has been considered in detail in an earlier chapter, and though neither Alt nor Noth was ever able to produce any really compelling evidence to support it, it is a plausible way to imagine ancient Israel functioning.

Others have argued that professional judges were a later development, perhaps originating in the southern kingdom of Judah with the political and religious reforms of Jehoshaphat (875–851 BC) documented in 2 Chronicles 19:4–11. They believe that the king always had an important part to play in both establishing and maintaining the Law, and that when Jehoshaphat set up a system of professional judges he was merely formalizing a state of affairs that had existed for a long time.

The king

The king certainly had a central role in the legal affairs of his people. All the ancient law codes known to us are associated with kings, though quite often their function was limited to classifying customary procedures rather than actually originating the Law. Since the laws of a state are a vital part of its self-understanding, it was necessary for the king to be involved in this way if his own position was to be maintained. But the Old Testament gives no real indication that the kings of either Israel or Judah operated in this way. Josiah perhaps came closest to publishing a law (2 Kings 23:1–3), though that story makes it clear that he was acting as an intermediary in a covenant renewal ceremony between God and the people in much the same way as Moses (Exodus 24:3–8) and Joshua (Joshua 24:1–28) had done earlier, and as Ezra was to do later (Nehemiah 8:1–12). When the Old Testament explains the function of the king, there is no mention of lawgiving, and he is himself clearly stated to be subject to the Law of the covenant (Deuteronomy 17:14–20; 1 Samuel 8:10–18).

Some scholars suggest that all this reflects the ideals of Old Testament kingship rather than what actually happened in practice, though incidents in which the king overturned the normal course of justice always seem to be regarded as the exception rather than the rule. There is no substantial evidence that the king was in control of the legal process unless we are prepared to set aside almost the whole of the deutero-nomic history as worthless and unreliable. This need not mean that kings never issued law codes as part of their duties. Josiah was certainly involved in re-establishing the laws of Deuteronomy, and there is also good reason to think that the book of the covenant may have been collated and issued in the time of David and Solomon almost as a constitution for their kingdom. But this did not make it 'state law', because it ultimately rested on a religious understanding of the life of the nation. It could just as easily be argued that when kings became involved in promoting the Law they were acting in a religious capacity rather than as purely political leaders.

Nevertheless, kings did have a judicial function. The kingship itself apparently originated within the general framework of family and tribal life (1 Samuel 8:4–5), and in that context the king would automatically be one of the 'elders' of the extended family of Israel. As such he would have a part to play in the administration of the Law, probably acting as a final court of appeal (2 Samuel 12:1–6; 14:1–11; 1 Kings 3:16–28; 7:7).

The priests

Deuteronomy makes a close connection between judges and priests when it provides for a court of appeal in Jerusalem staffed by both, apparently operating on a rota basis (Deuteronomy 17:8–12). Priests and judges are mentioned alongside one another elsewhere (Deuteronomy 19:17; 2 Chronicles 19:8–11), and in other ancient states priests often had judicial functions. In Israel, the close connection between Law and the covenant made it inevitable that priests would be involved in interpreting and applying the Law. No doubt this priestly function went back to a very early period of Israelite history. Whatever may be the truth about the nature of the 'minor judges', there can be little doubt that, like the 'major' judges, they had a religious as well as a political and social function. Samuel, who is presented as their successor, was essentially a priest operating from the shrines of Bethel, Gilgal and Mizpah, though his typical activities at these centres of worship clearly had judicial overtones (1 Samuel 7:16).

The precise judicial function of the priest is unclear. Priests would certainly pronounce on religious affairs (Leviticus 10:10; 13:1 – 14:57), and there are also hints that they could operate in a wider legal context (Leviticus 10:10–11; Deuteronomy 21:5; Ezekiel 44:24), though apart from the stories of Samuel there is no evidence of them ever doing so. Their more usual function would be as guardians of the final court of appeal, namely God. For the Law allowed that in cases where a normal court could reach no verdict, God should be called in as the final judge. God's will would then be ascertained either by a procedure of judicial oaths (Exodus 22:7–13) or by drawing lots – something probably associated with the manipulation of urim and thummim (sacred stones or dice) by the priests (Joshua 7:1–19; 1 Samuel 14:41–43).

Individuals and the community

The Old Testament lays great emphasis on groups: the family, the clan, the tribe, and ultimately the nation, are all of fundamental importance both religiously and morally. The covenant itself is a relationship between God and the whole people of Israel, and salvation and judgment are both corporate experiences. The processes of justice also take account of this corporate solidarity. When Achan stole some goods from the Canaanite city of Jericho, his entire family and all their goods shared in his punishment (Joshua 7:1–26), and some passages appear to elevate this to a general principle, that children will always be punished for the wrongs of their parents (Exodus 20:5; Deuteronomy 5:9). As a matter of common experience, it is true that any generation inevitably carries some burden from the past, but the Old Testament makes a very specific connection between past and present, the individual and the community. The prophets also emphasize corporate responsibility, pronouncing judgment on the whole nation because of the wrongs of some of its members (Amos 3:12–15; 5:16–24).

This emphasis was perhaps inevitable in a faith which was anchored to the events of history. If the exodus was to be relevant to later generations, then they had in some way to identify themselves with the experience of their forebears, and when they went along to organized worship at the shrines, they often did precisely that (Deuteronomy 26:5–10). This same connection between the experience of an individual and the state of the community also comes out in some of the psalms, though the best example of it is in the passages referring to the suffering servant. For here, this one person both represents the community and fulfils its true destiny in his or her own spiritual experience (Isaiah 42:1–4; 49:1–6; 50:4–9; 52:13 – 53:12). This way of thinking has often been described as 'corporate personality', and it has been assumed that the Old Testament has a unique way of looking at people and their relationships. On this view, the idea of personal responsibility only came into the faith of Israel at a relatively late stage, when the group was in danger of disappearing altogether as an identifiable national entity. Jeremiah 31:29–30 and Ezekiel 18:4, 20 certainly emphasize that each person is responsible to God, but their statements do not really contradict the earlier Old Testament position. In their day, the people were blaming all their problems on past generations, and in response to that Jeremiah and Ezekiel both emphasized that it was not quite as simple as that, for each individual must accept some share of responsibility for the state of society as a whole. In any case, there is plenty of evidence that individuals were believed to have moral and spiritual responsibility long before that time:

● Many individuals in the earlier parts of the Old Testament story are praised for their own personal response and commitment to God. Enoch (Genesis 5:21–24), Noah (Genesis 6:9–12) and Hannah (1 Samuel 1:9 – 2:11) – as well as the prophets – are all specifically described in terms of their own personal spiritual experience.

● Individuals are also condemned and judged for their own wrongdoing. When David committed adultery with Bathsheba, he himself suffered the penalty (2 Samuel 12:1–23), and when Jezebel met her death beneath the ramparts of Jezreel, that was considered a fair punishment for her malicious judicial murder of Naboth (2 Kings 9:30–37). Moreover, the law codes are full of instructions about how individuals are to be dealt with in the light of their own behaviour. The case of Achan, whose entire family was punished for his theft, is in fact exceptional, which implies that it was almost certainly considered to be a specifically religious crime, and for that reason was punishable under different rules.

● Amos seems to have condemned the whole nation without regard for personal responsibility, though he may have expected some to repent and avoid judgment (Amos 5:4–7, 14–15). But other prophets clearly distinguished between the majority of the people who had broken the covenant and a small group who had not and who for that reason would escape punishment (Isaiah 10:20–22; Micah 5:7–8; Zephaniah 2:3; 3:11–13).

The idea of corporate solidarity is both less precise and less extensive than has often been thought. But it is also less distinctive than has sometimes been suggested. Many modern states have a parallel in their memorials to an 'unknown warrior', a military person who has been buried in a public place to be a lasting reminder of thousands of others who died in battle and were laid to rest in unmarked graves where they fell. When people pay their respects at such national monuments, they are not primarily honouring the soldier who happens to be interred there. Through that figure, they are honouring the memory of all those whom the monument represents. The analogy is not exact, for people in ancient Israel obviously felt this strong sense of solidarity at many other levels of everyday life. But a person's place in the nation never encompassed everything, and there was always a belief that people were morally and spiritually responsible to God as individuals.

12 Worshipping God

Worshipping a holy God

A term often used in the Old Testament to explain why God should be
worshipped is the word 'holy'. In ordinary usage, to describe someone or
something as 'holy' can often mean little more than 'religious'. But when
the Old Testament describes Yahweh as 'holy' it is saying some very
specific things about God's relationship with people.

God is infinite

In the Old Testament story, God is best known to the people of Israel
through the events of their history and of their own everyday life.
Because of this, there are many graphic, and often intimate, insights
into God's nature and personality. But this never meant that ordinary
people could know everything about God. For example, when Job was
trying to make sense out of his own frustrating life, he was forced to
admit that in the last analysis there are hidden depths to God's
workings that defy human understanding (Job 42:1–6). Aspects of God's
character might well have been revealed clearly in events such as the
exodus, but there are still other dimensions of God's being that remain
deeply mysterious. Job was not the only one to feel this way, for both
poets (Psalm 139:6) and prophets (Isaiah 40:13–14). knew that God was
different from people. In earlier chapters we have repeatedly noticed
how God's apparent 'hiddenness' was a major part of Israel's experience
on both a personal and a national level. This feeling of perplexity and
wonder in the face of an awe-inspiring divine presence is, of course,
common to religious people the world over. So, also, is the use of the
word 'holy' to describe the difference between God and people. The
literal meaning of the Hebrew word translated 'holy' is not certain,
though many scholars believe it is linguistically related to a word that
means 'to divide'. When people describe the gods they worship as 'holy',
they often think of the universe being divided into two quite different
modes of existence. There is the place where God belongs, and people,
things and events connected with that can be called 'holy'. Then there
is also the world where human beings operate, and that is 'profane' or

'common'. In this context, the words 'holy' and 'profane' do not indicate moral judgments, nor for that matter is there necessarily a spatial implication, as if God literally exists in some other place than people. These expressions are simply terms used to convey the fact that God and people are not the same. The Old Testament shares this widely held view with other nations of both the ancient and the modern world (Leviticus 10:10).

Within this frame of reference, one aim of worship is to enable these two domains to meet and relate to each other. Even apparently 'common' things can be made 'holy' – places, times, people and objects. But once they have been set apart to God in this way, special care must be taken by 'common' people in dealing with them. 'Holiness' is often spoken of in the Old Testament as if it were a great power or invisible forcefield, emanating from the very person of God. It is not easy for modern people in a technological society to understand this way of thinking. But a parallel might be found in our own respect for the contents of the core of a nuclear reactor. Though most of us do not understand its workings, we all know that at the centre of the process are materials emitting out invisible rays of energy that, if not properly contained and controlled by those competent to deal with them, could be disastrous for us all. The Old Testament often uses similar sorts of imagery to describe God's holy presence. When God's will was revealed to Moses at Mount Sinai, God's communication was accompanied by an awesome sense of divine presence that ordinary people needed to avoid. The place became so saturated with this divine power ('holiness') that only specially equipped people were able to cope with it (Exodus 19:9–25). Ordinary people such as Moses could readily be set aside and made holy themselves, but if they came into contact with such holiness before that the results could be catastrophic. The Philistines later learned this to their cost when they tried to meddle with the ark of the covenant (1 Samuel 5:1 – 6:19). But even Israelites could suffer the same fate when they as 'common' persons came into contact with the 'holiness' of the divine presence (2 Samuel 6:1–8). God's majesty and power must be respected, and to call God 'holy' is one way of emphasizing that. Though there is some considerable emphasis on the fact that God can be known in a direct and personal way by ordinary mortals, God is still different, and to be esteemed and treated with due reverence (Exodus 15:11; Job 11:7–12; Psalm 139:6–12).

God is good

Many religious people think of their gods only in terms of awe-inspiring power. But Israel's covenant faith led to a distinctive and more carefully nuanced understanding of what it means to be holy. In the wider world of religions, the mysterious, numinous, all-powerful kind of holiness has often been advanced as an explanation for the irrational and capricious actions of the gods. But the events of Israel's history had shown that the

God of the Old Testament was faithful and trustworthy, not fickle and unpredictable. In the light of that, God's holiness was a way of behaving, as well as a state of being. To say that God is holy also implies that God is good, and since people do not always manage to live by God's standards, it can imply a confession of human failure (Isaiah 55:8).

These two aspects of God's holiness – the numinous and the ethical – are brought together most clearly in the description of the call of the prophet Isaiah as he went to the Temple to worship (Isaiah 6:1–7). By definition, what went on in the Temple was holy in the numinous sense, for the Temple was a holy place, set apart for God's own use, and only those who were ritually holy themselves were able to cope with it. As the prophet stood there with the other worshippers, he had an awe-inspiring experience of God's greatness and power – but in response to this revelation, he at once recognized that a state of ritual cleanness was not enough by itself to equip him for God's presence. God's majestic holiness and moral goodness could not easily be separated from each other, and Isaiah instantly knew that he was unfit to encounter God because of his own sinfulness. This recognition was one of the greatest insights of the Old Testament prophets. In traditional Canaanite spirituality it was widely assumed that divine holiness had only a cultic, numinous dimension, and that people could be made fit to deal with the gods by means of appropriate rituals. The people of Israel were constantly tempted to think the same way, but the prophets insisted that they were wrong and that God was concerned with everyday behaviour, not just with ritual at the shrine (Amos 5:21–24; Micah 6:6–8). Personal and social wrongdoing were incompatible with true worship.

The prophets were not the only ones who saw wrongdoing as a barrier to acceptance by God. The writers and editors of the law codes made the same connection between morals and worship, and the very words that worshippers used in the Temple itself often reminded them of precisely the same fact: 'Who has the right to go up Yahweh's hill? Who may enter God's holy Temple? Those who are pure in act and in thought' (Psalm 24:3–4).

Some details of Israelite worship echoed the cults of the surrounding peoples, though Israel's monotheism made the central thrust quite different. This Philistine cult stand showing musicians dates from the early tenth century BC.

God is love

For Isaiah, the painful awareness of God's moral holiness was inextricably linked to his own need for forgiveness (Isaiah 6:5). A way had to be found by which the sinful prophet could be made fit for the presence of such a holy God. In numinous terms, a person could be empowered to deal with holiness by undergoing the required ritual procedures. But how could moral reformation be brought about? Like others both before and after him, Isaiah knew only too well that human effort, while not insignificant, was unlikely to be able to achieve this ultimate transformation by itself, and if he was to be morally right with God, this was

something that only God would be able to accomplish. So the means of
Isaiah's spiritual reconciliation comes from God, carried directly from the
altar, and through this symbolic act he is told 'your guilt is gone, and
your sins are forgiven' (Isaiah 6:7). The book of Isaiah frequently calls
God 'the holy one' precisely because God forgives wrongdoing and
brings salvation to the lives of the people. God is almighty and infinite,
as well as morally perfect, but God also cares for ordinary, struggling
people. To describe God as 'holy' not only defines God's awesome power,
but also implies God's perfect love. At the same time as God's holy
presence highlights human failure, it provides the means whereby
wrongdoing can be forgiven and new life can be born: 'I am the high
and holy God, who lives for ever. I live in a high and holy place, but I
also live with people who are humble and repentant, so that I can
restore their confidence and hope' (Isaiah 57:15).

This is the background against which Old Testament worship needs
to be understood. Sincere worship reflects the response of God's people
to the revelation of God's nature, and the nature of God's holiness in
turn determines the character of the human response. Because God is
almighty, true worship must always respect the barriers between the
sacred and the secular, the holy and the profane. Because God is good,
true worship must honestly face up to the reality of human wrongdoing.
But because God is love, the repentant worshipper can always look for
God's forgiveness and anticipate the promise of a renewed life. The
precise way in which these themes are related to each other varies from
one occasion of worship to another. But all worship begins from the
recognition that God is holy and people are not. It is a celebration of the
many ways in which they can be made fit for God's presence.

Places of worship

A place of worship in the ancient world was not a space for people to
gather and hold meetings, but a place set apart for the use of the deities,
in which people would celebrate and bring offerings. Later Jewish
synagogues and Christian churches were essentially places for people to
meet one another, whereas traditional Israelite places of worship were
places where people could encounter God. A place of worship could not
therefore be constructed just anywhere, to suit the convenience of those
who might wish to go there. It needed to be a recognizably 'holy' place,
a spot at which God had been revealed in some specific way, and which
men and women could, therefore, assume was a place where the
holiness of God's presence might safely intersect with the profane life of
the world. When Moses encountered the burning bush in the desert, he
recognized it as just such a place (Exodus 3:5–6). That particular spot
never became a regular place of worship, presumably because of its
distance from the main centres of population in later Israel. But later
generations had many such places where they could legitimately

worship, because God had previously met there with the leaders of their nation. Inevitably, the most popular places of worship changed with the passage of time, and as we read the Old Testament story we can trace a number of significant stages.

The tabernacle or tent of Yahweh's presence

The stories of the earliest days of Israel's history depict the tribes who escaped from Egypt worshipping at a special tent placed in the centre of their camp. A variety of terms are used to describe this tent, though it is most often referred to as the tent of Yahweh's presence or tabernacle. The practice of having such a place for worship is not unusual among nomadic peoples in the Middle East even today. God's presence in this sanctuary ('holiness') was symbolized by the cloud which covered it.

During the Israelites' time as desert nomads, the central place in their camp was given to the 'tent of the Lord's presence' or 'tabernacle', with the ark of the covenant in its holy of holies. The altar for sacrifice stood on open ground outside the tent itself.

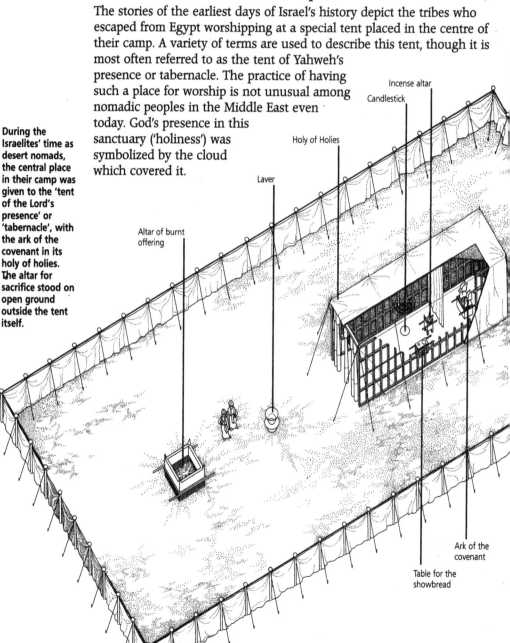

Incense altar

Candlestick

Holy of Holies

Laver

Altar of burnt offering

Ark of the covenant

Table for the showbread

The movement of this cloud provided the signal for the tribes to move on. The Old Testament provides detailed instructions for the construction and use of this portable sanctuary. There is considerable debate among scholars as to the precise origin of these instructions, but the general picture they give is typical of many ancient places of worship. A central enclosure marked the most holy part of the tent (the holy of holies), and this in turn was surrounded by various other enclosures until the boundary of the shrine was reached. Beyond this were the tents of the priests and those of the people. Such an arrangement was found in every place of worship throughout the whole of the Old Testament period. In the words of Ezekiel, it was designed 'to separate what was holy from what was not' (42:20), and to ensure that only those who were properly qualified would come into contact with the awesome holiness of God's presence at the very centre of the sanctuary. The sacred tents of Bedouin tribes would often contain a visual representation of their gods within this most holy place, but Israel never portrayed God in that way. Instead, the holy of holies contained the ark of the covenant. There is a good deal of uncertainty about the precise significance of this ark, but it was certainly identified very closely with God's personal presence in the midst of the people (Numbers 10:35–36; Joshua 4:5–13).

We do not know for sure what happened to either the ark or the tabernacle. The ark features in the Old Testament narratives a number of times after the desert period. It was present at the crossing of the River Jordan (Joshua 3:1 – 5:1). Later it was kept at Bethel (Judges 20:18–28), but was then captured from the sanctuary at Shiloh by the Philistines in the time of Samuel (1 Samuel 4:1 – 7:1), and later again it was taken to Jerusalem by David (2 Samuel 6:1–23), where Solomon finally installed it in the Temple (1 Kings 8:1–13). References in the liturgies of the psalms suggest that it was regularly used in religious festivals at Jerusalem (Psalms 24:7–10; 48:12–14; 132:1–18), and it was probably either destroyed or taken away by the Babylonian king Nebuchadnezzar when he overthrew Jerusalem in 586 BC. In any event, after the exile its place in the Temple was probably occupied by a gold plate, and by New Testament times Josephus says that the holy of holies was completely empty (*Jewish Wars* 5.5.5).

The tent of Yahweh's presence disappears from the narratives even earlier than the ark of the covenant, and there are no clear references to it after the tribes had settled in the land of Canaan. Some passages seem to imply that it was at one stage based in Shiloh (Joshua 18:1; 19:51; 1 Samuel 2:22), but if that was the case it cannot have lasted for long, and by the time Samuel had grown up Shiloh had a permanent building for worship (1 Samuel 1:7, 9; 3:15). 1 Chronicles 16:39 contains a reference to 'the tent of Yahweh' at Gibeon in the time of Solomon, though there is some uncertainty over the precise meaning of that phrase. David placed the ark of the covenant in a tent when he first took it to Jerusalem, but though this was undoubtedly intended to evoke images of the tent of Yahweh's presence, there is no suggestion that the tent he used was anything other than a new construction (2 Samuel 6:17; 7:2; 1 Kings 1:39).

Both ark and tent played an important role in the development of Israel's faith. By their very nature they were a challenge to the widespread view that gods were restricted in power and influence to specific places and peoples. From the earliest period of Israel's emergence as a nation, there was much debate as to whether Yahweh's power was territorial, extending only over the desert, and as a result the people generally included in their worship the traditional Canaanite deities as well, just to be on the safe side. Later on, in the time of Jeremiah, just before the final collapse of the kingdom of Judah, the people of Jerusalem went to the opposite extreme, and concluded that their city could never fall to their enemies because God lived there, in the Temple (Jeremiah 7:1–15). Both attitudes were understandable, but to the spiritual leaders of the nation both were false, and when Isaiah of Babylon declared that Israel's God was in reality the God of the whole world, he was articulating something that had been implicit in the Old Testament faith from a very early period (Isaiah 44:1–8).

Local sanctuaries

People always like to worship where they live, and the local sanctuaries in towns and villages throughout the land had an important part to play for most of the Old Testament period. Almost every settlement must have had its own place of worship, though not all of them would have been buildings. A majority may have been

little more than altars in the open air at which regular sacrifices could be offered. A great many such altars have been discovered by archaeologists throughout Palestine, sometimes constructed from heaps of stones, though at other times a natural feature of the landscape or a particularly striking rock would be used for the purpose.

Almost every settlement had a local place of worship. This model shrine has two pillars at the front similar in style to Solomon's temple.

The stories of Israel's earliest ancestors depict them worshipping at a great number of such local sanctuaries right across the country – places like Hebron, Mamre, Beersheba and Mizpah (Genesis 13:18; 18:1–15; 26:23–25; 31:43–55). These places were all traditional Canaanite places of worship, though the final editors of the Genesis stories generally point out that it was really the covenant God Yahweh whom they worshipped there, even if they did not realize it at the time. On other occasions the ancestors are depicted establishing new centres of worship. When Jacob had an unusual dream in the open air, he recognized the place of his dreaming as holy because he met God there (Genesis 28:10–22). As a result, he called it 'Bethel', meaning 'house of God', and later generations of Israelites regarded it as a particularly holy place (Judges 20:18–28; 1 Samuel 7:16; 10:3). After the collapse of Solomon's united kingdom, Bethel became one of the major sanctuaries of the northern kingdom of Israel (1 Kings 12:29 – 13:32; Amos 3:14; 4:4; 5:5–6; 7:10–13).

Local places of worship play an important part in the historical narratives. The stories about Samuel associate him with the sanctuaries at Shiloh, Bethel, Gilgal, Mizpah and Ramah (1 Samuel 1:1 – 3:21; 7:16–17). The shrine at Shiloh was evidently of sufficient importance to be called a temple, though after its destruction by the Philistines in about 1050 BC the centre of attention moved to other places, notably Gilgal (1 Samuel 11:14–15) and Mizpah (1 Samuel 13:8–15), both of which are connected with significant stages in Saul's career as king (1 Samuel 10:17–27). Later, King Solomon was a regular visitor to a sanctuary at Gibeon, and it was there that he had his famous dream in which he was promised the gift of wisdom (1 Kings 3:4–15). In that story, Gibeon is described as the place 'where the most famous altar was', but that was not to last for long, for soon afterwards Solomon built his great Temple in Jerusalem (1 Kings 5:1 – 6:38). After that, the local sanctuaries must have been put in the shade by the splendour of Temple worship. The large staff of priests and other officials there made worship so much more impressive and exciting than what went on in smaller towns and villages, and it was not long before substantial crowds were making regular pilgrimages to Jerusalem. This was what Solomon had wanted, for political as well as religious reasons, but it inevitably meant that smaller shrines had to struggle to survive. Many local places of worship probably fell into disuse at this period, while many more reverted to the traditional Canaanite forms of worship that the prophets denounced as departures from the true covenant faith. Such worship was certainly widespread, for looking back at this period Jeremiah could later comment, 'On every high hill and under every green tree you worshipped fertility gods' (Jeremiah 2:20). This complaint had particular relevance to the sanctuaries of the northern kingdom, but even in Judah every later attempt at religious reform involved the forcible closure of these local sanctuaries which had become centres of alien worship (2 Kings 18:4; 21:2–7; 23:1–20).

The sanctuary at Shiloh was of national importance to Israel until its destruction by the Philistines in about 1050 BC.

The Temple

The Temple in Jerusalem came to occupy a special place in the devotion of the people. Its unique position was celebrated in much of ancient Israel's best-loved poetry. It symbolized all the distinctive features not only of Israel's faith, but also of the self-consciousness of the nation, uniting the political and religious aspirations of the people, centred on the kings who ruled from Jerusalem as the successors of David. Devotion to the Temple could sometimes lead to misplaced nationalism, as it did in the days of Jeremiah when the inhabitants of Jerusalem were certain that nothing could happen to their city because the Temple was there (Jeremiah 7:1–15). The prophets had to remind them that God's holy presence in the Temple could become a sign of judgment as well as salvation, and it was possible to preserve the external appearance of true worship when in reality God's presence was no longer there (Ezekiel 10:1–22).

The Hebrew Bible contains some comprehensive accounts of the building of the Temple by Solomon (1 Kings 6:1–38; 7:12–51; 2 Chronicles 2:17 – 5:1), though the details of the design are never clearly spelled out, and when scholars have tried to construct models of the Temple they have come up with a number of different proposals. It is clear that the general layout was similar to many other temples throughout the ancient world, though no precisely identical temple has been found elsewhere in the region. This similarity is not surprising, as Solomon needed to import workers from Phoenicia to design and build it, presumably because Israel had no previous experience of a large-scale building project (1 Kings 5:1–12; 7:13–14). In general terms, the layout of the Temple was similar to the design of the tent of Yahweh's presence, with a central holy of holies surrounded by other spaces and enclosures. Indeed, most scholars believe that the Old Testament's descriptions of the tent are actually derived from the design of the later Temple. The basic structure consisted of three rooms: an entrance hall, a main room and, at a slightly higher level, the holy of holies. Whereas the entrance hall and main room were rectangular, with the doors on the shorter sides, the holy of holies was a square, and this was where the ark of the covenant was kept, with two large golden cherubim suspended from the ceiling above it.

Most of the worship took place not in the holy of holies, but in the other parts of the Temple building and courtyards. The actual contents of these areas varied from time to time, and the religious symbols and altars used there were often as much an indication of the nation's political alliances as of its spiritual commitment. When Ahaz wanted to seal his alliance with Assyria, he adjusted the Temple contents to prove his good intentions (2 Kings 16:10–18). His successor Hezekiah, on the other hand, wished to reassert Judah's independence, and set about removing such signs of external religious influence (2 Kings 18:4), only to have Manasseh later bring them all back again (2 Kings 21:1–7), until

Josiah eventually inaugurated a thoroughgoing religious reformation, and completely refurbished the Temple as well as closing down local shrines throughout the country (2 Kings 23:1–20). There was obviously a close connection between the kings of Judah and the Temple. Solomon played a major part in building it and in organizing worship there. But he also had his own palace next door, linked to the Temple by a private pathway (2 Kings 16:18). The Temple was more than a national place of worship: it also symbolized the power of the royal family of David. In the ancient world, politics and religion were often two sides of the same coin, and David and Solomon had political reasons for wanting to build a temple in Jerusalem. Various buildings mentioned on the perimeter of the Temple precinct may well have housed the king's personal treasury. Certainly, much of the nation's wealth must have been kept there, for invaders regularly went to the Temple to plunder it (1 Kings 14:25–28; 15:15; 2 Kings 16:7–8; 18:15–16; 24:12–13).

As well as priests, the Temple had a large staff, including administrators (Ezra 2:40–42) and Temple servants who kept the fires burning on the various altars used in worship (Joshua 9:27; Ezra 2:43–54; 8:20). Some of these workers may well have been non-Israelites, for the prophet Ezekiel later complained about the practice of allowing foreigners to be involved in the life of the Temple (Ezekiel 44:6–9). Not everyone, however, was happy with the Temple. There were always radicals who felt that it was a backwards step in Israel's spiritual pilgrimage, and that the covenant faith would be better served by adherence to the less settled ways of worship represented by the tent of Yahweh's presence (2 Samuel 7:5–7; Isaiah 66:1; Jeremiah 35:1–19). But most people were committed to it, and though they knew well enough that God did not literally 'live' in the Temple (1 Kings 8:27–30; Psalm 11:4), this was still the place where they felt most directly in God's presence (Psalms 26:8; 63:1–5; 84:1–4; 122:1). Their anguish was real and deeply felt when it was destroyed by the Babylonians (Psalm 137). After the exile, a replacement was built, of which we know only very little – but it was obviously a much less impressive place than the original had been (Ezra 1:2–4; 3:1 – 6:18).

The synagogue

The exile was in every way a great watershed for the people of Israel, and from that point onwards their worship was never again to be quite the same as it had been in the days of the kingdoms of Israel and Judah. The Temple was rebuilt in Jerusalem, and it continued to occupy a special place in the affection of the Jewish people. But the effective centre of worship shifted to the synagogue. By the start of the Christian era there were synagogues in all the important towns of the Mediterranean world, and Jewish people went there week by week for regular worship. Synagogue worship was quite different from Temple worship. For one thing, it was on a much smaller scale, and in addition, it never included sacrifice. Prayer, and the reading of the Law and Prophets, came to be all-important. Naturally, there was no ark of the covenant or a holy of holies, though later synagogues had their own 'ark of the law' which contained the sacred scrolls of the Hebrew scriptures.

Almost all the evidence for life and worship in the synagogues is later than the Old Testament period, much of it a lot later. It shows that the synagogues were more than places of worship: they were also social and educational centres for the many Jewish communities scattered throughout the world in the early centuries of the Christian era. The synagogues emerged to fill a need which had not existed when Israel was an independent nation with their own land. There is no certainty about how and when the synagogues originated, though several possibilities have been suggested:

■ Some believe they began in Judah itself even before the exile. We know that in the course of his religious reforms, Josiah made a concerted effort to close down the local sanctuaries throughout his kingdom and to centralize all worship in Jerusalem. Of course, that could not eliminate the need for people to worship where they lived and so, the argument goes, they went to Jerusalem only when they needed the sort of sacrificial worship that took place there. At other times they met for more informal local worship, which was the precedent for the emergence of the synagogue. There is, however, no evidence to support this view. Indeed, it is doubtful whether Josiah's reformation was quite as successful as that, for less than twenty years later Jeremiah provides plenty of evidence for worship continuing at traditional sites throughout the country.

■ It seems undeniable that the synagogue must have originated after the Temple at Jerusalem was no longer available for worship. After the destruction of Jerusalem by Nebuchadnezzar, the remnants of the

The Temple belonged to the whole Jewish nation, but the synagogues belonged to each local community. They began to play an important part in regular worship from the time that the Jews returned from Babylon. These remains are of the synagogue at Capernaum in Galilee.

population left in Judah probably worshipped on the Temple site from time to time (Jeremiah 41:4–5), but those who were transported to Babylon had no further access to Jerusalem. Possibly, therefore, synagogues began as places of prayer and contemplation for these exiles in Babylon itself. These people certainly took a close interest in the gathering together of the books of the Law and Prophets. But again there are no real facts to go on, and a certain amount of evidence to the contrary. In Psalm 137, for example, the exiles bemoan their predicament, but no reference at all is made to the possibility of synagogue worship as a way of compensating for the loss of the Temple. Comparatively few remains of synagogue buildings have been unearthed in Babylon, none of them relating to the Old Testament period.

■ It has also been suggested that the synagogue began in Palestine after the return of some of the exiles under Nehemiah and Ezra. There is a good deal of archaeological evidence for the existence of synagogue buildings in Palestine, though again none of it goes back to this period. Perhaps the most we can say is that the need for regular worship, combined with Ezra's strong emphasis on the reading and interpretation of the Law, could have provided suitable conditions for this new form of worship to evolve (Nehemiah 8:1–12).

Wherever the synagogues came from, the simple worship carried on there was an authentic reflection of an important strand in the spirituality of ancient Israel. For though the people rejoiced in the splendid magnificence of the Temple at Jerusalem, it had always been recognized that God's presence could not be restricted to one place. The consciousness that God was with them (symbolized by the ark of the covenant) was more fundamental than the need for a holy place like the Temple. There are many stories which show that God's presence could be enjoyed anywhere: Joseph met God in a prison (Genesis 39:21); Jeremiah at the bottom of a well (Jeremiah 38:1–13). When the Jewish people began to worship in synagogues throughout the world, not only were they coming to terms with the political realities of their national life, they were also exploring new dimensions in the covenant faith itself. Perhaps that is why Jewish writers such as Philo of Alexandria (*Life of Moses* ii:39) and Josephus (*Against Apion* 2.17) insisted that the synagogue began with Moses. Historically, they were certainly wrong, · but ideologically they were giving expression to an important aspect of the Old Testament faith.

The character of worship

What was worship like in Old Testament times? Reference has already been made to prayer in the synagogue and sacrifice in the Jerusalem Temple. Other passages mention the use of incense (Jeremiah 6:20) and the giving of monetary offerings (Amos 4:4), though the Hebrew Bible contains no fully detailed account of a complete celebration of worship. The most specific instructions refer to the offering of sacrifices, but worship obviously included a lot more than that (Leviticus 1:1 – 7:38; Numbers 15:1–31; 28:1 – 29:40). What went on in the local sanctuaries and in the Temple was probably so familiar a part of life that it was unnecessary to spell it all out in detail. Of course, it was inevitable that the Old Testament in its final form should ignore some aspects of worship in ancient Israel, for we know from the prophets that the people regularly worshipped their own God Yahweh using the rituals of the local Baal religion – and though this was popular, it was regarded as a denial of the true covenant faith.

In spite of the absence of any comprehensive set of instructions for the conduct of public worship, scholars agree that the Old Testament

This mosaic from the synagogue at Beth Shan includes pictures of the ark of the covenant, menorah (seven-branched candlestick) and shofar (ram's-horn trumpet).

does contain a good deal of material that was regularly used in that context, especially in the book of Psalms. This has been called 'the hymn book of the Second Temple', and it may well have been compiled at that time, for some psalms clearly refer to the exile and the events that followed it. Not all psalms are hymns in the normal sense. Some of them are more personal and individual expressions of piety, while others refer to the great ceremonial events of

Understanding the psalms

At one time, scholars tried to understand the psalms either as purely personal poetry, or as poems composed on particular historical occasions in the course of Israel's history. But more recent study has suggested that most of them had their roots in the worship at Solomon's Temple, and quite possibly in the worship at local sanctuaries as well. There are a number of reasons for accepting this:

● At least one Old Testament passage shows psalms being used in the course of worship. When David first brought the ark of the covenant into Jerusalem, its arrival was accompanied by dancing and singing (2 Samuel 6:5). One account of this incident includes an example of the songs that were sung on the occasion, and this turns out to be surprisingly similar to several of the psalms (1 Chronicles 16:8–36).

● Other Old Testament passages also confirm the important part played in worship by religious songs and poetry of the type found in the book of Psalms (Amos 5:23).

● Much of the imagery used in the psalms is very similar to imagery used in specifically religious poetry and songs elsewhere in the ancient cultures of Palestine. There are particularly close linguistic connections between many of the psalms and the songs used to worship Baal as depicted in the texts from Ugarit. The theological ideas are completely

national life. But whatever their form, the psalms provide an invaluable glimpse into the way God was worshipped in the Temple at Jerusalem in the period before the exile. Sometimes we see individuals at worship. In others, we can catch sight of great national occasions involving the whole community. Some psalms centre on the king and God's promises to the royal family of David. One thing we do not find, however, is worship related to rites of passage such as birth, marriage and death. Most nations celebrate these events in the context of religious worship, but in ancient Israel they were all essentially family matters, and in the time before the exile they had no particular connection with formal worship at all.

When we analyse the psalms and other references to worship, we soon discover that it included many different activities.

Singing and music

This was a vital element in all worship, and it appears throughout the Old Testament as an appropriate way for people to praise God. It was, of course, an important activity in many ancient religions. So, for example, when Elijah confronted the prophets of Baal on Mount Carmel, the Baal worshippers used music to stir themselves up into a frenzy (1 Kings 18:27–29). On occasion, prophets of Yahweh could use it for the same purpose (1 Samuel 10:5, 10–13). Not all religious singing was necessarily pleasing to God (Amos 5:23), but without it, proper praise could not take place. God's holy character found its natural response in this kind of worship (Psalm 22:3), and the awareness of God's presence most naturally led to worshipping with 'glad songs of praise' (Psalm 63:5). Singing became especially important after the exile, and the names of several choirs are mentioned in this connection (1 Chronicles 16:4–7;

---

different, of course, but a judicious comparison of the psalms with these other texts has led to enormous advances in our understanding of the meaning of many obscure Hebrew words used in the Old Testament.

● The Jerusalem Temple and its worship provide many of the basic themes of the psalms, reflecting the centrality of the Temple as a symbol of God's presence (Psalms 11:4; 46:4–6; 50:2), and the eager longing of the people to share in its worship (Psalms 26:8; 84:1–4; 111:1). Indeed, some of them even seem to refer directly to sacrificial worship (Psalm 36:8) and to the various days over which the great national festivals would be held (Psalm 118:24).

● The structure of some psalms seems to indicate that they were used as comprehensive liturgies for worship on particular occasions (e.g. Psalm 118:1–4). Some depict a number of participants in the worship, asking questions and receiving responses (e.g. Psalm 24). It is quite likely that many of the obscure references in the psalm titles are really instructions about how they were to be used in worship, and the Hebrew word selah, which appears in a number of psalms, is almost certainly an instruction to the Temple singers to increase the volume and sing louder.

Music played a central part in worship, and a great variety of instruments were used, just as they were among Israel's neighbours. The leading musician on this relief from Zinjirli is playing a eight-stringed lyre, the second a six-stringed lyre, and the two others are playing on hand drums.

25:1–31; Ezra 2:40–42). Some of the psalms have refrains, which suggests that one part of the song would be sung by the worshippers, and the rest by the choir (Psalms 42:5, 11; 43:5; 46:7, 11). Musical instruments are also mentioned in connection with the praise of God: tambourines, harps, lyres, drums, trumpets, rattles, horns, flutes and cymbals (2 Samuel 6:5; 1 Chronicles 25:1–6; Psalms 43:4; 68:25; 81:1–3; 98:4–6; 150:3–5; Isaiah 30:29). Worship was obviously a joyful business, and the carnival atmosphere of the Temple is captured in one of the psalms which speaks of 'a happy crowd, singing and shouting praise to God' (Psalm 42:4).

Prayer

This was to become one of the characteristic activities of the synagogue, and by the start of the Christian era there were also regular daily times of prayer in the Temple at Jerusalem. It is unclear whether this custom originated in earlier times, though prayer was certainly a vital element in worship right from the start. The belief that ordinary people could have direct access to God was a fundamental part of Israelite spirituality. Not only prophets such as Elijah (1 Kings 18:36–37), or kings such as Solomon (1 Kings 8:22–61), but ordinary people such as Hannah (1 Samuel 2:1–10) could bring their everyday concerns to God. The Torah contains prayers to be said on special occasions (e.g. Deuteronomy 26:5–10), and the book of Psalms contains many examples of prayers that were no doubt used by individuals, as well as by groups of worshippers, to give thanks and to express their trust and confidence in God. Physical movement was always an important part of prayer, emphasizing the essentially embodied nature of Old Testament spirituality. Sometimes the worshipper would kneel to pray (1 Kings 8:54), or bow low to the ground (Psalm 5:7). At other times prayers might be said in a standing position (1 Samuel 1:26), occasionally with hands raised up above the head (1 Kings 8:22, 54; Psalm 63:4; Isaiah 1:15). But while posture was important, it needed to be accompanied by 'a humble and repentant heart' (Psalm 51:17).

Dance and drama

Given the importance attached to singing and music in biblical worship, and the emphasis on the use of the body in prayer, it is no surprise to discover that dancing was also regularly used in the praise of God. Some of the psalms seem to presuppose it (e.g. 26:6), and others specifically encourage it (e.g. 149:3; 150:4). On one occasion even King David himself took part in public dancing as the ark of the covenant was brought into the city of Jerusalem. Indeed, he danced so vigorously that his wife thought his behaviour was indecent, and rebuked him for making a fool of himself (2 Samuel 6:1–22).

There is also evidence for the use of drama in worship, with many indications of occasions on which worshippers would process in and out of the Temple and around the city of Jerusalem (Psalms 26:6; 42:4; 48:12–14; 118:19, 26–27). Sometimes, God is depicted accompanying the worshippers as they go, perhaps in the form of the ark of the covenant, carried at the head of the procession (Psalms 68:24–27; 132:7–9). Other passages suggest that God's mighty acts in the past could be re-enacted in the course of worship, to bring home their lessons to new generations (Psalms 46:8–10; 48:8; 66:5). At the annual Passover festival – celebrated in the home rather than at a public event – drama also played an important part, for at the most solemn moment the worshippers ate a meal together dressed ready to go on a journey, just as the slaves in Egypt had done at the time of the exodus (Exodus 12:21–28). Symbolic actions could also play an important part in more ordinary acts of worship (Psalm 26:6). Drama has always been a powerful medium through which people can express their deepest convictions, and when the worshippers of ancient Israel reminded themselves of God's goodness to their nation they did so in action as well as in word.

Sacrifice

To many people, this is the most characteristic activity of Old Testament worship. Certainly, it was a daily ritual in the Temple, but it was only one element among many. Modern Western people tend to give so much attention to it simply because it is generally remote from their own experience. To us, the gratuitous death of animals in the course of religious worship is something repugnant, and our understanding is not helped here by the fact that the Hebrew Bible never explains exactly why this form of worship was used. As with so many other things, it simply takes it for granted that everyone would know why sacrifice was an appropriate way to worship.

Sacrifice is a worldwide phenomenon, and is not restricted either to the Old Testament or the Middle East. Anthropologists have tried hard to understand the need for sacrifice in different cultural contexts around the world, and the general consensus is that to appreciate the importance of it, we need to return to the observations about 'holiness' with which we began this chapter. Wherever it is practised, sacrifice is always understood as a means of relating the visible, tangible world in which people exist to the invisible, intangible (and often uncontrollable) world in which God or the gods exist. It is a means whereby people can encounter the powerful 'holiness'

that radiates out from the presence of God, without suffering the horrific consequences that would normally be expected to follow such an encounter. This is why animals (particularly domestic animals) were appropriate as sacrifices, for they are themselves living, have a close relationship to people, and could therefore serve as a suitable symbol of the worshippers.

Different faiths will have different understandings of the nature of sacrifice. For example, in many contexts it is thought of as a way of feeding the deities, though this is a view that the Old Testament rejects. The Israelite understanding of sacrifice was dominated by their perception of the meaning of holiness, which meant that an important function of sacrifice was concerned with securing ritual purity (Leviticus 11:1 – 15:33). At the same time, the moral dimensions of God's character were never far from view, and as time went on and the events of history made the need for forgiveness of wrongdoing more obvious, this came to be the predominant meaning that was attached to sacrifice (Ezekiel 45:18–25). This does not mean

that sacrifice and the forgiveness of wrongdoing were linked only at a late date, for at an earlier period, even sacrifices that were not identified as 'sin offerings' could be accompanied by great repentance (Judges 20:26; 21:1–4; 1 Samuel 7:2–9; Job 1:5). The prophets and others often reminded the people of the need for true confession and repentance to accompany sacrificial worship (Psalm 51:16–19; Amos 5:21–24; Micah 6:6–8). As in so many other things, the actual practice of ancient Israel varied according to time and place, and there is no shortage of evidence indicating that traditional Canaanite styles of worship continued, even though they were opposed by the prophets as being alien to Israel's true faith (Jeremiah 44:24–25; Amos 5:25–27).

The Old Testament mentions many different types of sacrifice. In some ways, they defy comprehensive analysis, though anthropologists have identified three major types of sacrifice in more general use, and it will be helpful to use these divisions in our discussion here.

The Israelites and their neighbours sacrificed animals as part of their worship. The small group of Samaritans who remain today still practise the sacrifice of animals.

GIFT SACRIFICES

Sacrifices would often be given to God as a way of returning thanks for some particular benefit that the worshipper had received. The very first sacrifices mentioned in the Hebrew Bible were of this type (Genesis 4:3–4), as also was the sacrifice of Noah after the great flood had subsided

Understanding sacrifice

Sacrifice was practised in many ancient cultures, and was a way of reaffirming the structures of organized life. This drawing, inscribed on shell, is of a worshipper carrying a kid. It comes from Mari, and dates from the middle of the third millennium BC.

So far, we have looked at the ways in which sacrifices were used in the worship of God in the Old Testament. But what is sacrifice all about? Just what did the worshippers think they were doing when they engaged in this sort of activity? At one time, it was thought that sacrifice was based on superstition and ignorance, and that it was only relatively late in Israel's history that it came to have any theological significance attached to it, as it came to be understood as a way of making amends for wrongdoing. But the anthropological study of sacrifice in many different cultures has shown that, whatever else it is, sacrificial worship certainly is not unsophisticated.

Wherever it is practised, sacrifice is a means of reaffirming the structures of organized life: it declares that God and people are united in a relationship of mutual interdependence, and, by means of the meal which often follows a sacrifice, it affirms the importance of good social relationships as the basis for a contented life. In the context of Israelite faith, those affirmations are central. Peace and harmony with God are fundamental requirements for a good life, and these things can be found only in a living relationship with God. Sacrifice, therefore, needed to be offered at those points in a person's life when they were out of tune with the 'holiness' that characterized God's own being.

Sacrifice and holiness

Just as God's holiness was defined in a number of ways, so sacrifices could be offered for a number of purposes:

● In relation to the mysterious, numinous holiness that radiated out from the divine presence, sacrifice was the means by which a person who was 'unclean' could be made 'clean' and fit to encounter God's holy power. In this context, the notion of 'unclean' was not related to morality or behaviour: things such as illness, touching a dead body, giving birth, menstruation – even having mildew in houses or clothing – all rendered a person 'unclean' in this ritual sense (Leviticus 11–15). This might well appear to be an odd collection of things, but what unites them seems to be the fact that they are all things that happen occasionally, and are not a part of everyday life. In this context, those things that are 'clean' are perhaps what we might call 'normal' – and any unusual occurrence renders a person 'unclean'. The precise reasons for this are no doubt lost in the mists of antiquity, but before a person could approach the holy presence of God in the sanctuary, such uncleanness had to be dealt with by the offering of appropriate sacrifices.

● There was also a moral side to the way God's holiness was understood in Israelite society. Wrongdoing was another thing that made people 'unclean', and therefore unfit to deal with God. An inadequate understanding of this led to many problems in the history of ancient Israel. The people were naturally inclined to think that worship was concerned only with the ritual aspects of holiness, and the prophets were continually reminding them that ritual worship and everyday behaviour could not be separated. There can be no doubt that the nation as a whole took a long time to

(Genesis 8:20). At the other end of the story we find the exiles who returned from Babylon offering the same sort of sacrifices (Ezra 6:16–18), while they are also mentioned in many of the psalms (e.g. 54:6–7; 56:12–13). On other occasions, gift sacrifices might be offered in order to secure God's guidance for the future (1 Samuel 7:9), though quite often a gift sacrifice would be

---

learn this lesson, which probably explains why offerings for sin came to assume more importance as time went on. For sacrifice was also the way that sin could be forgiven, and people could be restored to fellowship with God.

Making a sacrifice

The worshipper who made a sacrifice in ancient Israel did so out of a consciousness of being alienated from God, for whatever reason. Reconciliation with God had to be achieved in order for life to proceed as God intended it to. This sense of alienation is familiar enough to modern people, as also is the usefulness of some visible, tactile, symbolic way of dealing with it. Protestant Christianity has tended to place all the emphasis on internal spiritual change as the means of addressing personal dysfunction, but in the Old Testament (as in other Christian traditions) this change of internal disposition was always displayed externally. Here, sacrifice became a visible symbol of change in a person's life, and the actual act of sacrifice was designed to correspond with the stages whereby such change could be brought about.

First of all, the worshipper would approach the altar of God with their sacrifice, and would then lay their hand on the animal's head, to indicate that they wished to be identified with the animal. This was most important, for it meant that from this point onwards the animal was to be symbolic of the worshipper: whatever happened physically and outwardly to the animal was to happen to the worshipper spiritually and inwardly. Four things then took place:

● The animal was killed. In this action, the worshipper was reminded of the consequence of uncleanness: death, and separation from fellowship with God. The worshipper would perform this action personally, thereby declaring that he or she was ready to undergo some radical change.

● The priest then took the blood of the sacrifice (which now represented the worshipper's life offered up to God) to the altar. Depending on the identity of the person, different altars would be used. For an ordinary person, it was the altar of burnt offerings in the Temple courtyard; for a priest, the altar of incense in the Temple itself; and for the whole nation (on the day of atonement), the lid of the ark in the holy of holies. This action constituted the moment when the worshipper's uncleanness was removed (Leviticus 17:11) – the moment of reconciliation, or 'atonement' as it is sometimes called. God and people had been reunited in fellowship.

● After this, the animal's body was placed on the altar in the Temple, as a sign that the worshipper was now offering their whole life to God. In the case of a gift offering, the entire sacrifice would be burned there.

● Finally, depending on the nature of the sacrifice, some of the meat still left was eaten in a meal. Not only were things right between God and the individual worshipper: true fellowship with other people had also been restored.

We can see from all this that sacrifice was a very important part of worship. It both represented basic aspects of the Old Testament faith (people made for fellowship with God and with one another), and also externalized the faith in such a way that no one would be left in any doubt about what it meant to address Yahweh as a 'holy' God.

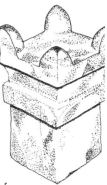

A horned altar found at Megiddo. It may have been used for burnt offerings, or as an incense altar, with the four corner projections supporting a bowl of incense.

given as a simple expression of joy on the part of the worshipper
(1 Samuel 6:14; 2 Samuel 6:17; Psalm 96:8). Such offerings would usually
be given in their entirety to God, by being burned on the altar of the
sanctuary – hence the alternative term that could be used to describe
them, 'whole burnt offerings' (Leviticus 1:1–17). Offerings of grain could
also serve the same purpose (Leviticus 2:1–16), while the annual offerings
of the first-fruits of the crops were, in effect, gift sacrifices given to
celebrate a successful harvest (Leviticus 23:1–25).

FELLOWSHIP OFFERINGS

Not all sacrifices were presented completely to God as whole burnt
offerings. Often, only a part of the animal was burned on the altar, and
the rest was eaten in a fellowship meal at the sanctuary, shared by
worshippers and priests (Leviticus 3:1–17). A shared meal is a symbol of
friendship throughout the world, but in this instance the worshippers of
ancient Israel were doing more than simply expressing their mutual
affection. For the most important event of their history, the covenant
ceremony at Mount Sinai, had been accompanied by a fellowship offering
like this (Exodus 24:1–8), and whenever this event was celebrated, a
fellowship offering was usually at the centre of things (Joshua 8:30–35;
2 Samuel 6:17; 1 Kings 8:63–64). No doubt the same themes would be in
the worshippers' minds whenever fellowship offerings were made. In
these meals the people were constantly reminded of the keynote of their
covenant faith: that they and God enjoyed a personal relationship, whose
repercussions influenced the whole of life.

FORGIVENESS OF SINS

The Old Testament mentions two sacrifices that were designed to
remove the barrier of wrongdoing that made fellowship between people
and God impossible: the sin offering (Leviticus 4:1 – 5:13) and the guilt
offering (Leviticus 5:14 – 6:7; Numbers 5:5–8). The precise difference
between these two classes of sacrifice is not very clear, but in view of
the way that God's holiness was equated with moral perfection, it is not
surprising that sacrifice and forgiveness should have been related to
each other in this way. Human wrongdoing broke the covenant
relationship between God and people, but fellowship could be restored
by the offering of an appropriate sacrifice.

An awareness of the seriousness of wrongdoing seems to have
developed most fully in the later stages of Israel's history. The earlier
prophets had found it difficult to convince the people that worship and
behaviour belonged together, but then when the awful events of the exile
had proved them right, everyone could see that disobedience to God was a
real problem that needed to be dealt with. The Hebrew Bible never
specifically discusses how a sacrifice was believed to deal with sin, but it
seems to have been assumed that those who did wrong deserved to die
(Ezekiel 18:20), and that a sacrifice could in some way substitute for the

condemned sinner. Certainly, the blood of these sacrifices (representing the life of the animal) played an important part (Leviticus 17:11) and it was as this was daubed on the altar that the worshipper was pronounced to have been forgiven. Depending on the identity of the sinner, different altars would be used. There was one occasion when the whole nation was united in seeking forgiveness: the annual day of atonement (Leviticus 16:1–34; 23:26–32; Numbers 29:7–11). On this day, the blood of the sacrifices would be taken into the holy of holies itself, and applied to the top of the ark of the covenant. This was why the lid of the ark came to be known as 'the mercy seat'. After the exile it was replaced by a gold plate which served the same purpose. When the main sacrifices had been offered, a second ritual took place. This involved the selection of two goats, one to be

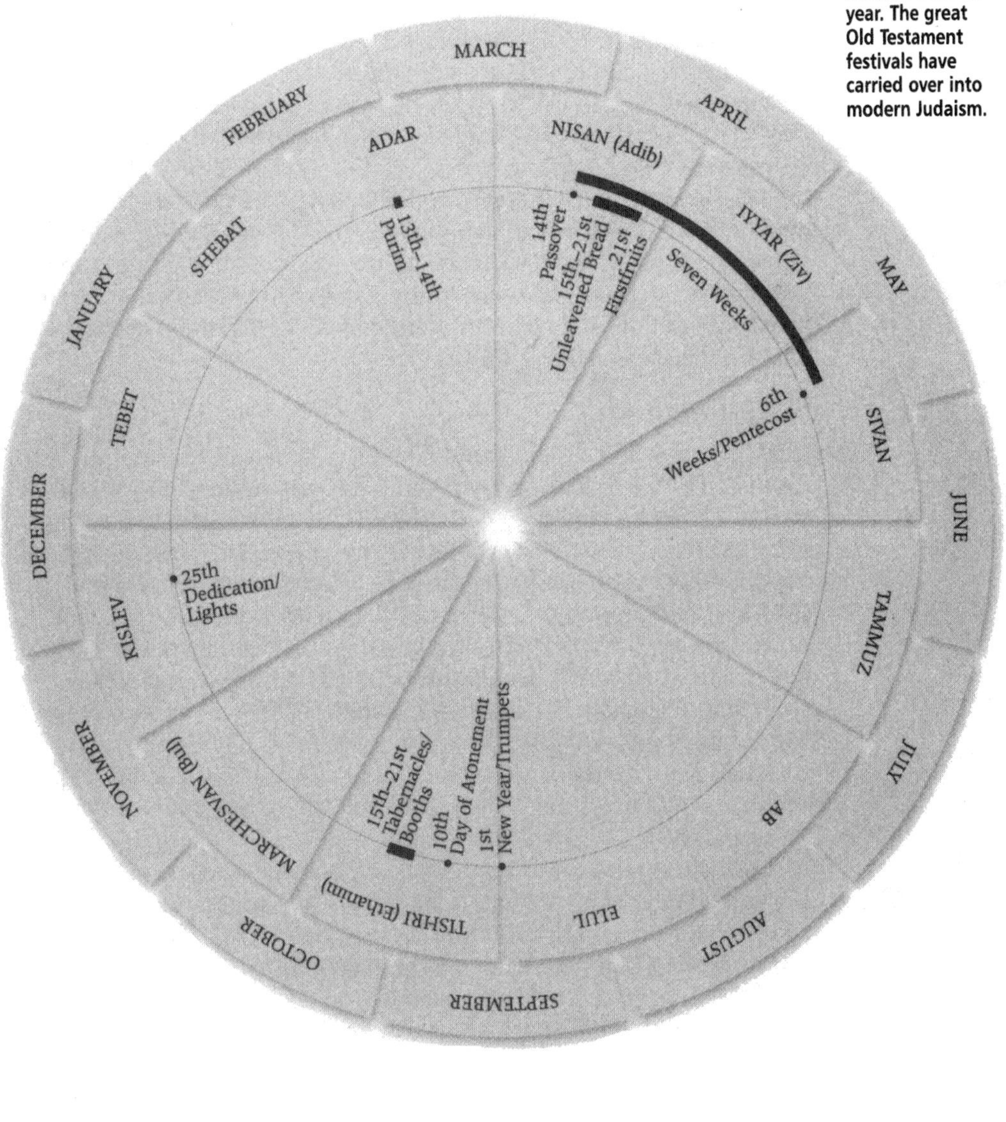

The annual festivals of Israel's year. The great Old Testament festivals have carried over into modern Judaism.

MARCH

FEBRUARY

APRIL

ADAR

NISAN (Adib)

IYYAR (Ziv)

SHEBAT

14th Passover

15th–21st Unleavened Bread

21st Firstfruits

Seven Weeks

MAY

JANUARY

13th–14th Purim

SIVAN

TEBET

6th

Weeks/Pentecost

DECEMBER

JUNE

KISLEV

25th Dedication/ Lights

TAMMUZ

NOVEMBER

JULY

MARCHESVAN (Bul)

15th–21st Tabercacles/ Booths

10th Day of Atonement

1st New Year/Trumpets

AB

TISHRI (Ethanim)

ELUL

AUGUST

OCTOBER

SEPTEMBER

sacrificed in the Temple and the other to be sent away into the desert beyond the boundaries of the inhabited land. The priest's hands were laid on the head of the goat which was to be sent out, and at the same time the sins of the nation would be confessed. These two procedures were quite different, but they both emphasized the same underlying conviction: that wrongdoing is a serious business as it disrupts fellowship between God and people. They were also a dramatic declaration that wrongdoing could be forgiven and obliterated from the lives of God's people just as surely as the goat was driven out into the desert, never to be seen again.

Times for worship

We have already seen that worship involved a whole style of life, including daily behaviour as well as what went on at the sanctuaries. It was, therefore, a continuous activity. One of the major themes of the Old Testament faith is that God is available to people at every time and in every place. Formal worship was one way of expressing this, and the sanctuaries would be open every day. But there were also special times when the great national festivals would interrupt the normal run of things and the people would join together to celebrate God's goodness to them corporately, usually in relation to some particular event in the nation's history. The significance of the different festivals changed with the passage of time, but we can trace a number of important occasions that would be celebrated in this way.

The sabbath day

Many nations in the ancient world had a regular day of rest, and the celebration of the sabbath every seventh day was an important part of Israelite life from a very early date. There is no one single passage which describes what a sabbath should be like, but it probably began as a day of rest, so that every member of the population (including slaves and foreigners) could renew themselves for their daily work (Exodus 23:12; 34:21). Worship was a part of this renewal process, and no doubt it was an occasion when crowds would throng to the various sanctuaries throughout the land (Leviticus 19:30; Numbers 28:9–10), though what they did there was not always approved of (Isaiah 1:13). On the sabbath, no regular work would be undertaken (Jeremiah 17:21–22; Amos 8:5), though it would not necessarily be a day of complete rest for everyone (2 Kings 11:5–8).

The main emphasis was on the sabbath as a day when people could look back to their nation's roots, celebrate God's goodness and greatness, and renew their commitment to the covenant faith. This is no doubt why its observance is required in the ten commandments (Exodus 20:8–11). The whole day was specially dedicated to God ('holy', Exodus 31:12–17), because it was a reminder of God's greatness both in creation and history

(Exodus 20:11; Deuteronomy 5:15). It was also a reminder that belief in God implied concern for other people (Deuteronomy 5:13–14). In the period after the Babylonian exile, the sabbath became very important in the synagogues, though eventually it turned out to be a day that was rigidly controlled by many prohibitions. But in the Old Testament period it was a day for joyful celebration (Isaiah 58:13–14).

The Passover

The greatest event of all to which the people looked back was God's deliverance of the slaves from Egypt (the exodus). This was marked in an annual festival at which an animal was sacrificed and a meal was shared. In this respect, the Passover was just a special form of fellowship offering, celebrating the relationship inaugurated between God and people in the exodus events. These events themselves had a profound impact on the way the festival was celebrated, as the people dressed up in the same way as their ancestors had done: 'with your sandals on your feet and your stick in your hand', as if ready for a long journey (Exodus 12:11).

According to the story of the exodus, the people prepared to leave Egypt in their family groups and this is how the Passover was celebrated in the earlier part of the Old Testament period. A lamb was sacrificed in the home, with none of the splendour of worship found in the sanctuaries, and the animal's blood was then daubed not on an altar, but on the doorposts of the house. At this time, the animal was always a lamb roasted for the fellowship meal, a custom perhaps going back to the origin of the festival in the days when Israel had been a nomadic sheep-rearing people. Later, it became a national occasion, centred on the Temple in Jerusalem, with all the impressive pageantry associated with worship there (Deuteronomy 16:1–8; 2 Kings 23:21–22; 2 Chronicles 30:1–22; 35:1–19). The ritual naturally changed to suit the different circumstances. Both sheep and cattle could be used in the celebrations, boiled rather than roasted. There was also a provision whereby anyone who missed the Passover because they were ritually unclean could celebrate it a month later than the proper date (Numbers 9:1–14; 2 Chronicles 30:23–27). It has been suggested that

This Jewish family are celebrating Passover, recalling their ancestors' deliverance from slavery in Egypt.

the worshippers in the Temple may have recited the story of the first Passover and exodus, perhaps acting out the events and culminating with the singing of the 'song of Moses' (Exodus 15:1–18). By the start of the Christian era, both the family and the national elements of the occasion were united, with the sacrifices being killed in the Temple, but the fellowship meals then being eaten in a family home.

The harvest festivals

The Old Testament mentions three major religious festivals that relate to the agricultural year (Exodus 23:14–17; 34:18–23). These celebrations had probably always been a part of the traditional cycle of Canaanite life, but the Old Testament links each of them to the great and unrepeatable events of Israel's history, and not to the cycle of the seasons and the inevitable concern of farmers for the continuing fertility of their land.

This limestone tablet, dating from about the time of King Solomon, has written on it a kind of children's rhyme that describes the farmer's year.

THE FESTIVAL OF UNLEAVENED BREAD

This was apparently related to the barley harvest and the offering of the first-fruits (Leviticus 23:9–14; Numbers 28:17–23), but was celebrated at the same time of year as Passover, which, together with the fact that unleavened bread features in the Passover story, meant that the two festivals came to be closely connected, and together served to commemorate the escape from Egypt.

THE CORN HARVEST (OR FEAST OF WEEKS)

This celebrated the end of the wheat harvest. Special offerings would be made in the sanctuaries, though the central action was the ceremonial presentation of the first sheaf that had been cut (Numbers 28:26–31). Following this, individual worshippers could bring offerings from their own crops (Leviticus 23:15–21). The events of the exodus were also in the minds of the worshippers on this occasion (Deuteronomy 16:12), though after the exile the harvest festival came to be used as a time for celebrating the giving of the Law at Mount Sinai.

THE FESTIVAL OF SHELTERS (OR TABERNACLES)

This came at the very end of the growing season, and was a celebration of the fruit harvest from vineyards and orchards (Leviticus 23:33–43; Deuteronomy 16:13–17). This was a particularly joyful festival, and took its character from the practice of the farmers who would stay out all night to guard their crops, with only flimsy huts to protect them. For the seven days of the festival, the worshippers lived in similar structures. The main feature of this occasion was the simple expression of joy at the safe gathering of the harvest. But there also seems to be a close connection between the festival of shelters and the renewal of the covenant faith, for Leviticus 23:33–43 identifies the temporary shelters with the tents in which Israel lived in the desert. Some have suggested that this association only came in later, when the shelters traditionally used at this time of year no longer had any practical relevance to the essentially non-agricultural life of the exiles. But many more are of the opinion that the covenant theme was always an important part of this festival, even from the earliest days of Israel's emergence as a nation in the land of Canaan. Allegiance to the covenant certainly seems to have been the bond that united the various tribes in the days of the judges. It is likely that they renewed their commitment to God and to one another in annual ceremonies which would include the reading of the covenant law (Exodus 24:7; Deuteronomy 27:9–10; Joshua 24:1–28). There are also indications that this covenant law could be read out as a part of the festival of shelters (Deuteronomy 31:9–13; Nehemiah 8:13–18), and many scholars therefore believe that this would have been followed by a solemn moment when the people committed themselves once again to the demands of God's covenant and Law.

Old Testament worship was clearly a varied experience, though one thing not found in it was preaching. The Torah was regularly expounded during organized worship after the exile (Nehemiah 8:7–9), but in the earlier period the main emphasis was always on praise and celebration.

The Festival of Shelters is in direct continuity with the Jews of Ezra's day. As well as celebrating the fruit and vine harvest, it reminds participants of the Israelites' wilderness days and the beginning of their covenant faith.

Like daily behaviour, worship was a response to God's revelation through the events of Israel's history and in the everyday experience of ordinary people. As the joyful worshippers went to the sanctuaries, they were reminded of God's past goodness, and given fresh inspiration for their own lives. But they were also challenged by God's holiness, as they faced the central need for repentance and forgiveness, and offered sacrifices in order to secure it. As time went on, it was this repetitive nature of much traditional worship that led prophets and others to question its lasting effectiveness, and to see it as but one stage on the road to a closer relationship with God. Could God not forgive sin in a more comprehensive way, they asked, so that humankind really could celebrate as those who were 'pure in act and in thought' (Psalm 24:4)?

The Old Testament never really gives an answer to that question, though some of its writers looked forward to a time when the covenant would be renewed in such a way that the past would be forgiven, and the future could hold out the hope of real victory over the power of evil in all its many forms (Jeremiah 31:31–34). They never spelled out the meaning of that in detail, but they were sure that God could be trusted to work for the benefit of the whole world, which was both God's creation and the object of God's continuing love. Whenever people commit themselves to God in humble trust, whether it be in great corporate acts of worship or in the private recesses of their own lives, they will always learn more about the true meaning of life and faith:

> *Don't you know? Haven't you heard?*
> *Yahweh is the everlasting God,*
> *who created all the world*
> *and never grows tired or weary.*
> *No one understands God's thoughts,*
> *but this is the One who strengthens those who are weak and tired.*
> *Even those who are young grow weak;*
> *young people can fall exhausted.*
> *But those who trust in Yahweh for help*
> *will find their strength renewed.*
> *They will rise on wings like eagles;*
> *they will run and not get weary;*
> *they will walk and not grow weak (Isaiah 40:28–31).*

Kings, priests and prophets in worship

The existence of a regular system for public worship inevitably requires full-time officials to look after the places of worship, and to supervise what goes on there. In the Old Testament a number of figures appear to be important in this connection. As we would expect in a patriarchal society, the vast majority of them were men, though there are references to 'the women who served at the entrance to the tent of meeting' in Exodus 38:8 and 1 Samuel 2:22. Unfortunately, next to nothing is said about their function, though some have assumed it to have been sexual, in view of the fact that Eli's sons are said to have had intercourse with them. The narrative, however, makes it clear that this kind of behaviour was an abuse of their priestly office, and it is just as likely that they carried out some kind of recognized role in worship at the shrines. It

may be relevant that this narrative is set in the earliest period of Israel's life as a nation, at a time of considerable upheaval and social disruption. It is a well-attested fact that women and other marginalized members of society are more likely to hold public office in such circumstances than in times of peace and stability, and several of them feature in the stories of the book of Judges. Generally speaking, though, religion – like the rest of life – was dominated by men throughout the Old Testament period.

The kings
Kings everywhere had a special role in religious affairs, though their precise function varied from place to place. In Egypt, for example, the pharaoh was often thought to be himself a divine being, while in Babylon the king was more likely to be regarded as a messenger of the gods, a special intermediary though not himself divine. Although some have argued

otherwise, it is unlikely that the kings of either Israel or Judah were ever thought of as being divine. Indeed, when the Syrian general Naaman assumed that one of them was, he was quick to disclaim it (2 Kings 5:7). The psalms contain ample evidence to show that the people prayed not to the king, but to God on his behalf (Psalms 20; 72:1–19). From the earliest days of Israel's arrival in the land of Canaan, God had always been regarded as the nation's true ruler. The tension between this belief and the political need for a militant leader was recognized in the stories of Saul's appointment (1 Samuel 8:1–22; 10:17–27), and occasionally features in the messages of the prophets (Hosea 8:4). But even when the idea of the monarchy was accepted, God was still regarded as the supreme sovereign of the people, and the king was God's servant (Deuteronomy 17:14–20).

The special nature of the king's position was symbolized in the fact that he was anointed. This ritual signified his close relationship with God, and declared that he was, in effect, a 'holy' person. David recognized this quality even in Saul (1 Samuel 24:5–7), and when he was killed in the heat of battle his murderer had to be punished for killing 'the one whom Yahweh chose to be king' (2 Samuel 1:14–16). This special relationship between God and the king was expressed in the idea of a 'covenant' existing between God, the royal family of David and the people of Judah (2 Samuel 7:8–16), and the king could on occasion even be called God's 'son' (Psalm 2:7).

The king could also be called a priest (Psalm 110:4). Kings in general often had an important part to play in organized worship, and the kings of both Israel and Judah are shown engaging in such activities. David established centres of worship (2 Samuel 6:17; 24:25), and Solomon, of course, built the Temple itself (1 Kings 5:1 – 6:14). The first king of the northern kingdom of Israel also set up sanctuaries in his own land, and decreed

Kings everywhere had a special role in religious affairs. In Egypt, the king (via the priesthood) provided for the gods, and in return the gods showed favour to the king. In this painted limestone relief, Pharoah Seti I makes an offering to the god Thoth.

Kings, priests and prophets in worship *continued*

the sort of worship that should be carried out there (1 Kings 12:26–33). As a result, these shrines were thought of as 'the king's place of worship, the national temple' (Amos 7:13). But the same was true of the Temple in Jerusalem, for the kings of Judah controlled the worship there too, and the priests were effectively members of the royal household, under the control of the king (2 Samuel 8:17; 20:25; 1 Kings 2:26–35; 4:4; 2 Kings 12:4–16).

The responsibility of priests in any ancient culture was to offer libation to the gods. This plaque from Babylon shows at the top a priest before a god, and on the lower half, men driving animals, possibly for sacrifice.

The kings also took charge of religious policy-making. Asa (1 Kings 15:11–15), Joash (2 Kings 12:1–18), Ahaz (2 Kings 16:1–18), Hezekiah (2 Kings 18:1–7), Manasseh (2 Kings 21:1–9) and Josiah (2 Kings 22:3 – 23:23) are all specifically credited with having reorganized Temple worship in one way or another. As well as being responsible for the general tenor of organized worship, the kings could also on occasion lead the people in their worship. Saul (1 Samuel 13:8–10; 14:34–35), David (2 Samuel 6:13; 24:25), Solomon (1 Kings 3:3–4; 8:62–63), Jeroboam I (1 Kings 12:32 – 13:1) and Ahaz (2 Kings 16:1–16) all offered sacrifices regularly. Kings could also pray on behalf of the nation, and issue blessings in God's

name (1 Kings 8:14–66; 2 Kings 19:14–19). On one occasion, David offered sacrifice and gave a blessing while clothed in the apparel of a priest (2 Samuel 6:12–19).

The kings obviously had an important role in the religious life of their people. Since they were believed to be appointed by God, this is not surprising, for they had the power to encourage their people to maintain the covenant faith – and, on occasion, to corrupt it. There have been many arguments as to the precise nature of the kingship, in view of the many 'priestly' functions that kings could carry out. But a number of factors suggest that we need to be cautious in claiming that the king's main function was religious rather than political:

● Religion and politics were always closely related in the ancient world. In particular, the various superpowers of the day often expected defeated nations to adopt their own religious practices, as a means of demonstrating appropriate subservience. This fact alone explains why the kings of Judah were so often involved in changing the furniture and equipment used in the Temple. Restoration of the covenant faith meant reasserting Judah's independence.

● The exclusive functions of the priests were not as well defined during the time of the monarchy as they were later to become after the exile. As we shall see below, any head of the family could offer sacrifices or establish a new place of worship – and when the kings engaged in such activities they could well have been acting mainly in that capacity.

● It is perhaps significant that the only occasions from which we have specific reports of kings conducting worship were specially important times in the life of the nation. No doubt, in general, the day-to-day conduct of worship in ancient Israel would be left in the hands of other religious officials, appointed by the king for the job.

Priests

We have already seen that during the period of the monarchy the priests often had a close relationship with the king himself. Some experts have suggested that the priesthood only emerged at this period, but it is more likely that its existence and functions go back much further than that. It is certainly true that the Old Testament shows a lot of flexibility in worship at an earlier time. A number of stories show the heads of families offering sacrifices (Genesis 22:13; 31:54; 46:1; Judges 6:19–27; 13:19–23; 1 Samuel 1:3; 2:12–13; 9:12–13), though this is not of itself evidence that there were no priests, for even much later the actual act of sacrifice was always performed by the individual worshipper and not by the priest. More surprising, perhaps, is the way that in this early period it was apparently possible for clans and other groups to appoint and dismiss their own priests at will (Judges 17:1 – 18:31). Again, however, incidents of this kind might well have been exceptions, for it would have been odd for Israel to have had no organized priesthood at this time. Other nations certainly had well-developed priesthoods, and the Old Testament mentions some of them: the Canaanite priest Melchizedek (Genesis 14:17–24), the Egyptian priest Potiphera (Genesis 41:45–46), the Midianite Jethro (Exodus 18:1) and the Philistine priests of Dagon (1 Samuel 5:5). In the context of the religious ideas of the time, the existence of the ark of the covenant and the tent of the Lord's presence would almost certainly have necessitated the existence of professional priests to take care of them.

So what did priests do, and how did they operate? The answer to that question naturally changed over time. After the exile, with the disappearance of the kings, the priests came to occupy an important political place. But in the earlier period, they must have operated in a more restricted religious capacity, at least in the great national sanctuaries that were closely controlled by the kings. Some aspects of their work are unclear, especially the

relationship between priests and Levites, though information is given about several of their functions:

● Priests cared for the sanctuaries throughout the land (Judges 17:1–13; 1 Samuel 1:1 – 3:21; Amos 7:10–13). They would get their living from the gifts of worshippers and, of course, they also had their share of the meat from the sacrifices (Numbers 18:8–32; 1 Samuel 2:12–17). They could also have their own lands and property (1 Kings 2:26; Amos 7:17).

● People would also consult the priests in order to get advice for particular situations. One story tells how Saul first met Samuel while he was searching for some lost donkeys (1 Samuel 9:3–26). The account does not say precisely how Saul expected Samuel to know where they were, but other passages seem to imply that the priest would use a set of special dice (Urim and Thummim) to give the answer to such questions (Exodus 28:30; Deuteronomy 33:8; 1 Samuel 14:41–42). It is not known how this procedure operated, but it seems to have died out quite early in any case. After the time of David, it was the prophets who gave direct advice and instruction of this kind (1 Kings 20:13–14; 22:6; 2 Kings 3:11–19).

● More generally, the priests would give instructions (Torah) on questions relating to worship. They were able to pronounce on whether things, places or people were clean or unclean, holy or profane, and so give guidance to the worshippers (Leviticus 10:8–11; 13:1–58; Ezekiel 22:26; 44:23; Haggai 2:11–14). Some scholars believe that moral law such as the ten commandments may also have been 'preached' in this way by the priests. After the exile, the Levites had the job of teaching, but their 'Torah' was different from the earlier priestly teaching, since it now consisted of exposition of parts of the written books of the Hebrew Bible (Nehemiah 8:7–9). Priests could also have certain judicial functions, as we saw in a previous chapter.

● Priests were involved in the offering of sacrifices. It would be the worshipper who

Kings, priests and
prophets in worship
continued

actually killed the animal, but the priest gave advice about the appropriate form of sacrifice to be offered on different occasions, and it was always the priest (as a specially 'holy' person) who took the blood to the altar. In this context, the priest served as a mediator, representing God to the people, and the people to God.

● The priest could also mediate between God and people in giving answers in God's name to the prayers of the worshippers (1 Samuel 1:17), or pronouncing a blessing upon them (Numbers 6:22–26). It was this function as mediator which was most characteristic of the priest's work. A priest was specially consecrated to God, and as such was able to deal with the awesome holiness of a place of worship. Through the presence of the priest, God and people could be brought together in a tangible way.

Prophets

When the people of Jerusalem were planning to get rid of Jeremiah, they commented that even if they disposed of him, 'There will always be priests to instruct us, the wise to give us counsel, and prophets to proclaim God's message' (Jeremiah 18:18). At one time, scholars were surprised to see prophets and priests mentioned in the same breath, as if they were complementary to each other. Indeed, by the end of the nineteenth century it was an 'assured result' of Old Testament study that priests and prophets were implacably opposed to each other. They were believed to represent different kinds of religion: priests being concerned with the arid and mechanical performance of pointless ritual, and prophets with the communication of a vital and life-giving message from God. It was widely supposed that the great Old Testament prophets were moral preachers, with no interest in organized religion at all, and that it had only been after the exile that a lesser breed of prophets emerged, who then became involved in formal worship because the fire of the original prophetic message had been all but extinguished.

It is certainly true that some of the prophets were outspoken in their criticism of empty formality (Isaiah 1:10–17; Hosea 6:6; Amos 5:21–24; Micah 6:6–8), but we can now see that it was wrong to dissociate them altogether from the organized worship. Closer study has shown that the prophets as a group often were closely linked with the shrines. A number of factors have led to this conclusion:

● As we have seen throughout this book, formal worship and everyday behaviour were closely linked in Israelite spirituality. Both of them were part of the people's response to God's goodness. The prophets could not have denied outright the importance of organized worship without also denying the very foundations of the covenant faith.

● The general picture often shows priests and prophets working alongside each other. Samuel and Elijah are the only prophets whom we know to have carried out priestly functions (1 Samuel 7:9; 11:15; 1 Kings 18:36–39), but other passages connect them quite clearly (Jeremiah 5:31; 23:11; 26:7, 16; 29:26; Lamentations 2:20; Zechariah 7:1–3), and there is mention of at least one prophet who had his own room in the Temple at Jerusalem (Jeremiah 35:3–4).

● The prophets often delivered their messages in the context of organized worship, and the themes of their teaching were related to the great festivals. For example, when Amos spoke of the coming 'day of Yahweh', he was probably taking up the popular expectations in the minds of the worshippers as they approached the climax of one of the regular festivals – though Amos then proceeded to turn their expectations upside down (Amos 5:18–24). When the priest Amaziah challenged Amos, he suggested that he should go and proclaim his message somewhere else, because he could not expect to be employed in Bethel, thereby implying that prophets would on occasion be employed there (Amos 7:10–13). Then we also need to take account of the fact that both Jeremiah (Jeremiah 1:1) and Ezekiel (Ezekiel 1:1) were themselves members of priestly families. Observations of this kind have been taken to indicate that Jeremiah, Ezekiel and others were actually on the staff at various places of worship, though that is going beyond the evidence, which shows them going to the Temple only to speak and to attend worship. It made good sense for them to take their message to where the people were, and to use familiar motifs to present a message. In any case, the prophets never restricted their preaching to ritual occasions, but went into the market place, the fields and anywhere else that people would listen.

● Certain psalms seem to imply that someone spoke in the name of God during the liturgy of worship. A number of psalms that begin as lamentations end in thanksgiving – implying that at some point during the prayer the worshipper has been reassured of God's continuing presence (Psalms 20; 22; 86). Others contain messages of reassurance said to have come directly from God (Psalms 12:5; 85:9–13; 91:14–16). One psalm clearly says that such messages were delivered by 'an unknown voice' in the course of Temple worship (Psalm 81:5–16). Since worship often included drama, and since other parts of the Old Testament show the prophets to be not only speakers on God's behalf, but also dramatists and mime artists, who better than a 'cultic prophet' of this kind to play such a part in worship? There is some evidence for this in the work of the Chronicler, who in one passage gives the title 'Levites' to people who were designated 'prophets' in the earlier account of Kings (compare 2 Chronicles 34:30 with 2 Kings 23:2). In other passages, these same 'Levites' are expressly given prophetic functions, including the deliverance of messages on God's behalf during worship (1 Chronicles 25:1–6; 2 Chronicles 20:13–19). Scholars have naturally speculated on the exact tasks performed by such prophets who played a

regular part in the Temple worship, but apart from these rather vague references in Chronicles, and the implications of certain psalms, there is unfortunately no specific information that could help to define their role more exactly.

Several prophets compared themselves to lookouts in their watchtowers, set to give warning when the people left God's ways. The prophets hated empty, formalized worship with no moral content.

13 From Hebrew Bible to Old Testament

The Hebrew scriptures have always been of the highest importance for Christians, and are quoted on nearly every page of the New Testament. Yet the Hebrew Bible (in the form of the Christian Old Testament) has also presented them with a problem, and even in the very earliest days of the church its meaning and relevance were among the most hotly debated subjects, sparking off endless controversy that lasted over generations. The death and resurrection of Jesus was the one issue that, in the years immediately following it, caused most friction and dissension in the emerging churches. Jesus himself had claimed that his own life was in some way a 'fulfilment' of the Hebrew scriptures (Matthew 5:17), yet many of his actions seemed to set aside its most distinctive teachings, not only on subjects such as sabbath-keeping (Mark 2:23–28) and the food laws (Mark 7:14–23), but also some of its moral teaching (Matthew 5:21–48).

In the very first chapter of this book I emphasized that it has been written from a self-consciously Christian perspective, and it is therefore appropriate that we should conclude by taking a look at some matters related to the kind of authority that the Old Testament is supposed to have in the context of Christian faith. This question is, in turn, related to even more extensive matters of understanding and interpretation, many of which are of significance no matter what the presuppositions of those who enquire about them. For the Old Testament has not only played an important part in the evolution of the Christian tradition, it has also been an influential text in the development of recent Western civilization, and its stories have often been quoted as the inspiration and justification for many aspects of the expansion of Western values throughout the world during the last two or three centuries.

Questions of belief

The very first generation of Christians were also Jews, and for them there was no particular sense of discontinuity between the Hebrew scriptures and their own belief in Jesus. For the most part they continued to observe the way of life in which they had been brought up, based on the Greek Septuagint as it was understood in first-century Judaism. But once it became clear that the Christian message was for non-Jewish people, and that Romans and Greeks could also become followers of Jesus Christ, the question of the authority of the traditional scriptures presented itself in an altogether more pressing form. Was it necessary for a Gentile person to become a Jew in order to be a Christian? Paul and other New Testament writers answered that question with a firm, 'No,' though they still valued the Hebrew scriptures, and often used these ancient books as a basis for their own exposition of the Christian faith. Therein lies the problem, for if certain parts of the Old Testament can be set aside as being no longer relevant to Christian faith and action, how can we tell which those bits are, and what should we do with the rest of it?

Searching for solutions

The question of the relationship between Old Testament and New was expressed in an outspoken way by a second-century Christian called Marcion. Not only did he see the ambiguities in the position evidently taken by the apostles, but he also noted other problems that the Old Testament posed for Christian belief. Jesus had spoken of a God of love who was concerned for the well-being of all men and women. However, as Marcion read the Old Testament he often saw there a rather different picture of God, one which seemed to be associated with extreme savagery and cruelty, appearing to imply that, far from seeking the salvation of people, God was more often connected with their annihilation. Of course, Marcion presented an oversimplified picture, underestimating the extent to which stern judgment was an important part of Jesus' teaching, and playing down the fact that God's love was never absent from Israelite spirituality. Nevertheless, the contradiction to which he drew attention is definitely there, and most modern readers would probably feel much the same as Marcion did. Even the most ingenious interpreter would find it exceedingly difficult to reconcile the sentiments of Psalm 137:8–9 with the statements about loving enemies in Jesus' Sermon on the Mount (Matthew 5:43–48), and in addition to that kind of issue there are topics like sacrifice which (at least to Western people) seem primitive and cruel, if not completely incomprehensible.

Marcion's solution to all this was simple: tear up the Old Testament and discard it altogether as an unworthy part of the Christian scriptures. But his view found no widespread support in the early church, not least because Marcion wanted to dispose of much of the New Testament as well, and that seemed to put a serious question mark against the reality of his Christian faith. Nevertheless, the leaders of the early church could understand well enough the point that Marcion was making. There was a real question about the Old Testament. For if (as they believed) the coming of Jesus was God's new and decisive action in the life of the world, then what relevance could the history of an ancient people have for faith in him? The usual answer was that when the Old Testament was correctly understood it could be seen to be saying exactly the same thing as the New Testament. But in order to demonstrate this, it was necessary to interpret the Old Testament in such a way as to show that its real meaning was somehow hidden from the casual reader.

By coincidence, Jewish scholars had already faced this question in a different context. A century and more earlier, Philo (c. 20 BC–AD 45), a member of the Jewish community in the Egyptian city of Alexandria, had taken up the challenge of reconciling the teaching of the Hebrew scriptures with the thinking of the great Greek philosophers. There were few obvious connections between them, but by applying a mystical allegorical interpretation to the Old Testament, Philo had succeeded in demonstrating (at least to his own satisfaction) that Moses and other Old Testament writers had actually declared the same ideas as Greek philosophy, only they had done it several centuries before the Greeks thought of them. Some of the early Christian leaders, especially those based in Alexandria, adopted this approach with enthusiasm, and in a very short time were using the same techniques to demonstrate that the Old Testament books also contained everything that was in the New Testament, for those with the eyes to see it. Even apparently insignificant details in its historical narratives could be understood as symbols of the

A Roman schoolmaster with his pupils. Paul writes in Galatians of the law as 'our tutor to bring us to Christ'.

Christian gospel. Anything red, for example, might be interpreted as a reference to the death of Jesus on the cross (for example, the red heifer of Numbers 19, or Rahab's red cord in Joshua 2:18). References to water soon became pictures of Christian baptism, and the story of the exodus, with its combination of blood (on the doorposts at Passover) and water (in the crossing of the Sea of Reeds), engendered many complex explanations of the relationship between the cross and Christian salvation, as well as the two Christian sacraments of baptism and the Lord's supper.

Hilary, bishop of Poitiers in France (AD 315–68), explained this way of reading the Old Testament in the following terms:

> *Every work contained in the sacred volume announces by word, explains by facts, and corroborates by examples the coming of our Lord Jesus Christ... From the beginning of the world Christ, by authentic and absolute prefigurations in the person of the patriarchs, gives birth to the church, washes it clean, sanctifies it, chooses it, places it apart and redeems it: by the sleep of Adam, by the deluge in the days of Noah, by the blessing of Melchizedek, by Abraham's justification, by the birth of Isaac, by the captivity of Jacob... The purpose of this work is to show that in each personage in every age, and in every act, the image of his coming, of his teaching, of his resurrection, and of our church is reflected as in a mirror (Introduction to* The Treatise of Mysteries*).*

Not all church leaders, even in those early centuries, were happy with this approach to the Old Testament, especially those connected with the other great Christian centre at Antioch in Syria. But it was generally taken for granted that the Old Testament was basically a Christian book, and in one way or another its contents had to be related to the fundamental beliefs of Christian theology.

During the Protestant Reformation the whole subject was once again opened for fresh examination. Martin Luther (1483–1546) and John Calvin (1509–64) both emphasized the need to understand the Old Testament in its historical and social context, and in that respect their approach was not dissimilar from that of many modern scholars. But

Martin Luther

Luther wanted to distinguish the value of Old and New Testaments by seeing the Old as 'Law' and the New as 'Gospel'. This gave him a neat tool with which to separate out the wheat of the pure gospel (which for him was found in Paul's New Testament letters) from what he regarded as the chaff of a superseded legalism (identified with the Old Testament, and Jewish Christianity more generally). This thinking has had a profound influence on biblical scholarship right up to our own day, often further fuelled by the inclination of Protestant (especially Lutheran) scholars to see what they regarded as Jewish legalism as a foreshadowing of medieval Catholicism, and even, in the early twentieth century, by the kind of anti-Semitism that flourished under the Nazis. But it is misguided in at least two fundamental ways:

■ It ignores the fact that 'law' is not actually the basis of the Old Testament faith – nor for that matter is it entirely absent from the New Testament either. In both of them, law is placed in the context of a covenant understanding in which God's love is the foundation principle.

■ Luther quite misleadingly identified Judaism with a moralistic legalism. This was unfair even to the Pharisaic viewpoint which the Christian Paul so clearly rejected, and there is no question that Luther allowed his own negative experiences of Roman Catholic Christianity to colour his view of Old Testament spirituality.

Calvin recognized some of these deficiencies, and instead he emphasized the importance of the covenant theme in both parts of the Christian Bible. By a careful comparison of God's relationships with people in ancient Israel and the Christian church, he was able to claim that the two testaments hang together as a 'progressive revelation' in which the ancient promises made to Israel in the Old Testament found their culmination in the ongoing life of the Christian church. This view is not without its own problems, but it does at least try to take the faith

of Israel seriously, and Calvin's position is still widely held today by
many conservative Christians.

After the Reformation, the question of whether the Old Testament is
a Christian book was effectively shelved until our own generation. The
European Enlightenment, with its emphasis on understanding the Old
Testament as a collection of ancient books in the context of its own
times, directed scholarly endeavours elsewhere, but the theological
question could not be banished for long, not only because of its
relevance to the events of the early twentieth century in Nazi Germany,
but also because of the way in which the Old Testament seems to have
been used as a justification for anti-Palestinian sentiments in the Middle
East and movements of ethnic cleansing in places as
far separated as South Africa and the Balkans.

John Calvin

Christians adopt various attitudes to the value
of the Old Testament:

■ Some insist on giving the Old Testament an equal
value and authority to the New, on the grounds that
every word of each is the direct utterance of God.
But considerable caution needs to be exercised
before accepting this outlook, for there are whole
sections of the teaching of Jesus himself where he
makes it clear that his message involved either a
rejection or a very radical revision of some
fundamental aspects of Old Testament teaching.

■ Others argue that the Old Testament is completely
replaced by the New, and so can be discarded. Here
again, we need to preserve the kind of careful
balance we find in the teaching of Jesus himself, for he also described
his ministry as in some sense a 'fulfilment' of the Old Testament. There
can be legitimate argument about what that means – but it must
certainly involve the assumption that the Old Testament has something
to say to Christians, and therefore has a place in a Christian Bible.

■ Some try to distinguish between various parts of the Old Testament,
perhaps by separating out things such as laws about priests, sacrifices
and purity (which Christians no longer observe) from other parts such as
the ten commandments and the moral teachings of the prophets (which
are still considered relevant). Calvin made a similar division to this, but
it is a good deal easier to make such distinctions than it is to justify
them. By removing such apparently irrelevant elements, we are in fact
displacing some of the most basic aspects of Old Testament spirituality.
In addition, it is precisely in such concepts as sacrifice that the New
Testament itself most often finds some intrinsic connection between the
Old Testament faith and Christian beliefs about Jesus.

■ It is also common for Christians to speak of a 'progressive revelation'
of God's will and character running through both testaments. On this
view, God's will is revealed in a number of stages, roughly corresponding

with the growing spiritual capacity of people to understand. This allows some of the more difficult parts of the Old Testament to be explained as being appropriate to a primitive age, but subsequently replaced by other more sophisticated notions, culminating in Jesus' teaching about a God of love. This also raises more questions than it solves. Not only is it based on an outmoded evolutionary idea of an inevitable moral progress in human affairs, but it also confuses statements about how God really is with statements about how people think of God. In addition, it contains the dubious implication that modern people invariably know more about God's will, and are more obedient to it, than were the prophets and other leading figures in the Old Testament story.

Making connections

There are obvious difficulties involved in interpreting the Old Testament within the context of the Christian scriptures. We need to recognize that it is in many ways a strange and alien book, to Christians as well as to others. Whatever assessment we may make of Israelite spirituality, it is not the same thing as Christian faith, and in practice when Christians read the Hebrew scriptures they often find them hard to understand because they belong to a completely different world from their own faith experience. Much of this strangeness can be dispelled once the Old Testament is placed in its proper historical and social context, which is why so much attention has been given to doing that in this book. At the end of it all, we may not find things such as sacrifice any more appealing, but at least we can begin to appreciate their significance when they are viewed in the total context of Israel's faith.

In practice, however, the relationships between Judaism and Christianity are more complex than that, and it is impossible to articulate an adequate Christian faith without reference to the Old Testament. At the most fundamental level, it is a simple fact that we will not get far in making sense out of the New Testament itself if we are ignorant of the Old. Jesus and his disciples were practising Jews, who were thoroughly immersed in Old Testament ways of thinking about God and the world. For them the Old Testament faith was a living and vital part of their total existence. Of course, in many respects they grew out of Judaism, as they found it necessary to discard or develop some things in the light of the exciting newness of God's actions in Christ. But for all that, they continued to think of their new Christian experience very much in terms of the faith with which they had been brought up. The earliest Christian churches used the Old Testament in its Greek translation as their Bible, and the language of the New Testament itself has a good deal more in common with that than it does with the secular literature of Greek and Roman culture. Inevitably, that language influenced the way the first Christians articulated their understanding of their own faith. Indeed, Old Testament language still permeates Christian thinking today, and those who have never seen an animal sacrifice (and would be horrified if they did) still talk about the 'sacrifice' of Jesus on the cross and continue to call a part of their church building an 'altar', even though no blood has ever been shed there. In the broader scheme of things, it is arguable that all this kind of imagery needs to be translated into different concepts in order for it to be effectively contextualized within today's culture, but to do that successfully it needs to be properly understood first, otherwise there is a constant danger that some significant aspect of Christian belief will be thrown out along with the language of sacrifice, altar and atonement. The place to find a proper understanding of all these notions is certainly the Old Testament.

But the Old Testament provides more than just a linguistic and cultural background to the thinking of the New Testament writers. It also contains important statements about God's relationships with humankind and the world that are as valid now as they were then. Each of the key concepts which we have used in this book to explore Israelite spirituality and beliefs forms an indispensable theological foundation for the Christian faith as it is presented in the pages of the New Testament. There is such a close interconnection between both testaments at this point that it is no exaggeration to claim that the Christian faith itself would make imperfect sense if we were to remove the basic affirmations of the Old Testament faith from the Christian Bible.

THE LIVING GOD
Nowhere is this more strikingly obvious than in the case of beliefs about God:

■ The belief that there is only one God, who is both all-powerful and yet personally interested in the welfare of ordinary people, is fundamental to both testaments. Nowadays, theologians often talk of these two aspects of God's character in terms of 'transcendence' and 'immanence'. We can be quite sure that this language would have meant little to the people of Old Testament times. Indeed, it is unlikely that these facets of God's character would have been perceived with equal clarity by all sections of the people of Israel at all periods of their history. But they were certainly implicit in the very earliest creedal confessions which exhort the people to worship only one God (Exodus 15:11–18), even if it was several centuries later that God's sole control of the world and its affairs was systematically asserted by one of the great prophets (Isaiah 40:12–31; 41:21–29; 44:1–20).

■ Bound up with the fact that God is unique is the belief that God's demands on people are primarily moral rather than being connected to religious services or ritual taboos. We have already noticed the distinctiveness of this idea in a world where religions were generally more interested in sacrifices and ritual than in morality. Yet the whole Old Testament understanding of worship makes no sense at all if these two aspects are separated – and again, the combination of these two is fundamental to the New Testament.

A popular image of God in the Bible is that of a shepherd.

■ Then there is the notion of God's grace, the fact that God gives undeserved gifts to people. The entire Old Testament story is given coherence by the knowledge that God had done great things for the people of Israel, and on that basis could challenge them to loyalty and obedience. Every stage of the narrative shows God's active concern to work for the salvation of the people, and this covenant principle is still basic to any Christian understanding of God's ways. The Old Testament, just as much as the New Testament, depicts God working in love for the good of humankind, and though the focus in the New Testament shifts from events such as the exodus or the exile to centre on Jesus, there is still an underlying assumption that God is an active and loving God, whose workings can be seen by ordinary people in the course of their everyday lives.

■ We have observed more than once that the Hebrew scriptures do not describe God 'metaphysically', by asking about the stuff of which God is made, but 'functionally', by reflecting on the ways in which God behaves. The New Testament shares this approach, when it says, in effect, 'Look at Jesus: this is what God is like.'

GOD AND THE WORLD

It is not too difficult to show that important aspects of God's character are common to both testaments. But without the Old Testament, the Christian faith would also be seriously lacking a perspective on the way God relates to the natural world.

■ In the world of the earliest Christians, it was commonplace to believe that the natural, physical world in which we live was intrinsically evil, and any sort of meaningful salvation would therefore need to involve an escape from this world to some other, more 'spiritual' and therefore more perfect world. This was part and parcel of the Greek outlook, and as the Christian church moved out from Palestine into the wider Roman empire it was always a temptation for Christians to incorporate it into their own thinking. Though there were fierce arguments on this very point, Christians never did accept the view that physical existence in this world is second best. But they were able to assert the basic goodness of life only because of the strong Old Testament conviction that informed their thinking. As a consequence, instead of regarding salvation in terms of escape from this world, the Christian writers of the New Testament declared that the world itself had its own part in God's plan of salvation: the coming of Jesus meant vitality and renewal for the very stuff out of which the world is made (Romans 8:18–25; Colossians 1:15–20; Revelation 21–22). In incorporating the physical world into their expectations of salvation, the New Testament writers were quite firmly grounded in the Old Testament faith that had gone before them, which saw the whole creation as blessed by God. Christians have not always taken this as seriously as they ought, but without this they would have little theological foundation for saying anything at all on major issues such as care for the environment and the use of the world's natural resources.

■ When the New Testament sets out to explain how Jesus Christ relates to people, it again does so on the basis of the Old Testament view of people and their relationship to God. It takes for granted the basic theological concepts that we have located in the creation stories, and sees human fallenness as a barrier between God and people that needs to be dealt with if open relationships between people and God are to be restored. This whole structure of thought is so crucial for Christian theology that without the Old Testament insight it is doubtful whether the apostolic faith could have developed at all in the way it did.

LIVING AS GOD'S PEOPLE

New Testament ethics also owe a good deal to the Old Testament:

■ The notion of natural law and a creation-centred spirituality, as we have discussed it in relation to the Old Testament, is a fundamental prerequisite of the Christian faith, and Paul takes it up as a key element in his explanation of how the life, death and resurrection of Jesus applies to all men and women, whatever their social or ethnic origins (Romans 1:18 – 2:16).

■ Equally central to the New Testament is the covenantal framework within which much Old Testament morality operates. The coming of Jesus was viewed as a further great act of God's love, comparable with the exodus and calling for a similar response of obedience and commitment. But the whole pattern of the Christian ethic is also based on the fundamental Old Testament assertion that people should behave in the same way as God (Matthew 5:48). The only difference is that the divine pattern is made even more explicit because of the model provided by Jesus himself, and which Christians are called on to follow (2 Corinthians 8:8–9; Philippians 2:5–11).

■ There is also the whole question of a Christian social ethic, which depends so much on the Old Testament heritage. For a variety of reasons, the New Testament has very little to say about how God deals with nations, and without the Old Testament the Christian faith would undoubtedly be considerably impoverished at this point. For the Old Testament provides the foundations for a Christian philosophy of history. No doubt the Old Testament position requires modification here and there in the light of the teaching of Jesus himself, but it is no coincidence that when modern Christians make pronouncements on social and political affairs, they often depend on the insights of the prophets and lawgivers of ancient Israel.

WORSHIPPING GOD

Here, too, the New Testament faith owes more to its Old Testament antecedents than is sometimes appreciated:

■ The style of worship of the early church grew out of the patterns of praise and joyful celebration that we have seen in the pages of the Old Testament.

■ Even more striking is the correlation between the understanding of what worship means in both testaments. For the undergirding principle of both Old Testament and Christian worship is that though God can be described as 'holy' – in every sense of that word – God is also open and accessible, and the reality of that can be represented in the events of worship in the presence of God's people.

■ We can hardly ignore the vast importance that the theme of sacrifice has come to assume in Christian thinking. The New Testament writers asserted that in Jesus' life, death and resurrection, all that was promised by the sacrificial worship of the Old Testament had been brought to fulfilment. It was impossible to speak of what Jesus could do in the lives of his people without some reference to the hopes and aspirations of the worshipper in ancient Israel. Indeed, the whole concept of sacrifice is so significant in the Christian tradition that at least one large section of the church thinks of it not only as a series of theological metaphors and images, but also as a continuing symbolic part of the ongoing liturgy of the worshipping Christian community.

Questions of behaviour

Reference has already been made to the question of the way in which the Hebrew scriptures not only report, but also seem actively to approve and promote repeated brutality and ethnic cleansing. Once we move away from aspects of theological belief, this is one of the major issues that contemporary readers of the Old Testament need to deal with. The question comes to a focus most clearly in relation to the stories in the early parts of the deuteronomic history, concerning the settlement of Israel in the land of Canaan. The books of Numbers and Deuteronomy – and, to a lesser extent, Joshua and Judges – express an intense hatred for the indigenous people of the land, insisting that they are so worthless that virtually any kind of barbarity against them can be justified. Ethnic cleansing and genocide are not merely reported, but apparently seem to be applauded as being God's will. Moreover, this is not just a historical issue that can be dismissed as belonging to a world far removed from our own, for throughout much of the last 1,000 years of Western history, these stories of how Israel attempted to annihilate

One of the great formative experiences of Israel's history was their entry into the promised land, seen here from across the north end of the Dead Sea. The people were called to remember that their land was held in trust from God.

the Canaanites have provided the ideological underpinning for imperialist adventures including the Crusades, the European invasion of the Americas and of Australasia, as well as being a major inspiration for the development of the Afrikaner mythology that led to apartheid in South Africa, and the emergence of a militant Zionism in the Middle East. Viewed in this light, the Bible appears not only to tolerate, but also to actively promote practices which, if they happened today, would be regarded as war crimes. Those who are familiar with the Bible, and read it regularly, often fail to appreciate the extent to which the presence of such elements leads others to question the value of its message, if not to disregard it entirely. In order to have integrity, these moral issues need to be addressed.

Possession of land as a sign of God's favour is mentioned more than 1,700 times in the Hebrew Bible, and the idea that 'success' is to be defined in terms of possession of land has been the driving force behind all colonial Western oppression of indigenous peoples. Christians read the accounts with the eyes of liberated slaves finding new land for themselves, but the liberating God of the exodus story can be made to

The Hebrew scriptures report, and appear to approve of, the destruction of entire communities in the process of settling the promised land. The thriving Canaanite city of Hazor lay in an important strategic position, and was taken by Joshua's army. The population was slaughtered and the city burnt to the ground.

look considerably more menacing when viewed from the perspective of those who are conquered. Nor is any of this just a matter of interpretation, for the oppression seems to be in the text, and racism and genocide are not only taken for granted, but are morally accepted as well. By comparison even with other religious literature, where deities are violent but unpredictable, there is something especially abhorrent to modern readers about the carefully planned massacres of ancient Canaanites, where some parts of the narrative portray Yahweh as not just allowing it, but actually requiring it. There is a serious moral and spiritual question here, for what kind of a God will recommend behaviour that falls well short of regular secular values? If it was not for the religious provenance of the Bible, Christians themselves might easily be campaigning to have passages like these banned as racist propaganda.

So much for the question, which has been deliberately spelled out here somewhat starkly in order to emphasize its importance. How can it be dealt with, from the perspective of the Christian reader of the Old Testament? Several points can be made.

Revisiting history

In previous chapters, a good deal of space was allocated to exploring what exactly it was that happened at the time when Israel was in the process of emerging as a recognizable nation in the land of Canaan. From all the evidence that has been surveyed there, two things seem absolutely certain, namely that there was no single cause that led to, or explanation for, the establishment of an Israelite state, and that the relationship between Israelite culture and traditional Canaanite ways was a good deal more complex than the presentation of the deuteronomic history seems to imply. In terms of cultural change, all the

available evidence indicates that the values identified with the notion of 'Israel' existed alongside and in competition with the traditional values of the Canaanite city states for a very long period of time, centuries rather than decades. The relevant archaeological data shows this, as does the evidence of the Old Testament itself, with its constant references to the way in which Canaanite practices never really disappeared from the culture of either Israel or Judah. While there is no reason to doubt that some elements within the people of Israel looked back to the exodus as an actual event experienced by their own forebears, there is also evidence that some other elements of the nation were attracted to the new state by its egalitarian ideology. We can discount the idea that a peasants' revolt would have been sufficient by itself to account for the emergence of Israel, but the biblical story provides evidence indicating that this happened in some cases, and that these people, therefore, far from being ethnically different from others in the land, were in effect converted Canaanites.

Earlier chapters have highlighted the fact that the narrative histories of the Old Testament are edited versions of traditional stories, and while this again does not necessarily undermine or question their usefulness, that does mean it is important to be aware of the editorial spin that has been placed on them. In the case of the stories of the conquest, it is not the accounts of individual episodes that contain the incitements to genocide, but the connecting tissue of editorial comment. The stories themselves describe a number of smallish military skirmishes, at the end of which the Canaanites are still a major force to be reckoned with, which is why Israelite settlements are then described as emerging predominantly in the poorer hill country. The editorial stance, however, taking in the whole subsequent history of Israel and Judah, right through to the effects of the Babylonian exile and beyond, traces the disastrous events of the exile back to the perceived failure of these earlier generations to annihilate the Canaanites. In other words, the kind of wholesale genocide which can seem to be such a pressing moral problem did not actually happen at all, but was the product of the kind of thinking about racial purity that had its origins in later history, particularly after the exile.

Moral tensions

Interestingly, the kind of moral dilemma that modern readers can identify in these stories is also to be found in the Hebrew Bible itself. Taken as a whole, and understood in relation to its theological and moral consequences, the Old Testament adopts a position that is the exact opposite of the one just highlighted. At the very beginning of the story, in the promise to Abraham and Sarah, God tells them that they were being chosen 'so that you will be a blessing… and in you all the families of the earth shall be blessed' (Genesis 12:2–3). The same theme had featured already at the beginning of the book of Genesis, with the insistence that all people – with no mention of race – were made 'in the image of God' (1:26–27), and the subsequent lists of people groups depict them as all being related to one another and, by implication, suggests that race is an artificial construct.

There is no doubt that in the post-exilic age, xenophobia was rife, as was observed in our discussion of the work of Ezra, who refused to have any dealings with the people of Samaria even to the point of insisting that Judahites who had married outside their own families and clans should divorce their partners. But even in that context, there were dissenting voices. It is hard to miss, for instance, the contrast between the universal message of God's love in Isaiah 40–55 and the more narrow-minded jingoism of Ezra. Moreover, the books of Jonah and Ruth, both of them probably written at roughly the same time, also stand in stark contrast to some strands of thought within the post-exilic community, with their overt insistence not only that people of different races would be accepted by God, but also that they could play a significant part in the purposes of God. The spirituality and commitment of the people of Nineveh turned out to present a radical – and divinely inspired – challenge to Jonah's more restricted vision of things, while the non-Israelite Ruth became one of the ancestors of King David, the most powerful icon of national identity for the kingdom of Judah and its successors.

The same uneasiness about the violation of human rights also surfaces elsewhere in the prophetic books, in at least one case taking the form of an outright challenge to the spin placed on a story by the deuteronomic editors. This is the case of Jehu, whose merciless massacre of Jezebel and the royal household of Israel (itself largely inspired by racial considerations) is singled out as a praiseworthy venture in 2 Kings 9:17–37, but was, according to Hosea, so contrary to standards of covenant-inspired decency that God would personally deal with it: 'in a little while I will punish the house of Jehu for the blood of Jezreel, and I will put an end to the kingdom of the house of Israel' (Hosea 1:4). Amos's condemnation of the systematic abuse of human rights is very similar (Amos 1:3 – 2:8).

Texts and readers

This entire debate highlights some underlying matters related to the way in which we read texts, for in considering the way in which the narratives about early Israel have been understood and applied within a more recent colonialist culture, it is obvious that the context of their interpreters has been at least as important as the contents of the text itself, for it appears to have blinded readers to the more subtle nuances that can be found in the Old Testament when viewed from a more holistic perspective. Looking at the history of Western imperialist expansion over the last 1,000 years and more, it is obvious that the main driving force has not been texts from the Bible. While it would be impossible to deny that these narratives have sometimes played a part in the formulation of expansionist policies, they have only done so in a context whose essential characteristics were formed through other influences. The main forces within that context were drawn from quite different sources, not least the increasing secularization of Western culture as a result of the Enlightenment, and selected aspects of the Hebrew scriptures were used more as the ideological icing on the cake than as any of its essential ingredients.

From the point of view of the victims of genocide, the most dangerous context is not that of the Hebrew Bible, but of those who would interpret and apply it in this kind of way. This is one reason why it will be worth spending a little more time reflecting on the relationship between texts and their readers. For the last two centuries or there-abouts, study of the Bible has been dominated by what was called the 'historical-critical method', in which all the emphasis was on getting back to ancient writers and their texts, trying to understand them in their own contexts, and assuming that if we can somehow imagine ourselves into their skins, we will be better placed to get to grips with what they have written. There is no question that the conclusions which have emerged from this way of studying the Bible have provided many valuable insights into the Bible and its world, and much of this book has been taken up with such matters, if for no other reason than that the world of professional biblical study still regards them as very important. However, reading and understanding the Bible is a far more subtle business than that, for it is not a one-way process in which we hear today what the ancient text and its author were saying in their world – it is, rather, a two-way process in which we are speaking to the text as well as listening to it. It is a fallacy to imagine that there is some truly 'objective' way of comprehending the Hebrew Bible (or indeed the Christian New Testament) which relies on self-validating 'scientific' procedures. There is no such thing, for we all bring our own presuppositions, our personal baggage and filters, to bear on everything we read. It is a pointless exercise to try to deny that, and those who do so lack credibility as well as integrity. Interpretation is a dynamic process, in which we bring something to these books, at the same time as we expect to receive something from them.

Questions related to biblical interpretation have a full chapter to themselves in the companion volume to this one, *Introducing the New Testament*, and readers who wish to understand all this more fully are recommended to consult that, for the same principles of reading and interpretation apply equally to both sections of the Christian Bible. But the point to be made in this context is that, if the stories of the Hebrew Bible are used to justify violence and genocide (as they have been), that is hardly something intrinsic to the text, but arises out of the social and cultural preferences and prejudices of readers of the text. The reality of this can easily be illustrated by reference to those millions of Jewish and Christian people in all times and all places (and notably, among today's Christians, in the non-Western world) who have read its stories and, far from being inspired to indulge in ethnic cleansing and racism, have been moved in exactly the opposite direction, to oppose those colonialists who, often, were the very ones who claimed the Old Testament as the justification for their own actions. A classic example would be the struggle against apartheid in South Africa during the second half of the twentieth century, for both the proponents of that political theory, and those who campaigned for its downfall, were motivated by their reading of the Bible. In its origins, apartheid was essentially a disagreement among Christians about the meaning of the Old Testament, which was then transformed into a racial policy. If there is any case to answer, it is not the Bible *per se* that stands in the dock, but those advocates of the historical-critical method who have insisted that understanding the Bible is a neutral project, and who have therefore tended to ignore altogether the moral and spiritual consequences of certain ways of using it. What is now needed is, on the one hand, a recognition that the Hebrew scriptures originated in a patriarchal society, and reflect all that goes on in such a context – and that could include horrific brutality in the ancient world, just as it often does in today's world. On the other hand, we need to be honest about the need for incorporating matters of faith and morality into our understanding, and recognizing that what we as readers bring to the text is at least as likely to determine our conclusions as what the text itself appears to say in abstraction. These texts are not meant to be models for human behaviour, so much as a sort of two-way mirror, through which we can come face to face with ourselves as well as catching a glimpse of the world as it is, and the world as God intends it to be. What we then do with those images is a matter of our own moral choice.

Glimpses of a different future

In the opening chapter, it was made clear that this is a Christian book about the Old Testament, and at various subsequent points the same emphasis has been repeated. If the contribution brought by the reader to the text is to be taken seriously, it is important – indeed, essential – that we all come clean about our starting points. The starting point here has been motivated by the conviction that the books of the Hebrew Bible, and its Greek translation, have an authentic place within the Christian scriptures, and that when viewed from this perspective the two testaments of the Christian Bible are coherent one with another, and have an inner integrity in their message. So how can we define what that integrity and coherence might be?

The early sections of this chapter have already drawn attention to some significant points of continuity between a Christian world-view and the Old Testament, and while few would wish to dispute the reality of the various connections traced here between the two, it is legitimate to ask whether some of this is not just wishful thinking from the Christian's point of view. After all, it is easy enough to look at the Old Testament with the benefit of hindsight and convince oneself that this or that element of Old Testament spirituality is somehow related to Christian thinking. Are we perhaps in danger of falling into the same kind of subjectivism as those more ancient expositors who looked at things such as Rahab's scarlet cord and saw in them a clear reference to the blood of Jesus on the cross? We are certainly not in the same predicament as the medieval scholars, for we have restricted our discussion here to features in the Old Testament which were an integral part of its historical development, and which were clearly perceived by the Old Testament writers themselves. But we still need to explain how we can be so sure that the Christian interpretation we want to place on these facts is not an alien intrusion into the Old Testament's essential message. In the final analysis, the truth is that it is only our Christian conviction that Jesus is God's final word to humankind that enables us to see both Old and New Testaments as parts of the same story. But we could certainly qualify that by drawing attention to the obvious fact that the Old Testament writers themselves seem to have regarded their faith as incomplete in itself, and therefore requiring some kind of future 'fulfilment'.

In many important respects, the Old Testament faith was anchored in the past. Some of its most distinctive insights emerged out of reflection on the great events of Israel's history, as they were reported by traditional tribal storytellers and then eventually incorporated into the historical narratives of the Hebrew Bible. When men and women wanted to know what God was like, they turned for an answer to events such as the exodus or the exile, as explained and interpreted by the prophets and others. But they never thought that God was locked up in the past. Quite the opposite, for one of the Old Testament's fundamental convictions is that God can be known by ordinary people in the everyday events of their present life. The prophets extended this conviction to its logical conclusion, observing that if Yahweh was the God of the past, who is also still active in the present, then this same God must also be working to create a new future. The Old Testament historians express this view right at the beginning of their long story, with their reference to the fact that the covenant made with Abraham and Sarah and their family was to be a blessing for all the nations (Genesis 12:3). At the time the final touches were being put to the Hebrew scriptures, this blessing of the nations was certainly not a reality, but represented a future hope that had yet to be accomplished, and as the Old Testament story proceeds, this hope is expanded and combined with other themes until a coherent future expectation emerges. There is a sense of growing anticipation that Israelite spirituality will be completed, which is expressed in at least three fundamental concepts.

This 'Good Shepherd' is from a painting by Christians in the catacombs of Rome. The idea of God as a shepherd is taken straight from the Old Testament.

A new covenant

A notable articulation of this hope is to be found in the expectation that there would need to be a 'new covenant', which would take up and fulfil all the unfulfilled commitments of the original Sinai covenant, and at the same time herald the beginning of a new era of relationships between God and humanity. This hope first emerged about the time of the exile, when it was clear that the original covenant had been a failure because of the disobedience and disloyalty of the people. For all its God-given potential, they had been unable to keep its terms, and as a result leading thinkers began to see that a complete change would be needed in the lives of God's people if ever they were to do God's will. This change would be based on forgiveness for what was past, but its most striking feature would be a radical transformation of the human will in such a way that God would empower people actually to keep the covenant: 'The new covenant that I will make with the people of Israel will be this: I will put my law within them and write it on their hearts' (Jeremiah 31:33). The key to success is found in the new initiative personally undertaken by God to enable people to live according to new values: 'I will give them a new heart and a new mind. I will take away their stubborn heart of stone and will give them an obedient heart... I will put my spirit in you' (Ezekiel 11:19; 36:27).

A messiah

The Hebrew word *mashiach*, like its Greek equivalent (*christos*), means 'an anointed person'. In the ancient world kings and priests were both anointed with oil, and attention has already been drawn to the significant part played by the king, especially in the southern kingdom of Judah. As the representative of God to the people, the king could be referred to as 'God's anointed', even as 'God's son' (Psalm 2:7), and this close relationship between God and the king in Jerusalem was cemented in the covenant made with the royal family of David (2 Samuel 7:1–17). Because of that, the king was in a very real sense the focus of the people's hopes as they looked for God's will to be done in their midst.

In the ancient world, priests and kings were anointed with oil. This mural, from Dura-Europus, shows Samuel anointing David as king.

If Israel's social relationships were to reflect the character of God's own person, then it was through the king that this would be put into practical effect. At least, that was the theory, though the reality was often different, as one king after another showed himself to be quite unfit, both morally and spiritually, to lead the people in ways that would reflect God's values and standards. The prophets generally hoped that the next king would be better, which is one reason why so many of them (at least in the early period) became involved in plots to overthrow even their own rulers. But from about the time of Isaiah onwards they were to become increasingly disillusioned with David's family. Though the prophets greeted each new king with optimism, their hopes for the future came to be expressed in more idealistic terms that show their expectations moving away from the actual kings in Jerusalem and towards an ideal king who would be commissioned directly by God to lead their people (Psalms 89:1–4; 132:10–12; Isaiah 9:6–7; 11:1–5; Jeremiah 23:5–6; Micah 5:2–5). It was out of this frustration that the hope of a messiah was eventually born, and by the end of the Old Testament period it was widely believed that God would once more intervene in history, and send a new king who would perfectly fulfil the hopes and aspirations of a genuine Israelite spirituality.

A new world

The Old Testament also looks forward to a time of physical renewal for the world itself. Since failure in the lives of people had often been linked to corruption in the world of nature (Genesis 3:17–19; Amos 4:6–12), it is not surprising that future personal and social renewal should also include plans for a revitalized world. This, too, became an important part of the Old Testament's view of the future, and many passages depict the material world sharing in the rejuvenation of the human world (Isaiah 11:6–9; 25:6–9; 51:3; 62:1–5; Ezekiel 47:1–12; Amos 9:13–15; Micah 4:1–4). The Old Testament faith is not a closed system, but a dynamic living spirituality that always expects God to do new things. This message was given its most comprehensive expression by Isaiah of Babylon who, in encouraging the exiles, exhorted them to direct their attention away from sentimental assessments of the past, and to look for God to do new things in their midst (Isaiah 43:18–19). He knew they could trust God not only because of all that God had done in the past on their behalf, but also because their trust was in 'the first, the last, the only God', one who could claim that 'there is no other god but me' (Isaiah 44:6). He also identified God's action on behalf of humankind with the work of a figure he called 'the servant of Yahweh'.

It has become customary in Old Testament studies to refer to four 'servant songs' which describe the work of this person (Isaiah 42:1–4; 49:1–6; 50:4–9; 52:13 – 53:12). Though there has been much discussion about the literary character of these songs, there is no doubt that 'the servant' had an important place in the prophet's message, for this person is portrayed as one who fulfils in his or her own life and experience all those aspects of God's will that Israel as a nation had been unable to accomplish. This figure has never been identified with the Messiah in Jewish readings of the scriptures. One of the distinctive features of these poems is that the servant undergoes great suffering, something that seemed incompatible with a messianic expectation of an all-powerful conquering king. But it was this very feature of the servant's work that led the early Christians to see here an expectation which they believed had been fulfilled in Jesus himself. In the final servant passage in particular, there are two themes that correlate very closely with the facts of Jesus' own life: the servant, though innocent, suffers for the wrongdoing of other people (53:4–9); and following that, God will vindicate the servant in such a way that the great and powerful will be astonished while those for whom the servant suffers will realize that this suffering was in their place (53:10–12). The correlation between the image of the servant here and the experience of Jesus is remarkably striking, and for Christians is perhaps the one theme above all others that helps to define the continuity between Old and New Testaments. Many efforts have been made to identify the consistency of the Christian Bible, with terms such as the covenant, or the idea of 'salvation

Nowhere in the Bible is the believer thought to have arrived at moral perfection. Paul, in his letter to the Philippians, takes an image from the chariot races and writes of 'pressing on' to reach that goal.

history' being put forward as the glue which binds together such apparently discordant literature into one coherent block. But the only real continuity in the midst of such diversity and discontinuity is God, whose personality and values appear throughout all the books, ultimately finding their very specific focus in the person of Jesus, who is presented as the definitive image of God. God constantly occupies the centre of the stage, searching for people, making new relationships with them, motivated only by undeserved and generous love. God is ultimately the unifying factor in the message of the Bible, engaged from beginning to end in the establishment of order out of the chaos which so easily engulfs the life of society and of the physical world, as well as the personal experience of individuals. For Christians, that process culminated in the life, death and resurrection of Jesus, and the gift of the Holy Spirit at Pentecost, though those stories themselves contain an insistent looking forward, and the belief that God will continue to work to empower future generations to reach their full potential as human beings, as they rediscover the nature of true faith in God. The New Testament itself is no more a closed book than the Old Testament, and it is this flexible quality of its spiritual understanding, expecting God to continue working in the world, and therefore allowing itself to be endlessly reinterpreted to address new situations and concerns, that has ensured not only its survival, but also its continuing appeal to those of all times and places who search diligently for the truth.

Other Books on the Old Testament

There are many series of books on the Old Testament which, in different ways, will provide a good introduction to the current state of play on any given topic among the scholars. The following are particularly recommended as being easily accessible to beginners in this field, and most of them have separate volumes on different Bible books:

Guides to Apocrypha and Pseudepigrapha, Sheffield: Sheffield Academic Press.

IBR Bibliographies, Grand Rapids: Baker.

Old Testament Guides, Sheffield: Sheffield Academic Press.

The Old Testament Library, London: SCM Press.

Old Testament Readers, Sheffield: Sheffield Academic Press.

Word Biblical Commentaries, Dallas: Word Publishing.

General

Brotzman, Ellis R., *Old Testament Textual Criticism*, Grand Rapids: Baker, 1994.

Coggins, R.J., *Introducing the Old Testament*, Oxford: Oxford University Press, 1990.

Friedman, Richard E., *Who Wrote the Bible?*, New York: Summit, 1987.

Gottwald, Norman, *The Hebrew Bible in its Social World and Ours*, Atlanta: Scholars Press, 1993.

Knight, D.A. and Tucker, G.M., eds, *The Hebrew Bible and its Modern Interpreters* , Chico: Scholars Press, 1985.

Moorey, P.R.S., *A Century of Biblical Archaeology*, Guildford: Lutterworth Press, 1991.

Rogerson, J., ed., *Beginning OT Study*, London: SPCK, 1983.

Rogerson, J., *Old Testament Criticism in the Nineteenth Century*, London: SPCK, 1984.

The History of Israel

Miller, J. Maxwell and Hayes, John H., *A History of Ancient Israel and Judah*, London: SCM Press, 1999, revised edition.

Pixley, J., *Biblical Israel: A People's History*, Minneapolis: Fortress Press, 1992.

Soggin, J. Alberto, *An Introduction to the History of Israel and Judah*, London: SCM Press, 1999, 3rd edition.

Historical and Cultural Background

Beyerlin, W., ed., *Near Eastern Religious Texts Relating to the Old Testament*, London: SCM Press, 1978.

Coogan, Michael D., ed., *Stories from Ancient Canaan*, Philadelphia: Westminster Press, 1978.

Dothan, Trude and Dothan, Moshe, *People of the Sea: The Search for the Philistines*, New York: Macmillan, 1992.

Fritz, V., *An Introduction to Biblical Archaeology*, Sheffield: JSOT Press, 1993.

Mazar, Amihai, *Archaeology of the Land of the Bible 10,000–586 BCE*, New York: Doubleday, 1990.

Moran, William, ed., *The Amarna Letters*, Baltimore: Johns Hopkins University Press, 1992.

Pritchard, J.B., *Ancient Near Eastern Texts Relating to the Old Testament*, Princeton: Princeton University Press, 1969, 3rd edition.

Redford, Donald B., *Egypt, Canaan and Israel in Ancient Times*, Princeton: Princeton University Press, 1992.

Sandars, N.K., *The Sea Peoples: Warriors of the Ancient Mediterranean 1250–1150 BC*, London: Thames and Hudson, 1985, 2nd edition.

The Emergence of the Nation

Coote, Robert, *Early Israel: A New Horizon*, Minneapolis: Fortress Press, 1990.

Gottwald, N.K., *The Tribes of Yahweh*, Sheffield: Sheffield Academic Press, 1999, 2nd edition.

Harrelson, Walter J., *The Ten Commandments and Human Rights*, Macon GA: Mercer University Press, 1997.

Hoffmeier, James K., *Israel in Egypt: The Evidence for the Authenticity of the Exodus Tradition*, Oxford: Oxford University Press, 1997.

Hopkins, David, *The Highlands of Canaan: Agricultural Life in the Early Iron Age*, Sheffield: JSOT Press, 1985.

Lemche, Niels Peter, *The Canaanites and Their Land*, Sheffield: JSOT Press, 1991.

Shanks, H., ed., *The Rise of Ancient Israel*, Washington: Biblical Archaeology Society, 1992.

Stiebing, William H., *Out of the Desert? Archaeology and the Exodus/Conquest Narratives*, Buffalo NY: Prometheus, 1989.

Thomson, T.L., *Early History of the Israelite People*, Leiden: Brill, 1992.

de Vaux, Roland, *The Early History of Israel*, London: Darton, Longman & Todd, 1961.

Kingdom and Nationhood

Alberts, R., *A History of Israelite Religion in the Old Testament Period*, London: SCM Press, 1994, 2 vols.

Brueggeman, W., *A Social Reading of the Old Testament: Prophetic Approaches to Israel's Communal Life*, Minneapolis: Fortress Press, 1994.

Dearman, J.A., *Religion and Culture in Ancient Israel*, Peabody: Hendrickson, 1992.

Frick, Frank S., *The Formation of the State in Ancient Israel*, Sheffield: Almond Press, 1985.

Fritz, Volkmar, *The City in Ancient Israel*, Sheffield: Sheffield Academic Press, 1995.

Gunn, D. and Ferrell, D.N., *Narrative in the Hebrew Bible*, Oxford: Oxford University Press, 1993.

Exile and After

Ackroyd, P.R., *Exile and Restoration*, London: SCM Press, 1968.

Christensen, Duane L., ed., *A Song of Power and the Power of Song: Essays on the Book of Deuteronomy*, Winona Lake: Eisenbrauns, 1993.

Clines, D.J.A., *The Theme of the Pentateuch*, Sheffield: JSOT Press, 1978.

Collins, J.J., *Jewish Wisdom in the Hellenistic Age*, Louisville: Westminster John Knox Press, 1997.

Jellicoe, S., *The Septuagint and Modern Study*, Oxford: Clarendon Press, 1968.

Noth, Martin, *The Deuteronomistic History*, Sheffield: JSOT Press, 1981, 2nd edition.

Porten, B., *Archives from Elephantine*, Berkeley: University of California Press, 1958.

Weinfeld, M., *Deuteronomy and the Deuteronomic School*, Oxford: Oxford University Press, 1972.

Theology

Allen, R.J. and Holbert, J.C., *Holy Roots, Holy Branches: Christian Preaching from the Old Testament*, Nashville: Abingdon Press, 1995.

Brueggeman, W., *Old Testament Theology: Essays on Structure, Theme and Text*, Minneapolis: Fortress Press, 1992.

Brueggeman, W., *The Psalms and the Life of Faith*, Minneapolis: Fortress Press, 1995.

Childs, B.S., *Biblical Theology of the Old and New Testaments*, Minneapolis: Fortress Press, 1993.

Clements, R.E., *Wisdom in Theology*, Carlisle: Paternoster Press, 1992.

Craigie, C.P., *The Problem of War in the Old Testament*, Grand Rapids: Eerdmans, 1978.

Crenshaw, James L., *Old Testament Wisdom*, Louisville: Westminster John Knox Press, 1998, 2nd edition.

Day, J., et al., eds, *Wisdom in Ancient Israel*, Cambridge: Cambridge University Press, 1995.

Eaton, John, *Mysterious Messengers*, London: SCM Press, 1997.

Gowan, Donald E., *Theology of the Prophetic Books*, Louisville: Westminster John Knox Press, 1998.

Hasel, G.F., *Old Testament Theology: Basic Issues in the Current Debate*, Grand Rapids: Eerdmans 1991, 4th edition.

Hubbard, R.L., et al., eds, *Studies in Old Testament Theology*, Dallas: Word, 1992.

Knierim, R.P., *The Task of Old Testament Theology*, Grand Rapids: Eerdmans, 1995.

Koch, K., *The Prophets*, London: SCM Press, 1982/83, 2 vols.

Mays, J.L., *The Lord Reigns: A Theological Handbook to the Psalms*, Louisville: Westminster John Knox Press, 1994.

Murphy, R.E., *The Tree of Life: An Exploration of Biblical Wisdom Literature*, Grand Rapids: Eerdmans, 1996, 2nd edition.

Ollenburger, B.C., et al., eds, *The Flowering of Old Testament Theology*, Winona Lake: Eisenbrauns, 1992.

Perdue, L.G., *Wisdom and Creation: The Theology of Wisdom Literature*, Nashville: Abingdon, 1994.

Preuss, H.D., *Old Testament Theology*, Louisville: Westminster John Knox Press, 1995, 2 vols.

Simkins, R.A., *Creator and Creation: Nature in the Worldview of Ancient Israel*, Peabody: Hendrickson, 1994.

Terrien, S., *Till the Heart Sings: A Biblical Theology of Manhood and Womanhood*, Philadelphia: Fortress Press, 1985.

Wolff, H.W., *Anthropology of the Old Testament*, Mifflintown: Sigler Press, 1996.

Wright, C.J.H., *God's People in God's Land*, Grand Rapids: Eerdmans, 1990.

Methods and Interpretation

Alter, R., *The Art of Biblical Poetry*, New York: Basic Books, 1985.

Barton, J., *Reading the Old Testament*, Louisville: Westminster John Knox Press, 1997.

Charlesworth, J.H. and Weaver, W.P., eds, *The Old and New Testaments*, Valley Forge: Trinity Press, International, 1993.

Clines, David J.A., *The Bible and the Modern World*, Sheffield: Sheffield Academic Press, 1997.

Duggan, M., *The Consuming Fire: A Christian Introduction to the Old Testament*, San Francisco: Ignatius, 1991.

Exum, J.C. and Clines, D.J.A., eds, *The New Literary Criticism and the Hebrew Bible*, Sheffield: JSOT Press, 1993.

Goldingay, J., *Theological Diversity and the Authority of the Old Testament*, Grand Rapids: Eerdmans, 1987.

Goldingay, J., *How to Read the Bible*, London: SPCK, 1997, 2nd edition.

Grabbe, L., ed., *Can a 'History of Israel' be Written?*, Sheffield: Sheffield Academic Press, 1997.

Long, V.P., *The Art of Biblical History*, Leicester: Apollos, 1994.

Niditch, S., *Folklore and the Hebrew Bible*, Minneapolis: Fortress, 1993.

Perdue, L., *The Collapse of History: Reconstructing Old Testament Theology*, Minneapolis: Fortress Press, 1994.

Petersen, D.L. and Richards, K.H., *Interpreting Hebrew Poetry*, Minneapolis: Fortress Press, 1992.

Steck, O.H., *Old Testament Exegesis: A Guide to Methodology*, Atlanta: Scholars Press, 1995.

INTRODUCING
THE ❖ NEW
TESTAMENT

14 The Beginning of the Story

The New Testament documents the rise of one of the most remarkable religious and social movements the world has ever seen. In their own day, the first Christians were accused of turning the world upside down with their message (Acts 17:6), and they have influenced every subsequent generation in history. The twenty-seven books of the New Testament contain stories of their deeds, accounts of their activities, together with letters and other occasional writings produced by this innovative group of people in the process of taking their message to the furthest reaches of the world as they knew it. It provides its readers with a unique archive of social history, for this is no domesticated, disinfected collection of writings: it bears testimony to the debates and disputes among the first followers of Jesus as they wrestled with the significance of his unique life and ministry, and even the stories of Jesus' own life are presented not in one agreed version, but through the perspectives of four different writers, each of whom displays their own characteristic insights into the meaning of the events they describe.

It is no exaggeration to claim that no other book from the ancient world has made such a lasting impact on world civilization. New Testament passages like Jesus' Sermon on the Mount (Matthew 5 – 7) or Paul's great hymn in praise of love (1 Corinthians 13) are acclaimed as outstanding literary compositions, even by those who have little time for their essential message. This is all the more surprising in light of the relative unsophistication of the New Testament writers. Not more than one or two of them can have had any sort of formal Greek education, and some of their books (Mark's Gospel, for example) would not be highly rated among scholars of ancient literature. Yet that has not dismayed the millions of people all over the world who still read the New Testament regularly and discover in its pages a personal inspiration for their daily living. It has the capacity to speak to people of different cultures, and at all periods of history, in a way that is highly distinctive, maybe unique. Though written in generally remote places of the ancient Roman empire, by people who were an oppressed and persecuted minority, its message still speaks with great power to spiritual searchers in all times and places.

Its contents can seem disparate and unconnected, and indeed it is

The world of the New Testament.

like a small library, containing diverse types of literature, compiled by many different authors, at different points during the first century AD. But, for all its diversity, the New Testament has one central focus. These books are all part of the same story. They reflect the fervour and devotion of the first followers of Jesus Christ, but more than that: they claim that the story of Jesus is the grand metanarrative of all history – the one big story that gives meaning and significance to all the small stories of everyday human experience and insight. Through their faith in this one person, the New Testament writers found the fragments of their own experience transformed into something more glorious than they could possibly have imagined. Regardless of the cost – and it often included suffering and death – they were determined to share this life-giving story with others. The shared conviction that this was the way to find true fulfilment and meaning lies at the back of all their writings. But behind their accounts of their own faith experiences stands the life of just one remarkable person, Jesus of Nazareth.

From Jesus of Nazareth to early Christianity

Jesus was born about 4BC into an ordinary working-class Jewish family, but (unusually for someone with no formal religious training) he went on to make a name for himself as a religious teacher (Matthew 2:1; Luke 2:1–7). He was in the public gaze for little more than three years before his life was tragically cut short by his execution on a Roman cross (Luke 23:33), yet in that short time he delivered a message that was to exert a crucial influence not only on his own people, but on the subsequent course of world history.

In one sense, Jesus' lifestyle was not particularly remarkable in the context of the Palestinian countryside where he lived and worked. There were hundreds of wandering teachers ('rabbis'), all of them men (never women) of exceptional gifts and insight who would gather round them small groups of disciples to perpetuate their teachings after they were gone. The stories about Jesus in the New Testament gospels describe how he himself followed this pattern, with twelve special followers to whom he entrusted the essentials of his teachings (Matthew 10:1–4), though they also report that on more than one occasion thousands of people flocked to listen to him (Mark 6:30–44; 8:1–9). However, what really distinguished Jesus from other rabbis of his day, was the fact that it was not among simple peasants on the shores of the inland Sea of Galilee that his teaching made its greatest impact. In a very short time after his death, his personality and his beliefs were having a profound effect in places far removed from the shores of Palestine.

A new faith

Within twenty years of Jesus' crucifixion, every major centre of Roman civilization could boast at least one group of his followers. The list of nationalities present in Jerusalem to hear Peter's first public sermon reads like a roll-call of most of the cities in the ancient world: 'We are from Parthia, Media, and Elam; from Mesopotamia, Judea, and Cappadocia; from Pontus and Asia, from Phrygia and Pamphylia, from Egypt and the regions of Libya near Cyrene. Some of us are from Rome, both Jews and Gentiles converted to Judaism, and some of us are from Crete and Arabia...' (Acts 2:9–11) – and their inclusion at this point in the Christian story was obviously not just wishful thinking, for in a very short time we have hard evidence of thriving Christian communities in Rome, Corinth, Ephesus, Philippi, Antioch in Syria and many other Mediterranean cities, not to mention far-flung places such as Ethiopia, Byzantium, and Alexandria in Egypt (Acts 8:26–39).

It was not long before these new followers of Jesus began to exert an increasingly powerful influence on life even in Rome itself. Writing of events in AD49, less than twenty years after the death of Jesus, the Roman historian Suetonius described a series of riots that led the emperor Claudius to expel the Jewish population from the city. According to him, the cause of all the trouble was a person whom he calls 'Chrestus' (Suetonius, *Life of Claudius* 25.4). There has been much debate as to who Suetonius believed this 'Chrestus' actually was, but there seems little doubt that the events he was describing were brought about by arguments over the teaching of those Roman Jews who had

Fishing on Lake Galilee: most of Jesus' followers were ordinary people from rural Galilee.

become followers of Jesus, and were hailing him as the expected 'Messiah' (a Hebrew term, whose equivalence in Latin was *Christus, Christos* in Greek, and hence the eventual common reference to 'Jesus Christ').

Opposition

It was not long before the popular media of the Roman world turned their attention to these followers of Jesus, describing their activities in lurid terms and portraying them not only as people with weird religious ideas, but people who were a threat to the safety and security of the Roman state:

> *The Christians form among themselves secret societies that exist outside the system of laws... an obscure and mysterious community founded on revolt and on the advantage that accrues from it... They form a rabble of profane conspiracy. Their alliance consists in meetings at night with solemn rituals and inhuman revelries... They despise temples as if they were tombs. They disparage the gods and ridicule our sacred rites... Just like a rank growth of weeds, the abominable haunts where this impious confederacy meet are multiplying all over the world... To venerate an executed criminal and... the wooden cross on which he was executed is to erect altars which befit lost and depraved wretches (Origen,* Against Celsus *8.17; 3.14; Minucius Felix,* Octavius *8.4; 9.1–6).*

The Christians themselves naturally saw things differently. Far from worshipping 'an executed criminal', these men and women who were causing such social upheaval firmly believed that their Jesus was not dead, but was really and truly alive, and was with them wherever they went (Acts 2:32). This was perhaps the one crucial factor which ensured the lasting success of the whole Christian movement. Because they believed that Jesus was not dead, but alive, his first followers were prepared to take the most incredible risks in spreading their message. Beatings, imprisonments, shipwrecks, and persecutions of all kinds – even death – were commonplace in the life of the early churches (Acts 12:1–5; 2 Corinthians 11:23–27). But the spectacular results that accompanied their endeavours made even the suffering infinitely worthwhile.

Changing the world

Of course, we look back on all this with the wisdom of hindsight. We know that the church did in fact survive and spread. But if we put ourselves in the position of those first followers of Jesus, it is very obvious that their success was by no means a foregone conclusion. Indeed, quite the opposite, for by normal standards everything was against them. Jesus himself was a Jew, as were all his original disciples, and though in some circles in the Roman empire the Jewish faith was respected, anti-Semitism was common. There was particular disdain for those Jews who lived in Palestine, who were often regarded by the Roman establishment as an incomprehensible, fanatical and unbalanced race. In addition, neither Jesus nor his followers were of high social standing, coming as they did from rural Galilee. It was hard enough for such people to gain a hearing even in their own religious capital, Jerusalem, let alone to communicate effectively with educated Greeks and Romans in the wider world beyond their own limited experience. Yet this is precisely what they did, as a movement that began spontaneously in a country on the edge of Roman civilization suddenly became an important social and political, as well as religious, force at the very centre of life in the empire. So what was their secret? What did Jesus and his teaching really mean – and why did his followers feel compelled to take it to the furthest corners of the world they knew? Why did they not stay at home instead, to be a reforming movement in their own Jewish religion? And just how did these hill-billies from the backwoods of Palestine manage to communicate the message of Jesus so successfully to the cultured inhabitants of ancient cities in Italy and Greece?

To find the answers to these questions, we need first to understand the world where they lived.

The Greek heritage

There is no such thing as a culture that comes from nowhere. We are all heirs to the past. In the world of the first Christians, the outward forms of administration and government were those of the Roman empire, but its cultural roots were embedded in a different world altogether. The way people spoke and thought, their aspirations and achievements, and their hopes and fears all went back to pre-Roman times. For though the Romans had shown themselves to be skilled in technology, building impressive roads and water-supply systems wherever they went, the underlying ideology of their empire had its real origins some 300 years before the time of Jesus, in the vision of Alexander the Great (356–323BC).

Alexander rose to fame almost overnight. He began as the son of a little-known local ruler in Macedonia, but he was such a brilliant general that, within a very short time, he was able to defeat armies much more prestigious than his own, and establish himself as undisputed emperor of the whole of the world that was then known to people living in the Mediterranean lands. The great Persian empire fell to his troops, followed by Egypt, and ultimately by other lands even further to the east. Just ten years after his first major success against the Persians, Alexander died at the early age of only thirty-three. But by then his empire stretched from Greece in the west to the Indian sub-continent in the east.

Alexander the Great (356–323BC), whose policy of Hellenization created a world in which it was easy for Christianity to spread.

Politically, it did not survive his death intact. After much squabbling among Alexander's generals, his territories were divided, and it was nearly 300 years later that they were finally reunited, when the Roman Octavian (63BC–AD14) eventually secured the eastern end of the Mediterranean Sea for his own empire.

Hellenism

Octavian was himself a brilliant strategist. But he owed much of his lasting success to the fact that there was already a far-reaching cultural unity among almost all the nations he had conquered. In spite of their diverse national traditions, people throughout the Mediterranean world were deeply conscious of being part of a wider world. In both east and west, people had common hopes, similar educational opportunities, and much the same way of understanding life. They even spoke the same language: Greek.

All this sprang directly from the genius of Alexander the Great. Unlike many other dictators, Alexander was not addicted to the exercise of power just for its own sake. He was not a brutish, uncultured person. In his youth he had been a student of the great Greek philosopher Aristotle, and he never forgot what he had learned from him. Alexander was a fanatic for

The triumphal arch at Palmyra in Syria. It was in Hellenistic cities that Christianity spread most rapidly.

his own native culture, and was genuinely convinced that civilization had reached its ultimate goal with the Greek way of life. He was determined to share it with the whole world, and he took steps to ensure that Greek customs, religion and philosophy – even the Greek language – would all be adopted throughout his domains. Cities were built everywhere in the Greek style, incorporating Greek temples, theatres and sports arenas. The way of life that resulted – 'Hellenism' – was to last for nearly 1,000 years after Alexander's death, and have a profound impact on the future course of the whole of Western civilization. Throughout its early centuries, the Christian church could not afford to ignore this massive cultural and ideological edifice. Church leaders eventually found themselves forced to articulate, even redefine, their faith in terms of the Hellenistic world-view, and the consequences of their doing so are still affecting the Christian church today.

The degree to which any particular nation accepted this Hellenistic culture naturally varied from place to place. Sometimes the changes were only superficial. The names of local gods and goddesses might be changed into Greek forms, but their worship often continued on in much the same way. In addition, ordinary working people had little time or opportunity for philosophical debates and sports activities, and it was generally the ruling classes who became most involved in such pursuits. They were also the ones who most often used the Greek language, for it meant they could make international contacts without the tedious necessity of learning several languages. But the Greek influence was everywhere, and in one way or another it penetrated to all sections of society.

It was in this Greek-dominated world that the earliest Christians proclaimed their message. For all its size and diversity, it was a world that was easy to reach with the good news about Jesus. There were few language problems; cultural barriers were minimal; and by the Roman age great roads were being built which would make it easy to travel from one part of the empire to another. But these were not the only factors that moulded the world of the first Christians. For by the first century AD many people also had other concerns.

Philosophy

Alexander had been inspired by a love for the great classical Greek philosophers. But by the time of the New Testament, their heyday was long past. Those who succeeded the original generation of creative thinkers were not of the same intellectual calibre, and much philosophy was concerned with detailed arguments about things that to ordinary people seemed trivial and irrelevant. But there were some whose ideas were more accessible than others, and who therefore attracted a following among many ordinary citizens.

Alexander the Great portrayed as a god on a coin minted by Lysimachus, king of Thrace from 306 to 281 BC.

THE STOICS

These were quite an influential group in the New Testament period. This school of thought was founded by Zeno (335–263 BC). He was a native of Cyprus, but went to Athens and eventually set up his own school in the *Stoa Poikile* ('the Porch'), from which the name 'Stoic' was derived.

Stoic philosophy was based on a belief that both the world and its people ultimately depend on just one principle: 'Reason'. Since the world itself operates by this standard, people who want to enjoy a good life must 'live in harmony with nature'. They could do this primarily through following their conscience, for that itself was also inspired by 'Reason'. This was something people could only do for themselves, and Stoics therefore laid great emphasis on living a life of 'self-sufficiency'. Many of them were widely respected for their high standards of personal

The Parthenon in Athens, home to many of the ancient Greek philosophers, and still a place of influence in New Testament times.

morality. It was not uncommon for them to be prepared to commit suicide sooner than lose their self-respect and dignity. Chrysippus (d.c. 206BC) ensured Stoicism's survival as an influential school of thought, and in the following centuries it went through several phases. In the early Christian period its most famous advocates were Seneca (4BC–AD65, Epictetus (AD55–135) and Marcus Aurelius (AD121–180).

Inevitably, this way of understanding life did not convince everyone – not least because it did not seem to tackle the social realities of the day. If 'Reason' filled and inspired everything, then why were all people not the same? Why were there so many slaves condemned to eke out a wretched existence? The Stoic could reply that, in their minds, slaves were equal to the emperor, a claim that provided very little consolation either for slaves or those who were concerned for their welfare.

THE EPICUREANS

These were another popular philosophical group in the Hellenistic age. They too had an ancient pedigree, tracing their origin back to the Greek Epicurus (341–270BC). Epicureans adopted a totally different view of life. Though many Greeks had debated what happens at death, they would have none of it. Death is the end, they said, and the only real way to make sense of life is to be as detached as possible from it. A good life consists in 'pleasure'. For Epicurus, this had meant things like friendship and peace of mind. But many of his followers interpreted it differently, and gained a reputation for reckless living.

These and other philosophical groups had many followers among the intellectual classes in New Testament times, but they never had much appeal for ordinary people. They were seldom able to stem the fears of the working classes, and in any case it was time-consuming and intellectually demanding to organize one's life this way. As a result,

THE BEGINNING OF THE STORY 377

Greek philosophy had few points of contact with the mass of the people, who were not highly intellectual and had little opportunity for the leisurely pursuit of personal morality.

Religion

Many people found it more natural to make sense of life in terms of religion, but for those who took Hellenism seriously, few certainties could remain. While the philosophers had produced systems of thought that were often incomprehensible, they had also questioned many traditional religious beliefs. There were those who still worshipped the old Greek and Roman gods, but they knew that many educated people had claimed to be able to prove that such deities did not really exist. International movements of trade and people had also made Europeans more conscious of the existence of other gods and goddesses in the eastern part of the Roman empire. Did they exist – and if so, how could they relate to life in the great urban centres of Greece and Italy?

Such ambiguities eventually led to what can appropriately be described as a failure of nerve in the Hellenistic world. While the philosophers had discredited traditional ways of making sense out of life, they had failed to establish a plausible alternative, and as a result huge numbers of people found themselves in a moral and spiritual vacuum. There was no shortage of religious ideas that could fill the gap, and people whose confidence in their inherited spiritualities had been eroded were ready to try anything that might give them new hope in an uncertain world.

Countries on the eastern fringe of the Hellenistic world had their own ancient religions, which were largely unknown to those living in the urban centres of the western empire. What little was known of them seemed to suggest they were more 'spiritual' than the rationalistic and materialist world-views of western thinkers. These factors, combined with a natural curiosity about the unknown, generated an increasing interest in non-western faiths. The fact that some of them at least looked as if they were compatible with the more accessible conclusions of Greek philosophy only served to heighten their appeal. Two aspects of western philosophy seemed especially congenial to these eastern faiths:

■ In order to explain the existence of evil in the world, philosophers had often argued that this world is neither the only world, nor is it the best. There is, they suggested, another world of goodness and light, and that is the most important sphere of existence. People belong to it because they have a 'soul', a spark of light that is related not to bodily existence in this world, but to spiritual existence in the other world. Our brief existence here is merely an unfortunate encumbrance, and to find true meaning and fulfilment it is necessary to escape the body (which had been castigated as 'the prison of the soul' by Pythagoras).

■ Alongside the moral philosophy of people like Plato, another major strand in Greek thinking had been concerned with natural philosophy –

what would now be referred to as science – working out how things work, and how the universe fits together. As Roman and Greek thinkers explored the mysteries of the universe, they found themselves fascinated by the movements of the planets and the stars, which seemed to operate with such precision and regularity that many believed the key to the whole of life was somehow locked up within them.

So the way was prepared for the penetration of many oriental religions into the Roman empire. For a long time astrology had been of great interest to eastern sages. So had the possibility of reincarnation. It was not long before these speculations were combined with the conclusions of Greek scientists to produce a new kind of religious movement in the Hellenistic world.

GNOSTICISM

This is a term often used to describe this movement today. There is a good deal of uncertainty about its precise origins, and a lot of disagreement as to whether it existed in the early first century, or whether it developed only later as a result of the spread of the Christian message itself. There is positive evidence of its existence in the second

---

Traditional Greek religion

Greek and Roman religion were very similar, indeed the same gods feature in each under different names. By the fifth century BC twelve gods and goddesses were identified by name as the key deities in the pantheon. They each had their own quite narrow sphere of influence, and worshippers would not follow their own favourites, but would pay some homage to them all in order that every aspect of human experience might be blessed by divine attention.

The twelve major deities were generally thought of as living in an extended family at Zeus' palace on Mount Olympus (hence the term 'Olympians' by which they were often known). Other deities existed, and were known as the 'chthonians' (from the Greek word *chthon*, meaning 'earth'), though they were not imagined to be in opposition to the Olympians, either morally or spiritually. The chthonians were not entirely negative influences, though gods of the underworld and of death were

certainly prominent among their number. But there were also positive gods within their ranks: food, for instance, grows in the earth, and even Zeus could have an earthbound, chthonic aspect to his character. Indeed, most of the leading gods had an endless list of adjectives applied to them, which defy neat classification. Individual communities constantly sought to define the qualities and powers of their particular deities as being in some way distinctive and different from the wider spirituality that was shared with other people throughout the Hellenistic world. Thus, for example, the 'Zeus of mountain tops' had qualities not possessed by 'Zeus of the city', or (to give an example that features in the New Testament, 'Artemis of Ephesus' (Acts 19:28) would bestow blessings and favours that would not be available to devotees of Artemis as she was revered in other Hellenistic cities.

Though gods might be portrayed in human form and, like people, originated from Mother Earth, they were never born, nor did they eat regular food, or grow old,

and third centuries AD, from Gnostic documents as well as from the writings of church leaders who wrote to denounce it. At that time it was obviously a widespread religious movement. It is unlikely that Gnosticism existed in any organized form in the New Testament period, though these later groups did not construct their systems out of nothing but incorporated materials that had been in circulation for a long time. Several New Testament books appear to refer to notions that later became central to Gnostic thinking, and it is obvious that these ideas were floating around independently in the religious atmosphere of the earlier Hellenistic age.

Gnostic thinking was based on the belief that there are two worlds: the world of spirit, where God is, which is pure and holy; and the world of matter, where people are, and which is evil and corrupted. A God who is holy and pure, Gnostics argued, can by definition have no involvement in what goes on in the material world. Salvation (however it might be defined) cannot be related to life here, but can only be a quality to be found in the other, spiritual world. A person's best chance of finding ultimate meaning is therefore to escape from this material world into the spiritual one, and discover true fulfilment there. For most Gnostics, this chance to escape came at death, when the soul left the

---

or die. If there had been a golden age when gods and people mingled freely with one another, that time was long since past, and for now there was a great gulf between the two modes of existence. There was however a third group, namely the heroes, who might also be worshipped, though being lower than the gods. A hero was typically a mortal who had died, having achieved great things, and whose tomb might become a centre of devotion.

Hellenistic religion had no organized central structure that could impose a uniform belief system at all the many local shrines. Though individual deities had their own priests, there was no recognized professional priesthood, and being a priest was not a full-time job. Authority in religious matters generally rested with those who had secular power, which in the household meant the father, while in the city-states it would be the local magistrates, or even the assembly of all citizens. The most important religious functionaries were often seers, who would deliver oracles

interpreting the divine will to any who asked their opinion – which they did, on matters as diverse as personal guidance, healing, the development of national

Mount Olympus, traditional home of the gods in Greek mythology.

body behind. But not everyone would be automatically qualified to reach the world of spirit. To do so, a person must have a divine 'spark' embedded in their nature, otherwise they would simply return to this world to start another meaningless round of bodily existence. Even those who possess this spark of deity can never be absolutely certain of finding ultimate release, for the evil creator of this world (the *Demiurge*) and his accomplices (the *Archons*) jealously guard every entrance to the world of spirit. To get past them, the spark must be enlightened about its own nature and the nature of true salvation. For this, 'knowledge' (the Greek word was *gnosis*) was required. When Gnostics spoke of 'knowledge' they did not have in mind an intellectual knowing of religious dogmas, or indeed of science. They referred to a mystical experience, a direct 'knowing' of the supreme God.

In practical terms, this kind of belief could lead to two quite opposite extremes. Some argued that their aim of complete liberation from the grasp of the material world could best be achieved by a rigorous asceticism which would effectively deny the reality of their bodily human existence. But there were others who believed that, by virtue of their mystical 'knowledge', they had already been released from all material ties, and therefore what they did in their present life

---

Traditional Greek religion *continued*

The sanctuary of Apollo at Delphi. The oracle in residence here was consulted by all Greek and many foreign states before embarking on major undertakings.

policies, or military campaigns. The oracle at Delphi was one of the most highly respected sources of such spiritual insight.

This was a religion of observance, in which the need to ensure ongoing security and prosperity in the various spheres of everyday life was the dominant factor, rather than (as in Christianity) matters of belief about God or the nature of the world and its people. Devotion was expressed through acts of respect directed towards the deities, with different gods or goddesses being recognized for their

influence in different circumstances and at different stages of life. For this reason, to speak of Greek or Roman religion as if it was some special sort of ritual or belief system, is misleading. Religious observance, in which the intrinsic reality of the gods and goddesses was recognized, was simply an everyday part of life, intended to preserve social stability, whether it be in the context of rites of passage, or of legal transactions, or military expeditions, or any other concern that people might have. Hellenistic spirituality was therefore not at all individualistic, and the notion of having a personal relationship with one of the gods would not have been a regular part of it. From a sociological point of view it was all about maintaining the well-being of the community, by observing the correct social forms at the right times and in the right places. This could easily be done, for example, by the head of a household acting on behalf of all members of a family, or by local magistrates as representatives of an entire community.

was totally irrelevant to their ultimate spiritual destiny. They saw it as their duty to spoil everything connected with life in the material world, including especially its standards of morality and what were regarded as conventional forms of behaviour. They might therefore promote anarchic and undisciplined behaviour as part of their spiritual quest.

It is not difficult to trace connections between this outlook and various groups who are mentioned in the New Testament, though we must remember there is no evidence that it had all been worked into a comprehensive system at this period. Nevertheless, Paul's letters to the church in Corinth often seem to be criticizing views that would certainly be congenial to later Gnostics, while Colossians, 1 John and Revelation also seem to be concerned with debates about people who were seeking to expound the Christian faith in similar terms.

MYSTERY RELIGIONS
Direct emotional experience of God also played a key role in the various mystery religions which sprang up in the Roman empire. Mithraism was one of the best known of these, and was very popular especially among the officers in the Roman army. But there were many others, associated with the gods of Asia Minor and Egypt as well as traditional Greek

---

Appropriate sites for devotion did not need to be special shrines or temples, and many thousands of *herms* (stone pillars with the head of the god Hermes on top and a phallic symbol in front) have been discovered at roadsides, or on street corners, inviting passers-by to seek the god's protection, and in the process recognizing their solidarity with the community in which the *herm* was located.

Sacrifice was the usual way to win the favour of the gods – usually of animals, though corn or fruit could also be offered. Far from being a gloomy occasion, this was generally a time for festivity and celebration, for only the poorest parts of sacrificial victims were actually offered to the gods, with the best cuts of meat then being eaten in a communal banquet. There was of course a serious side to it all, and worshippers regularly made offerings in order to win some particular favour from the deity. This was understood not so much as an attempt to bribe the gods, but more as a way of affirming that the human–divine relationship was a two-sided

affair operating in a cause and effect way that was predictable, and therefore orderly.

With the increasing influence of the philosophical thinkers, questions were inevitably raised about this belief system. In the earliest period, it had been taken for granted that the stories about the gods and their doings were about real deities, and what was described in these stories had actually happened. Under philosophical influence, the gods and their stories had been explained as symbols of some first force or abstract principle that lay behind the world, and while that did not invariably lead to an intellectual atheism or a discontinuation of the traditional forms of devotion, by the New Testament period cultural change (which included a fresh awareness of alternative religious traditions) was combining with growing spiritual uncertainty to undermine the easy acceptance of traditional Hellenistic beliefs – though they never disappeared entirely until they were eventually supplanted by Christianity itself centuries later.

practices. Like Gnosticism, these groups were by definition secret societies, and our specific knowledge of them is therefore inevitably limited. It seems likely however that many of them arose as developments from the various fertility religions which had been popular for thousands of years throughout the ancient Middle East. Their mythologies certainly seem to reflect the cycle of the seasons, as the new life of spring follows the barrenness of winter, all of it symbolized by the death and rebirth of the gods of fertility.

The ancient religions of Egypt and Palestine had generally celebrated this cyclical world-view in annual festivals in which priests and priestesses would act out the role of the deities, often in rituals with strong sexual overtones, and, in the Hellenistic mysteries, such rituals became mystical experiences for the individual worshipper. Their original mythology was transferred from the ongoing life of nature into the experience of individual people, who themselves spoke of undergoing the death and rebirth that had been so important to the prosperity of the ancient farmer.

Mithraism was the most powerful mystery religion in the Roman empire in Paul's time. Worshippers believed that the god Mithras would save the faithful and help them to reach heaven. Here Mithras, a Persian god, is killing the bull as a sacrifice (Roman temple of Mithras, Wallbrook, London, England).

A person could gain access to this mystical experience by way of an initiation ceremony. One account of the consecration of a priest tells how the subject was placed in a pit in the ground, covered with a wicker framework (Prudentius, *Peristephanon* X.1011–50). On this a bull (symbol of life and virility) was slaughtered, and its blood ran down and soaked the initiate. When the priest emerged, those around would fall down and worship him, for he himself had now been made divine through being drenched in the life of the bull. No doubt the initiation of a priest differed in some details from that of an ordinary person, but it is a safe guess that a similar pattern would be followed, while there is plenty of evidence to show that sexual rites of various kinds would often play a central part.

The Mysteries gave a sense of hope and security to their initiates, in both personal and social terms. Individuals gained a sense of personal meaning and purpose in life. They also became part of a distinctive group which shared the same secret experiences, and often operated as a mutual aid society in times of difficulty or hardship.

JUDAISM

This was also very popular in the Hellenistic world. There were a number of reasons for this, not least the fact that large numbers of Jews lived in most of the major towns and cities of the Roman empire. Wherever they went, they took their distinctive beliefs and lifestyle with them. While the Jewish communities were always conscious of a deep difference between themselves and their Gentile neighbours, they were not generally exclusive groups, and were usually more than happy for others to join them. Many Greeks and Romans were attracted.

From the perspective of city dwellers in the western empire, Judaism was essentially an eastern religion, and held all the attractions of mystery and intrigue that such an origin implied. But unlike the esoteric mystery cults, Judaism was not difficult for outsiders to understand. They could see its practical outworking in the everyday life of their Jewish friends, for its relevance depended not on secret experiences, but found expression in the ordinary life of the home. More important, enquirers could read the Jewish scriptures for themselves in their own Greek language, and make up their minds about it before committing themselves to involvement in the life of the Jewish community of faith.

Jewish teachers were not slow to exploit this openness to Judaism among those people who were not ethnically Jewish. Even in the time of Jesus, the persistence and enthusiasm of Jewish rabbis in sharing their faith with others, crossing land and sea to do so, was legendary (Matthew 23:15). Moreover, the Jewish emphasis on rigorous standards of personal and social morality found a warm reception among many thinking Greeks and Romans, who were dissatisfied with the permissiveness of their own culture. Some of them became full members of the Jewish faith, accepting all the demands of the Old Testament law to become 'proselytes'. Others merely accepted the Old Testament's moral teaching, and were given a lesser status as 'God-fearers'. These groups played a significant role in the developing life of the early Christian church. One of the first non-Jewish Christians mentioned in the New Testament – Cornelius, the Roman centurion – was a 'God-fearer' (Acts 10:1–48), and as the first Christian missionaries took their message into the wider Roman empire, they often found an enthusiastic response among such people. Indeed, Paul felt it was so important to share the message with these people that he made it a specific policy always to go first to the Jewish community in every town he visited.

Menorah carved on a column of the synagogue at Capernaum, dating from the end of the 2nd century AD.

CHRISTIANITY

This, then, was the world into which the first Christians brought their message about Jesus. It was a world that had been cut adrift from its roots, a world that was in search of a new self-understanding, and a world full of competing faiths and ideologies, all of them claiming to have the answers to the big questions of the day.

There are many ways in which the phenomenal success of the Christian faith in this context can be explained. But one of the key facts is simply that the Christian message addressed the key concerns of people in that culture at that point in time, and it was shared by people who had a clear understanding of what they needed to do in order to demonstrate its relevance to the everyday concerns of ordinary people. As the original followers of Jesus moved from their homeland on the fringes of the empire into the large urban centres of the western Mediterranean, they met people at their point of need. Not only were they able to engage with the questions that people were asking on an intellectual level, but in addition – and, if anything, even more significantly – the groups of Christian believers which they established throughout the empire demonstrated in a practical way the sense of purpose and meaning in life for which so many were searching.

Jesus' claim to be the fulfilment of the Old Testament faith gave

Traditional deities of Greece and Rome

Jupiter

Apollo

Zeus
Chief god, father of other gods; Roman Jupiter (Jove)

Hera
Sister and consort of Zeus; Roman Juno

Athena
Goddess of war, wisdom and the arts; Roman Minerva

Apollo
God of sun, prophecy, music, medicine, poetry; Roman Apollo

Athena

Artemis
Virgin goddess of chastity, the hunt and the moon; twin sister of Apollo; Roman Diana

Poseidon
God of sea, earthquakes, horses; brother of Zeus; Roman Neptune

Aphrodite
Goddess of love and beauty; Cytherea; Roman Venus

Hermes
God of commerce, invention, cunning, theft; messenger for other gods; patron of travellers and rogues; conductor of the dead to Hades; Roman Mercury

Hephaestus
Disabled god of fire and metalworking; Roman Vulcan

Ares
God of war; Roman Mars

Demeter
Goddess of agriculture, fertility, marriage; Roman Ceres

Dionysus
God of wine, ecstasy and orgasm; Roman Bacchus

Demeter

his followers a head start. Greeks and Romans – and expatriate Jews – naturally wanted to know what the Christians had to say, and because the Old Testament had already been translated into Greek, the earliest Christian missionaries had no difficulty at all in explaining their message in specific terms. In addition, Christianity had a certain curiosity value to the western city dwellers, as one of the many religions that were moving in from the east. Palestine itself was widely regarded as the very edge of the civilized land, and anything coming from that quarter would always be given a hearing by those who were disillusioned with their own religious heritage.

The early Christians could also appeal to those who were attracted to Gnosticism and the mystery religions. The whole thrust of Jesus' teaching was quite different from these world-denying systems of thought. But for that very reason it gave a more convincing explanation of life as it is in this world, rather than encouraging people to opt out and dream of the possibilities of life in some other world. The Christian message was firmly based on events that had taken place in the real

Jews and Judaism in the Roman empire

Most people assume that Palestine was the major homeland of the Jews in New Testament times. But in fact there were probably more Jews living in a city like Alexandria in Egypt than there were in Jerusalem itself, and overall there were significantly greater numbers living scattered throughout the major urban centres of the Roman empire than there were in Palestine. Josephus quotes the Latin author Strabo's comment that the Jewish nation 'has already made its way into every city, and it is not easy to find any place in the habitable world which has not received this nation, and in which it has not made its power felt' (Josephus, *Antiquities of the Jews* 14.7.2).

In Old Testament times, the land and people of Israel had been thought of as a self-contained geographical and national entity. Indeed, the Old Testament story is largely concerned with how Israel's ancestors had been gathered from various ethnic origins to be united in their common heritage, with its focus on their land, and the city of Jerusalem in particular. But by the time of Jesus the process was working

in reverse, and the Jewish people were living all over the world. This scattering, or *Diaspora* ('Dispersion'), had begun many centuries before in 586BC, when

River Euphrates near Babylon, home to a large Jewish population following Nebuchadnezzar's capture of Jerusalem in 586BC.

Nebuchadnezzar, king of Babylon, invaded the kingdom of Judah. As a way of imposing absolute control over the conquered nation, he took all the most gifted and influential inhabitants of Jerusalem off to a new life in Babylon. This was a disaster of immense proportions for the Jewish people. Politically, it was the final catastrophe, for never again were the Jewish people to enjoy an independent existence. Despite that, however, this Jewish exile in Babylon was to become one of the most creative forces in the whole history of Jewish religious history.

In the heyday of traditional Jewish

world of everyday experience – the life, death and resurrection of Jesus. It did not require believers to distance themselves from life as they experienced it, but to understand this material existence as the context in which God was active, and could be known in a personal way. Christians also affirmed that a good life could not be achieved by human ingenuity and, without denigrating the value of human rationality (as the mystery religions tended to do), they claimed that reason was not capable by itself of discerning the meaning of life. True satisfaction could only be found, they argued, through a close personal relationship with God, which through the work of God's Spirit shared some of the characteristics of the mystical experiences so popular at the time, but by virtue of being rooted in the life and teaching of Jesus of Nazareth was always grounded in the historical realities of life in this world. In addition, Christianity was not only concerned with individual self-fulfilment; through faith in Jesus believers found themselves part of a new social grouping – the church – that could offer a meaningful context for a corporate as well as an individual spirituality.

Jews and Judaism in the Roman empire *continued*

religion, the worship of the temple in Jerusalem had been of central importance. It was by regular visits to the temple and the offering of sacrifices there that people declared their loyalty to the God of Israel and their continued determination to obey the Law. But Nebuchadnezzar destroyed the temple, and though the remnants of the population who were left in Jerusalem still continued to worship in its ruins, even that consolation was not possible for those who had been removed to Babylon. Their feelings were expressed most poignantly in the words of Psalm 137:1–6:

> By the rivers of Babylon we sat down;
> there we wept when we remembered
> Zion.
> On the willows near by we hung up
> our harps.
> Those who captured us told us
> to sing;
> they told us to entertain them:
> 'Sing us a song about Zion.'
> How can we sing to the Lord in a
> foreign land?
> May I never be able to play
> the harp again
> if I forget you, Jerusalem!

In the event, Jerusalem was not forgotten, and it was not long before the exiles discovered that though at first it seemed inconceivable, they could indeed 'sing the Lord's songs in a foreign land'. It was in the synagogue that they did so. In a different social setting, some things just had to be different, and the local synagogue was not a replica of the temple back in Jerusalem. Worship in Jerusalem had been concerned with sacrifices, but this was no longer possible, and in the worship at the synagogue the central place of sacrifice had to be filled by something else. So a form of worship developed which allowed no place for sacrifice but instead placed a new emphasis on those traditional observances that could be carried out anywhere: prayer, the reading of the Torah, keeping the sabbath day, circumcision, and the observance of the ancient regulations concerning the preparation and consumption of food.

This adaptation of traditional Jewish worship was so successful that when Jews from Babylon were eventually able to return to their homeland, they took it with them. A bit later still, following the conquests of Alexander the Great, other enterprising Jews decided to emigrate

It is not difficult to see why and how the early Christians were able to fill the spiritual vacuum of the Hellenistic world so successfully. But the story of their faith is much more complex than just a haphazard coincidence of social factors in the ancient world. Indeed, it was not in this predominantly Greek world at all that the story had its beginnings and, to understand it fully, it is necessary to delve into the sometimes convoluted world of Jewish history and religion.

Palestine and its people

When Alexander conquered the ancient world, most nations went along with his policy of Hellenization. In many instances they accepted it only grudgingly, and quite often Hellenism made little impact on native customs. National institutions would be adjusted to conform with the Greek style, and the ruling classes in particular found it advantageous to adopt Greek habits, while the lives of ordinary people could remain virtually untouched by the Greek influence.

---

voluntarily to different parts of the Mediterranean world, and it was natural that they should adopt the synagogue as the central expression of their religious and national allegiance. By the time the first Christian missionaries were beginning to travel with their new message about Jesus, there was an extensive network of Jewish synagogues spread the length and breadth of the entire Roman empire.

Not all synagogues were exactly the same. In earlier times, the temple in Jerusalem had imposed a certain degree of central control over religious beliefs and practices, and it continued to do so in Palestine until its final destruction in AD70. But the synagogues were much freer to develop their own ways of thinking. The problems of being a Jew in Babylon were quite different from the challenges facing Jews in Rome, while the Egyptian city of Alexandria was different again. In each local centre, people had to work out for themselves how best to adapt their ancestral faith to the demands and opportunities of their new environments. Even within the same locality, different synagogues might reach different conclusions. In Rome, for example, some Jews were quite happy to go along with

many aspects of pagan society, even giving their children Latin or Greek names, and adopting the art-forms of Roman civilization, while others in the same city deplored what they saw as a dilution and betrayal of their ancestral faith, and stuck rigidly to a more traditional understanding of the laws of the.Hebrew Bible.

We also know of Jews who became deeply interested in the study of Greek philosophy. The most famous of these was Philo, a Jew from the Egyptian city of Alexandria. We know few details of his life, but he must have been born some time before Jesus, and probably lived until the mid-forties of the first century AD. He was a member of an influential Jewish family, and some of his relatives became deeply involved in politics both in Egypt and elsewhere. But Philo was most interested in explaining the thinking of Greek writers, especially the Stoics. He found many of their ideas congenial, and set out to show how the Hebrew scriptures and Greek philosophy were really saying the same things in their own distinctive ways. In order to demonstrate this, he had to regard the traditional stories of his people as a kind of allegorical or symbolic presentation of the truths expounded by

Most nations around the Mediterranean world would have preferred to retain full control over their own lives, but they knew well enough that the realities of international politics obliged them to go along with the superpowers of the day. In any case, even if Alexander's policy of Hellenization was more thoroughgoing than anything imposed by most other ancient empires, it was not a new concept. For centuries, subject nations had demonstrated their subordination by accepting the culture of their conquerors. It was taken for granted that this would include at least a token allegiance to the religions of their overlords. Modern states change the image on their postage stamps or currency when a new ruler comes to power: in the ancient world, they changed the statues and altars in their temples. It can have come as no surprise to discover that under Greek rulers, subject nations would be expected to find a place for the Greek gods.

Most were willing to do so, but not the Jews of Palestine. For them, practical politics and deeply held religious convictions could not be reconciled quite so easily. For one thing, their ancestral faith had always insisted that there is just one God, and that this one God must be

---

Jews and Judaism in the Roman empire *continued*

Philo of Alexandria (c. 20BC –c. AD50), whose writings interpreted the Jewish scriptures using Greek categories of thought.

the philosophers. Orthodox Jews elsewhere in the empire would certainly have regarded Philo as a traitor to his religion, but he saw himself as a faithful interpreter who was proud of his ancestral traditions, and had no doubt that what he was doing was both worthwhile and necessary.

There was, however, one thing on which all the synagogues of the Roman world were united. This was in their use of the Greek language. As one generation succeeded another it was not long before the vast majority of Jews in the Mediterranean world could speak no other language, and so it became important that the ancient Jewish scriptures, originally written in Hebrew, should be translated into the language that most Jews now spoke and understood best.

The actual origins of the Greek Bible that was produced are shrouded in obscurity. According to one ancient legend, the Jews of Egypt managed to persuade the Egyptian king, Ptolemy II Philadelphus (285–247BC) to sponsor the project. The story tells how he sent to Jerusalem for seventy men who knew both Hebrew and Greek, and locked them up in seventy cells while each one produced his own translation. When their work was finished,

to everyone's amazement the seventy men not only expressed the same ideas, but also used the very same Greek words to do so — whereupon Ptolemy was so impressed, that he was immediately convinced of the divine origins of their work! Not everyone believed that sort of story even in the ancient world, and another ancient source, *The Letter of Aristeas*, implies that the translators set the precedent for almost all subsequent translations, and worked as a committee.

Probably neither of these stories by itself reflects the full account of what actually happened, and many scholars now believe that the Greek Septuagint version of the Jewish scriptures (the LXX) just evolved gradually over many generations. But wherever it came from, it had enormous influence and importance. It was widely used not only by Jews all over the Roman empire, but was also read by intelligent Romans who wanted to know more about the Jewish faith. It also became the Bible of the first Christian churches, and its easy accessibility greatly assisted the Christians in sharing their faith throughout the Hellenistic world.

worshipped without visual representations, and according to carefully prescribed regulations. Other nations could declare their allegiance to Zeus simply by placing his statue alongside their own gods and goddesses, and including him in the rituals that were already taking place. But Israel would never do this, and regarded it all as a complete denial of some of the most cherished aspects of the Old Testament faith.

Hellenism and Judaism

These religious misgivings among the Jewish people never amounted to much in the time of Alexander himself. Indeed, it was some considerable time after his death before they were to become a real issue, under the Greek ruler of Palestine, Antiochus IV Epiphanes (175–164BC). Antiochus was a member of the Seleucid dynasty, whose predecessors had always allowed the high priestly rulers in Jerusalem a good deal of local independence. Unfortunately, the high priesthood itself became the subject of an internal power struggle at exactly the same moment as Antiochus suffered a humiliating defeat in Egypt at the hands of the Romans (168BC). This hurt Antiochus' pride, and he was determined to reassert his authority by whatever means he could. The Jews were an easy target, and Antiochus marched on Jerusalem determined to show who was in charge. He knew enough to realize that the factional arguments about the priesthood were not purely political, but involved differences of opinion among the Jews themselves about their own religion. He neither understood nor cared for their faith, but if it was causing trouble, then Antiochus knew that its power would have to be diminished.

Coin of Antiochus IV Epiphanes (175–164BC), who believed he was divine.

He responded by inaugurating a thoroughgoing policy of enforced Hellenization. All the things that were most distinctive about Jewish life were banned, including circumcision, keeping the sabbath day, and reading the traditional scriptures. Even worse, Antiochus decreed that the temple in Jerusalem, the focal point of traditional Jewish worship, should be dedicated to the Greek god Zeus. To rub salt into the wounds, he opened the temple up to the whole population of the land, which included people who were not themselves Jewish believers. This kind of cultural integration had always been desirable to the Greek rulers of Palestine, but whereas his predecessors had taken a more pragmatic view, Antiochus believed it was now essential to stamp out Jewish distinctiveness in order to ensure his own political survival. Whether they liked it or not, and regardless of the consequences, everyone in the land would be united under the Greek religion in a thoroughly Greek way of life.

Antiochus had seriously underestimated the strength of Jewish religious feeling. It was one thing to erect altars to Greek gods – but it would be another thing altogether to persuade the Jews to worship at them. Antiochus' efforts to enforce his new regime only increased the determination of the Jewish people to fight back. It was not long before an armed resistance movement was established by Mattathias, a priest from the village of Modein, along with his five sons. They came to be known as the 'Maccabees', and their tactics of guerrilla warfare were so successful that it took only three years for Antiochus' troops to be defeated and for his policies to be reversed.

Jews and Romans

All this took place nearly 200 years before the time of Jesus. In the intervening period, the Greeks had been replaced by the Romans as the dominant superpower. But the Jews of Palestine never lost their firm determination to resist religious compromise and, if possible, to preserve their own rights to political self-determination.

This fiercely independent posture was largely the result of their belief that they had been specially chosen by God to rule the world under the leadership of God's promised deliverer, whom they called the 'Messiah'. At one time it had been possible for them to expect that this might happen in the normal course of history. Ancient stories from the days of David and Solomon, almost 1,000 years before the birth of Jesus, depicted them as one of the great world powers. Their more recent successes against Antiochus had shown that they were still a force to be reckoned with, but it was obvious to most Jews living in Palestine in Jesus' day that something of almost supernatural proportions would have to take place if they were ever to be released from the iron grip of Rome.

At the same time, not all Jews wanted to be freed from Roman rule. There were some sections of society in Palestine who found it was comfortable to be friendly with the Romans, and even among those who saw freedom as an ideal, there were not many who were prepared to take practical action to secure it.

The Romans had an unenviable task in Palestine. For them, its continuing security was essential, as it was the main eastern frontier of their entire empire. Even so, they were on occasion prepared to make allowances for Jewish scruples. When they appointed Herod the Great as ruler of Judea in 37BC, they hoped he would be acceptable to Jewish public opinion, for as well as being a person whom the Romans felt they could trust he was also half Jewish, a fact which they assumed would commend him to the Jewish people, and lessen some of their resistance to foreign rule.

Herod the Great

The story of Herod's rise to power, and indeed of the rest of his reign, is a classic tale of intrigue and ruthlessness. As a king he was a combination of diplomatic brilliance and personal insanity. Though there is no record of it outside the New Testament, the story of how he

murdered the children of Bethlehem after Jesus was born (Matthew 2:16) is quite consistent with all that is known of his character and behaviour. Anyone who opposed his policies (or even just incurred his disfavour) could expect violent treatment. He never thought twice about killing even his own family: one of his wives, Mariamme, was executed on his orders, and he was involved in the murder of two of his own sons, Alexander and Aristobulus. Only five days before his death in 4BC he ordered the execution of yet another of his sons, Antipater, the one who had been expected to succeed him.

Yet Herod the Great was not called 'Great' for nothing, and in contrast to previous rulers Herod maintained peace and order throughout his territory. He was also responsible for a massive building programme: it was Herod the Great who started the building of a new temple at Jerusalem, which was still not finished during the lifetime of Jesus. He also built many other magnificent buildings in Jerusalem and Caesarea, and even in other Roman cities outside his own territory.

The three Herods

When Herod the Great died in 4BC the Romans divided his kingdom among his three remaining sons. With one possible exception, none of them was any better than his father.

Judea, the part of Palestine that included Jerusalem, was given to his

The Herodium is a fortress 7 m/12 km south of Jerusalem. Built by Herod the Great between 24 and 15BC, it stands on the spot where he achieved one of his most important victories over the Hasmoneans in 40BC.

son Archelaus. He was not allowed to call himself 'king' of Judea, as his father had been, but received the title 'ethnarch' instead. He ruled for only ten years: the Romans removed him from office. In AD6 Judea became a third-grade province of the Roman empire, under an officer of the upper-class equestrian rank, who was himself under the command of the Roman governor of Syria. These Roman rulers of Judea were later called 'procurators'. The best-known one, certainly in relation to the New Testament story, was Pontius Pilate, who governed Judea from AD26 to 36.

The northern part of Palestine was given to Antipas, another son of Herod. He was known as the 'tetrarch' of Galilee and Perea, and his territory included the village of Nazareth where Jesus grew up. Antipas was very much like his father, a crafty man who liked living in luxury. To make a name for himself he took great pride in the construction of massive public buildings. One of his major projects was the rebuilding of Sepphoris, a town only four miles from Nazareth. He also built the new town of Tiberias by Lake Galilee, and named it in honour of the Roman emperor Tiberius. It was Herod Antipas who had John the Baptist executed (Mark 6:17–29) and who was involved in the trials of Jesus (Luke 23:6–12).

A third brother, Philip, was given some territory to the north-east of Palestine when his father died. He founded the town of Caesarea Philippi at the foot of Mount Hermon. Of all the sons of Herod the Great, Philip was the only one who proved to be a balanced and humane ruler, and he survived as 'tetrarch of Iturea and Trachonitis' until the year AD34.

After Archelaus was replaced by a Roman governor, there were many revolts against the Romans in Judea. The Jews became more and more frustrated at not having control of their own affairs. The Romans for their part became less interested in trying to understand the special problems of the Jewish people. The oppression and corruption of many of the Roman rulers, encouraged by a rising tide of Jewish nationalism, continued to increase until eventually in the year AD66 a general revolt

Division of the kingdom on the death of Herod the Great.

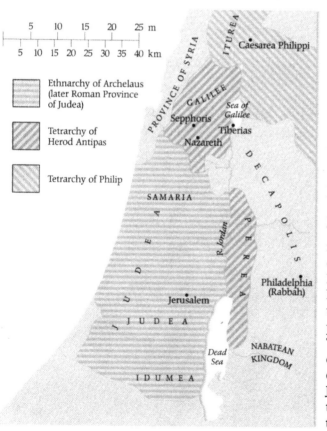

5 10 15 20 25 m

5 10 15 20 25 30 35 40 km

Ethnarchy of Archelaus (later Roman Province of Judea)

Tetrarchy of Herod Antipas

Tetrarchy of Philip

ITUREA

Caesarea Philippi

PROVINCE OF SYRIA

GALILEE

Sepphoris

Sea of Galilee

Tiberias

Nazareth

DECAPOLIS

SAMARIA

R. Jordan

PEREA

Philadelphia (Rabbah)

Jerusalem

JUDEA

Dead Sea

NABATEAN KINGDOM

IDUMEA

broke out. This revolt was finally crushed when Jerusalem was largely destroyed by the Roman general Titus in AD70.

Religious loyalties

The Jewish historian Josephus, who lived towards the end of the first century AD, and who was a friend of the Romans, reports that three main opinions were common among the Jews in Palestine: 'Jewish philosophy takes three forms. The followers of the first school are called Pharisees, of the second Sadducees, and the third sect, which has a reputation for being more disciplined, is the Essenes' (*Jewish Wars* 2.8.2). He also mentions a fourth group, called Zealots, but since he does not always include these among the philosophical sects, it seems likely that they formed a much looser kind of association (*Jewish Wars* 4.3.9). All these groups had their origins in the years following the Maccabean Revolt, and their actual membership was probably quite small, though most people would look to one of them for leadership, in much the same way as people nowadays might regularly vote for a particular political party, without joining it in a formal way as members. Three of these groups feature regularly in the New Testament: the Sadducees, the Pharisees and the Zealots.

Sadducees

The gospels of Matthew, Mark and Luke regularly mention the Sadducees along with the Pharisees, though in fact the two groups were not intrinsically related but were quite separate and actually held opposite opinions on almost everything. The Sadducees were only a small group, but were very influential because they consisted mainly of the more important priests in the temple at Jerusalem, and included only the most well-to-do classes of Jewish society. They were extreme conservatives in everything and disliked changes of any kind, especially changes which might affect the social status quo. Even if they believed theoretically in the coming of a Messiah, they generally had nothing to do with political protests, for that would only cause trouble with the Romans.

The name 'Sadducee' seems to mean 'son of Zadok', although the Sadducees were certainly not direct descendants of the priest Zadok mentioned in 2 Samuel 15:24–29. Other meanings for the name are also possible: either from the Hebrew word *sadiq*, meaning 'moral integrity' or 'righteousness'; or from the Greek word *syndicoi*, which could mean 'members of the council'. It is certainly true that the Jewish council of seventy (the Sanhedrin) had many Sadducees among its members, though since the remaining members were Pharisees, it is doubtful if this would be the origin of their distinctive name.

Sadducees were conservative not only in politics, but also in their understanding of Judaism. For them, the only religious teaching with any authority was the Law given by Moses in the first five books of the Hebrew Bible (the Pentateuch or Torah). They had no time either for

Facing page: Palestine in New Testament times.

the rest of the scriptures, or for anyone who tried to reinterpret or apply them in a more direct way to their own situation. This meant that they did not share with other Jews some of the beliefs of Judaism that were not explicitly contained in the Torah. For that reason, they did not generally believe that God had a purpose behind the events of history, while matters such as belief in a future life, resurrection, or a final judgment were regarded as unauthorized additions to the Jewish faith.

Pharisees

This was a much larger group, with maybe around 6,000 members at the time of Jesus. Many of them were professional students of the scriptures, but others had ordinary jobs. They were a national organization, with a large number of local groups found in most towns and villages throughout Palestine, each with their own officials and rules. They were probably the most influential religious group during Jesus' lifetime. The Sadducees disliked them because they believed and did things that went well beyond a literal understanding of the Law of Moses, but they were highly regarded by most ordinary people.

The Sadducees' chief complaint against the Pharisees was that they had collected many rules and regulations to explain what they saw as the real meaning of the Law. Though the Pharisees regarded the Hebrew scriptures as their supreme rule of life and belief, they also realized that

Modern Jews studying the Torah.

Tyre •

PROVINCE OF SYRIA

• Caesarea Philippi

ULATHA

5   10   15   20   25 m
5   10   15   20   25   30   35   40 km

L. Semechonitis
(L. Huleh)

GAULANITIS

♜ Fortress

PHOENICIA

GALILEE

R. Jordan

Ptolemais •

Chorazin •

Capernaum • • Bethsaida
Gennesaret •
Cana •
Magadan •
Dalmanutha

Sea of
Galilee

• Gergesa?

Tiberias •

Mt
Carmel △

R. Kishon

Sepphoris •

Nazareth •

• Gadara

Gabata •

The Great Plain
(Esdraelon)

• Nain

Agrippina •

Valley of Jezreel

D
E
C
A

Mt Gilboa △

Caesarea •

J U D E A

Scythopolis •

Salim •
Aenon •

Mediterranean Sea

S A M A R I A

Sebaste
(Samaria) •

P
O
L
I
S

Gerasa
•

Neapolis •

• Sychar

R. Jabbok

Plain of Sharon

Mt Gerizim △
• Mahnayim

Antipatris •

Alexandrium ♜

R. Jordan

P
E
R
E
A

Joppa •

Lydda •

Bethel •

• Archelais

Berea •

Jericho •

Philadelphia
(Rabbah)
•

Emmaus •
(Nicopolis)

Colonia Amasa
(Emmaus?)

Cyprus ♜

otus Paralius
zotus-on-Sea) •

Bethphage
Jerusalem • • Bethany

• Qumran

Azotus •

Bethlehem •

Hyrcania ♜

scalon
ee City) •

Herodium ♜

J U D E A

Terebinthus
(Mamre) •

Wilderness of Judea

Machaerus ♜

• Gaza

Hebron •

Engaddi •
(En-gedi)

R. Arnon

Dead Sea

Masada ♜

Bersabe
(Beersheba) •

I D U M E A

B
A
T
A
N
E
A
N   K I N G D O M

Malatha ♜

it no longer had any direct application to the kind of society they lived in, and to remain relevant it would need to be explained in new ways. For example, the ten commandments instructed people to keep the sabbath day holy (Exodus 20:8). But what did that really mean in everyday terms? What should people do and not do on the sabbath day? To provide a practical answer to that kind of question, the Pharisees had developed a list of simple rules that could be applied by anybody.

One of the writings influenced by them, the *Pirke Aboth*, opened with the advice to 'make a fence for the Law', which meant, 'protect the Law from infringement by surrounding it with cautionary rules which can act as a warning notice to stop people before they get within breaking distance of the actual God-given commandments themselves'. This intention was praiseworthy enough, but there can be no doubt that eventually it led to the multiplication of petty rules to such an extent that keeping the Law easily became an onerous burden, rather than the joyful celebration of God's goodness which it was meant to be. A typical example would be the rules concerning the sabbath. Tailors were not allowed to go out carrying a needle late in the day before the sabbath, in case they were caught with it still in their pockets when the sabbath began. But like everyone else, they could go for a walk on the sabbath day – provided it was no further than 2,000 cubits, roughly two thirds of a mile, a distance determined by reference to the space between the people of Israel and the Ark of the Covenant when they first entered Canaan! This became known as the 'sabbath day's journey'.

In spite of the apparent absurdity of some of these notions, there can be no doubt that many Pharisees did actually keep these rules, and Josephus comments that 'the people of the cities hold them in the highest esteem, because they both preach and practise the very highest moral ideas' (*Antiquities* 18.1.3). Jesus denounced them for what he called 'hypocrisy', which in this context seems to have been a complaint that the keeping of their own sectarian rules and regulations had become more important than they deserved to be. In that respect, their mistake was one common to many religious groups, namely the claim that the only possible way to know God is to be a member of the group.

Jesus also differed from the Pharisees on more substantive grounds, for it seems that a person's ability to keep the Law had also become a form of social stratification, something that Jesus repeatedly questioned with his insistence that God had a special love for the outcasts and marginalized members of society, and a corresponding disdain for those who were conventionally religious. All that is known of the Pharisees makes it doubtful whether they could ever have said with Jesus: 'I came not to call the righteous, but sinners' (Mark 2:17).

The Pharisees had distinctive views on other subjects, of course. They accepted the authority of the whole of the Hebrew scriptures, and . not just the Law of Moses. Unlike the Sadducees they had no difficulty in believing that there was a life after death. They might well have expected a Messiah to come and right the wrongs of their people, and though we have no record that they took part in open revolt against the Romans, they probably admired those people who did.

Zealots

These were the people who became most involved in direct action against the Romans. Conceptually, they probably shared many of the religious beliefs of the Pharisees, but their overriding conviction was that they could have no master but God, and for them that implied that driving out the Romans must be a top priority. Josephus identifies their founder as a man called Judas, a Galilean who led a revolt in AD6 at about the same time as Archelaus was removed from office by the Romans (*Jewish Wars* 2.8.1). He also reports that 'these men agree in everything with the opinions of the Pharisees, but they have an insatiable passion for liberty; and they are convinced that God alone is to be their only master and Lord... no fear can compel them to give this title to anyone else...' (*Antiquities* 18.1.6).

A Hebrew shekel, minted at the time of the first revolt against Roman rule, AD66–70.

The Zealots continued as a guerrilla movement until the siege of Jerusalem in AD70, and perhaps even after that. At least one of Jesus' disciples, a man called Simon, was a Zealot, and it is often thought that Judas Iscariot was as well (Mark 3:18). But more typical Zealots seem to

---

The apocalyptists

A source of particular insight into the religious expectations that probably formed the background to the life and teaching of Jesus is those works known as the apocalyptic writings. This is a disparate collection of writings compiled over a considerable period of time, all of them containing speculative visions of the future. The term 'apocalypse' literally means 'a revealing of secrets', and it is unclear whether their authors (referred to as 'apocalyptists') formed a distinctive religious grouping, or whether they were individuals who belonged to some of the other groups mentioned by Josephus. Since these people are mostly known only through their writings, it is hard to be sure, though it is certainly unlikely, that any of the apocalyptists would have been Sadducees. The apocalyptists' central claim was that they had received new revelations from God, something that by definition the Sadducees would

not countenance, as they considered Moses to be the only one who had ever received divine revelation. It is easier to equate the apocalyptic writings with aspects of Pharisaic belief, for they placed great emphasis on God's predetermined plan for the history of the world.

Whoever the apocalyptists might have been, their writings have a number of unusual characteristics which make them readily recognizable:

● They place strong emphasis on the life of heaven rather than the everyday world of human experience. Though events in this world are mentioned, they are important only insofar as they reveal something about events taking place in another, spiritual world. One apocalyptic writer states that 'the Most High has made not one world but two' (2 Esdras 7:50), and this viewpoint seems to have been widely shared by the apocalyptists. It was their job to reveal what was happening in God's world, and to assure their readers

have been people like Barabbas, whom the crowd chose to liberate in preference to Jesus (Mark 15:6–15), or the unnamed rabble-rouser with whom Paul was once confused (Acts 21:37–39).

Essenes

The Essenes are referred to by several ancient writers. Philo of Alexandria, the Latin author Pliny, and Josephus all mention them, though they are not explicitly named by any of the New Testament writers.

It is widely supposed that one section of the Essenes wrote the documents known as the Dead Sea Scrolls. This group had their headquarters at Qumran near the north-west corner of the Dead Sea. The people of Qumran probably had their origins among the religious supporters of the Maccabees, but became disenchanted with the corruption of their successors, the Hasmoneans. They chose to withdraw from mainstream society to live in an isolated community in the desert, where they could more easily preserve the traditions of religious and moral purity which they believed they could find in the Hebrew Bible.

Not all Essenes lived in this way, however, for Josephus says that they 'occupy no one city, but settle in large numbers in every town'. He also writes of others who, unlike the monastic groups, were married, though he does go to some pains to make it clear that they regarded

---

**The apocalyptists
continued**

that they had a central position in God's activities.

● The apocalyptic writings also emphasize dreams, visions and communications through angels. Since God is remote in a different world ('heaven'), intermediaries play a key role in dealings between people and God. A typical apocalypse is an extended report of how its writer received speculative visions and messages revealing what is happening in heaven.

● Corresponding with this is an unusual literary form. For the visions are not described in straightforward terms, but invariably use coded language. There are often references to esoteric passages in the books of the Hebrew prophets, and mythological beasts and symbolic numbers are used to represent nations or individuals.

● Apocalypses were normally written under the name of a great figure of the past. Enoch, Noah, Adam, Moses and Ezra are only a few of the ancient heroes who had apocalyptic works attributed to them.

This might have been necessary to protect the identities of their authors, because apocalypses were invariably written in circumstances of persecution. It could also have been the case that because the time of genuine prophecy was believed to have passed, prophets who wanted to get a hearing for their message had to attribute their work to somebody who had actually lived in the age when the Hebrew scriptures were in process of compilation. Revelation, the only New Testament book to use extensive apocalyptic imagery, is unique in this respect, and though there is a good deal of debate as to who its author actually was, he is named as a contemporary and friend of his readers, not someone from the distant past (Revelation 1:1–9).

Why did this kind of writing become so popular in the centuries immediately before the birth of Jesus? An attractive answer is that apocalyptic writing was a response to the difficult realities of life in

this not in relational terms, but only as a means of continuing the human race (*Jewish Wars* 2.8.2–13). There is also written evidence that another group lived in the desert near Damascus, whose organization was slightly different from the group at Qumran.

There is no clear account of the relationship between these various groups, nor any certain knowledge of how they might have been related to the Essenes apparently scattered throughout the towns and villages of Palestine. The community at Qumran is the best known, because of the

Qumran: view of the Essene settlement from the south west.

discovery of their writings, and at most points these documents are in harmony with the statements made by Josephus. The Dead Sea Scrolls reveal that the people of this community regarded themselves as the minority in Israel who were faithful to God's covenant. From their perspective, the rest of the nation, including especially the priests and religious leaders in Jerusalem, had wilfully jettisoned the true faith. Only their

---

Palestine at the time. The prophets had often suggested that the course of Israel's history was dependent on the nation's current spiritual attitudes. At times, it was almost as if they perceived a cause and effect relationship between religious faithfulness and political fortunes: when people were obedient to the Law of God they prospered and, if they weren't, they could expect hard times. These hard times had culminated most painfully in the capture of Jerusalem by Nebuchadnezzar in 586BC, and the exile of its population to Babylon. After only a short time in exile, the Jews had been allowed to return to their homeland, and those who returned were determined that they would not make the same mistakes as their ancestors.

A key part of the post-exilic reconstruction of the nation had been a rigorous reinterpretation of the Law, and an uncompromising application of its precepts to all aspects of national and personal life. As things turned out, however, these people did not prosper

either and, as time went on, the way to prosperity seemed to lie more in collaboration with outsiders such as the Romans than in remaining faithful to the ancient religious traditions. Those who tried to keep the faith alive found themselves more and more in a minority, while those who prospered often did so by sitting loosely to it, or even abandoning it altogether.

Apocalyptic writing might well have begun as an answer to this problem. Why did faithfulness not lead to prosperity? Why were good people suffering? Why did God not put an end to the power of evil forces? To these questions the apocalyptists answered that the present difficulties were only relative. Seen in the light of God's working throughout history, the good would eventually triumph and the oppressive domination of evil would soon be relaxed.

It is often asked whether Jesus had any connection with these apocalyptists and their visions of the heavenly world. Jesus

The first three columns of the Great Isaiah Scroll from Qumran, one of the oldest known manuscripts of a part of the Hebrew Bible.

own leader, the 'Teacher of Righteousness', and his faithful followers had preserved knowledge of the true meaning of the ancient scriptures.

Like some of the other religious groupings, the Essenes looked forward to a day of crisis in history. At this time God's sovereignty over all things would be reaffirmed, and in the process all heretics would be banished, along with foreign enemies such as the Romans. The members of the group, rather than the whole Jewish nation, would be recognized as God's chosen people, and they would take over and purify the worship of God at the temple in Jerusalem. They expected three leaders to appear in connection with these events: the coming prophet who had been predicted by Moses (Deuteronomy 18:18–19); a royal Messiah who

The apocalyptists
continued

was certainly familiar with the ideas that the apocalyptists put forward, and used much of the same imagery and language in his own teachings (Mark 13; Matthew 24 – 25; Luke 21). But there.are some important differences which should caution against a simplistic understanding which sees Jesus as just another apocalyptic visionary:

● Apocalyptic literature was always the report of visions and other insights into the heavenly world, given to humans through some special means. Jesus, however, did not base his teaching on visions and revelations of this kind, but spoke on his own authority. Moreover, his main concern was not with the affairs of some other, heavenly, world, but with life in this world. He did not reveal secrets; he made disciples and reminded them of their responsibilities to God, which always combined moral and social responsibilities as well as matters of belief.

● The apocalyptists were always concerned to encourage and comfort their readers by demonstrating that they were in the right, and their enemies would soon be overcome. But Jesus' teaching, even in what are called the 'apocalyptic discourses', was never designed to comfort his disciples. Nor did he suggest that they will automatically triumph over their enemies: on the contrary, Jesus made his teaching on the future an occasion to challenge his disciples' attitude to life, and regarded the time of God's intervention in human affairs as an occasion of judgment, for his disciples as much as for everyone else.

● There is no systematic view of the future in Jesus' teaching. This is quite different from the apocalyptic outlook, in which every detail of the future has already been mapped out in advance: there, it is all in God's predetermined plan, and those who hold the key to the coded language can know precisely what the future holds. Of course, there have been Christians who have produced systems of this kind on the basis of what they find in

would be a descendant of King David; and a priestly Messiah who would be the most important. In order to keep themselves in a constant state of readiness for these events, the Essenes of Qumran went through many ritual washings. Everything they did had some religious significance. Even their daily meals were an anticipation of the heavenly banquet which they believed would take place at the end of the age.

With the possible exception of the Sadducees, then, all the dominant religious groups in Palestine at the time of Jesus were hoping and praying that God would intervene to give new direction to the life of their people. They all had their own ideas about what God should do, and when and how it might all take place. Some, like the Zealots, were prepared to give God a helping hand when they thought it necessary. Others, such as the Pharisees and Essenes, believed that God's plan was fixed and predetermined and therefore could be neither changed nor enforced by human intervention. Over and above all this, no doubt many other people would be interested neither in political manoeuvring nor in theological disputes, but were still longing for a new direction in the fortunes of their nation. All these factors combined to produce a great sense of expectation, fuelled by much speculation about the meaning of the scriptures, and facilitated by the social and political ferment that ran like a metallic thread through the fabric that was life in Palestine at the time of the New Testament.

---

the New Testament, but the great variety of incompatible and contradictory understandings they have produced merely serves to emphasize the futile nature of such an undertaking. Jesus himself discounted the possibility that the divine plan might be uncovered so easily, and categorically asserted that he did not know it himself (Matthew 24:36; Mark 13:32). No apocalyptist would ever have said that.

● Apocalyptic writers were almost invariably pessimistic about the world and its history. Unlike the prophets of earlier generations, they despaired of God ever being able to work in the world. The forces of evil seemed too strong for that, and they saw the world running headlong to a final and tragic end. There was no point in trying to discover God at work in the midst of such evil, for God was not there. This is all in strong contrast to the outlook of Jesus, who made it abundantly plain that the 'kingdom of God' which he had come to inaugurate would affect the everyday life of ordinary people in this world (Luke 4:16–21). By both precept and example, he declared that God's will was not just something to be done 'in heaven', but was meant to impact the social and political realities of life here and now (Matthew 6:10).

There are then some fundamental differences between Jesus and the apocalyptists. He did not have an apocalyptic outlook on life. He occasionally gave his teaching in the language and imagery of the apocalyptic teachers, just as he referred to the 'golden rule' of the rabbis (Matthew 7:12). As a good teacher he realized that he needed to speak the language of his hearers, and it might well have been that many of the ordinary people of Palestine were most familiar with apocalyptic language. But, characteristically, Jesus took familiar concepts and gave them a new meaning.

Herod's Temple

Herod the Great began building the temple in Jerusalem in 19BC. The main building was complete by AD9 but work continued on it for many years after that. It was twice as high as Solomon's temple had been, and shone with gold decoration. This is an artist's impression of what it looked like.

The Holy of Holies, divided from the Holy Place by a curtain. The ark of the covenant stood here in Solomon's day, but no longer existed in Jesus' time.

The Holy Place, where the priests regularly burnt incense.

A bowl for ritual washings.

The temple area was a hilltop; Herod built a platform on it to make it level. It covered about 35 acres.

The altar where animals were sacrificed.

The court of the Gentiles. This was the only part in which non-Jews were allowed. The traders and money-changers worked here, and were turned out by Jesus.

Fort Antonia, where Roman soldiers were garrisoned.

The central buildings were surrounded by steps and another wall.

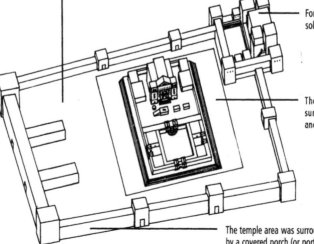

The temple area was surrounded by a covered porch (or portico).

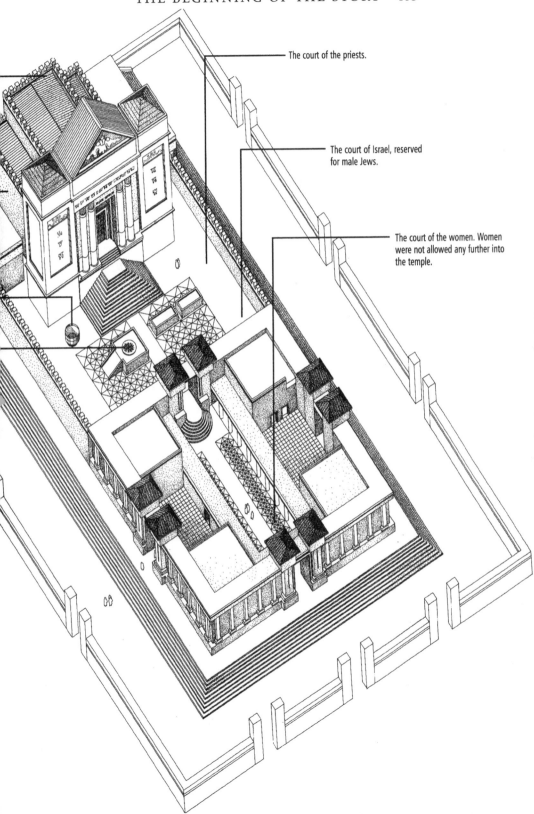

The court of the priests.

The court of Israel, reserved for male Jews.

The court of the women. Women were not allowed any further into the temple.

15 Jesus' Birth and Early Years

If there is one consistent theme that runs through all the stories of Jesus' birth, it is the repeated claim that ordinary people had more insight than religious experts when it came to understanding the significance of it all. The coming of the one who was later claimed to be the expected Messiah was recognized not predominantly by the great and the good but by those who, to a greater or lesser extent, were on the fringes of the cultured society of their day. The first chapter of Luke's Gospel paints a vivid picture of the little-known priest Zechariah and his wife Elizabeth praying expectantly for God to deliver their people, and being rewarded for their faithfulness by the announcement of the birth of their own son, later to be known as John the Baptist (Luke 1:5–28, 57–80).

Mary, the mother of Jesus, belonged to the same family. At the time of Jesus' conception and birth she was in the process of getting married to Joseph. This was an extended business, and it could take several months, with various betrothal ceremonies to get through before a couple were formally recognized as husband and wife. Joseph has traditionally been described as a carpenter, though the Greek word used to describe him (*tekton*) indicates that he was more likely a general builder, the kind of person who could turn his hand to just about anything in the construction industry. At the time, there was plenty of work in Palestine for such a person, so Joseph and Mary are unlikely to have been extremely poor. At the same time, they would not be rich. More importantly, from the religious perspective, as ordinary working people they would be regarded as quite unqualified when it came to understanding the Hebrew scriptures and applying them to the events of their own time in order to discern God's will for their people. They were part of the 'people of the land', whose endeavours were a necessary part of the national economy but whom the religious establishment would have considered incapable of spiritual insight.

The striking poetry of the hymn of praise sung by Mary, the Magnificat, emphasizes this theme (Luke 1:46–55), and all the leading characters in the nativity stories were lowly people. The first ones to hear the announcement of the fulfilment of the ancient promises with the birth of Jesus were some shepherds in the Judean hills (Luke

2:8–20), then Simeon and Anna in the temple (Luke 2:25–38). None of these people were of any significance to the world at large. The stories in the first chapters of Luke's Gospel emphasize that officialdom – whether political or religious – had no eyes with which to recognize Jesus. This lesson is repeated throughout the story of Jesus' life, as it becomes clear that to have a real understanding of God's actions in Christ even the most important people must become like little children (Luke 18:17).

When was Jesus born?

Deciding exactly when the birth of Jesus took place is not as simple a matter as it seems. The obvious thing to suppose is that Jesus was born between 1BC and AD1. But this has been known to be untrue for a long time, because of mistakes made as long ago as the sixth century in calculating the extent of the Christian era. In determining the likely date of Jesus' birth, there are four main pieces of evidence to be considered:

● According to Matthew 2:1, Jesus was born 'in Bethlehem of Judea in the reign of Herod the king', that is, before the death of Herod the Great in 4BC.

● Luke was much more interested in placing his story in the wider context of affairs in the Roman empire, and he says that Jesus was born during 'the first enrolment, when Quirinius was governor of Syria' (2:2). Josephus mentions an imperial representative called Quirinius being sent to Syria and Judea to take a census just after the beginning of the Christian era (Jewish Antiquities 18.1). This census, however, took place as part of the clearing-up operation after Herod the Great's son Archelaus had been deposed, which means it must have been in the year AD6 or 7 and could not therefore have been before the death of Herod the Great in 4BC. Because of this, it has been suggested that the person Luke calls 'Quirinius' might have been Saturninus, the imperial legate in Syria, who might have conducted a census in 6BC. However, there is no evidence that might explain how Luke could have confused the two, and in

the rest of his gospel, and also in his second volume, the book of Acts, he generally displays great care, and accuracy, in his use of the names and titles of Roman officials.

● At the same time, Luke's narrative does include other statements about the date of various important events in the life of Jesus. He records, for example, that Jesus was about thirty years old when he was baptized, and that this was 'in the fifteenth year of the reign of Tiberius Caesar' (3:1). Tiberius became ruler of the Roman empire in AD14, which would make the fifteenth year of his reign AD28. This calculation is complicated, however, by the fact that Tiberius had shared power with his predecessor Augustus from about AD11, which means that though he became emperor after Augustus died in AD14, for all practical purposes he had been the emperor for the previous three years as well. If, as is likely, Luke was reckoning the fifteenth year of Tiberius from AD11, that means Jesus would be thirty years old in AD25–26, which in turn would place his birth in either 5 or 4BC, and so before the death of Herod the Great.

● From time to time, some have tried to introduce a more scientific element into this debate, beginning with the bright star mentioned in Matthew 2:2 and calculating that there was a conjunction of certain planets about 6BC which might have been the same thing. Though such considerations cannot be entirely ruled out as admissible evidence, this kind of

A bronze head of Augustus (63BC – AD14) (Octavian), Roman emperor at the time of Jesus' birth.

Jesus grows up

Very little is known about Jesus' life as a child. His home was presumably the typical flat-roofed, one-roomed house of the time, built of clay. Joseph probably carried on his business from home, and various statements in the gospels imply that Jesus learned the same trade. Together they would make agricultural tools, furniture, and probably also worked on larger building projects. At the time when Jesus was

When was Jesus born?
continued

approach would require a lot of imagination to be convincing.

There are then two pieces of evidence (one from Matthew, the other from Luke) indicating a date for Jesus' birth around 4BC, with a third piece of information also provided by Luke concerning the census under Quirinius which seems not to agree with this dating. Three possible explanations have been advanced in the effort to solve this problem:

Luke has been misunderstood
Several scholars propose that the apparent 'problem' as it has been outlined here simply does not exist . They point out that, from a grammatical point of view, it is perfectly possible to translate Luke 2:2 to read, 'This enrolment was before that made when Quirinius was governor of Syria', in place of the conventional translation, 'This was the first enrolment, when Quirinius

was governor of Syria'. Linguistically, this understanding is certainly plausible, though it would hardly be the most obvious meaning of the statement, and it does involve an implicit assumption that the text has somehow been corrupted in the process of transmission. Still, though this explanation of the matter is by no means universally held, some notable New Testament scholars have supported it, and continue to do so.

Luke made a mistake
Many more scholars take the simpler way out of the difficulty by concluding that Luke was mistaken in the information he provides regarding Quirinius. This is perhaps the most obvious explanation to adopt, though it also leaves some unanswered questions. Notable among these is the way that elsewhere in his writings where Luke refers to people and events in the Roman empire, he shows himself to have checked his sources very carefully. He needed to, for one of his purposes in writing was to commend the Christian faith to upper-class Hellenistic citizens, and in that context it would be especially important for his facts to be correct in relation to the life of the empire. We may therefore assume that Luke believed this information to be correct. Moreover, he presumably thought it was compatible with the other indication about dates that he gives

Jesus' birthplace: the town of Bethlehem, 9 km south of Jerusalem.

growing up, the ancient city of Sepphoris was being redesigned and rebuilt only a short distance from Nazareth, and this project must have created a huge demand for the skills of people involved in the construction industry. The city was completed shortly before Jesus began his public ministry of teaching, and it is tempting to imagine that both he and some of his band of disciples might have been thrown out of regular work at that time as the massive project was completed. It could also be that Joseph died about this time. He certainly seems to

---

when reporting the date of Jesus' baptism by John, which presupposes that Jesus was born in the reign of Herod the Great, and therefore something like ten years before the rule of the Quirinius whom Josephus mentions. These considerations do not of course prove that Luke got it right, only that he thought he had checked his sources carefully and did not believe he was giving out contradictory messages.

Luke does not tell the whole story
A different way of dealing with this matter begins not from the bare facts as reported in literary texts, but with a sociological understanding of how things could be made to happen in the furthest extremities of the Roman empire. Ruling Judea from Rome in AD7 was not the same thing as it would be today, with instant communication from one part of the world to another. In ancient Rome things were very different. Even in ideal conditions, it could take months for a decree signed by the emperor in Rome to be delivered to a distant province like Judea, and there was always a good chance that it might be delayed or even lost in the process. Messengers could be robbed or shipwrecked, or just disappear on the journey. At a later period, for example, the Emperor Caligula sent orders that his own statue should be erected in the temple at Jerusalem. The local governor was wiser than the emperor, and realized that this would create great resistance from the Jews, so he wrote and asked the emperor to think again. Caligula insisted on his plan going ahead, and wrote back to the governor to tell him so. The ship carrying

his message took three months to make the voyage from Rome to Judea. In the meantime, however, Caligula was assassinated and another ship that left Rome much later bearing the news of his death and the end of his policies, arrived twenty-seven days earlier than the first one!

When we take account of such simple practical problems of communication and government, it is obvious that conducting a census would not be a simple matter. In addition, Roman enrolments were carried out for tax purposes, and for that very reason were regularly resisted throughout the empire. One such census in Gaul, for example, was so unpopular among the people that it took forty years to complete! When all these considerations are taken into account, it is virtually certain that a census completed by Quirinius in AD6 or 7 must have taken a long time to carry through, and would be based on information collected much earlier than the date when it was finished.

The emperor Augustus was very keen on gathering statistics, and he might well have persuaded Herod the Great to carry out a census. Quirinius was sent in AD6 to clear up the mess left by Archelaus, and it is quite possible that he would use information gathered earlier rather than beginning the same tedious process all over again. If this was indeed the case, then there is no convincing reason to suppose that Luke's information about the census is contradictory to the rest of the evidence that he and other writers supply, all of which suggests that Jesus was born about 5BC.

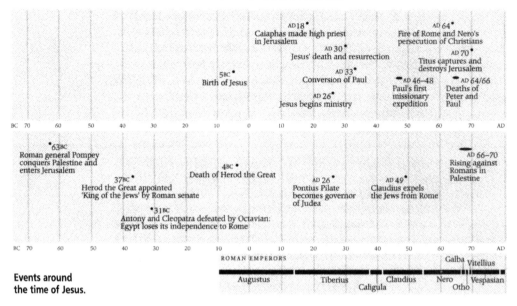

Events around the time of Jesus.

have disappeared from the scene during Jesus' early life, as he does not feature in the later stories of Jesus as an adult. Whenever Jesus' family are mentioned, it is only ever Mary and his brothers and sisters (Matthew 12:46; Mark 3:31; Luke 8:19). At his death, Jesus as the elder son of the family asked one of his senior disciples to take care of his mother Mary – another indication that Joseph was already dead (John 19:26–27).

Nazareth

Jesus obviously grew up in a simple home environment. But he also had the opportunity to gain some education. He was considered a suitable person to read the Old Testament in Hebrew in the synagogue at Nazareth, something that not everyone could do (Luke 4:16–20). There were organized schools in Palestine at this period, but most boys (never girls) would receive their education at the local synagogue. In addition, Nazareth itself must have been the kind of place where everyday life provided its own liberal education. It was not an important place, and is never mentioned in the rest of the Bible, or in any other contemporary literature. At one time, it was believed that Nazareth did not exist at the time of Jesus, but that is now known to be untrue, and various remains of water storage cisterns and other artifacts can be positively dated to this period. But it was never a large place, and even at its most expansive had a population of only about 200 people.

Its size alone would ensure that it was never mentioned in most official records, but in addition it was in Galilee – an area that was always despised by the strictest religious people, who felt that the inhabitants of Galilee were too relaxed in their dealings with explicitly non-Jewish culture. The reconstruction of Sepphoris as a Hellenistic city was not inconsistent in a place that was often called 'Galilee of the Gentiles', because it had more non-Jewish than Jewish residents. It was a great contrast to the southern province of Judea, whose people could more easily isolate their lifestyle from external influences – something that Jesus later criticized them for, claiming that they had too easily become introverted and self-centred, if not self-righteous and hypocritical. But Galilee was criss-crossed by major trading routes between east and west that ensured it would never be isolated from the wider life of the empire. Here Jesus would meet and mix with many people who were not Jewish, and he no doubt spent much of his time thinking and talking about the ideas of the Greeks and Romans as well as the religious heritage of his own people.

One of the special advantages of growing up in Galilee was that Jesus would probably be fluent in three languages. By now Hebrew was no longer the normal language of the Jewish people, and only continued in use because it was the language of the ancient scriptures. For several centuries, Aramaic had been the everyday language, and Jesus would use this at home and among his friends. This had originally been promoted by the Persian empire in the fifth and sixth centuries BC as its own international language, and had many similarities to Hebrew, which ensured its ready adoption throughout Palestine. However, since there were so many non-Jewish people in Galilee, Jesus must have spoken Greek as well, for this was the international language of commerce and government used everywhere throughout the whole of the Roman empire.

Jesus and his family

Apart from what we can infer from our knowledge of the kind of society in which Jesus was brought up, the New Testament tells us very little about his life before he was thirty years old. He was not the only child in his family. Mark 6:3 records how he returned to Nazareth as an adult teacher, and people found it hard to accept his message because they knew him only as 'the carpenter, the son of Mary, and the brother of James, Joseph, Judas, and Simon' – all of whom were still living in the village, along with some unnamed sisters. We know little about these brothers and sisters, though they were apparently believers in the very earliest days of the church (Acts 1:14), and James eventually became leader of the church in Jerusalem, though he was not a disciple during Jesus' lifetime. Mary herself is portrayed as constantly torn between discipleship and doubt, as she struggled to balance the needs of the various members of her family circle. But she was very firmly on Jesus' side, and features in the book of Acts as one of the leaders of the infant church (Acts 1:14).

Religiously, Jesus' family were obviously very committed to their ancestral faith. The one story about Jesus' childhood that the gospels do contain relates how on a pilgrimage to Jerusalem Jesus became separated from his parents, and when they eventually found him he was in the temple, discussing points of belief with the religious experts there (Luke 2:41–52). It is not easy to be more precise about the religious affiliations of Jesus' family, but some of them might have been Pharisees. James was certainly a conservative person later in life, even as a Christian, and according to one of his biographers he spent so much time in traditional Jewish prayers that his knees were like camel's knees! As a leader of the Jerusalem church he was able to stay in the city long after other Christians – including moderate Jewish believers like Peter – had been forced to leave. All these facts imply that he must have been quite traditional. Certainly, if some of Jesus' own relatives were Pharisees that could explain why he so often singled them out for special criticism, no doubt based on his first-hand experience of the way their theology had been applied in his own family circle.

Modern Nazareth: nothing now remains of the village that was Jesus' home.

The fact that the New Testament contains so little about Jesus' early life prompted later Christian writers to produce their own accounts of his childhood. From the second century and later, several such stories survive, with exotic titles like *The Gospel of the Nativity of Mary*, *The History of Joseph the Carpenter*, and *The Childhood Gospel of Thomas* (not to be confused with *The Gospel of Thomas*, which is a different kind of document altogether). Most of the stories contained in these 'gospels' are concerned with proving that Jesus had miraculous powers even as a child – powers, they claim, that he used to bring embarrassment both to his family and to the religious establishment. There is no reason to suppose that any of these accounts were based on authentic traditions about Jesus as a child: they were compiled in later generations by committed Christian believers who wanted on the one hand to satisfy natural curiosity about Jesus' origins, and also to enhance his reputation as a wonder-worker (something that, ironically, the New Testament gospels explicitly warn against).

John the Baptist

The next we hear of Jesus is when he was about thirty years old. His cousin, John the Baptist, had started a religious movement and had attracted quite a following. John lived a simple kind of life in the Judean desert, wearing clothes made of camel's hair and eating only the food of the desert, 'locusts and wild honey' (Mark 1:6).

John was by no means the only wandering prophet at that time. Many people were talking about the expected Messiah who would come to inaugurate some kind of new society. Further south in the same desert the people of Qumran were talking about similar things, and even later many rabble-rousers and prophets were able to attract people into the Judean desert in the hope of making a name for themselves and perhaps beginning a resistance movement that would banish the Romans from their land. One of John's most distinctive traits was that he quite specifically did not want to make a name for himself. He did not see himself as a messianic deliverer appointed by God to get rid of the political and social injustices of the time, but as 'a messenger', 'a voice' sent to bring the good news that the Messiah was about to come, and the nature of God's kingdom would soon be made plain (Mark 1:2–3).

Those who were familiar with the Hebrew scriptures knew that such a messenger would be like the Old Testament prophet Elijah (Malachi 4:5), and the gospel writers leave us in no doubt that they saw John the Baptist as this very person. Their descriptions of his way of life and of his message are closely modelled on the stories of Elijah in 1 Kings 17 – 19.

The New Testament and the Jewish historian Josephus both describe John's work as a call to the people to put their lives in order so that they would be morally fit to meet the person who was to establish God's new way of being (Josephus, *Antiquities of the Jews* 18.5.2). Earlier prophets had often condemned the people for their disobedience to the moral and spiritual standards God required of them, and declared that though they were still God's people, they could expect only judgment for their failure to live up to these expectations. Indeed, their judgment would be all the more severe because of the spiritual privilege they had enjoyed. John's message was exactly the same. He called on the people to be prepared to change their way of life, so they would be ready to meet God. Those who were willing to face up to the challenge showed their desire to change by being baptized. The Greek word from which this term is derived means 'to dip', and it was often used, for example, of the dyeing of clothes as they were immersed in a bath or tub. Baptism in the religious sense was just the same, except that it was people who were immersed, and they were dipped not in dye but in water. John's baptisms took place in the River Jordan.

Most Jews would have been familiar with baptism. It might have been used as a means of admitting Gentiles as proselytes or God-fearers into Judaism. It was certainly used in this way later. There is also ample evidence from the Dead Sea Scrolls that the Essenes used regularly repeated baptisms as a way of preserving their moral and religious purity. One of the most conspicuous features of the ruins of the monastery at Qumran is the incredibly complicated system of aqueducts and water tanks that was needed to provide sufficiently large quantities of water in the desert for the members of the community to undergo their baptismal rites. There were some differences, of course, and the rituals of people like the Essenes were not quite the same as the baptism of converts to Judaism. Unlike the ceremonial baptisms and washings that could be repeated over and over again at Qumran, proselyte baptism could only happen once, as it was not a rite of purification but of initiation, signalling the point at which a convert became a part of the faith community.

It is difficult to decide whether the background of John's ritual is to be found in repeated washings like those of the Essenes, or in the once-only baptism of Gentile converts. But the radical nature of John's message and the opposition he provoked would certainly be easier to understand if he was calling people who were already members of the covenant community to take part in something they would have regarded as appropriate only for those who were previously unbelievers. In John's view, however, some far-reaching changes of heart would be needed before his people could have any part in the new society that was about to dawn. They too would need to begin all over again, just as if they were Gentile people getting to know God for the first time.

Yet John did not see the full implications of what he was announcing. He saw the coming of the Messiah in conventional terms of judgment and condemnation, and described God's promised deliverer as a person who would chop down fruit trees that gave no fruit and burn the chaff away from the wheat (Luke 3:7–17). Admittedly, he appears to have seen with more clarity of spiritual vision than other religious people of his day, who took it for granted that the objects of God's anger would be the Romans. But he did not fully appreciate the true character of the 'kingdom of God', which in the teaching of Jesus turned out to be based less on damnation and judgment than on more generous qualities such as love, forgiveness and an unprejudiced concern for all kinds of people. This had always been the one thing that the ancient nation of Israel had found most difficult to understand, and it continued to cause problems even for Jesus' disciples, who could never quite grasp what it might mean for God's will to be done through self-denying service to others and suffering on their behalf (Mark 8:31–33). Though John announced the coming of the kingdom of God, the precise nature of what that might involve only became clear after the death and resurrection of Jesus.

Jesus is baptized

When Jesus came to John and asked to be baptized, John at first did not want to allow him to share in this symbol of repentance. After all, if Jesus really did have the special relationship with God which John believed he did, what could he possibly have to repent of? But Jesus assured John that he must take part in it, telling him: 'in this way we shall do all that God requires' (Matthew 3:15).

What did Jesus mean by saying this? The simple explanation is that Jesus felt he must identify himself with those who were ready to make sweeping changes in their lifestyles, and who would become his own first disciples. Far from separating him from other people, the gospels suggest that Jesus' special relationship with God was a powerful reason for becoming completely involved in the lives of the most ordinary folk. There are undoubtedly other undertones in these words, however, for in the context of the entire story of Jesus' life they link together the beginning and end of the story, implying that Jesus' baptism was in a sense the first step on the road to the cross, which was the climax and goal of his whole life. This is a theme that becomes more explicit when his death is later referred to as a 'baptism' in which God's will was more truly carried out than it had been in the days of John (Mark 10:38).

The gospels show Jesus' baptism by John as the start of an unfolding revelation of the exact nature of Jesus' relationship to God. According to Mark, on this occasion Jesus heard the words: 'You are my own dear Son. I am pleased with you' (Mark 1:11). This is a combination of statements found in two passages in the Hebrew Bible. First is an echo of Psalm 2:7: 'You are my son, today I have become your father.' In its original context, this statement referred to the kings of ancient Judah, who were regarded as reigning as the personal representatives of God, but by the time of Jesus it was widely understood as a prediction of the coming Messiah. In addition, however, there is a clear allusion to the poem of the suffering servant in Isaiah 42:1, where the servant is described as 'the one I have chosen, with whom I am pleased'. This concept of 'the servant of God' seems not to have been connected with the expectation of a Messiah before the time of Jesus.

The River Jordan. It was in this region that John the Baptist carried out his ministry.

The baptism stories, therefore, lay out two key themes that inform the rest of the story of Jesus. In them, Jesus is reassured of his own special relationship with God as the person who would inaugurate God's kingdom; and he was also reminded that to be this promised deliverer meant something very different from what most people expected. It was to include the acceptance of suffering and service as an essential part of his life, which would be a hard thing to work out in practical terms. But as he faced the challenge, the gospel writers remind their readers that Jesus was supported by God's personal presence, depicted at the baptism as the Holy Spirit symbolically coming to him in the form of a descending dove.

Jesus decides his priorities

The first three gospels tell how, immediately after he was baptized, Jesus was challenged to get his priorities right as God's promised deliverer, the Messiah. Mark mentions the temptations of Jesus only briefly, but Matthew and Luke both give more detailed accounts. They all place this period of self-appraisal at the very start of Jesus' public work, as a programmatic statement of his basic aims and objectives. But the issues raised in this story were continually cropping up in his ministry, for each of the temptations was an invitation to minister in a way that would bypass the suffering and humble service that Jesus ultimately knew to be God's way of doing things.

The first temptation was to bring about the messianic age by economic means, making stones into bread (Luke 4:1–4). There were certainly plenty of hungry people in the world who would have welcomed bread from any source. Indeed, Jesus himself was in the desert, and must have been hungry enough at the time. In addition, the ancient scriptures had often pictured the coming new age as a time of great material prosperity when the hungry would be fed and everyone's needs would be satisfied (Isaiah 25:6–8; 40:9–10; Ezekiel 39:17–20). Moreover, later stories show Jesus feeding the hungry on different occasions, so he was certainly not indifferent to the needs of starving people. There were therefore plenty of good reasons why Jesus should think it appropriate to be concerned with such matters. But he knew that the fame and popularity of an economic miracle-worker were not the same as suffering and service, and to establish a reputation on this basis alone would have been to deny the very essence of what God was calling him to do and be.

The Judean desert: traditional location for Jesus' temptations.

A word of God to the people of Israel at a crucial moment in their past history helped him to overcome the temptation: 'People cannot live by bread alone, but by every word that comes from the mouth of God' (Deuteronomy 8:3).

A similar temptation presented itself with the suggestion that he should throw himself down from one of the towers of the temple into the crowded courtyard below. Had he survived, that would certainly have been a dramatic demonstration to the whole nation that he was indeed endued with special powers. The miraculous and unusual had a special kind of appeal to the people whom Jesus knew best. Paul, who knew Judaism better than most, said it was characteristic of his people to 'demand signs' (1 Corinthians 1:22), though the same has been true of people in most cultures for most of history – including our own.

For Jesus, though, there was a more subtle underlying message here as well, for there was at least one ancient prophecy which seemed to suggest that the Messiah would suddenly appear in the temple in this kind of dramatic way (Malachi 3:1). This, together with a further promise that God would protect those who were ready to put their faith to the test (Psalm 91:9–16), presented a powerful argument for trying such a stunt. If Jesus was really God's Messiah, then should he not confirm his calling by trying out these promises to see if God really was on his side? Jesus was not afraid of the miraculous and the supernatural: there are many examples of that in the rest of his life. But he rejected the temptation to base his message purely on such sensationalism, again quoting the ancient scriptures to back up his judgment: 'You shall not put the Lord your God to the test' (Deuteronomy 6:16). The context of

Psalm 91 had made it clear that such promises of safety and security would be valid only for those who were prepared to live in obedient service to God's will – and for Jesus that was to mean service and suffering, not the arbitrary use of God's promises for his own ends.

The third temptation was to be a political Messiah. Luke places this one second, but Matthew puts it last, perhaps to emphasize its importance (Matthew 4:8–10). There is no doubt that this must have been the strongest of all temptations, for it was precisely what most people at the time were hoping that the Messiah would be. They also commonly believed that they would rule all the other nations in the new age that was coming, which no doubt explains the terms in which this temptation is presented to Jesus, to accept the authority of Satan in order to gain power over the world. The idea was made even more vivid by a vision of the splendour of the world's kingdoms. But Jesus realized again that this was far different from the kind of new society that he was to inaugurate. It was not that Jesus was unsympathetic to the deeply felt desire of his people for freedom: he had himself lived under the tyranny of Rome and had worked with his own hands to produce enough to pay Roman taxes. He was not unaware of the miserable condition of his people.

But he rejected political messiahship for two reasons. Firstly, he rejected the terms on which the devil offered it to him. According to the gospel narratives the devil offered to share sovereignty with Jesus. If Jesus accepted that the devil had authority over the universe as a whole, then he would be given limited political authority in exchange. That was something Jesus could not accept. His own commitment, and the commitment that he later demanded of his followers, was exclusively to God. To acknowledge the devil's power in any area of life would have been to deny God's ultimate authority. In addition, Jesus was offered the possibility of ruling by the 'authority' and 'glory' of an empire like that of the Romans. He knew that the nature of God's kingdom was to be quite different from the kind of authority to be found in an empire like that of the Romans. God's values and standards could never be imposed from outside, but would be nourished most effectively as people were set free to make their own choices not only about their relationship to God but also about how they could best create the new kind of social structures that would most closely reflect God's way of doing things.

It was not too difficult to reject this third temptation, and Jesus did so decisively. He would not try to impose a new authoritarianism on the world to replace the authoritarianism of Rome and the other empires that had preceded it. The 'kingdom of God' would not be the rule of tyranny and cruelty that some religious fanatics were hoping for, but something that would spring from the new, inner nature of those who were a part of it, as they discovered God in new ways and found themselves empowered to be the kind of people who would carry forward this new vision of a world transformed through the power of love and caring service.

The stories of Jesus' birth

The stories of how Jesus was born are certainly not the easiest parts of the gospels to understand. We have already seen that even the date of Jesus' birth presents a number of problems. But that difficulty is overshadowed by much larger questions about the whole nature of the stories, raised in a particularly pointed way by the repeated assertion in both Matthew and Luke that Mary was a virgin when Jesus was conceived (Matthew 1:18; Luke 1:26–27).

To be a virgin and pregnant is a contradiction in terms – so how are these stories to be understood? We can be sure that the gospel writers knew this well enough, which means that a key question surrounding the interpretation of their narratives relates to their genre or literary form. What kind of stories did the gospel writers think they were presenting here? The kind of literature a writer is creating has significant consequences for the way it is presented. In historical narrative, events are generally presented in a way that readers can imagine having happened, for while the details might be unique and distinctive, history writing depicts things that are similar to those we might expect to experience for ourselves. In poetry, however, things might be said that, as they are stated, are clearly untrue to historical fact. For example, when the English poet William Blake wrote his famous work *Jerusalem*, he described in graphic and realistic detail the miseries of the Industrial Revolution, and then imagined Jesus of Nazareth walking among it all. His readers got the point of his message, and appreciated it so much that his poem later became a classic definition of the self-understanding of the English – even though no one imagines for a moment that, in Blake's words, 'the Son of God' really did place his feet on 'England's green and pleasant land'. Similar examples could be found in the mythologies with which other nations around the world celebrate their distinctive identity.

So where would the gospel writers have placed their stories about the circumstances of Jesus' birth? Unfortunately, they never tell us, which is why their accounts have engendered so much debate and discussion. Inevitably, the debate focuses on the virginal conception of Jesus, if only because such a thing is so foreign to human experience. The very notion challenges our basic understandings about what is possible in this world, and highlights in a particularly stark way the role that our own presuppositions inevitably play in the interpretation of the New Testament texts. Those who begin by assuming that anything contrary to our own experience of life cannot exist will inevitably need to question, if not reject, the possibility that these birth stories are reporting anything that has a basis in historical fact. They will also have problems with other aspects of the gospels, notably the stories of Jesus' healings, and of course his resurrection from the dead. Following the arguments of scholars like the eighteenth-century philosopher David Hume, who claimed that there could be no such thing as the miraculous, generations of scholars have sought other ways to comprehend the apparently supernatural dimensions of the New Testament stories. In reaching such conclusions, they were inevitably working within the scientific paradigms of their day, which tended to be based on a mechanistic understanding of the cosmos, in which everything needed to be understood in a strict relationship of cause and effect. That was long before Einstein's articulation of the principle of relativity, not to mention the development of chaos theory, the uncertainty principle and other insights which have all made it plausible to imagine that unique events can, and do, happen randomly without any obvious rational explanation.

In today's more open atmosphere of New Age science and spirituality, the notion of the universe as a closed system has been abandoned, and people are more tolerant of the possibility of events that simply defy logical understanding. Indeed, whereas a century ago serious thinkers would have found it hard to believe anything beyond our own experience, there is an increasing trend in contemporary culture towards believing absolutely anything of an esoteric or unusual nature.

Neither of these approaches is particularly helpful, and a more appropriate way to tackle such questions is to keep an open mind about what is possible, while rigorously checking the alleged evidence in seeking to determine what might actually have happened in any given case. In this particular example, this means that the question of Jesus' conception should be addressed by asking: Does the evidence of the gospels make good sense? This involves examining the evidence on its own merits, scrutinizing its claims and possibilities, and being prepared to listen to its nuances, rather than prejudging its value on the basis of predetermined suppositions, whatever form they might take. Objectivity is notoriously difficult to pin down, but by weighing all the possibilities in this way, and recognizing our own starting points (while being prepared to go beyond them if necessary), we can at least hope to go some way towards a comprehensive appreciation of even the most perplexing issues.

As it happens, the stories of Jesus' virgin conception provide a particularly good example of the kind of concerns that are raised at many points in the New Testament gospels. Even a cursory examination of all the New Testament evidence as it relates to this story will demonstrate that it is not as simple a matter as we might imagine it to be. There are several aspects to be considered here:

● One of the most surprising things is that, apart from those references in the birth stories recorded by Matthew and Luke, there is no explicit statement in the whole of the rest of the New Testament regarding the circumstances of Jesus' conception and birth. There is no mention of it in the accounts of the teaching of the first disciples in the book of Acts. Paul never mentions it, nor is it found in the gospels of Mark and John (though neither of those gospels mentions Jesus' birth at all). It therefore seems certain that it was possible for the earliest Christians to have a complete understanding of the Christian faith without any mention of the virgin birth, and maybe without any knowledge of it. Later Christians have often argued that the virginal conception of Jesus was necessary in order for him to have been both divine and human, but the New Testament writers certainly believed all that without ever basing their arguments on the particular way that Jesus was either conceived or born.

This might appear to be a very strong argument for doubting that the stories in Matthew and Luke were intended to be understood factually. But in fact it is a double-edged argument. Since the idea of a virgin birth was not essential for a complete understanding of the precise nature of Jesus' person, why would Matthew and Luke want to invent it? Neither of them make any theological claims on the basis of their birth narratives: they simply present them as statements about the way Jesus was born.

● In certain passages of the gospels, Jesus is referred to as 'the son of Joseph' (Luke 4:22; John 1:45; 6:42), and the lists in both Matthew (1:2–16) and Luke (3:23–38) trace his ancestry through Joseph. It is therefore sometimes suggested that even within the gospels themselves there is no consistency, and Matthew and Luke have inserted these stories without noticing their incompatibility with other parts of their own narratives. For how could Joseph be Jesus' father if Mary was a virgin when Jesus was conceived? It is worth noting this, but it is not to be regarded as relevant to the issue of Jesus' conception. When Joseph married Mary he would be, in the eyes of both public opinion and of the Jewish law, the legal father of Jesus. Besides, there is no word for step-father in either Hebrew or Greek, and so the gospel writers were probably just recording the

The stories of Jesus'
birth *continued*

common description of Jesus as 'son of
Joseph'. Luke certainly thought this was
what he was doing (3:23).

● The notion of Jesus' conception by a
virgin has sometimes been traced back to
Greek or oriental stories about the gods
having intercourse with human women
and producing children. This notion is not
taken so seriously today as it would have
been two or three generations ago, not
least because the stories of the gospels
obviously move in a very different literary
atmosphere from the stories told of the
Greek gods. In addition, Luke's birth stories
as a whole have a distinctive style when
compared with the rest of his writings.
Though some scholars believe this to be a
deliberate device used by Luke in imitation
of the style of the Septuagint, others have
argued that Luke's Greek is of a sufficiently
consistent character to suggest that he is
here quoting or depending on an Aramaic
source. If that is true, it would imply that
he was incorporating traditional stories of
Jesus' birth that came to him from the very
earliest group of Christians in Palestine
itself, who were the only Christians ever
to speak Aramaic.

● Matthew's account raises a different
set of questions. In support of his story
he quotes from the Old Testament: 'All
this took place to fulfil what the Lord had
spoken by the prophet: "Behold, a virgin
shall conceive and bear a son, and his
name shall be called Emmanuel"'
(1:22–23). A significant fact to note in
this connection is that this passage from
Isaiah 7:14 has a different meaning in the
Septuagint (from which Matthew quotes)
than it had in the original Hebrew text.
Whereas the Greek version quite
specifically uses the term for 'virgin', the
Hebrew text calls the mother of Emmanuel
a 'young woman'. In the past, it has been
suggested that the whole idea of Jesus'
conception by a virgin arose out of this
apparent mistranslation of a passage from
Isaiah in the Septuagint. Three things need
to be noted in this connection:

In the first place this argument can
apply only to Matthew since Luke does not

quote this passage in his birth narratives.
So, even supposing this argument is
correct, it can only account for Matthew's
account, and not Luke's.

Then it is undoubtedly true that
Matthew's sole reason for accepting and
using the Greek version instead of the
Hebrew text was that it was appropriate to
his purpose in a way that the Hebrew was
not. But this is a common feature of
Matthew's Gospel, and he often selects
Old Testament texts and says they have
been fulfilled in Jesus' life and ministry
in a way that to modern readers seems
irrelevant and trivial. This was almost
certainly because he was writing mainly
for Jewish readers: since the Hebrew
scriptures were especially authoritative for
them, it was particularly important for
Matthew to use them to show how Jesus
was indeed the Messiah promised in their
pages. This is nothing like so important for
the other gospel writers, whose readers
were mainly Gentiles, with neither
knowledge of nor interest in the Old
Testament.

Thirdly, it is quite likely that it was not
the actual author of Matthew's Gospel
who selected this particular version of the
text from Isaiah. There is considerable
evidence to suggest that at a very early
stage of its existence the church began to
gather together Old Testament texts which
seemed to them to predict or forecast
some aspect of Jesus' life. These are the
collections of texts often called *testimonia*,
and there were probably several different
collections in existence not long after
Jesus' death. Again, these texts would
have a special appeal to Christians from a
Jewish background, but since the concept
of a virgin birth was quite unacceptable in
any form to orthodox Jews it seems
unlikely that they would have gone
searching for alleged scriptural references
to such a thing unless they had other
reasons for supposing it to be an
appropriate way to describe Jesus'
conception and birth.

In trying to reach a conclusion about
the nature of the birth stories in Matthew

and Luke, it is important to set them in the context of these gospels as a whole. It is hard to avoid the conclusion that Matthew and Luke treated them in the same way as the other traditions which were handed down to them, and which they incorporated in their own accounts. In terms of their genre, then, there is no reason to suppose they were in any way different from other narratives about Jesus, which probably places them in the context of Hellenistic popular biography. Indeed, some of their most distinctive literary and stylistic characteristics can be understood by placing these particular stories alongside traditional Jewish infancy narratives, such as those attached to Old Testament heroes like Moses, Samuel, and others. Luke's story in particular seems to be almost modelled after the stories of Samuel's conception and birth (1 Samuel 1 – 2), and Mary's song of praise, the Magnificat (Luke 1:46–55) not only parallels Hannah's song of thanksgiving following the birth of her son (1 Samuel 2:1–10), but is full of allusions to many other Old Testament passages. Matthew's story is also structured around many Old Testament texts, though in a completely different way, with subtle allusions and references to passages that Matthew saw as having been fulfilled in Jesus. In framing their accounts like this, Matthew and Luke were following in a long tradition of Jewish exposition of the ancient scriptures, known as Midrash – something that came in many different forms, but which was always loosely focused around an interpretative paraphrase of the scriptures. This is probably the most fruitful place to find literary models for what Matthew and Luke were doing, though not forgetting that the scope for wholly fictional elaboration of the stories must have been limited by the fact that they were both writing not more than a couple of generations after the events they purport to describe, at a time when (even in the 80s and 90s) there were still some who would remember how Jesus' birth had been reported from the very beginning.

John the Baptist and Qumran

In view of the similarities between the work of John the Baptist and some of the most distinctive activities of the Qumran community, it was inevitable that scholars would speculate about some possible connection between them. Two similarities between them are most obviously apparent.

In the Judean desert
Luke depicts John the Baptist living in the desert until he began his public work (1:80; 3:2). Since his baptizing took place in the River Jordan, it is natural to assume that the desert in question was the Judean desert surrounding the Dead Sea, into which the River Jordan flows, which in turn means he was probably living in the same desert as the Qumran people, and at about the same time. Since their monastery must have been one of the few places where it was possible to live in such an inhospitable region, it is suggested that John might well have known them, even that he might have been a member of their community.

It is certainly not difficult to believe that John would know of the existence of the monastery at Qumran, but some have gone much further by suggesting that he was a member of the group, and might even have been brought up by them from an early age. This argument is based on the statement in Luke 1:80 that as a child John 'grew and developed in body and spirit. He lived in the desert until the day when he appeared publicly to the people of Israel.' This statement can be put together with a piece of information given about the Essenes by Josephus, who comments that they often adopted other people's children in order to indoctrinate them with the ideas of their sect (*Jewish Wars* 2.8.2). This notion has many attractions, but in the end it creates more problems than it solves:
● The Greek words used in Luke 1:80 and 3:2 do not necessarily imply that John was actually brought up as a child in the

desert. It is certainly the case that he was in the desert reflecting on the nature of his life's work immediately before he began baptizing, but the most natural way to read the story about his birth is that he was brought up at home by his parents.

● It is also doubtful whether his parents would have allowed a group like the people of Qumran to adopt their child. Not only were they longing to have this son, but John's father Zechariah was a priest. One of the distinctive beliefs of the Qumran sect was that the Jerusalem priests were corrupt, and it is difficult to think that John's parents would have given their child to a group who were so hostile to all that they themselves stood for. It might make sense to imagine that John was kidnapped by the sect in order to rescue him from his family, but there is absolutely no evidence for that, either in the New Testament or anywhere else.

● The Judean desert was a big place, and by no means everyone who lived there would need to have been associated with Qumran. The shores around the Dead Sea are full of caves that would make ideal lodgings for hermits, as they did for the Zealots who continued to resist Rome after the destruction of Jerusalem in AD70. Even Josephus records an episode in which he once joined a hermit called Bannus who was living a solitary life in the desert (*Life of Josephus* 2). The appeal of this kind of life has always been strong to people of a particular disposition, and there must have been plenty of individuals living like this in the desert surrounding the Dead Sea.

Reconstructed pottery jar from Qumran. The scrolls and manuscripts were originally stored in pots like this to hide them from the Roman armies in the period following the fall of Jerusalem.

Baptism

If it is difficult to make any direct connection between John and the Essenes through their style of life, it is certainly no easier to do it through their religious rituals. John and the Qumran people both made use of water in their religious rites, but they had little in common beyond that. There were in fact several striking

differences between John's concept of baptism and the ritual washings that were practised at Qumran:

● The recipients of baptism were different. John baptized people who wanted to change their way of life, while the community at Qumran accepted only those who could prove that they had already changed their way of life. An initiate often had to wait for a year or two before being allowed to take part in the ritual washings at Qumran, whereas John was prepared to baptize immediately anyone who was willing to declare their intention to change.

● The character of the two rituals was also different. A person baptized by John was baptized only once, and the rite could not be repeated. By contrast, the ritual washings at Qumran were repeated over and over again. Indeed, 'baptism' in the sense that word is usually understood is not really an appropriate word to describe what went on at Qumran. Essene 'baptisms' were a means of effecting a ritual purification in the lives of those who were members, rather than being a rite of admission to the sect.

● The overall significance of the rituals was different. John's baptisms were carried out as part of the preparations for the arrival of the expected Messiah. But the Qumran washings were not connected with the expectation of a Messiah, or indeed of anyone else. They were more a means of expressing in symbol the moral and spiritual purity which the community hoped to preserve among its members.

If John the Baptist ever had been a member of the Qumran community, he had certainly changed his outlook quite radically by the time he began his public work. But arguments in favour of such a connection are not very strong, and it makes better sense to think of both John and the people of Qumran as offering different forms of response to the growing political, moral, and spiritual crisis that was facing their nation at the start of the first century.

16 Who was Jesus?

After he had met John and been baptized, most of Jesus' life was spent as a religious teacher. It was quite normal for Jewish religious teachers to adopt an itinerant lifestyle, wandering about from place to place, often accompanied by their disciples. Jesus plainly fitted into this pattern. He had his disciples, and the term 'Rabbi' or 'Teacher' was regularly applied to him (John 1:38; 3:2; 9:2). Like other religious teachers he carried out much of his work in the synagogue, the place where Jews met for worship each sabbath day (Mark 1:21; Luke 4:16; 6:6). He also spoke with people wherever he met them (Mark 1:16–20). He called his first disciples from their fishing boats, and regularly taught out in the open countryside where large crowds could gather round him.

It was Jesus' teaching that really caught the imagination of the people. As they listened to him they sensed that this was no ordinary rabbi, not least because he was not just someone else's disciple passing on what he had heard from others. He was saying totally new things about people and their relationship with God, and doing so in an especially provocative way that almost forced his hearers into making a decision about him. All the gospels document the rapid emergence of somewhat polarized opinions about him. On the one hand many ordinary people declared that 'he taught them as one who had authority' (Matthew 7:29), while many religious experts dismissed him as an impostor and a cheat.

The teaching that caused such a sharp division among his hearers focused especially on two subjects. On the one hand the gospels depict Jesus making many bold claims about his own person and significance, and while he never actually claimed in so many words to be the Messiah of ancient prophecy, that is the clear implication of the way the narratives present him. Alongside the various claims about his own destiny and importance, there are also numerous statements about the exact nature and meaning of the 'kingdom of God' whose arrival Jesus announced. The kingdom is a sufficiently significant subject to require a whole chapter to itself. But first we will consider the claims that Jesus apparently made about himself, not least because his teaching about the kingdom is shot through with the assumption, either stated or implied, that he himself was to play a central role in its coming.

The Son of man

It was not long after the death of Jesus that his followers everywhere were openly claiming that he was the long-awaited Messiah of traditional Jewish expectation, and by the time groups of his followers were established in Gentile communities around the Roman world the Greek term 'Christ' – the equivalent of the Hebrew 'Messiah' – was widely used almost as a second name for Jesus. It is therefore surprising how infrequently that terminology is used in the gospels themselves. Mark's Gospel was probably the first one to be written, and the word for 'Messiah' or 'Christ' is used only seven times there. One of them is in the title of the gospel (1:1), and of the other six only three could be taken as a reference to Jesus being the Messiah or Christ (8:29; 9:41; 14:61–62). In only one of these (14:61–62) is Jesus shown making a direct personal claim to be the Messiah, and it is striking that even in that instance Mark shows Jesus immediately going on to identify the Messiah with someone he calls 'the Son of man'.

The meaning of 'Son of man'

The exact meaning of the term 'Son of man' has been one of the most hotly disputed subjects in recent study of the New Testament, and what can be said here is only the barest summary of what some of the experts are saying.

One point on which all scholars are agreed is that the most helpful question to ask is: What would come into the minds of those people who actually knew Jesus when they heard him use the term 'Son of man'? Since his first hearers were Jews, it is natural to look to the Jewish religious tradition for an answer. In the Hebrew Bible, the expression 'Son of man' is typically used in two ways. More often than not, it simply means human beings as distinct from God. In this context, it usually emphasizes the weakness and poverty of ordinary mortals in contrast to God's might and power (Numbers 23:19; Job 25:6; Psalm 8:4; 146:3; Isaiah 51:12). Prophets could on occasion be addressed by God as 'son of man', and this was a means of emphasizing the difference between them and the ultimate source of their message (Ezekiel 2:1; Daniel 8:17).

But the term is also used in a quite different way in Daniel 7:13–14. In this passage, far from indicating the weakness of men and women as opposed to the greatness of God, 'one like a son of man... came to the Ancient of Days and was presented before him. And to him was given dominion and glory and kingdom, that all peoples, nations and languages should serve him.' Moreover, 'his dominion is an everlasting dominion, which shall not pass away, and his kingdom one that shall not be destroyed'. The book of Daniel was an apocalyptic work, which no doubt explains the somewhat exaggerated nature of some of its imagery. But the same character also seems to feature in other apocalyptic writings that might have been current at the time of Jesus. In *The Similitudes of Enoch*, 'the Son of man' again appears as a supernatural figure sent from God as the future judge of humanity (1 Enoch 37–71), while the reference to an individual more cryptically described as 'the Man' in 2 Esdras 13 might also be intended to carry the same connotation. It is not easy to trace more direct connections between the gospels and these usages of the term. There is no certainty that either of these books was actually written by the time of Jesus, and they are only known through

So who was the Son of man? The actual term is used fourteen times in Mark's Gospel; in the longer account of Matthew it occurs no less than thirty-one times. This term is used more often than any other to describe Jesus and his work, and in addition it is only used in sayings actually ascribed to Jesus himself: there is only one clear example of others using it of Jesus (John 12:34, where his listeners are requesting clarification of his own use of it). Moreover, it is only found once outside the gospels (Acts 7:56). The unambiguous testimony of the entire New Testament therefore is that this is a term that Jesus used for himself, and one that was never widely used of him either by his contemporaries or later generations of his followers. So what did it mean?

One commonsense view would be that when Jesus spoke of himself as 'Son of man' he was simply wanting to emphasize that one part of his nature was ordinary and human, while another side of his character could be described in grander terms by epithets such as 'Son of God'. Even if something of that kind might on occasions be included, the term has to mean more than this, however, because the Son of man can be

---

relatively late texts that might in any case have been subject to later emendation and corruption. It is certainly not possible to use them with any confidence to show, for example, that the term 'Son of man' could have been a widely recognized title of any sort in the time of Jesus.

In addition to these uncertainties, it has also been claimed that in Aramaic the phrase 'son of man' would either convey nothing sensible at all, or would at best be some kind of generic way of referring to people in general (like the English term 'humankind'), rather than a specific way of describing a particular individual. This particular consideration is complicated by the fact that, though Jesus must undoubtedly have used an Aramaic term, the gospels were all written in Greek and, though they do occasionally preserve the actual Aramaic words used by Jesus, they do not do so in this case, though scholars generally assume that the Aramaic phrase would have been *barnasha*.

Three factors then need to be considered in trying to decide what the significance of this term 'Son of man' was meant to be when used by Jesus:

● The actual Aramaic words 'son of man' might well have had no specific meaning, but were possibly just a circuitous way of saying something like 'human being'.

● In the Old Testament, the term 'son of man' had been used to describe human beings and their difference from God.

● In the book of Daniel and other Jewish apocalypses, the 'son of man' was a transcendent, heavenly figure who shared in God's own power.

It is not necessary to choose between these possible backgrounds to the way Jesus used the term: probably all of them are relevant. If the term 'Son of man' had no very clearly definable meaning in the Aramaic that Jesus spoke, then it could easily have been used for that very reason: with no ready-made significance, Jesus would have been free to make it mean exactly what he wanted it to mean. If the term 'Messiah' had featured in his teaching, it would have been far more difficult for him to explain precisely what he understood his role to be, since people had so many preconceived ideas of what the Messiah was supposed to do and say. Though it can hardly have clarified things, the ambiguous term 'Son of man' at least offered the potential for avoiding that particular problem.

described as 'coming in clouds with great power and glory' (Mark 13:26), or 'seated at the right hand of the power of God' (Luke 22:69). Statements like that can hardly have been intended to emphasize Jesus' human character over against his claims to have some special significance in the plans of God!

The Messiah

It is unnecessary to spend long examining Jesus' claims to be the Messiah, for it was not a title Jesus used for himself. In Mark, the first gospel to be written, there is only one instance where he might have been doing so (9:41), though there are four very significant occasions when other people called Jesus 'the Messiah', and he apparently accepted the title:

■ When Peter finally began to articulate his embryonic beliefs about who Jesus might be, and told him 'You are the Christ', Jesus replied that he was 'blessed' to have received such a special insight (Matthew 16:16–17).

The meaning of 'Son of man' continued

At the same time, for those with the perception to see it, the background of the term in the Jewish scriptures and other religious writings did provide some clues to the things Jesus wanted to say about himself. For it seems that he did want to claim both that he was an ordinary human being, and that in some way not clearly defined he was specially sent from God – and these are both concepts that could be found in the traditional use of the 'Son of man'.

In the first three gospels (Matthew, Mark and Luke) Jesus is shown using the name 'Son of man' in four distinct ways:

● There are some instances where the term 'Son of man' appears as the equivalent of the personal pronoun 'I', simply as a means of describing Jesus' ordinary human existence. Certainly that is how the gospel writers understood some passages, for in places where different gospels have the same sayings, one gospel can use 'Son of man' where another writer uses the pronoun 'I'. Examples can be found by comparing Mark 10:45 and Luke 22:27; or Mark 8:27 and Matthew 16:13; or Matthew 19:28 and Luke 22:30.

● In other places, 'Son of man' is used to emphasize Jesus' claim to have special

authority to speak in the name of God – as, for example, when he claims to forgive sins (Mark 2:10) or assumes the right to set aside the traditional sabbath commandments (Mark 2:28).

● At other times, Jesus uses the title 'Son of man' with reference to a future coming on the clouds of heaven and to his exaltation at God's side where he then plays a key role in a future judgment. This is the same use as in Daniel 7, and features particularly in Matthew (for example, 10:23; 13:41; 19:28; 24:27, 37), though it is also found in Mark (8:38; 13:26; 14:62) and Luke (17:30; 18:8; 21:36; 22:69).

● Most often, however, the term is used with some reference to the suffering and death that was to be part of Jesus' experience. In nine out of the fourteen uses in Mark, 'Son of man' is used to refer to Jesus' coming death. This characteristic use might appear to be all but incompatible with the previous reference to triumph and glory. But, in fact, the precedent in Daniel 7 had identified the 'one like a son of man' as a representative of 'the saints of the Most High', who in the context were clearly undergoing great suffering and persecution. Some passages (for example, Mark 9:12;

■ Another occasion was during his trial before the Jewish authorities, when Jesus acknowledged to the high priest that he was the Messiah (Mark 14:61–62).

■ There is also the story of how Jesus healed someone who was thought to be possessed by demons. Not only did he allow this man to address him as 'Son of the Most High God'; he also told him, 'Go home to your friends, and tell them how much the Lord has done for you' (Mark 5:1–20).

■ On another occasion Jesus was going along a road near Jericho when a blind beggar called Bartimaeus shouted out and addressed him as 'Son of David'. Though others who were standing around evidently told the man to be silent, Jesus did not do so, and therefore by implication seems to have accepted this title for himself (Mark 10:46–52).

From these four instances it is clear that the gospels do not consistently show Jesus expressing the same attitude towards the claim that he was the Messiah, 'the Son of David', on every occasion. By the time he appeared before the high priest it was obvious that he was to be

10:45) use 'Son of man' language alongside allusions to suffering persons in the Old Testament (for example, Psalms 22; 69; 118:22; Isaiah 52:13 – 53:12), thereby combining different traditional images to show Jesus as the one foretold in the ancient promises, who would achieve glory and vindication through suffering and service.

The phrase 'Son of man' also occurs in John's Gospel, with some of the same connotations as in the others, though here there is additional emphasis on the Son of man as one who came from heaven to earth and will return thence (3:13; 8:28), as well as a connection between his suffering and the celebration of the Christian eucharist (6:53). It is also used to refer to Jesus being 'lifted up', a term that is used in John to refer to suffering (in the crucifixion, 3:14; 8:28; 12:34) as well as to glory and exaltation (12:23; 13:31).

The Last Judgment, woodcut by Albrecht Dürer (1471–1528).

condemned anyway, and so he apparently had no qualms about claiming to be the Messiah (though even on that occasion he at once went on to redefine the concept of 'the Messiah' in terms of the more nebulous 'Son of man'). But when Peter confessed that he was the Messiah, Jesus told him and the other disciples to keep it secret and not to tell anyone else about it. On the other two occasions he apparently accepted a messianic title from other people without making any further comment – and in the case of the man possessed with demons he told him to share his experience with his friends and relatives. Jesus' attitude to letting people believe he was the Messiah apparently varied according to the circumstances, and was partly dependent on the question of whether or not this claim should be publicized. How is such apparent inconsistency to be understood? Two possible explanations have dominated discussion of this issue:

JESUS NEVER CLAIMED TO BE THE MESSIAH

One way to solve the problem is to say that Jesus never in fact claimed to be the Messiah at all, and that Mark and the other gospel writers have written their stories of Jesus' life and teaching with an eye more to what they believed about Jesus than to what he might have claimed for himself. In the light of all they had learned from Jesus, and especially after his death and resurrection, it seemed only natural to conclude that he was indeed the Messiah who had fulfilled the prophecies contained in the Old Testament. When they came to write their gospels, they knew that Jesus himself had been ambivalent about claiming to be the Messiah, but by then it was more important for the church's mission that it should be made perfectly clear just exactly who Jesus really was. So Mark (the writer of the earliest gospel, and who was followed by Matthew and Luke) bridged the gap between his own beliefs and the reality of Jesus' more cautious self-perception by creating the literary motif of a 'messianic secret'. This phrase was first coined by W. Wrede to explain why it is that whenever Jesus is depicted talking to his disciples about his position as Messiah he always tells them to keep it a secret.

The difficulty with this notion is that although it fits in with some of the evidence, there are other pieces of information which do not fit. There are, for example, the incidents involving the demon-possessed man at Gerasa and Bartimaeus at Jericho. Then there is also the undeniable fact that, while different people no doubt understood it in different ways, Jesus was actually condemned to death because he claimed to be 'king of the Jews', that is, their Messiah. It is difficult to see how Mark could have left these stories in his narrative in this form if he had been so intent on making the idea of the 'messianic secret' convincing.

JESUS BELIEVED HE WAS, BUT NEVER CLAIMED TO BE THE MESSIAH

We seem to be left with the implication that Jesus thought he was the Messiah, but that he did not explicitly claim he was. This idea itself raises some awkward questions, though three facts are particularly relevant to any consideration of such a possibility:

■ It needs to be remembered that, while the preservation of the story of Jesus' life and teaching for posterity was undoubtedly one reason why the gospels were written, it was not the only one. Indeed, a more important purpose was to provide a resource for Christians at the time (mid to late first century) that would facilitate their own spiritual nurture as well as their mission in calling others to join them. Like today's readers, those who first received the gospels had a broader perspective than those who were with Jesus during his lifetime. Their starting point was their own experience of faith, their reception of the Holy Spirit, and behind that their knowledge of the end of the story in Jesus' death and resurrection. They had no difficulty in recognizing that Jesus must be the Messiah, sent by God to inaugurate that new way of being which he called 'the kingdom of God', for they knew their own lives had been so changed by following him that they believed themselves to be already living according to the new standards and values which Jesus had announced. The more time that passed, the more certain they were of this fact, which perhaps explains why the word 'Christ' is used so many times in John's Gospel, whereas it is hardly ever used in the other three, for it is generally thought that John was writing later than the others, by which time Jesus' messiahship was so self-evident that he could simply be called 'Christ' (Messiah) without the need for further definition or qualification.

■ Another relevant consideration is that the gospels themselves make it clear that Jesus and his contemporaries were at cross-purposes when they spoke of the Messiah. To most people, the Messiah was to be a political king, something that Jesus constantly sought to deny and redefine; for him being the Messiah meant humble service and obedience to God's will. Arguably therefore for Jesus to have spoken openly of being the Messiah, far from being a clarification of his message, would actually have concealed the real significance of what he was trying to say. It would certainly have brought about an early encounter with the Romans. Even the disciples, including Peter who declared his belief that Jesus was the Messiah, seem not to have fully understood all the ramifications of that until much later. Despite their close relationship with Jesus, they displayed their ignorance of his intentions on more than one occasion (Mark 8:14–21; 9:30–32; 10:35–45). There can be no doubt that this is an accurate picture of their faith, or lack of it, for by the time the gospels were written these same disciples were the church's heroes, and no one would have made up stories that gratuitously portrayed them in a bad light.

■ It makes overall sense to conclude that Jesus' attitude did in fact vary, and that his whole life and work was a mixture of revelation and secrecy. This comes out in the way he liked to call himself 'the Son of man', which had no ready-made meaning. To those who were not prepared to think very deeply about it, it was a name that could only confuse, and conceal Jesus' claims rather than reveal them. At the same time, many incidents in Jesus' life – including the miracles, but also occasions such as his baptism (Mark 1:9–11), his temptations (Luke 4:1–13) and his entry into Jerusalem (Mark 11:1–11) – would lose their meaning if Jesus was not claiming to be the Messiah.

Many of the things he did and said were exactly the things that the Messiah was expected to do and say when he came.

The most satisfying overall conclusion seems to be that Jesus did not use the word 'Messiah' of himself because of the way it would have suggested to his hearers an earthly king and a new political state. Jesus certainly had no intention of being that kind of 'Messiah', as Matthew and Luke highlight by showing that possibility being so decisively rejected right at the start of his ministry in the temptations. So he cast his whole ministry in a mould that would conceal his claim to be Messiah from those who did not want to understand it in the same way as he did, but that would provide enough clues to his identity as Messiah for those who were prepared to think about it more deeply.

The Son of God

The belief of the Christian church from the very earliest times has always included the statement that Jesus was 'the Son of God'. This too was an expression that would be familiar to the people of Jesus' day. In Hellenistic culture, it was often used to refer to some heroic human figure, and this is probably the way it was used by the Roman centurion at the cross who said of Jesus, 'Truly this was the son of God' (Matthew 27:54). That is certainly how Luke understood it, for in his account he has the centurion say, 'Certainly this man was innocent' (Luke 23:47).

Like the terms 'Son of man' and 'Messiah', the term 'Son of God' had also been used in the Hebrew scriptures. It could be applied to the nation of Israel (Exodus 4:22; Jeremiah 31:9; Hosea 11:1), to leading individuals within the nation (for example, Deuteronomy 14:1; Isaiah 1:2; Jeremiah 3:22), to angels and other heavenly beings (Genesis 6:2–4; Job 1:6–12; Psalm 29:1), and to the king (2 Samuel 7:14; Psalm 2:7). Partly as a result of the way this title was applied to the kings, especially those descended from David, it came to be applied to the Messiah as well (2 Esdras 7:28, and in the Qumran texts at 1QSa 2:11–12; 4QFlor 1:10–13; 4QPsDan A). Within the Jewish context, this phraseology did not indicate a divine figure descending from heaven as the bearer of salvation, except insofar as angels were thought of as messengers from God. The status of 'son of God' was more often understood as a recognition by God of some particular achievement by the individual who received the title.

In the gospels, however, the notion of Jesus' divine sonship is quite explicitly used to indicate that Jesus enjoyed a special relationship with

God. Notwithstanding all the debates about the authenticity of various sections of Jesus' teaching, one thing on which virtually all scholars are agreed is that Jesus consistently used parent-and-child language to refer to his relationship with God. Even at the early age of twelve, Luke depicts him referring to the temple at Jerusalem as 'my Father's house' (2:49), and the story about the wicked tenants of the vineyard makes it clear that he himself was the heir whom the owner had sent to put things in order (Mark 12:1–11).

Jesus clearing the temple – an episode that clearly implied some claim to special authority (Mark 11:15–19; John 2:13–22). Illustration by a 19th-century artist.

The claims implied by such stories are also made explicitly on the lips of Jesus, most strikingly in a statement recorded by both Matthew and Luke: 'All things have been delivered to me by my Father; and no one knows the Son except the Father, and no one knows the Father except the Son...' (Matthew 11:27; Luke 10:22). It is clear that Jesus was understood to be claiming a unique relationship with God, with very little room for misunderstanding.

So what did it mean for Jesus to be spoken of in this way? This is, of course, one of the great questions that theologians have thought and talked about for centuries, and it is only possible here to give a very sketchy response to it.

■ In any discussion of the nature of God, it should never be forgotten that to describe Jesus as 'the Son of God' is to invoke a familiar analogy to describe something that is, by definition, indescribable. When Jesus took the human relationship of child to parent, and said, 'My relationship with God is a bit like that', this was never intended to be a literal statement about the being of God. Talk of God as 'father' is not to be understood as a claim that God is male, though generations of Christians have uncritically made that assumption. Nor indeed is even the parent–child image meant to be applied inflexibly. There is no suggestion that every aspect of human family relationships can be matched to relationships with God, not least because many people have unhappy relationships with their parents. The gospels themselves warn against this kind of literal understanding, for though children might on occasion be able to say in a normal family that 'Whoever hates me hates my Father also' (John 15:23), no human could ever say 'I and my Father are one' (John 10:30).

■ Like the other titles reviewed here, this one had also been used in the Old Testament. The term 'son of...' was a common idiom of the Hebrew language. For example, the Israelites could be called 'sons' or 'children' of Israel, though modern translations often disguise the wording (Deuteronomy 1:1; Judges 1:1). Wicked people are regularly referred to as 'sons of wickedness' or 'sons of Belial' (Deuteronomy 13:13), while the Hebrew word equivalent to 'human beings' is 'children of men' (1 Samuel 2:12).

Though we would not now use the exclusively male-oriented language of the Hebrew Bible, if we described ourselves as 'children of our parents' we would be saying that we share precisely the same characteristics and nature as our parents before us. So when the New Testament says that Jesus is 'the Son of God' it is stating that Jesus shared the actual characteristics and nature of God. He was claiming to be really and truly divine; to make a narrow distinction between the nature of 'God' and the nature of 'the Son of God', as has been done by, for example, the Jehovah's Witnesses, is to disregard the way that the analogy is being used here, as well as to ignore the natural idiom of the linguistic context in which the New Testament was compiled.

■ In John 1:1–18 and Revelation 19:13, this relationship between Jesus and God is expressed in another way. There Jesus is called the 'word' or *logos* of God. God's word is, of course, the way that God communicates. But when the New Testament calls Jesus 'the word' it says something more than that. For John says that 'the Word was God' (1:1) – that is, God's message to humankind was not just written in a book, it was displayed in the very person of God. He also says that 'the Word became a human being': God was personally embodied in 'the Word', in Jesus (1:14). Moreover, because of the way the concept of the 'logos' had been used in circles inspired by Greek philosophy to denote the fundamental principle of the universe, it seems likely that some cosmic claim about the significance of Jesus was also being made when such language was used.

Whether Jesus is described as 'the Son of God' or 'the Word of God', the implication is the same: the earliest Christians were all saying that through Jesus it is possible to gain a perfect image of what God is like. That is why it is worthwhile giving careful attention to uncovering the nuances of what Jesus was actually saying and doing, for the New Testament claims that in his life and teaching it is possible to see and hear what God is really like.

The servant

The way Jesus depicts God is challenging and disturbing to conventional views, most of which owe a great deal to images inherited from the Greek philosophers, in which 'God' was portrayed as a being of great splendour, majesty and, above all, power. This final title – 'the servant' – overturns that conception, and it seems to be the image that Jesus most readily applied to himself and his work. It is true that nowhere in the gospels do we find Jesus actually calling himself 'the servant of God', yet it is hard to get away from the impression that Jesus' perception of himself was so very different from current expectations precisely because he understood his mission in terms of the suffering servant of the book of Isaiah (Isaiah 52:13 – 53:12).

The gospels make many references to Jesus' conviction that it was to be his lot to suffer, not least in the distinctive use of the term 'Son of man' in that connection. From the time he was baptized, and perhaps before that, Jesus saw that the course of his life was to be one of suffering. The voice at his baptism, echoing words from one of the passages in Isaiah about the suffering servant (Mark 1:11; Isaiah 42:1), made it clear to him that his life's work was to consist of humble self-denial, and this conviction was vigorously reiterated in his responses to the temptations. According to Mark, Jesus warned his disciples at a very early stage in his ministry that the day was near when he, the bridegroom, would be taken away from his friends (2:20). Immediately after Peter declared his belief that Jesus was the Messiah, Jesus again repeated that 'the Son of man must suffer many things' (Mark 8:31), something reinforced by the further statement that 'the Son of man also came... to give his life as a ransom for many' (Mark 10:45).

Most of the titles applied to Jesus are difficult to understand in detail, largely because they all had varied meanings and implications within their original Jewish context. But all have one very clear implication. There is no doubt that by applying them to Jesus, the gospel writers were wanting to claim that he had a unique relationship with God, and a unique authority. This authority was expressed in his claim to forgive the sins of other people, which the religious teachers of the day correctly recognized as a claim to exercise power that belongs only to God (Mark 2:1–12). But Jesus also demanded from his followers a loyalty and devotion that no ordinary human being could ever have the right to claim. He told would-be followers: 'Whoever does not bear their own cross and come after me, cannot be my disciple' (Luke 14:27). This claim to a unique relationship with God is expressed in John's Gospel in terms of a complete identification between Jesus and God: 'I and the Father are one... whoever has seen me has seen the Father' (10:30; 14:9), and a virtually identical claim is found also in the gospels of Matthew (11:27) and Luke (10:22).

There continues to be a good deal of discussion about the extent to which these elevated claims go back to Jesus himself. There is no question that the full significance of who Jesus was, and how that significance might best be articulated, only emerged as his followers reflected on their own experience of him, in the light of the total picture of his life and ministry that was only possible after his death and resurrection. In the past, scholars have often attempted to distinguish some core tradition consisting of the actual words Jesus might have used from the further reflections on him that emerged as the gospel writers and others worked through the wider consequences of his life and teaching. Such an enterprise is not altogether misguided, and in a later chapter we will need to give some further consideration to this matter. But when all is said and done, the gospels are the only portrayals we have of the life and teaching of Jesus, and it is ultimately a pointless exercise to try to find within them a simple religious teacher who had no awareness of his own possible significance in the divine scheme of things. Who would wish to crucify such a harmless person? It is a waste of time trying to separate the supposedly human figure, the 'Jesus of history', from the Christ and risen Lord who was soon regarded as equal with God in early Christian theology. Jesus is depicted making grand claims for himself in the very earliest records about him, and it is not possible to find in the New Testament a Jesus who did not make supernatural claims for himself, without in the process so discrediting the overall reliability of the texts that it would scarcely be worth reading them for any purpose at all. If Jesus' followers later made new claims about his importance, these were all firmly grounded in his own teaching about himself and his understanding of his place in the plans of God.

17 Understanding Jesus' Death

Why did Jesus die? Of all the questions that might be asked about Jesus, perhaps no other can be answered in so many different ways. To a certain extent, the answer given will depend on the way the question is approached. We can see this quite clearly, even in books written as long ago as the first century AD.

Josephus, for example, says very little about Jesus, but he does say that 'he was the Messiah; and when Pilate heard him accused by the most highly respected men amongst us, he condemned him to be crucified' (*Jewish Antiquities* 18.3.3). He was obviously convinced that Jesus died as a result of political intrigue and collaboration between Pilate, the Roman prefect of Judea, and the religious establishment in Jerusalem. This is also clearly stated in the stories of Jesus' death in the gospels. But if we look at some other parts of the New Testament and ask the same question, 'Why did Jesus die?', we find a somewhat different emphasis in some of the answers. According to the book of Acts, Peter said on the day of Pentecost that though Jesus was 'crucified and killed by the hands of lawless men', he was also 'delivered up according to the definite plan and foreknowledge of God' (Acts 2:23). Paul expressed a similar understanding when he explained his most deeply held convictions to the Christians in the Greek city of Corinth by saying that 'Christ died for our sins in accordance with the scriptures' (1 Corinthians 15:3).

The New Testament itself then answers the question, 'Why did Jesus die?' in two different ways. One answer is based on the historical facts that led to Jesus' crucifixion, while the other is based on the claims Jesus made about himself, and on the beliefs of the early church about his significance in God's plan for humanity. Jesus' death can be understood as a simple matter of history, but at the same time the very nature of his death, executed in the company of criminals, raises its own questions when placed alongside the claims made for him. For how could someone who was God's own representative have come to meet his end in such a way? Surely if Jesus was in some way divine, it would be a contradiction in terms for him to die at all, let alone on a cross.

Opposition and conflict

All the gospels are unanimous in showing that, from the very start, Jesus' actions and words created divisions among those who met him. John explains this in a theological way by saying that when Jesus came, God's light had come into the world, and this fact itself demanded that people make some kind of decision about him, to be with Jesus on God's side, or against him (John 3:16–21). Elsewhere in the gospel traditions, Jesus himself makes the same strident demands: 'No one can serve two masters; for a slave will either hate the one and love the other, or be devoted to the one and despise the other. You cannot serve God and wealth' (Matthew 6:24). There are many stories about Jesus which show how he enjoyed great popularity as a teacher and healer, but was also opposed by the religious and civil authorities of the day.

The Jewish and Roman calendars.

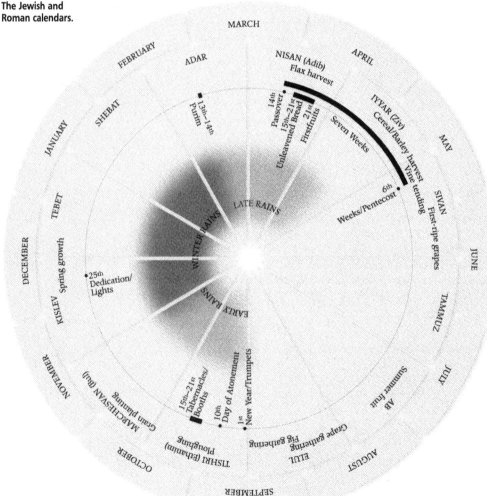

The Roman rulers of Palestine were always suspicious of anyone who became too popular, just as people today are often suspicious of politicians who appear to be too successful. According to Josephus, Herod Antipas got rid of John the Baptist because he was afraid of political revolts, and it must have been difficult for the authorities not to think of Jesus in the same way. After all, he attracted very large numbers of people, and on at least one occasion a crowd of 5,000 wanted him to become their king and lead a revolt against the Romans (John 6:15).

The gospels show Jesus resisting such political power time and again. But they also show that he had no such qualms about getting on the wrong side of the religious authorities. Right from the very start, the crowds declared that his teaching was different from that of their own religious experts, and Jesus evidently accepted this. What is more, he had no hesitation in condemning the Pharisees and Sadducees outright, describing them as 'blind leaders of the blind', who had perverted and denied the word of God (Matthew 23:16–24). Though they appeared to be very religious and holy, he said that deep down inside they were as rotten and worthless as a grave full of old bones (Matthew 23:27).

What is more, Jesus' criticism of these people appears to have been a deliberately planned policy. Though Jesus is portrayed spending a short time in more remote areas teaching his disciples, all the gospels suggest that there was a specific moment at which he decided the time had come to confront the authorities in Jerusalem itself. Different explanations have been given of this step:

■ The oldest view is that Jesus realized the time for his death had come, and so he set himself to go to Jerusalem to fulfil God's will. This is clearly implied in what Jesus said to his disciples according to Luke's account: 'Behold, we are going up to Jerusalem, and everything that is written of the Son of man by the prophets will be accomplished' (Luke 18:31).

■ It was at one time fashionable to think that Jesus made a deliberate gamble that did not pay off. According to this view, which was popularized by Albert Schweitzer (1875–1965), Jesus expected God to intervene in history in a dramatic and more or less immediate way, and his visit to Jerusalem was an attempt to force God's hand. When God did not act, Jesus found himself unexpectedly dying on the cross.

■ Others have suggested that Jesus went to Jerusalem simply because he had been to most other parts of Palestine and he wanted to continue his teaching in the religious capital of the nation. The fact that he became involved with the political authorities there was just an unexpected and unfortunate miscarriage of justice.

We will return to the views of Schweitzer in a later chapter. The other two explanations of Jesus' visit to Jerusalem probably both have some truth in them. No doubt Jesus did want to share his teaching with the people of Judea as well as those in other parts of Palestine – though according to John's Gospel, he might well have done so on more than one occasion before his final visit there. But if we allow for the possibility that Jesus was in any way at all conscious of some kind of special relationship with God, it is inevitable that he cannot have been totally ignorant of the growing opposition he was arousing among the religious leaders of his people. A visit to Jerusalem was bound to bring him into direct confrontation with them.

If there had previously been any doubt as to who Jesus was claiming to be, his entry into the city of Jerusalem made it plain, for the manner of his arrival brought to a focus several underlying messianic themes in his lifestyle and teaching. In effect, Jesus entered Jerusalem in a way that amounted to an open declaration that he was the Messiah. He came on an ass, in accordance with a prophecy in Zechariah 9:9, and the crowd acclaimed him as their king entering his capital city. Immediately after this he went to the temple, the place from where the Messiah was popularly expected to begin the task of expelling Gentiles from Jerusalem (Mark 11:10; John 12:12–19). Jesus hardly fulfilled that particular expectation, for instead of putting the Gentiles out he made a symbolic attempt to restore to them the only court of the temple in which they were allowed to worship, and in the process banished the Jewish bankers who had turned it into a place of business (Mark 11:15–17).

Jesus obviously knew what he was doing, and he can hardly have been surprised to discover that the religious leaders soon put a price on his head. He does not even appear to have been surprised when one of his own followers, Judas Iscariot, picked up the money offered by the high priests (Mark 14:43–52), and he found himself betrayed, arrested, and put on trial for his life.

Jesus on trial

The gospels appear to report two different trials of Jesus. One was before the religious authorities, when of course he was charged with a religious offence. The other was before the Roman prefect Pontius Pilate, where he was naturally charged with a political offence. It is widely believed that the religious authorities had no power to carry out a death sentence themselves, which was why they needed the support of the Romans, though there are different opinions about this, and also about the precise relationship of the different trials to one another. It certainly makes good sense to suppose that Jesus' enemies would make much of the charge of blasphemy before a religious court, and then change to a charge of political revolt as the one most likely to secure some action by the civil authorities.

John's Gospel shows the trial beginning in the house of Annas, father-in-law of Caiaphas, the high priest (18:12–14). Annas had no official position, but as a former high priest and a leading Sadducee he was obviously someone of great influence. Perhaps this trial was an informal investigation held to formulate proper charges. The supreme religious court of seventy members, the Sanhedrin, could not officially meet until daylight, but as soon as it was morning the members were summoned to Caiaphas' house (Mark 14:53 – 15:1; John 18:15–27).

After Jesus had refused to answer questions about his teaching, and the witnesses had failed to agree in their evidence, Caiaphas asked Jesus a direct question under oath: 'Are you the Christ, the Son of the Blessed?' To this Jesus not only replied 'I am', but added, 'and you will see the Son of man sitting at the right hand of Power, and coming with the clouds of heaven' (Mark 14:61–62). This confession apparently convinced the Sanhedrin that Jesus was guilty, though not all of them can have been opposed to what Jesus stood for. Many of them would certainly have welcomed a messianic leader who would strike a blow against the Romans, while Joseph of Arimathea, who subsequently arranged for Jesus' body to be interred in his own tomb, is specifically identified as a member of this Council (Mark 15:42–47). But for others, Jesus had already shown that he was ready to challenge too many of their inherited religious traditions, including not only ritual matters but even central institutions such as the sabbath. By the time Jesus was brought to trial, the ultimate outcome was a foregone conclusion no matter what was said.

The next step was to bring Jesus before Pilate. Here the charge of blasphemy was dropped, for a charge based on religious scruples would never have appealed to a Roman official. It appears that Jesus' accusers first tried to get Pilate to confirm their own sentence without stating a charge at all, but when Pilate then insisted on a charge, three accusations were made:

■ Jesus was perverting the Jewish nation. The religious leaders, of course, thought of this in terms of perverting the nation from their own brand of Judaism. But they no doubt wanted Pilate to think of it in terms of undermining the nation's loyalty to the emperor.

■ Jesus had forbidden the payment of taxes. This was the usual charge made against Zealots.

■ Jesus had claimed the title 'king' – something that only the Roman senate could give.

After Pilate had interviewed Jesus, he realized that, though Jesus might have upset the sensitivities of some religious leaders, he was scarcely guilty of any crime under Roman law. If he had claimed to be a king, he was obviously not the kind who could rob Caesar of his power (Luke 23:13–16). But Pilate also realized that to upset the Jerusalem establishment was a very serious thing. He was caught in a cleverly contrived trap. On the one hand he could acquit Jesus and risk a riot – something which would be looked upon very seriously by his own superiors. On the other hand, he could condemn Jesus, and have to live with a guilty conscience for the rest of his life. It was the fear of riots that eventually forced his hand, as the crowd told him: 'If you let this man go you are no friend of Caesar's' (John 19:12). The last thing Pilate could face would have been bad reports of his conduct going to Rome.

A model of the Fortress Antonia, the place where Jesus appeared before Pilate. It abuts and overlooks the Temple wall.

So Jesus was crucified, and as often happened in such cases, a placard was nailed to the cross to show his offence. In this instance the inscription read: 'Jesus of Nazareth, the King of the Jews'. No doubt that satisfied Jesus' religious opponents, who could understand kingship in terms of a claim to be the Messiah, while the Romans for their part would be satisfied that Jesus was worthy of death as a revolutionary opposed to their own power. None of this would be exceptional or noteworthy. Jesus died in the same way as many other messianic claimants and Zealots. The only difference noted by the gospels is that Jesus' death took a little less time, only six hours, something that facilitated the religious systems that had opposed him so effectively, for the sabbath day was fast approaching and in order to be ritually pure in time it was necessary for his accusers to see his body disposed of as fast as they could.

In purely historical terms there is little more to be said about the crucifixion of Jesus. But for the earliest Christians, the true significance of this event went well beyond the apparently straightforward happenings of that day.

Understanding the death of Jesus

The first generation of Christians, like all Christians ever since, were convinced that Jesus' death on the cross had a meaning that affected not only their own experience, but also had consequences for the whole of the cosmos. Their starting point was the knowledge that their own lives had become meaningful in a new and fresh way because of what Jesus did on the cross. They expressed it in many different ways: some said their sins had been forgiven, others that they had found peace of mind, or that they had been reconciled to God. But all of them were convinced that what had happened to them as a result of Jesus' death was real – as real as the fact that Jesus had died. Indeed, in one way they knew it better. For whereas their knowledge about Jesus' death came from hearing the reports of other people, each one of them had personally experienced this dynamic change in his or her own life.

But how could such a thing be explained in terms that other people would understand, and that would bear some relationship to the reality of what had actually taken place on the cross? The one thing that was clear from the outset was that this was not something that could easily be expressed in logical, analytical terminology. If its meaning could be encapsulated in words at all, they would need to be symbolic and pictorial words, language that would use the familiar and ordinary to describe a reality that was quite extraordinary. The New Testament uses many different figures of speech to describe what Jesus was actually doing when he died on the cross. He was sacrificed (1 Corinthians 5:7); he took the punishment for human sinfulness (1 Corinthians 15:3); he paid the ransom for the human race (1 Timothy 2:6); he justified believers (Galatians 2:16). Each of these statements, and many others, brings out some of the things the early Christians understood about Jesus' death. But in using such statements, two things should never be forgotten:

■ They are all pictures, or analogies. Just as it was important not to press too literally the metaphors and images that were used in talking about Jesus' personal claims, so it is important to bear in mind the essentially illustrative nature of the language used in the New Testament to describe his death. Failure to do that can lead to absurdity, if the details of a particular analogy are used in ways that the early Christians never contemplated.

■ In pictorial terms, the theology of the New Testament can more usefully be compared to a landscape than to a portrait. Just as a landscape is made up of any number of different items, so the New Testament's explanation of Jesus' death consists of many different images. It is possible to consider certain parts of the landscape separately and in greater detail than others, and in some circumstances it might be both necessary and legitimate to do so. But it is always important that the details are not isolated from their overall context as components in the bigger picture. Every one of the metaphors used in the New Testament to describe Jesus' death played an indispensable part in the early church's articulation of its meaning. But no one of them by itself was believed to contain the whole truth. For that it is necessary to consider them all, and place them within the context of the entire experience and theological understanding of the early church.

Five particular images seem to be central to what the New Testament says about Jesus' death on the cross.

Jesus' death as a battle

The gospels show the whole of Jesus' life and ministry as a battle against those forces that might oppose God's will. Sometimes (as in the temptations) these forces can be imagined in dualistic fashion as embodied in the figure of the devil, who represents the opposite force to God. At other times particular individuals can be identified with the forces opposing God, even Jesus' own closest friends (Peter, in Mark 8:33). Jesus' miracles were often described in terms of releasing people from the power of evil, while Jesus appears to have regarded his whole life as an effort to win a victory over the kind of negative influences represented by unjust suffering, sin and death. Paul regarded the cross as God's final and decisive struggle against the powers of evil, believing that in spite of Jesus' apparent defeat, his resurrection actually signalled a complete victory over sin and death (Colossians 2:8–15). The same view is found in the gospels (John 12:31), and the image of the cross as a battle with the forces of evil is one that has regularly appeared in the Christian tradition ever since, not least in its Easter hymns.

To understand Jesus' death only in these terms leaves unanswered a very obvious question. If Jesus triumphed over sin in his cross and resurrection, why is there still so much evil in the world today? One set of images that has been used to explain this was taken from the events of the end of World War II. The decisive moment that settled the outcome of the war came on D-Day, but the final day of victory (V-Day) came some time later. The day of Jesus' crucifixion can be thought of as the D-Day of God's warfare against sin – but the V-Day is still to come, in the future when evil is finally conquered. This is by no means the full answer to the problem of evil, but it is a partial answer to it when Jesus' death is understood in terms of a battle. Of course, viewing Jesus as a military leader is a very one-sided image, not least because he went out of his way to redefine messiahship in completely different terms. Ultimately, Jesus did not see the way to the world's salvation through power and control, but through love and humility. This particular metaphor has often been given more importance than it deserves, as it has had a natural appeal to those generations of Christians who were also empire builders and conquerors. Arguably it has led to some of the worst atrocities ever committed by Christians, from the medieval Crusades against the Muslim world to the colonialism of more recent times.

Jesus' death as an example

Many well-known Christian hymns describe Jesus' death as an example. This stems from the belief that on the cross Jesus revealed God's love for the world. Jesus himself never spoke of the cross as a revelation of God's love, but both Paul and John did (Romans 5:8; 1 John 4:10). They also suggested that as Christians consider Jesus' sufferings, they ought to be challenged to share such sufferings themselves. The writer of 1 Peter used this as a powerful motivation to encourage Christians who were being persecuted for their beliefs: 'to this you have been called, because Christ also suffered for you, leaving you an example, that you should follow in his steps' (1 Peter 2:21).

This is a concept that is easier to understand, for there are many examples of people who have selflessly given their lives for a good cause. Others admire and respect them, and might even be moved to take up the cause themselves. This particular image has been especially inspirational to those who suffer, either for their faith or from the effects of economic and political oppression. Many Christians of the developing world find it speaks to them in a way that the military image of power never can, reminding them that the Jesus who found the most acceptance among the poor and the marginalized also died among the same people, at the hands of the rich and powerful. Again, this metaphor does not exhaust all that the New Testament wants to say about Jesus' death, for he was not simply an innocent man dying at the hands of his oppressors – and if it was in some sense God who was there on the cross, there is a correspondingly limited sense in which people can take up and share that experience.

Jesus' death as a sacrifice

One of the most natural images for people with a Jewish background was the picture of sacrifice. Animals were sacrificed as part of the regular ritual in the temple, as they were more generally in the ancient world. Sacrificial language is used to explain and comment on the death of Jesus throughout the New Testament. When John the Baptist saw Jesus he exclaimed: 'Behold the lamb of God...' (John 1:29). Paul wrote of 'Christ our Passover lamb' (1 Corinthians 5:7), while 1 Peter described Jesus as 'like a lamb without blemish or spot' (1:19), and the book of Hebrews went to extraordinary lengths to compare Jesus' death with the sacrificial rituals of Judaism and to present it as in some way the fulfilment of them all.

This image raises particular questions for today's readers of the New Testament, largely because it is so alien to their experience of either religion or life. Reflecting on two questions might help to explain it:

WHAT WAS 'THE LAMB' TO WHICH JESUS WAS COMPARED?

The New Testament writers generally connect Jesus' death as a sacrifice with the consciousness that their sins had been forgiven, so the most obvious connection of the imagery is likely to be with the various sacrificial procedures of the Old Testament that were designed to procure forgiveness from sin. These sin offerings are documented in Leviticus 5:17–19. There was also, however, the well-known event of the first Passover, at which the people of Israel were delivered from slavery in Egypt, and in which the sacrifice of a lamb played a large part (Exodus 12). In the context of the last supper, Jesus himself seems to have made a deliberate connection between his own death and the annual death of the Passover lambs, reminding his disciples that what he was to do on the cross was to be as great a turning-point in their own lives as the Passover had been in the experience of their forebears (Mark 14:22–25). There is no need to choose between these two somewhat different sacrificial images. When the New Testament describes Jesus' death in terms of a lamb being sacrificed, either or both of them could be in view at different times. The lamb of the sin offering and the lamb of the Passover were each regarded as relevant images for the death of Jesus.

WHAT DID THE ACT OF SACRIFICE MEAN?

Relatively few people today have seen an animal sacrifice, even in those cultures where it is still practised. The majority probably tends to think of it as a rather barbarous ritual from an uncivilized past. But in sacrificial contexts, its real importance is generally located not so much in the physical brutality as in what the action as a whole can be understood to represent or symbolize.

Worship in ancient Israel was based on a strong concept of difference between ordinary people and God. This difference could be understood in both spatial and moral terms. Spatially, 'uncleanness' disqualified people from dealing with the 'holiness' that was equated with religious shrines, so that only certain specially equipped people (usually priests) could touch, or even come into close contact with, the presence of God. Morally, 'sin' – whether deliberate or accidental wrongdoing – similarly disqualified a person from acceptance by God. Both forms of alienation could be dealt with by the offering of appropriate sacrifices. Not all sacrificial procedures were exactly the same, but a typical sacrifice might begin with the worshipper approaching the altar (representing God's presence) with the sacrifice, hand placed on the animal's head. This identified the worshipper with the animal, indicating that what happened physically and outwardly to the animal was understood to be happening to the worshipper inwardly and spiritually.

After that, the animal was killed, usually according to carefully laid-down regulations. In the context of sin offerings, this action itself reflected the seriousness of sin, reminding the sinners that they too deserved to die. The priest would then take the blood of the sacrifice (which now symbolically represented the sinner's life given up to God) to the altar. This act of reconciliation, or 'atonement', indicated that the sin had been dealt with, and God and the sinner had been reconciled to each other. At this point the animal's body could be placed on the altar in the temple, signifying that the forgiven worshippers were offering their whole being to God. Finally, much of the meat would be eaten in a meal shared with others, thereby showing that sacrifice not only reconciled people to God, but also to one another.

This, in general terms, is what the New Testament writers had in mind when they described Jesus' death as a 'sacrifice'. The book of Hebrews in particular goes further, however, and argues that there was some intrinsic connection between the inherited Jewish understanding of sacrifice and the death of Jesus, with Jesus' death being the actual fulfilment of the Old Testament rites. His death was the reality, the sacrifices the picture. Other writers applied the imagery in a looser way, comparing the beneficial effects of the cross (reconciliation to God) with the outcome of animal sacrifices, but without necessarily drawing detailed parallels between them.

Jesus' death as a ransom

One of the few statements about the cross and its meaning in the gospels is found in Mark 10:45, where Jesus himself is reported as saying that his intention was to be 'a ransom'. This figure of speech is much easier to understand, for the idea of kidnappers demanding the payment of a ransom in exchange for the safe release of their victims is well understood. The background to this picture in the New Testament was not, of course, the hijacking of planes or the kidnapping of diplomats, though the general concept was the same. The 'ransom' in this case would be the price paid to set a slave free. In the Roman world, this ransom was often paid by a third party, who would accompany the slave in an act of worship at the shrine of their local god. There the ransom was paid to the slave's owner in a religious ceremony. The legal explanation of what took place was that the slave had been bought by the gods, and so could no longer be owned by another human.

When the emphasis is on the resulting freedom, this is a very appropriate way of describing Jesus' death. The New Testament frequently affirms that a person set free by Jesus is redeemed in order to belong to God. So Peter could speak of Christians as 'ransomed from... futile ways' (1 Peter 1:18), and Paul reminded his readers: 'you are not your own; you were bought with a price, so glorify God in your body' (1 Corinthians 6:19–20). He even linked this image to sacrificial language by exhorting those who were set free 'to present your bodies as a living sacrifice, holy and acceptable to God' (Romans 12:1).

Crucifixion, engraving (1511) by Albrecht Dürer.

However, like all the other images used to illustrate the meaning of Jesus' death, this one is open to misunderstanding, even reduction to absurdity, when it is understood in a literalistic way, for example by asking to whom Jesus paid the ransom. But accepted in the way that the New Testament presents it, it is perhaps the most comprehensive of all the pictures used in the New Testament to describe what Jesus did on the cross: he set free those who were oppressed.

Jesus in the place of others

To say that Jesus died as a sacrifice, or to pay a ransom, is basically to say that he died in the place of other people. On the cross he did something that the human race could not do for itself. This representative nature of Jesus' death is expressed in 1 Peter 2:24, by the statement that Jesus 'bore our sins in his body... that we might die to sin and live to righteousness'. The statement in Mark 10:45 that Jesus came 'to give his life as a ransom for many' also conveys the same idea. It is a powerful image, but once again it is important to clarify what is meant by saying that Jesus suffered in the place of others, if this picture is not to end in absurdity.

It is not difficult to imagine a legal scene like a law court, in which the judge is God the Father, a harsh, authoritarian figure demanding that justice not only be done, but be seen to be done. Instead of the human race as a whole being on trial for the way the values and standards of God's kingdom have been disregarded, Jesus finds himself there. Even though he is guilty of nothing, and certainly not worthy of the death penalty, he is to become the unfortunate victim of God's harsh and unbending demand for justice. From time to time, the imagery has indeed been understood in this way, but if that is the picture then it is very difficult to see how it can be an adequate account of early Christian convictions about the death of Jesus. It implies, for example, that God is actually less just than a human judge, for how many of us would consider justice to be satisfied if an innocent person were punished in place of a guilty one? It suggests that God has a perverted sense of justice and moral responsibility – for how many of us would agree that it is always good for a repenting sinner to escape all the consequences of their wrongdoing? In addition, how can this view be reconciled with the fact that God does seem sometimes to allow people to suffer the consequences of their misdeeds – indeed, that they can on occasion suffer for no apparent reason at all?

What is really wrong with this caricature is its image of God. In the Hellenistic world, it was not difficult to find people who thought of God as a terrible and awesome figure, remote from the everyday concerns of ordinary people, and generally more interested in punishment than in forgiveness. The idea that God is like that has been perpetuated by more recent generations of Christians. The use of exclusively male language to refer to God has often created the impression that God behaves like the worst sort of macho warrior, and this secularization of the biblical image has in turn made it all too easy for the values of Jesus' teaching to be corrupted and replaced by an essentially unchristian world-view. If there is anything distinctive about

This unusual rock formation in Jerusalem has often been compared to 'the place of a skull' (Golgotha, John 19:17). Though it is unlikely that this was the site of the crucifixion, it perhaps gives an idea of the kind of terrain in the area.

the teaching of Jesus, it has to be in the way he redefined God, replacing the harsh confrontational image of judgment and condemnation with the language of family love and acceptance. It might place question-marks against some deeply held inherited beliefs, even among Christians, but there is no escaping the fact that the image of God offered by Jesus is not about domination, power, control, and exploitation, but has at its centre vulnerability, weakness, and affirmation of the human condition. This is the point at which incarnation and cross come together, for when the New Testament speaks of Jesus suffering on behalf of others, those others have already been redefined as members of Jesus' own family. His suffering for the wrongdoing of others was not something imposed by a stern judge to fulfil the demands of some abstract notion of justice, it was suffering in the way that a person might suffer for the wrongdoing of a member of their own family. In that context, the reality of evil is certainly not diminished: indeed its long-term consequences need to be taken much more seriously than might be the case in an exclusively legal context. But when it is addressed in the context of a family, it is always going to be with a view to unconditional acceptance of those who have done wrong, and a progression towards forgiveness and new life in the context of a supportive group.

Each of these ways of talking about Jesus' death has its inadequacies, for they are all only pictures, and even to the writers of the New Testament the cross remained a great mystery. But two aspects of God's relationship with the human race run through all these images:

■ One of the most pressing problems in life is the problem of evil. If God is really loving and forgiving, why is there so much evil in the world? If God is a forgiving God, then surely the universe should be arranged differently so that the stupidity of people will not cause so much suffering? There is no easy answer to such questions. In biblical terms they are part of the frustration of a world that has been so spoiled by sin that Paul could speak of 'the whole creation… groaning in travail' as it waits to be released from its suffering (Romans 8:18–25). The cross shows that, even if the suffering so endemic in human experience is not removed, God shares it with us. If Jesus was divine, as the earliest Christians believed, then in the cross God personally was somehow sharing the final and extreme consequence of human sinfulness.

■ The cross highlights the cost of forgiveness and, therefore, of discipleship. Forgiveness is often costly, especially when it involves relationships within a family. It is often more demanding to forgive a close friend than someone who is otherwise a stranger. Grace does not come cheap. Forgiveness is not an arbitrary thing, and its price is seen in the crucifixion.

Of course, ultimately all these statements are figures of speech, pictures, metaphors, analogies. Some of them seem remote, even irrelevant to the images we would most naturally adopt today. It is natural to ask ourselves why the first Christians found it necessary to reflect on Jesus' death in such complicated terms. Could they not have contented themselves with regarding him as a good man dying a bad death? Was it really necessary to turn a sad story into a theological analysis of the meaning of life? The answer to questions like that is to be found in what they believed to have happened three days after the cross. For they were convinced that Jesus came to life again. If they had not believed that, then the cross would have meant nothing to them. But because of their belief in the resurrection and their experience of the risen Christ at work in their own lives the earliest Christians were totally convinced that Jesus really was who he had claimed to be, and that meant his life must have consequences that went well beyond the few years of his own ministry on the fringes of the Roman empire. But were they right? That is perhaps the most crucial question of all, and one to which we must turn our attention in the next chapter.

Palestinian politics and justice under the Romans

When Herod the Great died in 4BC, both the country and his own family were left in chaos. The semi-independence of Judea was at an end, for though Herod left a will, it was subject to the approval of Augustus, who naturally divided the country up as he pleased. Behind the scenes, Rome had always been the real ruler of Palestine since Pompey's invasion in 63BC, but with Herod's death it asserted its sovereignty more directly. Herod's son Antipas disputed the terms of the will, and along with his brothers Archelaus and Philip was called to Rome to see the emperor. While this consultation was taking place, the whole country was torn apart by revolts, all of which were crushed by Roman troops. Augustus decided that, in the circumstances, it made sense to divide Palestine between the three of them. Archelaus got Samaria, Judea and Idumea, while the rest was split between Philip and Antipas.

This was a compromise arrangement. Had Augustus given the kingdom intact to any of the three, it could easily have provoked all-out war. Yet to introduce direct Roman government would have incensed the Zealots and other nationalists. In the event, Archelaus proved to be so incompetent that even the long-standing rivalry between Jews and Samaritans was laid aside so they could present a united complaint about him to Augustus. As a result, in AD6 Archelaus was recalled to Rome, and sent off into exile in Gaul. Augustus could have appointed one of the other two brothers in his place, but he knew that whoever was not appointed would almost certainly plot the downfall of his brother. In any case, he really trusted neither of them, and so Quirinius, the imperial legate of Syria, was sent to take a census of the taxable property of Judea, as the first stage in its organization as a province within the Roman empire.

Judea became one of the imperial provinces of the empire, and was governed by a procurator of equestrian rank, a man called Coponius. We know very little about how these procurators were allowed to govern their provinces. Indeed, there is some doubt as to whether they should be called 'procurators' at all. Tacitus certainly applied this title to Pontius Pilate, but there is some evidence that 'prefect' was the correct title at the time. In *The Jewish War*, Josephus states that Coponius 'was entrusted by Augustus with full powers and authority to inflict the death penalty' (2.8.1) – which seems to imply that the governor had the equivalent of the *imperium* exercised by the proconsuls in other parts of the empire. There is no ancient definition of what this *imperium* amounted to, but it apparently conferred supreme power in administration, defence, the dispensation of justice, and the maintenance of public order.

The maintenance of order would certainly be a major concern in a province like Judea, with such a volatile population in a strategic position on the edge of the empire. As a judge, the procurator had absolute authority in matters of life and death within his province, and even Roman citizens could appeal to Caesar only in special circumstances. Very few cases would actually come to the procurator. Most minor affairs would be settled in the various local courts, or in the Jerusalem Sanhedrin where traditional religious law was properly understood and dispensed. Only crimes involving capital punishment would be referred to the procurator, since he was the only one with power to prescribe the death sentence. The Sanhedrin was concerned with matters relating to traditional Jewish law, in civil and criminal cases, as well as matters relating to religion. In Judea, it could make arrests, try, and condemn criminals to any punishment apart from death, without any recourse to the procurator – though on occasion this prescription was ignored, and mobs took matters into their own hands by lynching criminals after only a Jewish trial.

The procurator's court was formally run, with charges being presented against the accused by any private parties with an interest in the case. There was no inquisition by the court, and cases were heard by the holder of the *imperium* on his tribunal, generally assisted by his *consilium* of friends and officials, who constituted a panel of reference rather than a jury. All these features can be found in the trial of Jesus.

There was a whole network of local courts to deal with other matters. Judea was divided into eleven toparchies, or districts, and each village within a toparchy had its own council, presided over by a village clerk. They would deal with civil cases and certain less important criminal ones. Since this was the official structure of the land, it is surprising to find no reference to it in the gospels. Neither village clerks nor the commandants who controlled each toparchy feature in them, though the tax collectors who do would be part of the same system of administration. At a time when their independence was suspended, it was natural for Jews to want to use their own ancient procedures, even if it had only a theoretical significance. As a result, the authority of the village congregation, the rulers of the synagogue, was widely respected, even though it had no officially recognized jurisdiction.

Little is known of the way that Philip and Antipas organized things, except that their territories did not fall under the jurisdiction of the procurators. They had the right to mint their own coins, and Philip went as far as to put his own head on them – a thoroughly un-Jewish action. But the area he ruled was well away from the mainstream of Jewish life. Antipas was the local ruler of Galilee, which is why Pilate sent Jesus to him for trial (Luke 23:6–12). Maybe he hoped that there would be some loophole in the law of Galilee that would enable Antipas to take responsibility for a citizen of his own territory. But Jesus had already described this same Antipas as a 'fox' (Luke 13:32), and he was certainly far too crafty to allow himself to be duped in this way. As a result of his clever manoeuvring on this and other issues, he managed to stay in power until AD39, long after Pilate had been removed from office.

Did the Jews condemn Jesus?

Who was it who actually conspired to bring about the death of Jesus? What was the precise relationship between the various Jewish leaders who feature in the gospel stories, and the Roman Pontius Pilate who eventually condemned Jesus? That might sound like the sort of historical conundrum that would interest only a minority of people. But in reality it has been one of the hottest subjects in discussion of Jesus' death for many generations. Down through the centuries, the belief that the Jews were responsible for the crucifixion of Jesus has led to the most horrific persecution of that nation. Even the Nazi holocaust can, in some respects, be traced back to religious roots. Reading many of the books written by leading Bible scholars in pre-war Germany, it is not difficult to see how their apparently abstruse historical and theological theories actually gave encouragement to those who for political and racial reasons already hated the Jewish people. The claim that Judaism was a dead and lifeless religion, designed only to keep people in bondage rather than setting them free to live life to the full, can only have fuelled the fires of anti-Semitism that swept across Europe in the 1930s. And the certainty that Jewish leaders were in the vanguard of the opposition to Jesus merely fanned the flames to even greater intensity.

In point of fact, the New Testament nowhere suggests that either Jews or Romans should carry all the blame, in any absolute sense. At one time, it can seem as if 'the residents of Jerusalem and their leaders' were instrumental in Jesus' death (Acts 13:27), while at another it is attributed to Judas or Pilate, or the devil, or other cosmic forces (1 Corinthians 2:7–8). The fact is that, for the earliest Christians, the precise identity of the players in this drama was not all that important, though it is absolutely clear that the death of Jesus was not an ethnic issue,

Did the Jews
condemn Jesus?
continued

and the arguments about his teaching did not have a racial basis, but were concerned with the kind of religious attitudes that have surfaced frequently in both religious and non-religious societies. The kind of bigotry, narrow-mindedness, and intolerance that Jesus opposed is by no means an exclusively Jewish trait, and never has been. The kind of goodness represented by Jesus makes us all uncomfortable, and many others would have reacted to him in exactly the same way as some of his contemporaries did.

In addition to these general matters, however, there has been a good deal of discussion about historical issues related to the trials of Jesus. In what sense can it be claimed that there ever was a Jewish trial at all, in the sense of a formal legal procedure conducted by a group such as the Sanhedrin? The problem is that there is no contemporary evidence about Jewish customs and practice at this time. Our only knowledge of the subject comes from the Jewish law book, the *Mishnah*, which dates in its present form from about AD200. This contains traditions that are much earlier than the time when it was written down, but it is impossible to know how far these regulations were in force at the time of Jesus.

Judged according to these later standards, a trial such as that which the gospels describe would certainly have been very irregular. The leading members of the Sanhedrin were the prosecution as well as the judges, and they had already been involved in the plot to have Jesus arrested. The trial appears to have begun with no definite charges, and no evidence was called for the defence even though the key prosecution witnesses contradicted each other. Moreover, two very important rules of later Jewish law were ignored completely. These laid down that twenty-four hours had to elapse between a death sentence being passed and carried out; and that a trial should not be held on the day before the Jewish holy day, the sabbath.

Because of these irregularities many Jewish writers – often motivated by their understandable concern to undermine the kind of anti-Semitic propaganda that regarded them as Christ-killers – have insisted that there is no historical truth in the gospel narratives at this point. In terms of the social dynamic of Palestinian society at this time, however, it is hard to find convincing reasons for regarding this trial as fiction. Though the Jews had very little real influence over their political society, their leaders were always keen to apply their own law whenever they could. This was not only a kind of psychological prop to nationalist aspirations: it was also a useful means of gaining the support of the mass of the Jewish people for their policies. A death sentence passed on Jesus under traditional Jewish law by a religious court would certainly have influenced ordinary people against him, and it might even have been expected to exert a certain moral pressure on the Roman judge who was to have the final word.

It is, however, not very likely that this Jewish trial was as illegal as it can be made to appear if compared with the rules of the *Mishnah*. Quite apart from the doubt over whether these procedural rules were in operation at the time, it is especially significant that, of all the charges made by the first Christians against the religious establishment, they never accused them of breaking the law in order to have Jesus executed. In addition, there is no reason to imagine that the members of the Sanhedrin were anything other than people of high moral ideals, some of whom had considerable sympathy with Jesus' message. Perhaps a majority of them met with their minds already made up, and to that extent were unable to give Jesus a fair hearing. But even these people were genuinely convinced that their view of things was right, and that Jesus was nothing but a messianic pretender and a troublemaker.

Pontius Pilate

Pontius Pilate was the fifth Roman prefect of Judea, coming to power in AD26 in succession to Valerius Gratus. He ruled for ten years. Little is known of him before he received this appointment, though legend has it that he was born at Fortingall, a remote spot in the highlands of Scotland which his father allegedly reached while serving with the legions on the northern edge of the empire. As procurator of Judea, Pilate's normal residence would be in Caesarea, and his name has been found there on an inscription, which confirms that he was known by the title of 'prefect'. Pilate was accompanied by his wife (Matthew 27:19), which was a relatively recent innovation introduced by the Roman senate only five years before his appointment.

Pilate's only claim to any sort of fame relates to his involvement in the death of Jesus. The Roman author Tacitus (*Annals* 15.44) only mentions him in this connection, though the Jewish writers Josephus and Philo both supply more information about his general disposition. They had a low opinion of him, and describe him as a brutal and callous man who cared little either for Jewish religious scruples or for common human values. One passage in the gospels refers to an occasion when he ordered the death of certain Galileans, and 'mingled their own blood with their sacrifices' (Luke 13:1). This was probably the occasion described by Josephus, when Pilate had raided the temple treasury for cash to build an aqueduct, only to face demonstrations from crowds of outraged believers when he made a visit to Jerusalem, presumably for one of the festivals. In retaliation, Pilate sent his troops into the crowd in disguise, and a considerable number were killed while he himself sat and watched the gory spectacle (Josephus, *The Jewish War* 2.10.4). It could well be that this was why Antipas never had much time for Pilate (Luke 23:12), and it might have been

This inscription from Caesarea mentions the rule of Pilate as 'prefect' of Judea.

sensitivity to this situation that led Pilate to send Jesus to him for trial.

Eventually, Pilate's cruelty and careless disregard for religious sensitivities led to him being summoned to Rome to give an account of himself. What happened then is unknown. Some traditions claim that he and his wife later became Christians, and the Coptic church honours them both as saints and martyrs. But Eusebius reports more plausibly that he eventually committed suicide during the reign of Gaius (AD37–41). His rule was the second longest of all the procurators, which suggests he might well have been an efficient administrator. But the gospels present him as a weak man, and an opportunist who condemned Jesus to death, not out of any respect for the Jews, but only as a means of preserving his own reputation with the authorities back in Rome who had already had to endure enough problems during his rule in Judea.

The last supper

All four gospels give an account of what is generally called the 'last supper' of Jesus. They relate how Jesus acted as host to his disciples in a room loaned by a friend in Jerusalem, on the evening before he was crucified (Matthew 26:20–30; Mark 14:12–26; Luke 22:7–39; John 13:1–30). The first written account of this meal is contained not in the gospels but in the writings of Paul in 1 Corinthians 11:23–26, though his account of it agrees in its main details with the stories told in the synoptic gospels (Matthew, Mark and Luke). John's Gospel gives a fuller account of some aspects of the meal, and includes the story – not mentioned by the others – of how Jesus washed his disciples' feet. At the same time, John omits to mention the central feature of the other accounts, the institution of the Lord's supper, or eucharist.

At this last meal with his disciples, Jesus followed the normal Jewish custom and gave thanks to God for the meal. He then proceeded to break the bread that was on the table, and handed it to his disciples, saying, 'This is my body which is for you. Do this in remembrance of me' (1 Corinthians 11:24; compare Matthew 26:26; Mark 14:22; Luke 22:19). After this, he handed them a cup of wine, telling them: 'This cup is the new covenant in my blood. Do this, as often as you drink it, in remembrance of me' (1 Corinthians 11:25; compare Matthew 26:27–28; Mark 14:24; Luke 22:20).

Times and dates

The disciples, like all other Jews, would be quite familiar with the idea of a 'covenant'. The last supper took place at about the same time as the Jewish people were preparing to celebrate one of the most important religious festivals, the Passover. The Passover festival celebrated and recalled the inauguration of God's 'covenant' with their ancestors. They remembered how, long ago, God had delivered Israel from slavery in Egypt, and in gratitude for this deliverance Israel had given their obedience and devotion to God (Exodus 12 – 23). Ever since that time they had regarded themselves as 'the people of the covenant', and the 'covenant' was simply the fact that God had done something for the people as an act of undeserved love, and they had responded in love and obedience.

When Jesus compared his own death to the inauguration of a 'new covenant', he was suggesting to his disciples that through him God was performing a new act of deliverance, and that a similar promise of loyalty and devotion would be required of those who would share in its benefits. God's new kingdom makes demands of those who would be part of it, and Paul says that Christians ought to repeat this meal regularly as a constant reminder of the fact that their new life of freedom was won by Jesus on the cross. Because of that, they owe him their unfailing loyalty and obedience.

Paul, of course, was not intending to give an historical account of the last supper; he mentions it more or less incidentally. His main intention was to emphasize that the eucharist (as it came to be called) was a continuing reminder to Christians of how much they owe to God. But in the case of the gospel accounts of the last supper, the matter is much more complex. They were clearly intending to give some sort of historical account of the last supper, and it is therefore legitimate to ask historical questions of them. The most important question is whether the last supper was a celebration of the Jewish Passover, or whether Jesus was observing some other kind of feast with his disciples.

This in turn resolves itself into two further questions:

Do Jesus' actions at the last supper suggest that he was observing the Passover with his disciples?
Here we shall restrict our discussion to what Jesus and his disciples actually did.

The traditional 'Passover plate' contains foods symbolizing different aspects of the story of Israel's deliverance from slavery as told in the book of Exodus.

The question of what the gospel writers *thought* he was doing is dealt with separately. Within the gospel stories it is possible to find arguments both for and against the idea that Jesus was observing the Jewish Passover. The following facts seem to favour the view that it was a Passover meal:

● The meal of the last supper was eaten in Jerusalem, and not at Bethany where Jesus was staying at the time (Mark 14:13; Luke 22:10). With growing opposition from the religious leaders, this can hardly have been a sensible time for Jesus to make unnecessary excursions into Jerusalem. But if Jesus was intending to share in the Passover festival, he would have to do so, since the Passover feast could only be eaten within the walls of the city. This could explain the emphasis on the disciples' concern to find a room in a suitably located house (Matthew 26:17–19; Mark 14:12–16; Luke 22:7–13).

● According to John 13:23–25, Jesus and the disciples took their meal reclining on couches. This was not the invariable Jewish custom, but it was obligatory at the celebration of the Passover. The instructions for celebrating Passover (the Passover *Haggadah*) say: 'On all other nights we eat and drink either sitting or reclining, but on this night we all recline.' The *Mishnah* adds that even the poorest person in Israel must not eat the Passover feast except while reclining (*Pesahim* 10:1).

● The meal took place at night. This was also a distinctive custom associated with the Passover. The usual custom was to eat the main meal of the day in the late afternoon. But the Passover was always at night, the time when the events it commemorated had taken place.

The last supper
continued

● The dipping of pieces of food into a sauce (Mark 14:20; John 13:26) was definitely a custom used only at the Passover. The Passover *Haggadah* does not refer to bread being served in this way, but it does say: 'all other nights we do not dip… even once, but on this night twice'.

● The disciples sang a hymn before they left the room (Mark 14:26). The singing of the so-called 'Hallel' psalms (Psalms 113–118) was a special feature that marked the end of the Passover meal.

Despite all these similarities between the last supper and the Passover, however, there are other aspects of the gospel narratives that suggest the last supper was not a regular Passover feast:

● It is most unlikely that Jesus would have been judged, condemned and crucified in the middle of such an important feast as the Passover. In particular, it is unlikely that a Roman governor would have been so foolish as to take the great risk involved in the public execution of a popular figure at a time when Jerusalem was crowded with pilgrims. To have done so would have defiled the day of the great festival, and could easily have sparked off a riot among the Jews.

● It would have been against Passover laws for Jesus to be tried in the middle of a festival. All forms of work were prohibited on the Passover, and that included the work of the Sanhedrin. In addition, religious leaders would have risked ritual defilement by having anything to do with Pilate at this time (John 18:28). The whole business of the trials, and especially the element of urgency about them, is better explained if the Passover was to begin shortly than if it was already taking place.

● A number of circumstantial details do not easily fit with the assumption that Jesus was observing the Passover. There is, for example, no mention of a lamb or of unleavened bread, though these were the single most important items of the

traditional Passover meal. It would also have been surprising to find Simon of Cyrene coming in from the fields at the height of such an important festival when work was strictly forbidden (Mark 15:21). It is also surely significant that the earliest Christians observed the Lord's supper once a week and not annually, as they might have been expected to do had it originally been a Passover celebration. Taken by themselves small details like this would not prove very much. But when considered along with the other evidence they can be given some weight in the argument.

Faced with these apparently conflicting pieces of evidence, equally reputable scholars have made different judgments. Many have argued strongly in favour of the view that Jesus was actually keeping the Jewish Passover, though a significant minority have argued just as strongly that he was not. They suggest that what he was celebrating was a *Kiddush*, a type of feast with which committed believers would often prepare for the beginning of the weekly sabbath. It has also been understood as a feast of a more general nature known as a *Haburah*. Such feasts are well known in later Judaism, and still form a part of modern Jewish observances, but there is little evidence to show that they existed at the time of Jesus, and even less to show what might have taken place at them.

Did the gospel writers think Jesus was observing the Passover with his disciples?
Judged purely on the basis of the evidence reviewed so far, there is much to be said on each side of the argument. But the really awkward questions begin here, for the three synoptic gospels say quite definitely that the last supper was a Passover meal – though, as we have seen, not every detail of their description of the meal fits in with this assumption (Matthew 26:18; Mark 14:12; Luke 22:15). On the other hand, John says equally clearly that

	Synoptics	John
Thursday		
evening	Passover	Last supper
	Last supper	Arrest
	Arrest	
Friday		
morning	Trials and	Trials and
afternoon	crucifixion	crucifixion
evening	Beginning of sabbath	Beginning of sabbath and Passover
Saturday	Sabbath	Sabbath and Passover
Sunday	Resurrection	Resurrection

The relationship of Passover to the last supper, according to the synoptics and John.

the last supper was not the Passover, but took place on the day before the Jewish festival – yet here also, not every part of his description of the occasion matches that statement (John 13:1; 18:28).

At one time, it would have been easy to solve this problem by assuming that John, in particular, made a mistake in his story. There are some scholars who still take that approach today, but it is now generally recognized that this is too simplistic a solution, and even if John's Gospel was one of the latest books of the New Testament to be written, it is by no means a later fabrication of the life and teachings of Jesus. On the contrary, though the fourth gospel does present its own problems of interpretation, the accounts preserved by John are clearly based on authentic, reliable and early traditions.

In order to grasp the precise nature of the difficulty, some knowledge is necessary of the way times were calculated in Jewish culture. Ancient Jewish chronology is notoriously difficult to understand, and in this case the matter is made more complex by the fact that the Jewish day begins at sunset, whereas the Roman day (like our own) began at midnight. So, for example, while for the sake of convenience the weekly Jewish sabbath might be referred to as Saturday, it actually lasts from sunset on Friday evening until sunset the next day (Saturday).

The gospels all agree that Jesus was crucified on a Friday afternoon, and his empty tomb was discovered on the Sunday morning. In between this was the sabbath, which was always a holy day – but on the particular week in question, the Passover was also being celebrated, and this was an even more holy day. Putting this calendrical information alongside what is reported in the gospels, it seems that the synoptic writers thought that the Friday was the Passover festival, whereas John believed that the Passover fell on the sabbath in that particular year. On this understanding, there is no problem with the statements made about Jesus: the difficulty rather is concerned with the chronology of these various religious festivals.

This is one of those matters on which caution is probably the wisest course. There is certainly no one answer that could claim to be the generally accepted consensus of opinion. But one possible way of understanding the awkward distinction between John and the synoptics is to suppose that the two traditions were using different calendars, and that what was in one calendar the day of the Passover would be another day in a different calendar.

Nowadays we would find it impossible to believe that there could be different opinions about something as basic as the date, but in the context of first-century Judaism this is not such a far-fetched explanation as it sounds. There was constant speculation on such matters, and the existence of the various sectarian

The last supper
continued

movements within first-century Judaism was to a large extent related to differing opinions on this very subject.

One of the most striking differences between the Essenes of Qumran and the Pharisees in Jerusalem, for example, was on the question of their religious calendar. The mainstream Jewish calendar was based on calculations related to the movements of the moon, whereas the Qumran people appear to have used another calendar as well, based on calculations about the movements of the sun. This same calendar features in the *Book of Jubilees*, and according to it the Passover meal was *always* on the day that began on the Tuesday evening. If Jesus used this same calendar, then he could have celebrated a real Passover with his disciples on the *Tuesday* evening, but still have been crucified as the official Passover was about to begin on the Friday evening. This ingenious solution, however, still leaves unanswered a number of vital questions:

● There is no reason to suppose that Jesus did in fact use anything other than the official calendar. He appears to have moved in the mainstream of Judaism rather than in any sectarian movements, and is often depicted taking part in the regular worship of the synagogue. If, as John suggests, he had often attended the great temple-based festivals in Jerusalem, it would be more natural to suppose that he kept the same calendar as the Jerusalem authorities, otherwise he would not have attended the festivals at the same times as everyone else (John 7:1–39). In addition, we know that Jesus was often in conflict with the Pharisees about the observance of religious festivals, and was regularly accused of doing things that were not allowed on the sabbath – yet he never claimed that he did them because he used a different calendar. He explained his actions by reference to the fact that he believed himself to be 'lord even of the sabbath' (Mark 2:28).

● The Passover lambs had to be ritually slaughtered in the temple, and this would obviously be done according to the official calendar. It is therefore difficult to see how the disciples could have had a lamb available in Jerusalem on the Tuesday evening – yet without the lamb, there could be no Passover meal.

● This alternative calendar would mean that Jesus was held in custody for two days before his crucifixion, which is difficult to reconcile with the unanimous testimony of all four gospels that the trials took place in a hurry so that Jesus could be condemned and executed before the beginning of the sabbath.

Despite its attractions, this theory rests on rather shaky foundations, though it is not impossible to imagine that new evidence to strengthen it could be discovered in the Qumran texts or elsewhere. In the present state of our knowledge, however, it is difficult to accept it as a sufficient explanation of the difference between the synoptic gospels and John. A more likely possibility is that these dating indications were inserted into the narratives by their respective authors consulting the calendar at the time and place when they were actually writing. John's Gospel was written from the perspective of the Jews of Palestine: could it be that on the year in question, they celebrated the Passover on the sabbath, while Mark (followed by Matthew and Luke) followed the customs of the Jews of the Dispersion, and on their reckoning the Passover was held on the Friday in the year that Jesus died? Many more speculative theories have been advanced from time to time, all with something to commend them. Perhaps this is one of those topics on which the wisest approach is to admit that we simply do not know for certain – though the explanation is highly likely to be related to calendrical confusion. In any case, this one detail should not be allowed to hide the fact that all four gospels are in complete agreement on everything else. Nor can it be concluded that because there is no obvious answer at present, that means there is no answer. But if an explanation lies in the arcane speculations of religious experts on their calendar, it will be a long and tedious process before a widely acceptable answer is found.

The New Covenant

In any case, we will never find a full explanation of the last supper if we only ask what sort of Jewish feast Jesus was keeping. What Jesus was doing at the last supper fits in with many Jewish customs. That is hardly surprising, since he and his disciples were Jewish believers. But the precise nature of what he was doing cannot be fitted exactly into any specific occasion in the Jewish religious calendar. It seems unlikely, for the reasons already given, that the disciples were celebrating the Jewish Passover, though at the same time it seems obvious that their last supper with Jesus followed fairly closely the formal setting of the Passover meal.

Perhaps a little more room should be allowed for the creative originality of Jesus himself. In the nature of the case the Passover lamb was absent, but in this supper that was of little importance. By this point, Jesus had a pretty clear idea of what would happen next, and was bold enough to claim that God was already providing a lamb, and he was here offering himself in symbol to his disciples as 'the Lamb of God who takes away the sin of the world' (John 1:29). It was no coincidence that he was crucified at the very same time as the symbols of God's past deliverance were being sacrificed in the temple courts.

At the same time, there was a strong sense that Jesus' death was not to be just a reinterpretation of an ancient ritual, but would usher in something quite different and revolutionary, that would both sum up and supersede the events associated with the first Passover. This was the inauguration of the kingdom of God and in the last supper, surrounded by those who would become the nucleus of this new way of being, Jesus was symbolically offering himself for their freedom in the bread and the wine. This is why these things became within the church the external symbols of that freedom from sin and its consequences which Jesus had announced, and which his death and resurrection were about to bring to birth.

18 The Resurrection

All the New Testament writers agree that Jesus was raised to life on the third day after his death. The reactions of other people to this claim will of course depend to a large extent on their basic presuppositions about the supernatural. Those who begin from the assumption that anything beyond our normal experience is impossible will obviously have to find some other explanation for what the first Christians thought was the resurrection of Jesus. Those who accept the possibility of unique occurrences which seem to go beyond regular human experience will no doubt find it worthwhile to pay serious attention to some of the claims of the New Testament. With the general collapse of the rationalist-materialist world-view in recent years, and the emergence of so-called 'New Age' postmodern spirituality, the dominance of an unbridled scepticism in Western culture has gradually been eroded, so that there is probably a greater openness about such matters at the start of this new millennium than has been the case for some time. That should not be used as a substitute for critical consideration of the evidence, such as it is, though it certainly changes the atmosphere in which such examination can take place.

There can be no question that the earliest Christians were completely convinced that the resurrection event, or complex of events, was a real, historical happening that had taken place in their own world, and which had exercised a profound influence on their own lives. Whereas it is unclear just how widespread was belief in the conception of Jesus by a virgin, the resurrection was a different matter altogether. Paul spoke for the whole of the early church when he declared that, if the reality of Jesus' resurrection was denied, the Christian faith would be emptied of its meaning: 'If Christ has not been raised, your faith is futile and you are still in your sins' (1 Corinthians 15:17). By way of unpacking that conviction, Paul proceeded in the same passage to give a list of people who could verify that Jesus had come to life again, so he obviously thought of the resurrection event as something that could be attested by witnesses – an outward, public happening rather than a private, mystical experience. At the same time, one of the other dominant features of the New Testament accounts is that nowhere do they provide an account of the actual act of rising again, only of the results of that act as demonstrated through the appearances of the risen Jesus, and the fact that his tomb was found empty.

The belief of the early church

The earliest evidence for the resurrection almost certainly goes back to the time immediately after it is alleged to have taken place. This is the evidence contained in the summaries of Christian faith found in the first part of the Acts of the Apostles. Of course, these are now contained in a document that was compiled in its present form at least thirty years after the death of Jesus, and perhaps as much as fifty years later, but there is a widespread consensus that the first few chapters of Acts preserve material from very early sources. The language used in speaking about Jesus in the early speeches in Acts is quite different from that which was in common use when the book was compiled in its final form. It is even quite different from the letters of Paul, which were certainly written long before the book of Acts. So we may be reasonably confident that here we have very early sources.

The Resurrection of Christ, woodcut (1510) by Albrecht Dürer.

These early speeches indicate a largely Jewish type of Christianity, showing a set of simply expressed beliefs about Jesus, and providing a generally believable account of what life might have been like in the first days of the church. According to this picture, the central feature of the early Christian church's message was the story of Jesus himself – how he had come to fulfil God's promises, how he had died on the cross, and how he had come back to life again. This message was so consistently expressed that it has been possible to discern a regular pattern of statements that were apparently made about Jesus from the very earliest times. C.H. Dodd, who first identified this pattern of statements, called it *kerygma*, a Greek word meaning 'the declaration'. Every authentic account of the Christian message contained these statements:

■ Jesus has fulfilled the Old Testament promises;
■ God was at work in his life, death and resurrection;
■ Jesus has now been exalted to heaven;
■ The Holy Spirit has been given to the church;
■ Jesus will soon return in glory;
■ All who hear the message must respond to its challenge, showing a willingness to change their lifestyle and follow Jesus.

If the resurrection was to be removed from this *kerygma*, then most of it would no longer make sense. The whole existence of the early church was based on the belief that Jesus was no longer dead, but was alive.

It also seems likely from the evidence in Paul's letters, as well as from Acts, that the recognized qualification for an apostolic leader was that he or she had seen the risen Jesus. This was explicitly made a condition when the apostles came to appoint a successor to Judas Iscariot (Acts 1:21–22), and Paul also claimed that his own vision of Jesus on the road to Damascus gave him the same status as those who had been apostles before him (Galatians 1:11–17).

The evidence of Paul

The second main piece of evidence regarding the resurrection is provided by Paul himself in 1 Corinthians 15. If there is room for differing opinions on the importance of the evidence of Acts, there is no such room in the case of Paul's evidence. He was certainly writing his letter no more than twenty-five years after Jesus was crucified, and his statements might well form the earliest piece of documentary evidence for belief that Jesus had risen again. It is obvious, both from the contents of 1 Corinthians and from its context, that Paul's main intention there was not to give a reasoned argument for believing in the resurrection of Jesus. He was, rather, trying to help his readers to overcome a specific set of problems that had arisen in their local faith community. The information he included about how Jesus rose from the dead is more or less accidental, which in itself makes it all the more impressive, for he reminded the Corinthians that what he was saying was something they had always known and believed. Even though he sketched the details in just a few sentences, his account shows that at a very early date Christians, even in Greece, were quite familiar with the full story of how Jesus had died and come back to life again.

In this account Paul refers to an occasion when the risen Jesus was seen by more than 500 disciples at one time, most of whom he says were still alive when he wrote and could confirm what he said (1 Corinthians 15:6). He also mentions an appearance to James, the brother of Jesus, and includes his own conversion encounter with the risen Lord among these resurrection appearances (1 Corinthians 15:7–8). Though they were all written later than Paul's letters to Corinth, the gospels never mention these appearances of the risen Jesus at all, which suggests that the fact of Jesus' resurrection was so widely believed among the first generations of Christians that the people who wrote the gospel stories did not even think it important to marshal *all* the evidence for it. As with the rest of the narratives, they used only a small selection of the material that was at their disposal.

The gospel traditions

The stories found at the end of each of the four gospels are of course the main source of information about Jesus' resurrection. There are certain distinctive features about these stories:

■ They all emphasize two main facts: that the grave of Jesus was found empty, and that the risen Jesus was seen by different people on several different occasions. Both these pieces of evidence were important. By itself, the fact of the empty grave would prove nothing except that Jesus' body was not there. Without the empty grave, the visions would prove nothing objective, though they might reveal something about the mental state of the disciples. But the combination of the two facts, if they are indeed correct, would be strong evidence in support of the claim that Jesus was alive.

■ When the resurrection narratives are compared with many of the other stories about Jesus, they are told in a relatively simple and uncomplicated way. For example, they contain no symbolism requiring special insight to understand, nor are there many subtle allusions to the Old Testament, nor any real attempts to bring out the theological significance of the events they describe. If they are compared in this respect with, say, the accounts of how Jesus was baptized, the contrast is very marked indeed.

After his crucifixion, Jesus was placed in a tomb carved from the solid rock. Tombs of this kind often had a heavy stone which could be rolled across the entrance.

The disciples

The fourth and final piece of evidence relating to the resurrection event is the indisputable fact that a thoroughly disheartened band of disciples, who should by all the rules of historical probability have been depressed and disillusioned by their leader's crucifixion, was, in the space of seven weeks, transformed into a strong band of courageous witnesses, and the nucleus of a constantly growing church. The central fact of their witness was that Jesus was alive and active, and they had no hesitation in attributing the change in themselves to what had happened as a result of his rising from the dead. They themselves were obviously convinced that this was what had actually happened, for the resurrection was not just something they talked about: it was something they were willing to die for. It is beyond doubt that no one dies for something unless they are totally convinced of its truth.

Facts and faith about the resurrection

So much, then, for the various pieces of information supplied by the New Testament. What can be made of them? Firstly, three general observations are worth making:

Why do the accounts differ?

Despite the fact that the information given in the gospels is narrated in a simple way, the gospel accounts are not easy to reconcile with one another. Though many people have tried, no one has been completely successful in producing an 'agreed version' of how the New Testament says it all happened. It is unlikely that anyone ever will. Throughout their work, the gospel writers were selective. They used only those stories and teachings of Jesus that would be helpful to their first readers. This is one of the reasons there are four different gospels:

because people in different parts of the empire had their own varied concerns. This process of selection was clearly applied to the resurrection stories, as can be seen from the fact that Paul preserves some pieces of information not mentioned by any of the gospels.

At first sight, this might appear to be an argument against the resurrection having happened at all, but it can also be claimed as a strong argument on the other side. Eye-witnesses often give very different accounts of what they have seen, especially when they see things that do not fit in with their expectations of how things should be. The disciples themselves had no expectation at all that a dead person might come to life again. Mark 9:9–10 suggests they had no idea what 'resurrection' could possibly mean; it was something quite alien to their way of thinking. It is not surprising then that the disciples did not tell a logical and coherent story. The story of someone rising from the dead would be much more difficult to believe if all four gospels had given exactly the same account. Yet, despite minor discrepancies in detail, all the

An ossuary. After a body decomposed, the bones were gathered together and placed in this kind of container.

■ There is no evidence that the risen Jesus appeared to anyone apart from his own followers, though it is possible that he might have done so. Those who wrote the gospels were writing for a specific readership, which was either a Christian readership or people who were already sufficiently interested in the Christian faith to want to know more about it. In this context, the first concern of the gospels was to describe what it might be like when disciples encounter the living Jesus.

■ Evidence about somebody who appeared and disappeared in a room with closed doors is obviously quite a different kind of evidence from that historians normally deal with. That is not to say it should be inadmissible, but it certainly does not fit into the ordinary rules of evidence.

■ The fact that Mary Magdalene, the married couple on the road to Emmaus, and the disciples in the boat on Lake Galilee all failed to

---

accounts are agreed on the main parts of the story. In all of them the tomb is empty and Jesus appears to the disciples.

In Mark, the earliest gospel, the account ends at 16:8, and what follows in some English versions as 16:9–20 is generally considered to be a later addition. In this account, some women who came to the grave on the Sunday morning to finish the process of embalming Jesus' body found that the stone slab used as a door to the rock tomb had been rolled back, and were terrified by the sight of a young man in white sitting inside. This 'young man' (who is clearly intended to be understood as an angel) said, 'Do not be amazed; you seek Jesus of Nazareth, who was crucified. He has risen; he is not here, see the place where they laid him. But go, tell his disciples and Peter that he is going before you to Galilee; there you will see him, as he told you' (Mark 16:6–7). At that, the women ran terrified from the graveyard, and because of their fear they told no one of what they had seen and heard.

Luke includes the story of a couple returning to their home in the village of Emmaus, who met the risen Jesus without recognizing him. They spoke of women visiting the grave and seeing a vision of angels, who assured them that Jesus was alive (Luke 24:22–24). But no reference is made here to Jesus going to Galilee. Many sophisticated explanations have been proposed for this, though it is not inconceivable that the women did not deliver this message for the simple reason stated by Mark: they were afraid to go back there, for they thought that the king of that area, Herod Antipas, would now be ready to get rid of any of Jesus' followers who were found there.

Matthew repeats Mark's account, though with some additional details, mostly directed towards heightening the supernatural trappings of the event. He speaks of a great earthquake on the Sunday morning, and also mentions the terror of the guards at the tomb (Matthew 28:1–4). In this account, the women are still central but left the grave in a mixed mood of fear and joy, and were met by Jesus himself, who repeated the message about going to Galilee (Matthew 28:5–10). Matthew includes a story showing how the disciples followed this instruction at once, and describes how they met with the risen Jesus on a mountain in Galilee, where they were commissioned to take his message to all nations and invite others to join them in a life of discipleship (Matthew 28:16–20). This appearance of Jesus seems not to be the same as the ascension story told by Luke. Though Jesus is reported as making

recognize Jesus, though they knew him well and had seen him only a few days before, suggests that his physical appearance must have changed in a way that would certainly be confusing to any ordinary witness in giving evidence.

What, then, can be said on the basis of these various pieces of evidence? There can be no question that the earliest church believed that Jesus had come back to life again. The disciples and their followers knew that something had happened to change their lives after the crucifixion of their master, and they explained this change by the fact that he had risen from the dead. But to speak of this kind of 'resurrection faith' is one thing; to speak plausibly of a 'resurrection fact' is quite another. Obviously there must have been something that can be called the 'resurrection fact' which called forth the disciples'

Why do the accounts differ? *continued*

some similar statements on each occasion, the ascension took place not in Galilee but in or near Jerusalem (Luke 24:44–53; Acts 1:6–11). In effect, Matthew brings the story begun by Mark to its logical conclusion: Jesus' appearance in Galilee and commission to the disciples to proclaim the good news about him.

Luke's story has certain differences from Mark's: there were two angels in the tomb, and Galilee is mentioned not as the location where Jesus would meet the disciples later, but as the place where he had originally foretold his death and resurrection (Luke 24:1–11). When the women told the disciples their story, it was not believed. In some old manuscripts of Luke, there is at this point a story of how Peter and John visited the tomb to confirm what the women reported, but this is probably a later effort to harmonize Luke's story with the incident recorded in John 20:1–10. After telling of how Jesus met the couple on the road to Emmaus, and then appeared to all the disciples in a room in Jerusalem (Luke 24:13–43), Luke goes on to record the ascension on the road to Bethany, as if it followed immediately after the resurrection (Luke 24:44–53). But in Acts he makes it clear that the ascension took place after an interval of forty days (Acts 1:3). He does not mention an appearance in Galilee.

John's Gospel, on the other hand, describes appearances of Jesus both in Jerusalem and in Galilee. Of the women named in the other gospels as having discovered the empty grave, only Mary Magdalene is mentioned here, though the fact that she uses the plural pronoun 'we' in reporting the event to Peter implies that others were with her (John 20:1–2). They found the tomb empty and returned to tell the disciples, whereupon Peter and John then went to the tomb and found the grave clothes lying undisturbed – proof that the tomb had not been robbed (John 20:3–10). At this point Mary saw two angels in the tomb and was greeted by Jesus, whom she mistook for the gardener (John 20:11–18). An account then follows of two appearances to the disciples in Jerusalem. During the first of these Jesus breathed on them and gave them the Holy Spirit (John 20:19–29), while the last chapter of John, which is almost certainly a later addition, albeit by the same author, describes Jesus' appearance to the disciples on the shore of Lake Galilee, and how he had breakfast with them before recommissioning Peter (John 21:1–25).

The 'Garden Tomb'. Though this is certainly not the actual place where Jesus was buried, it gives an idea of what his tomb might have looked like.

'resurrection faith'. But what was it? It does not have to begin with the actual rising of Jesus' physical body from death, and it is not difficult to think of alternative explanations:

The 'resurrection fact' was a subjective experience

A natural reaction to the evidence about the resurrection is to suppose that the so-called 'resurrection appearances' were purely subjective. The pious might call them visions; psychologists would be more inclined to call them hallucinations. If we could assume that this is what happened, it would solve the problem. But it is not quite so simple:

■ The fact that the tomb was empty, and that neither friend nor enemy produced the body of Jesus is so strongly emphasized in the gospels that it must be accounted for. Both the Romans and Jesus' religious opponents had an obvious vested interest in producing a body, for that would have squashed the Christian movement once and for all. It is therefore safe to assume that neither of these groups had removed it. The disciples, on the other hand, were prepared to stake their lives on the fact that Jesus was alive. Many of them were brutally murdered for their faith, including Peter and other members of Jesus' inner circle, who would be prime suspects for removing the body. It is highly improbable, if not impossible, to imagine that they would have willingly suffered in this way, if all the time they knew where they themselves had hidden Jesus' body.

■ Although an individual experience like that of Peter or James might be reasonably regarded as subjective, and an appearance to a crowd of 500 might sound like a mass hallucination, an encounter such as that on the road to Emmaus, with the absence of excitement and the gradual recognition of the stranger by two people, has all the marks of an authentic account. The statements that the risen body could be touched, that the risen Jesus ate food with his disciples, and that he breathed on them, show the disciples were convinced they were in contact with a real physical body and not a vision.

■ Unlike the other disciples, Paul was what might be called 'psychically experienced'. He writes of having had visions and revelations of a mystical nature on several occasions (1 Corinthians 14:18; 2 Corinthians 12:1–4), but he placed his Damascus road experience in a different category altogether. For him it was quite distinctive, to be compared only to the appearances of the risen Jesus to the other disciples. All the accounts describe encounters with the risen Jesus as an apparently unique kind of experience – neither purely subjective like dreams, nor purely objective, but with some of the characteristics of both.

The 'resurrection fact' was a theological creation

It has been argued that the 'resurrection faith' arose because the disciples saw some theological reason that required it. Because they believed Jesus to be God's Messiah it would be natural for someone who claimed this position to rise from the dead. This explanation, however, raises more questions than it answers:

■ There is no evidence from any source at all to suggest that the Messiah was expected to rise from the dead. On the contrary, the Messiah was popularly expected to kill other people and, if he suffered and died himself, by definition he was not going to be regarded as the Messiah.

■ The Old Testament expresses a very negative attitude to the idea of resurrection, and many Jews simply did not believe it was possible. The disciples themselves appear not to have known what it was earlier in the ministry of Jesus (Mark 9:9–10).

■ It is also difficult to see how the idea of resurrection can have come from an interpretation of Old Testament expectations, since the resurrection stories are completely lacking in scriptural quotations. In this respect there is a sharp contrast with the stories of the crucifixion, which are full of such allusions. In addition, there was no consistent expectation of life after death in the Hebrew tradition, let alone any preconceived notion of what it might be like.

The 'resurrection fact' was a later belief

It has also been argued that belief in Jesus' resurrection was a late idea, only coming to prominence after the Christians had been forced to leave Jerusalem at the time of the Jewish revolt against the Romans (AD66–70). Up until then, they regularly met for worship at the tomb of Jesus. But what could they do once they had been barred from entering the city? To answer that question, the story of the empty tomb was put together to explain why, after all, they did not need to worship there.

Worship at the tombs of heroes is a common practice. It happened in Jesus' day (see Matthew 23:29), and Christian pilgrims of later generations have certainly visited Jesus' traditional burial site in the Church of the Resurrection, or its rival, the so-called 'Garden Tomb'. But to suggest that the discontinuation of such a practice in the first century led to belief that Jesus was alive is completely far-fetched. For one thing, there is no evidence that anybody at all was interested in the place where Jesus was buried, earlier than the fourth century. In addition, there are the statements made by Paul in 1 Corinthians, written at least ten years before AD66. By that time, one gospel had certainly been written and, furthermore, the gospel accounts were undoubtedly based on stories that went right back into the earliest days of the church. It makes no sense at all to suppose that belief in the resurrection was a late development. The fact is that Christians did not venerate the tomb of Jesus because they believed there was nothing in it – and they held this belief right from the start.

Many other more fanciful suggestions have been made from time to time to account for the 'resurrection fact'. But the overwhelming weight of all the evidence suggests that, however it might be described in cognitive abstractions, the 'resurrection fact' was a real, historical event. No other hypothesis gives an adequate account of so much of the evidence.

What does the resurrection mean?

To talk of describing the 'resurrection fact' in abstract terms, not to mention the language of scientific enquiry, moves well beyond the categories of thought of the first disciples. One of the most striking things about the evidence of the New Testament is that the disciples appear to have had no interest at all in probing the whys and wherefores of the 'resurrection fact'. They knew it was a real fact, because of their own experience of Jesus Christ and the evidence of the empty tomb – and that was all they needed to know. This no doubt helps to explain why there is no description anywhere in the New Testament of how the resurrection actually took place. Some Christians in the second century regarded this as a deficiency in the New Testament, and produced their own vivid descriptions of what the body of Jesus looked like, how it came out of the grave, and how those who saw it were affected by the experience. But for the first witnesses such details were not the main focus of interest. For them, the resurrection was not just a happy ending to the story of Jesus; it was the natural climax of the whole of his life, and the vindication of the high claims made for him during his ministry. It was also a guarantee that the life and teaching of Jesus was not just an interesting chapter in the history of human thought, but was the way through which men and women could come to know God. This is why the proclamation of a living Jesus became the central part of the message the disciples declared throughout the known world.

But why was it so very important? Why did Paul claim that without the resurrection of Jesus the whole of the Christian message would be meaningless? A good way to answer this question is to put it the other way round: rather than asking negatively what would be lost if the resurrection could be disproved, asking what positive place the resurrection held in the beliefs of the first Christians. Three claims are made in this respect:

The resurrection and Jesus' identity

Jesus' claims to be the Son of God were shown to be true. Peter said on the Day of Pentecost that the resurrection was a clear proof that 'God has made this Jesus, whom you crucified, both Lord and Messiah' (Acts 2:36). Paul wrote to the Christians of Rome that Jesus was 'declared Son of God by a mighty act in that he rose from the dead' (Romans 1:4). In spite of Jesus' authority displayed in his teaching and actions, and the implied claims about his central role in God's plan, without the resurrection he might have been thought of simply as a great and good man. But after he had risen from the grave, his followers knew for certain that he was who he had claimed to be. They could now see and appreciate his whole life on earth in a new and fuller way, as the life of God personally lived out among ordinary mortals.

The resurrection and new life

The resurrection was more than just a new light on the crucified Jesus. It is emphasized throughout the New Testament, and especially by Paul,

The ascension

The ascension as such features only in Luke's story of Jesus' life. It is unclear whether Luke 24:50–53 tells of it, for in some ancient manuscripts the crucial words 'and was taken up into heaven' are missing. But Luke certainly documents it in more detail in Acts 1:6–11. This story marks the point at which the regular resurrection appearances of Jesus ceased. As such, it is merely the culmination of several occasions when Jesus had disappeared from his disciples' gaze in the forty days following the resurrection. From the time of the resurrection itself, Jesus was understood to have been exalted into the presence of God. When he left the couple at Emmaus, he did not return to some kind of earthbound limbo, but to the heavenly glory which, as the risen Son of man, he had now entered. The actual story of the ascension presumably reflects some particular occasion when he left the disciples in a dramatic and memorable way – and after which, they saw him no more. Though the ascension story itself is only recorded by Luke, the idea is referred to in several passages in John (20:17; 13:1; 16:10; 17:11), while Matthew's Gospel concludes with the conviction that Jesus had received precisely the kind of universal authority that the ascension story seems to imply.

The notion that Jesus was taken 'up into heaven' has sometimes been problematic for modern readers of the gospels. Certainly, we no longer share the perception of ancient people, that the universe is a three-tiered construction, with the earth sandwiched in the middle between the heavens and the underworld. In this frame of reference, it would be natural to think of Jesus being taken 'up to

that the resurrection, as well as the cross, was an indispensable part of the arrival of God's kingdom and all that entailed. The first Christians were practical people rather than theorists. What they wanted was something that would work in real life. They were longing for some kind of personal empowerment that would enable them to be the best people they could possibly be. They understood this in terms of living at peace with God, and being delivered from their self-centredness to live in harmony with other people and, indeed, with the natural environment. They realized that this was unlikely to be achieved either by formal religious observance or by their own efforts at self-improvement, and what was needed was some fresh, energizing life-force that could transform the human personality.

Paul found this new life-force in Jesus, and expressed it in a mystical way as a union between the deepest recesses of his own person, and the Jesus who had been crucified and raised from death. It was such a striking reality for him that he could even write, 'It is no longer I who live, but Christ who lives in me' (Galatians 2:20). This was not just conventionally religious language, for Paul seems to have meant what he said in the most literal sense: Jesus was now living in him in such a way that even the details of his life were determined not by him but by this living Christ. In trying to express all this, Paul used imagery in which he compared the baptism of Christians to the death and resurrection of Jesus (Romans 6:1–10). In baptism, Christians were covered with water as a physical symbol of something that would also happen inwardly and

---

heaven'. But even today, that could easily be a natural, common sense way to describe such a disappearance. Acts 1:12 seems to place the ascension on the Mount of Olives, and Constantine subsequently built a church there, around a cave that he believed marked the spot. Later tradition identified an open space as the more likely site of the ascension. In AD384, Egeria joined in a celebration of the ascension on a small hill a little further up the Mount of Olives, and some six years later a pilgrim called Poemenia had a shrine constructed there – around a rock which bears a mark allegedly made by Jesus' right foot as he said farewell to his disciples.

The New Testament's concern, however, is not with spatial definitions as such, but with the fact that Jesus himself had returned to be exalted in glory with God. This was always implicit in the 'Son of man' title, for in the book of Daniel this character received 'authority, honour, and royal power' (Daniel 7:14). In the context of imagery depicting the cross as Jesus' final battle with the forces of evil, and his resurrection as the proof that he had triumphed, then the ascension demonstrated that this victory was absolute. It was a way of affirming the cosmic dimensions of Christian salvation, declaring that the life, death and resurrection of Jesus were good news not only for people, but also for the world of nature, and indeed for everything in the entire universe. It brought order out of chaos and, in theological terms, represented the reversal of all that had gone wrong in the primeval fall, and both declared and inaugurated the possibility of renewal and rebirth.

spiritually, so that being drenched with water was like being buried, as Jesus was, and coming out of the water was like being raised again, as Jesus was. The essence of Paul's understanding of these events was that becoming a Christian involved a willingness to 'die', in the sense of shedding a self-centred existence, in order to be 'raised' again and receive a new existence, the life of Jesus Christ himself living within.

So the resurrection of Jesus was crucial, for if Jesus had only died on the cross, he might well have been understood to have set an example, or offered a sacrifice, or paid the price of human freedom – but his suffering would have had no power to affect everyday living. Without the resurrection, the cross might have been an interesting theological talking point, but would have been powerless to have any lasting effect on the lives of ordinary people. Because of the resurrection, however, Paul had discovered a new life: 'For to me, life is Christ' (Philippians 1:21). Moreover, he was confident that this was to be the normal experience of everyone who was a Christian: Jesus Christ actually living in those who commit themselves to him.

The resurrection and future hope

The resurrection of Jesus has a further implication for those who already have Christ's life within them. An important part of Jesus' teaching in John's Gospel was that his followers would share in 'eternal life' (John 3:15; 4:14; 17:3). This 'eternal life' included two things. On the one hand, the phrase indicates that Christians were expecting to enjoy a new quality of life: 'eternal life' is 'God's life' and, when Paul wrote of his own Christian experience of Christ living within him, he was reflecting a similar conviction.

On the other hand, to have the kind of life that God has does not just mean that Christians have a new dynamic for life in this world; it also implies that their relationship with God inaugurated by faith in Christ will never end. This distinctive aspect of Jesus' teaching was reinforced and emphasized by Paul when he wrote that the resurrected Jesus should be regarded as 'the firstfruits of those who have fallen asleep' (1 Corinthians 15:20). He understood this to mean that Jesus' rising again was a pledge and a promise that his disciples, too, would survive death. Those people who shared in Christ's sufferings and resurrection in a spiritual sense had the assurance of a life beyond the grave which, like their present lives, would be infused by the personal presence of God. But it would also be distinctive and new, for this resurrection life takes its character from the fact that Jesus is risen, and therefore shares the incomparable nature of that kind of renewed existence now enjoyed by Jesus – a life in which suffering, death and oppression are gone for ever and replaced by the new ways of God's kingdom (1 Corinthians 15:57).

To understand more fully what the implications of that might be, we now need to move on to consider Jesus' teaching about God's way of doing things, that different way of being which is called 'the kingdom of God'.

19 What is God's Kingdom?

The kingdom of God is the major theme of Jesus' teaching in the gospels of Matthew, Mark and Luke. This concept, expressed in various ways, had been a central part of Jewish religious aspirations for generations. At the time of Jesus, it was popularly anticipated as a time when the promises of the Hebrew scriptures concerning the place of Israel in God's plan would be fulfilled in a dramatic way: the hated Romans would once and for all be driven out of their land, and the people would enjoy a new period of political and religious freedom, and self-determination.

It is no wonder, then, that when Jesus emerged as a travelling prophet after his baptism and the temptations, and declared that 'the time is fulfilled, and the kingdom of God is at hand' (Mark 1:15), people of all kinds showed great interest in what he had to say. This was what they were waiting for: a new kingdom of God that would finally crush the old kingdom of Rome. Moreover, they fully expected that they, the Jewish people, would have a prominent part in this coming kingdom under the leadership of their long-awaited Messiah.

From the very beginning of Israelite history, God had always been regarded as 'king' of the people (Psalms 96:10; 99:1; 146:10). The Hebrew Bible declared that the whole world belonged to God, because God made it – and Israel as a nation belonged to God because God had rescued its ancestors from slavery in Egypt and led them to a new land. When they wanted to appoint Saul as their own king a century or two later, some people opposed the move on the grounds that God was the only true king the nation should ever have (1 Samuel 8:1–18). Subsequently, when David became king in Jerusalem, the two ideas were brought together: David and his successors were the rightful rulers of the nation, because God had chosen them (2 Samuel 7:1–17). Their duty was to do God's will, so that the kingdom would reflect the standards of God's law. In reality, things were rarely that simple. As one king succeeded another, it was painfully obvious that many of them were interested only in power and self-fulfilment, and the earlier ideals gradually disappeared. They certainly disappeared as practical politics, though they never quite vanished altogether, for they were transformed into a hope for the future: that at some time God would step in to put things right and establish a kingdom of justice and righteousness. The prophet Zechariah was only one of many who fervently looked for that time to come, a day on which 'the Lord will become king over all the earth' (Zechariah 14:9). By the time of Jesus, there was a widespread expectation that the arrival of the Messiah would herald the coming of this kingdom.

The kingdom of God

But what did Jesus mean in speaking of 'the kingdom of God'? Today, the notion of 'kingdom' most obviously denotes a state or territory that, if not actually ruled by a king, is nevertheless a political entity of some kind. In the ancient world, things would have been no different, and there can be no doubt that it would have been perfectly understandable for Jesus' contemporaries to conclude that he was announcing the establishment of a new state which, in contrast to the countries around, would somehow be ruled by God in person.

That idea is so obviously contrary to what Jesus taught about the kingdom of God that, right from the beginning, it is clear that he must have been using the phrase in some other way. If Jesus was talking about a new state, then he must have seen himself as the agent of a new political dynasty, in effect a Zealot. Yet both his words and his actions seemed to deny that. So what was Jesus really talking about? Some Christians have concluded that, in spite of all the indications to the contrary, Jesus must have been mainly concerned with starting a society that was to be ruled by God, distinct from those ruled by ordinary mortals. Many theologians of the Middle Ages, for example, followed St Augustine in identifying the kingdom of which Jesus spoke with the organized society they knew in the church. Throughout the days of Christendom, the concept that the church was a legitimate successor to the Roman empire, with a political mandate to expand its own empire, motivated Western exploration of other parts of the world, and played its part in the emergence of colonialism. Even today, it is not difficult to find Christian leaders who will speak as if 'the kingdom' is just another word for 'the church', while many more are prepared to talk of it as if it is a kind of political manifesto. Here, we will suggest that Jesus' use of the term 'the kingdom of God' cannot be limited to any of these things, but is in fact more comprehensive than all of them. A good definition of it is 'God's way of doing things'. It begins from those values and standards that most adequately reflect God's own character, though as Jesus expounds the significance of that, he inevitably provides insights into how all this might be applied in practical terms to different life situations. That means that we can expect to find models for how discipleship might impact politics, economics, or other tangible social

Augustine of Hippo (AD354–430). Unattributed engraving copied from a 15th-century

realities. But these things do not exhaust the meaning of 'God's kingdom', which is both wider and deeper than that: wider because it is a way of being that was to be applied to the whole of life, both private and public, and deeper because it would address not only material but also spiritual realities, giving those who committed themselves to it a fresh understanding of true freedom and justice, and the renewed experience of God's presence in their lives.

A new way of being

There were already clues pointing in this direction in the actual words that Jesus probably used to articulate his teaching. Though Jesus might well have been able to speak two or three languages, it is very likely that most of his teaching was given in Aramaic, for that was the language that most people in Palestine knew best. The gospels were written in Greek, of course, like the rest of the New Testament, and we therefore have no direct record of the actual Aramaic words used by Jesus. But even the Greek word that is translated into English as 'kingdom' (*basileia*), more often means the activity of a king rather than the territory over which a sovereign might rule. The Aramaic word that most scholars think Jesus himself would have used (*malkutha*) certainly had that meaning. So we are justified in supposing that Jesus was talking about what might be called 'the kingship of God', rather than 'God's kingdom'. 'Kingship' would be about God's style, the way that God operates, and the example that God sets to others. This helps to explain why Jesus was concerned more than anything else about the quality of human life, and the nature of meaningful relationships, rejecting attitudes of power and control in favour of love, acceptance and mutual service. For him, these qualities were to characterize the life of his disciples because he perceived them as central to the person of God.

This helps to explain some of the apparently more difficult things that Jesus said. For example, he told the Pharisees, 'The kingdom of God does not come in such a way as to be seen... because the kingdom of God is within you' (Luke 17:20, 21). On another occasion he told his disciples, 'whoever does not receive the kingdom of God like a child shall not enter it' (Mark 10:15). It would have been nonsensical to speak of a political territory existing in the lives of individual people: there is no sense in which a person could 'receive' a state, nor could it be 'within them'. But Jesus was saying that from the moment God is recognized as sovereign in someone's life, then the 'kingdom of God' has really arrived. He could say this kingdom was already 'among' his hearers, because he himself was there, and he was completely committed to exploring and putting into practice the values and standards that God represented.

In a similar way, Jesus compared 'entering the kingdom' to 'entering into life' (Mark 9:43–47). Those people who 'inherit the kingdom' also 'inherit eternal life' (Matthew 25:34–46), and the gate leading to the kingdom is 'the way that leads to life' (Mark 10:17–23). The well-known story of the son who ran away from home also emphasized the fact that to be a member of the kingdom is to share in God's family life, and to experience God as a loving parent (Luke 15:11–32). In the same way, Paul reminded his Christian readers in Corinth that 'the kingdom of God does not consist in talk but in power' (1 Corinthians 4:20), the empowerment of God that enables those who wish to change to live in ways that will truly reflect God's ways of doing things.

At the same time, it would be wrong to understand the kingdom exclusively in terms of an individual relationship between people and God, for there are many statements in the gospels which show that Jesus regarded the kingdom of God not only as the inward rule of God in the lives of his followers but also as some kind of tangible reality. For example, he spoke of people who would 'come from east and west, and from north and south, and sit at table in the kingdom of God' (Luke 13:29). At the last supper Jesus told the disciples, 'from now on I shall not drink of the fruit of the vine until the kingdom of God comes' (Luke 22:18). Matthew records him saying that his followers would 'inherit the kingdom prepared... from the foundation of the world' (Matthew 25:34).

Jesus seems, therefore, to have understood this idea of God's kingdom in at least two ways: on the one hand, as God's guidance in the lives of those who would be disciples, and on the other hand, as something that God would somehow display to the world at large. Both these concepts were already found in the expectations of the Old Testament writers. Though it is true that certain parts of ancient Judaism had expected God's sovereignty to be displayed in the form of an organized kingdom, which would replace the empires of the world, not all previous generations had seen God's future intervention in human affairs in the same nationalistic terms as some of Jesus' contemporaries. Circles inspired by apocalyptic thinking had a tendency to magnify the material aspects of 'the kingdom of God'. In Daniel, for example, 'the saints of the most high', represented by 'a figure like the Son of man', receive the kingdom of God and possess it for ever (Daniel 7:13–18), and this kind of expectation was heightened and magnified by later apocalyptic writers, some of them contemporaries of Jesus. It was an outlook expressed by some of Jesus' own followers when they wanted to make him their king after the miraculous feeding of the 5,000 (John 6:15) and it was by no means absent from the inner circle of his closest disciples. When James and John tried to claim the chief places on either side of Jesus' throne they were obviously thinking in crudely political terms (Mark 10:35–45).

Though Jesus rebuked them on that occasion, he never denied that God's kingdom would in some way affect society in a political sense. He sometimes suggested that it would do so in relatively undramatic ways, comparable to the way yeast makes bread rise, or a mustard seed quietly grows into a large tree (Matthew 13:31–33). But he was also quite convinced that God would act decisively and directly, not just in the lives of individuals, but also in the public affairs of nations and empires (Mark 13).

At the time of Jesus, many of the rabbis were emphasizing that God's kingship over Israel was already in existence, even under the Roman rule, and that it operated through the Torah, or Law. The rabbis sometimes referred to people 'taking upon themselves the kingdom of God', and by this they meant accepting and obeying the Torah as the instrument of God's rule over his people.

This tension between what God can do now in those who are prepared to order their lives according to God's standards, and what God will ultimately do through them in society at large, is found elsewhere in the New Testament, so that there is a constant balancing act between what God is accomplishing now, and what God might be expected to bring to pass in the future. Paul, for example, says that 'the kingdom of God is not concerned with material things like food and drink, but with goodness and peace and joy in the Holy Spirit' (Romans 14:17), thereby linking it inseparably with moral choices and personal spirituality. Elsewhere, however, Paul easily connects the arrival of God's kingdom with the events surrounding the end of the world: 'The end comes when Jesus delivers the kingdom to God... after destroying every other rule and authority and power' (1 Corinthians 15:24), making it clear that he also believed God would break into history and alter its course, and that this too was part of the coming of God's kingdom. This was made quite explicit in Revelation, in which 'The kingdom of the world has become the kingdom of our Lord and of... Christ, and he shall reign for ever and ever' (Revelation 11:15). It was also an important element in the teaching of Jesus himself, which needs to be considered alongside the more personal aspects of his message, in order to produce a rounded account of what he wanted to say.

'Eschatology' and the kingdom

This whole question of the different things that might be meant by 'God's kingdom' is generally called 'eschatology'. The actual word 'eschatology' is derived from the Greek words *eschaton* and *logos*, and means 'ideas about the end'. But eschatology is not just concerned with what might happen at the end of the world: it is essentially concerned with God's sovereignty, and with all the different means by which God's ways of doing things can make themselves felt, whether in the lives of individual people, in society, or in the ultimate meaning of the entire cosmic process. Over the last century or so, three main perspectives have dominated discussions about the meaning of Jesus' teaching on the kingdom of God.

'Futurist eschatology'

The first of these views Jesus' teaching as part of a 'futurist eschatology'. Used in this context, the word 'futurist' means in the future from Jesus' point of view, and not from the standpoint of the present day. There are many contemporary Christians who have a 'futurist eschatology' in the sense that they expect God's kingdom to come in a tangible, material form at a time that is still in the future from now, and they often further identify the coming of God's kingdom in this way with beliefs about the second coming (or *parousia*) of Jesus himself. But when scholars talk of the gospel traditions, they normally reserve the term 'futurist' for Jesus' own expectations about the kingdom, and not the expectations of modern Christians.

Albert Schweitzer (1875–1965) was a German musician and theologian who became a medical missionary in Africa, and

Albert Schweitzer was a doctor in Africa. His ideas about the kingdom have been widely influential.

in the early days of his career he did a great deal to promote the idea that Jesus was obsessed with a futurist eschatology. By that, he meant that Jesus held roughly the same expectations as the apocalyptic writers of his day, and that he believed God was about to intervene immediately and dramatically in the affairs of humanity, and his own life's work was to be the decisive climax of history. By definition, therefore, that climax would have to come within Jesus' own lifetime. On the basis of this perception, Schweitzer suggested that when, for example, Jesus declared that 'the kingdom of God is at hand', he really expected the cataclysmic end of the world to come almost immediately. More than that, Jesus also imagined himself to be 'the Messiah designate' who would assume a position of full authority once the kingdom had actually arrived. Like many other visionaries both before and after him, Jesus found the reality of life rather different from these idealistic dreams, and as life went on very much as before it began to seem as if the dream had been only an illusion.

Early in the course of his work, said Schweitzer, Jesus was sufficiently confident to announce to his disciples that the Son of man was about to appear in glory – so soon that they could expect his arrival in the course of a few days (Matthew 10:23). When it failed to happen, Jesus decided to try to force God's hand by going to Jerusalem and pressing his claims with the authorities there, and it was this move that resulted in him being arrested, tried and tragically sentenced to death. However, even this astonishing display of blind faith did not produce the desired result, but ended with defeat and a cry of despair from the cross, as Jesus realized that the God he served had abandoned him.

Surprisingly, perhaps, the fact that Jesus' ministry so evidently ended in failure did not invalidate his teaching, for Schweitzer claimed that an even greater power resulted from this incredible act of misplaced confidence than would have been the case if the hoped-for apocalyptic kingdom had actually arrived. The example of Jesus is something that can still exert a dynamic moral and spiritual influence over those who are willing to be obedient. Schweitzer himself certainly put into practice the lessons he saw there, though ironically his overall perspective on Jesus prevented him from taking his actual teaching very seriously, for he regarded even the Sermon on the Mount as an 'interim ethic', valid only for the very short period of Jesus' own ministry. Instead, he attached the greatest importance to Jesus' faithfulness to his convictions, even when those convictions were apparently seriously inadequate.

Schweitzer's views were published in a remarkable book that first appeared in English in 1909, under the title The Quest of the Historical Jesus. It is still regarded as one of the great theological classics, not least because of its comprehensive presentation of the course of scholarly debate over the decades preceding its publication, and the fact that Schweitzer put his finger on some key aspects of Jesus' life and teaching. The way he placed Jesus' teaching about the kingdom of God in the same frame of reference as the work of the apocalyptic writers opened up many new possibilities for understanding the impact that Jesus must have had in the cultural context of his day. He was also certainly correct in seeing that Jesus' style of life, and especially his death, could not easily be separated from his message, and that it was inappropriate to try to understand his teaching without also taking account of his personality.

But taken as a whole, Schweitzer's view failed to convince as a comprehensive account of the whole of Jesus' life and teaching. For one thing, he consistently underrated the claims made in the gospels about Jesus' own significance, preferring instead to confine his attention almost exclusively to the statements about the kingdom of God. But for a holistic view that takes account of all the evidence, these two parts of Jesus' teaching must be understood together, for what is said about the kingdom of God is complementary to the teaching about Jesus' self-claimed special relationship with God.

Unless we are prepared to deny all historical credibility of the gospel narratives, it is hard to believe that Jesus realized the importance of dying at Jerusalem only after the failure of all his previous efforts to bring about the kingdom. Nor is it necessary to believe with Schweitzer that Jesus' death also failed in its intended purpose, and left only a vague spiritual influence to affect the lives of those who take time to think about it.

Schweitzer made much of statements such as Jesus' words to his disciples just before his transfiguration: 'there are some standing here who will not taste death before they see the kingdom of God come with power' (Mark 9:1), something which, on Schweitzer's understanding, never happened. But he was able to reach this conclusion only because of his generally sceptical attitude to the evidence of the New Testament. The whole conviction of the early church, however, was that God *did* intervene in human affairs in a powerful and dramatic way with the resurrection of Jesus and the gift of the Holy Spirit to his followers – and that both of these were the direct outcome of Jesus' death on the cross. Since much of the New Testament was written less than a generation after these events took place, its evidence cannot be brushed aside quite as easily as Schweitzer thought.

'Realized eschatology'

The exact opposite of Schweitzer's theory was C.H. Dodd's idea that Jesus had what he called a 'realized eschatology'. According to Dodd (1884–1973), what Jesus was really saying was that the kingdom had already arrived in his own person. We could say, therefore, that the coming of Jesus was itself the beginning of God's reign; though the kingdom might need to grow and develop, the ultimate and decisive act has already taken place.

This proved to be an attractive view, especially to people of the mid-twentieth century who were still optimistic that the

'Eschatology' and the
kingdom *continued*

world could gradually be made into a better place, and generally saw this coming about through a scientifically inspired evolutionary process of moral improvement and education. Whereas the thought patterns familiar to first-century Jewish apocalyptists seemed bizarre and unbelievable, this image of the kingdom naturally commended itself to middle-class social activists in the Western world. Moreover, the idea that Jesus saw his own life and work as the coming of God's kingdom did actually shed new light on some aspects of the gospel narratives. The miracles, for example, are much easier to understand when they are viewed as signs and demonstrations that God was at work in bringing the kingdom to birth through the life of Jesus than they would be with the more traditional view that had regarded them as 'proofs' of Jesus' divine nature.

Dodd was a sufficiently careful scholar to recognize that not all the gospel materials can be easily understood in the context of a realized eschatology. What could be made, for instance, of those parables that appear to be concerned with the last judgment and some kind of future winding up of things – parables like the story of the ten bridesmaids or the sheep and the goats (Matthew 25:1–13; 31–46)? Dodd proposed that these should be interpreted not as images of a final judgment that would come at the end of the world, but as pictures of the kind of challenge that presents itself to anyone whenever they are confronted with the message about Jesus and God's kingdom. There is certainly plenty of evidence that Jesus regarded the declaration of his message as, in some sense, a judgment on those who heard it and did not respond. The terms in which he condemned the Pharisees often seem to imply that they had placed themselves beyond the possibility of salvation (Mark 3:28–30; Matthew 23),

C.H. Dodd, the English theologian who developed the idea of 'realized eschatology'.

and the author of the fourth gospel is surely giving an accurate representation of at least part of Jesus' message when he comments that 'Whoever believes in Jesus is not condemned; but whoever who does not believe is condemned already, because they have not believed in the name of the only Son of God. And this is the judgment, that the light has come into the world, and people loved darkness rather than light, because their deeds were evil' (John 3:18–19).

It is not difficult to find passages in Jesus' teaching that can give some support to most aspects of Dodd's theory. But the theory ultimately proved incapable of accounting for all the evidence. There were two major stumbling-blocks:

● Although there are many passages in Jesus' teaching which are consistent with a 'realized eschatology', there are a good many more which are not. In many cases Jesus refers to the Son of man coming 'with the clouds of heaven', and his whole outlook was undoubtedly coloured by the kind of apocalyptic imagery to which Schweitzer so strikingly drew attention.

● It is also necessary to consider what the rest of the New Testament reflects about the beliefs of the first Christians, and there can be no doubt that other writings reveal a mixture of a 'futuristic' type of eschatology and a 'realized' type alongside one another.

In the letters Paul wrote to the church in the Greek city of Thessalonica in the early 50s of the first century, there is a considerable emphasis on the expectation of the early Christians that Jesus would return in glory. Paul himself obviously shared this expectation, though not in the same extreme fashion as the Thessalonians (1 Thessalonians 4:13 – 5:11; 2 Thessalonians 2:1–12). In Corinth, on the other hand, the same Paul knew people who believed that the conventional descriptions of the end of things were to be taken as symbols of their own spiritual experience – and to them he again emphasized his own belief that Jesus would return in the future (1 Corinthians 15:3–57). At the same time – and paradoxically, perhaps – Paul himself was not totally one-sided in the matter, for in Galatians, one of his earliest letters, he suggested that in a very real sense the fullness of God's kingdom had come and was already at work in those who were Christians.

If Dodd's theory was completely correct and Jesus did actually think that the kingdom had already arrived in its final form, it is hard to see how and why the first Christians should have forgotten this emphasis so soon and turned instead to speculations about the future. This is an especially important question, since so many of these Christians were not Jews, and they would not naturally have thought of the future in terms of traditional apocalyptic teachings. We should also bear in mind that the gospel traditions themselves were preserved in the churches, and for the churches' use, and it is surely unlikely that such a glaring inconsistency between the teaching of Jesus and the actual beliefs of the church would have gone unnoticed.

'Inaugurated eschatology'

Because of the difficulties involved in both the futuristic and the realized views of Jesus' eschatology, there has been considerable support for a view that would take the best from both of them, recognizing that in a sense God's kingdom did actually come in the person of Jesus, but that its complete fulfilment was still seen in the future. Thus Jesus' teaching is what might be called an 'inaugurated eschatology'.

This is probably the best explanation of the matter. It is essential to recognize with Schweitzer that Jesus' background was that of first-century Judaism, and his teaching included a complete view of the future course of events, including last judgment and final resurrection, as part of the consummation of God's kingdom. But it is also important to recognize that Jesus claimed that the kingdom had arrived already in his own person, and so people

must make their own response to God's demands upon them here and now. If, as has been suggested here, 'the kingdom of God' is a way of speaking about 'God's way of doing things', then there is no intrinsic difficulty in bringing these apparently diverse understandings into dynamic relationship with each other: they are simply different aspects of the same divine will.

This rather complex subject can be summarized by noting four points which seem basic to understanding what Jesus had to say about the coming of the kingdom:

● Jesus certainly used the language and, perhaps to some extent, shared the views of those who expected the kingdom's imminent arrival through a direct intervention of God in human affairs.

● Jesus believed that the fundamental nature of the kingdom of God was being revealed in his own life and work. It is clear from the gospels that this proved to be very different from what most of his listeners had expected, for the kingdom was revealed not as a tyrannical political force that would take over from Rome, but as a loving community of those whose only allegiance was to God, whose values in turn were quite different from the norms of conventional society.

● God's direct intervention is to be seen not only in the life and teaching of Jesus, but also in his death, resurrection and gift of the Holy Spirit to the church. It might well have been in these events that some of Jesus' own predictions about the last things were fulfilled – for example, the statement that some of his disciples would see the kingdom coming with power before they died (Mark 9:1).

● Since there is so much variety in the language used by Jesus to describe the kingdom, its full understanding also requires a similarly broad and comprehensive interpretative framework. The kingdom can arrive secretly, like the yeast working in the dough (Matthew 13:33), or it can come by the sudden appearance of Christ in glory, as at the expected second coming (Mark 13).

The kingdom of God and the kingdom of heaven

One of the striking facts about Matthew's Gospel is that it consistently uses the term 'kingdom of heaven' to describe the subject of Jesus' teaching. The only exceptions to this are in Matthew 12:28; 19:24; 21:31 and 21:43, where we find the term 'kingdom of God', which is used throughout Mark and Luke.

On the basis of this distinction, some interpreters have thought they could differentiate two quite separate phases in Jesus' teaching. But, in fact, there can be no doubt that the two terms refer to the same thing. This can be demonstrated quite easily by comparing the same statements in Matthew and in the other two synoptic gospels. For example, whereas Mark summarizes Jesus' message as 'the kingdom of God is at hand; repent' (Mark 1:15), Matthew has, 'Repent, for the kingdom of heaven is at hand' (Matthew 4:17). The two statements appear in exactly the same context (the beginning of Jesus' teaching ministry), and it is obvious that they are different versions of the same saying. There are many other examples of the same thing.

The most obvious explanation of this variety of expression is the fact that Matthew was writing for Jewish readers, whereas Mark and Luke were both writing for a predominantly non-Jewish readership. The Jewish tradition had always avoided direct use of the name of God in case people should unwittingly find themselves breaking the commandment, 'You shall not take the name of the Lord your God in vain' (Exodus 20:7). To minimize the possibilities of this happening, they often used other terms instead, and 'heaven' was a favourite substitute for 'God'. Matthew, therefore, speaks of 'the kingdom of heaven' in order to avoid offence to his readers. Gentiles, however, had no such reservations, and to them a term like 'kingdom of heaven' would have been unnecessarily complicated, if not altogether meaningless, so Mark and Luke use the term 'kingdom of God' instead.

It might be thought that since 'kingdom of heaven' was the most natural term for Jewish believers to use, this would be the one originally used by Jesus himself, and later adapted for non-Jews by Mark and Luke. But the likelihood is that Jesus actually spoke of the 'kingdom of God', and Matthew has adapted this to 'kingdom of heaven' for his own purposes. There are two reasons for thinking this:

● In general, Jesus never showed any reticence in speaking about God. Not only did he claim to know God in a close and personal way, he also dared to place relationships with God in the intimate context of family imagery, thinking of himself as a child and God as a parent.

● There are, as we have seen, four instances in Matthew where the term 'kingdom of God' is actually used. This can readily be understood if we suppose that Matthew overlooked these four occurrences of the word, but it is really impossible to think that in just these four cases he changed an original 'kingdom of heaven' into 'kingdom of God' for the benefit of his Jewish readers.

20 Understanding the Gospels

Up to this point, we have said a great deal about the life and teachings of Jesus, but very little about the sources of information through which he may be known. Naturally, what has been said about Jesus has been mostly based on those parts of the New Testament which tell of his life and work – the four gospels, according to Matthew, Mark, Luke and John. In using them, several assumptions have been made about their character as literature, assumptions that have inevitably coloured the picture of Jesus presented here. For example, it has been assumed that, though they display some characteristics of biographical writing, they are not comprehensive chronicles of his entire life but rather are selective presentations of those aspects of his life and teaching which seemed most important to the people who first wrote them down. In addition, we have assumed that there is a good deal of overlap and repetition in their various accounts, so that one gospel may legitimately be used to elaborate or clarify the teaching contained in another. Then we have also taken it for granted that it is actually possible to know something about Jesus from the study of the gospels – that, although they are indeed the products of the early church and therefore reflect the concerns and interests of their writers, it is still possible to distil from them a core of hard information about Jesus as he actually was. In this chapter and the two which follow, some of these assumptions will be examined in greater detail, as we seek to understand the reasons for holding them, and to explore their implications.

What is a gospel?

Discussion of this question dominated scholarship throughout the twentieth century. For most of the century, the gospels were regarded as unique documents, a distinctive form of literature created by the early church for the specific purpose of sharing their own faith in Jesus, and used in the celebrations of Christian worship as well as in the missionary endeavour of inviting others to follow him. By the end of the century, however, a strong case was being presented for understanding the gospels in the context of other literature of the Hellenistic world, and in particular for seeing them as a form of Graeco-Roman biographical writing.

It is obvious that the gospels are not 'biography' in the modern sense of that word. A contemporary biography usually begins with an account of the subject's childhood years, and progresses consecutively through adolescence and adulthood to show how the mature person has developed in response to the various influences of early life and environment. By contrast, the main emphasis in the gospels is not on the course of Jesus' life, but on the events of the last week or so. This is prefaced by reports of Jesus' teaching and accounts of a few incidents from the three years immediately preceding his death, with virtually no mention at all of his childhood and adolescence.

The gospels and Graeco-Roman biography

Applying today's standards to the gospels is not likely to be particularly enlightening, for questions about the style or genre of a piece of writing need to be addressed in relation to the actual context in which it was written, and what possible models might have been current in that time and place. In assessing the genre of a particular piece, among other things we need to take account of the structure and style in which it is written, the stated intentions of the author (if any), the process whereby the writing has been put together, the way the author expected or intended it to be used, and the contents. Knowing what kind of writing we are dealing with – even in the most general terms – can make a difference to the way in which we read it.

An example taken from a world perhaps more familiar might help to illustrate this. Television is a major source of information for most people today, and in that medium the same subject might be treated in several programmes that belong to different genres. The topic of world debt, for example, might be considered in a news bulletin, or in a documentary investigation, or in a piece of drama. Depending on which genre the viewers believe a particular programme belongs to, they will view it differently. The genre of a news bulletin creates an expectation that this will be a factual account of the subject, whereas if a programme is perceived as a documentary viewers will expect it to be more wide-ranging, probing the subject from different perspectives, and constructing an argument that requires viewers to form some assessment of what is being claimed. More often than not, there will be an accompanying expectation that, no matter how personally detached the programme makers might try to be, they will have their own angle on the subject, and to a greater or lesser extent they will be crusading for the wider acceptance of their conclusions or recommendations. A piece of drama, perhaps illustrating the impact of debt on poor countries by telling the contrasting stories of life for a typical family in the West and in the developing world, might easily combine features of the news bulletin and the documentary, but viewers would instinctively look at it with yet different expectations, and a major purpose might easily be seen as entertainment, even though it deals with some very serious issues. In each case, the viewers' expectations of a particular genre will shape the way they understand and interpret what they are watching. Things are not always quite so clear-cut, of course, as programme-makers can make subtle changes to their basic genre, thereby confusing the audience about what they are seeing. In some TV programmes it can be hard to distinguish fact from fiction, for the two are either deliberately combined (as in drama-documentaries), or (as in science fiction movies) the visual effects make even the most unbelievable possibilities seem factual. But the general point still stands: genre affects how we approach a programme, and at what level we seek to understand and respond to it.

The same is true of literature. The genre within which the New Testament gospels are placed determines to a significant extent how the reader will process and understand what is in them. As long ago as 1915, C.W. Votaw proposed that in the world of the Roman empire, the gospels could best be understood as part of the genre of popular biography. The emergence of form criticism, however, moved discussion in a different direction, and two form-critical insights in particular seemed to undermine the possibility that the gospels should be understood in this way:

■ Form critics generally saw the gospels as collections of traditions about Jesus' life and teaching that emerged from the life of the earliest Christian communities, rather than being the creative work of particular authors.

■ Form critics viewed the gospels as 'kerygmatic' documents, written to proclaim the primitive Christian message (*kerygma*), and if they provided any sort of portrait of Jesus as he might have been that was an unexpected bonus and not the primary purpose.

Further study – and in particular the emergence of redaction criticism (which is dealt with in more detail in the next chapter) – called these presuppositions into question. In particular, the gospel writers ('evangelists') came to be regarded as creative writers, not merely collecting traditions that were handed onto them, but actually shaping and presenting them in ways they believed would be most appropriate to their readership. In that light, the need to define what kind of literature they thought they were writing once again emerged as a key question. After several false starts, in which the gospels were occasionally compared to what turned out to be non-existent genres of literature in the Roman world, the popular biography now seems to be the category into which they might most easily be fitted. It is not difficult to find similarities between the gospels and such works:

■ In some instances, the gospels share particular stylistic characteristics of popular Graeco-Roman biographies. Luke's preface, for example (Luke 1:1–4) follows a common literary practice of ancient writings, while both Matthew and Luke provide genealogies of their subject, and Luke also includes some time indications placing Jesus in the context of events in the wider Hellenistic world (2:1–2; 3:1–2).

■ The continuous nature of the gospel narratives, albeit generally encompassing only a short period of time, places them in the category of biography, as distinct from the so-called apocryphal gospels of the second century, which contain disconnected sayings or stories, without any overall framework.

■ Though the early Christians wanted to say much more about it, the way in which the gospels portray Jesus' death as a heroic martyrdom was another regular feature of traditional biographies of the time.

■ The gospels regularly use some literary devices that were popular with biographers: for example, the placing of key events or significant teaching within the context of meals, or the descriptions of private conversations and discussions between Jesus the teacher and his disciples.

■ Though there are exceptions, both gospels and ancient biographies generally displayed no interest in the personal psychological growth and development of the subject (something which readily distinguishes them from modern biography).

At the same time, some features of the gospels serve to set them apart from Graeco-Roman biographies:

■ All four gospels were anonymous pieces of writing (the names of Matthew, Mark, Luke and John were attached to them only later, probably to distinguish them from one another once they were all circulating together). This was highly unusual among traditional Greek or Latin authors.

■ Luke is the only one who shares any significant stylistic characteristics with classical authors, though his gospel also raises other issues in relation to the fact that it is only the first part of a two-volume work, which included Acts. While it is not impossible to regard Acts as a continuation in the form of a biography, that is neither the most obvious nor the most plausible literary genre for it. It might be, though, that Luke (and, to a lesser extent, Matthew) represents a stage of gospel writing at which Christians were becoming more aware of the possibility of commending Jesus to educated Romans by conscious adoption of the literary conventions of the day.

■ All the gospels include extensive references to the Old Testament as a way of explaining their subject matter. This would not generally recommend them to the literary élite of their day, and might actually have prevented their recognition in such circles, where examples from the Greek and Latin classics would have been considered more appropriate, and also more widely known. At the same time, it perhaps indicates that a better place to search for literary antecedents for the gospels might be the Jewish tradition, if not the Old Testament itself.

■ While traditional biographers would have portrayed their subjects as models of particular virtues that were admired by society at large, the gospel writers say very little about Jesus' personal characteristics, and when they do it is not to affirm some existing assumptions, but to present Jesus as the originator of a new set of values altogether.

■ The gospels appear to have been written not for general circulation in the literary market place, but for the benefit of Christian groups who would use them in the context of their own worship and mission.

■ An additional complicating factor in this attempt to place the gospels within a literary context in the Hellenistic world, is the ongoing disagreement among experts in Graeco-Roman literature about the actual extent to which authors would follow the allegedly typical characteristics of a particular genre. There is some evidence that there was not necessarily a rigid demarcation between different genres, and that any given author might actually choose to combine a variety of styles in a particular piece of writing, for example by incorporating into a biographical narrative features that would have been more at home in a novel, especially in elaborating the details of private conversations or in describing events that took place behind closed doors.

In the light of all these considerations, the best conclusion still seems to be that, while the gospels show a much greater acquaintance with the conventions of ancient literature than was once believed – especially with the category of popular biography – they have too many distinctive features for it to be plausibly concluded that their authors were self-consciously compiling works of literature that would take their place alongside the writings of classical authors. It is more likely that the evangelists had an awareness of the styles in which others were writing about their own heroes at the time, and were influenced by the conventions of the day only in the general sense that they were themselves part of Hellenistic culture, and had a general familiarity with the way in which literature might be constructed. Though their works undoubtedly display some of the characteristic features of biography, they are rooted within a distinctive set of purposes that more closely related to the needs of the evangelists and the Christian communities for which they wrote.

Gospel writers on the gospels

In the end, we are still left with the necessity of turning to the gospels themselves in order to ascertain their nature. What did their authors think they were doing as they wrote? The obvious place to begin is with Mark, which is commonly thought to be the earliest of the four, and therefore to a large extent provided a model for the others, especially Matthew and Luke, which in different ways may be regarded as revised versions of Mark. Mark 1:1 describes this work as 'The beginning of the gospel of Jesus Christ', a statement which stands as a kind of title or heading to what follows. Two words are relevant here in relation to understanding the purpose of the gospel: the words 'beginning' and 'gospel'. 'Gospel' is simply the English equivalent of Mark's Greek word *euangelion*, and it was originally chosen because the two words had the same meaning: 'good news'. Mark, then, was writing about 'the beginning of the good news', which was not something detached or distant from Mark and his readers, but could actually be a way of referring to their own spirituality.

Mark and the other gospel writers had heard the 'good news' about Jesus, and their own lives had taken a totally new direction as a result of their acceptance of it and their decision to follow Jesus. For them, an important part of discipleship was the need to make known to others the message that had changed their own lives. Their preaching and teaching did of course have a cognitive element within it, along the lines of those basic statements of faith identified by C.H. Dodd as the earliest *kerygma* (chapter 5). But for Mark and his contemporaries this message was far more than just a bare statement of propositional truths about Christian belief: it was also in an important sense the 'good news' of their faith, which had expressed itself in their own lives as they opened themselves to the possibility of changing values and standards, and experienced the empowerment which came to them as they sought to follow Jesus and put into practice God's ways of doing things.

When Mark described his gospel as 'the beginning of the good news', he was therefore saying that his purpose was to describe the first stage in the development of the message to which he and others had responded. The story he told was not a historical curiosity, but was an integral and important part of their own story and experience as Christians. Luke had a similar intention, and in his preface informed his readers that his narrative was designed to enable them to know the full implications of the Christian message which they had heard so often (Luke 1:4). Indeed, Luke felt an even greater compulsion than Mark to emphasize the continuity of the life of the church with the life of Jesus by writing a second volume (the Acts of the Apostles) to bring the story more fully up to date.

When the writers of the gospels are called 'evangelists', therefore, this is a very precise definition of their intention. For they were primarily concerned to deliver the message about Jesus to their own contemporaries, and the normal interests of a biographer were very much a secondary consideration. This observation has at least three important consequences for our understanding of the gospels they wrote:

■ The gospels must be regarded as *selective accounts* of the life and teachings of Jesus. On occasion, incidents from Jesus' life and teaching might have been used as illustrations to explain more abstract theological points, though we may be sure that the stories would also be told for their own sake, as self-contained presentations of the Christian message requiring no further explanation. Indeed Papias, a leader of the church at Hierapolis in the early second century, claimed that Mark's

Gospel consisted of summaries of the stories told by none other than Peter himself (Papias, quoted in Eusebius, *Ecclesiastical History* III.39.15).

The fact that the information contained in the gospels was first presented in this way goes some way towards explaining the apparent incompleteness of the gospel accounts. All four of them put together would hardly contain enough information to document three years of anyone's life, let alone someone as active as Jesus. But when we realize that the information they contain has been preserved because of its relevance to the life of the earliest churches, we can readily understand why so much that we would like to know has been left out. This probably explains why the New Testament has no mention of the early childhood of Jesus, nor for that matter any descriptions of what he looked like, or the kind of person he was. Had the evangelists been writing merely to satisfy people's curiosity about Jesus, they might have included that sort of information. But that was not their intention. They were primarily concerned to nurture the faith of their Christian communities, and to invite other people to follow Jesus, and for these purposes such details were quite irrelevant.

■ If the gospels are illustrations of the apostolic preaching, this means that their contents cannot be regarded as simple stories about Jesus. They must be closely related to the beliefs of the evangelists. At one time it was fashionable to suppose that it was possible to recover from the gospels a picture of a simple Galilean teacher which had later been altered by Paul and others into a theological message about the Son of God. But it is now widely recognized that the gospels are themselves among the most important theological documents of the early church, and we can never in fact discover a picture of Jesus as a simple Galilean teacher. As far back as it is possible to go, the Jesus found in the pages of the New Testament is always a person who is at the centre of great claims about his significance and who utters definitive pronouncements on the relationship of people to God. All his teaching and every incident recorded in the gospels has a specifically theological dimension to it.

■ If, as we have suggested, the authors selected their materials to serve their own purposes in writing, then it follows that we can probably discover something about them and their readers by comparing their relative selection and use of information about Jesus. In the case of the first three gospels this can be done quite easily, for they tell roughly the same story in the same order, and each of them repeats large sections of the material that is found in the others. By comparing the different ways that Matthew, Mark and Luke have used the deeds and teaching of Jesus in their narratives, it is possible to learn something about them and the situation in which they lived and worked.

So to understand the gospels fully is a rather complex business. We need to know why the evangelists wrote as and when they did. Then we need to try to understand the way they assembled their material, and why they used it in one particular way rather than another. In addition, we must always bear in mind that their gospels were intended to serve the ongoing purposes of the church, which means that in the final analysis they were not written as biography, history, novels, or even theology in the usual sense.

Preaching and writing

Where did the evangelists get their information, and what did they do with it? This question has occupied much scholarly attention since about the mid-nineteenth century. It has at times led investigators down many tedious blind alleys, though that should not be allowed to conceal its usefulness and relevance to developing a considered understanding of the nature of the gospels. The way authors use their sources can provide helpful clues to the purpose of their writings, and to know what a writer is doing can be an essential part of grasping his or her message. Method and message are more closely connected than many readers appreciate.

Since the gospels developed in the context of the mission and worship of the early church, we can expect to find clues to their origin by examining the church's message, which typically centred around three major themes: the promises of the Old Testament, information about Jesus and his significance, and a personal appeal to those who heard about these things to respond by choosing to follow Jesus for themselves.

Old Testament texts

A major underlying assumption of the beliefs of the early church was that the promises of the Old Testament had been fulfilled in the life of Jesus. In the New Testament summaries of the church's message, this statement is often made in a rather generalized way, but in real-life situations it must have consisted of a more specific declaration, whether in a predominantly Jewish or a mainly Gentile context. Anyone who was already familiar with the Old Testament would not have been content to know that, in some general way, Jesus was the fulfilment of the ancient scriptures: they would have wanted a clear explanation of precisely which prophecies Jesus was supposed to have fulfilled, and on what evidence such a claim might be based. At the time, a favourite preoccupation of several groups within Judaism was the compilation of lists of Old Testament promises which the Messiah would fulfil when he came. Several such lists have been found at Qumran, but they were not the only people who had such an interest. These lists are generally referred to by scholars as *testimonia*, referring to their function in providing scriptural testimonies to the coming of Christ.

The New Testament contains several indications that suggest these text-lists were probably in regular use among Christians from the earliest times. Matthew and John both refer to a considerable number of texts from the Old Testament, with an indication that they were fulfilled in some particular incident in the life of Jesus. The passages they quote are often relatively obscure, and it is striking that Matthew and John hardly ever used the same ones – perhaps because they were using different collections of *testimonia*.

Some of Paul's letters also string Old Testament texts together in continuous passages in what often seems to be a rather arbitrary fashion, and here again it is reasonable to think that Paul must originally have found these grouped together under the same headings in a collection of Old Testament texts to which he had access. It could easily be that the collection of these texts from the Old Testament was the very earliest form of literary activity in the Christian church. They would be assembled for the convenience of those who were engaged in sharing the Christian message so that they could give specific examples to support their claim that Jesus had fulfilled the traditional expectations concerning the Messiah.

Words of Jesus

The central element in the *kerygma* was a series of statements about Jesus himself. No doubt in the very earliest days of the church's existence it would be possible to proclaim the message with no more than a passing reference to Jesus' life and teachings, particularly in Palestine in the years immediately following the death of Jesus himself, for many could be assumed to know something about Jesus and his teaching, even if they had no personal experience of him. But, before long, Christian missionaries were spreading out far beyond Palestine and carrying their teaching to parts of the Roman empire where Jesus was quite unknown. In this different environment it would have been essential for the Christian message to include some kind of information about Jesus himself, if only a skeletal outline of the most significant events such as death and resurrection.

Once people had become Christians they would require further instruction in their new faith, which would presumably include the kind of information about Christian beliefs and behaviour that could also be found in the various New Testament letters. One obvious and important source of such teaching must have been the remembered statements of Jesus himself. This would not necessarily be separately identified as information about Jesus, but would be incorporated into the developing tradition of the churches. For instance, in Romans 12 – 14 Paul gives advice that is so reminiscent of some of the most distinctive aspects of Jesus' teaching in the Sermon on the Mount that it is most natural to

Paul's use of only small sections of Jesus' teachings known from the gospels raises many questions. However, this diagram highlights the fact that it is only possible to trace the exact source of a particular passage when it occurs in more than one text. In other places, Paul could have been using Jesus tradition, but we have no way of recognizing it as such.

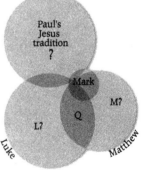

suppose that the two derive from the same source, even though Paul never actually says that he was quoting from, or alluding to the teaching of Jesus. Other parts of Paul's writings also show that traditions related to Jesus' life and teaching were familiar to the early Gentile churches (1 Corinthians 7:10–11; 11:23–26; 15:3–11).

It is therefore quite likely that long before the gospels were written in their present form the sayings of Jesus had already been collected together to form the basis of teaching for new converts in the early church. No doubt there would be a number of such collections of Jesus' teaching (generally referred to as *logia*, a Greek word meaning 'sayings'), compiled for different purposes and occasions.

In addition to these general considerations, other indications also support the belief that this would be one of the earliest types of Christian writing about Jesus:

■ There certainly were later collections of this kind, even long after the writing of the New Testament gospels. A number of papyrus fragments dating from the third century AD, found at Oxyrhynchus in Egypt, contain sayings of Jesus, some of them different from those found in the gospels, while the various Gnostic gospels also generally consist of sayings, as distinct from narratives. They were all compiled for different purposes than the New Testament gospels, and contain sayings of Jesus not found there, which might or might not be authentic. But quite apart from arguments about their genuineness, the existence of such documents shows quite clearly that the collection of sayings of Jesus was an ongoing activity in Christian circles.

■ The organization of the material in the gospels often seems to suggest that Jesus' sayings had been grouped together before they were placed in their present context. There are many groups of sayings which are only loosely linked together and do not form any kind of consecutive argument. For example, the sayings about salt in Mark 9:49–50 appear to have no intrinsic thematic connection with each other apart from the fact that they all mention salt: possibly they had already been gathered together on that basis alone before Mark incorporated them in his gospel. The same can probably be said for even quite extensive sections such as the Sermon on the Mount. Here too, there is no very obvious consecutive argument running through these chapters (Matthew 5 – 7), and it seems certain that the sermon as such was gathered together by Matthew, as the same sayings appear in quite different contexts in Luke's Gospel. No doubt the fact that these particular teachings of Jesus all deal with issues of Christian behaviour was a major reason why they were put together in this way, to provide a compendium of ethical teaching that would be easily accessible to new converts.

■ A strong reason for assuming the existence of collections of Jesus' sayings early in the church's history has been the fact that Matthew and Luke have a large amount of material that is common to both their gospels, but which is altogether absent from Mark's Gospel. This material consists almost entirely of Jesus' teachings, but it also includes the story of his baptism and temptations (Matthew 3:13 – 4:11; Luke 3:21–22; 4:1–13) and the story of one miracle, the healing of the centurion's servant (Matthew 8:5–13; Luke 7:1–10). The generally accepted explanation of this common material is that Matthew and Luke both used the same collection of Jesus' sayings and incorporated it into their respective gospels.

This sayings collection is referred to as 'Q', a convenient abbreviation of the German word *Quelle*, meaning 'source'. It is widely believed to have been a written document, whose original order has been generally preserved by Luke when he incorporated its material into his own gospel. For this reason, it has become conventional to refer to Q material by using the symbol Q followed by the chapter and verse reference from Luke. So, for example, the original Q story of the healing of the centurion's servant (as distinct from the edited versions of it contained in Matthew and Luke) might be referred to as Q 7:1–10. A few scholars argue that Q did not exist in written form, but was a looser collection of traditions existing in oral form. Its existence in some more or less fixed form is certainly credible, not least because its alleged contents are quite similar in their arrangement to the collections of prophetic oracles that we find in the Old Testament. Prophetic books generally contained predominantly the prophet's spoken messages, gathered together and edited by disciples, but supplemented by an account of the prophet's call and just one or two representative incidents from his life. The tradition called Q seems to have adopted the same literary model: an account of the baptism and temptation of Jesus (which can reasonably be equated with his call), and an illustration of the most typical of his activities (a healing miracle), but with the main emphasis on his teaching.

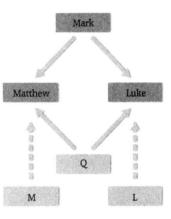

Synoptic gospels

The synoptic gospels and their sources.

From the evidence assembled so far, it may be concluded that from the very earliest times the church's main interest was in two kinds of literature: the *testimonia*, and the *logia* of Jesus. They might also have had a commonly agreed outline of the course of Jesus' life and teaching, though that is less certain. In any event, it was not long before it became necessary to gather all this material together in a more permanent form, perhaps in the first instance by the rewriting of *logia* in the light of the *testimonia*, supplemented by an outline narrative to give coherence and form to the enterprise. It is difficult to be sure for how long this process continued, but the end product was to be the four documents we now know as the gospels of Matthew, Mark, Luke and John.

Putting the gospels together

The first three gospels are referred to as the synoptics because they are so much alike: when they are set out in columns alongside one another, it is obvious that much of their material is a variation on a common theme shared by the others, though each of them is too distinctive in its emphases for the relationship between them to be understood merely as different editions of the same information. The precise way in which these three gospels are related to one another is at the centre of the 'synoptic problem'.

Many of the resemblances between these gospels could be explained by imagining that their authors had used the same collections of sayings, which had been circulating in slightly different forms among different groups of Christians, but a close examination of them shows that this would be too simplistic a solution. There are so many instances where the three synoptics use precisely the same language, vocabulary and grammatical constructions in the same contexts that the only reasonable conclusion is that they must have shared written sources.

As early as the fourth century, Augustine was proposing that Matthew must have been written first, Mark then made a summary of Matthew's work, and eventually Luke came along and wrote his gospel on the basis of both Matthew and Mark. This view was widely held until the late nineteenth century, though from time to time variations on it were proposed – most notably by J.J. Griesbach (1745–1812) who accepted Augustine's view on the priority of Matthew, but argued that Luke came next, and Mark eventually abbreviated both of them to write his own gospel.

With only a very few exceptions, no one today would accept any of that. To suppose that Matthew or Luke was the first gospel raises more questions than it answers:

■ Why would anyone have wanted to condense Matthew and Luke in order to make a gospel like Mark? Compared with the two longer gospels, Mark's short narrative can hardly be regarded as comprehensive. It has no mention at all of Jesus' birth or childhood, comparatively little about some of his most distinctive teaching, and only a very abbreviated account of the resurrection. Since the gospel writers selected their materials according to the interests and concerns of their readers, we must allow that in principle there would be no reason why an abbreviated version of Matthew and Luke should not have been produced. But given the absolute centrality of precisely those elements which are either missed out or underplayed in Mark, it is virtually impossible to envisage any Christian group that would have been satisfied with Mark's account of Jesus if they already had access to Matthew and Luke. Indeed, it was not long before Christians almost universally ignored Mark and preferred Matthew and Luke for this very reason. If Mark was written last, in full knowledge of the other two synoptic gospels, it is very difficult to explain why it was written at all.

■ Much of Mark's language seems to point to the same conclusion. If Mark used the polished accounts of Matthew and Luke, why did he so often write Greek that is virtually unintelligible? The parable of the mustard seed is a good example: Matthew and Luke are similar to each other, and both contain eloquent Greek expressed in a sophisticated style (Matthew 13:31–32; Luke 13:18–19). Mark 4:30–32, by contrast, contains a very complicated Greek sentence which is lacking any verb, and which makes imperfect sense as it is. If Mark was copying Matthew's or Luke's account, then it looks as if he went out of his way to avoid using their grammatically correct words, substituting a construction that is all but meaningless. It is very difficult to think of a good reason for doing that.

■ It is almost as difficult to believe that Luke read and used Matthew's Gospel. If he did, then here again he seems to have adopted some unexpected literary procedures. From a literary standpoint, Matthew contains one of the greatest masterpieces in any of the gospels, the Sermon on the Mount. If Luke had that before him as he wrote, why did he break it all up, using some of its content in his own Sermon on the Plain, but scattering the rest of it in small sections all over his own gospel?

There are many other examples of similar problems at other points in these three gospels, which is why most scholars have preferred a rather different explanation of their relationships to one other. The more generally accepted explanation of the resemblances between the synoptic gospels is that Matthew and Luke both used two source documents in writing their own accounts of Jesus' life and teaching. These were the sources we now know as Mark's Gospel and the hypothetical document Q. It is, of course, certain that Luke, at least, used a variety of sources in composing his gospel, for he explicitly says that he had sifted through the work of other people, selecting those parts of their record that were suitable for his own purpose in writing, and in view of its close literary connections with Mark and Luke, it seems highly likely that the author of Matthew must have used the same method in his work.

Five major considerations point to the conclusion that Matthew and Luke used Mark.

WORDING

A comparison of the words used in different texts is a very simple way of determining their literary connections. More than half of Mark's actual vocabulary is contained in Matthew and Luke, and both of them have identical sections not found in Mark. So it seems that there was one source known to them all, and another source used only by Matthew and Luke.

ORDER

If the order of events in a narrative contained in more than one gospel also corresponds with those sections that have the same wording, it is reasonable to go a step further and assume that a common source lies behind them, whose order as well as wording has been substantially reproduced by all three evangelists. Again, there is much evidence for this. Matthew, Mark and Luke all follow the same general order of events, beginning with John the Baptist's prophetic ministry, followed up by a time when Jesus taught in Galilee, all the while provoking increased opposition from the religious authorities. During this period, Jesus is shown making journeys to remote northern areas to give teaching privately to his disciples, before finally they go to Jerusalem, and Jesus' last days, his trials, crucifixion and resurrection. It is not just that the same general narrative framework appears in all three synoptics, for within this framework particular incidents are also often recorded in the same order.

This feature of the synoptic gospels is easiest to explain if Matthew and Luke were using Mark, and not the other way round. For it is striking that when Matthew departs from Mark's order, Luke has the same order as Mark; and when Luke departs from Mark's order, Matthew follows Mark (for specific examples, compare Mark 3:13–19 with Matthew 10:1–4 and Luke 6:12–16). There is only one incident which both of them place differently from Mark: the appointment of the twelve disciples. Sometimes Matthew or Luke will leave the pattern of Mark's narrative in order to add something new, but after their addition they usually return to the point in Mark at which they left off. This is one of the strongest arguments to support the conclusion that Matthew and Luke must have copied Mark, and not the other way round.

CONTENT

An analysis of the content of the narratives also reveals the use of different sources. If one writer records the same story in the same words and order as another author, then it is reasonable to suppose either that both have used the same source, or that one has used the work of the other. This is what happened in the case of the synoptic gospels: of the 661 verses in Mark, 606 are found in Matthew in a virtually identical form, and about half of them are also contained in Luke.

STYLE

This is a very difficult criterion to use satisfactorily, for an author's style can depend on so many things: the situation in which he or she is writing, the readership that is in mind, whether a secretary was used, and so on.

There certainly are some marked stylistic differences between Mark and the other two synoptists, and on the whole Mark's Gospel is written in a poorer Greek than the others. For example, he very often describes incidents in the historic present tense (using the present tense to speak of something that happened in the past). Even in the same passages, however, Matthew and Luke always have a past tense, which is, of course, the correct literary form. This argument for dependence of Matthew and Luke on Mark is not as strong as it is sometimes imagined to be, for it relies on the assumption that the evangelists would of necessity use their sources in a rather wooden way, simply copying out word for word what they had before them. In reality, not many authors would follow a source closely enough for its style to obscure their own, and if Mark was poor at writing Greek, then his grammar would tend to be poor whether or not he was copying from some other source. But other considerations all point to Matthew and Luke having used Mark, not the other way round. For example, in eight cases where Mark records sayings of Jesus in Aramaic there is no trace of this in Luke, and only one example in Matthew. It would certainly be more likely that Matthew and Luke would have omitted the Aramaic sayings than that Mark would have deliberately introduced them.

IDEAS AND THEOLOGY

If it could be shown that one gospel narrative contains a more developed theology than another, then it might seem reasonable to regard it as the later of the two. There are certainly some discernible differences of emphasis in the gospels. For example, Matthew and Luke appear to have modified or omitted certain statements in Mark that could be thought dishonouring to Jesus. The blunt statement of Mark 6:5, that in Nazareth Jesus 'could do no mighty work' appears in Matthew 13:58 as 'he did not do many mighty works there', while Luke omits it altogether. Similarly, Jesus' question in Mark 10:18, 'Why do you call me good?' appears in Matthew 19:17 as, 'Why do you ask me about what is good?'

Surely, then, the more primitive a statement, the earlier it must be? This can be made to seem like a simple test, but it is not so simple to apply in practice. It is not always easy to determine whether an apparent difference in attitude is a real one, nor is it altogether straightforward and self-evident how a particular view should be described as 'developed' as opposed to another view that is characterized as 'primitive'. Even supposing it might be possible to make such a differentiation with some degree of certainty, why should a 'developed' theology be regarded as chronologically later than a more 'primitive' outlook? Throughout the history of the church – and still today – simplistic beliefs have existed alongside more sophisticated and complex ones, and the acceptance of one or the other is more clearly related to personal choice and temperament than it is to any kind of time considerations. In terms of the first century, the theology of Paul (highly 'developed' by any standards) was certainly in existence long before the gospels were written, and there is also some evidence to indicate that there was considerable diversity of theological expression in all the major centres of Christianity at the time. Had there not been, most of the rest of the New Testament would never have been written at all! The question of theological diversity will be taken up in a later chapter; here it is simply important to note that equating theological difference with an extending timeframe is, at best, a very subjective business.

Not all these five factors are of equal importance, and it is not hard to pinpoint real or imaginary difficulties with some of them. But taken together, the cumulative effect of their evidence is most easily explained if we suppose that Matthew and Luke used Mark's account, rather than that Matthew was the original gospel which Mark summarized and from which Luke made selective extracts.

New light on old problems

Much of the emphasis in New Testament scholarship is now moving away from a mechanistic analysis of the gospels, towards a more holistic effort to understand their origins in the total context of the social

Two sources or four?

What has been said so far about the way the gospels came to be written represents the broad consensus among New Testament scholars; though there might be differences of opinion on points of detail, this solution to the synoptic problem is, in general outline, universally held by virtually everyone.

But in addition to the idea that the synoptic gospels depend mainly on the two sources Mark and Q, it has been suggested that these are not the only sources that can be discerned behind these gospels. Perhaps the classic statement of this solution to the synoptic problem (certainly in the English-speaking world) was set out by B.H. Streeter in his 1924 book, *The Four Gospels*. He not only proposed that Matthew and Luke used Mark's Gospel and Q, but suggested that in addition it was possible to trace two further sources which he called M and L. In effect this material was simply what is left of the accounts of Matthew and Luke once the Marcan and Q material has been removed, but Streeter's identification of them was important, because he believed that these two collections of material were themselves separate and coherent sources of independent origin, and therefore could be used alongside the others when it came to matters of the historicity and value of the traditions.

Streeter began his observations from the fact that Matthew and Luke each seem to have used Mark in rather different ways. Matthew followed Mark's order and general framework very closely, though at the same time he frequently rewrote the actual material, and often condensed material from Mark to make more room for additional information. The result is that Matthew's Gospel looks rather like an enlarged edition of Mark. But Luke is different, for whereas Matthew made use of almost all the material contained in Mark, Luke's Gospel contains only about half of Mark's material. What is more, Streeter discovered that if all the Marcan material is removed from Matthew, what is left has no coherence and the book simply falls to pieces. But if the same thing is done with Luke, what is left is a reasonably consistent and continuous story. This is particularly true of the stories of Jesus' death and resurrection in Luke, which seem to have a different underlying shape than the stories in Matthew and

experience of the early Christian communities. Though the two-source theory of gospel origins is still widely accepted, new angles are constantly being explored, some of which might well have a decisive influence on future understandings of the way the New Testament came to be written.

Did Q really exist?

Questions continue to be asked about the two-source hypothesis itself. Debates that seemed to have been settled in principle almost 100 years ago are now being reopened, and much of the evidence for the two-source theory is being looked at again. Was Mark really the first gospel to be written? Did Q ever exist independently as yet another 'gospel'? If so, why was it originally written, and what was its distinctive message? Is it really necessary to suppose that Q represents a fixed collection of *logia* rather than just a looser collection of traditions known by both Matthew and Luke? Several reasons have been advanced for doubting the existence of Q:

Mark, and appear to have been supplemented by information from Mark, rather than being based on Mark's story.

In the light of these observations Streeter suggested that, before Mark was written, Luke must have compiled a first draft of his gospel, based on the sayings collection Q and the material labelled L, which he had obtained from the church at Caesarea where he stayed while Paul was in prison (Acts 23:23 – 27:2). Streeter called this first draft of the gospel 'Proto-Luke'. Then, he suggested, when Luke was living in Rome at a slightly later date he got to know of Mark's Gospel, which had been written in the intervening years, and he fitted extracts from it into his own already existing Proto-Luke. At the same time, he might also have added the preface (Luke 1:1–4) and the stories of Jesus' birth in chapters one and two.

Several considerations certainly give plausibility to this theory. For example, Luke often contains a different version of a story from Mark's. The story of Jesus' rejection at Nazareth is a good example (Mark 6:1–6; Luke 4:16–30), in which it is obvious that both evangelists are reporting the same incident, but Luke's account is so much fuller that it seems likely that he

must have had a different source of information. Streeter also drew attention to the way that small sections of Mark's narrative, often in Mark's exact wording, appear to have been inserted into the middle of other material in Luke, creating the impression that they were later additions. It is also striking that a great deal of information contained in Mark is simply omitted in Luke, and Streeter argued that if Luke had known of Mark's Gospel when he first wrote his own, he would have included more of Mark's material in it.

Another feature of Luke's Gospel which Streeter's theory seemed to explain is the way in which Luke appears to have two beginnings. The preface at 1:1–4 is followed by the stories of Jesus' birth, but then the flow of the narrative is interrupted at 3:1, which reads like another beginning, with its careful dating of the opening of Jesus' ministry, followed by the list of his ancestors in 3:23–38. If 3:1 was the original beginning of Proto-Luke, to which Luke later prefaced what is now chapters 1 and 2, that could provide a credible explanation of this unusual feature.

The importance of Streeter's theory about the way Luke wrote his gospel lies

■ There is no hard evidence of its existence. In spite of the confidence with which scholars have reconstructed Q, and even claim to be able to give an account of its own literary history and development, no one has ever seen it. There is not even a fragment of any ancient manuscript of Q, nor is there a single reference to its existence anywhere in ancient literature. Nineteenth-century scholars believed that Papias was referring to Q in his statement that Matthew 'compiled the *logia* in the Hebrew language, and each one interpreted it as he could' (quoted in Eusebius, *Ecclesiastical History* III.39). But Papias used the very same word *logia* to describe the whole of Mark's Gospel, so there is no reason to imagine he was referring to a collection of the sayings of Jesus rather than the completed Gospel of Matthew – still less that Q could have been the specific sayings collection he had in mind.

■ There are no other ancient documents that look like Q. Though some Gnostic gospels (especially the *Gospel of Thomas*) provide a kind of parallel for interest in collecting sayings of Jesus, and though such interest seems inherently likely among his followers, Q is not actually like

---

Two sources or four?
continued

in the fact that if there ever was a Proto-Luke, this would form another independent and early source of knowledge of the life and teachings of Jesus. It has not, however, commanded anything like universal assent, though it continues to have its advocates. One of its major weaknesses is the assumption that Streeter made about the nature of the gospel traditions in the early churches. He assumed that the gospels were written in a neatly defined, linear way, and tended to think of the evangelists as if they had been newspaper editors, sitting down with reports from several sources and extracting various sections from different written documents. This was a popular concept in the early twentieth century, and was widely applied to the study of both Old and New Testaments, often combined with an evolutionary perspective on literary development which supposed that tradition develops from more or less primitive forms to more sophisticated ones. Subsequent research has shown that this was a considerable over-simplification of the matter, at several different levels. It could well have been, for example, that Luke was familiar with the Marcan material, but not through Mark's Gospel in its present form.

This is also a weakness in other suggestions that Streeter put forward. He argued not only that four identifiable sources can be traced behind the synoptic gospels, but that each of them represented the traditions of the life and teaching of Jesus as they had been preserved in the four most important centres of early Christianity: Mark was written in Rome, Q in Antioch, M in Jerusalem and L in Caesarea. If it could be demonstrated, this would be a neat way to understand not only the gospel traditions, but also some aspects of the life of the early Christian communities. But it was based on flawed assumptions, not least the idea that what Streeter called M and L were coherent documents. In reality, however, this is hardly the case: when the Marcan and Q material is taken away from Matthew, what is left is not a coherent collection at all, and the same is true to a lesser extent of L, which is just Luke's Gospel minus the Q and Marcan material.

Thomas in that it contains some narrative material as well. It is therefore difficult to identify a specific genre to which Q might belong. This is not a conclusive argument, as the early Christians do seem to have been remarkably creative in the way they produced their literature. For people who actually invented a new type of book (the codex) by fastening single pages down one edge, in place of the more cumbersome use of lengthy scrolls, departing from literary and stylistic norms would hardly be an adventurous move. Yet it would still be surprising that there should only be one single example of a Q-style writing, especially when we know that the early church was not embarrassed to preserve multiple diverse accounts of Jesus, as for example in the finished gospels themselves.

■ In a considerable number of passages, Matthew's and Luke's texts agree over against Mark's, in either wording or order. This can generally be explained by the assumption that, at some points, there was overlap between Mark and Q, and that Matthew and Luke preferred the fuller version generally believed to be contained in Q. However, some of these agreements of Matthew and Luke against Mark are found in the story of Jesus' death (compare, for example, Matthew 26:67–68 / Luke 22:63–64 with Mark 14:65), and since every account of the scope of the hypothetical Q has concluded that it did not contain a passion narrative, some scholars want to argue that this phenomenon can more easily be explained on the assumption that Luke used Matthew than by reference to the traditional view that both of them used Q.

■ The existence of Q has also been questioned on the basis of considerations related to the way in which ancient authors might have operated. It has been claimed that when a writer is using a source, while the information might be sharpened up and reshaped at the beginning of the day, as tiredness sinks in there will be a tendency to revert to the underlying patterns of whatever source is being used – and that in the case of the so-called Q material, such evidence always shows Luke reverting to Matthew's forms of expression. For example, in the parable of the talents (Matthew 25:14–30; Luke 19:11–27) Matthew has three servants, and Luke has ten. But as the story is told, Luke mentions 'the first', 'the second', and then 'the other' servant (19:16, 18, 20), which is easier to understand if Luke knew Matthew than if both of them were using the hypothetical Q. Those who wish to dispose of Q also argue that the very notion of gospel writers using sources in this way is a legacy from a previous generation which adopted a 'scissors and paste' approach to literature, which can no longer be sustained – and if M and L as separate written sources should be jettisoned, then so should Q.

In spite of all this, the consensus still favours the two-document hypothesis, according to which Mark was written first and Q had a more or less fixed form, in which it was used by Matthew and Luke independently. A major reason for this is that, while some of the arguments against Q carry some weight, the traditional view still seems to be more capable overall of answering more questions than the view that Luke used Matthew. Given the nature of the argument, there will always be room for disagreement on the details, but for the present at least, most scholars are still prepared to believe that the balance of probability lies in believing that Q was a real gospel source, whose existence solves more problems than it creates.

Who were the gospels for?

Ever since the rise of form criticism in the early part of the twentieth century, a major assumption on the part of scholars was that the four gospels were each written for quite specific readerships, and emerged within particular Christian communities. The reason for there being four gospels, rather than just one, has been explained in terms of the different challenges faced by Christians in different social and religious contexts, and the need for these diverse questions to be addressed using the stories and teachings of Jesus. Just as Paul and other Christian leaders

Form criticism

Once the two-source theory had been widely accepted as the most likely explanation of the 'mechanics' of gospel writing, a whole series of new questions began to present themselves. For the isolation of the various sources used by the evangelists in composing their accounts of Jesus' life and teaching only answers the question, where did the gospels come from? But there is also the further question, where did their sources come from? What was happening to the traditions about Jesus between his death and resurrection and their preservation in writing in the gospels?

These questions had occurred to a number of scholars in Germany even before B.H. Streeter had published his classic work on gospel origins – *The Four Gospels* – in 1924, and in trying to answer them, they came up with a new method of analysing the Bible literature. This was largely the creation of Hermann Gunkel (1862–1932), who began his academic career as a professor of New Testament, though his most lasting reputation has been as a scholar of the Old Testament. His interests, however, also included the study of other traditional literature, as well

as psychology and other emerging social science disciplines. He realized the Bible was not written in a cultural vacuum, and concluded it would be worthwhile to compare the way its authors worked with what was known of the way other similar writings came into being. In particular, he observed that the literature of nations and movements always develops not in a self-conscious literary way, but as a natural part of everyday life. That means the lifestyle (not to mention the temperament and disposition) of those who write and read it plays a key role in its formation. Gunkel studied literary forms in the hope of being able to reach beyond the text to see how the books had been used in real life, and in the process to shed new light on the history of the text itself. This procedure was reflected in the term he used to describe his work, *Formgeschichte*, which literally means not 'form criticism', but 'form history'.

Gunkel's application of this method to the Psalms broke new ground, and New Testament scholars soon began applying it to the gospels, most notably K.L. Schmidt, Martin Dibelius, and Rudolf Bultmann. Two well-established conclusions on the writing of the gospels seemed to make it natural to explore this new methodology:

wrote letters to inform and inspire faith in their readers, and to address their questions about lifestyle and beliefs, so the evangelists wrote their gospels for roughly the same purposes. Therefore, while their main intention might not have been to document the experiences of the various communities to which they belonged, it is nevertheless possible to discern within the nuances of the different gospels the distinctive concerns of the churches for whose use they were written. These assumptions arose from the form-critical belief that social function can be read out of the literary form of a narrative, and this in turn encouraged the development of redaction criticism as a discipline which would try to give a coherent account of the communities which produced the gospels in their final form.

This way of understanding the gospels has been questioned, on several grounds:

■ It is argued that the gospels are a different kind of literature from the New Testament epistles, and that to apply the same methodology

---

● Before the rise of critical study, the gospels had been understood as straightforward lives of Jesus, written to preserve a historical account of his deeds and words. That position had been abandoned at an early stage in critical study, to be replaced by the view that the evangelists wrote for essentially pragmatic purposes, to meet the needs of the early Christian communities. These needs mostly related to evangelization (sharing the Christian message with others), liturgy (regular worship), catechesis and paranesis (the teaching of Christians about their faith), and conflict resolution (on such topics as Christian attitudes to observance of the Jewish Law). On this understanding, the gospels were not comprehensive accounts of either Jesus' deeds or his words, but were selective recollections about him extrapolated from a much larger pool of available material – and the sole basis on which the stories about Jesus were selected and preserved was their relevance to significant questions and debates in the life of the early Christian communities. Two of the gospel writers actually said this (Luke 1:1–4; John 20:30–31;

21:25), but the full implications of that had never previously been noticed.

● Within this frame of reference, creating a continuous story of Jesus' life from start to finish was neither necessary nor appropriate. This is the sense in which it might be said that the early Christians had no particular interest in the 'historical Jesus'. To claim, as some have done, that it would have made no difference to their faith whether or not Jesus ever existed is absurd. But the evangelists were less interested in constructing a 'life of Jesus' than in saying something to demonstrate his relevance to the everyday experience of his followers. Again, Luke and John spelled this out clearly and there is no reason to suppose Matthew and Mark operated in any different way. This practical purpose had repercussions for the way the evangelists (particularly the synoptists) arranged their material in short paragraphs or sections (pericopes), with no obvious continuity of either narrative or argument running from one to the other. The apparent lack of connection from one pericope to the next is so striking that K.L. Schmidt could refer to the individual sections as 'pearls on a string'. Even where stories seem to have been gathered together in blocks prior to their inclusion in

to understanding them is a fallacy. In order to understand the epistles, it is undoubtedly necessary to have at least some knowledge of the various communities to which they were addressed, even if the epistles themselves may then be used to develop even more detailed perceptions of the concerns of those same communities. But in the case of the gospels, no such prior knowledge seems to be required.

■ The idea that the evangelists would write only for other Christians implies a parochial mentality that other evidence does not support. Roman society as a whole was remarkably mobile, and Christian leaders travelled extensively, seeing the church as a worldwide movement and encouraging the various Christian communities not to remain separate, but to communicate regularly with one another in order the more effectively to encourage one another's faith.

■ It has also been argued that the only reason why scholars would have wished to identify the gospels so closely with specific communities was

---

**Form criticism
continued**

the gospels, the basis of such collation was invariably topical rather than historical or biographical. So, for example, the material in Mark 2:1 – 3:6 consists entirely of stories about controversy, while Mark 4:35 – 5:43 is a collection of miracle stories and Matthew 5 – 7 is a block of teaching (the Sermon on the Mount). The only possible exception seems to be the story of Jesus' death, which has an internal argument and organization that might imply it was always preserved as one continuous story – though even that was probably related to apologetic concerns, namely the need to explain how a respected teacher could meet such an unexpected end.

The forms

Building on these established results of scholarship, form critics speculated that individual stories would be preserved in different 'forms', depending on their context and purpose. This 'life situation' (in German, *Sitz im Leben*) would then determine the way in which things were expressed. The term 'form' referred to features such as the length of a particular *pericope*, its structure, way of organizing material and so on. This methodology had already been well tested in relation to the

traditional folk literature of northern Europe, but form in this sense is still a familiar part of modern life. Think, for example, of the difference between a TV documentary and a game show. They might easily deal with the same subject (say, sport), but their approach is quite different. In fact, just by observing the structure of each programme, viewers can instantly distinguish between the two, without needing to know anything at all about sport. In the same way, form critics suggested it is possible to identify the context in which particular sections of the gospels had been used in the life of the early church just by looking at their form.

If this could be done reliably, it would of course be an invaluable aid to understanding the gospels, for if it were possible to know the use to which the various traditions were put in the early church, that would in turn illuminate their relevance to the church's life, and potentially reveal new dimensions of their essential meaning. Unfortunately, however, the form critics have failed to agree on this essential point, and though Martin Dibelius gave what has come to be regarded as the classic analysis of gospel forms in 1919, his five main forms have by no means been universally accepted by others.

A fragment of the Egerton papyrus (first half of the 2nd century), containing scraps of the text of a non-canonical gospel.

However, it is worth reviewing them here as they illustrate the kind of things that form criticism looks for.

Paradigms

Different scholars gave different names to these stories. Rudolf Bultmann called them 'apothegms', while Vincent Taylor more prosaically called them 'pronouncement stories'. Whatever they are called, they certainly do form a distinctive group of stories, distinguished by the way they all culminate with a punch-line. Some of them contain narrative, but the key thing is the pithy statement that comes at the end, and all other details are secondary. Several examples are found in the early chapters of Mark (see 2:1 – 3:6). This literary form was common in both Greek and Jewish literature of the time, and provided Christians with memorable slogans to describe significant aspects of their beliefs. Dibelius believed that this form originated in the earliest Christian preaching, in which such stories would be used as examples and illustrations. In addition to the use of a striking saying as the culmination of such stories, they were also characterized by their tendency to minimize pictorial description in order to focus attention on the most important element, which was the saying of Jesus. When a story is handed on orally, two things may typically happen to it. Either it can be worn down by frequent repetition, so that little remains apart from the most essential facts expressed in as succinct and striking a way as possible – or the opposite can happen, with extra details being added to make it more realistic and interesting. Most form critics regarded the paradigms as having been worn down to their bare essentials, rather than being elaborated as they were handed on.

Tales

Dibelius defined these as stories told for the sake of being a good story, and he included many (though not all) of the miracle stories in this group. Vincent Taylor actually called this form 'miracle stories'. Again, there were similar forms elsewhere in the first-century milieu, and it is not hard to imagine Christians utilizing them to highlight Jesus' own powers as a means of authenticating his message. In these stories Jesus' deeds are much more important than his words. Dibelius believed they were the work of professional storytellers in the early church, whose job was to cast stories about Jesus into the same form as the

related to a loss of confidence in them as historical sources for the life and teaching of Jesus himself. This topic is dealt with in a later chapter. But, the argument goes, if the gospels tell us little or nothing about Jesus, they must still contain information about something – and that something must therefore be the life of their own communities, presented in quasi-allegorical form through the narratives about Jesus. If such scepticism was rejected, there would be no reason to suppose that the gospels were written for other Christians in specified locations: instead, they can be understood as general literature written for the same reasons as anyone might write a book, to communicate a message to as many people as possible.

Arguments like this have caused a stir in the world of New Testament scholarship, though the idea that the evangelists saw themselves as literary artists writing for anyone who would read their books raises its own questions:

Form criticism continued

stories of the Greek gods, in order to win converts to the Christian faith by demonstrating that Jesus was superior to other deities. The New Testament never explicitly mentions storytellers in the early Christian communities – perhaps because this way of sharing faith was so common that its existence could be taken for granted. Certainly, given the general popularity of storytelling in the ancient world, not to mention the fact that Jesus' own most characteristic method of communication was in the telling of stories, it would be surprising if his followers did not self-consciously use the same approach. To suppose that the stories of Jesus were carefully crafted by professional storytellers is not to imply any particular view of the reliability of their picture of Jesus. In view of the fact that the gospels themselves were written down in something less than a generation after the events they describe, there cannot have been too much scope for the free creation of fictitious details about him. But there can equally be little doubt that the stories of the gospels have, for the most part, been carefully crafted so as to capture the imagination of those who would read or hear them.

Legends
Dibelius chose this term because of its common use (in his day) to describe traditional stories about the lives of the saints, the main point of which was typically to provide a moral example for others to follow. By using this terminology, he was not intending to make any value judgment about the historical reliability or otherwise of these stories, though he was of the opinion that they would often be fictitious. Their main function was to glorify the person they describe, rather than to report any factual information about him. Examples of this 'form' in the gospels would be Matthew 14:28–33; 16:13–23; 27:3–8; Luke 2:41–49.

Myths
For Dibelius, this term indicated stories in which a human person interacted with some other spiritual or supernatural world. He included only three gospel stories here: Jesus' baptism (Mark 1:9–11 and parallels), temptations (Matthew 4:1–11 and parallel in Luke), and transfiguration (Mark 9:2–8 and parallels).

Exhortations
By exhortations Dibelius meant teaching. There is of course a lot of teaching in the

■ The suggestion that the evangelists saw themselves as producing literature for wide circulation depends to some extent on the view that their gospels fit neatly into the category of Graeco-Roman biography – which was usually composed for general circulation. But, as we have already noticed, the gospels do not represent a pure form of this genre. They are more accurately described as religious works written with some of the style of biography than as biographical works written about a religious subject. In the case of the only two evangelists who explicitly spell out their purposes in writing, both of them quite specifically say they were writing to encourage and nurture Christians in their already-existing faith (Luke 1:1–4; John 20:31).

■ The gospels for the most part do not actually speak a language that would automatically have been accessible to any readers who cared to pick them up. They assume a community of common understanding, whose ways of expressing things was in many respects very different from the wider Hellenistic world. For example, the extensive use of the

---

gospels, and there are very many diverse forms of it. But since he believed it was all used in the same context in the life of the church (i.e. the instruction of converts) Dibelius lumped it all together. The parables would obviously belong here, along with other sayings.

Criticisms of form criticism

Throughout the twentieth century, the methodology as well as the conclusions of form criticism have been subjected to extensive appraisal. In the process, the method has been refined to meet some of the objections. The following are the main points of debate:

● Some have questioned the appropriateness of the entire method. They point out that the early development of form criticism owed a great deal to theories about the compilation of north European folklore, which was not only separated by time and distance from the biblical writings, but also originated in a very different cultural context which was arguably alien to the Semitic mindset. How relevant is it to extrapolate principles and theories from one culture and apply them to another at a different period of history? Rudolf Bultmann addressed this concern by drawing attention to what he considered

parallels to New Testament 'forms' in the works of Jewish rabbis – but virtually all his examples suffered from the same weakness, dating from a time much later than the New Testament. However, subsequent research has shown that the concept of literary forms was indeed known in Hellenistic writing both before and after the first century, and though some earlier claims might have been exaggerated, the general models provided by form criticism are still of value, provided their limitations are recognized.

● Even supposing that forms were a common device, have form critics sometimes been over-enthusiastic in their assumption that the biblical writers were so consistently and exclusively influenced by convention and custom in the way they spoke and wrote that a particular genre (or *Gattung*, the German term) always had the same terminology, style and *Sitz im Leben*? While this is in general a safe assumption, form criticism did not always make enough allowance for the distinctive and particular. In reality, passages that clearly share the same general form often also show considerable variation in detail, and by emphasizing the common elements it is all too easy to miss the distinctive intention of particular speakers or writers. One of the

Hebrew scriptures, not only in general terms but through the citation of specific quotations, presupposes some prior knowledge on the part of readers. The many nuances in the descriptions of Jesus, in which he can be compared to Old Testament characters, not to mention the use of technical terms, all implies an original readership with some knowledge of such matters. When, as in John's Gospel, the Jewish background is explained, it is done in a self-conscious way that implies it was not normally necessary – and, indeed, in the case of John was quite likely done at a time when the gospel was being reissued for somewhat wider circulation than it had originally enjoyed.

■ Though it was a worldwide network, with many of its leaders travelling regularly around the churches, who must therefore have known of each other's existence, the early church was also a threatened minority group. In such circumstances, the preservation of the story of its own origins for its own internal support would have been a perfectly natural thing to do. With the likely exception of Luke, at least one

---

Form criticism continued

few things that all sources seem to testify to is Jesus' difference from other teachers, not his similarity to them.

● Form and content cannot be separated as easily as some form critics have supposed, and to concentrate on form alone can be misleading. In theory, once the 'pure' version of a form has been identified (by, for example, comparative study of Greek, Latin or Jewish literature), it should then be possible to check the extent to which any particular New Testament example departs from it, and thereby to identify some of the distinctive aspects of the New Testament's message. In practice, it is not at all easy to identify such pure forms. Dibelius and Bultmann both argued strongly in favour of using pure forms as the starting point, but in practice their categories were often not based on form at all, but on content. Dibelius' legends, myths and exhortations were all classifications of content, not of form, and it is arguable that tales were as well (they are all miracle stories, though in this case the content does seem to be accompanied by a distinctive form). The only category which was unambiguously based on literary form was the paradigm. To take account of the obvious diversity of forms found in the New Testament,

scholars today operate with a much more elastic definition of forms than Dibelius or Bultmann. But this raises a different set of problems, because the more flexibility there is, the less useful the whole analysis of forms becomes.

● Form criticism has sometimes become a circular and self-validating form of study. A scholar's prior understanding of how forms develop does affect exegetical judgments on particular passages. Dibelius and Bultmann believed that over time the forms became more complex, while Taylor argued the exact opposite – that the stories and teachings were worn down with much repetition so that what is left now is the bare essentials. To see the difference these different assumptions can make, we might think of study of the parables. It has generally been assumed that the parables all follow one form, and only ever make one single point. If so, it is a foregone conclusion that any additional points or 'explanations' of a parable's meaning must be later additions to the text. But if there was diversity in the forms, or if the evangelists were creative writers and not merely collectors of traditions, then this understanding would be at least questioned, and might be undermined completely. Self-validating arguments like

purpose of the gospels was to provide reassurance and support to groups who were either suffering persecution or were feeling threatened in some way by others, and who would value the specific support that could be given to them by the writing of their own gospel, which would show how their particular predicament was rooted in the origins of their group, and might be addressed by resources drawn from the experience of their founder, Jesus himself.

No doubt the gospels, like other Christian literature, did circulate among communities other than those for whom they were first compiled. There is evidence for the exchange of epistles, though only within local areas (Colossians 4:16), and it was not until nearer the end of the first century that wider collections of Christian writings were made. Of course, if the two-source theory of the origins of the synoptic gospels is correct, it also assumes that the evangelists had access to the writings of other people. But it is important to remember that though travel in the Roman empire

---

this are not intrinsically without value: the formulation and testing of a hypothesis is a proven procedure in many fields of research. But the constant challenging of the hypothesis is important, and this is what has often been lacking in New Testament study. In its original version, form criticism depended on the accuracy of Schmidt's notion that the evangelists were only stringing pearls together. Redaction criticism has now shown that the string is at least as significant as the pearls, and that needs to modify the method.

● Form criticism has also been criticized for paying too little attention to other kinds of evidence, notably historical commentary. For example, it was too easy to move from the observation that exhortations were preserved in a catechetical context in the early church, to the conclusion that much . of the teaching of Jesus was invented by early Christians to answer their own ethical or theological questions. Ernst Käsemann went as far as to comment that form criticism 'was designed to show that the message of Jesus as given to us by the synoptists is, for the most part, not authentic, but was minted by the faith of the primitive Christian community in its various stages.' Moreover, it is not as easy as it seems to identify particular forms

with specific life contexts. Klaus Berger has questioned whether life settings do actually give rise to literary forms, and insists that it is rarely possible to correlate individual *pericopes* with particular life situations. Even granting that such an enterprise is possible, how can we be sure that we have identified the most useful parallels? For example, what assurance can there be that stories of Jesus' miracles had the same function as Hellenistic stories of divine wonder workers that share the same literary form? How do we know that the forms of the Jewish world operated in the same way – particularly given the traditional Jewish concern for the accurate transmission of the teachings of the rabbis? In the hands of Birger Gerhardsson, this Jewish concern for accuracy in preserving the teaching of rabbis became a powerful reason for rejecting form criticism altogether. He clearly overstated his case: the mere fact that the early church preserved four different gospels shows that they were able to live happily with some diversity in the traditions about Jesus. The form-critical quest is still worth following, but with greater sensitivity to the nuances of the cultural context than has been the case in the past.

was relatively easy, it would still only be the upper classes who were easily mobile, and that itself is probably sufficient to explain how Matthew or Luke could have laid hands on Mark's work or the hypothetical Q. The majority of Christians were unlikely to have been literate, and when they discovered the stories of the gospels, it would be as they heard them read out in their own church community. If others beyond the churches learned these stories, most of them would do so by being introduced to such reading and storytelling sessions by their Christian friends in the places where they lived, which itself underlines the likelihood that, as the stories developed, they would be told in ways that had direct local relevance.

Study of the gospels does not stand still for long. The assured results of one generation are constantly being probed and questioned, if not abandoned, by those who come after them. Whether today's questions will continue to be as important as they seem to be right now, remains to be seen. No doubt new questions will present themselves, many of

---

**Form criticism
continued**

The value of form criticism
● At the time of its development, form criticism was a corrective to the findings and attitudes of historical and literary criticism. There were some questions that these methods had been unable to address. They could not construct a literary history of the New Testament, nor were they able adequately to understand all the diverse contours of New Testament faith. The picture painted by historical and literary criticism turned out to be too simple and unilinear, partly because it studied the early church in isolation from its wider cultural and religious context, and partly because it tended to impose a rigid evolutionary framework in which theological ideas could only develop in one direction, from simple to complex. Form criticism at least identified the right questions that would give access to the pre-literary period of the gospels, even though it now seems that time might have been much shorter than was once imagined.
● Form criticism highlighted the fact that serious study must begin with understanding the kind of literature we are reading, the literary category to which it belongs, and its characteristic features. This is particularly important when we recall that Jesus was operating in a cultural context with its own long literary history and traditions.
● Form criticism set out to discover the function of literary genre in the life of the community or the individual, how and when it was used and for what purpose. This is one of its features that is both a weakness and a strength. There will certainly always be room for legitimate disagreement on this, as it is inevitably a circular argument to use our present understandings of the forms to determine the needs that existed in the churches, and then to use these needs as a way of understanding and interpreting the forms. But as long as we remember such conclusions are tentative, there is nothing wrong with this. In any case, the rest of the New Testament gives at least some glimpses into what was going on in the early church, and can be used as a check.

Those who want to reject form criticism out of hand are being too extreme. On the other hand, if form criticism is applied as if it were the only possible way to understand the gospels, then it can lead to unreliable – even absurd – conclusions. Past generations have sometimes made that mistake, and it is not for nothing that

them of a different kind from those asked by earlier generations. One of the major shifts during the course of the twentieth century was a recognition that, wherever the evangelists obtained their own information, each of them has written what is essentially an original composition, distinctive in important respects from the work of any of the others. Much of the interest is now focused on what the evangelists were doing, rather than on revealing the mechanics of how they were doing it. As a result, theological insights need to be used to supplement the earlier findings of the literary critics.

---

more recent scholars have supplemented it with redaction criticism, rhetorical criticism, and other reader-oriented methods of understanding texts. No one method by itself can possibly answer all our questions in relation to the writing of the gospels. But that is not a reason for rejecting it outright. Form criticism is an important part of the jigsaw – but it is the whole picture that is ultimately significant, not merely the individual pieces. When combined with other methods of investigation, form criticism's positive outcomes far outweigh whatever weaknesses it might have. Understanding just how a form is being used and reshaped gives important clues to a writer's purpose – but a satisfactory analysis and evaluation of those clues will only emerge out of a more comprehensive investigation, in which form criticism is just one of several possible methods that must be used.

21 Four Portraits of Jesus

Mark

Mark's Gospel is considered first because it is now recognized as a basic source for the other two synoptic gospels. It is, however, only in fairly recent times that Mark has received careful attention. It was generally neglected by the church in earlier centuries, in favour of the longer accounts of Matthew and Luke. This is hardly surprising, for they contain most of Mark's information and a lot more as well, and so Mark soon came to be regarded as an abbreviated version of Matthew. But the situation has now changed and, with the knowledge that Mark's Gospel was almost certainly the first to be written, it has achieved an eminence it has probably never enjoyed since the time of its first compilation.

Ancient evidence

There is, however, some evidence to show that it was valued in certain Christian circles not long after its composition. Papias (c. AD60–130) identified Mark as 'Peter's interpreter', and reported that 'he wrote down accurately, but not in order, as much as he could remember of the things said and done by Christ' (quoted in Eusebius, *Ecclesiastical History* III.39.15). Irenaeus (*Against Heresies* I.1.1) and Clement of Alexandria (in Eusebius, *Ecclesiastical History* VI.14.6ff) also associated Mark's Gospel with Peter's preaching, and in more recent times the contents of the gospel have often been thought to support the belief that Peter was the source of much of it.

A number of stories are told with such vivid details that it is natural to regard them as first-hand accounts of the events they describe. The story of Peter's call (1:14–20) and of Jesus' first sabbath in Capernaum, when Peter's mother-in-law was healed (1:29–34), are good examples of this. In addition, some of the references to the disciples, and to Peter in particular, are highly unfavourable. The disciples are consistently portrayed as ignorant and obtuse, repeatedly failing to understand what Jesus was trying to teach them (4:35–41; 5:25–34; 6:37–38; 8:14–21, 31–33; 9:2–6, 32; 10:35–45). In Mark's Gospel the disciples are not at all the kind of people the later church liked to think they were, and it is unlikely that they would have been depicted in such an unfavourable light had Mark not had good information, perhaps coming from Peter himself, to support such a picture.

The author

Mark, or Marcus, was a very common name, and he could have been anybody. In considering matters of authorship, our starting point has to be the fact that none of the gospels actually names its writer. John's Gospel comes nearest to doing so, but even then it is only an enigmatic reference to a witness to the crucifixion (John 19:35), and though this person is often identified with the 'beloved disciple', it is far from clear who that might have been. In this respect the gospels are quite different from most of the rest of the New Testament, for they are presented as anonymous writings. The traditional ascriptions to Matthew, Mark, Luke and John were of course added at an early stage, but they represent the opinions of the early church about the authors of the gospels, rather than any sort of claim by the authors themselves.

It is clear from the evidence that the author of the second gospel was generally associated by the early church with a person called John Mark who is known from other parts of the New Testament (Acts 12:12). According to Acts, a group of Christians regularly met in his mother's house in Jerusalem, and John Mark himself is named as the companion of Paul and Barnabas in their earliest missionary work (Acts 12:25; 15:37–41). Though Mark deserted them, Paul mentions him favourably in two of his later letters (Colossians 4:10; Philemon 24), so they must have patched up their differences. He is also spoken of with affection in 1 Peter 5:13 and that (depending on one's view of the authorship of 1 Peter) may be taken as evidence for associating him with Peter as well as with Paul.

It is more difficult to be certain that this same Mark was actually the author of the gospel, though in view of the tendency of second-century Christians to associate books of the New Testament with key figures in the early church, it might well be that the tradition connecting Mark with the second gospel is not altogether untrustworthy. John Mark was a comparatively insignificant person, and not the kind of individual who would be credited with writing a gospel unless there was good reason to believe that he did in fact do so.

The readers

It is generally thought that Mark's Gospel was written in Rome, to serve the needs of the church there. Irenaeus and Clement of Alexandria disagree on the precise circumstances of its composition, but both agree it was written in Rome. If the author of the gospel was indeed John Mark, then references to him in the New Testament also place him in Rome.

The gospel was certainly written for a non-Jewish readership. Aramaic phrases such as *talitha, koum* or *ephphatha* are translated into Greek for the benefit of Mark's readers (5:41; 7:34). Jewish customs are also explained in a way that suggests they were unfamiliar (7:3–4). There are also a number of Latin technical terms in Mark, which suggests that the gospel originated in a part of the Roman empire where Latin was spoken (4:21; 12:42; 14:65; 15:19). In view of all these pieces of evidence Rome certainly seems to be a plausible place of composition.

The date

Dating the gospel, however, is not so easy, for a number of reasons:

■ The evidence of the church fathers is contradictory. Clement of Alexandria says that Mark wrote the gospel under Peter's dictation, and that the final draft of it was approved by Peter himself. But Irenaeus

places the writing of the gospel after the deaths of both Peter and Paul. This means that we have to try to decide from the evidence of the gospel itself when it might have been written, which is no easy task.

■ It is often thought that the many references to trials and persecutions in Mark suggest that his readers were suffering for their faith in Christ (8:34–38; 10:33–34, 45; 13:8–13). If this is so, it could date the gospel somewhere between AD60 and 70, during which period Nero tried to blame the Christians for problems in the city of Rome. But of course, persecution was such a common feature of church life in the first century that it is not essential to connect Mark's Gospel with one of the more well-known persecutions. There must have been many local persecutions that have left little trace in literary sources, though they would be real enough to those who had to suffer them.

■ Then there is the question of whether the apocalyptic section in Mark 13:1–37 presupposes that Jerusalem had already fallen to the Romans when it was written. Since this took place in AD70, an answer to this question would at least date the gospel on one side or the other of that event. Here again opinion is divided, though a majority of scholars place the gospel's composition between AD60 and 70, or even a little later.

Peter dictating the gospel to Mark. From an 11th-century Italian ivory relief.

Mark's purpose in writing

Mark's intention in writing is revealed in the key themes which appear in his gospel:

■ If, as the early traditions suggest, this gospel had some connection with Peter, one reason for its composition could well have been the desire to preserve Peter's reminiscences as a lasting testimony for the church. This would be especially easy to understand if Mark wrote at a time immediately preceding, or just after, Peter's death. To this extent,

Mark probably did have some kind of biographical purpose in view. The theme of persecution also features in several passages relating to the nature of discipleship. The disciples and their faith, or lack of it, form a significant literary motif in the structure of Mark's narrative. Stories about them are used to introduce new aspects of Jesus' ministry in the main section of the gospel (1:16–20; 3:13–19; 6:7–13), and in the second half of the narrative the disciples are the focus of continual attention, playing a key role even in the final enigmatic paragraph of the entire gospel (16:7–8).

■ The failure of the disciples to appreciate that following Jesus would involve suffering is related to the way Mark presents Jesus as Messiah. The opening sentence confirms the importance of messiahship for Mark's presentation of Jesus (1:1), and this theme is expounded in different ways throughout, sometimes in association with the title 'Son of God' (1:1; 1:11; 3:11; 5:7; 15:39), while at other times the 'Son of man' terminology is more prominent (occurring no fewer than thirteen times between 8:31 and 14:62). Mark's understanding of Jesus' divine significance ('Christology') is always related to the themes of suffering and the cross: ultimately, it is through the cross that Jesus' true nature as Messiah is revealed.

■ Alongside the elevated descriptions of Jesus as Messiah, Son of God, and Son of man, Mark also presents Jesus as a very human figure: he can be angry on occasions (1:43; 3:5; 8:12; 8:33; 10:14); he is unable to perform miracles if the appropriate conditions of faith are absent (6:1–6); and he suffers physically in a way that might be thought incompatible with his position as the Son of God (8:31–33; 9:31). At one time these things were thought to be signs of Mark's 'primitive' theology, though that is not the only possible explanation. A better one might be to place it in the context of first-century debates about what it meant for Jesus to be regarded as both human and divine. Under the influence of a metaphysical dualism inherited from Greek philosophy, many Christians struggled to understand how God (a spiritual being) could have any contact at all with this material world, and resolved their problem by supposing that the divine Christ-spirit only entered the human Jesus at his baptism, and left him again before the crucifixion. Such people came to be known as Docetists, because they held that Jesus only seemed to be human (from the Greek verb *dokeo*, 'to seem'). The writer of 1 John was certainly concerned to correct such people, and John's Gospel might have been as well. But Mark could also have been intended as a corrective to this idea: in response to those who were asserting that Jesus' humanity was illusory, Mark emphasized its reality by depicting him as the divine Messiah whose origin and significance was both hidden and revealed in the life of a truly human person.

Mark's ending

The best ancient manuscripts have Mark ending at what is now designated 16:8, which appears to be part-way through a sentence, and

therefore an odd way to conclude a book. There is no evidence that Mark's narrative was originally longer, though there have been suggestions that the final page was torn off at an early stage and lost, which would explain the efforts of later writers to make good the omission by adding either what is now known as the 'longer ending' of 16:9–20, or a somewhat shorter one which is indicated in the footnotes of most Bible versions. Mark 16:8 is certainly a dramatic and unexpected ending, especially since it means there are no resurrection stories in Mark, and indeed the resurrection is only hinted at in the most general way possible. This certainly cannot have been because Mark did not either believe or expect a final glorification of the crucified Jesus, for there are several passages elsewhere which point forward to precisely such an outcome for his ministry (9:2–8; 13:26–37; 14:62). It might be that the explanation is to be found in the secrecy motif that pervades Mark's narrative, alongside the many stories that show the disciples failing to comprehend the full meaning of all that Jesus was saying, though some have argued that Mark was influenced by the classic structure of Greek tragedy, and this conclusion was intended to be a particularly striking form of the *denouement* that regularly ended such literature, after catastrophe had befallen the hero.

Was Mark influenced in writing his gospel by the classic structure of Greek tragedy? The scene shown on this vase is from the tragedy *Choephoroi* by Aeschylus.

Luke

Traditions associating the third gospel with a person called Luke date from as early as the second century. The Muratorian Canon and the anti-Marcionite Prologue to Luke, as well as Irenaeus, Clement of Alexandria, Origen and Tertullian, all identify Luke as its author. The exact value of these traditions is, however, uncertain, since most of what they contain could just as easily have been deduced from the New Testament itself, and so they are not necessarily of any independent worth. The evidence of the New Testament is in fact more useful in identifying the author.

■ A distinctive feature of Luke's Gospel is that it is not complete in itself: it is the first volume of the two-volume history of early Christianity which is continued in the Acts of the Apostles. The style and language of these two books is so similar that there can be no doubt they were both the product of one writer. Both are addressed to the same person, whose name is given as Theophilus (Luke 1:1–4; Acts 1:1).

■ In Acts there are certain passages known as the 'we passages'. They are given this name because at these points the narrative changes from using 'they' and 'he' to the pronoun 'we' (Acts 16:10–17; 20:5–15; 21:1–18; 27:1 – 28:16). Though it is never clearly stated who the 'we' are, the use of this pronoun clearly implies that the writer was present on these occasions, and therefore was a companion of Paul. Since the style of these passages is the same as that of the book as a whole, it seems likely that the author has used his own travel diary as a source of information, and a careful scrutiny of the narratives shows that Luke is the person who best fits the evidence.

■ This Luke is identified as a doctor by Paul, and it has occasionally been proposed that the author of Luke and Acts displays a particular interest in the diagnosis of illness – though it is likely that the limited medical terminology used would be familiar to any intelligent person in the Roman world. But there are one or two points in the gospel at which Luke seems to show himself to be more sympathetic than Mark to the work of doctors. This comes out very noticeably in the story of how Jesus healed a woman with an incurable haemorrhage. Mark 5:26 records that she had been treated by many doctors, and then comments, somewhat cynically, 'She had spent all her money, but instead of getting better she got worse all the time,' while Luke 8:43, on the other hand, simply comments that 'no one had been able to cure her'.

Part of a collection of instruments used by a Roman doctor.

Luke is mentioned three times in the New Testament. On each occasion he is said to be a companion of Paul, and in Colossians 4:14 Paul says that he was not a Jew (see also Philemon 24; 2 Timothy 4:11). That would probably make him the only Gentile writer of the New Testament. The Greek style of Luke–Acts certainly suggests that their author could have been a native Greek speaker.

According to Eusebius (*Ecclesiastical History* II.4.6) Luke came from Antioch in Syria, and one ancient manuscript of Acts 11:28 implies that he was in Antioch when the church there received news of the impending famine. But the generally accepted text of Acts has Luke join Paul when he entered Europe for the first time. He also accompanied Paul on his final journey to Jerusalem, and then on to Rome itself. According to Streeter and others, Luke might have collected some material for his gospel during this period from the church at Caesarea – though his final version of it might well have been written in Rome.

The date

It is not possible to be certain of the exact date when Luke finished his gospel. Since he incorporated in his own account some material from Mark, he must have written the final draft of his own book after Mark's

Gospel was written and in circulation, so the date given to Luke will depend to some extent on the date we assign to Mark. It has been suggested that Luke 21:5–24 displays a knowledge of the fall of Jerusalem to the Romans in AD70, and if so the finished gospel would need to be dated sometime after that.

Luke's purpose in writing

Why did Luke write his gospel? There has been extensive discussion of this, in relation to Luke in particular, and some key themes can be identified:

■ Luke articulates his purpose in the prologue to the gospel (1:1–4), where he indicates that he was writing for a person called Theophilus, 'so that you will know the full truth about everything which you have been taught'. Moreover, he states that he undertook this work in a consciously literary manner, studying the accounts written by other people, and then on that basis compiling what he describes as 'an orderly account'. While Luke was not solely motivated by biographical concerns, he emphasizes his concern for historical record more clearly than any of the other evangelists.

■ Partly arising from this, Luke continually emphasizes that the events he describes are part of a much larger divine plan for the whole of history. The notion that God has a plan is repeated many times (1:14–17, 31–35, 46–55, 68–79; 2:9–14, 30–35; 4:16–30; 13:31–35; 24:44–49, and in many other places). Luke makes explicit connections between his story of Jesus and the history of Judaism, and goes out of his way to demonstrate the continuity of Christianity with the Old Testament, while also insisting that Jesus was the fulfilment of all God's promises, and so the old ways had been superseded. Right from the outset, he makes it clear that those who follow Jesus do not first need to become Jews in order to be Christians, but that Jesus had come to be 'a light... to the Gentiles' (2:32). By the time Luke was writing, there were many more Gentile Christians than Jewish ones, and the relationship of Judaism and Christianity had become a significant issue. Luke portrays them both as part of a much bigger picture: in his account, the story of salvation (often referred to by the German term *Heilsgeschichte*) spans the whole of time, though the life, death and resurrection of Jesus is presented as the mid-point of all time: the event to which the Old Testament was pointing forward, and from which all subsequent human life could take its meaning (2:11; 4:21; 5:26; 13:32–33; 23:42–43).

Luke used this observation to bridge the gap between the events of Jesus' life and the concerns of the Christians for whom he was writing. He stressed this connection especially by his emphasis on the role of the Holy Spirit as a key player in the entire drama of salvation. The Spirit features at significant points in the story (1:35; 3:15–18, 21–22; 4:1, 14, 16–18), and by underlining the way in which the Spirit operated both in the life of Jesus and in the ongoing life of the Christian community

(24:49), Luke links together the two volumes of his writings, and in the process assures his readers that though Jesus the Messiah might seem to be dead, and therefore absent from the scene, he is very much present through the continuing work of the Spirit. It might be that Luke emphasized the continuing presence of Jesus with his followers as a corrective to some of his contemporaries who were becoming impatient because the second coming of Jesus, the *parousia*, had not yet taken place. He reminded them that although his final appearance in glory is yet in the future, Jesus is with his people in a real way through the presence of the Holy Spirit in their lives.

■ Another notable feature of Luke's Gospel is its emphasis on the nature of the community that was established by Jesus, and continued through to his own day. In particular, he stresses the inclusive nature of that community of disciples: the Christian message is for everyone. In recounting the story of the infant Jesus, Luke included the statement that he was to be 'a light to reveal God's will to the Gentiles' (2:32). In tracing Jesus' ancestry, Luke 3:23–38 went back to Adam, the common ancestor of all, in contrast to Matthew 1:1–17, which traced it back only to Abraham, the forebear of the Jewish race. In Luke's account of the sermon in the synagogue at Nazareth, Jesus' message was concerned with the Gentiles (4:16–30), and Luke also tells of Jesus' special interest in the Samaritans, whom the Jews hated even more than the Romans. Throughout this gospel Jesus is characteristically presented as the friend of the outcasts of society (9:51–56; 10:25–37; 17:11–19). These are the people whom God is happy to welcome, an attitude that is also recommended to Jesus' followers. The happiness of being a Christian is emphasized over and over again. Luke's account begins with the angels telling 'glad tidings of great joy' (2:10), and ends with the disciples returning to Jerusalem after the ascension 'with great joy' (24:52). In between these events, many of the most appealing of Jesus' parables end on the same note of happiness. The parables about lost things (15:1–32), and many others, emphasize the joy that is given to Jesus' disciples, while at the same time encouraging them to show the same openness to others as God had shown to them when they were themselves outside the kingdom.

Matthew

Matthew's Gospel is very different from either Mark or Luke, and there are a number of special characteristics that need to be considered before we can say anything about its origin, date or authorship.

The structure of the gospel

The one thing that is immediately obvious about Matthew's Gospel is that it is much more carefully crafted as a piece of literature than either of the other two synoptics. Its structure presents a very well-organized arrangement of the material, which is generally set out in topics. That much is agreed by all interpreters. However, there is nothing like a consensus on what the structure might be, or even on the actual nature of the topics which are used to give it shape. Several suggestions have been put forward.

One particularly popular way of understanding Matthew's structure was proposed in the early part of the twentieth century by B.W. Bacon, who identified a series of five blocks or 'books' of material, arranged between the prologue of the birth stories and the epilogue of the passion narrative. Each of these sections of the gospel concludes with the statement that 'when Jesus had finished these things...', and they were characterized by a well-balanced combination of narrative and teaching material which Bacon suggested was intended to present Jesus as the new Moses, with the five central sections corresponding to the five books of the Law in the Old Testament (ascribed to Moses in Jewish tradition). On this understanding, the structure of the gospel would be as follows:

Introduction	1:1 – 2:23
Book 1 The new law: following Jesus	3:1 – 7:29
Narrative (Galilean ministry)	3:1 – 4:25
Teaching (Sermon on the Mount)	5:1 – 7:29
Book 2 Discipleship and Christian leaders	8:1 – 11:1
Narrative	8:1 – 9:34
Teaching	9:35 – 11:1
Book 3 The revelation of the kingdom	11:2 – 13:53
Narrative	11:2 – 12:50
Teaching (parables)	13:1–52
Book 4 The church and its administration	13:54 – 19:1a
Narrative	13:53 – 17:27
Teaching (order, discipline, worship)	18:1 –19:1a
Book 5 Judgment	19:1b – 26:2
Narrative (controversies in Jerusalem)	19:1b – 22:46
Teaching (judgment on the Pharisees, apocalyptic teachings)	23:1 – 26:2
Conclusion	26:3 – 28:20

The main weakness with this proposal is that the story of Jesus' death and resurrection does not feature as a central part of the gospel's message, and appears only as a concluding postscript, as it were, to the major part of the book. The idea also failed to convince others because, though it does correspond to what appear to be natural divisions in Matthew's work, there is no compelling reason for adopting it other than the fact that it is possible to find a plausible understanding of the gospel on this basis. Nowhere does Matthew say that Jesus is the 'second

Moses', nor do the individual sections of the gospel correspond in any very exact way to the five books of the Pentateuch: arguably the only thing common to both is the number five.

Others have made different suggestions, pointing out that if the gospel is analysed not on the basis of literary style, but of content, quite different conclusions may be reached. By using the statements of 4:17 and 16:21 ('From that time on, Jesus began to...') as structural markers, it has been suggested that Matthew has not five divisions, but only three. J.D. Kingsbury accordingly proposes that Matthew's main concern was to show how Jesus was God's Son and Messiah, and that the gospel is arranged topically around this theme as follows:

■ The person of Jesus as Messiah and Son of God (1:1 – 4:16).
■ The proclamation of Jesus' messiahship (4:17 – 16:20).
■ The suffering, death and resurrection of the Messiah and Son of God (16:21 – 28:20).

This has the advantage of understanding the passion narratives as a central element in Matthew's Gospel, though it is open to question whether the statements in 4:17 and 16:21 are intended to bear the structural weight thereby placed upon them, while there is also the fact that they are not specifically unique to Matthew, for both of them are taken over from the Marcan account. In the absence of other evidence that Matthew accorded them particular significance, it does not necessarily follow that they reflect a particular Matthean emphasis, as opposed to just being a part of the tradition that Matthew inherited.

A number of more speculative attempts have also been made to explain the structure of the gospel by means of Jewish lectionaries, or various linguistic and mathematical formulas. It is of course true that the gospel's teaching is often grouped in series of threes and sevens, but this might have been intended as an aid to Christians who wished to memorize Jesus' sayings, rather than as a cryptic clue to the organization of its material.

Matthew's purpose in writing

While the exact nuances of Matthew's structural procedures might be elusive, there are several clear and unequivocal emphases that are distinctive to this gospel.

■ When compared with the other gospels, Matthew has a clear orientation towards the Old Testament and its relationship with the Christian message. This is of course true in general terms of just about the whole of the New Testament. But Matthew presents the life and teaching of Jesus as the fulfilment of the ancient promises made to Israel, not just in the general sense that Jesus is 'the son of David', but with extensive and specific reference to Old Testament texts. It seems that Matthew wanted to assert that Jesus had fulfilled in his experience all that happened to the nation of Israel, and to prove it he often quotes scriptural passages in ways that can seem to stretch credulity. For example, when Matthew reports Jesus' return from Egypt to his homeland as a baby, he quotes Hosea's statement about the exodus of Israel from Egypt: 'Out of Egypt have I called my son' (2:15; see Hosea 11:1). The methodology whereby the Old Testament is being used might be unclear (in fact, it reflects typical Jewish exegetical practices of the time), but the message is clear: everything that was central in the relationship of God with the people of Israel has now found its true and final expression in the life of Jesus.

■ It is therefore rather surprising to find that alongside this strong Jewish interest there is a great emphasis on the universality of the Christian message. The faults of Judaism are not passed over in silence. Indeed Matthew contains the most scathing criticisms of the Pharisees found in any gospel (23:1–36), while there are other passages indicating that Israel's day as God's people has now passed (8:10–12; 21:43). But this is all balanced by a striking emphasis on the missionary work of the church. This becomes most explicit in the great missionary commission given by Jesus to his disciples in 28:16–20, but it is implied from the very beginning, in the story of eastern rulers travelling to pay homage to the infant Jesus (2:1–12).

■ There is also a distinctive interest in eschatology here, and the teaching on this subject in Matthew 24 and 25 is considerably fuller than the corresponding sections of the other synoptic gospels. Matthew has a number of parables on the subjects of the second coming and last judgment that are not found elsewhere, most of them concerned to encourage Christians to live in a state of constant readiness for Jesus' return, because 'you do not know the day or the hour' (25:13). Perhaps some of Matthew's readers were beginning to doubt that Jesus would return, and for them parables like that of the ten bridesmaids would emphasize that such an attitude could lead to even those who thought they were disciples being unexpectedly excluded from the kingdom.

■ Another striking characteristic of Matthew's Gospel is its concern with Christian community and discipleship. It is the only gospel where the actual word church (Greek *ekklesia*) occurs (16:18; 18:17), and this fact alone probably contains the clue to the purpose of the whole gospel.

Matthew was making a collection of Jesus' teachings in a form that could be directly utilized in the ongoing life of the church. It was a compendium of authoritative advice for both new converts and older believers as they tried to put their Christian faith into practice in their everyday lives. It undoubtedly succeeded in this last aim, for it was not very long before Matthew's Gospel was the most widely used and respected. It contained Jesus' teaching in a form that could easily be understood by new converts, and would provide the basis of their instruction in the Christian faith. It also demonstrated the continuity between Jesus and the Old Testament in a very direct way, and so could be a useful handbook for dealing with questions raised by enquiring Jews, as well as helping Christians from a Jewish background to integrate their new faith with their heritage. Though it is not the longest of the gospels, it had the added advantage of being the most comprehensive of the synoptics: since it contained almost all of Mark, and much of Luke, its position as the most important gospel was soon assured in the early church.

The author

There is no widespread agreement on who wrote the gospel, and when. Many scholars today find no difficulty in accepting the early Christian traditions that identify Mark and Luke with the other two synoptics, but with Matthew the position is rather different. For the Matthew whose name was associated with this gospel by later church leaders was a disciple of Jesus, and therefore an eyewitness of the events described. It is not easy to see why one of the twelve disciples should have relied so heavily on Mark's Gospel, which was written by someone who was not a witness of the events of Jesus' life, especially when Matthew's own call to discipleship is told in 9:9–13 in a version that is largely copied from Mark 2:13–17. Other arguments against Matthean authorship are less substantial. For example, it has been claimed that, as someone obviously steeped in Jewish ways, Matthew would not have known enough Greek to compose such an impressive work in that language. But he was a tax collector, and therefore a close partner with the Romans – and in any case Greek was much more widely known and spoken even in Palestine than was at one time thought likely. Others have proposed that Matthew must have been written by a Gentile, because of its universalism and a handful of apparent misunderstandings of Jewish practices. However, the complaints against traditional Jewish attitudes are very much in line with statements made by the Old Testament prophets, while the kind of mistakes allegedly found here (misunderstanding of the nature of Hebrew poetry in 21:5–7, the idea in 18:34 that torture was a Jewish practice, which it was not, and others like them) are hardly evidence for a Gentile author.

Though some leading scholars continue to believe that the apostle Matthew was the author, it is worth pointing out that, as with all the other gospels, knowing the exact identity of the author is not going to be crucial for understanding it. The book itself is anonymous, and makes no claim at all about its author. We can be fairly certain it would be a man, but whether he was associated with the apostle Matthew, and at what stage or in what way, is impossible to say with certainty.

The date

The date of the gospel is also in doubt, and depends on the answers to a number of other questions.

■ If the two-source hypothesis about synoptic origins is correct, then Matthew must have been written after Mark, and after the collection of sayings known as Q was in existence.

The dramatic events of AD70, when the Roman armies destroyed Jerusalem and plundered the temple, are depicted on the triumphal arch of Titus, in Rome.

■ It is widely believed that Matthew was written later than Luke, because 22:7 and 24:3–28 appear to contain direct references to the fall of Jerusalem in AD70. This presumption of course depends on the belief that there can never be such a thing as genuine predictive prophecy, and therefore if Jesus appears to have foretold an event in the future this means the early church must have rewritten the tradition in the light of later circumstances. Even if the possibility of such foresight is allowed, though, Matthew was clearly an intentional literary stylist of some skill, and might easily have formulated the actual phraseology to reflect the details of what happened when the temple was destroyed in fulfilment of an earlier prediction.

■ It has also been argued that the type of church organization envisaged in Matthew is well developed, and therefore reflects a stage towards the end of the first century. Like all arguments based on the notion of 'development', this one is easier to put forward than it is to substantiate. When the details of this gospel's teaching on the church are compared with, say, Paul's letters to the church at Corinth in the mid-fifties of the first century, it is very difficult to find any substantial differences between the two.

The majority verdict is that, taking all these factors into account, Matthew is probably to be dated sometime in the period between about AD80 and 100.

John

John is quite different from the other three gospels. Its style of writing is more reflective than the immediacy of the others, while its presentation of Jesus is distinctive. Instead of spending most of his life in the relative obscurity of Galilee, Jesus is a regular visitor to the festivals in the temple at Jerusalem, where he continually debates and discusses with the religious authorities the finer points of Jewish scriptural interpretation and spirituality (2:13; 5:1; 6:4; 7:2; 10:22; 11:55). Instead of speaking about his possible identity as Messiah in a hesitant way, he makes openly messianic claims from the outset, and in a series of seven sayings introduced by the words 'I am' he appears to take for himself the traditional authority that was reserved in the Old Testament for God alone (where God's personal name *Yahweh* had been defined as meaning 'I am who I am'). Instead of speaking in parables about the kingdom of God, he talks in extended discourses about 'eternal life' – discourses in which (since ancient Greek had no equivalent of modern quotation marks) it is incredibly difficult to decide where the speech of Jesus is meant to end and the reflections of the evangelist himself might begin. Some familiar synoptic episodes such as the casting out of the money changers from the temple are placed in a different context, while others are not mentioned, though the meaning of them seems to be referred to.

So, for example, the last supper is dominated by the washing of the disciples' feet by Jesus (13:1–20), while the idea that bread and wine are the body and blood of Christ is expounded in a discourse following the feeding of the 5,000 (6:25–58). The other gospels to varying degrees present the cross as tragic, albeit inevitable, but in John it is depicted as Jesus' final glorification, the one thing above all others that demonstrated his oneness with God and his place in God's plans for the cosmos – a universal aspect of his significance that is also emphasized in the opening paragraphs, where Jesus is identified with the universal *logos* (word, or reason) of Greek philosophical speculation (1:1–14).

Structure

All this is set out in a carefully constructed narrative, with three easily recognizable sections sandwiched between a prologue and an epilogue, as follows:

THE PROLOGUE (1:1–18)
In which the scene is set, perhaps with references taken from some early Christian hymn or confessional formula, but certainly with allusions to the story of creation in the book of Genesis, to the Old Testament figure of Wisdom as a mediator of God's presence on the earth, and drawing connections between these themes and the concepts of Greek philosophy – all of them designed to highlight the universal significance of the person of Jesus.

THE BOOK OF SIGNS (1:19 – 12:50)
Within which the key events of Jesus' ministry are organized by themes and topics, highlighting in particular his growing conflicts with the religious establishment in Jerusalem, and in the process affirming the

fact that as Son of God he was the fulfilment of all the expectations of the Old Testament.

THE BOOK OF GLORY (13:1 – 20:31)
Where through a series of private meetings with his disciples, including extensive discourses, he prepares them to be leaders of the infant church, nurturing their own faith and entrusting them with guidelines for the future life of the Christian community. As the culmination of all this, the stories of Jesus' death and resurrection gather up the other themes of this gospel, and whereas sacrificial overtones are present in the synoptic accounts of the cross, here it becomes yet another manifestation of Jesus' divine nature.

EPILOGUE (21:1–25)

The character of the fourth gospel
The striking nature of the differences between this gospel and the others has, not surprisingly, led to heated debates about the relative value of their respective accounts of the life and teaching of Jesus. In his monumental study of gospel origins, B.H. Streeter described John as deriving 'not from the original authorities, but from the vivid picture… reconstructed by [the author's] own imagination on the basis of contemporary apologetic'. For him this could lead to only one possible conclusion: John must be a second-century theological interpretation of the life of Jesus – a kind of extended imaginative sermon, based on a muddled misunderstanding of the synoptic traditions, and therefore of no value at all as a reliable account of Jesus as he might actually have lived and taught.

This verdict has now to be regarded as a most inadequate account of the matter, for several reasons:

FACT AND FICTION IN THE TRANSMISSION OF STORIES
To suppose that, if the synoptics give a 'true' picture of Jesus, John's picture must be 'false' is to set up an artificial dichotomy between the two that, if it ever did have validity, would have been more appropriate to the mechanistic view of science popularized by the rationalist-materialist philosophy of the European Enlightenment than to the understanding of literary compositions. We have already seen that the New Testament gospels cannot be simply categorized as ancient biography – though John undoubtedly has more of the characteristics of that form than the other three – but they are certainly carefully crafted narratives aiming to tell the story of Jesus' life and teaching. As such, they are to be judged not by the standards of scientific enquiry, but according to the practices of storytelling, in which the 'truth' of a narrative is to be judged as a whole on its own terms, rather than in relation to notions of truth and falsehood drawn from some other sphere of human endeavour. The early Christian communities clearly had no problem in accepting that within the gospel

traditions there would be a subtle combination of factual and fictional elements. Had they not done so, they would certainly not have tolerated the existence of four gospels which, for all their similarities, are sufficiently different from one another as to defy all attempts at producing one harmonized, 'factual' version of the life and teaching of Jesus from them. They knew what more recent interpreters have often forgotten, that both artists and historians operate under similar constraints as they seek to balance bare fact with fictional elaboration, and that the telling of a good story that will speak to the hearts and minds of its hearers or readers depends on the coherent combination of both these elements. While all four gospels contain both factual and fictive elements, the fourth gospel appears to have a greater preponderance of the latter. Perhaps, it might be suggested, this is one reason why, of all the gospels, it seems to have had the power to speak more profoundly to a greater variety of people in different times and places than the other three – because it presents its subject matter from more angles than the synoptics. We return to this topic in the next chapter, when we discuss more extensively the reliability of the gospel traditions.

Some of the great scholars of the early church who wrote about the Gospels:

Irenaeus, Bishop of Lyons (from AD175–195), known for his writings against Gnosticism.

John and the synoptic gospels

At one time, it was widely assumed that the author of John's Gospel knew the synoptic gospels, because a number of stories are common to both. The story of how Jesus fed the 5,000 (6:1–15; see Mark 6:30–44 and parallels) and the story of his anointing at Bethany (12:1–8; see Mark 14:3–9 and parallels) are examples. Even in the earliest centuries it was therefore supposed that John was writing a kind of 'theological' interpretation of the 'factual' stories of the synoptic gospels: Clement of Alexandria, for instance, characterized John as a 'spiritual gospel' in comparison to the 'physical' or 'bodily' accounts of the synoptics (quoted in Eusebius, *Ecclesiastical History* VI.14.7). This inevitably led to the conclusion that the fourth gospel must be late in date and inferior in quality to the synoptic gospels.

This assumption has, however, been questioned at two points. In the light of more recent study it is obvious that it is too simplistic to set the 'history' of the synoptics over against the 'theology' of John, for the synoptic writers were themselves theologians and did not write their gospels for purely biographical reasons but because they had a message for their readers. It is also now widely (though not universally) believed that the fourth gospel is not dependent on the other three, and it might well have been written without any knowledge of them.

Closer examination of the stories found in all four gospels shows that though there are similarities, there are also a number of differences, and these differences are not the kind that can easily be explained on theological or ideological grounds. John's variations are much easier to understand on the assumption that he had access to different reports of the incidents known also to the synoptists. When this hypothesis is

tested in detail, it can be seen not only that John's account comes from a different source, but also that there are a number of pieces of information in John which can be used to supplement the information of the other gospels in such a way as to make the whole story of Jesus' life and ministry more understandable.

For example, John 1:35–42 mentions that some of Jesus' disciples had previously been followers of John the Baptist, an observation that can help to explain the exact nature of the Baptist's witness to Jesus in the synoptics, and especially the emphasis placed there on his role in 'preparing the way of the Lord'. John's account also helps to answer the question (not obvious from the synoptics) of what Jesus was doing between his baptism and the arrest of John the Baptist. The synoptics report that Jesus began his ministry in Galilee after John's arrest (Mark 1:14; Matthew 4:12; Luke 4:14–15). This is the only ministry recorded in the synoptic gospels, though during his last visit to Jerusalem Matthew and Luke (Q) report that Jesus said of its inhabitants, 'How often would I have gathered your children together...' (Matthew 23:37; Luke 13:34), which suggests that Jesus had visited Jerusalem on a number of previous occasions. John 2:13 – 4:3 tells of just such an occasion, right at the beginning of Jesus' ministry, when he worked alongside John the Baptist in Judea before going back to Galilee when John was arrested.

John 7:1 – 10:42 fills out the synoptic material at a later point, when it records another visit by Jesus to Jerusalem some six months before his entry on Palm Sunday. John records how Jesus left Galilee and went to Jerusalem for the Feast of Tabernacles (September) and stayed there until the Feast of Dedication (December) after which, because of growing hostility, he returned to the area where John the Baptist had worked (10:40), only making a brief visit to Bethany when he heard that Lazarus had died (11:1–54). A little later, six days before the Passover (April) he returned for his final visit to Jerusalem (12:1, 12). This is the only one recorded in any detail in Mark, though the others are perhaps implied by Mark's summary statement: 'he left [Galilee] and went to the region of Judea and beyond the Jordan' (Mark 10:1).

John also provides a number of smaller details which help to explain and clarify some points in the synoptic narratives. At the end of the feeding of the 5,000, Mark 6:45 records that Jesus compelled his disciples to escape on a boat while he himself dismissed the crowd, while John 6:14–15 fills in some of the detail, explaining that Jesus had to take this action because the crowd were eager to kidnap him and make him their king. We have already noticed in an earlier chapter how the stories of the last supper and of Jesus' trials can be fully understood only in the light of information contained in John's Gospel.

In view of evidence of this sort, it is now coming to be realized that John's Gospel is a source in its own right. The information it contains is independent of that in the synoptic gospels, but at many crucial points John complements the other three.

THE BACKGROUND OF JOHN IN JUDAISM

It is also now recognized that the background of much of John's Gospel is Jewish, and not exclusively Greek. Early traditions place the origin of this gospel in Ephesus, which made it inevitable that scholars should look for an exclusively Hellenistic background, especially in view of the prologue (1:1–18) which explains the incarnation in terms of the word or *logos*. Apart from the fact that Hellenism is now known to have been all-pervasive throughout the Roman empire, even in Palestine, it is interesting to note that if the prologue is removed from John there is little in the rest of it that demands a Greek background. Not only is there an emphasis throughout the gospel on the fulfilment of the Old Testament, but the evangelist states his purpose in a very Jewish form: 'these things are written that you may believe that Jesus is the Christ [Messiah], the Son of God' (20:31).

This impression is confirmed by a closer analysis of the actual language of the gospel, for at many points the Greek shows a close connection with Aramaic sources. The writer often uses Aramaic words – for example, *Cephas* (1:42), *Gabbatha* (19:13), or *Rabboni* (20:16), and then explains them for the benefit of Greek readers. Even the meaning of the word Messiah is given a careful explanation in 1:41. There are also places where the Greek of the gospel follows the rules of Aramaic idiom. Though the distinction is not generally made in modern translations, such an instance occurs when John the Baptist says of Jesus, 'I am not worthy *that I should untie* the thong of his sandals' (1:27; the other gospels have a different and correct Greek expression, meaning 'to untie').

Jesus' sayings in John are also on occasion expressed in the typical parallelism of Semitic poetry (12:25; 13:16, 20), while other sections of his teaching can be retranslated into Aramaic to form completely realistic Aramaic poetry (for example, 3:29–30). It is not likely that John is a direct translation of an Aramaic document, though some have suggested this. But these facts do suggest that the teaching in John has the same Palestinian background as the material of the synoptic gospels, while the curious use of Aramaic grammar in Greek writing might well suggest that Aramaic was the author's native language.

NEW DISCOVERIES

There is now a considerable and important body of evidence drawn from archaeology which has rendered the idea that John was a late Hellenistic gospel untenable:

■ The Dead Sea Scrolls have shown that the apparently odd combination of Greek and Jewish ideas found in John was current not only in Greek cities like Ephesus in the second century AD, but also in Palestine itself, in strict Jewish circles, in the pre-Christian era. Many phrases familiar from John are also found in the scrolls, such as 'doing the truth' (3:21), 'walking in darkness' (12:35), 'children of the light'

(12:36), or 'the Spirit of truth' (14:17). Moreover, the contrasts made in John between light and darkness, truth and error, are also typical of the Qumran scrolls – and in both contexts this dualism between light and darkness, truth and error is an *ethical* dualism, in contrast to the metaphysical emphasis of most Greek and Gnostic philosophies.

■ The discovery of Gnostic gospels has had a different kind of impact on study of John. Prior to the discovery in the late 1940s of the Coptic Gnostic library at Nag Hammadi in upper Egypt, knowledge of Gnosticism was based largely on information given by a number of church historians and theologians who wrote books to refute it, and from their statements it was not too difficult to imagine that John's Gospel could have been written in the second century as a part of the

The author of John's gospel is now known to have had personal knowledge of the city of Jerusalem in the period of Jesus' lifetime. Some have identified this site near St Anne's Church as the location of the Pool of Bethesda (or Beth-Zatha) mentioned in John 5:1–18.

battle between Gnostic and 'orthodox' Christians. But the knowledge derived from the writings of Gnostic teachers themselves has demonstrated quite categorically that there was a vast difference between the world of John's Gospel and the world of classical Gnosticism.

■ Archaeological excavations in Jerusalem have also provided evidence to illuminate the traditions of John's Gospel. One of the unusual features of this gospel is its proliferation of names and descriptions of places, and it was widely thought at one time that these names were introduced either as a theological device (as symbols), or to give the impression of authenticity in otherwise fabricated accounts. But it is now clear that most of this geographical information rests on real knowledge of the city as it was before AD70. Since the Romans completely destroyed Jerusalem at that time, a later visitor to the city would not have been able to observe the ruins and imagine what it must have looked like beforehand. Excavations in Jerusalem have now shown that descriptions of the Pool of Bethesda (John 5:1–15), for example, or 'the Pavement' where Jesus met Pilate (John 19:13) are based on intimate knowledge of the city at the time of Jesus.

John's purpose in writing

In one sense this is an easy question to answer, for 20:31 spells out the purpose: 'that you may believe that Jesus is the Christ, the Son of God, and that believing you may have life in his name'. Though that can be understood as a statement of some evangelistic purpose, which would mean the gospel was written for those outside the church, the first clause could also be translated 'that you may continue to believe', and other factors also seem to indicate that it was written with the needs of Christians in view:

■ There are extensive references to the concerns and interests of second-generation Christians who were not eyewitnesses of the events described (20:26–31), with specific mentions of persecution (15:18–25; 16:1–4), mission (14:12–14; 15:26–27; 17:15–19), the need for continued faithfulness (15:1–11; 17:11–12), unity and love within the community (15:12–17; 17:20–23), as well as extensive teaching throughout chapters 14 – 16 on the role of the Holy Spirit in the ongoing life of the church.

■ There is a strong emphasis on the distinction between 'Jews' and Christians here, which is not so much an ethnic distinction as a religious one ('Jews' are not contrasted with Gentiles). In view of the lack of racial overtones and the emphasis on religious differences, it is going too far to describe this as anti-Semitism, though the acrimony of a passage such as 8:42–47 is unmistakable, while 9:22, 12:42 and 16:2 clearly imply a total break between Judaism and Christianity, and some believe they reflect the situation around AD85–90 when Christians were expelled from the synagogues as a consequence of a prayer against heretics formulated by Rabbi Gamaliel II. If so, this experience was clearly in the past at the time the gospel was written, though its recipients (who seem to have included Gentiles as well as Jews) were still living with the painful memories of such an event.

Author and date

The question of authorship has always been rather confused. Early church traditions mention two Johns in connection with the gospel: the apostle, and a John whom they call 'the Elder'. In the gospel itself, the 'beloved disciple' seems to be portrayed as a source of some of the information, though it is never made clear who this person was. Irenaeus identified the beloved disciple with John the apostle (*Against Heresies* I.1.1), though

---

Redaction criticism

Whereas source and form criticism are concerned to uncover the very earliest beginnings of the stories about Jesus, and to trace the history of the material before it was incorporated into the gospels themselves, redaction criticism sets out to discern how the individual authors actually used the materials that were handed down to them, and from which they constructed their gospels. All the claims about the aims, purposes and special interests of Matthew, Mark, Luke and John that are outlined in this chapter are based on the conclusions of redaction criticism.

Redaction criticism begins from the assumption that it is possible to distinguish between the traditions that the evangelists used, and the way they themselves actually shaped and wrote up those traditions in the process of compiling their own distinctive accounts of the life and teaching of Jesus. It then assumes that the way the individual evangelists have used their materials can reveal something about their own concerns, insights and theological perspectives.

The ability to compare how different evangelists have used the same material is obviously an important part of this process, which is why it is much easier to discern the redactional concerns of Matthew and Luke than it is of Mark or John, because we know that Matthew and Luke were working with the same sources (Mark and Q). By identifying changes of wording, and analysing which materials an evangelist has included, and which have been left out, as well as the editorial connecting phrases that are used to link it all together, it is possible to discern patterns and then to conclude that those patterns must correspond with some particular concern of the author. For example, Luke not only contains more material on prayer than the others, but he also inserts references to prayer in passages which in Mark make no mention of it (compare, for example, Mark 3:7–19 with Luke 6:12–19). When such features keep on recurring, it is reasonable to suppose that they reflect a particular theme which the evangelist wanted to emphasize (as Luke does with prayer).

It is obviously easier to be certain of some conclusions than others. For example, discerning trends in how Matthew and Luke have used Mark will always be easier than doing the same for their use of Q, since there is no independent access to what Q might have been in its original form, as there is for Mark. But that should not be used to question the method, which when judiciously applied has often led to significant and creative insights into the evangelists and their overall concerns. Far from being the kind of wooden 'scissors-and-paste' editors that Streeter imagined them to be, all four of them were obviously creative literary artists, carefully constructing their narratives so as to have maximum impact on their readers.

some interpreters believe he might just be an ideal figure, symbolic of the true follower of Christ, while others have pointed out that Lazarus is the only person of whom it is specifically and consistently said that Jesus loved him (John 11:5, 36). In addition, 21:24 appears to distinguish the final editor of the gospel from this 'beloved disciple', while implying that he was the source of much of its information.

One way of explaining all this is to suppose that John has gone through two editions. Apart from the prologue, it does focus on issues related to the Jewish background and heritage of Christianity, whereas with the prologue it takes on the appearance of a book more suited to the wider Greek world. Could it be that the prologue was added after the completion of the original work, to commend the gospel to a new readership, facing relational issues with the synagogues, but well beyond the original context of Palestine?

This possibility might be supported by the odd connection between chapters 20 and 21. The last verse of chapter 20 appears to be the logical conclusion of the book, though it is then followed by the post-resurrection instructions of Jesus to Peter in chapter 21. This final chapter could perhaps have been added at the time when the book was adapted to serve the needs of a new group of people, though its style and language is so close to that of the rest of the gospel that it must have been added by the same person or persons. It seems at least possible that the gospel was first written in Palestine, to demonstrate that 'Jesus is the Christ' (20:31), perhaps over against the views of sectarian Jews influenced by ideas like those of the Qumran community, and then when the same teaching was seen to be relevant to people elsewhere in the Roman empire, it was revised, with Jewish customs and expressions being explained, and the prologue and epilogue added. The advice to church leaders in chapter 21 suggests that the final form of the gospel might have been directed to a Christian congregation comprised of both Jews and Gentiles somewhere in the Hellenistic world, perhaps at Ephesus.

The date of the gospel is not easy to ascertain, partly because (unlike the case of Matthew and Luke) there is no other evidence against which to set it. Traditions from the second century onwards suggest that it was written by John the apostle at the end of a long life, and most scholars continue to date it somewhere between about AD85 and 100, though opinions differ regarding the possible connection of it all with the apostle John. He cannot have been the final author, for that was a group of people who identify themselves as at least second-generation Christians (21:24). Nor are there are any specific indications that he was the 'beloved disciple', though a plausible case can be made out for that. However, there is no widely accepted opinion on the author's identity, and the consensus at this point in time can best be described as an open-minded agnosticism, with many scholars willing to allow some direct connection between John the apostle and the fourth gospel, though few wish to be more precise than that.

22 Engaging with the Wider World

After the resurrection of Jesus, his followers were faced with some hard choices. The previous two or three years had been the most exciting time of their lives. They had been captivated by his teaching, and watched with growing expectancy as Jesus' actions made it plain that God's kingdom had really and truly arrived. Then came the crucifixion, and with it all they had hoped for seemed doomed to certain failure. Even the resurrection left them afraid and disillusioned, and when they realized that Jesus would no longer be physically present with them they must have been under intense pressure simply to forget him, or at least to regard those three years as a temporary interlude, and to return home to pick up the threads of their working lives where they had left off before they joined Jesus. By doing that, they would still be able to share their memories of him, and perhaps even try to put some of his teaching into practice in the local synagogues of rural Palestine – but their lives would no longer be dominated by him in the way they had been before.

Yet the more they thought about it, the more they knew how impossible such a reaction would be. Jesus had demanded their radical and wholehearted obedience when they first met him, and his final message to them was just as challenging and uncompromising: 'Go, then, to all peoples everywhere and make them my disciples... you will be witnesses for me in Jerusalem, in all Judea and Samaria, and to the ends of the earth...' (Matthew 28:19; Acts 1:8).

Back to Jesus

Jesus had never really been an establishment figure. People who met him often recognized him as a 'rabbi', and gave him that title (e.g. Matthew 26:25; Mark 9:5; 10:51; John 1:49; 4:31), but right from the very beginning they all knew that he was different and that his message was distinctive. In his very first report of Jesus' public teaching, Mark comments: 'The people who heard him were amazed at the way he taught, for he wasn't like the teachers of the Law; instead, he taught with authority' (1:22).

That does not mean to say that his teaching was completely new and unique. It has been rightly pointed out that almost everything in Jesus' teaching had been said before him by the Jewish rabbis. Since both he and they were setting out to explain the significance of the Hebrew scriptures for their own generation, it is hardly surprising that they discussed the same issues, and even on occasion reached similar conclusions. But what was so different about Jesus – and what was to set his followers radically apart from Judaism – was the framework in which he set his teaching. For on two crucial matters Jesus adopted a fundamentally different stance from other religious teachers of his day.

Keeping the Law

The Law, or Torah (the first five books of the Old Testament), was central to Judaism, as keeping the Law in all its details was the way that faithful believers could demonstrate their obedience to God and commitment to the covenant with Israel. It is often difficult for a non-Jew today to understand the almost mystical significance of the Law for a faithful Jewish believer in the time of Jesus, and no doubt that is part of the reason why some of the most influential Protestant biblical scholars of the last 100 years or so have found it easy to misrepresent Jewish spirituality as a harsh and unforgiving legalistic system. Jewish believers in the time of Jesus must have had a far more positive attitude to faith than the kind of blind obedience credited to them by some Christian writers in more recent times. But no matter what their motivation, keeping the Law and its precepts had always been a central plank of Judaism, and it would have been unthinkable that anyone might please God without also observing the many detailed requirements of the Torah.

There had always been more than one way of understanding what might be entailed in keeping the Law, of course. The prophet Amos, 700 years before the time of Jesus, had condemned his contemporaries for their eagerness to keep the minute details of the ritual and ceremonial regulations, while ignoring the central moral requirements that were also laid down in the Torah (Amos 5:21–24). The same tendency could be found in Jesus' day, and his strongly worded condemnation of the Pharisees was not so very different from Amos' complaints: 'You hypocrites! You give to God a tenth even of the seasoning herbs, such as mint, dill and cumin, but you neglect to obey the really important teachings of the Law, such as justice and mercy and honesty' (Matthew 23:23). Such behaviour was presumably not uncommon, for when Jesus was asked why his disciples did not keep every detailed requirement of the Law, he pointed out to his questioners their own inconsistency in avoiding moral obligations to their parents by using a legal loophole that would allow them to use their wealth for more 'religious' purposes (Mark 7:1–13).

The adoption of such double standards is of course by no means an exclusively Jewish problem, and to label it as such is to import an ethnic dimension into Jesus' teaching that was never there. Jesus never actually questioned the validity of the Law, nor did he deny that it had been given by God, though he did suggest that with his own coming, it was no longer relevant (Luke 16:16). More than that, in a series of remarkable statements he contrasted his own teaching with that of the Torah, and elevated his own authority to a higher status than that of Moses, the traditional Hebrew Law-giver: 'You have heard that people were told in the past [by Moses] but now I tell you...' (Matthew 5:21–22, 27–28, 31–47). It is also significant that, according to Mark's account of his trial by the religious authorities, Jesus was first charged with blasphemy against the temple (Mark 14:57–59). The charge failed, but from the authorities' viewpoint it was not totally without foundation, as can be seen from his statement in Matthew 12:6, 'I tell you that there is something here greater than the temple.'

It is therefore not surprising that, though he seemed to be an ordinary rabbi, Jesus was soon outlawed by the religious establishment. This radical teaching about the Law and the temple struck at the very foundations of their most firmly held convictions. Other rabbis had asked awkward questions before, but generally in the context of polite debate about points of interpretation of the Law. If Jesus had been content to do the same, perhaps the system could have assimilated him more easily. It was not totally inflexible, and had survived many changes before and would undergo many others after the time of Jesus. But Jesus was above all an activist, and detached scholarly argument was not his style.

The way he behaved was, if anything, even more scandalous than his teaching. Mark 2:23–28 tells how he and his disciples picked grain as they walked through the fields, an action that was forbidden because it was regarded as harvesting by the legal experts of the day, and therefore an infringement of the law about not working on the sabbath. Jesus' reply to their criticism of this behaviour was to justify his disregard of the Law with the declaration that 'the sabbath was made for humankind, and not humankind for the sabbath.' On another occasion when he was asked why his disciples ignored the conventions about ritual washing before eating a meal, he also dismissed that criticism by appeal to a higher principle: 'whatever goes into a person from outside cannot defile... it is what comes out of a person that defiles... it is from within, from the human heart, that evil intentions come, leading people to do immoral things, to rob, kill, commit adultery, be greedy...' (Mark 7:18–22).

Not only did Jesus challenge the precepts of the Law in this way, but he also insisted on taking his message to all sorts of people who were regarded as unclean. Lepers, prostitutes, tax gatherers (Roman collaborators) and others feature regularly and prominently in the gospels, and Jesus himself was described as 'a glutton and a drinker, a friend of tax collectors and other outcasts' (Matthew 11:19). Instead of making his friends among the conventionally religious, Jesus chose those who were despised for their inability to keep the Law. Indeed, he made a virtue out of it, reminding his questioners on one occasion that, 'I have not come to call respectable people, but outcasts' (Mark 2:17).

A number of stories in the gospels explain why Jesus felt like that, but perhaps none sums up his attitude more succinctly than the parable of the Pharisee and the tax collector who went to pray in the temple at the same time. The Pharisee prided himself on his moral and religious attainments – and told God so. The tax collector, on the other hand, was so conscious of his own unworthiness to speak to God at all that he could only cry out, 'God, have pity on me, a sinner.' 'But,' said Jesus, 'the tax collector, and not the Pharisee, was in the right with God when he went home', because he recognized his own sinfulness and came to God with no spiritual pretensions (Luke 18:9–14). The Pharisees were emphasizing the importance of showing commitment to the covenant by faithful observance of the Law, whereas Jesus believed it was possible to keep all that was in the Law – and more besides – and still not please God. Whereas the religious establishment was concerned with actions that could be assessed and regulated by rules (as religious establishments always are), Jesus was much more concerned with what a person is than with what he or she does. Paradoxically, perhaps, he did not go on to dismiss behaviour as unimportant, but he emphasized that how people behave depends on their inner nature, and for him the secret of goodness was therefore to be found not in obedience to rules, but in the spontaneous activities of a transformed character: 'A sound tree cannot bear evil fruit, nor can a bad tree bear good fruit' (Matthew 7:18).

Religion and race

There was another element in Jesus' conflicts with the religious establishment. Many people in the Roman empire admired the moral precepts of the Old Testament, and the principles enshrined in the ten commandments and other parts of the Torah commanded the respect of many upright Romans and Greeks. But admiring the Law was not quite the same thing as pleasing God, and before they could be fully incorporated into the people of God, Judaism demanded that Gentiles must be circumcised and accept the various detailed regulations of the Law. In effect, Gentiles had to become Jews before they could be accepted by God: there was no salvation outside the Jewish nation. This stringent requirement of converts did not stop the Pharisees and others from engaging in missionary activity among non-Jews, and Jesus himself commended them for their enthusiasm (Matthew 23:15). But he evidently did not approve of their insistence that in order to please God such people should accept all the detailed regulations of the Torah.

The precise extent of Jesus' own involvement in a mission to those Gentiles is somewhat unclear. He certainly made no concerted effort to preach the good news to them, though all four gospels show him accepting and respecting the faith of such people whenever he met

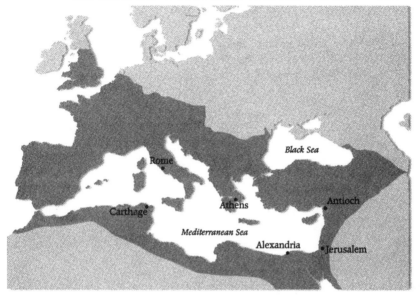

The extent of the Roman empire at the time of Jesus.

them. He was not unwilling even to assist a Roman officer, remarking in the process that, 'I have never found anyone in Israel with faith like this' (Matthew 8:5–13). A number of incidents show his acceptance of various non-Jewish groups within Palestinian society (Mark 5:1–20; 7:24–30), while one of his best-known parables praised the virtues of a Samaritan, the one race that was despised perhaps more than any other by religious Jews (Luke 10:25–37).

In the light of this, some readers of the gospels have found a contradiction in Jesus' instruction to his disciples in Matthew 10:5–6, 'Do not go to any Gentile territory or any Samaritan towns. Instead, you are to go to those lost sheep, the people of Israel.' But this advice was given in respect of a limited mission tour which the disciples were to undertake for a short period only, during Jesus' own lifetime, and Matthew himself certainly did not regard it as more widely applicable, for he is the only gospel writer to record the great commission of Jesus, exhorting his disciples to 'Go... to all peoples everywhere and make them my disciples...' (28:19). Other passages such as Matthew 8:10–12 and 21:43 make the same point, as do many passages in Luke's Gospel. The best way to understand the advice of Matthew 10:5 is to set it alongside another commission given, according to Luke, after the resurrection: '... you will be witnesses for me in Jerusalem, in all Judea and Samaria, and to the ends of the earth' (Acts 1:8). It was natural that the first followers of Jesus should take their message in the first instance to the Jewish community, for they were themselves Palestinian Jews, but Paul later adopted the same strategy in cities far removed from Palestine, and regularly gave the Jewish community the opportunity to respond to his message before he took it to Gentiles. In Romans 11:13–24 he insisted there was a theological basis for this priority, related to the ancient history of Israel as the recipients of the Law and people of God's covenant.

The church is born

As they met behind closed doors in Jerusalem in those early days after Jesus' resurrection, the disciples knew that it was easier to talk about changing the world than it would be to go out and do it. But it was not long before something happened that not only altered their thinking, but gave them a courage and boldness to share their faith that was to send shockwaves throughout the Roman world.

Only fifty days after the death of Jesus, Peter found himself standing before a large crowd in the streets of Jerusalem, fearlessly proclaiming that God's kingdom had arrived, and that Jesus was its king and Messiah. At the time Jerusalem was full of pilgrims who had come from all parts of the empire for the Festival of Pentecost – and as Peter spoke they not only understood his message, but, when he invited them to become disciples of Jesus themselves, 3,000 accepted his challenge and declared their willingness to live according to the values and standards of God's kingdom (Acts 2:14–47).

What had happened to bring about such a transformation in the lives of Jesus' followers? The answer to that is contained in the opening

Peter's audience on the Day of Pentecost had travelled from far and wide, indicating the extensive spread of Jewish people throughout the ancient world.

section of Peter's address. For as he stood up to speak with the crowd, he reminded them of an Old Testament passage that had described the coming new age as a time when God's Spirit would work in an exciting new way in the lives of men and women. As the Hebrew prophets had looked to the future, some of them realized that the human predicament would never be resolved until a new relationship was set up between people and God, in which God would not just ask for obedience but would actually give people a new moral power that would enable them to be what they were intended to be (Jeremiah 31:31–34). In Joel 2:28–32, this new power for living had been associated with the gift of God's Spirit, and Peter took that passage as his text and claimed that it was now coming true in the experience of Jesus' disciples. Through Jesus' death and resurrection, ordinary people could enjoy a new level of personal relationship with God. Peter was prepared to testify to that on the basis of his own experience.

For Peter and the others, that day had begun like any other. But as they faced the enormity, and the apparent impossibility, of the task Jesus had left them, they were taken by surprise as a new life-giving power burst into their lives. It was a moral and spiritual dynamic that equipped them to bear witness to their new faith – a power that would make them like Jesus. It was not easy to describe in words exactly what they experienced, but they identified it as the power of the Holy Spirit. As a consequence of what happened to them, their hesitating and uncertain trust in Jesus and his promises was remarkably confirmed and from that moment onwards they had no doubt that God's promises to previous generations were actually coming true in their own lives. The church was in the process of being born. More than that, they themselves were being reborn for, in addition to Peter's new-found ability to speak in a powerful way to the crowds gathered in Jerusalem, he and the others discovered that they now had the ability to carry out remarkable deeds in the name of Jesus. If they had ever entertained any residual doubts, the power that swept over them was so overwhelming that they needed no further argument to persuade them that Jesus was alive and at work in their lives in a unique way.

As a result of all this, the apostles and their converts were so totally dominated by their love for the living Jesus and their desire to serve him that the humdrum concerns of everyday life were forgotten. Instead, the Christians 'spent their time in learning from the apostles, taking part in the fellowship, and sharing in the common meals and prayers' (Acts 2:42). As a first step towards beginning to live the way Jesus had spoken of, they even sold their goods and pooled the proceeds. Making money was no longer the most important thing in life: the only things that really mattered were serving God, and taking their life changing message to other people.

The church grows

During these early days in Jerusalem, the open friendship and simple lifestyle of the early church must indeed have seemed like the dawning of a new age. But it was not long before other more complex questions reminded Peter and the others that God's kingdom had not yet arrived in all its fullness. Their newly established community of mutual acceptance and sharing was itself proof that the new society had begun but, as time passed, the tension between present and future that was so fundamental in Jesus' teaching was to have disturbing repercussions for the ongoing life of the embryonic Christian church. During the lifetime of Jesus, the new messianic movement which he founded was for the most part a local sect within Palestinian Judaism. All the disciples were Jews and, though both the logic of Jesus' message and the example of his own practice made it clear that Gentiles were not to be excluded, the issue simply did not arise to any great extent. Those Gentiles whom Jesus encountered were isolated individuals, few in number, and in any

The Day of Pentecost

The precise nature of the disciples' experience on the Day of Pentecost has been much discussed. It has sometimes been suggested that it never happened, and that the whole of the story in Acts 2 was intended by Luke to convey some theological lesson rather than to report an actual incident. A typical explanation along these lines would be to seek a background for the narrative in the fact that the festival of Pentecost was traditionally connected to the giving of the Old Testament Law at Mount Sinai. According to the late second-century Rabbi Johanan, the one voice of God at the giving of the Law had divided into seven voices, which had then spoken in seventy different languages. That, together with the fact that wind and fire were present both at Sinai and at the events of Pentecost, is said to be enough to explain the picturesque language used by Luke.

This kind of explanation seems far less plausible today than it would have done in the nineteenth or twentieth centuries, when the rationalist-materialist world-view of the Enlightenment was still dominant, with its underlying assumption that there

is no such thing as religious experience, and therefore phenomena like speaking in tongues, visions or other mystical manifestations can only be explained by being reduced to categories of psychology or anthropology. But even on its own terms it is possible to challenge the idea that the Acts narrative is a gloss on traditional Jewish beliefs. There is no evidence at all to show that the rabbis linked Sinai and Pentecost before the second century, which was long after the particular day of Pentecost to which Luke refers, and indeed much later than the lifetime of Luke himself. The narrative presents a realistic account of what the disciples might have been expected to do under the circumstances, and it is perfectly believable that after the unexpected events of the previous Passover they would have gathered in the way Luke describes, apprehensive about what might happen next. It is probably unlikely that their expectations included what did actually take place, and they might well have been naïvely thinking that, after the death and resurrection of Jesus, there was nothing else left except the end of the world. If so, they were in for a surprise, for the new age of which Jesus had spoken did indeed

case many of them were probably either God-fearers or actual converts to Judaism, and so not totally outside the boundaries of traditional Jewish spirituality (Mark 7:24–30; Luke 7:1–10).

But it was not long before the church was forced to give considerable attention to the whole question of the relationship between Jewish and Gentile followers of Jesus. Though they did not realize it at the time, the events of the Day of Pentecost recorded at the beginning of the book of Acts were to be a watershed in more ways than one. For when Peter stood up to explain the Christian message to the crowds in Jerusalem, he faced a very cosmopolitan audience of 'religious people who had come from every country of the world' (Acts 2:5). Naturally, they must all have been interested in Judaism, or they would not have travelled to Jerusalem for a religious

A typical street in old Jerusalem.

dawn, but not in the way they imagined it might, even if Peter did later connect it with what the prophet Joel had expected in 'the last days' (Acts 2:17–21).

Like all mystical happenings, their experience defies neat classification. It certainly had some of the common features of visions, as the disciples saw 'what looked like tongues of fire' (but were not fire), and heard 'a noise from the sky which sounded like a strong wind blowing' (but was not the wind). But the result of this experience was clear for others to see: 'They were all filled with the Holy Spirit and began to talk in other languages, as the Spirit enabled them to speak' (Acts 2:2–4). The most natural understanding of this is that they were speaking in tongues, or 'glossolalia' as it is sometimes called. This phenomenon is mentioned elsewhere in the New Testament as one of the gifts of the Spirit (1 Corinthians 12:10; 14:5–25), and is also widely known and practised today in churches of many traditions. It is generally agreed that such speaking in tongues is not the speaking of foreign languages otherwise unknown to the speaker, but a kind of ecstatic speech, quite different from the form and content of actual languages. Paul certainly

perceived a difference, for he contrasted the speaking of ordinary languages with tongues, which he called 'the language of angels' (1 Corinthians 13:1).

Some still argue that the experience of the Day of Pentecost was not the speaking of tongues, but the speaking of foreign languages. But if that was the case, it is hard to see why some who heard it should have concluded that the disciples were drunk (Acts 2:13), while others heard God speaking to them quite clearly in terms that they could understand. No doubt the explanation for this lies in the fact that what Luke reported he had learned from others who had been there, and whose lives had been changed as a result of what they had heard. Whatever kind of inspired speech the apostles were using, those who were present found themselves caught up by what the followers of Jesus called the power of the Spirit, and the message they heard came to them as clearly as if it had been expressed in their own everyday languages.

festival. But not all the Gentiles among them would be full converts who had accepted the whole of the Law, while even those who were from Jewish families in various parts of the Roman empire must have had a rather different background and outlook from those who had been born and bred in Palestine itself. Most of those listening to Peter's address were probably Greek-speaking Jews who had made a pilgrimage to Jerusalem for this great religious festival. Many of them would have been visiting Jerusalem for the first time. Though their homes were far away, such Jews of the Dispersion always had a warm regard for Jerusalem and its temple. This was the central shrine of their faith, just as it was for their compatriots who lived much nearer to it. Peter and the other disciples had no doubt that the good news about Jesus must also be shared with people like this. Indeed, they had much in common. The disciples themselves were regular supporters of the synagogue services. They too observed the special festivals, and on occasions they could even be found teaching within the temple precincts (Acts 3:1–26). This was something that Jesus himself had not been able to do without fear of the consequences, and though Peter and John were subsequently arrested and charged before the religious authorities, they were soon released and the only restriction imposed on them was that 'on no condition were they to speak or to teach in the name of Jesus' (Acts 4:18). Apart from their curious belief in Jesus, their behaviour was generally quite acceptable to the Jewish authorities.

The conflict begins

It was not long before all this was to change, when an argument arose between some Jews who spoke Greek ('Hellenists') and others whose main language was Hebrew or Aramaic ('Hebrews'). They had all become Christians, perhaps on the Day of Pentecost itself, and some of these 'Hellenist' Christians were probably visitors to Jerusalem from other parts of the Roman empire (Acts 6:1) – though many Jews in Palestine also spoke Greek, and some of them might have been permanent residents. At any event, those whose main language was Greek felt they were getting an unfair deal in the distribution of funds within the church, and as a result of their complaints seven people were appointed to supervise the arrangements for these Hellenistic Christians, in addition to the apostles who had the care of the more conservative Hebrew Christians. Though most of those who are named are otherwise unknown, one of them – Stephen – soon demonstrated that he was at least as gifted in theological argument as he was in the administration of funds (Acts 6:2–6).

According to Acts, it all started as an argument within the 'synagogue of the Freedmen' in Jerusalem. It is not

A Christian symbol carved on the steps of the Hellenistic Temple of Apollo at Didyma in modern Turkey.

certain just who these 'Freedmen' were, but it is a fair guess that they would have been Jews who had come from other parts of the Roman empire, released from some form of slavery, and had then formed their own synagogue in Jerusalem. Acts says that this synagogue congregation 'included Jews from Cyrene and Alexandria', and that they sided with others 'from the provinces of Cilicia and Asia' in debates with Stephen. Stephen himself was presumably a member of this synagogue, and no doubt he supposed that by sharing his new insights into the scriptures with other members of it he would be able to influence them to recognize Jesus as the promised Messiah. But it was not to be. Far from persuading his fellow Hellenists of the truth of the Christian claims, all he managed to do was to convince them that he was himself a heretic, and before long he found himself accused before the court of the Sanhedrin.

The narrative in Acts suggests that in order to bring effective charges, Stephen's accusers had to tell lies: 'This man', they said, 'is always talking against our sacred Temple and the Law of Moses. We heard him say that this Jesus of Nazareth will tear down the Temple and change all the customs which have come down to us from Moses!' (Acts 6:13–14). This accusation has a familiar ring about it, for according to

Stephen's speech

The address of Stephen before the Sanhedrin (Acts 7:1–53) is one of the longest speeches reported anywhere in the New Testament, and at first sight it seems hardly to be a response to the charges that had been made against him. Because of this, some have suggested that what is contained in Acts 7 was a free composition by the author of Acts to provide an appropriate theological explanation for why the Hellenist Christians began to move away from Jerusalem and to loosen their allegiance to Judaism. This question is not of course restricted to the story of Stephen: it is also relevant to the speeches reportedly delivered by Peter, Paul and others in later sections of Acts. Were these speeches based on verbatim reports that were handed down to the author of Acts? Or did he follow the example of a writer like Josephus, who seems to have inserted speeches at will into the mouths of those whose exploits he describes? A number of points may be made:

● Obviously, none of the speeches reported in Acts can be verbatim accounts. They are far too short for that, and in any case people in the ancient world were not obsessed with the desire for accurate quotation which is so important today. This can be seen quite clearly in the way some New Testament writers refer even to the Old Testament scriptures. Though they had supreme authority for them, they often quote from no known version, but refer to them from memory, regularly introducing inaccuracies as a result. In the case of Stephen's trial, it is unlikely that anyone would have taken down extensive notes of what was actually said. The narrative gives the impression that the whole thing took place with great urgency.

● At the same time, it should be borne in mind that not all ancient historians were like Josephus, and the Greek tradition of history-writing would be better represented by an author like Thucydides. He also felt that the inclusion of speeches

Thucydides (460–400BC).

Mark 14:57–59 it was one of the charges brought against Jesus at his trial. But whereas on that occasion the false witnesses failed to agree, and so other charges had to be found, in the case of Stephen he went on to condemn himself out of his own mouth.

In his long speech before the Sanhedrin, Stephen not only admitted the truthfulness of the vague accusations made against him by the witnesses; he also went on to make very specific statements about the subjects in dispute (Acts 7:1–53). With a carefully detailed survey of the history of Israel, he argued that the temple ought never to have existed at all. Illustrating his case with copious quotations from and allusions to the Hebrew scriptures, he pointed out how Moses had received instructions for the construction of a simple tent as a place of worship in the desert, and this had continued in use long after the time of Moses. Things had begun to change only with the accession of Solomon to the throne, when increased wealth and a new international political stature had inspired him to build a central sanctuary in Jerusalem (1 Kings 5:4–5). The Old Testament suggests that Solomon had divine approval for his actions, though strenuous religious and moral conditions were also imposed to ensure the continued existence of the temple (1 Kings 9:1–9). But quoting Isaiah 66:1–2, Stephen argued that the temple had

---

Stephen's speech continued

at appropriate points in his narrative would help to highlight the important points, but he was not in the habit of simply inventing such speeches, as he explains in the beginning of his *History of the Peloponnesian War* (1.22.1): '... some speeches I heard myself, others I got from various quarters; it was in all cases difficult to carry them word for word in one's memory, so my habit has been to make the speakers say what was in my opinion demanded of them by the various occasions, of course adhering as closely as possible to the general sense of what they really said.'

● On more general grounds, Acts would appear to fit into the Thucydidean mould rather than following the traditions of a person like Josephus. Though its story of early Christianity is undoubtedly selective, when it can be tested against external evidence from other sources, it appears to be generally trustworthy.

● All the speeches in Acts at least have the appearance of authenticity. In subject matter, language and style they are varied

to suit the people who make them. Certainly, as far as the Stephen speech is concerned, the content of the speech does fit in admirably with the kind of occasion that is described. Whenever dissidents of any kind are on trial for their lives, they often choose to defend not themselves, but the ideals for which they stand, and that is precisely what Stephen did. No doubt he had argued like this many times before within the synagogue itself, and others would likely repeat the same arguments on many subsequent occasions. To that extent, his speech was a confession of faith. It is not unrealistic to imagine that he would be determined to take his own last chance of standing before the highest religious authority and making sure his message was heard there too. It is certainly the sort of thing one can imagine having taken place, and in this respect it is quite different from the verbose and often irrelevant speeches which Josephus inserted into the mouths of many of his characters.

been a mistake from the start, for 'the Most High does not dwell in houses made with human hands' (Acts 7:48). He then went on to accuse the religious leaders of wholesale disobedience to the very Law that they professed to uphold (Acts 7:53).

Not surprisingly, all this was too much for them, and when Stephen committed what they regarded as the final blasphemy by asserting that he could 'see heaven opened, and the Son of man standing at the right hand side of God', he can hardly have been taken aback when he was dragged out of the council chamber and stoned to death (Acts 7:56–60).

Stephen's speech is almost unique in the New Testament. With the exception of the book of Hebrews, no other New Testament person or book has much to say about the temple and its services. But outside the New Testament there is evidence of others who disapproved of what was going on there. At a much later date, the *Epistle of Barnabas* adopted a

---

Stephen's death

The manner of Stephen's trial and death . raises some of the same questions as we have already dealt with in relation to the conviction and crucifixion of Jesus. Indeed, it seems likely from the way Luke describes the two episodes that he was consciously intending to draw some connections between the two, maybe to remind his readers that, whatever their undoubted successes, the followers of Jesus could expect to share in the same rejection at the hands of the religious establishment as Jesus himself had suffered. But whatever the literary motif behind the story might be, the same underlying historical issue arises, namely whether or not the Sanhedrin had the right to execute Stephen in the way Luke describes. At the time, Judea was a Roman province, and in Roman provinces generally the right to execute even convicted criminals was reserved for the Roman governor and no one else. This point was brought out quite clearly in the stories of Jesus' trials and execution in the gospels, and according to John 18:31 the same religious leaders who were implicated in Stephen's death had been forced to admit earlier to Pilate that 'we are not allowed to put anyone to death'.

This was not the full story, however, for there seems to have been one circumstance in which the Sanhedrin was allowed to carry out a death sentence without reference to the Roman authorities. This was in the case of a person who violated the sanctity of the temple at Jerusalem, and Josephus reports that anyone, even a Roman, who entered the temple unlawfully could be executed on the orders of the Sanhedrin (*Jewish Wars* 6.2.4). But this has all the appearance of having been a special arrangement, which simply serves to emphasize the weak position of the religious court, for if it already had general powers of jurisdiction in such cases, it would not have required this kind of special dispensation.

In view of the way that Stephen had spoken, it is always possible that he might have been deemed to have violated the temple and its rights in some way, though it is more likely that his death was not the result of a formal sentence, so much as a mob lynching. Acts 7:54–60 does not suggest that any legal verdict was given, but rather that his accusers spontaneously stoned him in their fury. There is evidence of at least one other example of such behaviour, namely the execution of James of Jerusalem in AD62.

very similar radical position on the temple, and some of its strongly anti-Jewish sentiments could easily have been inspired by the story of Stephen (there can be no question of the influence being the other way round, for *Barnabas* was not written until the early second century).

But some scholars have suggested that Stephen's thinking could have been influenced by two religious groups in Palestine who did exist at the same time as him, and who also rejected the temple in Jerusalem. These were the people of Qumran, who wrote the Dead Sea Scrolls, and the Samaritans, neither of whom took part in the worship at the temple, though they each had their own reasons for not doing so, neither of which coincided with the convictions that Stephen apparently held.

The Qumran community had imposed on themselves an enforced isolation from Jerusalem. Believing the temple and its priesthood to be corrupt, they had moved out to establish their own monastic community by the shores of the Dead Sea. But they fervently believed that this state of affairs was only temporary: they looked for the messianic age to dawn very soon, and believed that when it did they themselves would be able to return to Jerusalem and restore the temple and its worship to its original purity. Unlike Stephen, though, they did not despise the temple as an institution, but deplored what they regarded as its temporary corruption.

The Samaritans were also unable to take part in the temple worship at Jerusalem, though for rather different reasons related to their status as a renegade group within Jewish culture, with their own sanctuary on Mount Gerizim and their own version of the scriptures, which was substantially shorter than that used by the Jews themselves. There are obvious points of contact between the thinking of the Qumran community, the Samaritans and Stephen, and the way that Stephen expounded the Old Testament is not unlike the way some of these other sects would have used it. But it is problematical to suppose that Stephen had ever been a member of either group. If he had been, it is hard to see how and why he could have been in Jerusalem in the first place. It is more likely that his thinking on the temple, which was derived from the Old Testament, developed spontaneously as a result of the events of the Day of Pentecost and what followed. Through the presence and power of the Holy Spirit in the church, Christian believers felt they now had direct access to God in person, and for them that was a major reason why the temple was redundant. It had at best been an indirect means of worshipping God, and once people had direct access for themselves then the temple and its rituals became an unnecessary encumbrance for those who were following Jesus.

In Luke's narrative, the story of the death of Stephen plays a pivotal role as one of the crucial events in the life of the early church, with repercussions for the church and its development that were not restricted to Jerusalem, or even Palestine, but ultimately throughout the Roman empire.

Moving beyond Jerusalem

One of the immediate consequences of Stephen's death was a widespread persecution of the Christians in Jerusalem. There is no evidence that a majority of them had adopted the same radical attitude towards the temple as Stephen, but it was perhaps inevitable that people should suppose that most, if not all Christians would share his opinions. It was entirely predictable that the religious establishment should resist this kind of teaching, for Stephen was striking at the very heart of their power base. But the persecution that followed was counter-productive, for it led to the dispersal of Christians from Jerusalem itself, especially those elements who were perceived as the most liberal. Caesarea, Antioch and Damascus – not to mention other, more far-flung cities from which the Hellenist Christians had originally come – all witnessed a considerable influx of these people, who were not just the first Christian refugees, but turned out also to be the first Christian missionaries. This can hardly have been what their opponents intended, but the oppression of the church in Jerusalem only encouraged it to spread to other parts of the land.

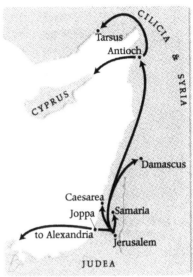

The spread of the early church.

Not all Christians felt they had to leave Jerusalem, and the Acts narrative suggests that those who continued in faithful observance of traditional religious practices were able to stay, even in the face of such intense opposition. Luke mentions by name only the apostles, but it is certain that others must have stayed behind too, all of them characterized by their commitment to uphold the Jewish faith, while incorporating within it their belief in Jesus as the Messiah. This inevitably meant that the church in Jerusalem became more conservative and more conventionally Jewish, a fact that in due course led to its demise and the extinction of all Judaistic forms of Christianity.

But Acts has very little to say about the church in Jerusalem at this time. Instead the attention shifts to the exploits of various Christian leaders elsewhere in Palestine.

Into Judea and Samaria

Philip is one of the Hellenist Christian leaders singled out for special mention in Acts, and he was no doubt typical of many others. Relatively little is known about him, but he was obviously very successful in communicating the Christian message, especially in Hellenistic cities like Caesarea. Some years later, he and his daughters were leading figures in a prosperous Christian community there (Acts 21:8–9), but before settling in Caesarea he had a successful mission among the Samaritans too. From this period, Luke includes the story of how Philip met and baptized an African, an Ethiopian government official who was presumably an adherent of Judaism, since he was on his way home from visiting the temple in Jerusalem when Philip met him in the desert. After an extended conversation about the meaning of the Hebrew scriptures, the man declared his faith in Jesus as the Messiah, and was baptized there and then (Acts 8:26–40).

Philip had been a member of the same group as Stephen, appointed to oversee the funds for Hellenist Christians, and his close association with Stephen might have been the reason he left Jerusalem. But it was not long before some of the original disciples of Jesus also began to tour the countryside of Palestine with their message. People such as Peter and John would probably never have felt at home in Jerusalem anyway, for they were themselves from the country, and the urban culture was foreign to them. Moreover, though Jesus had no doubt visited Jerusalem on several occasions during his own lifetime, the main centre of his activity was not among the conventionally religious people there, but among the marginalized 'people of the land' in rural Palestine, so it would be natural for the remaining disciples to follow his example.

Luke tells of Peter and John together visiting the Samaritans who had come to believe in Jesus as a result of Philip's mission (Acts 8:14–17). Whether or not they initially went as some kind of official delegation to check out what Philip was doing, they found themselves making a public affirmation of his work. Not only did they recognize his Samaritan converts as true disciples, but they also engaged in teaching among the Samaritans themselves (Acts 8:25). Before long Peter had become involved in an itinerant ministry over a wide area of the Palestinian countryside, visiting Lydda, Joppa and even Caesarea (Acts 9:32 – 10:48).

Widening horizons

It was in the course of such travelling that Peter was to become convinced of the importance of non-Jewish people for the future of the Christian church. Of course, he himself had probably never been as religiously conservative and traditional as some of the church members whom he left behind in Jerusalem. The very fact that he was prepared to take his message to the more Hellenized parts of Palestine is itself evidence of that. It is also significant that in the course of this tour, 'Peter stayed in Joppa for many days with a leather-worker named Simon' (Acts 9:43) – something that no strictly orthodox Jew would have been prepared to do, for workers in leather were generally regarded as being ritually unclean, since they were in constant contact with the skins of dead animals (Mishnah, *Kelia* 26.1–9). But in this case, Peter was simply following the example of Jesus himself, who had never had much time for such prohibitions, and was not afraid to have close dealings with all kinds of outcasts of Jewish society (Luke 15:1–2).

Joppa, modern-day Jaffa, was the scene of a radical about-turn in Peter's attitude to preaching the gospel to non-Jews.

While staying with this man, Peter had an experience that was to change his life. In a dream, he saw a large sheet full of 'all kinds of animals, reptiles and wild birds', many of them ritually unclean by the standards of the Old Testament food laws (Acts 10:1–23). When a voice told him to help himself to a meal from some of these creatures, all his religious instincts told him not to do so – until he was rebuked by the voice (which he now recognized to be God's) telling him, 'Do not consider unclean anything that God has declared clean' (Acts 10:9–16). This was another lesson that Peter must have heard from the lips of Jesus himself (Mark 7:14–23), though in the tense atmosphere of Jerusalem after the death of Stephen he had adopted the more expedient course of following the normal practices of the culture. But he was about to become caught up in something far larger than arguments about food, and what followed eventually had far-reaching implications for the rest of his life's work.

No sooner had Peter woken from his dream than messengers arrived at the door of the house asking that he accompany them to their master, Cornelius (Acts 10:17–22). This man was a Roman centurion in Caesarea, which was the main garrison town and the headquarters of the Roman procurators. Peter must have realized the serious implications of going there, both politically and religiously. But after the vision he had little choice, and so not only did he see Cornelius, but he entered his home and accepted the Roman's hospitality – something that would have been quite unthinkable to the Christians back in Jerusalem. Moreover, as Peter spoke with Cornelius and the members of his household the seriousness of their spiritual search was too obvious to ignore. They not only heard what he had to say, but they responded warmly to his message and when they began to speak in tongues just as the apostles themselves had done on the Day of Pentecost, Peter knew he could not deny the reality of their commitment to Christ. As a result they were baptized and welcomed into the community of the church and – as if to underline his own acceptance of them – Peter stayed in their home for a few days more, no doubt instructing them further in their new faith (Acts 10:24–28).

This was a turning-point for Peter. On his return to Jerusalem, the more conservative Christians were not at all pleased, and though his own account of the affair gave them some reassurance, the rest of Acts shows that this incident had a deep and lasting effect on Peter's relationship with the church at Jerusalem (Acts 11:1–3). Peter would never be leader of the Jerusalem church, but before long was displaced by someone who had not even been one of the original twelve disciples: James, the brother of Jesus. In addition, it was not long after Peter's visit to Caesarea that Herod Agrippa I, the ruler of Palestine at the time, instituted an official persecution of the Christians in Jerusalem. As a result of this, James, the brother of John, was martyred, and Peter himself put into prison (Acts 12:1–5). Peter's willingness to reach out to Gentiles with the Christian message might have given Agrippa the opportunity he was looking for to gain the sympathetic support of the religious establishment for his actions against the church, and if so, that would be an added reason why Peter soon fell from prominence among those Christians who also wanted to maintain their traditional Jewish allegiances.

Very little of a specific nature is known about Peter's activities after this point, but what evidence there is connects him not with the Jewish churches in Palestine, but with the Gentile churches that were soon to emerge all over the Roman empire. Paul provides evidence of an occasion when Peter visited Antioch in Syria (Galatians 2:11–14), and he also seems to have had some kind of contact with the church at Corinth in Greece (1 Corinthians 1 – 4). He seems to have travelled extensively, often accompanied by his wife (1 Corinthians 9:5), and according to well-attested traditions he had strong connections with the church at Rome, and it was there that he was put to death during the persecution of Christians by Nero in about AD64.

The church in Galilee

Apart from occasional visits to Jerusalem, Jesus spent almost all his life in Galilee. The majority of his followers lived there – many thousands of them, according to the gospels – and yet Galilee hardly ever features in the remainder of the New Testament. The story of Acts deals exclusively with the exploits of the followers of Jesus in Jerusalem and in the Gentile cities of the Roman empire, while the New Testament letters mostly relate to the same set of circumstances and none of them can unequivocally be connected with continuing communities of disciples in Galilee.

It is not difficult to see the reasons for this. Luke is the only New Testament writer to have produced anything like a history of the church, and he himself was a Gentile which ensured that his main interest – and that of his readers – would be in the work of Paul and others like him who had been instrumental in spreading the gospel to the major centres of Hellenistic population. For these people, Palestine was a little-known remote outpost of the empire, and small internal distinctions such as the difference between Galilee and Judea must have been relatively insignificant to Gentiles who scarcely knew the location of either of them. In his gospel, Luke did not always distinguish the two areas with as much precision as the other evangelists, and in Acts the only real distinction that he makes is between Jewish Christians and Gentile Christians. A native of Palestine would not have seen it like that. The Judeans had little time for the people of Galilee: it was too open to Gentile influences for their liking, and the fact that Jesus originated there was to many people a good reason for paying no attention to him (John 1:46).

In spite of the fact that followers of Jesus in Galilee would tend to be ignored by Gentile Christians and despised by those from Jerusalem, it is reasonable to assume that they must have continued to flourish. Popular movements like that built up by Jesus do not vanish overnight, especially in a rural area. But what happened to his thousands of followers in Galilee? Some have suggested that they simply dissipated and eventually went out of existence altogether. Some of them had certainly accompanied Jesus to Jerusalem, convinced to the very end that he was about to set up a new nationalist government that would overthrow the Roman rule. Judas Iscariot seems to have thought that way, and when Jesus died in apparent defeat such people probably just went back home to look for another leader. But not all Jesus' followers went with him on his last journey to Jerusalem, and not all of them had an exclusively political view of his message. These others presumably continued the work that Jesus had started in Galilee, and might easily have developed their own continuing communities of his followers independently of what was going on in Jerusalem. There are certainly some indications to support such a view:

● Galilee had always been quite different from Jerusalem, with its own ways of doing things, and its own religious traditions, most of which were despised by the more orthodox and conservative religious leaders in Jerusalem. In view of this background, it is not especially likely that the church in Jerusalem would have wanted any involvement with affairs in Galilee, and still less probable that the Galilean followers of Jesus would automatically have been prepared to accept the authority of the Jerusalem church and its leaders.

● The very character of these leaders must have been an influential factor in the development of the Galilean church. After the expulsion of the Hellenists, the church in Jerusalem seems to have taken a very conservative direction. Members of some of the very same religious groups that had been so strongly opposed to Jesus actually rose to positions of influence in the church itself (Acts 6:7; 15:5), and there are compelling reasons for thinking that James,

The church in Galilee
continued

the main Jerusalem leader, was himself a Pharisee. Presumably in aligning themselves with the Christian cause they had acknowledged Jesus as the Messiah, though that seems to have made little difference to their general outlook and behaviour. They were still firmly committed to upholding traditional rituals and customs, as can be seen from the reception they gave Peter after he had stayed with Cornelius (Acts 11:1–4). It can have been no coincidence that Peter and the other original disciples did not stay long in Jerusalem. Persecution from the authorities and resistance to their more liberal ways from within the church itself soon forced them to leave the city: did most of them return home, to Galilee?

● The assumption that they did fits neatly with the evidence relating to Peter, and provides a plausible explanation for what he might have been doing between the time when he left Jerusalem and the slightly later stage at which there is evidence for him travelling the Roman empire as an itinerant evangelist. Was it in the familiar surroundings of Galilee that he worked out his own approach to the questions raised by the admission of Gentiles to the church? If there is any truth at all in those traditions which have connected Peter to Mark's Gospel, then it is noteworthy that one of Mark's essential themes is the way in which the people of Galilee are depicted giving a warm welcome to the Christian message, while the inhabitants of Jerusalem consistently reject it. Could this emphasis reflect Peter's thinking about the development of the church at Jerusalem during this period?

● Two other New Testament books have from time to time been connected with the Galilean churches: James and Hebrews. Both of them have clear Jewish connections, and both are difficult to identify with what is known of the kind of beliefs that were held in the church at Jerusalem. James has a very uncomplicated understanding of the Christian message, with many connections in both style and

substance to the message of Jesus himself as it is reported in the gospels, while Hebrews not only seems to show some acquaintance with the traditions about Jesus, but also sets out to demonstrate the irrelevance of Jerusalem and its temple – something that would be welcomed by Galileans. Both these books are discussed in more detail in chapter 23.

No one will ever know for sure exactly what happened to the followers of Jesus in Galilee, for their story was never written down. There does however seem to be enough evidence to suggest that the movement started there by Jesus did not die out, but probably grew and flourished, at least for the lifetime of his original disciples.

The Acts of the Apostles

The book of Acts is the sequel to Luke's Gospel. The two books obviously belong together: they were both written to the same person, 'Theophilus', with the gospel intended to tell the story of the life and teaching of Jesus while Acts continues the story to describe how his small band of disciples had developed into a worldwide Christian movement.

Despite its title, Acts does not in fact tell the story of all the apostles. Only some of them are mentioned extensively, and the book has most to say about Peter and Paul, together with a few incidents from the lives of other early Christian leaders such as Philip, John, James the brother of Jesus, and Stephen. The story is told in two parts. The first is concerned mainly with events in Jerusalem and elsewhere in Palestine, and here Peter is the leading character (chapters 1 – 12). The second section of the book tells the story of Paul (chapters 13 – 28), though there are some integrating features in the narrative: Paul makes his first appearance at the stoning of Stephen (Acts 7:58), while Peter is still a major player in Luke's story of the Council of Jerusalem, which is essentially a part of the story of Paul (Acts 15:7–11).

The author

Who wrote the book of Acts? Or, to put the question more accurately, who wrote the two volumes, Luke and Acts? There is no doubt they were both written by the same person. They are both addressed to Theophilus, and their style and language are identical. Other considerations have already been outlined in the earlier discussion of Luke's Gospel, where it was concluded that all the evidence points to the author being Luke, the Gentile doctor who accompanied Paul on some of his travels.

The date

The date of Acts is a more complicated matter and three main suggestions have been put forward:

The second century

Scholars of the nineteenth-century 'Tübingen School' believed that Acts must have been written sometime after AD100, and though this view has by no means won a majority following it still has some supporters. Two main considerations are usually advanced:

● Acts 5:36–37 refers to two individuals called Theudas and Judas, and 21:38 mentions an Egyptian troublemaker. Since Josephus' *Antiquities of the Jews* 20.5.1 seems to describe the same events, and since this was not published until AD93, Acts, it is claimed, must have been written later than that. But there is no textual or stylistic evidence to support the idea that Luke used Josephus' account as a source for his own, and his description of these people actually has significant differences from what Josephus says, which means it is only possible to connect the two by making the further assumption that Luke misunderstood Josephus' story when he read it.

● It is also suggested that Acts was written in about the middle of the second century to counteract the influence of Marcion. Among other things, Marcion was suggesting that the first disciples of Jesus had misunderstood the point of his teaching, and that Paul was the only true interpreter of Jesus. It is certainly true that Acts was read with renewed interest at the time of Marcion, for its story shows little sign of the kind of misunderstanding that Marcion emphasized. But there is no real trace of second-century concerns in Luke's writings, while there are plenty of indications to connect it with the period that it purports to describe.

AD62–70

At the opposite extreme of what is historically plausible, other scholars have suggested that Acts was written almost at the same time as the events it describes – either immediately after the arrival of Paul in Rome (AD62–64) or shortly after his death (AD66–70). The following

The Acts of the
Apostles *continued*

The Roman
emperors exacted
heavy taxes both
from their own
people and
those in subject
provinces. In this
3rd-century relief
from Germany,
the collector sits
with his ledger
and heaps of
coins.

arguments are said to favour such an
early date:

● By any standards, Acts ends very
abruptly. Paul has arrived in Rome, and
the last we see of him he is 'teaching
about the Lord Jesus Christ quite openly
and unhindered' (Acts 28:31). This is not
as odd as it can be made to seem, for
from another viewpoint it is the natural
climax of Luke's narrative. The prologue
of Acts 1:8 indicates that Luke's intention
was to explain the progress of the
Christian message from Jerusalem to
Rome, and that is what he does by
ending the book once Paul has arrived
there. It was no doubt inevitable that
some readers would be curious to know
what eventually happened to Paul: did he
appear before the emperor's court, and
what was the outcome? Eusebius
supplemented Luke's story with the

information that 'after defending himself
the apostle was sent again on his
ministry of preaching, and coming a
second time to the same city suffered
martyrdom under Nero' (*Ecclesiastical
History* II.22), and *1 Clement* 5 (written
about AD95) suggested that Paul visited
Spain during this short time of freedom,
which has convinced some that it was
during this period that Paul penned the
'pastoral epistles' of 1 and 2 Timothy and
Titus. Whether or not Paul went on such
further travels, all the evidence indicates
that he was beheaded during Nero's
persecution in about AD64.

In view of all this, it is argued that if
Acts was written after Paul was dead,
then the statement about him preaching
openly and unhindered is an odd note on
which to finish the story of his life. This is
the kind of argument that can be turned

on its head, though, for since Paul was obviously Luke's hero it is just as likely that he would want to show his life ending in triumph rather than the apparent defeat of martyrdom.

● A more substantial argument is that the book of Acts adopts a generally favourable attitude to the Roman authorities. Paul's Roman citizenship is constantly highlighted as an invaluable asset which gave him freedom to travel in peace all over the empire. When he meets Roman officials they are always on his side: Sergius Paulus, the proconsul of Cyprus who became a Christian (Acts 13:6–12); Gallio, the proconsul in Corinth who gave him a fair hearing (Acts 18:12–17); even the Roman commander in Jerusalem who rescued him from a hostile mob (Acts 21:31–40). They all look favourably on Paul's mission, and

Acts gives the impression that, if the empire was not exactly supporting the church, it certainly was not its sworn enemy. All that changed in AD64, with the persecution started by Nero, and official persecution of one sort or another continued spasmodically right through to the end of the first century. On this basis it is argued that Acts must have been written prior to AD64. Like the other one, this proposition ultimately depends on a more or less subjective estimate of what an ancient writer might have been expected to do in the circumstances. In reality, there is no way of telling whether or to what extent any author might allow his or her perception of historical events to be affected by what later took place, and if Acts can be regarded as a reasonably faithful presentation of the period it describes, then its apparent pro-Roman bias might simply reflect the facts of the situation. It might also reflect Luke's own experience as a member of the Roman upper classes.

● Acts does not seem to contain any hint of the fall of Jerusalem in AD70, and if Jerusalem had been destroyed before the work was written, it is claimed that we would have expected a mention of the fact, for it would have been a striking vindication of Luke's viewpoint on Judaism and indeed on Jewish Christianity. Again, this argument depends on the assumption that it is possible to know precisely what was in the mind of an ancient author, and what he or she might be expected to write in given circumstances.

● Another relevant fact is that Acts makes no mention at all of the letters that Paul wrote to his churches. This almost certainly implies that Acts was written before the letters were collected together and circulated more widely, which certainly would date Acts earlier than a writing like 2 Peter, which mentions Paul's letters as a part of the Christian scriptures (2 Peter 3:16).

AD80–85

The consensus would be to reject both a very late second-century date for Acts and a very early date in the sixties of the first century. On this understanding, it was probably written sometime between AD80 and 90. Two substantial reasons have been put forward for this:

● Acts 1:1 begins with the words: 'In my first book I wrote about all the things which Jesus did and taught', and this 'first book' was Luke's Gospel. When he wrote the gospel, Luke incorporated stories and sayings of Jesus derived from Mark, which seems to have been written between 60 and 65. On this reckoning, Luke's first volume can hardly be placed much earlier than about 65–70, which in turn means that Acts, as the second volume, cannot have been written as early as 62–64. This is a persuasive argument though it is not the final word, for it has at least two weak spots.

Firstly, it depends on the date assigned to Mark, which to some extent is a matter of scholarly guesswork, though good reasons can be put forward in support of the generally held view.

Secondly, it is also possible that the prologues of both Luke and Acts were added last, when the two books were in their final form. If Luke's Gospel existed in some other form before its final one (whether or not that can be identified more specifically as Streeter's 'Proto-Luke'), then maybe that reflected Luke's way of working, and Acts also might have been written in stages. The passages where Luke uses 'we' rather than 'they' could have been just the first of several editions of Luke's story of the early church, an original account that was later expanded to include stories about the early Jerusalem church, perhaps brought to Luke's attention during his stay in Caesarea while Paul was in prison there. It is therefore always possible that the basic core of Acts could have been written before the gospel, with only the prologue being added later to commend it to Theophilus.

There is however a more substantial reason for dating Acts later than the lifetime of Paul. Luke's writing often seems to show signs of attitudes and beliefs which were common in the post-apostolic age. Indeed, Luke and Acts together have been regarded as a kind of manifesto of what scholars refer to as 'early Catholicism'. This subject is dealt with in some detail in chapter 22, where it is argued that the emergence of so-called 'Catholic Christianity' was a natural, almost imperceptible development of certain elements within the teaching of the apostles themselves. Whatever the outcome of that debate, however, Luke does have a distinctive outlook that in many respects corresponds to a form of church life that was more prevalent in the late first century.

For instance, by reading only Acts it would be quite easy to get the impression that the early church had a largely uncontroversial existence, whereas Paul's letters (all of them borne out of controversy) paint a different picture. No doubt it was a part of Luke's intention to stress that there was fundamental agreement between all sections of the early church, and up to a point Paul himself wanted to argue as much, for he went out of his way to emphasize his own continuity with the earliest disciples. But that is only a part of the picture, and Paul's letters more typically reveal him as a person who had profound disagreements not only with his enemies, but on occasion with his friends as well. Of course, Paul's letters also show him as a very impulsive person, and it is quite possible that some of the issues he wrote about with such passion turned out to be less serious than he thought at the time, and Luke, writing some time later, could take a more detached view of these things, and see them in their proper perspective, both in the life of Paul and in the ongoing experience of the church.

This does not mean that Luke was any less a friend or even a disciple of Paul, for good teachers do not turn out students who are clones of themselves, but encourage them to develop their own distinctive thinking. In any case, as we shall see below, the positions that Luke adopts in Acts differ from Paul in the details rather than on the fundamentals.

The real choice for the date of Acts is between the sixties and the eighties of the first century. The evidence on the one side is just about as problematic as that on the other, though the balance of probability seems to favour a date in the eighties, perhaps around AD85.

The value of Acts

What sort of book is the Acts of the Apostles? We have occasionally referred to it as a history of the early church, but of course it is not a comprehensive history: there are so many things it does not include that it is clearly not the full story of early Christianity. Instead, it is a selective story, drawing attention to those people and movements which Luke believed to be especially significant. In writing his gospel, Luke had adopted exactly the same procedure, selecting those aspects of the life and teaching of Jesus which would be most relevant to the concerns of his readers, and in Acts he covers those incidents which for him typified the trend of events among the first generation of Christians. He wanted to show how Christianity spread from Jerusalem to Rome, and everything that he included was intended to illuminate that transition. In the process, he omitted many things that today's readers might have wished to know about. What happened to Peter? How did James get on in the church at Jerusalem? What became of Jesus' other disciples? Luke simply ignores these questions because they were not relevant to his purpose.

This means that his story is also an interpretation of the progress of the early church. All history, of course, is an interpretation of past events, and the book of Acts therefore raises many of the same questions as we have already dealt with in connection with the gospels. Much of what has been said in chapters 10 and 12 can also be applied to the understanding of the historical nature of Acts, and there is no point in covering the same ground again here. It is however worth repeating that by characterizing Acts as a Lukan interpretation of early church history nothing is being either said or implied that would not be true of any kind of second-hand knowledge we might have. It is not to suggest, for example, that Luke simply invented his stories: indeed, if nothing had happened, there would have been nothing for him to interpret. Acts, however, reflects the way that Luke, from his own presuppositions and background, saw the history of the earliest church.

There are in fact a number of reasons for thinking that the picture which he painted was an essentially authentic reproduction of life in the period which it describes:

● In the prologue to his gospel (Luke 1:1–4) Luke gives some indication of his procedures: he read all that he could find, sifted through it and then wrote his own considered account of what had happened. In the case of the gospel it is possible to see pretty clearly how he went about it, for the end product can be directly compared with Mark, which was one of his major source documents. The way he has used Mark shows that Luke was a very careful writer, aware of the need to reproduce his sources accurately and without distortion. There is no comparable direct access to whatever sources he might have used in the writing of Acts, though it is widely surmised that he relied on written information for at least the stories of early events in Jerusalem and Samaria (chapters 1 – 9). The natural assumption would be that he would have exercised the same care in compiling the narrative of Acts as he had previously taken with the gospel.

The Acts of the Apostles *continued*

The inscription from one of Thessalonica's gates mentions the rulers of the city as 'politarchs' – the term used in the account of Paul's visit in Acts. It helps reinforce the authenticity of the account in the Bible.

In addition to that, he was himself personally present for at least some of the events in Acts (the 'we' passages).

● The picture Luke paints of life in the earliest Palestinian churches is consistent with what might be expected. Much of the theology which he attributes to those earliest Christian believers has a far less sophisticated character than the theology either of Paul or of the church later in the first century. For example, Jesus is referred to as 'the Messiah' (Christ) in Acts 2:36; 3:20; 4:27, and he can be called 'the servant of God' (Acts 3:13, 26; 4:25–30), or even in one instance 'the Son of man' (a title much used by Jesus himself but found nowhere in the

and its officials. He always uses the right word to describe Roman administrators, and sometimes uses terminology that would only be familiar to people living in particular cities. Sergius Paulus and Gallio are correctly designated 'proconsuls' (Acts 13:7–8; 18:12). Philippi is accurately described as a Roman colony, ruled by the *Strategoi* (Praetors), which is an unusual word to find in a literary source, but has been discovered on inscriptions which show that it was the colloquial term used in Philippi itself (Acts 16:12, 20–22). At one time, Luke was believed to have been mistaken in using the term 'politarchs' to describe the rulers of Thessalonica (Acts 17:8), because it

rest of the New Testament except Acts 7:56). The Christians are called simply 'disciples' (for example, in Acts 6:1–7; 9:1, 25–26), and the church itself is 'the Way' (Acts 9:2; 19:9, 23; 24:14, 22). Norman Perrin, whose scepticism about the reliability of the gospels was reviewed in chapter 12, describes all this as 'extraordinarily realistic... the narratives of Acts are full of elements taken directly from the life and experience of the church'.

● This same realism can be seen in Luke's description of the Roman world

is found nowhere in the rest of Latin or Greek literature. However, subsequent archaeological discoveries have shown that Luke was quite right to describe the authorities at Thessalonica in this way, though only someone who had actually been there would have been likely to do so, for it was a local term not common elsewhere. There are also many other points at which Luke's stories can be shown to depend on direct and reliable knowledge of the Roman world as it actually was at the time he purports to be describing.

● The same concern for authenticity can also be seen in Luke's representation of the problems of the early church. The only real controversy that appears in Acts is concerned with the relationship of Jewish and Gentile Christians. This argument rapidly diminished in importance, and after AD70 was of no significant concern at all, except as a theological debating point. At the time when Luke was writing, other issues were far more prominent – efforts to define heresy and orthodoxy, and various power struggles between different factions within the church – though these later concerns are never incorporated into the Acts story.

● There is just one point which may at first sight appear to undermine confidence in Luke's general trustworthiness as a historian, and this is his treatment of Paul. Paul's letters do seem to present a somewhat different angle on Paul's life and teaching from the picture of him in Acts – indeed, Acts does not even mention the fact that Paul wrote letters at all! A number of points are relevant in explaining this apparent discrepancy.

Firstly, Luke's failure to mention Paul's letters is not all that serious. He might quite possibly have regarded them as personal letters, and therefore of no great importance for his own purpose. We must also remember that though we rightly regard Paul's letters as primary evidence for his activity, they are to some extent evidence without a context and it is therefore easy for us to overestimate how their significance would be seen at the time of their composition.

More seriously, however, it is pointed out that the sort of things Paul concerns himself with in Acts are usually significantly different from his normal concerns in the letters. Again, this is not specially surprising. When Paul wrote letters, he was writing to Christians, whereas when he speaks in Acts he is usually addressing non-Christians. There has been plenty of speculation about the content of Paul's initial preaching to the Galatians, Corinthians, Thessalonians and others, but it is impossible to know for certain what he would typically have told them. One thing we can be sure of is that he would present his message in a different way to engage the attention of the unconverted than he would when trying to correct the errors of those who were already Christians. It is noteworthy that in the only instance where Acts reports an address to Christians by Paul (Acts 20:17–38), the substance of his message is not materially different from the typical content of his letters. Even his message at Athens (Acts 17:22–31) is not significantly different from what he wrote on the same subject in Romans 1:18 – 2:16.

A third consideration, however, is that significant differences are said to emerge in relation to what many believe to have been the central feature of Paul's thinking: 'justification by faith'. But this is not a strong argument, for it depends on the prior assumption that 'justification' was in fact the centre of Paul's thinking. For scholars of the Lutheran tradition (German Lutherans in particular), this assumption is beyond question. But it is equally plausible to argue that, far from being the central core of Paul's theology, this topic assumed such large importance in letters like Galatians and Romans only because, either really or potentially, a particular kind of Judaizing opposition was in view. In any case, where 'justification' does feature in Acts (for example, 13:39, the sermon in the synagogue at Antioch in Pisidia), the way it is used is not at all inconsistent with Paul's arguments in Galatians or Romans, even though it might be less comprehensively worked out. Luke was generally less interested in theological matters than Paul was, and though it has become fashionable to speak of Luke as a 'theologian', he was not a professional and he would not have had the same concern for detail that Paul himself no

The Acts of the Apostles *continued*

doubt had. The kind of theology Luke attributes to Paul is exactly what we would expect in the circumstances, and he shows his knowledge of key phrases and ideas that Paul used, while displaying less interest in the detailed arguments that could be brought out in their support.

The purpose of Acts

Though he does not address their problems directly, Luke must have hoped that his first readers would learn something from his story to help their own Christian thinking. He might therefore have had at least three primary aims in view:

● Perhaps the main thing that comes out clearly from Acts is the conviction that Christianity is a faith with the potential to change the world. Indeed, through Paul and others it *did* change the world, and the secret of its success was the endowment of the Holy Spirit bestowed on them by the risen Jesus Christ. Luke sought to encourage his readers to follow the example of those who had been Christians before them, and to do for their generation what Paul had achieved in his.

● Luke also seems to go out of his way to emphasize that Christianity could enjoy good relationships with the Roman empire. On the one hand, he commended the Christians to Rome itself, by his emphasis on the fact that their faith was the true successor of Judaism – and Judaism, of course, was a recognized religion within the empire. But he also encouraged his readers themselves to take a positive attitude towards the empire by stressing that its officials were good, honest people, and implying that a maniac like Nero was the exception rather than the rule.

Nero (AD37–68). Roman emperor from AD54 until his suicide.

● In view of the claim made at the beginning of his gospel, we must also take seriously the position of Luke as the first historian of Christianity. His two books were addressed to Theophilus in order that he might be informed about the facts of the Christian faith, and the procedure that Luke adopted for compiling his story suggests that he had a historian's interest in finding out about the past for its own sake. As the church developed into a significant community within the Roman world, it was important for its members to know their origins and history, and Luke was perhaps the first person to set some of it out in a systematic form.

The missing apostles

All three synoptic gospels, together with Acts, list twelve special disciples of Jesus, yet apart from Peter, James, John and Judas Iscariot, none of them feature prominently in the gospels, and they are not mentioned at all in the rest of the New Testament. We do not really know what happened to these people but there are a number of stories about them in early Christian writings outside the New Testament.

Thomas supposedly went to India, where he died as a Christian martyr, though not before he had persuaded a notable Indian ruler and his family to believe in Jesus. The Mar Thoma church in southern India claims that he was its founder, but it is more likely that it was established by other missionaries from the church in Edessa, by the banks of the River Euphrates. Eusebius says that Thomas himself went to India, and perhaps that is why the Indian Christians regard him as their patron saint (Eusebius, *Ecclesiastical History* III.1.1).

Andrew is said to have travelled extensively throughout Greece and Asia Minor, even crossing to the northern shore of the Black Sea. His life was allegedly characterized by miraculous deeds, including the resurrection of thirty-nine dead sailors washed up from a shipwreck! However, when the proconsul's wife in the Greek city of Patrae became a Christian, her husband was so enraged that he had Andrew crucified on a cross shaped like the letter X. Other legends claim that sometime between the fourth and ninth centuries, his arm-bone was taken by Regulus to Scotland, where Andrew became the patron saint and his cross the national flag.

Thaddaeus is mentioned in the New Testament only by Matthew and Mark. According to Eusebius (*Ecclesiastical History* I.13), a person of that name was connected with the establishment of the church in Edessa. The story tells how Agbar, king of Edessa, had written a letter to Jesus asking that he be healed of a disease, and in his reply Jesus said that after his ascension, Thaddaeus would be sent to heal him. But other traditions connect Thaddaeus with Africa.

Philip and *Bartholomew* feature in stories about their travels around Asia Minor, accompanied by Philip's sister Mariamne. The *Acts of Philip* tell of encounters with dragons and beasts who speak to them, with Philip finally being martyred in Heirapolis, though Clement of Alexandria suggests that he lived to old age. Bartholomew has also been connected with a mission to India.

Matthew is said to have preached in Judea for eight years after the ascension, before going off to Ethiopia and Arabia. According to Papias, he had something to do with Matthew's Gospel.

James, the son of Alphaeus is mentioned in Spanish traditions that tell how Theodorus, Bishop of Iria, discovered his tomb at Santiago in 835, apparently guided there by a star.

Simon the Zealot travelled to England, according to some stories, together with Lazarus and Joseph of Arimathea.

We cannot trust any of these traditions about the 'unknown' apostles. Some of them might conceivably be based on vague recollections of their exploits, but on the whole their stories are just designed to fill in the gaps in the New Testament story, and have no independent historical value.

23 Introducing Paul

After the early chapters of Acts, the centre of interest moves away from Peter and the other disciples of Jesus to another important figure in the life of the early church: Paul, the Pharisee. He was not the only Pharisee to become a Christian (Acts 15:5), but he was certainly the best known of them. Unlike the first generation of Christians, Paul was not born in Palestine, though he was a Jew. His home was in the city of Tarsus in the Roman province of Cilicia, and he was also a Roman citizen (Acts 22:3, 27).

Paul's early life

There were probably two distinct periods in Paul's early life: his childhood, spent in Tarsus, and his adolescence and early adult years, which were spent in Jerusalem. The words translated 'brought up' in Acts 22:3 could indicate that Paul was only a baby when he moved from Tarsus to Jerusalem, though it is more likely that they refer to the period of his formal education, which would mean he was resident in Jerusalem predominantly during his teenage years, or perhaps a little earlier. Since he returned to Tarsus after he became a Christian, this seems the most obvious meaning of the expression.

First and foremost, Paul was a Jew, and incredibly proud of it – as he was of the reputation of Tarsus, which was a notable university town and centre of government and trade. Though efforts have been made, from time to time, to discover the influence of formal Greek rhetoric behind the structure of some of his letters, there is little evidence that he had any specialized Hellenistic education, and the general cultural ethos of this kind of city is probably sufficient to explain the three references to Greek literature which are contained in Paul's letters and sermons: references to the poets Epimenides (Acts 17:28), Aratus (Titus 1:12), and Menander (1 Corinthians 15:33). Since Paul's parents were Roman citizens, they must have been fairly liberal in their attitude towards non-Jewish culture, and Paul's letters reveal a similar outlook on his part. Though he did not necessarily find all aspects of the lifestyle of Hellenistic culture equally appealing, Paul had a robust appreciation for life in the urban centres of the empire, and a sympathetic understanding of the pressures faced by those who became Christians from such a background.

Quite early in his life, Paul's parents decided that he should become a student and teacher of the Jewish Law. As a small child in Tarsus, he would have learned the traditions of his people through regular instruction at the local synagogue, though as a Jew of the Dispersion his first Bible was probably the Septuagint rather than the Hebrew Bible. Paul also learned the art of tent making, for all students of the Torah were expected to have a practical trade as well as doing their studies. This skill played a significant part in Paul's mission strategy later in his life, for not only did it enable him to live in financial independence of the churches he founded, but it also gave him an opportunity to share his message in the market place while plying his trade.

As a young man, Paul was soon sent away from Tarsus to the centre of the Jewish world, Jerusalem, where he became a student of the learned Rabbi Gamaliel, who was the grandson and successor of Hillel, one of the greatest rabbis of all time. Hillel (60BC – AD20) had taught a more advanced and liberal form of Judaism than his rival, Shammai, and many interpreters believe that what Jesus said about divorce might have been provoked by arguments between the followers of these two rabbis (Mark 10:1–12). Hillel was of the opinion that a man could divorce his wife if she displeased him in any way – even if she burned his dinner – whereas Shammai took the view that divorce was justified only in the event of some serious moral sin. What Paul himself later wrote on this subject suggests he must have changed his mind after he became a Christian. Paul gained at least one great benefit from his education in the tradition of Hillel. Shammai had refused to see any place for the Gentiles in the purposes of God, whereas his rival had welcomed them, positively setting out to invite them to consider the Jewish faith. No doubt it was through Gamaliel that Paul first came to appreciate the enormous spiritual potential for introducing the God of the ancient scriptures to the Gentile population of the Roman empire.

This Jewish boy has portions of the Law in a tiny leather 'phylactery', in literal obedience to the instruction in Deuteronomy 6:8 to tie the commands of the Lord 'on your arms and wear them on your foreheads'.

Paul progressed well in his studies at Jerusalem, and by all accounts was a highly successful student (Galatians 1:14). Though the exact position to which he rose in Judaism is never clearly spelled out, he had sufficient influence that when Christians were being tried for their faith he found himself in a position to 'cast his vote' against them, either in a synagogue assembly, or even possibly in the supreme religious council, the Sanhedrin (Acts 26:10).

Significant influences in Paul's life

Like that of any other young person, Paul's character was formed by many diverse influences in his early life, and their complex interaction with his inherited, temperamental disposition and his religious upbringing hold many clues to the person he became, both as a Jew and as a Christian.

Paul and Judaism

Paul himself never explicitly mentions Hellenistic influences, but he makes many statements about his Jewish background and upbringing. In particular, until the end of his life, he remained proud of the fact that he was a good Pharisee, and his many letters reveal that, even as a leading Christian, he never rejected the fundamental world-view and beliefs of his teachers. The differences of opinion on matters of faith between the Pharisees and the Sadducees appear at several points, both in the narratives of Acts and in his own letters, and on every point of dispute between these two groups, Paul always took up, and often elaborated upon, the viewpoint of the more liberal Pharisees.

A key Pharisaic belief seems to have been the conviction that history had a goal and a purpose, and the Pharisees held that God was ordering events according to a specific plan which would culminate with the coming of the Messiah to lead the people. Paul warmly embraced this view as a Christian, and used it in Romans 9 – 11 to deal with one of the things that caused him considerable personal pain – the rejection of Jesus as Messiah by the mainstream of the Jewish world. He argued that God was ordering the course of history with a view to the ultimate salvation of both Gentiles and Jews, who would be incorporated into the one community of God's people.

Pharisees also had distinctive beliefs about a future life, and Paul stressed this to his own advantage when on trial before the Sanhedrin (Acts 23:6–10), and again before Herod Agrippa II (Acts 26:6–8). But, as a Christian, Paul went further, for he wanted to add that no one could guarantee there would be a resurrection without acknowledging the fact that Jesus Christ had risen from the dead.

Pharisees believed in the existence of angels and demons, while the Sadducees did not. Again, Paul retained the Pharisaic belief as a Christian, but transformed it in the light of his experience of Christ by linking it to the cross, on which he claimed Jesus had vanquished the powers of evil. Because of this, he could describe Christians as 'more than conquerors through the One who loved us' (Romans 8:37). Though Paul had a developed angelology, he always understood angels to be heavenly beings serving as God's messengers: they could never rival the living Christ, in whom 'all the fullness of God was pleased to dwell' (Colossians 1:19).

It was not only in terms of specific beliefs that Paul continued to respect and celebrate his Jewish heritage. The very way he wrote and

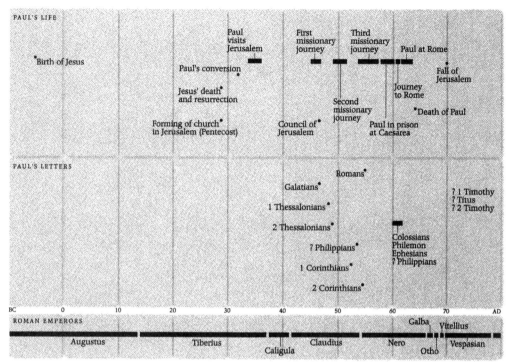

reasoned, using the Hebrew scriptures to 'prove' his theological points, was taken directly from his training as a Pharisee. No one who reads his letter to the Galatians can fail to be amazed, and sometimes surprised, by the way Paul draws what can seem to be very unusual meanings from apparently quite straightforward Old Testament passages. For instance, he was arguing like a Jewish rabbi when he claimed that the promises made to Abraham referred to a single person, Jesus Christ; the Greek word for 'offspring' (like its English equivalent) is a collective singular word and not plural in form (Galatians 3:16). Like the rabbis, Paul argued from single isolated texts, and could link up texts taken from completely different, and unrelated, parts of the Old Testament.

These specific points of agreement between Paul's upbringing as a Pharisee and the beliefs he continued to hold as a Christian are, however, relatively trivial compared with what Paul appears to have regarded as a major break between his own original beliefs and his convictions as a Christian. In recent years there has been very considerable discussion of the nature of Paul's relationship to Judaism, all focused on his attitude to the Torah. Put simply, when Paul compared and contrasted Christianity with Judaism – as he did especially in Galatians and Romans – was he being fair to Jewish beliefs about the Law, or was he setting up a misleading caricature which was then predictably easy for him to dismiss? The overall impression that Paul gives is that Jews in general, and the Pharisees in particular, were narrow-minded legalists who insisted on detailed observance not only of the actual Law of the Hebrew scriptures, but also of traditional laws and customs for which there was no biblical authority. What is more, Paul can be understood as implying that it was claimed those who did not observe all of these regulations in every particular could never attain to full salvation, and that he himself had been all but destroyed as he vainly tried to do so.

The problem is that Jewish sources themselves tend to present a rather different picture – not of oppressed people struggling hard to keep a Law that was always beyond their moral grasp, but of committed believers joyfully observing the Law as part of their total response to the love of God as they had experienced it. We take a longer look at this matter in a later chapter. Here, it is worth making three general observations:

■ Direct and specific information about Judaism in the first century is very limited, and the most comprehensive accounts of Jewish theology come from the period of the Mishnah (mid-second century onwards) and even later. After the fall of Jerusalem in AD70, Judaism was forced to reimagine itself without the temple, and underwent a considerable period of uncertainty and radical change. All the evidence relating to Jewish thinking dates back to this time. Of course, it would be unreasonable to conceive of the second-century rabbis inventing their views from nothing, and we can be certain that, to a large extent, the structure of the faith that emerged then would have been largely a systematic reordering of traditional beliefs that went back much further. Nevertheless, the lack of hard evidence that is itself contemporary with the New Testament should at least introduce a note of caution into the debate, for Paul's evidence is indisputably first-hand.

■ When we enquire about Paul's overall attitude to his Jewish heritage, the picture that emerges is more complex and more carefully nuanced than it can be made to look on the basis of some of the texts. Paul never actually stated that Judaism had not worked for him as an intellectual system; indeed, in more than one place, he claimed that he was very satisfied with it (Galatians 1:14; Philippians 3:6). Moreover, he never abandoned the belief that, somehow, the Jewish people would remain central to God's plans right to the end, and though he expressed considerable anguish that his compatriots refused to recognize Jesus as their Messiah, this did not prevent him from remaining committed to them (Acts 21:17–26), and anticipating that they would ultimately share in the benefits of God's kingdom (Romans 9 – 11). It is too simplistic to portray Paul as having abandoned Judaism, still more so to imagine that he could be described as anti-Semitic. The thing that really made a difference, as we shall see in the next chapter, was his personal encounter with the living Christ on the Damascus road. This was the ultimate source of his Christian faith, and the rest of his life was spent struggling to understand how, if Judaism was based on a revelation of God's will, it could be reconciled with what happened to him on that day.

■ Since Paul had a personal vested interest, not in seeing Judaism undermined, but in seeing it transformed as a result of the new insights he believed had been entrusted to him, it is inherently unlikely that he would have deliberately misrepresented it. Regardless of what the rabbis thought Judaism ought to be about, it is hard to get away from the conclusion that Paul himself did actually know Jewish believers who were self-righteous legalists. In any book-based religion there will always be a problem with narrow-minded bigots who pervert the spiritual essence of the faith in order to establish their own power base. The Christian church has had its fair share of such people: one need only think of the Crusades, and much of what followed them, to appreciate that, while the clearly stated essence of Christian faith in the teaching of Jesus allows no place for the imposition of the 'kingdom of God' by militaristic means, this has not deterred those who claim to follow him from making the effort to do just that. If there were first-century Jews who similarly corrupted some central aspects of their own faith, this should hardly be a cause for surprise. More unusual would be the fact that, later, rabbis were able to make a break with this and rediscover something of the more generous spirit that had always pervaded their traditional scriptures.

Paul and the philosophers

Of the many philosophical schools of the time, Stoicism was probably the most congenial to Paul. One or two of the great Stoics came from Tarsus, and Paul might have remembered something about their teachings from his youth.

Some scholars have suggested that Paul's acquaintance with Stoic philosophy was closer than this. Paul's style of debate and argument sometimes resembles the Stoics' procedures: both use rhetorical questions, short, disconnected statements, an imaginary opponent to engender debates, and frequent illustrations drawn from athletics, building, and urban life in general. It is even possible to find phrases in Paul's teaching that are not inconsistent with Stoic doctrine, even if they do not overtly support it, for example, the description of the cosmic Christ in Colossians 1:16–17: 'all things were created through him and for him. He is before all things, and in him all things hold together.' There is also the fact that, in his address at Athens, Luke reports that Paul had actually quoted from Aratus, who was a well-known Stoic poet (Acts 17:28). Some of Paul's letters also often reflect Stoic terminology, as when he describes morality in terms of what is 'fitting' (Colossians 3:18; Ephesians 5:3–4). No doubt Paul would know and sympathize with many Stoic ideals, but at a deeper level there are outstanding and quite fundamental differences between Paul's world-view and Stoicism:
■ Stoicism was based on philosophical speculation about the nature of the world and its people. Insofar as there was one, the real 'god' of Stoic thinking was abstract human reason. By contrast, Paul's faith was very

firmly based on the notion of direct revelation coming from God to humankind, most notably (though not exclusively) through the life, death and resurrection of Jesus Christ (1 Corinthians 15:3–11).

■ The Stoic 'god' was an ill-defined abstraction, sometimes associated with the whole universe, sometimes with reason, and sometimes even with the element of fire: 'What god we know not, yet a god there dwells' (Seneca, *Letters* 41.2, quoting Virgil). Paul, however, always regarded God as a personal being, definitively – though not exclusively – revealed in Christ.

■ Stoics found 'salvation' in self-sufficiency. They sought to win mastery of themselves so they could live in harmony with nature: 'The end of life is to act in conformity with nature, that is, at one with the nature which is in us and with the nature of the universe... Thus the life according to nature is that virtuous and blessed flow of existence, which is enjoyed only by one who always acts so as to maintain the harmony between the daemon within the individual and the will of the Power that orders the universe' (Diogenes Laertius, *Lives of the Greek Philosophers* vii.1.53). Paul's understanding of salvation and personal fulfilment was completely different from this, and was to be found not in dependence on himself, but in a mystical identification with Jesus Christ: 'I have been crucified with Christ, it is no longer I who live, but Christ who lives in me; and the life I now live in the flesh I live by faith in the Son of God, who loved me and gave himself for me' (Galatians 2:20).

■ Stoicism had no future hope or expectation. It was a philosophy of hopelessness, in which most people were considered incapable of reaching any moral maturity, but would be destined to be destroyed as one cycle of the world's history followed another, only to be reborn, or reincarnated, again so that the whole cycle could be repeated. Paul's theology was quite different, for he believed that the world as it now is would end decisively with the future, personal intervention of Christ himself, after which he expected a completely new world order to emerge (1 Corinthians 15:20–28).

The influence of the Stoics on Paul must be reckoned to be minimal. No one can avoid using words and phrases, even religious ones, with which they are familiar in other contexts, and on those occasions when Paul used the language of the Stoics, it was because it had a wider currency in Hellenistic culture. He certainly endowed it with new meanings, for his own message of salvation through Christ was a long way from the Stoic message of salvation through self-discipline.

Paul and the mystery religions

There are several superficial resemblances between the mystery religions and the Christian faith: both came to Rome from the east, both offered 'salvation' to their followers, both used initiation rites (Christian baptism) and sacramental meals (the Christian communion), and both referred to their saviour god as 'lord'. Undoubtedly, the two often became intertwined as converts from the mysteries entered the church and, naturally enough, used the familiar categories of their mystery beliefs as a vehicle for articulating their new faith. It was probably this tendency that was the cause of much of the trouble in the church at Corinth, about which Paul wrote in his letters to the Corinthians.

Because of these resemblances between Christianity and the mysteries, some scholars of the late nineteenth and early twentieth centuries proposed that Paul changed the simple, ethical teaching of Jesus into a kind of mystery religion. This view was rejected by the scholarly community because there is no real evidence in its favour, though it still surfaces occasionally in more popular presentations of Paul. What evidence there is tends to show quite the opposite:

■ The mysteries were always syncretistic – ready, and even eager, to combine with other religions. This was something that Christians always rejected, believing that they alone had the full truth revealed to them by Christ.

■ Much of the evidence that was claimed to show Paul was a mystery adherent is now known to have been either false or misleading. For instance, when the title 'lord' was applied to Jesus it certainly did not come from mystery religions, but from the Old Testament. The Christian

The dining room or *triclinium* in the 3rd-century Temple of Mithras under the church of San Clemente in Rome. The small altar in the foreground has a carving of Mithras killing the bull.

confession of faith, 'may our Lord come' (recorded in 1 Corinthians 16:22 in its Aramaic form, *Maranatha*) shows that the very earliest church in Jerusalem, the only one to speak Aramaic, must have given Jesus that title long before Paul came on the scene.

■ What always impressed the Graeco-Roman world was not the similarity of Christianity to other religions, but its difference from them. The accusation most often made against Christians was of atheism, because they would not admit even the possibility that other gods might exist.

No doubt Paul knew of the mystery religions and their resemblances to Christianity. They told of deities coming into the world in the guise of humans; of salvation as 'dying' to the old life; of a god giving immortal life; and of the saviour god being called 'lord'. It is possible that Paul, who was ready to be 'all things to all people' (1 Corinthians 9:22), sometimes deliberately used their language. But, as with Stoicism, it is more likely that he used it unconsciously, for the terminology of the mystery religions was widely known, and would be used as easily and uncommittedly as people today might use the language of the New Age. Paul shows no detailed knowledge of the mystery religions, and makes no clear reference to any of their ceremonies.

Paul's background included three worlds of thought: the Jewish, the Greek and the mystery. Each one of these can shed a certain amount of light on his personality and his teaching. But Paul cannot be regarded as merely the natural product of his cultural surroundings. He understood himself primarily in terms of his faith relationship to Jesus Christ, and whatever he might have gained from these other sources, the consciousness of having found new direction on the Damascus road was always dominant in his thinking.

Paul and the earliest church

But what about Paul's relationship to the other leaders of the early church? In reading the New Testament, it is not difficult to get the impression that only two people really mattered in the early church: Jesus himself, and Paul. The stories of Jesus in the gospels and the writings of Paul together account for something like three-quarters of the whole New Testament, and though we occasionally meet Peter, James, and other lesser characters such as Silas or Timothy on the pages of Paul's letters, even in the book of Acts they take a back seat to Paul himself. Of course, there are reasons for this, no doubt connected with the purpose for which Acts was written in the first place. It is, by any account, a selective story of the beginnings of Christianity: for example, if we only had Acts to go by, we might suppose that Paul was the first Christian to take the gospel to Rome, though his own letter to this church demonstrates that a large and thriving Christian fellowship existed there long before he ever visited Italy (Romans 1:6–7). Paul's work, though of fundamental importance, was clearly complementary to that of many other figures in the early church, whose names and exploits have not been recorded in any detail.

But is 'complementary' the most appropriate way to describe Paul's relationships with Peter and other early Christian leaders – or was he instead establishing a different brand of Christianity altogether, different from the original church at Jerusalem not just in character, but in belief as well? That suggestion was first put forward in the middle of the nineteenth century by the members of the 'Tübingen School' in Germany, orchestrated by Ferdinand Christian Baur. They argued there was a vast difference between Paul's type of Christianity and that of churches founded by more self-consciously Jewish Christians such as Peter, or James of Jerusalem. They understood the whole of the first generation of Christianity as a conflict between these rival forms of Christian belief – a conflict that was resolved only with the emergence of the Catholic Church in the second century. This was not a new idea and, even in the second century, the anonymous authors of *Clementine Homilies* and *Clementine Recognitions* had suggested there were irreconcilable differences between Paul and the original apostles.

Is this a fair picture, either of Paul or of the others? Was he really independent of the original base of the church in Jerusalem? Or did that become a convenient conclusion for twentieth-century scholars to reach because, on the whole, they found his open-minded view of the gospel more congenial, or even – as has been suggested – because their anti-Semitic bias required them to marginalize Jewish elements in the early church, while their Protestant bias naturally inclined them to reject anything that could be made to resemble Roman Catholicism? There is a good deal of truth in such suggestions, as we shall see in later chapters when we return to these themes. Here, it is appropriate to point out that, when the New Testament is examined more closely, whether Paul's own writings or the stories of Acts, it soon becomes clear that Paul was much more conscious of his own Jewish origins and background than the majority of early twentieth-century scholars were prepared to allow. At a number of points Paul went out of his way to establish some sort of continuity between his own Gentile churches on the one hand, and the earliest Jewish churches – even Judaism itself – on the other.

Christians and the Old Testament

It is significant that whenever Paul defined Christian faith, he consistently did so in relation to Judaism. In his letter to the Galatians, for example, the argument of which is also closely followed in Romans, the interpretation of the Old Testament is a crucial element in what he says. In one way, this is understandable, for the Galatian churches were being infiltrated by people claiming that, before being admitted to the church, Gentile believers in Jesus first needed to become Jews. Paul found this argument unacceptable for, he claimed, a living relationship with God through Jesus Christ depended on simple trust (Galatians 2:15–21). Yet, instead of merely stating this, he still held the Old Testament in sufficiently high regard to feel it was important to demonstrate the position he was taking was fully in accord with the teaching of these ancient scriptures. He argued that, long before the Old Testament Law had even come into existence, Israel's ancestor Abraham had trusted God's promises, and had found acceptance with God on that basis. Therefore, anyone who now wished to be a member of God's covenant people need only to follow the example of Abraham, and trust God, for the Law was in some ways an aberration from the original simplicity of the relationship between Abraham and God (Galatians 3:6–9).

Modern readers can find the argument of Galatians somewhat convoluted and unnecessarily complicated, but that is only due to Paul's insistence on taking the Old Testament seriously. Though he disagreed with the argument that, in order to please God, a person needed to accept the Jewish Law and customs, he accepted without question the more fundamental premise that, in order to please God, a person must become a part of the covenant nation which traced its historical origins back to the Old Testament stories of Abraham's calling. Far from dismissing those who were saying that Gentiles must become Jews in order to be Christians, he was agreeing with them. But, while they supposed that obedience to the Law was the hallmark of the real Jew, Paul redefined 'Jewishness' to lay all the emphasis, instead, on continuity with Abraham. For him, to be a child of God was to be a member of Abraham's family and, to join that, faith in God was the only required qualification (Galatians 3:6–25; 4:21–31).

This line of argument was continued in his letter to the church at Rome, in which he added the comment that 'the real Jew is the person who is a Jew on the inside... and this is the work of God's Spirit, not of the written Law' (Romans 2:29). In saying this, Paul stood in the same tradition as Stephen, and the Old Testament prophets before him, who had consistently tried to restore the covenant faith to what they believed its original position to have been, namely that obedience to God's will, and not ethnicity, was its core value. No matter how he redefined the Old Testament faith in relation to the Judaism of his own day, Paul always felt it was important that Christians, whatever their ethnic origins, understood their own spirituality within the context of the continuing actions of God in history, which had begun with Abraham, and would receive their final fulfilment and consummation at some unspecified future time (Galatians 3:29). Unlike some of his later admirers, Paul never suggested that the Old Testament was irrelevant for the Christian, but instead viewed even Gentile Christians as part of a great line of faith stemming from Abraham himself, and insisted that this was what qualified them to be a part of 'the Israel of God' (Galatians 6:16).

The church and Israel

One of the most difficult passages in the whole of Paul's writings makes all this even more explicit (Romans 9 – 11). There is no consensus on how this section of Romans relates to its context, with some commentators arguing that this is the key that unlocks the door to the rest of the letter, and others believing it was an afterthought, representing Paul's uncertain speculations on the fate of the Jewish people, rather than any kind of carefully developed thinking on the subject. Whichever view is correct, what Paul actually says is clear enough: that in his understanding, to be born a Jew still carried a distinct advantage. The whole 'people of God' (ancient Israel and their descendants, together with the Gentile Christians) can be compared to an olive tree, whose roots extend deep into the Hebrew scriptures, and onto which Gentile Christians have been grafted like a new branch (Romans 11:13–24). In the meantime, it might seem as if some of the original – Jewish – branches have been broken off, but this is only a temporary situation and they will be restored. Though it might seem to some that 'the people of God' now comprises only Gentile Christians, God had allowed them to enter the covenant only to encourage the further obedience of those who belonged to it by birth: 'Because they sinned, salvation has come to the Gentiles, to make the Jews jealous of them... the stubbornness of the people of Israel is not permanent, but will last only until the complete number of Gentiles comes to God. And this is how all Israel will be saved' (Romans 11:11, 25–26).

Paul uses the imagery of an olive tree to describe the Jewish naton, onto which Gentile Christians have been 'grafted'.

Paul concludes discussion of the subject on that somewhat cryptic note, and there are many difficulties in understanding precisely what he meant. But however he thought this was all to be accomplished, Paul clearly believed the Jews had an important part to play in the whole history of salvation, something which in itself suggests he was by no means as implacably anti-Jewish as some have suggested.

To the Jews first

Paul's missionary practice reveals the same emphasis, for whenever he went to a new town in some hitherto unvisited part of the Roman world he always went first to the Jewish synagogue (Acts 13:14; 14:1; 17:1–2). Of course, there would be good tactical reasons for doing so: since he was concerned to declare that Jesus was the Messiah, it was only natural that he should speak first to people who had some notion of who and what the Messiah might be. The fact that they had rather different expectations from Paul himself usually became clear fairly quickly, and he found himself thrown out of one synagogue after another. But that did not prompt him to abandon the strategy, for in addition to its practical advantages he also had a strong

Orthodox Jewish boy with teacher.

theological reason for operating this way: 'the gospel... is God's power to save all who believe, first the Jews and also the Gentiles' (Romans 1:16).

Jews and Gentiles

Despite this, Paul believed he was specifically called to take the gospel to Gentiles rather than Jews. According to his letter to the Galatians, this special commission was recognized by the Jewish church leaders in Jerusalem: Paul would go to Gentiles, they to Jews (2:7–9). Obviously this was not a hard and fast rule, for Paul often met and spoke with Jews, while Peter in particular was to become involved in missionary activity among Gentiles. But as a rough arrangement, it was a satisfactory division of labour. Its origin could well have been in social and economic considerations rather than purely theological ones, for Paul was a single person and therefore had more freedom to engage in long and arduous journeys than the Palestinian apostles, who had dependent families and needed regular financial support from the churches. Paul also probably had inherited wealth from his family, and could easily stay long enough in a place to take casual employment to support himself as the need arose (Acts 18:3; 2 Thessalonians 3:8).

There are many complex problems involved in understanding the accounts of Paul's dealings with the leaders of the Jerusalem church. But the fact remains that Paul evidently had regular and not unfriendly contacts with the leaders of the church there.

Paul and Jerusalem

But was it more than that? Was Paul, as some have argued, almost under the control of the Jerusalem leaders? Do his letters not conceal the truth, by making him appear much more independent than he actually was? This suggestion has gained some support from the fact that, towards the end of his third missionary tour, Paul put a great deal of effort and energy into taking a collection among the Gentile Christians of Greece and Asia Minor, which was to be for the benefit of the church in Judea (1 Corinthians 16:1–7). Hellenistic Jews throughout the empire sent an annual tax to the authorities in Jerusalem, to support the temple and its services there – so does this collection imply that the Jerusalem church exercised a similar central control over the whole Christian movement?

It seems unlikely, for Romans 15:26–27 describes the collection in the following terms: 'the churches in Macedonia and Achaia have freely decided to give an offering to help the poor among God's people in Jerusalem. That decision was their own'. Paul added that 'as a matter of fact, they have an obligation to help them. Since the Jews shared their spiritual blessings with the Gentiles, the Gentiles ought to use their material blessings to help the Jews.' In other words, conscious of his own deep indebtedness to the Jewish Christian church, Paul had organized this collection as a kind of thank offering and spontaneous expression of love for the Christians in Jerusalem (2 Corinthians 8:8–14). That would not necessarily prevent some of the Christians in Jerusalem seeing it in a different light, of course, and it has been suggested that they might have regarded it as the fulfilment of the ancient prophecies of Isaiah 60:11 in which 'the wealth of the nations' would be brought to Jerusalem by Gentile messengers 'bowing down to show their respect'.

If that were the case, however, we might expect them to have received Paul and his Gentile Christian companions with open arms. In fact it is not at all clear what happened to the collection when it finally arrived in Jerusalem, and it has been plausibly suggested that the Christians there actually refused to accept it. It is certainly notable that when Paul was subsequently arrested in the temple, it was not the Christians who sprang to his defence, but a Roman officer (Acts 21:27–40). Perhaps the more conservative Christians there had not gone as far as to lead him into a trap, but still they were not sorry to see the last of him. The same cannot, however, be said of Paul's attitude to them, and the very fact that he had made the effort to return to Jerusalem at this time shows his deep and lasting indebtedness to the leaders of the first Christian church.

Paul and the teaching of Jesus

This indebtedness also comes out in the way Paul's letters often display knowledge of and familiarity with the teachings of Jesus himself. One of their most intriguing features is the complete absence from them of any direct references to the life and teaching of Jesus. At one time it was fashionable to suggest that Paul had no time for Jesus, and that his own brand of Christianity was based instead on Greek and Roman concepts. But there are just enough references to Jesus to make that proposition unacceptable.

Occasionally, Paul says explicitly that he is quoting from or referring to 'words of the Lord' (1 Corinthians 7:10; 9:14; 1 Thessalonians 4:15), but there are many other places where his own advice is so close to the teaching of Jesus, as it is known from the gospels, that Paul must have been referring to it. An example is in the practical advice given to the church in Rome, where some key gospel themes recur:

Love your enemies	Matthew 5:43–48	Romans 12:14–21
Love God and your neighbour	Mark 12:29–31	Romans 13:8–10
'Clean' and 'unclean' foods	Mark 7:14–23	Romans 14:14
Responsibility to state authorities	Mark 12:13–17	Romans 13:1–7

Paul's knowledge of the words and deeds of Jesus had not come from personal contact with Jesus, but from those who had been Jesus' first disciples – especially, perhaps, from Peter with whom Paul spent two full weeks after his conversion (Galatians 1:18). Paul must have known a great deal more about Jesus' teaching than can be inferred from his letters, but there are probably good reasons for his apparent silence on the matter. For one thing, his letters were all occasional writings rather than considered and carefully worked out accounts of his whole theology. In addition, his readers would have been likely to know a lot about the life and teaching of Jesus already, for it is reasonable to suppose that such information would have been included in the initial communication of the Christian message. It is certainly improbable that Paul could have spoken meaningfully about Jesus either to Gentiles or to Hellenist Jews without at the same time giving them some explanation about who Jesus was. To be able to do that with conviction, he needed the cooperation and friendship of the original Jewish disciples.

Taken together, these six points suggest that, far from being an eccentric individualist, Paul was fully integrated into the Christian movement as it began among the first Jewish disciples of Jesus. But, in addressing some of these matters, we have already anticipated the course of much of Paul's life, and before going further it will be necessary to pause and consider how and why Paul the Pharisee became a Christian in the first place.

24 Paul the Persecutor

One of the most cherished beliefs of Judaism, and one that Paul no doubt shared, was that God would soon intervene in history to rescue the chosen people of Israel from the domination of alien political forces. A popular expectation was that at this time God would re-establish them as one of the great nations of the world; the Messiah would arrive in dramatic fashion, march on Jerusalem with his followers, enter the temple, and drive the hated Romans from the land. According to the gospels, Jesus had fulfilled all this and more, though not along the lines of the traditional expectation. Far from being royal, he was of obscure origins (Luke 1 – 2; John 1:46), with no army, and an obvious contempt for physical violence (Matthew 5:38–42). Though his entry into the temple (Mark 11:1–19) could be depicted as the fulfilment of the prophecy of Zechariah 9:9, it heralded not victory over the Romans but humiliation and death at their hands.

Paul felt an intense contempt for this crucified 'Messiah' and, if anything, he despised even more the activities of the followers of this pseudo-Christ who were soon claiming that after his degrading execution he had risen from the dead, and God had recognized him as the true Messiah by giving him a place of high honour (Acts 2:22–24). Paul might conceivably have had some respect for Jesus himself, for he had been an ethical teacher and said many things with which other rabbis could agree. But his followers were ignorant and uneducated and had nothing at all to commend them (Acts 4:13). What right had they to tell the religious leaders of the day that they had been mistaken, and had done nothing to prevent the death of God's own son?

Persecution

When Stephen dared to say in public that the days of the temple and its traditional religious practices were over, Paul and other religious leaders knew that the time had come for action (Acts 7:2–53). It was no longer acceptable to dismiss these followers of 'the Way', as they called themselves, as if they were amiable eccentrics, for they were beginning to pose a dangerous threat to the whole religious system. No doubt it was this fear that led to Stephen being stoned to death by a Jerusalem mob while, according to Acts 7:54 – 8:1, Paul himself stood by guarding their coats.

This is how the reader of Acts is introduced to Paul, but as the narrative unfolds it becomes obvious that he was more than just a coat minder. When he saw that the Christians were beginning to move out of Jerusalem to other places, he realized that, far from having solved the problem, the way Stephen and others were being persecuted was only helping the Christian cause to spread to other parts of the Roman empire more remote from Jerusalem and where, if it took hold, it would be correspondingly more difficult to restrict or control.

One of the places where the Christians were congregating was Damascus, an independent city within the Nabatean kingdom. At this period Aretas IV (9BC–AD40) ruled over the Nabatean kingdom, though he had no direct authority over Damascus itself (2 Corinthians 11:32–33). This was not the first time that Damascus had served as a haven for religious refugees from Judea. According to the *Zadokite Fragments* (documents that stem from a Jewish sect associated with the Essenes) a large number of Jews had fled there just before 130BC. Since these people had been able to live independently of the authorities in Jerusalem, the early Christians probably thought they could do the same. In addition, the faith communities formed by these earlier migrants might be expected to provide an ideal audience, which would be interested in hearing the Christian claims that Jesus was the awaited Messiah. Without Paul's astute mind, they might have got away with it. But he remembered that, at an earlier time in the nation's history, the Romans had given the high priest in Jerusalem the right to have Jewish criminals extradited from other parts of the empire (1 Maccabees 15:15–24), and so he went to the high priest to ask for a letter that would authorize him to pursue the Christians to Damascus, and bring them back to Jerusalem for trial and sentence (Acts 9:1–2). It was while doing so that Paul had a remarkable experience which was to alter the course of his whole life.

The Damascus road

This experience is described in detail in three different places in the book of the Acts, which shows just how important it was not only in Paul's life, but in the entire history of the early church. In Acts 9:3–19 there is Luke's summary account of what happened, then 22:6–16 presents a personal account given by Paul when defending himself before a Jewish mob in Jerusalem, and finally in 26:9–23 there is yet another account given by Paul, this time in his defence before Herod Agrippa II.

The three accounts do not agree precisely in every detail, and it is clear that Luke used them to build up a composite picture, exploring the different nuances of the experience that would be specially relevant to the concerns of the different circumstances depicted in his narrative.

In all essential points, the three accounts tell the same story. Paul was travelling along the road to Damascus, intent on wiping out the Christians there, when 'a light from heaven, brighter than the sun' (Acts 26:13) shone down on him, and he was challenged by the voice of the risen Christ asking, 'why do you persecute me?' (Acts 9:4; 22:7; 26:14). Paul's life was to take a radical about-turn, as he was presented with the possibility of understanding the world in a way more different than he had ever imagined. His inherited assumptions were not only challenged, but also shown to be false, as he realized that what was happening was, in his own words, 'a revelation of Jesus Christ' (Galatians 1:12). The one whom Paul had so despised, and whose followers he was bent on punishing, was standing before him, thereby revealing his identity as Messiah, and inviting Paul to believe in him. Though the narratives are unclear as to the precise moment of Paul's conversion, they leave no doubt that he became a new person as a result of what happened both on the roadside and, subsequently, in Damascus itself. From this moment onwards, the Pharisee who had hated the Christian faith was to be one of its greatest advocates, and he was to place his traditional faith in a different perspective altogether as a result of what happened that day.

Like most notable events, Paul's conversion did not spring from nowhere. Unquestionably, he already knew a great deal about the life and teachings of Jesus of Nazareth – indeed, on the basis of what he later wrote in 2 Corinthians 5:16, some have concluded that he might have been personally acquainted with Jesus during his lifetime. That seems unlikely, but what is certain is that he must have taken a considerable interest in the kind of interpretation that was being placed on the scriptures by Hellenist Jewish Christians like Stephen. By depicting him as a bystander, watching the coats at the stoning of Stephen, Luke was probably intending to suggest that, even at that time, Paul had a hesitating sympathy with what was being said. Either way, there can be little doubt that such thinking had an enormous and profound influence on his own life for, in many respects, the later teaching of Paul on the place of Old Testament Law and covenants in the Christian life was but a logical extension of the teaching of those Hellenist Jews who were Christians before him.

Paul gives several accounts of the decisive events on the Damascus road, when the risen Christ spoke to him. The encounter meant a radical change in Paul's life.

Though Paul's letters show him to have been mostly concerned about the Law as a source of morality, and not much interested at all in its ritual and ceremonial aspects, much of what he later wrote about the temporary and passing nature of the Law bore a striking similarity to Stephen's arguments about the Law and the temple (Galatians 3:1–25).

When Paul arrived in Damascus after his remarkable experience, he was unable to see, and was overwhelmed by it all for three days, during which he neither ate nor drank. But when Ananias, a Christian living in Damascus, went to visit Paul his sight was restored, Paul was baptized, and then introduced to the Christians in the city (Acts 9:10–19; 22:12–16). Like Peter at the household of Cornelius, Paul discovered that, within the community of the church, he would find acceptance among people who, on any other ground, would have been abhorrent to him. In many ways, his experience was even more radical than that of Peter, for the people who welcomed him so generously were the very ones he had been intent on hounding to death. In the light of this, it is hardly surprising that, when he wrote to advise the Galatian Christians, who were struggling with the consequences of ethnic diversity, he should have emphasized his conviction that people of different social and religious backgrounds could come together only through living a shared commitment to Jesus Christ: 'there is no difference between Jews and Gentiles, between slaves and free men, between men and women; you are all one in Christ Jesus' (Galatians 3:28).

The different accounts of Paul's conversion

There are three main differences in points of detail between the accounts of Paul's conversion:

● In Acts 9:7 Paul's companions heard the voice of the risen Christ, but saw no *person*. They might have seen the bright light. In 22:9 Paul says they 'saw the light but did not hear the voice of the one who was speaking to me'. What they heard was presumably a sound, but not an intelligible voice. The account in chapter 26 does not refer to the companions either seeing or hearing.

● In Acts 9:4 and 22:7 the only person mentioned as falling to the ground is Paul, the central figure in the drama, though this need not exclude the possibility that the others fell to the ground, as in 26:14.

● In Acts 9:6 and 22:10 Paul is told to go on to Damascus, where he will be instructed what to do, whereas in 26:16 his commission to be an apostle is given at the time of the vision. As he reflected on it later, Paul generally identified the entire experience as the occasion of his call, and Galatians 1:11–12 seems to imply that the actual content of his message was given to him on the Damascus road.

These distinctions are not of great importance and can be easily explained by reference to the different purposes of the narratives in each case. Indeed, the fact that these variations in emphasis have been preserved by Luke instills greater confidence in his abilities as a credible historian. If he had invented the story he would have been more likely either to have told it only once, or to have made sure that each account of it was identical with the others in form and language.

It was this burning conviction that inspired Paul to carry the Christian message not only to the cities of Palestine – places like Damascus itself, Antioch, and even Jerusalem – but also to the furthest corners of the world as it was known to him. In doing so he displayed an amazing vitality and, through his many letters, he has provided an invaluable series of snapshots of what it was like to be a Christian in the wider Roman world of the first century AD. It was not all easy going, even for an apostle, and Paul's long journeys must have been physically exhausting and highly dangerous. But Paul was undaunted for, from the time of his conversion, he was quite convinced that he was not alone in his endeavours, but the Christ whom he had encountered on the Damascus road was living within him and empowering him for this work. Paul's references to his achievements in Judaism show him to have been a fanatical believer, and, from that moment onwards, all his energy was redirected into serving Christ. Writing towards the end of his life, he put it like this: 'I count everything as loss because of the surpassing worth of knowing Christ Jesus my Lord' (Philippians 3:8).

Paul did not forget his original purpose in coming to Damascus, which had been to visit the Jewish synagogues of the city. He went straight to the Jewish community, where his arrival was undoubtedly expected. But his message was not what they expected, for instead of denouncing the Christian faith he proclaimed it, and made known his new allegiance to Jesus the Messiah (Acts 9:20–25). In Galatians 1:17 Paul mentions a brief visit to a place he refers to as 'Arabia' (probably an area near Damascus) before returning to Damascus for three years. Though Luke never mentions it, this is not inconsistent with the narrative of Acts, where it is stated that he remained in Damascus for 'many days' (9:23). He might have retreated to 'Arabia' immediately after meeting Ananias, or he might have gone there after some initial teaching in the synagogues.

Eventually, Paul found it impossible to stay any longer in the city of Damascus. Religious and civil authorities were both eager to get rid of him, so his friends secretly let him down over the city wall in a basket (Acts 9:23–25; 2 Corinthians 11:32–33).

Paul and the Jerusalem Christians

At this point, Paul paid a visit to Jerusalem, which was probably the one described in Galatians 1:18–24. Not surprisingly, his arrival struck terror into the disciples in Jerusalem until Barnabas, one of the leaders of the church, told them of Paul's conversion and witness in Damascus (Acts 9:26–30). After this, Paul went out and shared his new message with such boldness in Jerusalem itself that the apostles sent him away to Caesarea for his own safety, and from there he returned to his original home in Tarsus. Paul later explained that his main motive for visiting Jerusalem at this time had been to meet Peter, with whom he stayed for fifteen days. He also met James, the brother of Jesus, though he did not meet many of the other Christians, and most churches in the area only knew of him by reputation (Galatians 1:18–24). He then spent the next eleven years in Cilicia and Syria, probably still unknown to many of the original believers in Jerusalem and the surrounding area.

Though the Christians in Jerusalem might justifiably have forgotten Paul, Barnabas did not and, when he found himself becoming involved in the work of the church in Antioch, in the Roman province of Syria, he sent for Paul to come back from Tarsus to help (Acts 11:19–26). Paul and Barnabas had been working together for about a year in the church at Antioch, when a prophet named Agabus arrived from Jerusalem and declared to the church that a great famine was coming, which would adversely affect the well-being of the Christians in Jerusalem (Acts 11:27–30). The largely Gentile church in Antioch decided to send aid to their fellow believers, and delegated Barnabas and Paul to take the relief fund in person. Luke's narrative places this visit to Jerusalem in AD43, when the persecution of Christians in Jerusalem, begun by Herod Agrippa I in AD42, was still continuing. It was probably this visit that Paul referred to in Galatians 2:2; the 'revelation' of which he speaks was presumably the prophetic message of Agabus about the famine. Paul added the further information that, on this visit, he only saw the church leaders in private, which would be easy to understand if there was persecution going on at the time.

Antioch, on the River Orontes, was the third largest city in the Roman empire. It was the capital of the Roman province of Syria, and an important centre of commerce. The church at Antioch was fast-growing and dynamic. The town is now Antakya in south-east Turkey.

Paul and the Gentiles

Paul's own account of all this makes it clear that his meeting with the leaders of the Jerusalem church was crucial for the emergence of his own ministry, for at this time the original apostles indicated their willingness to recognize his mission to the Gentiles as a valid extension of the Christian message (Galatians 2:1–10). This was an important issue for the early church.

Some Jews, mostly those living in the Dispersion and Pharisees of the more liberal school of Hillel, had shown considerable missionary zeal in winning converts to Judaism. But their converts were required to obey the traditional law in its entirety, both ritual and moral. Though it was possible to join in Jewish worship as 'God-fearers', without taking upon themselves the whole burden of the Jewish Law (like Cornelius), a central requirement for those who sought full admission to the Jewish faith community was the rite of male circumcision. The church leaders in Jerusalem, who were all practising Jews and probably regarded themselves as a reforming movement within Judaism rather than a separate faith, naturally took it for granted that any Gentiles who wished to become Christians would first become Jews, by being circumcised.

The experience of Peter with Cornelius had convinced them that it was possible for a Gentile to be converted and receive the power of the Holy Spirit (Acts 10:1 – 11:18), but when Paul and Barnabas inaugurated a mission among the Gentiles in Antioch it raised different questions altogether. For one thing, Cornelius had been an adherent of Judaism and, though he was a 'God-fearer' and not a full proselyte, his case was, therefore, somewhat different from that of converts with no previous connections to Jewish spirituality. In addition, there does not appear to have been a widespread Christian movement connected with Cornelius at the time of Peter's visit, whereas in Antioch a church of Gentile believers was formed. The Jerusalem leaders were willing to recognize that Paul and Barnabas were engaged in a commendable enterprise, but they refused to accept any responsibility for it.

When Peter visited Antioch afterwards, he at first followed the custom established by Paul, and ate with the Gentile converts. Peter himself had previously eaten a meal in the home of Cornelius, but this would not normally have been an acceptable practice for an orthodox Jewish believer. When less liberal Christians arrived in Antioch from Judea, Peter was easily persuaded to abandon the practice, and Barnabas joined him. This inconsistency led to a severe rebuke from Paul, and the evident tensions running through this episode provide the first example of something that was to trouble Paul throughout his ministry. Although he knew that his own special mission was to Gentiles, Paul could never forget his people. He was proud of having been born into the Jewish faith community, and constantly went out of his way to affirm the advantages it had given him. Yet, in his heart, he believed the religious leaders had been mistaken in not recognizing Jesus as the Messiah. He felt so passionately about it that in Romans 9:3 he went as far as to declare, 'I could wish that I myself were accursed and cut off from Christ for the sake of my own people, my kindred according to the flesh'. But he never quite came to terms with the extent to which the issue of Gentiles becoming Christians would divide the church. As Paul began to fulfil the terms of his calling, inviting Gentiles to follow Jesus without ever considering the long history of the faith tradition they would enter, it took only a short time for the rumblings of discord first heard in Antioch to develop into a full peal of thunder.

Who were the prophets?

When Paul was giving advice to the Christians at Corinth about the use of spiritual gifts within their church, he advised them to desire all the gifts that had appeared among them, but especially 'prophecy' (1 Corinthians 14:1–5; 12:4–11). What was this prophecy, which is mentioned not only in 1 Corinthians, but also throughout the book of Acts?

It is clear that there was, in the early church, an important group of men and women known as prophets. They are regularly listed immediately after the apostles (1 Corinthians 12:28–29; Ephesians 2:20; 3:5; 4:11), while the tasks of evangelist, pastor and teacher, to which later Christians have always given a high priority, are regularly placed after the prophets in order of importance (1 Corinthians 12:28–29; Ephesians 4:11; Acts 13:1; Romans 12:6–8).

These prophets seem to have been people with particularly close access to God's will, which enabled them not only to forecast certain specific events in the future (as Agabus did, Acts 11:28; 21:10–11; see also Revelation 22:6), but also to deliver other authoritative guidance for situations that arose within the church. In Acts 13:1–4 the prophets of the church at Antioch, inspired by the Holy Spirit, gave directions that Paul and Barnabas should be 'Set apart for... the work to which I have called them,' while the four daughters of Philip the evangelist regularly acted as prophets in the church at Caesarea (Acts 21:8–9). The deliverance of prophecy was also involved in the appointment of Timothy (1 Timothy 1:18; 4:14), while at other times prophets could be found rebuking Christians who were lazy, or encouraging those whose faith was under attack (see for example Acts 15:32; 1 Corinthians 14:3).

In addition to such practical activities within the Christian community, prophets also had an important theological task. 1 Corinthians 13:2 equates being a prophet with understanding 'all mysteries and all knowledge', while Ephesians 3:5–6 indicates that the prophets had a particular part to play in explaining how Gentiles could be incorporated within the community of God's people, which had its beginnings in Old Testament times. At the same time, however, prophets could get things wrong, and Paul laid considerable emphasis on the need for prophetic utterances to be scrutinized by the further gift of 'discernment' whereby the true and the false might be distinguished (1 Corinthians 12:10).

Nevertheless, the prophets were highly regarded in the churches of the New Testament period, as charismatically inspired individuals who enjoyed particular insights into the Christian message, and through whom God's will could be made known to the church.

What happened after Paul's conversion?

In describing what happened after Paul's conversion on the Damascus road, we have taken information from Acts and Paul's letter to the Galatians and, by combining these two sources, it has been suggested that the order of events was as follows:
● Paul's conversion (Acts 9:3–19; 22:6–16; 26:9–18; Galatians 1:11–17).
● A brief stay in Damascus (Acts 9:19b).
● A visit to 'Arabia' (Galatians 1:17–18).
● Work in Damascus for something like three years (Galatians 1:17; possibly Acts 9:20–22).
● Paul's first visit to Jerusalem after his conversion (Acts 9:26–30; Galatians 1:18–20).
● Paul's stay in Tarsus (Acts 9:30; 11:25; Galatians 1:21).
● Barnabas joins the Christian movement among the Gentiles in Antioch (Acts 11:20–24).
● Paul joins Barnabas in Antioch (Acts 11:25–26).
● Paul and Barnabas visit Jerusalem with famine relief for the church there, fourteen years after Paul's conversion (Acts 11:29–30; 12:25; Galatians 2:1–10).

This interpretation is by no means universally accepted, and is only one possible way of understanding the various time references provided by Acts on the one hand, and by Paul himself on the other. There is a major dispute concerning whether Paul's own account of his contact with the Jerusalem apostles can be reconciled with Luke's narrative in Acts.

From Galatians 2:1–10 it is obvious that Paul regarded the visit he describes there as absolutely crucial for his entire ministry to the Gentiles. In trying to connect this with Acts, it is natural to look for an account of a visit which had the

same kind of far-reaching significance for Paul's ministry to the Gentiles, and the occasion that most obviously appears to meet this requirement is depicted in Acts 15:1–29. This is the occasion often known as 'the Council of Jerusalem' when Paul and Barnabas, sent to Jerusalem as official delegates from the church in Antioch, met in some kind of formal session with the other apostles and church leaders to try to decide once and for all what was to be required of Gentile Christians in relation to

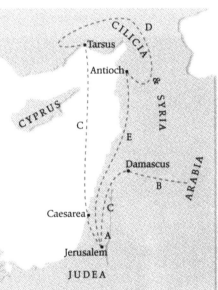

paul's movements between his conversion and the Council of Jerusalem.

the Jewish Law. While the traditional view has, therefore, been to regard Acts 15:1–29 as an account of the same meeting as Paul describes in Galatians 2:1–10, this identification raises two major problems:
● According to Acts 15:1–29, this visit resulted in a thorough and wide-ranging discussion of the very issues with which Paul was dealing when he wrote Galatians, namely the question of the status of Gentile Christians, whether they should be expected or required to observe the Torah, and if so whether they needed to keep the Law in its entirety, or only certain aspects of it. Acts 15:23–29 records the details of a compromise

What happened after Paul's conversion?
continued

worked out by the Council, with the agreement of Paul and Barnabas, which was apparently accepted by all concerned as an appropriate basis for the admission of Gentiles to the Christian church. Yet, in Galatians 2:1–10, Paul makes no reference to any such agreement having been made, even though it would have been crucial in this defence of his own position. In Galatians 2:6 he confidently declares that the Jerusalem church leaders 'added nothing to me', which is a very different story from that in Acts 15:1–29, where they insisted that he should stick to the

same position as everyone else, which he evidently agreed to do.

● If Acts 15:1–29 refers to the same events as Galatians 2:1–10, there is a further historical discrepancy between the two accounts. Between Paul's conversion and the Council visit, Acts tells of two earlier visits to Jerusalem (Acts 9:26; 11:30; 12:25), while Paul mentions only one (Galatians 1:18). It is virtually unimaginable that Paul could have been mistaken, for the whole of his argument in Galatians depends for its validity on the assumption that he was describing every

The church at Antioch sent Paul and Barnabas with relief funds to help the Christians in Jerusalem. This early Byzantine structure in Antioch has been claimed as the first Christian church building.

single meeting he had ever had with the Jerusalem leaders. To have omitted one of them – especially such a significant one – would have undermined everything he was arguing for. It would, therefore, be necessary to suppose that Luke was mistaken in his account in Acts, either by describing the same incident twice, or out of sheer ignorance of what really happened.

Besides these difficulties in correlating Acts 15:1–29 with Galatians 2:1–10, several smaller points of detail can also be interpreted to suggest the alternative possibility that, in fact, these two accounts are not describing the same meeting:

● In Acts 15:2, Paul and Barnabas were 'appointed' by the church at Antioch to go to Jerusalem and meet with 'the apostles and the elders'. In Galatians, however, Paul quite specifically uses different language, saying that he 'went up by revelation' (Galatians 2:2).

● The conference of Acts 15:1–29 seems to have been a semi-public, and certainly formal event with the apostles and elders and 'the whole church' involved in it (Acts 15:22). In Galatians, however, Paul makes a special point of mentioning that the meeting was held in private (Galatians 2:2); and only James, Cephas (Peter) and John are mentioned by name in connection with it (Galatians 2:9).

● The outcome of the meeting of Acts 15:1–29 was a decision ('the Apostolic Decree') allowing Gentile converts to remain uncircumcised, while also insisting that they ought to observe certain traditional dietary customs, which would make it easier for Jews to eat meals alongside them (Acts 15:28–29). The outcome of the Galatians conference, on the other hand, was a mutual recognition of Paul and Barnabas as apostles to the Gentiles, and of Peter and the others as apostles to the Jews (Galatians 2:9–10), with no mention at all of the relational complexities between the two groups within the church.

In view of these differences between Acts 15:1–29 and Galatians 2:1–10, it seems better to suppose that Galatians 2:1–10 records the same events as Acts 11:29–30 and 12:25. There are at least four factors in favour of this:

● The claim that Paul went to Jerusalem 'by revelation' (Galatians 2:2) would be a natural way to refer to the prophecy of the famine by Agabus, which was the immediate occasion of the Jerusalem visit of Acts 11:28.

● Galatians 2:2 suggests that the meeting with the church leaders was a private one, and Acts dates the famine either during, or shortly after, the persecution of Herod Agrippa I, which could easily explain the need for such secrecy. The absence of James and other Christian leaders from the meeting mentioned in Acts 12:17, which took place during this visit, is also consistent with this reconstruction.

● It is possible to translate Galatians 2:10 as follows: 'Only they asked us to go on remembering the poor, and in fact I had made a special point of doing this very thing.' On this understanding, Paul could have been making a direct allusion to some such visit as is recorded in Acts 12:25, when he took famine relief to the Jerusalem Christians.

● Since Paul obviously intended to recount every visit he made to Jerusalem, from the time of his conversion to the time he was writing, and if Acts 11:29–30 refers to the same event as Galatians 2:1–10, this provides a simple explanation for his silence regarding the terms of the Apostolic Decree: the Apostolic Council had not yet taken place.

On this interpretation, Paul's letter to the Galatians must have been written sometime between the events of Acts 12:25 and Acts 15:1–29, though this in turn raises other important questions about the date of Galatians which will be dealt with in the next chapter.

25 Into All the World

Not long after they had returned from Jerusalem to Antioch, Paul and Barnabas entered a new phase of their work, as the Gentile church there, following guidance from its prophets, set the two friends apart and sent them off on their first real missionary expedition (Acts 13:1–3).

From Antioch to Cyprus

When they left Antioch, they firstly went to Cyprus, which was Barnabas' home country. In the story of Paul's meeting with the Roman proconsul, Sergius Paulus, in the capital, Paphos, Luke introduces one of the central themes of the book of Acts, namely the warm acceptance of Paul's message by representatives of the Roman empire (Acts 13:6–12). Significantly, too, from this point in his narrative Luke abandons the use of the Hebrew name Saul, and exclusively refers to him by his Roman name, Paul. This narrative also introduces another theme, in the form of Elymas, or Bar-Jesus, a Hellenistic magician who attempted to thwart Paul's efforts to convince Sergius Paulus of the truth of his message about Jesus. Just as the gospels depict Jesus himself as confronting the power of alternative spiritualities, so throughout Acts, Paul is faced with the same kind of challenge.

After a promising start, Paul and Barnabas left Cyprus and sailed to the south coast of Asia Minor, then crossed the mountains into Pisidia, to another town called Antioch (Acts 13:13–14). From there they pressed on eastwards to the region of Lycaonia, which was part of the Roman province of Galatia and, after successful missionary work in several towns of that region, they returned to Antioch in Syria by roughly the same route, except that they did not visit Cyprus again (Acts 14:21–28). In each town, the apostles began their work in connection with the Jewish synagogue. Probably they felt that in this context they were likely to meet the kind of Gentile 'God-fearers' who would be most open to their message. On the return journey, Paul and Barnabas made a point of revisiting each new congregation of Christians that had been formed, encouraging them in their new faith and helping their leaders to understand what might be required of them (Acts 14:21–23).

At some stage during this trip Paul seems to have fallen ill, for in writing to the Galatians he referred to a disease which gave him a repulsive appearance when he was with them (Galatians 4:13–15). He also mentions elsewhere that he suffered from a 'thorn in the flesh', which might well have been the same ailment (2 Corinthians 12:7). The way it is described in Galatians suggests it must have been some kind of eye disease.

The first Gentile churches

As a result of Paul's visits to these cities, many Gentiles came to believe in Jesus Christ. Besides Jewish proselytes and God-fearers, there were many others with no previous connection at all with Judaism. Paul began to realize how much potential there was for sharing the gospel with Gentile people, and the significance of his own calling in that respect. His experiences at this time also convinced him that Gentile believers should be admitted to the Christian community on the basis of their faith in Christ, and with no further obligation to be circumcised, or to observe other conditions derived from the Jewish Law. One of the first discoveries Paul made after his own conversion had been that his new understanding of Jesus Christ helped him establish a new relationship with other people, including those whom he might previously have looked down on. In the same way, he now found that, though he himself continued in his Jewish observance, a shared belief in Jesus enabled him to enjoy a new level of meaningful relationship with Gentiles of all sorts. This was what Paul had come to expect, following his experience on the Damascus road, for it had been made clear to him then that he was to fulfil a very special role in spreading the Christian message through the wider Roman empire. When he and Barnabas returned to Syrian Antioch, they were welcomed by the church there, who agreed with their strategy of taking the gospel directly to Gentile people, and celebrated their success in evangelizing the inhabitants of southern Asia Minor.

Judaizers

But this happy situation did not last for long. Emissaries from the Jerusalem church soon arrived in Antioch with a very different attitude. What was worse, from Paul's point of view, they also visited the new groups of Christians which he and Barnabas had just established in the course of their first missionary expedition (Galatians 2:11–14). Their arrival created havoc among the new Christians as they told them that Paul had only delivered to them a very deficient account of the Christian message. According to Paul, if Gentiles were willing to accept the claims of Christ over their lives they would be given power by the Holy Spirit working within them to live the kind of life that was pleasing to God. To many more conservative Jewish Christians, this idea was blasphemous. Their understanding was that God's will had been revealed in the Old Testament, where it had been clearly taught that, in order to be a part of the community of God's people, a person must be circumcised and observe many other regulations. So how could Paul claim that these Gentiles were proper Christians when they had never even considered the full implications of God's ancient revelation? How dare he suggest that an acceptable standard of Christian morality could ever be attained by any means other than careful observance of the rules clearly laid down in the Torah?

The new converts were thrown into confusion by such teaching. All they knew was that they had accepted the message

Paul's first missionary journey.

Paul declared, that their own experience of Christ matched what had happened to Paul on the Damascus road, and that they could expect to be empowered by the Holy Spirit to live in a way that would be pleasing to God. The majority of them had never been followers of Judaism, and had no idea what was in the Old Testament. Paul had given them no indication that it was necessary for them to find out in order to be acceptable to God.

But when these new Christians began to read the Old Testament under the guidance of the Judaizers who had now visited their churches, they found themselves faced with a mass of rules and regulations, many of which seemed irrelevant to the reality of life in the average Hellenistic city, and which they had no real inclination to fulfil, even if it was necessary to do so for salvation. Some of them decided to make a brave attempt, and began by keeping the sabbath and possibly certain other traditional festivals as well (Galatians 4:8–11). A number of them even started thinking seriously about being circumcised, in order to fulfil what seemed to be the requirements of the Old Testament (Galatians 5:2–12). But the great majority simply did not know what to do.

This was the point at which news of the situation reached Paul, and he was infuriated by what he heard. It was not practical for him to visit these new converts again just at that particular time, so in the heat of the moment he decided that he must write them a letter. This was the letter known to us as the epistle to the Galatians.

Paul the letter writer

When Paul wrote letters to the Christians who were under his care, he naturally followed the common style of the day. An ancient letter usually had a more or less set pattern, and Acts 23:26–30 contains a typical example of such a letter in the form of the message sent by Claudias Lysias to Felix at the time when Paul was committed for trial. Paul always adopted the same structure in the letters he wrote to churches:

■ Unlike a modern letter, an ancient one would always begin with the name of the writer, and only then would it name the person to whom it was sent. Paul follows this quite closely.

■ Then followed the greeting, usually a single word. Paul often expanded this to include the traditional Hebrew greeting, *shalom* ('peace') together with a new, Christian greeting ('grace' – in Greek very similar to the normal everyday greeting).

■ The third part of a Greek letter was a polite expression of thanks for the good health of the person addressed. This was usually expanded by Paul into a general thanksgiving to God for all that was praiseworthy in his readers.

■ Next followed the main body of the letter. In Paul's letters this was often divided into two parts: doctrinal teaching (sometimes in response to questions raised by his readers), followed by advice on aspects of the Christian lifestyle.

■ Personal news and greetings came next. In Paul's case this was more often news of the churches and prominent individuals in them, though occasionally there might be news of Paul himself.

■ There was often also in Paul's letters a note of exhortation or blessing in his own handwriting, as a kind of guarantee of the genuine and personal nature of the letter.

■ Finally, ancient letters often ended with a single word of farewell, a feature which Paul almost always expanded into a comprehensive expression of blessing and prayer for his readers.

Paul writes to the Galatian churches

A quick look at Galatians reveals just how closely Paul kept to this pattern, even when he was writing what must have been a very hurried letter. He began by giving his own name, 'Paul an apostle', and he also associated with his letter 'all those of God's family who are with me'. He then named the people to whom he was writing, in this case a group of churches: 'the churches of Galatia'. The greeting followed, 'Grace... and peace', and was expanded into a brief sentence of praise to God (1:1–5).

Antioch in Pisidia, high in what is now central Turkey, was a Roman city with a strong Hellenistic Greek and Jewish culture – just the sort of place Paul chose for his visits. The aqueduct once carried by these arches provided Antioch's water supply.

One very significant omission is to be noted at this point. Nowhere in Galatians did Paul give thanks for the spiritual condition of his readers. There was nothing to be thankful for: they had not been Christians long enough for Paul to be able to refer to praiseworthy deeds done in the past (as he did, for example, in Philippians 1:3–11), and their condition at the moment of writing certainly gave Paul no cause for thanksgiving.

After that, the main body of the letter follows, divided roughly into a doctrinal and a theoretical section (1:6 – 4:31) and a practical description of Christian living (5:1 – 6:10). No personal news and greetings finish this letter, perhaps because of the haste with which Paul was writing, or because he had no time for such pleasantries with people who had so readily disregarded his teaching. He did, however, include a final appeal in his own handwriting, which contained the interesting information that his own writing was much larger than that of the secretary who had written most of the letter – an observation which, incidentally, gives added probability to the suggestion that Paul might have suffered from bad eyesight (6:11–17). Paul then drew his letter to a conclusion with a blessing which was also a prayer for his readers, assuring them that a power greater than their own was ready to their hand: 'The grace of our Lord Jesus Christ be with your spirit, brothers and sisters, Amen' (6:18).

The letter and its argument

That has covered only the bare bones of the letter. But what was Paul actually saying? Though Galatians is not an especially long and involved letter, it is not always very easy to understand Paul's meaning. This is partly because the letter was written hastily in the middle of a raging controversy, and in such circumstances people do not express themselves in the ordered way they would in calmer moments. But the complexity of his expression also stems partly from the subject matter, for Paul was very much at home in the Old Testament and was able to quote it with great freedom as he set out to expound the twin principles of liberty and equality within the Christian community.

Paul's letter falls conveniently into three main sections, as he deals in turn with what he regarded as three false ideas that were being propounded by the Judaizing teachers, who had visited the Galatian churches.

Where did Paul get his authority?

The first thing the Judaizers had said was that Paul was not a proper apostle, and because he was not one of the original twelve, nor had he been accredited by the original apostles in Jerusalem, he had no right to give any directions to new Christians, so they ought to pay no attention to what he said. Paul's reply to all this is in 1:10 – 2:21, where he argues strongly that he needed no authorization from Jerusalem or anywhere else, since he himself had met with the risen Christ on the Damascus road. Far from being inferior to the others, he had encountered Jesus face to face – indeed, he was in the same situation as James, the Jerusalem leader, who had a very similar experience to Paul (1 Corinthians 15:7). This was where he got his accreditation as an apostle (Galatians 1:11–12) and, though he had visited Jerusalem on several occasions, he had never felt it necessary to obtain the permission of the original disciples to carry on his work, nor had they suggested that he needed such permission (1:18 – 2:10). In fact, quite the opposite was the case, for 'when they saw that I had been entrusted with the gospel to the uncircumcised [i.e. Gentiles]; just as Peter had been entrusted with the gospel to the circumcised [the Jews]... and when they perceived the grace that was given to me [by my encounter with the risen Christ], James and Cephas and John... gave to me and Barnabas the right hand of fellowship; that we should go to the Gentiles and they to the circumcised' (Galatians 2:7, 9). Subsequent events at Antioch had proved conclusively that Paul was in no way inferior to Peter (Cephas), who was commonly reckoned to be the greatest of the apostles. When Peter had broken off eating with Gentile Christians merely because some Jewish believers arrived from Jerusalem, Paul had no hesitation in opposing him 'to his face' (Galatians 2:11). Paul implies (and we have no evidence to the contrary) that Peter accepted the rebuke delivered to him on this occasion, thereby implicitly recognizing Paul's apostolic authority.

Christians and the Old Testament

After dealing with this malicious attack on his own credentials, Paul went on to appeal briefly to the Galatians' own experience before proceeding to deal with the second piece of false teaching propounded by these Judaizing intruders. What they knew of Christ ought to have shown them that they had received the Holy Spirit (the mark of the true Christian, Romans 8:9) not because they had obeyed the Old Testament Law, but because they had exercised faith in Jesus (3:1–5). This then led straight into an attack on another part of their teachings. In the Hebrew scriptures the promise of the messianic kingdom had been given to Abraham and his descendants (Genesis 17:7–8), and this was the basis on which the Judaizers were arguing that anyone who wished to be in the messianic kingdom must become members of Abraham's family by circumcision and continued obedience to the Old Testament Law (Genesis 17:9–14). Paul addressed this contention in three ways, by appealing to the Old Testament itself:

■ He pointed out (3:6–14) that the blessings promised to Abraham apply to 'all who believe'. Abraham had faith in God, and this faith was the basis of his acceptance by God (Genesis 12:1–4; see also Hebrews 11:8–12, 17–19). At the same time, 'all who rely on works of the law are under a curse'. Human experience and scripture both proved that, in practice, it was impossible to be justified in God's sight by keeping the Law, because this was so hard to do.

■ But was not the Law God's highest revelation, surpassing all that had gone before it? No, says Paul; since the Torah only came into effect long after Abraham's time, it could not possibly alter a direct promise made to him by God. The 'inheritance' promised to Abraham could not be obtainable by both Law and promise (3:18). The Law had a different purpose in God's plan:

Firstly, it served to show up sin as a transgression against God's will (3:19; see also Romans 4:15; 5:13). Before the law was given, the only moral guidance that humankind had was the 'law of nature', expressing itself through their own conscience. But after the Law was given by Moses, people were able to understand wrongdoing for what it really was: defiance of God's will.

Secondly, the Law was given to be a teacher 'until Christ came, that we might be justified by faith' (3:24). Paul suggests that, as people tried to gain salvation by their own efforts at keeping the Law, they realized it was an impossible task, and so the way was prepared for God's new act of grace in Jesus Christ.

■ Paul then proceeded to take this argument to its logical conclusion (3:25 – 4:7). The Old Testament Law was only effective 'till the offspring should come to whom the promise had been made' (3:19) and, since this 'offspring' had come in Jesus Christ, that inevitably meant the era of the Law was ended and, to those who had faith in him, Christ would give freedom from the Law and its demands. Before, they had been slaves to 'the elemental spirits of the universe' (an expression which includes the Law, but is not restricted to it, 4:3), but now they were children and heirs of the promise made to Abraham (4:4–7).

Freedom and legalism

By placing themselves under the Law and keeping traditional Jewish holy days, the Galatians were trying to undo what God had already done for them in Christ. Paul was fearful that if they did this, he had wasted his time ministering among them (4:8–11). By way of explaining why, he went on to deal with another argument put forward by the Judaizing teachers, who had given 'scriptural' reasons to show that even Gentile Christians ought to keep the Torah and be circumcised, reasons which Paul counteracted in three ways:

■ Paul returned again to examine the status of the Law (4:21 – 5:1). Once more he appealed to the story of Abraham, this time using the incident of Sarah, a free woman, driving out Hagar, the slave. This, he said, was an allegory of the superior position of the good news in Christ over and against what might be perceived as the legalism of the Jewish Law.

A Jewish or Christian bronze stamp of Byzantine origin and dating from the 3rd or 4th century, showing traditional imagery: a seven-branched candlestick, a palm frond, and a cluster of grapes.

■ Paul also answered the queries about circumcision (5:2–12), making it clear that, in his view, circumcision was of no value either way to Christians: it simply made no difference whether Christians were circumcised or not. Their standing before God must depend not on such external signs, but on 'faith working through love' (5:6). In the case of people like the Galatians, he believed that to submit to circumcision would actually be a denial of what Christ had done for them (5:2). In any case, being circumcised also obliged people to observe the whole of the Jewish Law (5:3) – the very thing that Paul had just rejected, and which experience showed to be impossible. The freedom brought by Christ was clearly incompatible with the 'yoke of slavery' (5:1) associated with circumcision and the Law.

■ After this, Paul dealt with the question of Christian behaviour (5:13 – 6:10). One thing that marked Jews off from other people in the ancient world was their very high moral standards, which resulted from their close adherence to the Old Testament Law. The Judaizers who visited Galatia had argued that if Christians discarded the Law, they would have no guide for their conduct and be indistinguishable from other people around them. This was an important question, and one that was not easy to answer.

It seems Paul had told the Galatian Christians that, if they trusted Christ, the Holy Spirit would empower them to live as Jesus lived. This is the kind of thing he indicates in 2:20: 'I have been crucified with Christ, it is no longer I who live, but Christ who lives in me; and the life I now

Who were the Galatians?

In discussing the order of events following Paul's conversion, it was suggested that the letter to the Galatians can be dated about AD48, just before the visit of Paul and Barnabas to Jerusalem for the Apostolic Council. The arguments already set out provide good reasons in favour of this date and, if they are correct, Galatians would be the first letter that Paul ever wrote and probably, therefore, the first book of the New Testament to be written. But what has been said so far is not the complete story.

In addressing the letter, Paul says he is writing 'to the churches of Galatia' (1:2), and later calls his readers Galatians (3:1). The mention of people who could be called 'Galatians' would most naturally suggest the Celtic people of that name who lived in the region of Ankara in present-day Turkey, and who gave their name to an ancient kingdom there. But if these are the people referred to, then Acts indicates that Paul did not visit them until his second and third missionary expeditions (Acts 16:6; 18:23), which in turn means that he could not have written to them as early as AD48. It has also been argued that, since Paul's teaching in Galatians closely resembles what he says in Romans, which certainly was written towards the end of his third missionary tour, it would make more sense to suppose that this letter was written to the people of north Galatia some time between AD56 and 58. The scholarly consensus, in fact, favours this later date, and the view put forward here is a minority opinion, albeit one that has been, and continues to be, held by some very eminent scholars.

Sir William Ramsay was the first scholar of any importance to advocate this view of the matter. At the beginning of the twentieth century, he conducted extensive archaeological investigations in the very areas of Asia Minor of which we are speaking, in the course of which he revealed that the *Roman province* of Galatia included not only the ancient kingdom of the Galatians in the north of Asia Minor, but also the southern region of Lycaonia ('south Galatia'), in which Paul worked during his first missionary expedition, and where he had established churches at Lystra, Derbe and Iconium. This, at least, eliminates the argument that Paul did not visit a place that could be called 'Galatia' until much later, and makes it possible that Galatians could have been written about AD48 to the churches Paul had visited on his first missionary expedition.

The other argument often put forward to support a later date for the letter, that it is similar to Romans, is weak, and the evidence can be interpreted in more than one way. There are subtle distinctions between Galatians and Romans, with Romans certainly being a more sophisticated and rounded presentation of what are fundamentally the same arguments. The more detached tone of Romans suggests that it was written at a time and place when Paul was able to set the passion and acrimony of the Galatian situation in a wider context, which might suggest a longer period between them, rather than some immediate connection.

There are still many unanswered questions about the date and setting of Galatians, but on balance the early dating has the ability to answer more questions than a later date (including other issues previously discussed concerning the integration of the accounts of Paul's visits to Jerusalem in Acts), and therefore can plausibly be advocated as the most satisfactory option.

live in the flesh I live by faith in the Son of God, who loved me and gave himself for me.' But would it work? Paul dealt with the accusations of the Judaizers on this score by making four important statements:

Firstly (5:13–15), 'freedom in Christ' does not mean a freedom for Christians to do as they like. It is a freedom to serve one another in love and, since the Holy Spirit's purpose is to reproduce in Christians a Christ-like character, their freedom should obviously be demonstrated in ways that are consistent with this.

Secondly (5:16–26), though the Christian gospel does not prescribe particular actions, 'those who belong to Christ Jesus have crucified the flesh with its passions and desires' (5:24). That means the Christian's life will be marked out by the fruit of the Spirit. The demands of Christ are far more radical than the external imposition of ethical rules: the Christian's whole personality should be transformed, as attitudes and behaviour have been changed from within. This was the same lesson that Jesus himself had taught: 'A sound tree cannot bear evil fruit, nor can a bad tree bear good fruit' (Matthew 7:18).

Thirdly (6:1–6), Christians should beware of judging others. They ought to recognize that they themselves could have no moral strength to do what is right, apart from the power of the Holy Spirit. Insofar as they have a duty, it is to 'fulfil the law of Christ' by bearing 'one another's burdens' (6:2), which is something very different from the observance of a restricted collection of externally imposed rules and regulations.

Fourthly (6:7–10), Paul sums up his advice: in order to reap the harvest of eternal life, his readers must not cultivate the 'flesh' (their own self-gratification), but the 'Spirit' (their new life given by Jesus Christ).

Then, finally, in 6:11–18, Paul makes one last appeal to his readers, which includes two further points against his opponents, followed up by two balancing statements of his own belief and practice.

His opponents, in spite of their high pretensions, were in fact spiritually bankrupt (6:12), wanting to 'make a good showing in the flesh', the very thing that Paul had denounced in the previous section of his argument (6:8, 'those who sow to their own flesh will from the flesh reap corruption'). They are also inconsistent, even with their own starting points for, though they emphasize the outward sign of circumcision, they are not willing to accept the spiritual discipline involved in keeping the Old Testament Law.

After preaching in Perga, Paul and Barnabas completed their first missionary journey by sailing back from Attalia to Syrian Antioch. There they recounted their experiences to the church which had commissioned them. Attalia is now the modern resort of Antalya in southern Turkey.

Paul was driven by the conviction that what had been revealed to him by the risen Christ was of supreme authority, and so he concluded by affirming that the only real cause of boasting before God must be that the Christian is crucified to the world, through the cross of Christ. Talk of a cross in the first century meant only one thing: death, and that is what Paul meant when he wrote of Christians sharing in the cross of Christ (Galatians 2:20). He was not urging them to be martyrs, but was indicating in a more mystical, inner sense that Christians should die to themselves, by giving up their claims to final jurisdiction over their own lives and destinies, and applying the gospel and its values to every aspect of life. This kind of 'new creation' would be the only thing of any value in the sight of God, and constituted the sole qualifying mark of membership in 'the Israel of God' (Galatians 6:14–16). Paul himself may be criticized for being a traitor to Judaism, but as far as he was concerned he bore the mark of true spirituality before God: 'I bear on my body the marks of Jesus' (6:17).

This, then, is how Paul dealt with the problems of the churches of Galatia. One slogan used here neatly summarizes it all: 'in Christ, it is not circumcision or uncircumcision that counts, but the power of a new birth' (Galatians 6:15).

The Apostolic Council

No doubt it was in this fashion that Paul set out his arguments at the Council of Jerusalem in AD49. According to Acts even James, probably the most traditional of the Jerusalem leaders, had to agree with the main part of Paul's argument (Acts 15:6–21). The Jerusalem apostles accepted that there was no great doctrinal principle involved, though there was still the pressing practical problem of how Jews and Gentiles could meet together and share food at the same table.

In order to make this possible the Jerusalem leaders suggested that Gentile converts should abstain from those activities particularly offensive to Jewish Christians: things like eating food that had been offered in pagan sacrifices, eating meat from which the blood had not been drained, and sexual habits which did not accord with accepted Jewish Law and custom (Acts 15:19–21, 28–29). This arrangement was accepted by Paul, but it was a compromise, and it appears not to have been a very successful one, for when Paul faced the same problems again in Corinth, he never referred to the terms of the Apostolic Decree at all, but argued once more from the basic principles involved in the matter (1 Corinthians 8:1–13; 10:18 – 11:1).

There is, however, another question raised by Luke's account of the Apostolic Decree. If we are correct in thinking that Paul wrote Galatians just before he went to the Council, then the narrative of Acts 15 depicts him accepting something he had just vehemently rejected in Galatians, namely the application of some sort of 'law' to Gentile Christians.

Various explanations might be possible:

■ One solution is to suppose that the Apostolic Council never actually happened, and that it was invented by Luke for the purpose of showing that both Jewish and Gentile sections of the church were united in the early years of its history. This explanation is largely the result of supposing that the narrative of Acts cannot be reconciled with Galatians 1 – 2, whereas if the alternative correlation between the two proposed here is accepted, that difficulty largely disappears. There is also the more general consideration that, since Luke usually emerges as a trustworthy historian at those places where his story can be tested against external evidence, in the absence of specific indications to the contrary, there is no reason to suspect his overall reliability at this point.

■ Another possibility is to suppose that the Apostolic Decree was in fact addressed to just a small and relatively local group of churches, namely those specifically mentioned by name in Acts 15:36 – 16:5. If this was the case, there would be no difficulty over the fact that Paul did not quote the Decree in 1 Corinthians, for it would never have been intended to apply there.

■ Perhaps a better explanation still is that Paul was, at heart, a conciliatory and pragmatic sort of person. Having said his piece in Galatians, and having won the theological debate in Jerusalem, he was content to accept that, regardless of theological difficulties, Jews and Gentiles had to live together within the local church, and the acceptance of these guidelines was a straightforward means of achieving this.

■ As we proceed now to consider Paul's experiences in other churches, it is noticeable that, time and again, he bent over backwards to accommodate people whose viewpoint was different from his own (1 Corinthians 9:19–23). He realized that a divided church was a poor witness to the non-Christian world, and at this stage of his ministry the Apostolic Decree perhaps seemed the best solution to a pressing problem.

26 Paul the Missionary

Back to Galatia

After his crucial meeting with the leaders of the Jerusalem church, Paul went off again into the Gentile world, fired with a new enthusiasm. In the course of his earlier mission work, he had come to realize just how attractive the Christian message could be to the populations of the great urban centres of Asia Minor, and he could now see the potential for moving even further afield to invite others to follow Jesus Christ.

Paul's second missionary journey.

He began this second expedition with a new companion. Barnabas did not join him on this occasion because Paul was unwilling to give a second chance to John Mark (Barnabas' cousin) who had apparently let them down during their earlier trip (Acts 15:36–40). But Paul found a keen helper in Silas, one of the messengers who had been sent to Antioch to explain the decisions of the Jerusalem Council to the church there (Acts 15:30–33). In the course of their journeying, Paul was joined by two others in addition to Silas: Timothy, who met them at Lystra (Acts 16:1–3), and Luke who attached himself to them at Troas (Acts 16:10–12).

The first thing Paul wanted to do was to revisit some of the communities that he had founded in south Galatia during his first expedition from Antioch. He had been hoping to see them ever since he heard of the consternation created by the interference of the Judaizers, and during this further visit he no doubt explained that, although as Christians they were not required to fulfil all the detailed requirements of the Torah, it would nevertheless be desirable if they could agree to accept the arrangement that had been worked out in Jerusalem, because that would create an environment in which Christians from a Jewish background could feel free to meet with them (Acts 16:4).

After this, Paul and Silas went on with Timothy, who had joined them in Lystra, through Phrygia and Galatia – perhaps this time north Galatia. Paul had planned to go to the Roman province of Asia, which was the area round Ephesus in the west of Asia Minor, and also into Bithynia, the province to the north which adjoined the Black Sea (Acts 16:6–7). Neither of these intentions worked out, and indeed Luke specifically comments that they were 'forbidden by the Holy Spirit', though he gives no indication as to how this instruction might have been received. Paul and his companions, therefore, went on into Troas, ancient Troy, in the part of Asia Minor nearest to Europe.

During the night Paul had a dream of a Macedonian appealing for help, something which he recognized as a mandate directly from God inviting him to cross the Aegean Sea and enter Europe (Acts 16:9–10). In the context of the narrative of Acts, Paul's entry into Europe at this point is portrayed as a pivotal point in Luke's purpose to document the spread of the gospel from Palestinian beginnings to the centre of the empire in Rome itself. In terms of the expansion of the church, however, it was certainly not the first time that Christian missionaries had entered Europe, for at a later date Paul wrote to a large and flourishing church at Rome, which had not been founded by his own efforts.

The great Roman roads were of vital military and commercial importance. The stone slabs of the Egnatian Way were worn down by the heavy traffic. Paul's group used this route to travel from Philippi to Thessalonica.

Philippi

The first town the missionaries visited was Philippi (Acts 16:12). This was a Roman colony in the north-east corner of Macedonia, largely populated by retired soldiers from the Roman army. Although the city had such a large Gentile population, Paul still followed his earlier custom of first going to the Jews at their usual meeting place, which in this case was 'a place of prayer' by the riverside; there were so few Jews in Philippi that they did not even have a synagogue building.

Paul was summoned to Europe by a dream in which a Macedonian (a person from northern Greece) appealed to him. This Latin inscription from Philippi includes the name of the Roman province of Macedonia.

Converts

Among Paul's hearers at this place of prayer was Lydia, and she was the first to become a Christian in Philippi. If Paul had any lingering doubts about the wisdom of abandoning his earlier plans and moving instead into Europe, they must have disappeared with the conversion of this woman, for she was a native of Thyatira, a city located in the very area of Asia Minor where Paul had originally been intending to go (Acts 16:14–15). She might well have been the one who first took the Christian message to her home town, where there was soon a large Christian community (Revelation 2:18–29). In any event, her discovery of Jesus as the Messiah brought about an immediate and revolutionary change in her life, for though she was a woman of some importance, her own home was soon opened to Paul and his friends and became the headquarters of their activity. Once again Paul was learning that the gospel created a unity of friendship between men and women that could overthrow all normal social and racial barriers.

One thing that happened at Philippi provides a good illustration of why the Christian faith began to arouse so much antagonism in many parts of the Roman empire at this time. As he was going about his evangelistic work, Paul was continually pestered by a slave girl who, by means of some kind of clairvoyance exercised in a trance state, had brought a large income to her owners. Like Jesus before him, Paul had a keenly developed sense of both social and spiritual injustice, and could not pass up the opportunity to help this person find freedom from the spirit of divination, which was believed to possess her, as well as from the exploitation of those who owned her. Predictably this action was not well received, and her owners were so angry that they accused Paul and Silas of creating a public disturbance, by recommending customs that were unlawful for Roman citizens (Acts 16:16–21).

Imprisonment

Accusations of causing a public nuisance could always be guaranteed to arouse a Roman official to some sort of action, and the town officials responded swiftly. Paul and Silas were beaten and thrown into prison, where they spent the night singing praises to God. During the night an earthquake broke open the prison doors and, though they could have escaped, they chose to remain, along with the rest of the prisoners. The local jailer was ready to take his own life, assuming that in such circumstances all his prisoners would get out, and when he found they were still there he was amazed, and challenged by the realization that these prisoners were at peace with themselves in a way that he was not. On learning of the secret of their power, he became a Christian himself, along with his entire household. After the conversion of his jailer, Paul was determined to leave prison. In fact, he ought never to have been there in the first place, for he was a Roman citizen. He, therefore, claimed his rights as a citizen, and demanded an apology from the embarrassed city authorities, before leaving the city of Philippi altogether (Acts 16:22–40).

Luke stayed behind in Philippi to help the new Christians become established in their faith. They were drawn from all levels of society and included a prominent local trader, a spiritual healer and astrologer, as well as the city jailer and his family. Paul's reputation travelled fast and, at one of the next places they visited, he and his friends Silas and Timothy were described as 'people who have turned the world upside down' (Acts 17:6). The next towns to be visited were Thessalonica and Beroea. There were significant synagogues in each place, and many converts were made. In both places, however, there was also serious opposition stirred up from within the Jewish community, opposition which seems to have been directed specifically at Paul himself, as a former Pharisee, since Silas and Timothy were able to stay on there when Paul went to Athens (Acts 17:14–15).

Athens

Athens had for centuries prided itself on being the intellectual centre of the ancient world. By the time of Paul it was no longer an important political centre, but it was still a city of learning to which many young Romans were sent to study philosophy, or to be initiated into one of the many oriental mystery religions which found a home there.

Communicating his message in Athens was bound to require a very different approach from that used in most of the places Paul had visited up to this point. The people there had no Jewish or biblical background at all, therefore to introduce Jesus as the Messiah would have meant little or nothing to them. With ethnic Jews and Gentile proselytes or God-fearers, Paul could begin from the Hebrew scriptures and point out how the promises made there had been fulfilled in the life, death and resurrection of Jesus. At Athens, he was conscious of his own relative ignorance regarding the nature of the Hellenistic spiritual search, so his mission began not by speaking, but by observing what was going on there, and listening to the debates that were already in progress. It was only a matter of time before he was invited to go and address the court of the Areopagus. The Athenians had always enjoyed a good debate, and the city leaders believed that taking an interest in philosophy and religion was part of their job.

In speaking with them, Paul began from the Greek view of God as creator, benefactor and invisible presence within the universe, talking of the universal human search for God, who is 'not far from each one of us', and referring in the process to statements made by the Greek poets Epimenides and Aratus (Acts 17:27).

Athens symbolized the tradition of classical learning. The Acropolis, on which the Parthenon was built as a temple to the goddess Athene, served as both a focus of worship and a defensive stronghold.

He also spoke of the many shrines and altars which were located all round the city. This was fairly typical of Greek cities, which generally had an abundance of small statues and icons at strategic locations, to provide an opportunity for people to pay homage to the deities as they went about their daily business. The status of these gods and goddesses had been thrown into some doubt as a result of the thinking of previous generations of philosophers, and some of the language employed by Paul might have been alluding to arguments used to question this form of traditional observance since the days of Xenophanes in the sixth century BC. Paul was not specially concerned with condemning the traditional spirituality of his hearers, but with using it as an opening to present his own message. Since he had observed an altar 'to the unknown god', he identified Jesus with this unknown deity, and proceeded to explain the gospel from this perspective. Paul had a strong belief in a creation-centred spirituality, shared by all people by virtue of their common humanity, quite independently of their formal religious traditions (Romans 1:18 – 2:10), and this was his starting point in Athens. Of course, he also shared those aspects of Christian belief which were unique and distinctive, including belief in one God whose nature had been revealed in the life, death and resurrection of Jesus Christ.

A stone altar discovered at Pergamum. The top line reads, 'to unknown gods'.

His message was given a mixed reception, and Athens was not one of the cities where Paul immediately established a thriving Christian community. Nevertheless, this narrative plays a central part in the book of Acts, for while other stories can give the impression of a somewhat triumphalist progress of the gospel, this one reminds its readers that even Paul's mission work was not guaranteed instant success. It also – and more importantly – provides a model for contextualizing the Christian message in cultures where the salvation history of the Old Testament story was unknown. In doing so, Paul is shown affirming the spiritual starting points of his audience, and being prepared to journey alongside them, while at the same time challenging them to see things from the new perspective of belief in Jesus. In the process, he drew on resources that were already in his own Jewish tradition, particularly the creation-centred theology of the book of Genesis, and its developments in later Judaism.

Corinth

After this, Paul pressed on to Corinth, an ancient Greek city that had been rebuilt as a Roman colony in 46BC. Corinth had a unique location, at the narrowest point in the mainland of Greece, and therefore provided easy access to the Aegean Sea on the east and the Adriatic Sea on the west. Though the Romans had opened up extensive seagoing trade routes, and navigational methods were well advanced, ancient sailors still preferred to travel close to the coastline whenever they could, and Corinth took advantage of this to establish itself as one of the foremost centres of trade and transportation. Though there were plans to build a canal from the Aegean Sea to the Adriatic, even in New Testament times, it was many centuries later before the project was carried through. At the time when Paul visited the city, it had two separate harbours on each of its coasts – Lechaeum and Cenchreae – and between the two was an intricate construction like a conveyor belt, along which vast numbers of slaves would haul ships from one harbour to another. Corinth became an important transit point at which ships could pass from the Aegean to the Adriatic, without navigating the dangerous southern tip of Greece. Because of its strategic position, roughly midway between the eastern end of the Mediterranean and Italy, there was always a constant stream of traffic passing through.

Corinth had become a major interchange not only for commerce, but also for the many cultures of the empire. On the streets of Corinth, people of many different ethnic origins and religious convictions mingled naturally, and the city was a vibrant microcosm of the life of the entire empire. As a staging post for sailors, it was also home to one of the largest numbers of prostitutes anywhere in the empire, and its name became a byword for sexual experimentation of every imaginable kind.

Paul clearly recognized the strategic importance of Corinth, staying there for the next eighteen months (Acts 18:11), and even after that he took more interest in the nurture of the church there than he normally did with other Christian groups he founded. In Corinth, Paul made friends with Aquila and his wife Priscilla who, like himself, were Hellenistic Jews and tent makers. He followed his previous pattern of beginning his work in the synagogue, but he was forced to leave when he met the usual opposition. He then moved next door, to the home of one of his new converts, Titius Justus, and used that as the base for his mission to the city. Many citizens became Christians at this time, including Crispus, one of the synagogue leaders (Acts 18:8), and a very large and influential Christian community began to be established in the city.

After Paul had been there for about eighteen months, the synagogue authorities decided to make a concerted effort to have him chased out of town. This move coincided with the arrival of a new Roman magistrate, the proconsul Gallio, who was the brother of the well-known poet and philosopher, Seneca. The charge against him was that 'this man is persuading people to worship God in ways that are contrary to the Law' (Acts 18:13). Predictably, it came to nothing because Gallio would not judge Paul under the Jewish Law, and according to Roman law he had done nothing wrong. The major significance of this episode is that it is the only incident in Paul's life which can be given a fairly precise date. Gallio's period of office in Corinth is recorded in a copy of a letter sent from the emperor, and preserved on a stone inscription, which shows that he must have been proconsul either in AD51–52 or AD52–53.

We can date Paul's 18-month stay in Corinth by this inscription from Delphi. It shows that Gallio, who was proconsul at the time of Paul's visit, came to Corinth in either AD51 or 52.

Paul writes more letters

At an early point during Paul's stay in Corinth, Silas and Timothy (who had remained behind in Thessalonica) arrived with news of the Christians there. Their report was most encouraging for, though it had been little more than six months since their conversion to Christ, the example of their changed lifestyle had made such an impact on the surrounding area that others had also been attracted to Christian faith. However, there were also some problems in the church. The people in the synagogue had stirred up opposition, including physical violence, and several matters were leading to tensions within the Christian community itself. Questions needed to be answered about sexual relationships, about the nature of leadership, and about the fate of Christians who had died. On hearing of all this, Paul wrote to encourage them and to give them guidance on these particular problems. The letter he wrote was 1 Thessalonians.

However, the Thessalonians were soon diverted away from following Paul's advice in this letter, as what he had said about the state of Christians who died, and the expected *parousia* of Jesus became the occasion for apocalyptic speculation. It was not long before Paul had to write another letter to help sort out the difficulties which, to some extent, the Thessalonian Christians seem to have invented for themselves out of certain parts of his first letter, and so he penned 2 Thessalonians.

It was in Thessalonica that Paul had been accused of 'turning the world upside down', and the Christian community that he left behind him there continued this activity. As we read the letters Paul wrote to them, it is easy to conclude that the Thessalonian church was in serious difficulties, but we must not allow a few trivial criticisms to obscure the fact that this was one of the very few churches that Paul commended so warmly for its Christlike character. The encouragement he received from these people must have been a great help to him as he faced the next big test of his life's work.

1 Thessalonians

After his usual introduction, Paul begins by commending his readers for their faithfulness to the Christian message. They had worked carefully to follow all that Paul had taught them, with the result that a strong church had been established and, by the example of their changed lives, the claims of the gospel had been advanced within their wider social context. In Galatia, it had been suggested that Paul's message of freedom from the Law would lead to low moral standards, whereas the exact opposite seemed to have happened here, as the whole of Macedonia and Achaia saw the difference the Christian faith made to the way of life of these believers (1 Thessalonians 1:2–10). The way Paul describes all this raises some questions about the exact nature of his mission in Thessalonica, for he refers to his converts as having 'turned to God from idols' (1:9), which would imply they were predominantly Gentiles, whereas Acts 17:1–9 only mentions converts from within the synagogue community. But later sections of this letter cover apocalyptic concerns that are more likely to have been raised by converts from within Judaism, so perhaps the reality is that Paul's mission appealed to a broad cross-section of the Thessalonian population, including those of Jewish ancestry as well as Gentiles previously associated with the synagogue, and those with no such connection.

Paul and his converts
Paul goes on to reflect on his own mission strategy when he and his friends first arrived in the city. He reminds his readers that the apostles had been careful not to advertise themselves, but to draw attention to the essentials of their message; though they had been sent out with the personal authority of God, and with the backing of the earliest churches, in their attitude towards the people they were serving they followed the example of Jesus: 'we were gentle among you, like a nurse taking care of her children… we were ready to share with you not only the gospel of God but also our own selves' (2:7, 8). They felt they had been well rewarded for their efforts, for the Thessalonians had responded to the message, and had recognized its life changing potential: 'when you received the word of God that you heard from us, you accepted it not as a human word but as what it really is, God's word, which is also at work in you believers' (2:13). This knowledge, together with the news conveyed by Silas and Timothy, proved a great encouragement to Paul as he worked in difficult conditions in Corinth (2:17 – 3:8). Nevertheless, there was something lacking in their faith (3:10), and so Paul set out to try to give good advice on the various matters which Timothy had reported to him.

How should Christians behave?
The Judaizers were right when they suggested the one thing that would present the biggest challenge for Gentile converts was the question of personal morality. Hellenistic culture was generally very permissive, and few kinds of sexual activity were prohibited outright. Paul's hope had always been that, by relying on the empowerment of the Holy Spirit, converts would align their lifestyles with accepted Christian values and, in a majority of cases, that was what had happened among the Thessalonians. But

it was still necessary to reinforce what he had no doubt told them when he founded their church (4:1–8), and in doing so Paul naturally reflected on what he had written earlier in Galatians on the same matter: 'you were called to freedom... only do not use your freedom as an opportunity for the flesh, but through love be servants of one another' (Galatians 5:13). The Thessalonians had learnt this lesson well: 'you yourselves have been taught by God to love one another; and indeed you do love all the brothers and sisters throughout Macedonia' (1 Thessalonians 4:9–10). It was a lesson that could never be overemphasized. In a world in which the established order was rapidly changing, and in which people were frantically grasping at whatever spirituality came their way, one of the most important things the church could do was to display the love of Christ (4:9–12). Jesus himself had taught, 'By this everyone will know that you are my disciples, if you have love for one another' (John 13:35), and the advice is here repeated and reinforced by Paul.

What about the future?

One thing above all appears to have been troubling the church at Thessalonica. They understood well the relationship that ought to exist among the members of their community, but what about those Christians who had died shortly after Paul's departure from the city? Perhaps Paul's teaching on the *parousia* had been misunderstood, as some of these converts seem to have had the idea that no Christians would die at all before Christ returned in glory. Paul corrected this by providing a clear statement spelling out his beliefs on the matter, and emphasizing that, though Christ's presence was already operative in the church through the work of the Holy Spirit, Jesus would one day come back openly and in glory (4:13–18). Meanwhile, the Thessalonian Christians should not worry unduly about loved ones who had died: 'since we believe that Jesus died and rose again, even so, through

Jesus, God will bring with him those who have fallen asleep' (4:14).

Paul appreciated the potential pitfalls in emphasizing what God would do in the future, so he went on to remind the Thessalonian Christians that their belief in the future return of Jesus was no excuse for inactivity in the present. Though some people would not be prepared for 'the day of the Lord', Christians ought to be. Their business was not to try to calculate 'the times and the seasons' (5:1), but to 'encourage one another and build one another up' (5:11).

Living the Christian life

Finally, Paul gave some advice to his readers on a number of topics, summarizing all that he had said before (5:12–21).
● In the church, the Christians should:
– respect those who laboured among them, that is the leaders;
– be at peace among themselves (a repetition and reinforcement of what he had said in 4:9–12);
– encourage one another in their faith in Christ (5:14).
● In their everyday lives, Christians should:
– return good for evil (5:15), one of the most characteristic marks of the Christian (see also Matthew 5:44);
– 'rejoice always' (5:16).
● In their relationship to God, Christians must:
– live in an attitude of prayer (5:17);
– allow the Holy Spirit to direct their lives (5:19–20).

Paul signed off with his usual blessing and greeting, making a last appeal and promise to his readers. He reminded them that the secret of successful Christian living was to be found in the work of the living Christ continuing to operate through the lives of his followers, and 'the one who calls you is faithful, and will do this' (5:24).

2 Thessalonians

In this second, shorter letter to the Thessalonians Paul clarified three main points.

The church and its enemies

From what is said in 2 Thessalonians 1:5–12 it appears that the church had faced increasingly fierce opposition. He explained that this was to be expected, for the more widely known their love and Christian character became, the more their enemies would make life difficult for them. No one would ever bother about a religious faith that meant nothing to those holding it; but the revolutionary character of the life of the Thessalonian church naturally drew the attention of others to what was going on. It would be impossible to turn the world upside down without provoking some reaction from that world. Paul reminds these Christians that, though for the moment things might be difficult, God is on their side and will ultimately vindicate them.

The church and the future

A more subtle form of 'persecution' had also come into the church, with the appearance of forged letters claiming to have been written by Paul and his associates (2 Thessalonians 2:1–12). Apocalyptic enthusiasts of some kind had taken advantage of Paul's mention of the *parousia* of Jesus in his earlier letter, and used the occasion to put across their own point of view on the subject. Paul had to warn the Thessalonian Christians 'not to be quickly shaken in mind or excited, either by spirit or by word, or by letter purporting to be from us, to the effect that the day of the Lord has come' (2:2). The exact connotation of the claim that 'the day of the Lord has come' is difficult to establish. In 1 Corinthians there is a mention of people who thought that the resurrection (which was generally associated with the end of things and the *parousia* of Christ) had already taken place,

on the basis of which belief they indulged in what Paul deemed to be unacceptable sexual practices (1 Corinthians 15:12–58). It is difficult to make any specific connection between the two groups of people, but in any event Paul goes on to emphasize here that, in his view, the *parousia* and all it entails was not an event that could take place invisibly or mystically (which would need to have been the case if it had already happened). On the contrary, he places his own expectation firmly in a context of actual events by mentioning certain historical occurrences connected with 'the lawless one' (2:3–12) that would herald the return of Christ.

The church and society

The outcome of the interest in future events that had arisen in Thessalonica was that some of the Christians had stopped living a normal life. They had opted out of society and were idly waiting for Christ to return, an attitude which Paul criticized severely. For him, authentic Christian spirituality was unlikely to be demonstrated by becoming a religious hermit, but required people to play their full part in the life of the wider culture. People who did not do this, however 'spiritual' their motives, should be disciplined by the church. It was not very often that Paul instructed a church to take disciplinary action against one of its members, but this was one such case. Of course, the other Christians were not to do this with a judgmental spirit, but in a way that was calculated to lead to restoration: 'Do not regard them as enemies, but warn them as believers' (3:15).

Even with all their problems, however, the Thessalonians had learnt the true secret of the Christian way of life that Paul had shown them. They were rapidly becoming the kind of congregation of which Paul could be proud: 'your faith is growing abundantly, and the love of every one of you for one another is increasing' (1:3).

Did Paul write 2 Thessalonians?

In our analysis of 1 and 2 Thessalonians, we have assumed that Paul wrote them both, the second one in response to problems that had arisen subsequent to his first letter. There is room for debate regarding the actual order in which they were written, and some have proposed that 2 Thessalonians was actually written first. Not only does it seem to be addressing a circumstance in which persecution was an immediate concern, whereas 1 Thessalonians implies it was in the past, but it is also possible to understand the questions about eschatology in 1 Thessalonians as having developed on the basis of what is said in 2 Thessalonians, rather than vice versa.

There is no way to be sure of the order of the letters, but of more importance is the suggestion that the two letters are so individually distinctive that if Paul wrote one of them, he cannot have written the other. Since 2 Thessalonians is the shorter and less comprehensive, this one has most often been questioned, for a number of reasons.

A different eschatology

In 1 Thessalonians 4:13 – 5:11, Paul writes of the coming of Jesus as an imminent event, and Christians are warned not to be taken by surprise when it comes. But in 2 Thessalonians 2:1–12, Paul lists a sequence of events that will take place before the *parousia* and this, it is argued, removes the element of immediacy from it. Paul can hardly have held both views at once. But this argument is not as impressive as it seems, for two reasons:
● Though 'signs of the end' are not listed in 1 Thessalonians, they are implied in 5:1, where Paul writes, 'There is no need to write to you, brothers and sisters, about the times and occasions when these things will happen.' This statement seems to suggest that Paul thought they already knew about such matters, and when he proceeds to warn his readers not to be taken by surprise, it is precisely because

The Arch of Galerius, an impressive Roman structure, straddled the Egnatian Way at Thessalonica.

**Did Paul write
2 Thessalonians?**
continued

they, of all people, should have been able to recognize when Jesus was about to return.

● The two letters deal with different issues. In the first place, Paul had been asked a personal question about the fate of Christians who died – and he gave his answer on an appropriate personal level. But the question behind 2 Thessalonians is quite different, and concerns people who were saying that the 'day of the Lord' was there already. This was a quite different kind of argument, and it demanded a different sort of answer, not this time from a personal perspective, but on a broader cosmic level.

A different tone

2 Thessalonians is said to be more formal than 1 Thessalonians. Here again, the alleged differences are nothing like as great as some seem to think. The writer of 2 Thessalonians still has a deep concern for his readers and if, as we have suggested, 1 Thessalonians had been wilfully misunderstood by some people, it is hardly surprising that Paul should have been sterner with them the second time. Exactly the same change of tone can be traced in the later correspondence between Paul and the church at Corinth, and for the same reasons.

Too many similarities

This is almost the opposite argument – not that the two letters are different, but that they are too much alike! Some similar words and phrases are used in both, and this has been interpreted as an indication that 2 Thessalonians is just a rewritten form of 1 Thessalonians – rewritten, presumably, by someone else, later than the time of Paul. Again, this is a very slender basis on which to reach such a conclusion, for three reasons:

● Why would anyone wish to produce such a rewritten version of one of Paul's letters? The only plausible possibility would be to try to contradict, or correct, what was later seen as an erroneous idea

in 1 Thessalonians. If the eschatological perspective of 1 and 2 Thessalonians was different, then that could perhaps provide an explanation. But we have already seen that this is not the case.

● Why should an author not repeat himself or herself? Even today, someone engaged in a long correspondence will often refer to previous letters in the process of compiling later ones, and there is no reason to suppose that Paul could not have done the same. We certainly know that was the practice among other Greek letter writers. Especially when giving personal advice in a continuing situation, it is often necessary to say the same things more than once.

● The actual verbal similarities between 1 and 2 Thessalonians are not very extensive. At least two thirds of 2 Thessalonians is quite new, and much of the rest consists of standardized terminology which was part of the stock-in-trade of the letter writer – the equivalent of our 'Dear sir', or 'Cordially yours'.

All these problems are more apparent than real. Distinctions of this kind can be made to look significant when viewed as objects of detached analysis, but such variations and repetitions make good sense when placed in a wider social context, and are the sorts of things that happen every day in real life, especially in dealing with situations such as these letters presuppose.

Paul's strategy for evangelism

Paul was perhaps the most successful Christian missionary there has ever been. In less than a generation he travelled the length and breadth of the Mediterranean world, establishing growing and active Christian communities wherever he went.

What was his secret? Paul, of course, was always conscious that he was only a messenger, and that what really brought a change to the lives of those whom he met was the power of God's Holy Spirit. As he considered the many hardships that he had to endure, he described himself as a 'common clay pot', just a temporary container for the renewing power of God (2 Corinthians 4:7). But Paul was also a sophisticated strategist. His route was never haphazard, and his methods of communication were based on considerable insight into the ways people think and take decisions.

Paul was a frontier evangelist, but he himself never visited a geographical frontier! He could have spent months, even years, trekking through uncharted territory, or making his way laboriously across country paths to reach remote places. He did neither of these things. Instead he took advantage of the major highways the Romans had built across their empire. Combined with regular sea routes, they gave ready access to all the major centres of population, and these were the places Paul visited. He knew that he could never personally take the gospel to every man and woman throughout the empire, but if he could establish enthusiastic groups of Christians in some of the key cities, then they in turn would spread the good news into the more remote areas. Moreover, residents of rural districts often had to visit the nearest city, so they too could be reached with the gospel, which they could then take home to their own people. This was what had happened on the Day of Pentecost in Jerusalem, and Paul was well aware of the great potential that such a strategy offered. At least one of the churches to which Paul later wrote a letter – that in Colossae – was founded like this.

Paul was also aware of the need for variety in his presentation of the Christian message. The great secret of Jesus' success had been his ability to speak to people wherever he found them. When he was in the fields, he spoke of growing crops (Mark 4:1–9). With families, he spoke of children (Matthew 19:13–15). With fishing people, the subject was fish (Mark 1:14–18). Paul was the same. He went to people wherever they would listen – in the Jewish synagogues, in the market places, even in the shrines of traditional Greek deities. In the synagogue at Thessalonica, he began with the Old Testament (Acts 17:2–3); at Athens, he started from the 'unknown god' for whom the Greeks were searching (Acts 17:22–31); in Ephesus, he was prepared to engage in public debates about the meaning of the Christian gospel (Acts 19:9).

Readers of Paul's letters have often sought to understand them by reducing his message to a collection of abstract propositional statements about the human condition, but that was not how Paul communicated. He began where his hearers were, and was prepared to engage with their needs. Sometimes it might have been appropriate to deliver a formal address; at other times that would have been entirely the wrong method of approach. Paul and his associates were always ready to get alongside people to help them find new direction for their own spiritual journeys. This was part of the secret of success in Thessalonica: 'we were gentle when we were with you, like a mother taking care of her children... ready to share with you not only the good news from God but even our own lives' (1 Thessalonians 2:7, 8).

It was this sensitivity to people, and flexibility in his evangelism, that Paul was later to encapsulate by saying, 'I make myself everybody's slave in order to win as many people as possible... all things to all people, that I may save some of them by whatever means are possible' (1 Corinthians 9:19, 22).

27 Paul the Pastor

When Paul left Corinth he paid a short visit to Ephesus, and then returned directly to Caesarea in Palestine, from where he went straight to Antioch in Syria (Acts 18:18–22). After a short stay there he began what is often called his 'third missionary journey', which was not at all a missionary expedition in the same way as his two earlier tours had been.

This third expedition was more in the nature of a pastor's ministry, and centred on two main places, Ephesus and Corinth. Paul began with a short trip through Galatia and Phrygia (the districts where he had been during his second expedition), but instead of going north to Troas, as before, he went directly to Ephesus.

Paul's third missionary journey.

Ephesus

Ephesus was the capital of the Roman province of Asia and was, therefore, a centre from which, by road or sea, Paul could easily keep in touch with most of the young churches he had already established in Asia Minor and in Europe. It was also a location from which he and his colleagues could reach out into the whole province of Asia. His stay there resulted in churches being established in such places as Colossae and Laodicea, which Paul himself had not yet visited.

Ephesus was a large and cultured city. After the riots protesting at Paul's teaching, the citizens gathered at the theatre, which held 25,000 people. In the distance is the harbour, which has long-since silted up.

In the course of his three years' stay at Ephesus, Paul seems to have paid a short visit to Corinth. When he finally left Ephesus he went on to revisit the churches in Macedonia – probably those of Philippi, Thessalonica and Beroea (Acts 20:1–2). This might have been the occasion on which he went 'as far round as Illyricum', the region of Greece on the Dalmatian coast of the Adriatic Sea (Romans 15:19). For a further three months he stayed in Achaia (probably mostly in Corinth), then went back to Macedonia (Acts 20:3). There representatives of several churches, including Luke, joined him to take a gift from the Gentile congregations to the church in Jerusalem (Acts 20:4–6; cf. 24:17).

The impact of the gospel

Paul's long stay in Ephesus was undoubtedly the most important part of this period of his ministry – perhaps even the most significant time of his entire life's work. In addition to being the geographical centre of all the places Paul had previously visited, Ephesus was also a prominent centre of spiritual traditions, at the heart of which was the great temple of Artemis (Diana) which was renowned as one of the wonders of the ancient world.

Paul's ministry in Ephesus was so successful that the two mainstays of Ephesian religious life were seriously challenged. One of the things for which Ephesus was well known was its great number of magicians and astrologers, many of whom became Christians and actually burnt their books of magic spells. The silversmiths of the city found that their trade in selling small replicas of the temple of Artemis to pilgrims began to decline, which led Demetrius and some others to start a riot against the Christians in the city (Acts 19:23–41).

Prison again?

In spite of such successes, however, Paul endured great hardships at Ephesus – something he had come to expect when his ministry led to large-scale conversions to Christ. In 1 Corinthians 15:32 he states that he fought with 'wild beasts' there, which might suggest he was thrown into the Roman arena, though it is probably a figure of speech. In 2 Corinthians 1:8 Paul speaks of the afflictions he endured in Asia, and in Romans 16:7 (probably written just after he had left Ephesus) he describes Andronicus and Junias as 'my fellow prisoners'. References such as these are often taken to indicate that Paul was imprisoned during this stay in Ephesus. The evidence for such an imprisonment is considered in more detail in chapter 19.

Advising the churches

This third period of Paul's ministry is of most interest to us because it is the period when three of Paul's greatest letters were written: 1 and 2 Corinthians and Romans. They have often been interpreted as if they were theological tracts written in the form of letters but, like Paul's earlier letters, they follow the normal pattern of ancient letters, and each arose out of a specific historical situation.

Paul and the church at Corinth

The letters to Corinth in particular confront us with one of the most complicated historical puzzles of the entire New Testament. Galatians and 1 and 2 Thessalonians were fairly easy to fit into the picture of Paul's activities recorded in Acts. But in the case of 1 and 2 Corinthians we have no information at all from Acts, and in order to piece together the historical situation behind this correspondence we depend entirely on the vague hints and allusions that Paul made as he wrote. Since it was not his main purpose to give a consecutive account of his own movements, or of the state of the Corinthian church, any reconstruction of what was going on must be more or less imaginative. But there is general agreement among most scholars that Paul's dealings with the church in Corinth at this time can be summarized in six stages:

Bad news from Corinth

During his three years' stay at Ephesus, Paul received bad news of the state of the Corinthian church, in response to which he wrote a letter warning them of the dangers of immorality. This letter is referred to in 1 Corinthians 5:9, 11, where Paul says: 'I wrote to you in my letter not to associate with sexually immoral persons... but now I am writing to you.' Some scholars think that part of this previous letter could be preserved in what is now known as 2 Corinthians 6:14 – 7:1, since that section seems to be out of character with its context in 2 Corinthians, and it begins, 'Do not be mismatched with unbelievers.'

Paul writes 1 Corinthians

Members of Chloe's household also brought reports that the Corinthian church was dividing into different parties, and Paul's own authority as an apostle was being challenged (1 Corinthians 1:11). These reports had later been confirmed by Stephanas and two others (1 Corinthians 16:17), who brought with them a letter from Corinth asking certain definite questions. 1 Corinthians was probably Paul's reply to this letter.

Paul visits Corinth

After this, Paul learned, perhaps from Timothy who had returned from Corinth to Ephesus, that his letter was having no effect. At that point he decided to pay a short visit to Corinth to see for himself what was happening. No such visit is mentioned in Acts, but it is certainly implied in 2 Corinthians 2:1; 12:14 and 13:1. On this visit he must have come, as he had threatened in 1 Corinthians 4:21, 'with a rod', for he later referred to it as a 'painful visit' (2 Corinthians 2:1).

Another letter

After his return to Ephesus, Paul sent Titus with a much stronger letter, written 'out of much affliction and anguish of heart', as he puts it in 2 Corinthians 2:4. Some think this letter is now preserved in 2 Corinthians 10 – 13, where Paul launches a vigorous counter-attack on those who were questioning his apostolic authority, something which was almost certainly the subject of this third letter.

Good news from Corinth

Paul then left for Macedonia, having been forced out of Ephesus (Acts 20:1). In Macedonia he met up with Titus again, who brought welcome news of a change of attitude in the Corinthian church. He also carried an invitation for Paul to go to Corinth (2 Corinthians 7:5–16).

Paul writes 2 Corinthians

Paul sent back to Corinth with Titus a more compassionate letter, expressing his great joy. This letter is probably what we now know as 2 Corinthians 1 – 9. He also took this opportunity to write on other subjects: the relation of teachers and hearers; the hope of a life after death; the general theme of salvation; and the collection which he was organizing for the Jerusalem church. If 2 Corinthians 10 – 13 belongs to this same letter, Paul must have heard news of a further revolt against his authority at Corinth while he was actually in the process of writing to them, which led him to defend his own position as an accredited apostle of Christ. Some scholars think that 2 Corinthians 10 – 13, rather than being earlier than 2 Corinthians 1 – 9, or written at the same time, was actually sent later, when Paul's authority was again being undermined.

So much for the circumstances in which these letters came to be written. But what was Paul actually saying in them? In trying to answer that question, it will be best to pick out certain features of what Paul said, from which it will be possible to gain a picture of the situation in the church at Corinth. 1 Corinthians provides most information about this, and so we will focus particularly on that letter.

1 Corinthians

Life in Christ (1 Corinthians 1:10 – 4:21)

One of the things that characterized the city of Corinth was the diverse nature of its society. Its position as an important seaport on one of the busiest routes in the Mediterranean ensured this. In the streets of Corinth, military personnel from Rome, mystics from the east, and Jews from Palestine continually rubbed shoulders with the philosophers of Greece. When Paul had proclaimed the good news about Jesus in this city, it was a cross-section of people from this cosmopolitan society who responded and came together to form the Christian church in Corinth.

Not surprisingly, men and women from such different spiritual and intellectual backgrounds brought with them into the church some very diverse concepts and ideas. While Paul was there the various sections of the young congregation were held together, but on his departure these new Christians began to work out for themselves the implications of their Christian faith, and naturally began to produce different answers.

A DIVIDED CHURCH

As a result the church at Corinth had, for all practical purposes, been divided into four different groups, to which Paul refers in 1 Corinthians 1:10–17. Some were claiming that their spiritual allegiance was to Paul, others to Apollos, others to Cephas, while yet others claimed only to belong to Christ (1:12–13). These four parties clearly reflect the diverse backgrounds of the Corinthian Christians:

■ The 'Paul party' would consist of libertines. They were people who had heard Paul's original preaching on the freedom of the Christian and concluded from it that, once they had responded to the Christian gospel, they could live as they liked. This was exactly what the Judaizers, who opposed Paul in Galatia, had said would happen when the Christian message was declared without making people obey the Old Testament Law. Paul, in fact, always emphasized that, far from relieving Christians of moral obligations, his message actually made deeper demands of them. But this danger of lawlessness ('antinomianism') was always present in his churches.

■ The 'Cephas party' were undoubtedly legalists. They were people like the Judaizers, who believed that the Christian life meant the strict observance of traditional Jewish practices, both ritual and moral. Many of them had probably been members of the synagogue when they heard of Jesus the Messiah.

■ The 'Apollos party' were probably devotees of the classical Greek outlook. Apollos is mentioned in Acts 18:24–28, where he is described as a Jew from Alexandria, 'an eloquent man, well versed in the scriptures'. Alexandria in Egypt had a large Jewish population, and several influential and gifted teachers lived and worked there, both before and after the New Testament period. The best known among these was Philo (about 20BC–AD45), a Hellenistic Jew who specialized in interpreting the scriptures, in accordance with the concepts of Greek philosophy, to demonstrate that Moses and others had already anticipated what the philosophers said centuries later. As an educated Alexandrian Jew, it is likely that Apollos would have been steeped in this kind of scriptural interpretation. He would naturally be an acceptable teacher to those Christians at Corinth with a Greek philosophical background.

■ The 'Christ party' probably consisted of a group who considered themselves to be above the parties that had developed around the personalities of ordinary mortals. They wanted a direct contact with Christ, in the same way as they had experienced direct mystical contacts

Corinth was a city placed at a major junction of trade-routes. Prominent among its ruins is the Temple of Apollo, behind which rises the rock acrocorinth.

with gods in the mystery religions. If Serapis could be called 'lord', so could Christ. But Paul made it clear to them that in fact, 'no one can say "Jesus is Lord" except by the Holy Spirit' (1 Corinthians 12:3). What they were trying to do was exchange one mystery god for another. Since this kind of belief often led to libertinism in practice, these people might well have found themselves aligned alongside the 'Paul party' on some important ethical issues.

THE CONFUSION AT CORINTH

As we read through 1 Corinthians we can see how each of these groups was at work, spreading its own ideas and emphases. *The libertines*, who claimed to follow Paul, encouraged the whole church not to worry about moral norms (5:1–13). *The legalists*, claiming to follow Cephas' example, raised the old question of what kind of food Christians should eat, though this time the argument was over food that had been offered in sacrifice to traditional deities before being sold to the public (8 – 9). *The philosophers*, followers of Apollos, were insisting that they had a form of wisdom that was superior to anything Paul had spoken about (1:18–25). *The mystics*, claiming they were following Christ, were inclined to argue that the sacraments of the church acted in a magical way, and therefore they need not worry about any possible consequences of their lifestyle (10:1–13). The resurrection had already come, they claimed, and they knew it had because they themselves had been raised in a mystical way with Christ (15:12–19). They claimed they were now living on a super-spiritual level of existence, far beyond the grasp of the followers of Paul, Cephas or Apollos (see also 4:8).

Various strands in these different types of extremism led, in the second century, to the emergence of Gnosticism, and here in Corinth we can see the first stirrings in that direction. But at the time, Paul was not concerned with giving a name to this movement; all he saw was one of his largest churches being thrown into a state of considerable confusion by fanatics operating from at least these four different directions.

This was completely contrary to all that he understood the Christian message to be. He had told the Galatians that belief in Christ would create a new community of equality and freedom for all Christians, something that he had himself experienced as he moved from city to city, and found new friends among the unlikeliest of people simply because they had been united in Christ.

THE ANSWER IN CHRIST

He knew, therefore, that the answer to the Corinthian situation must be found in Christ. Neither Paul himself, nor Cephas, nor Apollos, nor the kind of 'Christ' that was being followed in Corinth, could achieve any lasting result. When he had first visited Corinth, Paul declared the cross of Christ and his resurrection to be 'of first importance' in the understanding of the Christian faith (1 Corinthians 15:3–7; 1:18–25). Whatever Paul, Apollos or Cephas had done in their own name was of no lasting consequence, for this was the only basis on which men and women of diverse cultures could be reunited. So Paul repeated his basic message as the answer to the problems of the Corinthian church: 'no other foundation can anyone lay than that which is laid, which is Jesus Christ' (3:11).

Having set out his own starting point, Paul went on to look at some of the specific problems of the church at Corinth – problems concerned with their attitudes to secular standards and institutions, and to one another in the gatherings of the church.

Life in the world (1 Corinthians 5:1 – 11:1)

Though Christians enjoyed certain privileges by virtue of their new life in Christ, they still had to live in the same social context as everyone else. In Corinth, three main areas posed problems concerning the Christian's relationships with non-Christians.

CHRISTIAN BEHAVIOUR

At least two of the 'parties' in the Corinthian church claimed to have a theological reason for ignoring the accepted Christian standards of morality and, in the central part of his letter, Paul mentions three specific matters which had come to his attention in this context:

■ **Permissiveness** One thing that particularly worried him was the report that 'there is immorality among you... of a kind that is not found even among pagans; for a man is living with his father's wife' (5:1). Paul was never one for taking drastic action against people with whom he disagreed, but this kind of behaviour was so serious that he felt he had no alternative but to instruct the church members not to associate with the individual concerned until he was prepared to change his lifestyle. He told them, 'When you are assembled, and my spirit is present, with the power of our Lord Jesus, you are to deliver this man to Satan for the destruction of the flesh, that his spirit may be saved in the day of the Lord Jesus' (5:4–5). The precise meaning of this instruction is not especially clear, but the main point is obvious: this kind of wrongdoing was, in Paul's view, so serious that it must be completely eradicated, and if the person concerned was not prepared to change, then he must leave the Christian community – though his final spiritual fate was not the business of the local church, but would be revealed 'in the day of the Lord Jesus'.

■ **Freedom** Once again Paul had to emphasize that freedom in Christ does not mean the freedom to be immoral (6:12–20). Christians are not free to do as they please, but free to serve God, to whom they belong (6:19–20).

An upper-class Roman couple.

■ **Marriage** One of the questions that the Corinthians had asked Paul was also concerned with marriage and divorce (7:1–40). In replying, Paul permits Christians to marry (7:1–9), though he himself was not married, and could 'wish that all were as I myself am' (7:7). He forbids divorce (7:10–11), except in a case where a non-Christian partner deserts a Christian (7:12–16), and he recommends that the Corinthian Christians should remain in their present condition, either married or single (7:17–24), though he recommends celibacy as the preferable state (7:25–40).

This was clearly advice given for a specific situation that had arisen in Corinth, and it is interesting to note the way Paul separates his own advice and opinion from what he believed to be the teaching of Christ. He felt that he had Jesus' authority for saying there should be no divorce among Christians (7:10–11), but of the other issues with which he deals, in one case he makes it plain that it is 'not the Lord' who is speaking (7:12), and in another he merely says, 'I think that I have the Spirit of God' (7:40).

This is the sort of passage that has given rise to much discussion, for Paul says some exceedingly odd things here. Why does he seem to place so little value on marriage? No doubt Paul's own experience has played its part, for as a rabbi he must have been married himself at one time (all rabbis had to be), though he clearly was not at this point. The most likely explanation of his own situation is that he was divorced, possibly as a result of becoming a Christian. But there was a more fundamental reason behind his advice here, and what he recommends was based on pure pragmatism: given the precarious and unstable state of the Corinthian church at the time (7:26), there were many more important things to be done than making arrangements for weddings.

Jesus himself had said something not altogether different: 'If any one comes to me and does not hate his own father and mother and wife and children and brothers and sisters, yes, and even his own life, he cannot be my disciple' (Luke 14:26), and there is a striking similarity between this and 1 Corinthians 7:29–31. Jesus was certainly not against marriage and family life, and other passages in Paul's writings demonstrate that he also held marriage in high regard. Here, it was a question of practical priorities and, in dealing with what he perceived to be a desperate situation, drastic action was called for.

CHRISTIANS AND THE CIVIL LAW

Another thing that concerned Paul was the way Christians in Corinth were quarrelling with each other, and then going to the civil law courts to sort out their grievances. Paul had to condemn this practice out of hand. For one thing, it was quite absurd that Christians, who claimed to be brothers and sisters, should go to secular courts at all; when a quarrel arises in a family, it should not be necessary to go to court with it, and surely some member of the church community ought to have been wise enough to sort out these problems (6:1–6). But what disturbed Paul even more was that such acrimonious quarrels were arising in the first place. Christians ought to follow the example set to them by Christ, and 'suffer wrong' rather than create division in the Christian community (6:7–8). In the light of what God has done for them in Christ, their petty bickerings fade into insignificance (6:9–11).

EVERYDAY LIFE

It was possible for Christians to live independently of the secular courts, but it was more difficult to avoid other religiously charged aspects of life in a city like Corinth. For the Corinthian church, this focused on the question of food, particularly meat. It became an issue because Corinth, in common with other Hellenistic cities, had no regular butchers' shops. No matter what its source, the purchase of meat almost always had religious connotations. The best and largest source of meat would be the traditional Greek shrines, where animals were sacrificed to honour the deities. In those cities with a substantial Jewish population, meat butchered according to the rituals of the Hebrew scriptures would also be available. Either way, some Christians found themselves with a problem. Relationships with the Jewish community were often difficult so, for the most part, Jewish butchers would not wish to supply them – nor, for their part, would Gentile Christians wish to buy from them, since that would look as if they were accepting the validity of the Torah's dietary prescriptions. But what about meat from Greek temples? Insofar

as they might have considered the possible religious ramifications of buying meat from this source, most Christians argued that, since the deities honoured there did not exist, the fact that animals had been offered to them in sacrifice was of no consequence. Others, however, were less certain, and felt that by buying meat of this kind they were somehow encouraging and sharing in the worship associated with it. What, then, were they to do? Paul took up this matter in 1 Corinthians 8:1 – 11:1, in which the following four points are central to his advice:

Some of the Christians at Corinth had scruples about eating the meat available, since it may have been offered at pagan temples. This inscription is from the meat market (*macellum*) in Corinth.

■ Christians are, of course, free to eat food that had been offered to honour Greek deities, since such gods do not exist. But those who understand this must also be sensitive to the concerns of those who might see the matter differently. Those Christians who are 'enlightened' should occasionally be prepared to forgo the freedom to eat food bought from local shrines, out of consideration for those others who might be offended by such behaviour (8:1–13).

■ This was the kind of concession that Paul himself had made, in a different context. As an apostle, Paul had the right to be supported by God's people, and he even alludes to the teaching of Jesus to prove it: 'the Lord commanded that those who proclaim the gospel should get their living by the gospel' (9:14). However, he reminds the Corinthians that he had given up his right to be maintained in this way, and instead had been willing to place himself under restrictions so that his message might be accepted by all kinds of people: 'though I am free with respect to all, I have made myself a slave to all, so that I may win more of them' (9:19).

■ Christians should also recognize that there could be real dangers in adopting an essentially magical attitude to spirituality. Some of the Corinthians apparently took the view that the Christian sacraments provided them with some sort of immunity from traditional Greek rituals, so that they could take part without necessarily endorsing all that was going on. Paul drew attention to several episodes in the history of Israel that showed this was not so, and argued that it was naïve to imagine they could share in the Lord's supper one day, and honour the local deities the next, without compromising their integrity (10:1–22).

■ The general principle to be followed in reaching practical decisions on all these matters was not to do anything that would lead others astray, even things that might be right in themselves, but to 'do all to the glory of God' (10:23 – 11:1).

Life in the church (1 Corinthians 11:2 – 15:58)

Paul had been asked the answer to several specific questions that were puzzling the church at Corinth. Some of them we have already considered, questions concerning marriage and divorce, and food bought from local shrines. But there were others, concerned with the church's worship (11:2 – 14:40) and beliefs (15:1–58).

THE CHURCH'S WORSHIP (1 CORINTHIANS 11:2 – 14:40)

As the Christians in Corinth met for worship, trying to put into practice what Paul had taught them, three practical difficulties had arisen:

■ **Freedom in worship** It seems that Paul had taught them very much the same things as he had passed on to the churches of Galatia. Two of the basic points of this message had been that in Christ there was to be no distinction of race, class or sex (Galatians 3:28); and that Christ had given Christians a new freedom (Galatians 5:1). In practical terms of the church's worship, this meant that Paul, contrary to the Jewish custom of the day, allowed women to play a full part in the Christian ministry. He had passed on 'traditions' to that effect to the Corinthian church (1 Corinthians 11:2), traditions which the church members had observed. But they misunderstood the character of Christian freedom, and some women, who were taking a leading part in the church's services, were doing in God's presence things they would not have done in front of their neighbours.

The prevailing social custom of the time laid down that respectable, modest women did not appear in public with their heads uncovered. The Corinthian Christians, however, argued that they were set free, even from the norms of their culture, and that they should be able to express this freedom before God in the church. For Paul, this was a similar situation to the one which had arisen over buying meat, except that in this case it was not other Christians who were being offended, but the wider community. Since Paul saw a major aspect of the church's responsibility to be calling others to follow Christ, he invited the Corinthians to adopt the same strategy as he himself had outlined previously: 'To the Jews I became as a Jew, in order to win Jews… To those outside the law I became as one outside the law… that I might win those outside the law… I have become all things to all people, that I might by all means save some' (9:20, 21, 22). Within this frame of reference, he advised that women taking a public part in the church's worship ought to follow the prevailing social custom and do so with their heads veiled, even if in an ideal world it might have seemed like a limitation of their Christian freedom (11:2–16).

■ **Morals and worship** The way the church was observing the Lord's supper (eucharist) also gave cause for concern (11:17–34). Instead of following the instructions which Jesus himself gave, and which Paul had delivered to them at an earlier stage (11:23–26), some of the Corinthians were making the service into an occasion for feasting and merriment by bringing along their own food, and having private feasts – feasts which they ought to have held in their own homes (11:22).

The party divisions that Paul was so much against were even rearing their ugly heads at the Lord's table (11:18–19), because different groups were happy with eating different foods and, in addition, those who were richer had much more to eat than those who were poor, who were being left on the sidelines. All this division, not to mention the accompanying revelry and drunkenness, was dishonouring both to the purpose of their gathering and to the Christians themselves. They were giving no thought to what they were doing, and some of them had brought upon themselves the judgment which they deserved (11:29–32).

■ **Charismatic gifts and worship** Another very important feature in the Corinthian church was the exercise of spiritual gifts. Basic to Christian experience in the apostolic churches was the conviction that Christians were people empowered by the Holy Spirit. They were 'charismatics', people with *charismata* (a Greek word which literally means 'gifts of grace'). These spiritual gifts included speaking in ecstatic tongues (*glossolalia*), the interpretation of such tongues, prophecy (as in Acts 13:1–2), and the working of miracles by the apostles (Acts 19.11–12).

The Corinthian Christians possessed all these gifts and many more in abundance, and they were so eager to exercise them that several people could be taking part in church worship at the same time. This was clearly an unsatisfactory way of going on, and Paul had to remind them that 'God is not a God of confusion but of peace' (1 Corinthians 14:33), which meant that, when the gifts were being used, it could be taken for granted that, if God was truly inspiring them, this should occur in a way that would lead to the building up of the whole church (12:7).

Paul had no problem with recognizing the validity of all the various charismatic manifestations that had appeared in Corinth. He emphasized that every one of them was God-given and each, therefore, had its rightful place in gatherings of the congregation. Just as the human body has different parts, each of which must make its contribution to the smooth operation of the body, so it is in the church: each of the gifts possessed by different members of the church should contribute to the smooth running of the whole (12:14–31).

Not every Christian would be given one of the more spectacular gifts, such as speaking in tongues, but they were all of value. Over and above this, one gift should be common to all of them, namely love, which was the only basis on which the other charismatic endowments should be either desired or sought after (14:1–2).

THE CHURCH'S BELIEF (1 CORINTHIANS 15:1–58)

Finally, Paul turns to what he regarded as the core of essential Christian belief which, coincidentally, also happened to be one of the most contentious issues engaging the Corinthian Christians: the resurrection of Jesus.

Some members of the church were claiming that, in their mystical experiences, they had already been raised to a new spiritual level above that achieved by more ordinary Christians, a notion that Paul believed to be linked with a fundamental misunderstanding about the resurrection of Jesus. He deals with it in two ways:

■ Firstly he reminds the Corinthians of the firm historical foundation on which belief in the resurrection of Jesus was based (15:3–11). In doing this he provides the earliest New Testament account of belief in the resurrection of Jesus.

■ Secondly, he goes on to show how, if the resurrection of Jesus was a material occurrence (as he and the other apostles believed it was), this must be a guarantee that Christians also will be raised on the last day, in the same way as Jesus was raised from the dead. Therefore, in view of the centrality of Jesus' resurrection to the whole of Christian belief, those who denied its material reality, by re-imagining it as a series of mystical experiences, were actually denying the basis of the Christian faith, for 'if the dead are not raised, then Christ has not been raised. If Christ has not been raised, your faith is futile and you are still in your sins... we are of all people most to be pitied' (15:16–17, 18).

More arguments in Corinth

This was not the end of Paul's correspondence with the Christians at Corinth, though he must have been at least partly successful in persuading them to change their minds, for we hear nothing more of questions about the resurrection, marriage, or things like meat purchased in the local shrines. But there were still problems, this time especially connected with the arrival of messengers claiming to be 'apostles' sent from the church in Jerusalem (2 Corinthians 11:1–15). Paul had already dealt with people like this in the churches of Galatia, but those who came to Corinth were not 'Judaizers' in the strict sense. They were not trying to persuade the Corinthians to become Jews by accepting circumcision and the Old Testament Law. Rather they were aiming to persuade them to transfer their allegiance away from Paul to the more conservatively inclined leaders of the original church in Jerusalem.

Paul had apparently chosen to visit the church at Corinth while these people were in residence there, and this is the 'painful visit' to which he refers in 2 Corinthians 2:1. It was certainly painful for Paul, for he was insulted by these false apostles and their claims that his authority was questionable. He left in a hurry, something he later recognized as a mistake for it seemed to confirm what his opponents were saying about him (2 Corinthians 1:12–22). As a result the Corinthian Christians were left in a turmoil. Who were the real apostles, and how could they tell the difference between true and false? Their loyalty swung from one to the other and, in order to clarify the issues, Paul wrote to them yet again. The letter he wrote this time was 2 Corinthians.

While 1 Corinthians has a clear line of argument from beginning to end, 2 Corinthians has quite a different feel to it, and often reads more like an anthology of Paul's advice on different subjects than the kind of progressive discussion we find in other letters. For this reason, some interpreters think this is just what it is: a collection of two or three letters that were originally written quite independently, and later joined together by an editor. This would not be an unusual procedure in the ancient world and, in principle, there is no reason why a collector of Paul's letters should not have done this. The train of thought in 2 Corinthians certainly does seem to change direction rather abruptly at several points:

■ 2:14 – 7:4 is quite different from what precedes and follows it. Moreover, 7:5 makes quite good sense if it is read as the continuation of 2:13. Even within this section itself, however, 6:14 – 7:1 seems to break the sense of what goes before and after it. Could it be that this section in particular contains what were originally separate letters, perhaps including some of those which we know Paul certainly wrote to Corinth, but which are not separately identified anywhere in the New Testament?

■ Chapters 8 and 9 seem to deal with the same topic (the collection for the church in Jerusalem), but with no reference to each other. In particular, chapter 9 seems to introduce the subject quite independently of what has already been said about it in the previous chapter. Could 2 Corinthians 9:1–15 be another separate letter, this time written before all the troubles began, to recommend Titus and some others to the church at Corinth and to encourage the Christians there to give generously for Jerusalem?

■ Chapters 10 – 13 are in sharp contrast with chapters 1 – 9. At the end of chapter 9, Paul expresses satisfaction that the Corinthians have sorted out their problems, yet at the beginning of chapter 10 he is on the offensive again. So were chapters 10 – 13 originally written as a separate letter at a time when the situation was more desperate?

■ All these suggestions make good sense, especially since we know that Paul wrote more than just two letters to Corinth. The major argument against supposing that 2 Corinthians is this kind of compilation is the somewhat random way in which these other shorter sections seem to be incorporated into the present text. For example, why would a collector of Paul's letters have mixed them all up with each other, inserting separate, shorter letters halfway through longer ones in such a way as to disrupt the sense of both? Would it not have been more natural to have included them in sequence, one after the other? For this reason, a majority of commentators find themselves convinced only that chapters 10 – 13 are a different letter, later than chapters 1 – 9, on the grounds that this is preferable to the only other possible explanation for the change in tone from 9:15 to 10:1, namely that some other information had come to Paul's attention at the very moment when he reached the end of what is now chapter 9. But, because of the apparently illogical juxtaposition of the other material, the consensus is that the apparent changes of subject matter between 2:14 – 7:4, 8:1–24 and 9:1–15 are best understood as digressions in Paul's own thinking.

What, then, does 2 Corinthians have to say about these fresh problems faced by Paul in his relationships with the Corinthian Christians? The letter falls naturally into four main sections.

Facing up to problems (2 Corinthians 1:3 – 2:13)

Paul knew that he needed to explain the turbulent nature of his relationship with the Corinthian church. But there was also the question of true and false apostleship, and he clarifies his position on both these topics in his opening thanksgiving section (1:3–11). Here he draws attention not only to his affection for the church in Corinth, but also to his conviction that suffering and weakness are, in some way, an inevitable part of the true service of God. To cope with persecution, Paul needs to trust wholeheartedly in God, but he also needs the prayerful support of his readers. This is why he appears less self-confident and aggressive than his opponents, for he does not regard his relationship with his converts as a one-sided enterprise: he needs their prayers just as much as they need his guidance.

Paul also needed to reassure the Corinthians that he could be trusted. His unexpected visits and letters, and last minute changes of plan had given them the impression that he was unstable (1:12 – 2:4). They had concluded that he was afraid to visit them because he knew at heart the claims of the 'false apostles' were true. Paul obviously felt these criticisms deeply, and defends himself against the charge that he was acting selfishly. Nothing could be further from the truth: he had written a letter rather than making a visit because he hoped that would be a less painful way of correcting them: 'my purpose was not to make you sad, but to make you realize how much I love you all' (2:4).

Personal animosities must also be put right – and both Paul and the church should be prepared to forgive those who have been particularly offensive (2:5–11). Paul obviously refers here to a specific person – according to some, perhaps the man mentioned in 1 Corinthians 5:5, who was cohabiting with his own stepmother, but more likely someone else who had been especially abusive to Paul himself.

What is an apostle? (2 Corinthians 2:14 – 7:4)

The major point at issue was Paul's authority as an apostle, and he introduces this subject with an expression of his own gratitude to God for his experience as a participant in 'Christ's victory procession' (2:14). Yet, although he is in such a close personal relationship with Christ, this does not allow him to boast in a triumphalist way about his own abilities, for endowment with the Holy Spirit brings great responsibilities, and it is the recognition of this that Paul believed made him different from the other so-called 'apostles' who had arrived in Corinth: 'We are not like so many others, who handle God's message as if it were cheap merchandise; but because God has sent us, we speak with sincerity... as servants of Christ' (2:17).

Unlike those who had come from Jerusalem, Paul did not depend on official letters to establish his credentials, but was content for the validity of his work to be judged by its results in the changed lives of his converts, and the quality of his own personal lifestyle (3:1–18). If Christians are truly serving God, then God's presence should be visible for all to see: 'All of us... reflect the glory of the Lord... and that same glory, coming from the Lord, who is the Spirit, transforms us into his likeness in an ever greater degree of glory' (3:18), something that he identifies as one of the distinct advantages of Christian faith over other spiritual traditions (3:4–17). Even so, this provided no sort of guarantee that apostles could expect to live on a different plane from other people, unaffected by the ordinary problems of everyday life (4:1–15). For though the gospel is a powerful, life-giving message, God chose to entrust it to 'common clay pots', who are 'often troubled... sometimes in doubt... badly hurt' (4:7, 8, 9). Jesus himself had had the same experience, but after the cross had come the resurrection, and this for Paul provided the key to the Christian life. In Galatians 2:19–20 he had emphasized that the secret of his faith was the presence of the living Christ within him, and the same theme recurs here: 'we are always in danger of death for Jesus' sake, in order that his life may be seen in this mortal body of ours' (4:11). For Paul this was where the emphasis ought rightly to be placed: the messengers of the gospel must not be confused with the message itself, and the fact that the 'spiritual treasure' is in 'common clay pots' draws attention to the fact that 'the supreme power belongs to God, not to us' (4:7).

Reflecting on the various physical dangers that he had faced led Paul onto the subject of life after death. This had already been a major topic in 1 Corinthians, but here the perspective has changed and he asks different questions, no doubt as a result of his recent narrow escapes from death (presumably in Ephesus, 2 Corinthians 1:9). What he says in 5:1–10 makes this one of the most complex passages in all his letters, and has given rise to much speculation about the nature of his thinking on the subject. But two things are quite clear: he is still opposed to the views of those Corinthians who had been claiming that 'resurrection' was a matter of a person's inner spiritual experience; and he still clings to the Jewish belief in a bodily existence after death, rather than resorting to the Greek view of an immortal soul that would survive the disposable body. However, he continues to insist (as he had done in 1 Corinthians 15:42–57) that the resurrection existence is continuous with this life, though not identical with it, for he envisages that God will replace 'the earthly tent we live in' with 'a house not made with hands, eternal in the heavens' (5:1).

Throughout, he maintains the tension between present and future that is so familiar from the teaching of Jesus, insisting that even the final resurrection state would only be the final outworking of what God was already doing in the lives of Christian people. This is why the way Christians think, the way they behave, and their standards and values, should reflect here and now the reality of God's living presence: 'No longer, then, do we judge anyone by human standards... When anyone is joined to Christ, there is a new being; the old is gone, the new has come' (5:16, 17).

Looked at in this light, Paul's sufferings could in no way contradict his claim to be an apostle. On the contrary, he regarded them as the clearest possible demonstration of the truth of that claim (6:1–10). By now, Paul felt that he had explained himself in more detail than was necessary, and concludes by appealing to his readers to show the same degree of honesty about their own motivation (6:11–13).

He then moved on to warn them that the Christian lifestyle should be wholly different from a secular lifestyle. Christians must reflect God's own values and standards (6:14 – 7:1) by setting an appropriate distance between themselves and the prevailing values of the culture. It has often been supposed that Paul was here referring to matters of personal morality, especially marriage relationships. These would probably be covered by what he says, but his advice is far more wide-ranging, for he is encouraging his readers to be prepared to put God first in every area of life, not just where they find it convenient.

Looking to the future (2 Corinthians 7:5 – 9:15)

Paul now moves on to the effects of his painful letters, which had apparently led to a change of heart on the part of the Corinthians – a change which Titus had reported (7:5–16). It was presumably on this basis that Paul felt it was now appropriate to invite them to contribute to the collection he was organizing for the financial relief of the church in Jerusalem (8:1 – 9:15). This was not the first time the Corinthians had heard of this (1 Corinthians 16:1–4), but their stormy relationship with Paul had prevented anything being done about it earlier.

Paul urges them to be generous not simply out of a sense of duty, but as a loving response to what God had done for them. The coming of Jesus into their lives had been an unmerited act of God's goodness, and they should meet the needs of others in the same attitude: 'You know the grace of our Lord Jesus Christ; rich as he was, he made himself poor for your sake, in order to make you rich by means of his poverty' (8:9). He also believed that such an act of generosity would improve relations between the purely Gentile churches, which he had established, and the more Jewish congregations back in Palestine (9:1–15).

Authority and charisma (2 Corinthians 10:1 – 13:10)

In this section Paul again takes the offensive. If this was not a separate letter, it is necessary to imagine that he must have heard of yet further challenges to his authority, even while he was in the process of writing. This time it seems he was being criticized because of his personality. 'Paul's letters are severe and strong,' his Corinthian opponents were saying, 'but when he is with us in person, he is weak, and his words are nothing!' (10:10). Clearly, he lacked the charismatic appeal of the 'false apostles' who had come to Corinth. They did not suffer from self-doubt and persecution as he did, but were always boasting about their own mystical experiences and spiritual maturity. Paul does not answer these charges comprehensively. That had already been done in the previous discussion of the relationship between weakness and power in the lives of God's servants. He tackles the subject less systematically here, suggesting that these others only seem so impressive because 'They make up their own standards to measure themselves by, and they judge themselves by their own standards!' (10:12). Indeed, they do worse than that, for Paul accuses the Corinthians of accepting 'anyone who comes to you and preaches a different Jesus, not the one we preached; and you accept a spirit and a gospel completely different from the Spirit and the gospel you received from us!' (11:4).

He then launches into a wide-ranging attack on those who were questioning his own credentials on this spurious basis – dealing in turn with his relationship to the Corinthian church (11:1–6), his style of life (11:7–11), and the ultimate source of his authority (11:12–15). Far from showing him to be second-rate, his suffering and persecution actually demonstrate the reality of his calling (11:16–33).

The 'false apostles' also seem to have been claiming more spectacular manifestations of the Holy Spirit's gifts than Paul. There is plenty of evidence to show this was a recurring problem in Corinthian church life (1 Corinthians 12 – 14). Paul recognized that boasting about such things does no good, but he also needed to set the record straight, and point out that he too had 'visions and revelations given me by the Lord' (12:1). Nevertheless, he still returns to the theme of suffering and weakness as the cornerstone of his apostolic status, arguing that it is only as people recognize their own weaknesses and trust entirely in God that they can speak of being truly Christian (12:7–10).

Finally, Paul reminds them that he will be visiting Corinth again, and they would do well to put their lives in order before his arrival. Despite what his opponents have claimed, he is prepared to denounce them face to face, though it would be so much happier for everyone if they would get back to the basis of the gospel first, and recognize that it is only when they each acknowledge their human weaknesses that God's power can work effectively in their lives (13:1–10).

So Paul came to the end of the most complicated correspondence he ever wrote. Like Galatians, the Corinthian letters were written in the white heat of controversy, which only adds to our difficulties in understanding them. Paul was under attack from his friends as well as his enemies, something that must have given him considerable reason to pause and think out his gospel again. He wanted to avoid the pitfalls of the past, without in any sense compromising his basic position that in Christ all barriers of race, sex and social standing are removed, and all men and women stand equal in the freedom given to them by the Holy Spirit. It was probably thoughts of this kind that dictated the form of Paul's next major letter, which is quite different from any of those we have looked at so far.

Looking towards Rome

Towards the end of his extended dealings with the Corinthian church, Paul visited the area of Corinth, and spent some three months there. After this, he was intending to go to Jerusalem with the delegates from the Gentile churches, who were taking a gift to the Jewish church. Later, he hoped to visit Rome, before perhaps going further west to Spain. It was natural for Paul to wish to visit Rome, but the Christian situation there was quite different from that in other cities with which Paul had dealings, and would need some careful advance planning. For one thing, the Roman church had not been founded by Paul, which meant he needed to be careful about appearing to meddle in a situation which was none of his business. In addition, the church in Rome did not consist of one single congregation, but of a whole network of smaller groups, meeting in different people's homes around the city. This feature of Roman Christianity could almost certainly be traced back to the Jewish community there, which was similarly fragmented, with many different synagogues ranging from the most conservative to the most liberal. The Christian cause certainly had its origins in these synagogues, and no doubt the spectrum of Christian belief was equally wide, and largely defined along the same lines, except with the additional question of Gentile believers and their responsibility in terms of the Jewish Law and traditions. Though some Christians in Rome admired Paul, others must have been highly suspicious of him, particularly in relation to what they knew of his attitude to Jewish customs. For all these reasons, Paul felt the time was right for him to restate his message in a form that would not easily be open to misinterpretation, either by sympathizers or by opponents, and so he decided to prepare for his visit to the capital by writing a letter to the various factions within the Christian community there, containing a reasoned statement of his own beliefs. This was the letter to the Romans.

Romans

Though Romans has been regarded as a comprehensive summary of the whole of Paul's thinking, this is a misleading and unhelpful way of looking at it. He was certainly in a more reflective mood when he wrote Romans than when he penned Galatians, or any of the Corinthian letters. But there are several important aspects of Paul's thinking that do

not feature here at all. In particular there is no mention of his belief in the future return of Jesus, or of life after death – both subjects on which we know he had significant things to say. What he says on the nature of the church in Romans is also very limited when compared with his fuller exposition of the same theme in 1 Corinthians.

Romans is best understood as a more carefully articulated account of some of the major themes of Galatians and 1 and 2 Corinthians (1 Corinthians in particular). As we noted in an earlier chapter, Romans and Galatians cover so much of the same ground that it has often been supposed they must have been composed around the same time as each other. But Romans is more carefully nuanced than Galatians, and Paul takes greater care to spell out his arguments. It is probably more accurate to describe Romans as the argument of Galatians, as it looked when viewed through the spectacles of the struggles he had faced in Corinth. In writing it, Paul was conscious of two audiences. The

It is unclear how the Christian church in Rome began. It included people from different ethnic roots, and even some from the Emperor's household. The forum, seen here, was at the city centre. Rome at this time had a population of over one million.

most obvious one comprised the Roman Christians, to whom he would send it as a summary of his beliefs, to smooth the way for his expected arrival in the city. But before that, he was going to Jerusalem, where he knew he would come under attack from the Jewish establishment, both from those who followed Jesus as Messiah, and those who did not. Though he had forcefully dismissed the arguments of the Judaizers in Galatians, he realized that there was some substance to a few of the claims they had been making. Both in Galatia and Corinth, the way he expressed his beliefs had proved to be easily misunderstood and misrepresented. Now was the time to deal with this, and to refine those aspects of his message that needed clarification, while not watering down the essential elements of his thinking on the place of the Gentiles within the Christian community, and the significance of all that in relation to traditional Jewish observances. He knew that, on his arrival in Jerusalem with the collection, he would need to give a satisfactory account of himself to the church leaders there, and this time he was determined to be more precise than he had previously been in explaining his message. In that context, Romans was a draft of some of the things he intended to say to them.

Because Romans is so closely based on Paul's previous letters to the Galatians and the Corinthians, there is no need to summarize it in such great detail here. The arguments about the Law, and its place in relation to the ancient covenant, are exactly the same in Romans as they were in Galatians, and even the allusions to the Abraham story are repeated. Our discussion is, therefore, deliberately limited to those aspects of the argument that are distinctive or unique to Romans. The letter falls into three major sections.

HOW CHRISTIANS KNOW GOD

The first part of Romans, chapters 1 – 8, is one long theological argument starting with a text from the prophet Habakkuk: 'the just shall live by faith' (Habakkuk 2:4). Here, Paul argues in a way that is already very familiar from Galatians; indeed many of the points he makes are the same. Everyone, whether Jew or Gentile, is under the power of sin. Apart from Christ there is no way of escaping God's judgment (1:18 – 3:20), yet it is possible to receive 'the righteousness of God', that is, release from God's sentence of condemnation and the power to share in God's own goodness. This is something that can be obtained only through faith in Christ, and not by good works (3:21 – 4:25).

As in Galatians, Paul illustrates his theme by reference to the life of Abraham (4:1–25). He then goes on (5:1 – 8:39) to describe the results of this new relationship with God: freedom from God's judgment on sin; freedom from slavery to sin; freedom from the Law; and freedom from death through the working of the Spirit of God in Christ: 'In all these things we are more than conquerors through the one who loved us' (8:37).

These themes had featured before, in either Galatians or Corinthians, but Romans includes several new elements, all of them resulting from Paul's experience of seeing his message misunderstood and misapplied in the churches. This time he deals directly with the problem of antinomianism (6:1 – 8:39) by making it clear that although Christians are set free from the need to observe formal rules, in order to live in ways that would be pleasing to God, this does not mean they have no responsibility for their actions. Though set free from oppressive legalism, they have in fact entered into a new kind of service, not now as 'slaves of sin' (6:17) but 'slaves of God' (6:22). Christians are freed by Christ not so they can do as they please, but so that they may be 'conformed to the image of God's Son', something that is the work of the Holy Spirit empowering them to live in God's way (8:29). All this was already implied in Galatians, but it is spelled out here much more comprehensively, so as to minimize the complaints of the Judaizers against Paul. It is, in effect, the teaching of Galatians as reformulated by Paul after his experiences in Corinth.

ISRAEL AND SALVATION

In chapters 9 – 11 Paul moves on to discuss other aspects of his present understanding of the Law and Judaism more generally. In a very convoluted argument, he reaffirms his pride in his own people and their spiritual heritage, while at the same time struggling to understand why Jesus was not more widely recognized as the Messiah. He goes to some pains to affirm that, while it might seem he is arguing that the Jews as a nation have been completely rejected by God, things are more complex than that, for he still believes in the ancient promises, and also in God's sense of justice and fair play. If Jews seem to be on the sidelines of God's purposes, this is the result of their own choice in rejecting Jesus and the way of 'faith', preferring to stick with the way of 'works'. Even now, though, God's rejection of Israel cannot be final, for there is still a faithful remnant (presumably people like him, 11:1–10), and God's ultimate plan is to bring together people from all races, Jews included (11:11–36).

HOW CHRISTIANS SHOULD BEHAVE

Paul then moves away from strictly theological statements to write about the practical application of God's will in Christian living (12:1 – 15:13). Here, he deals with the Christian's relationship to the church (12:1–8), to other people (12:9–21), and to the state (13:1–10), summing up Christian duty as a whole in the words 'love is the fulfilling of the Law' (13:10). He thereby tried to emphasize again that standards of Christian morality are to be produced not by sets of rules and regulations imposed from outside, but by the power of the Holy Spirit working within the believer. Paradoxically, the outcome of the Spirit's work will be that the Law of God is in fact observed, and the key idea of this law is love. Paul illustrates this by reference to two live issues: the eating of vegetables in preference to meat (14:1 – 15:6) – not for vegetarian reasons, but out of similar concerns to those highlighted in Corinth by the issue of buying meat from Greek shrines; and the general attitude of Jews and Gentiles towards one another within the church (15:7–13).

The final chapter of the letter concludes with many greetings to the various home-based churches in Rome, which in themselves give an interesting insight not only into the diversity of the Roman church, but also into the general mobility of first-century Christians. Paul clearly knew personally many of those he mentions, having previously met them in other cities around the empire.

Paul and his Jewish roots

In recent years, scholars have expended a lot of energy in trying to understand exactly how Paul viewed his faith as a Christian in relation to his ancestral faith within the Jewish tradition. For centuries, it was taken for granted that Paul became a Christian at a point in his life when he was disillusioned with Judaism. Some passages in his letters seem as if they can be understood in that way, and when these were placed alongside strident statements contrasting God's freely given love with human efforts to achieve salvation, it was natural to conclude that Paul was saying dependence on God's grace was the Christian way, while the Jewish way was to try to earn God's approval by doing good things, identified with 'the works of the Law'. This understanding of Paul's thought goes back at least to Martin Luther, the German monk who became one of the leaders of the Protestant Reformation. He himself had been all but destroyed by the legalistic demands of the medieval Catholic tradition, and when he started to read Paul's writings (especially Romans) it was as if Paul was speaking directly to him. It was a truly liberating discovery to realize that achieving God's favour was not a matter of carrying out sufficient good works to merit God's attention, but instead was about recognizing that God had already accomplished all that was necessary for human salvation through the life, death and resurrection of Jesus Christ. As he read further, it almost seemed that Paul was not writing about his own spiritual experiences in first-century Judaism, but was describing with incredible accuracy Luther's own journey of faith many centuries later. For Luther, everything Paul said about Judaism could be read as if it was a detailed comment on the medieval church, and it was inevitable that Luther's own oppressive experiences in that church were in turn read back into the New Testament, so that a detailed correspondence was assumed between the beliefs of the church, and the beliefs of ancient Jews. Just as the church had come to believe that outward ritual by itself was the key to achieving salvation, so it was taken for granted that the Jews must have believed circumcision by itself was an act that could save people. Just as the medieval church leaders had played down God's love and kindness, so too had the Jews, and instead of accepting salvation as a gift from God, they had preferred to rely on external things like circumcision, keeping rules and regulations, and the performance of empty ritual. Since Paul had spoken to Luther's own needs so powerfully, presumably he was wrestling with the same issues himself in ancient Judaism, and therefore the Judaism he knew must have been reduced to the pitiful and pointless effort of trying to earn God's favour by building up religious merit through keeping the law, observing rituals, and so on.

There can be no doubting the profound impact that this insight had on Martin Luther and, through him, on the entire course of subsequent Christian history in the West. It was a correct perception of the problems facing medieval Catholicism. But was it also a true picture either of Paul or of the Judaism with which he was familiar? Protestant — especially Lutheran — scholarship certainly thought so and, for the next 400 years, it was taken for granted that Judaism was based on a very mechanical understanding of God, in which a person's religious duty was defined solely by the keeping of mindless rules and regulations. By contrast, Paul's spirituality was seen as a more spontaneous and immediate response to God, vital and relevant because it broke away from all that. Those sections of the Bible which seem to reflect a more structured approach to faith were questioned, or even rejected, for being secondary interpretations of the core of authentic spirituality. This is what led Luther himself to dismiss the epistle of James as having no value, and inspired more recent Lutheran scholars to draw such sharp distinctions between the life of the truly apostolic church, and what later

Paul and his Jewish roots *continued*

happened as the church became more institutionalized. In the study of the Old Testament also, it led to the prophets being much more highly valued than the priests, who were held to have been responsible for the development of the Law that Paul allegedly found so oppressive in his day.

From time to time, this understanding of Judaism was questioned, not least by Jewish scholars, who were also interested in the origins of Christianity but struggled to recognize their own faith in Paul's letters, as understood through the eyes of Luther. It is not as easy as it might sound to extract a systematic account of Judaism from the disparate writings of the various ancient rabbis – any more than it would be possible to construct a normative account of the whole of Christian belief from the writings of Christians from many times and places. Like the New Testament itself, the writings of the rabbis were addressed to different times and places, and consist of many different styles of literature, ranging from serious exposition of the Hebrew scriptures to jokes told over the meal table. Nevertheless, all the evidence seems to show that ordinary Jews, far from being oppressed by the Law, saw it as God's gift, and regarded the keeping of it not as an unnecessary burden, but as a delight. As the writings of the rabbis were scrutinized, it became obvious that many scholars who had made confident pronouncements about the nature of Jewish beliefs had never consulted any actual Jewish sources at all, but were simply repeating what they had heard from others, much of which was based on Christian opinions which themselves were heavily influenced by Luther's experience. In the early twentieth century, however, such observations were not welcomed. The great social and political upheavals that led to the emergence of the Nazis, and thence to the Holocaust, were already underway in

Carvings of menorah from the synagogue at Corinth.

Europe, and there can be no question that it was politically expedient for Judaism to continue to be portrayed as a primitive and oppressive faith compared with – especially – Protestant Christianity.

By the mid-1970s, the time was right for a reappraisal of these questions, and it came in 1977 with the publication of a book by Ed Sanders, entitled *Paul and Palestinian Judaism*. In it, he reviewed the arguments put forward by earlier scholars, but went on to insist that the most useful way to compare and contrast two faith traditions such as Judaism and Christianity is not so much by asking abstract theological questions about beliefs, but by identifying the inner dynamic of the respective communities through exploration of their 'patterns of religion', which includes two particular questions: 'How do people get into this faith community?' and 'How do they stay in it?' After exhaustive exploration of the Judaism of Paul's day, Sanders suggested that, for all its diversity, there was a common thread in what he called 'covenantal nomism'. This was based on the belief that God's loving actions on behalf of people ('grace') were the foundational starting point, and that the role of people was to respond in obedience to this expression of God's love. In discussing Jesus' ethical teaching in a previous chapter, we have already noticed the significant part played in the Hebrew Bible by this pattern of God's actions followed by human response. The Judaism of Paul's day was fundamentally the same, and on this basis Sanders argued that our starting point for understanding it should be the outworking of God's undeserved love and, therefore, keeping 'works of the Law' was not about 'getting into' the faith community, but was part of what was necessary in order to 'stay in'. On this view, the assumptions of Judaism, far from being diametrically opposed to Paul's Christian faith, were exactly the same.

That being the case, what can we make of Paul? In some passages at least, he does appear to imply that Judaism was about works, and not about faith – indeed, that Israel actively preferred the one to the other (for example, Romans 9:32). If he did not mean what Luther and traditional Protestant interpretation thought he meant, what exactly was he saying? Several possible answers to that question have been proposed:

● Some scholars have sought the answer in the fact that Paul's origins were not with the mainstream of Judaism, as it existed in Palestine, but among Jews of the Dispersion. It has been suggested that Jews living in the wider Roman empire faced different challenges, among which was the influence of Greek ways of thinking, often combined with the ridicule of the traditional Jewish practices that were recommended in the Torah. Under this kind of pressure, Jews had been forced to become more defensive about the centrality of practices such as circumcision, sabbath keeping, food regulations, and so on, which in turn had led to a narrow legalism in which the externals became more important than the faith. If it could be sustained, this would be a neat way of solving the problem, as it would enable both Jewish (Palestinian rabbis) and Christian (Paul) sources of written information to be correct, with the apparent confusion being blamed on a form of Hellenistic Judaism that no longer exists, and was never in any case the mainstream. However, the distinction between Palestinian and Hellenistic Judaism, which this presupposes, is highly problematic, as Palestine was an integral part of the Hellenistic world, and the New Testament itself attests to the presence and influence of Hellenistic Jews, even in Jerusalem.

● Sanders himself proposed a somewhat different way of looking at things, by suggesting that Paul's starting point was not actually Judaism, but Christianity. In other words, Paul looked at all the benefits he perceived himself as enjoying as a consequence of his Christian faith and, in looking back at Judaism, depicted this as the opposite. Since, as a Christian, Paul knew that, for himself, there was no

salvation except through Christ, then by definition there could be no salvation in Judaism. Similarly, if the empowerment given by the Holy Spirit enabled him to live in a way that was satisfying for him, and pleasing to God, then presumably Judaism had not helped him to do either of these

Ruins of the synagogue at Sardis.

things. And if Christ now gave him direct access to God, then the Law must have been unable to deliver this. By adopting this procedure, Paul produced a picture that, by definition, held Judaism up as the exact antithesis of Christianity – a picture that served his purposes in the context of the kinds of debates he became involved in, but which inevitably tended to simplify the relationship between the two, and therefore in the end helped to created a false and misleading caricature of Jewish spirituality. On this view, Paul was not actually reacting to any specific form of Judaism, but was rather meaning to articulate his understanding of Christian faith.

● Others have accepted this somewhat opportunistic view of Paul's intentions, but have argued that, in the end, Paul had an inconsistent and incoherent set of beliefs and attitudes. Yet others, however, have tried to disconnect Paul from actual Jewish practices and beliefs by proposing that his understanding of the Law was based on a bookish reading of the Old Testament, in which it can easily be made to seem that keeping the Law had a salvation-earning quality.

Several points can be made in relation to this debate:

● It is clear that the presuppositions of scholars have played a major part in this debate from start to finish. Luther himself was certainly more influenced by his own circumstances than by a dispassionate understanding of Paul in his first-century context, while much early twentieth-century scholarship was undoubtedly in tune with an anti-Semitic fascism, if not directly created by it. Likewise, Sanders' view is clearly motivated by the perfectly understandable desire to reimagine the New Testament in a form that will not perpetuate anti-Semitism and Christian persecution of Jews.

● In relation to Paul, it is important to remember that all his writings were occasional documents, written to address specific issues in particular circumstances. None of his letters was intended to be a reflective, comprehensive account of his thinking. All the negative references to Jewish practices and the Law were written in the context of acrimonious debates with those who wanted to insist that Gentile believers must first become Jews before being accepted as proper Christians. Though it has been argued that Judaism would never have produced such people as these Judaizers, this is hard to believe, if only because Paul clearly thought his letters were addressing a real group of people. Moreover, he expected the arguments of those people to be answered by what he had to say. Given his pragmatic intent in writing at all, it is difficult to see why he would have done anything other than attack the actual views being put forward by his opponents. His own credibility must have depended on dealing with what was actually being claimed. Since Paul's own letters are, in the end, the primary source material for his arguments with opponents, it is a curious logic that would dismiss their value, but still insist that modern readers of those sources can have accurate insights into what was going on. Whether they were being faithful to Judaism or not, the simple

fact seems to be that Paul did meet people who were legalists in the narrow sense. In that context (represented especially by Galatians, but also in certain sections of Romans), it was inevitable that Paul should play down the importance of the Law, in the face of those who wanted to do the opposite. In point of fact, however, not all of Paul's references to Jewish spirituality are negative, and some (for example, Galatians 2:14; Philippians 3:5–6; Romans 9 – 11) are very positive indeed. It might be that the problem is not so much with Paul, as with those who want to take his letters and distil from them some system of thinking that can be labelled 'Pauline theology'. Do we possess sufficient resources to systematize Paul's thinking in this way?

● Running through much of this debate is an underlying methodological assumption that is sceptical about the possibility of religious experience. In the final analysis, Paul was less against Judaism than for Christianity. In his experience on the Damascus road, Paul discovered that his existing spirituality was deficient: he was wrong in questioning Jesus' messiahship, and that discovery in turn led to further reflection on other aspects of his inherited belief system. His later statements about Judaism and the Old Testament did not emerge as the result of a process of abstract intellectual reflection, but out of his experience. But experience itself has tended to be a problem to theology, ever since the Enlightenment, and consequently there has been a need to reduce anything that seems like religious experience to other categories, usually taken from the discourse of social science. Inevitably, that leads to an exclusively cognitive, analytical perception of Paul's thought, on the basis of which it is impossible to trace a straight line from his Judaism to his Christianity. But if the validity of spiritual experience is allowed, there is no need for such a linear development from the one to the other, and Paul's own accounts of his conversion as well as the narratives in Acts all emphasize the sense of discontinuity between his earlier life and his work as apostle to the Gentiles.

28 Paul Reaches Rome

In Romans 15:23, Paul made the extraordinary statement: 'I no longer have any room for work in these regions.' There is no doubt that the whole of Asia Minor and the Balkan peninsula, where Paul had been working, certainly had not been fully evangelized by this time, but Paul viewed his own missionary task in a slightly different way. He regarded as his responsibility the formation of Christian congregations at strategic points throughout the Roman empire, from where others could reach out into the surrounding regions. At this point in his ministry, he felt he had completed that kind of work in the areas where he had been operating, and he would now set his sights on a different objective. Hitherto, he had worked almost entirely in the eastern part of the empire and, in moving westwards, Italy was the next most obvious place to aim for if he was to fulfil his dream of ensuring that, during the course of his lifetime, the gospel would be spread throughout the major cities of the Mediterranean world. But, since Italy already had churches at its most important centres, including Rome, Paul saw Spain as his next major objective, though he still believed that, as the 'apostle to the Gentiles', he had something to contribute to the church in the most strategic position of all: Rome, the capital of the empire. He was normally reluctant to enter what had previously been the sphere of other missionaries, but he decided to make an exception in this case, and so he planned to visit Rome before moving further west. Firstly, though, he had other urgent matters to deal with.

The collection for Jerusalem

In Romans 15:31, Paul had made what turned out to be a prophetic statement. He asked his readers there to pray 'that I may be delivered from the unbelievers in Judea, and that my service for Jerusalem may be acceptable to the saints'. Paul knew that he was hated in Judea more than anywhere else, even by some of those who were Christians. In the eyes of many, he was just a heretic and a traitor to his Jewish heritage. As a Pharisee he had been entrusted with the priceless privilege of interpreting the Old Testament Law, but as a Christian he had despised this privilege, appearing to regard the Law to be an inadequate channel of salvation, and powerless as a source of moral inspiration. In reality, Paul's view was not quite so straightforward: contrary to what his opponents thought, he held his own Jewish heritage to be very valuable, and in writing Romans he had given powerful expression to his feeling that God had not completely rejected the Jewish people. But he also believed that the whole point of the Old Testament was now summed up in what he had discovered about Jesus Christ, whom he regarded not only as Messiah, but also as the true fulfilment of all that the ancient scriptures had promised.

The collection, which Paul had organized in the Gentile congregations as a gift for the church at Jerusalem, was intended to be a sign of his own continuing care for his people, and an expression of solidarity between Gentile and Jewish believers. He hoped this generosity would show that, whatever theological differences might exist between the Jewish and Gentile Christian churches, they were united in care for one another.

So Paul set off for Jerusalem in the company of Christians from Beroea, Thessalonica, Derbe and Ephesus, along with Luke and Timothy. He must have known that, in some ways, he was taking a foolhardy step, for on the journey he stopped off at Miletus and sent for the elders of the Ephesian church. In the course of his conversations with them he made it clear that, while he hoped to return to them, it was more likely that he would suffer 'imprisonment and afflictions' in Judea. But he was still prepared to take the risk, because he saw the expression of unity between Jews and Gentiles as a fundamental part of his ministry, and something that was an essential witness to the gospel: 'I do not account my life of any value nor as precious to myself, if only I may accomplish my course and the ministry which I received from the Lord Jesus, to testify to the gospel of the grace of God' (Acts 20:24).

When he arrived in Jerusalem, Paul's fears and expectations were fully realized. Reports reaching Judea ahead of him had contained exaggerated accounts of Paul's break with Judaism, making no mention of those concessions he had regularly made to Jewish practices and expectations. James, who was now the leader of the church in Jerusalem, explained the situation to him more fully: 'You see, brother, how many thousands there are among the Jews of those who have believed; they are all zealous for the law, and they have been told about you that you teach all the Jews who are among the Gentiles to forsake Moses, telling them not to circumcise their children or observe the customs' (Acts 21:20–21).

James, like Paul himself, hoped the collection brought by Paul and his friends would pacify these hostile Jewish Christians. He also advised Paul to make a peace gesture to the wider religious culture, by paying the expenses involved in a ritual vow being undertaken by four Jerusalem Christians, and by sharing in their fast (Acts 21:23–24). Paul agreed to do this, for his policy had always been one of fitting in with all kinds of people: 'I have become all things to all people, that I might by all means save some' (1 Corinthians 9:22).

Towards the end of this fast, some Jews from the province of Asia spotted Paul in the temple, and convinced themselves that he had defiled the sacred site by taking some of his Gentile companions into its inner court. To do this was a very serious crime; indeed, it was one of the few misdemeanours carrying the death penalty that the Romans allowed the Jewish authorities to try, and punish, themselves. To ensure that no one committed this crime unknowingly, an inscription stood over the main gate of the temple in Paul's day, reading (in three languages): 'No foreigner may enter within the barricade which surrounds the temple and its enclosure. Anyone caught doing so will have themselves to blame for their ensuing death.' Two such inscriptions, in Greek, have been unearthed on the temple site in Jerusalem.

Under arrest

Those who spotted Paul in the temple wanted to act without the decision of a court by killing him there and then, but the Roman commander arrived and rescued Paul – not because of any sympathy for him or his message, but probably in the hope of avoiding a riot (Acts 21:30–36). This Roman officer assumed that Paul must be some sort of political agitator, and was about to have him beaten to get the truth from him when Paul claimed the immunity from such treatment which was his right as a Roman citizen (Acts 22:22–29). Because the accusation against Paul was clearly a religious matter concerned with the Jewish Law, the Sanhedrin was the proper body to deal with it. But, when they met to hear what he had to say, Paul started a quarrel between the two major groups on the council (Pharisees and Sadducees) by stating that he was still a good Pharisee as he believed in the resurrection of the dead (Acts 23:1–10).

The Romans always felt uneasy in Jerusalem, and when it was learned that a plan was afoot to kill Paul, he was taken under armed guard to Caesarea, the Roman headquarters on the coast of Palestine. There he would escape the direct notice of the Jewish authorities, and the matter could be dealt with under Roman procedures. Paul was again tried before the Roman procurator Felix, and this time the charge was not only that of defiling the temple, but also of provoking civil disorder wherever he went. There is a clear parallel here between the trials of Paul and the earlier trials of Jesus, for in both cases the original starting point was a religious dispute, which was redefined as a political charge before a Roman judge. Though Felix, like every other Roman official, disliked anything that might cause civil disorder, he was convinced of Paul's innocence. He postponed a decision on the case, partly in the hope of receiving a bribe, and partly for fear of arousing yet more trouble among Paul's accusers if he was formally declared to be innocent (Acts 24:1–26).

Anyone could enter the outer court of the Temple in Jerusalem, but Gentiles were forbidden to go through to the inner courts on pain of death. Inscriptions in Greek (like this one) and Latin warned visitors of the penalty.

At this point (about AD59) Felix himself was recalled to Rome to account for his own misconduct in relation to other matters. The new procurator, Porcius Festus, heard Paul's case again, and suggested another trial in Jerusalem. This had no attraction for Paul: he knew the risk of assassination there, and he could also foresee further delays. His imprisonment had already lasted two years, and he was impatient to reach his immediate goal by visiting Rome. If he was forced to go there as a prisoner, that would be better than not going at all, and so he decided to exercise his right of appeal to the supreme court of the Roman empire, the emperor himself (Acts 25:1–12).

Paul's decision to appeal to Rome took Festus by surprise, for he realized the weakness of the case against Paul and was at a loss to know what to write in a report to the emperor. When Herod Agrippa II visited Caesarea, Paul was again called to appear before both men in the hope that Agrippa, who knew more about Jewish affairs, would be able to suggest a solution. Both rulers appear to have been impressed with Paul's message, though they tried to pass it off by joking about it (Acts 26:1–32).

Destination Rome

At last Paul got his heart's desire, and he was sent off to Rome, accompanied by Luke and another of his friends, Aristarchus. He travelled on one of the prison ships that made regular voyages from Palestine to Rome at this time. The Romans imported criminals from elsewhere in the empire, who provided entertainment by fighting with one another, or with wild animals in the amphitheatres of Rome. Though it was a cruel death, many of those who were transported in this way preferred a 'heroic' death, with gladiators or wild animals, to the slow and painful process of crucifixion, which would have been their alternative fate.

Paul was apparently treated as a special case, no doubt related to his status as a Roman citizen, and also the fact that he seems to have been reasonably well off. Like any other rich Roman, he travelled with two companions, and was taken into the captain's confidence, even being consulted about details of the voyage. Luke's narrative account of the voyage to Rome (Acts 27:1 – 28:13), with its graphic descriptions of storms and shipwrecks, is widely perceived as a first-hand account of the journey, and is certainly one of the most gripping of such stories in the whole of ancient literature.

After many adventures on the way, Paul eventually landed at Puteoli in southern Italy, where he was warmly welcomed by the local Christians (Acts 28:14), and then as he got nearer to Rome, Christians from there came out some distance along the road to meet him. For two years, Paul remained a prisoner, under house arrest in a property which he rented for himself, and was protected by Roman guards, whom he would also have had to pay.

Even in such unusual circumstances, however, Luke did not lose sight of the significance of this in terms of his own intention to show the progress of the gospel, from the Palestinian fringe of the empire to its centre in Rome. He portrays this as the fulfilment of Paul's commission to be apostle to the Gentiles, and acknowledges that, though this is hardly

St Paul's Bay, Malta, fits the description of the site of Paul's shipwreck in Acts 27:39–41.

Route of Paul's voyage to Rome.

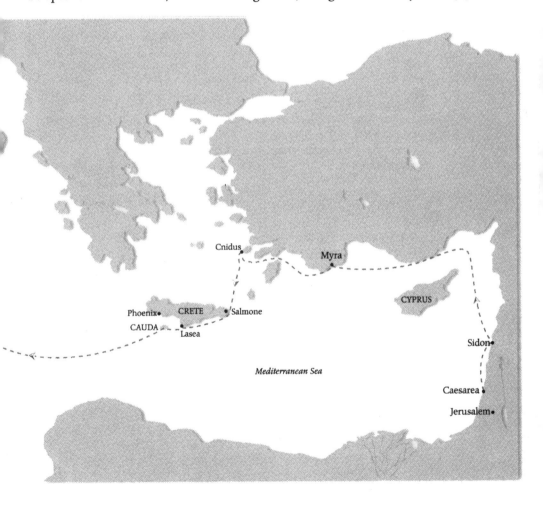

how Paul might have expected to arrive in the capital, this was all part of God's plan that he should have the opportunity to take his message to Rome. Accordingly, Paul soon got in contact with the leaders of the Jewish community there, who (as in many other places) heard his message, with some of them believing but the majority rejecting it. Again Luke portrays Paul turning to the Gentiles and, in spite of the limitations imposed by his house arrest, the final picture of him is 'preaching the kingdom of God and teaching about the Lord Jesus Christ quite openly

After Paul landed in Italy Christians came out from Rome to meet him at the Forum of Appius on the Appian Way. This famous road is still lined with Roman monuments.

When did Paul die?

Luke was more interested in recounting the progress of the Christian message, from Jerusalem to Rome, than in the messengers who spread the gospel, which no doubt explains why the story in Acts ends at the point it does. But all the traditions of the early church say that Paul met a martyr's death at Rome during the persecution ordered by Nero in AD64. We may suppose that, despite the long delays, he was ultimately brought to trial in Rome, and perhaps was sentenced to death immediately after this – though in view of the reluctance of Felix and Festus even to commit him for trial it is unlikely that Paul could have been found guilty on the charges under which he was sent to the emperor's court.

Since this trial would have taken place in about AD62, Paul presumably engaged in other activities until his final trial and death under Nero in AD64. This is certainly the view taken by early church tradition, and so Eusebius, for example, recorded that 'after defending himself the apostle was sent again on his ministry of preaching, and coming a second time to the same city, suffered martyrdom under Nero' (*Ecclesiastical History* II.22). There are two possibilities for his further activities:

● One is that Paul fulfilled his intention of going on to Spain. There is no biblical evidence to support this, though there are local traditions in Spain itself to this effect, and also a statement that he did so in *1 Clement* 5 (a letter written about AD95 by Clement of Rome to the church at Corinth). But it is more likely that the originators of these traditions based their statements on what Paul said in Romans 15:24, and assumed that since he wanted to visit Spain he must actually have done so.

● The other possibility concerning what Paul did after his supposed release arises from the references to Paul's travels in the pastoral epistles (1 and 2 Timothy and Titus). These letters might suggest that Paul revisited some of the places he had been to earlier in Asia Minor and Greece, and also some others of which there is no mention, either in Acts or in the earlier letters, such as Colossae, Crete and Nicopolis.

It is not essential to assume that such visits took place towards the end of Paul's life, for Acts by no means gives a complete account of all his earlier travels. In 2 Corinthians 11:23–27, for example, Paul mentions many incidents not included in Acts, but which had presumably occurred in the course of his pastoral ministry in Ephesus and the surrounding areas. Nevertheless, it would take a considerable degree of ingenuity to fit the travel references that are implied in the pastoral epistles into the Acts narrative. It is certainly easier to suppose that they represent further missionary exploits after his first visit to Rome – though even then it is no simple matter to fit all these references together to reconstruct a plausible journey. There are also other difficulties involved in understanding the pastoral epistles, which we shall come to shortly.

and unhindered' (Acts 28:31). Paul had achieved his objective. On the Damascus road he had been commissioned to be the apostle to the Gentiles, 'to open their eyes, that they may turn from darkness to light and from the power of Satan to God, that they may receive forgiveness of sins and a place among those who are sanctified by faith in me' (Acts 26:18), and Luke leaves him at the point where he had fulfilled the terms of this commission for, by this time, every strategic centre throughout the eastern empire had a Christian community which owed its origins to Paul's unceasing endeavours.

Letters from prison

In four of his letters (apart from 2 Timothy) Paul refers to himself as a prisoner, and it has traditionally been assumed that they must have been written during his period of imprisonment at Rome from AD60–62. These are the letters to the churches at Colossae, Philippi and Ephesus, and the personal letter to Philemon, who lived at Colossae.

The church at Colossae

Colossians and Philemon were written at the same time as each other, the former to the church and the latter to one member of it. Timothy is associated with Paul as the author of them both, and there are greetings in both from the same five people. Aristarchus, Mark, Demas, Epaphras, Luke and Archippus of Colossae are mentioned in both, and so is Philemon's runaway slave, Onesimus.

Though Colossae was not too far from Ephesus, where Paul had worked for three years, he had never visited the town. The church at Colossae had probably been founded by Epaphras, who might have been one of Paul's converts in Ephesus. The fact that such a thriving church had been established at Colossae by this time is striking proof of the wisdom of Paul's missionary strategy of establishing his own work in a central place from which other Christians could reach out to the surrounding areas.

Epaphras visited Paul during his imprisonment in Rome, and gave him a generally encouraging report of the Colossian church. But one thing that was causing him real concern was the emergence of a collection of opinions and practices that has often been labelled 'the Colossian heresy'. This appears to have combined some of the practices that Paul was opposing when he wrote Galatians, with beliefs that seem to have included some elements of the opinions held by the 'Christ party' in Corinth. The kind of ethnic superiority championed by people like the Judaizers had been combined with the intellectual exclusivism that was common in many Graeco-Roman religious cults, and the practical outcome was the emergence of a group of people in the Colossian church who considered themselves better Christians than the rest of the church members. As Paul understood it, these people were proposing that a complete and lasting salvation could not be achieved simply by faith in Christ, but required additional insights into divine things, which were to be obtained through a secret knowledge imparted in a mystical way.

This knowledge could be acquired by taking part in various ritual practices, such as circumcision, not eating certain foods, and observing traditional Jewish festivals and sabbaths. In practice, much of this must have seemed very similar to what was being demanded by the Judaizers in Galatia, who were also promoting the value of circumcision and other rituals, though the underlying ideology among the Colossian Christians was in fact established on quite a different foundation. For the Gentile

Christians of Galatia, the issue was whether to observe the requirements of the Torah as an integral part of obedience to the religious covenants of the Hebrew scriptures, whereas in Colossae such observances were being promoted for different reasons. These people seem to have been religious ascetics, and what they were looking for was something that would help them to check 'the indulgence of the flesh' (Colossians 2:23). They were not interested in the arguments raised by those who suggested that, in order to be good Christians, Gentiles should first become Jews, and the fact that they chose to achieve their asceticism by adopting certain practices and attitudes from the Old Testament Law was almost a coincidence. This becomes very clear from Paul's reply to them, for he mentions none of the issues that were so central to his argument in Galatians, but instead opposes them by highlighting the fundamental moral issues that are raised by any kind of ascetic practice.

Colossae stood in the broad fertile valley of the Lycus, near Laodicea. The ancient town is now buried beneath a mound.

The church at Ephesus

Uniquely among Paul's letters, Colossians makes explicit reference to another letter: 'when this letter has been read among you, have it read also in the church of the Laodiceans; and see that you read also the letter from Laodicea' (Colossians 4:16). Laodicea was another town quite near to Colossae, and Paul wanted the churches to exchange letters.

There is, of course, no 'letter to the Laodiceans' contained in the New Testament. Noting this omission, the church of the early centuries lost no time in producing such a letter, and there is indeed a *Letter to the Laodiceans* known in a Latin version. This letter is almost impossible to date accurately and, though it might also have existed in Greek, there is every reason to suppose that it is a very much later composition. It contains no real substance, and consists of a series of bits and pieces from Paul's other letters strung together in an aimless way. A more plausible suggestion regarding the identity of the letter from Laodicea to which Colossians refers is that it was the same as the New Testament letter known as Ephesians. This contains, in a fuller and more carefully argued form, the same kind of teaching about the person of Christ as in

Colossians

In his letter to the Colossian church, Paul deals with this false teaching by emphasizing again that in Christ believers can find all they need. Like the later Gnostics, some of the Colossians had been suggesting that they needed other supernatural agencies, and that Jesus was just one of several possible manifestations of God. Against this, Paul firmly asserted that 'In Christ all the fullness of God was pleased to dwell' (Colossians 1:19). Indeed, he went further than this by reminding his readers that in Jesus 'the whole fullness of deity dwells *bodily*' (2:9).

The Colossians claimed they needed to experience something deep and mysterious if they were to find full salvation, and Paul agreed with them. His own job could be described as the presentation of 'the mystery' – but, far from being something deep and hidden, this 'mystery' was the very thing that lay at the heart of all Paul's preaching, the simple fact of Christ's own life at work within them, empowering them to be the kind of people who could fulfil God's will (1:27). Whatever the Christian might have needed, it could all be found in Christ, for in him 'are hid all the treasures of wisdom and knowledge' (2:3).

Paul then went on to remind his readers of all the things they had as Christians, some of which they were now trying to obtain by other, mystical means:

● Were some of them claiming to be super-spiritual because they were circumcised? All Christians, said Paul, received 'a circumcision made without hands' (2:11) when they fulfilled the true meaning of the old ceremony by 'putting off the body of flesh', that is their old, sinful lives, that they might live a new life in the power of the Holy Spirit given to them by Christ.

● Were some claiming to have a new kind of life that other Christians did not have? Then they should recognize that all Christians have been made alive by God through what Christ did on the cross (2:13–15).

● What about ritual observances, designed to keep 'the flesh' in subjection? These also were of no real value and, even in terms of their own original purpose, they have been superseded, because they were but 'a shadow of what is to come'. Since the reality has now come in Christ, they are no longer valid. Quite apart from such theological arguments, though, they were a waste of time in practical terms, for though they might have 'an appearance of wisdom in promoting rigour of devotion and self-abasement and severity to the body... they are of no value in checking the indulgence of the flesh' (2:23).

Instead of fixing their attention on these things, Paul advised the Colossians to live up to their true position in Christ. Whoever they might be, and whatever experiences they claim to have, all Christians stand equal before God, all have the same temptations to face (3:5–11), and there is only one way for such temptations to be overcome: 'Set your minds on things that are above, not on things that are on earth. For you have died, and your life is hid with Christ in God... there is no longer Greek and Jew, circumcised and uncircumcised, barbarian, Scythian, slave and free, but Christ is all, and in all' (3:2–3, 11).

Instead of following a false set of values, based on mythological speculation, the Colossians ought again to remind themselves that the true ambition of the Christian must be to become like Christ (3:12–17): 'whatever you do, in word or deed, do everything in the name of the Lord Jesus' (3:17).

By their emphasis on asceticism and speculation those Colossian Christians who had adopted this outlook had actually removed Christian faith from the sphere of real life. But Paul was convinced, as always, that Christianity was essentially incarnational, and its spirituality was not rooted in some other esoteric world, but was to be grounded in everyday life in this one. So he ended his letter by showing how the power of Christ, which operates in the Christian (1:27), might be worked out in the family (3:18–21), at work (3:22 – 4:1), in the church (4:2–4), and in life in general (4:5–6).

Colossians, but without the pointed references to local persons and events. There are certainly indications that Ephesians was intended for a wider readership than just the Christians at Ephesus:

■ The words 'at Ephesus' in Ephesians 1:1 (the only indication that the letter was destined for that city) are not found in the best and oldest manuscripts of this letter. Some modern versions of the New Testament put the words 'at Ephesus' in the margin.

■ There are no personal greetings in this letter, which is especially surprising considering that Paul probably had more friends in Ephesus than anywhere else.

Philemon

Along with the letter to the church in Colossae, Paul also sent a personal note to one of its leading members, Philemon. He must have been quite affluent, for the Christians gathered for their regular meetings in his house (verse 2). Like everyone else in his position in the Roman empire, Philemon had a number of slaves, one of whom, Onesimus, had run away from Colossae, perhaps taking some of Philemon's possessions with him (verses 18–19). While on the run he had met Paul, and as a result he became a Christian himself.

Paul knew it was his duty – both as a citizen and as a Christian – to return Onesimus to his master. There were serious legal penalties in the Roman empire for anyone harbouring runaway slaves and, in addition, Paul appreciated that any other course of action would threaten the bonds of Christian friendship that existed between himself and Onesimus. For all these practical reasons, Paul sent Onesimus back to Colossae, along with this short personal letter. Of course Paul's action in doing this raises other questions about his attitudes to slavery as an institution, and modern readers might reasonably wonder how this episode fits in with Paul's categorical statements elsewhere that freedom is at the very heart of the Christian gospel (for example, Galatians 3:28; Colossians 3:11).

We shall deal with this and related

issues in chapter 21. Here it is worth noting that Paul did explicitly express the hope that he was not returning Onesimus to exactly the same position as he was in before, for he sent him back as 'not just a slave, but much more than a slave: he is a dear brother in Christ' (verse 16). Moreover, he instructed Philemon to 'welcome him back just as you would welcome me' (verse 17). There might indeed have been even more than that implied in Paul's request, for it has often been thought that Paul was actually asking Philemon to release Onesimus from his service so that he might return to work full-time with Paul as a Christian missionary (verses 11–14).

There is no way of telling what happened when Onesimus got back to Colossae, as he never features anywhere else in the New Testament. At the beginning of the second century, Ignatius mentioned a person called Onesimus who was leader of the church at Ephesus, describing him as 'a man of inexpressible love' and 'an excellent bishop' (Ignatius, *To the Ephesians* 1). If this was the same person, that could explain why a short personal letter to Philemon should have been preserved and included in the official collection of Paul's letters to churches. Depending on the date when Paul wrote the letter, this identification could be possible, but in any case it makes good sense to suppose that Philemon must have complied with Paul's request, otherwise this note would undoubtedly have been quickly forgotten.

This Roman slave badge reads, 'Seize me if I should try to escape and send me back to my master'. Onesimus' escape was a very risky venture.

Ephesians

In Ephesians, Paul again emphasized the central place of Christ in the plan of God and in the life of the Christian believer. He began by reminding readers of the great privileges they possessed in Christ. Though the people to whom he was writing had previously 'lived in the passions of their flesh' (Ephesians 2:3), God had put them in a new position. They had been 'made... alive together with Christ... and raised... up with him, and made to sit with him in the heavenly places' (2:5, 6). Every individual Christian had become a part of God's new creation in which God's plan was 'to unite all things in Christ, things in heaven and things on earth' (1:10).

Some of the people who read Paul's letter had been told these things before by Paul himself, for this was his special ministry: 'to preach to the Gentiles the unsearchable riches of Christ' (3:8) and to demonstrate how those 'riches' could be received and enjoyed in real life. Some of his readers might have been influenced by the kind of misguided ideas that had circulated in Colossae, but they would only find the true satisfaction they desired if they were willing to be 'filled with all the fullness of God' (3:19), which could be found nowhere else but in Christ.

After setting out this comprehensive and all-embracing description of the cosmic Christ as Saviour of the world, and as the source of all physical, mental and spiritual knowledge and activity, Paul went on to draw attention to its practical implications. If his readers were indeed members of Christ's body, new people and children of God, they must show by their actions who they really were:

● In the church they should be 'eager to maintain the unity of the Spirit in the bond of peace' (4:3). As in 1 Corinthians 12, Paul again claimed that they could expect the unity of the Spirit to be displayed by the giving of 'gifts of grace' to 'the body' for its growth and development (4:7–16). Because of the close relationships enjoyed by believers within the Christian community, any wrong done by one member would inevitably affect the others – something that would 'grieve the Holy Spirit of God' (4:30). In view of what God had done for them in Christ, Christians ought to 'be kind to one another, tenderhearted, forgiving one another, as God in Christ forgave' them (4:32). Paul could even advise them to 'be imitators of God' (5:1), by showing in their dealings with one another the same self-sacrificing love as God had shown to them in Christ.

● In personal morality Christians should 'Take no part in the unfruitful works of darkness' (5:11). What ought to characterize them instead was that they were 'filled with the Spirit' (5:18), the results of which Paul had listed in Galatians 5:22–23.

● In their social lives Christians must again be ruled by the principle of self-giving love, whether the matter at issue was in the family (5:21 – 6:4) or the workplace (6:5–9).

Finally, Paul reminded his readers that they could expect to encounter opposition, 'the wiles of the devil', against which they must 'Put on the whole armour of God' (6:11).

As an ethical theory, what Paul had put forward here would be impossible to carry out. How could anyone hope to be ruled by self-sacrificing love of the same kind that God had shown in Christ? Paul knew, from his own personal experience and his knowledge of the experience of others, that it was possible in only one way: if the Christian was 'strong in the Lord and in the strength of God's might' (6:10). This was one of the constant themes of all Paul's writings: it had appeared in what was probably the first letter he wrote, and a lifetime of work for Christ had only strengthened his belief that 'If we live by the Spirit', we ought also to 'walk by the Spirit' (Galatians 5:25).

■ In the middle of the second century, Marcion referred to Ephesians as 'the letter to the Laodiceans'.

It makes sense to suppose that Ephesians was a circular letter addressed to a number of different congregations. The words 'at Ephesus' in Ephesians 1:1 would have been found in the copy that went to that city, while the copy referred to in Colossians 4:16 would have had the words 'at Laodicea' instead.

The church at Philippi

With the exception of Philemon, Philippians is the most personal of Paul's letters. It was written to acknowledge a gift that the Philippian church had

---

Did Paul write Ephesians?

In most of Paul's letters we are always close to the heartbeat of the apostle, and usually not far from controversy. It takes little imagination to envisage the furious arguments that led to the writing of Galatians or 1 and 2 Corinthians, for example, but in Ephesians things are different. Here the discussion is much more serene and settled, and seems to progress independently of any direct involvement with opponents, or indeed any specific readers.

A number of other arguments can also be presented, which together support the suggestion that perhaps Paul himself was not the actual author of this letter, though its sentiments are not inconsistent with his known positions on any number of matters:

● **Language** A number of words found in Ephesians are not used elsewhere in Paul's writings. This includes some prominent features, such as the references to 'the heavenly world' (1:3; 1:20; 2:6; 3:10; 6:12) which is a key term here but occurs nowhere else.

● **Style** The way Ephesians is put together is also distinctive. Instead of the unplanned – and largely unrestrained – language of the other letters, Ephesians moves from one theme to another in more sedate fashion, generally using more complex sentence structures in the process.

● **Colossians** Ephesians has a close resemblance to Colossians. More than a

third of the actual words of Colossians also occur in Ephesians. Since Colossians has more of Paul's usual personal touch about it, many think this must have been the original letter, which was subsequently copied and adapted by the later author of Ephesians.

● **Doctrine and theology** At a number of points, Ephesians seems to reflect concerns that are known to have been especially typical of church life at a period later than the time of Paul. An example would be the use of the term 'church' to describe a universal movement that included all Christians everywhere (for example, 1:22–23), which is different from Paul's usage, for he generally thought of only local groups of Christians ('the church in Corinth', etc.). Then there is the position of 'apostles and prophets' as 'the foundation' of this church (2:20): does this (along with the list of church officers in 4:11) point to a time when church structures were more fully developed? There is also the apparent absence of any reference to the *parousia* of Jesus, and to the theme of 'justification by faith'.

So was Ephesians written not by Paul himself, but perhaps by one of his close friends, or a later admirer who wished to commend Paul's work to a wider readership? It has been suggested that Ephesians is a compendium of Paul's teaching, written as a concise introduction to the major themes of his theology, perhaps at a time when his letters were being collected together. The problem with this is that Ephesians is not really a summary of the whole of Paul's teaching at all, and it is precisely the absence of some characteristic themes that has cast doubt on its genuineness as a letter by the apostle himself. The same criticism applies if Ephesians is regarded as a synopsis of Paul's theology.

It has also been suggested that both the differences and similarities between Paul's other letters and Ephesians can be explained by his use of a secretary. It is a known fact that Paul regularly asked others to actually put pen to paper, only signing his own name to validate what had been written (for example, Galatians 6:11), and it might be that Luke, or some other person, could have been responsible for the final forms of expression in this letter. There are certainly a number of striking linguistic similarities between Ephesians and Luke–Acts.

Whatever is concluded about the person who actually wrote the words down, we should certainly not miss the weakness of the other arguments put forward against Paul's authorship. The close relationship between Colossians and Ephesians really proves nothing, as authors often base one book on something that they have written previously, and Paul had certainly done this before. The relationship between Galatians and Romans is a useful model here, and is in many significant respects similar to the relationship between Colossians and Ephesians, as both Romans and Ephesians take up points that had previously been made in the heat of debate, and refine and restate them in a way designed to make them more universally applicable to the concerns of a wider readership.

Viewed in this light, many of the apparent theological differences between Ephesians and earlier letters also appear in a different perspective. Nothing in Ephesians actually contradicts previous statements by Paul, and much of it is a logical development of things he had said elsewhere. So, for example, while there is no

instance in other letters of the use of the term 'church' to describe all Christians everywhere, the very fact that Paul could apply the term 'church' to Christians in Rome, or Corinth, or wherever, implies that there was something they all had in common and which bound them together. Paul certainly had a profound sense of solidarity between the various local Christian communities, as evidenced by the priority he gave to organizing the collection for Jerusalem – and to talk of all these groups together as 'the church' would simply give theological expression to that reality.

Many of the other alleged doctrinal discrepancies are not as impressive as they can be made to look. It might be true that the *parousia* is not found in Ephesians (though it must surely be implied in 4:30 and 5:26–27), but it is not mentioned in Romans either! The absence of 'justification by faith' would only be remarkable if it was indeed the central core of Paul's thinking, but if (as has been argued in a previous chapter) it only featured in particular situations of controversy, its non-appearance here would mean nothing. In point of fact, one of the major themes of Ephesians is the work of the Holy Spirit in the lives of Christians, a topic which almost certainly has a far stronger claim than justification to be the real centre of Paul's theology.

Ephesians is undoubtedly different, and the conclusions reached by various scholars on its authorship will tend to reflect their opinions on other subjects, most notably their understanding of Paul's temperament (was he the kind of person to engage in further reflection, or was he an impulsive, opportunist thinker?) and their understanding of the part played by pseudonymous writings in early Christianity. Whatever view is adopted, Ephesians represents a significant and mature reflection on some of the key themes in Paul's other letters and, even if it was written by a later admirer, it accurately captures the feel of Paul himself.

The Temple of Artemis (Diana) at Ephesus was four times the size of the Parthenon at Athens. This larger than life-sized Roman statue of the goddess is in white marble, and is decorated with symbols of sexual fertility.

sent to Paul to help him financially while in Rome. One of the Philippian Christians, a man called Epaphroditus, had brought the gift from Philippi and had been a great help to Paul during his short stay in Rome, and most of Paul's letter, which was sent back to Philippi with Epaphroditus, is concerned with personal matters affecting Paul's possible release, and expressing his warm affection for the generosity of the Philippian Christians.

In what was probably his first letter, one of the central features of Paul's

Philippians

Paul had always been especially close to the Christians in Philippi. It was the first church he established on European soil, and it was also apparently one of the few that had not been torn apart by damaging arguments about Christian faith and behaviour.

Paul's letter begins with an appreciative expression of thanks to God for all that these Christians had meant to him (1:3–11). Unlike some others, they had consistently 'helped me in the work of the gospel from the very first day until now' (1:5), which was why he felt able to accept their financial generosity (1:7) – something that had seemed unwise in the case of more volatile congregations such as that in Corinth (1 Corinthians 9:8–18). Because of their open and friendly attitude, however, he was confident that their Christian living would be marked by 'the truly good qualities which only Jesus Christ can produce, for the glory and praise of God' (1:11).

Paul continued to sound this note as he brought them up to date with his own situation in prison (1:12–30). His main ambition in life had always been to bring glory to Jesus – and even his imprisonment was doing that (1:12). Since Christians already have Jesus Christ living within them, Paul knows that physical death would only deepen that experience (1:21). Death might have been preferable to prison for Paul, but he could see good reasons why God would probably allow him to live a little longer: 'to add to your progress and joy in the faith' (1:25). To suffer for the cause of the Christian gospel

was not a sign of defeat, but of triumph, and so he advised them neither to be sorry for his present plight, nor afraid of persecution themselves (1:27–30).

There was, however, one thing that bothered Paul about the church at Philippi. Some of the Christians were quarrelling with each other, and Paul later named two particularly argumentative women, Euodia and Syntyche (4:2–3), though they were clearly not the only ones. In urging them to 'look out for one another's interests, not just for your own' (2:4), Paul quoted from an early hymn that was no doubt familiar to his readers, and perhaps to Christians in other churches as well (2:6–11). It is obvious that this passage is a quotation: it interrupts the flow of Paul's language; and it has the style of a hymn, with a definite rhythm, carefully balanced lines, and the 'parallelism' that was characteristic of Hebrew poetry. This 'Christ hymn' has been the subject of much scholarly debate. Who wrote it? Where did Paul get it from? How did he use it? And what did it mean? There is no agreed answer to all these questions, though it is clear enough why Paul inserted it here.

This is the only place in any of Paul's letters where he explicitly holds up the example of Jesus as a pattern for Christian behaviour, although 2 Corinthians 8:9 is very similar, and it is striking that the aspect of Jesus' life he chose was not his compassion, care or good works, but his relinquishing of divine status when he became a human person. This idea was very important for Paul, and lay at the heart of much of his thinking. In order to be a Christian at all, people must be prepared to give up their own claims to

self-understanding had been his conviction that 'I have been crucified with Christ, it is no longer I who live, but Christ who lives in me' (Galatians 2:20) and, as he faced the uncertainty of trials and possible death, he again set the dominant note in Philippians 1:21 by a similar statement, just five words in Greek: 'For to me to live is Christ.' From start to finish, Paul was motivated by his experience of the risen Christ, as he saw in his own life what might be possible for those who were willing to commit their time

---

determine their destiny, and instead offer all that they are to Christ for empowerment and transformation. This was a lesson he had himself learned on the road to Damascus, and it runs like a golden thread through the fabric of all his letters.

Paul then moves on to explain, in greater practical detail, what it means for a Christian's life to be infused with the life of the risen Jesus himself. For his readers, it should mean a lifestyle that would be distinctively Christian, shining like stars in a dark sky (2:12–16), while for himself it would eventually lead to a martyr's death. But that, too, was a privilege: 'If that is so, I am glad and share my joy with you all' (2:17–18). Epaphroditus (himself a member of the Philippian church) had recently experienced the same feelings, for he too 'risked his life and nearly died for the sake of the work of Christ' (2:30). He and Timothy would soon be going to Philippi to encourage the Christians there, and perhaps even to prepare the way for a visit by Paul himself (2:19–30).

At this point, Paul seems to digress and to write about troublemakers who were operating in Philippi (3:1 – 4:4). Some have argued that this section was originally a separate letter altogether though, if so, it is hard to see why a later editor would have inserted it at such an odd point in Paul's writing. There are plenty of examples of Paul writing impulsively and changing subjects quite unexpectedly, and it is not difficult to imagine that this is what has happened here. The people he writes about are 'those who insist on cutting the body' (3:2), which is code language for circumcizers. Paul does not spell out the reasons for their demand for circumcision, whether it was related to keeping the Law (as in Galatia) or as an ascetic practice (as in Colossae), though the former seems more likely, for he replies by reminding them of his own accomplishments in keeping the Jewish Law (3:1–11). This leads him into reflection on his achievements as a Pharisee, in which he was 'without fault' (3:6) – though he was prepared to reckon all that as 'complete loss for the sake of what is so much more valuable, the knowledge of Christ Jesus my Lord' (3:8). This 'knowledge' consisted not primarily in knowing facts about Jesus, but in enjoying a close, personal relationship with him, in which the resurrection life of Jesus himself gave Paul a new and meaningful dynamic for his own daily life: 'All I want is to know Christ and to experience the power of his resurrection, to share in his sufferings and become like him in his death' (3:10).

Even so, Paul was not claiming that he had 'arrived' spiritually, as some of his opponents in Corinth and Colossae believed they had. Unlike them, he was still on his way, like a marathon runner moving steadily towards the finishing line, and those who wanted to be spiritually mature should follow his example (3:12–21).

Finally, he brought to a close this most joyful of all his letters with advice on a number of varied topics, finishing by reminding his readers that, like him, they could have 'the strength to face all conditions by the power that Christ gives' (4:13), for 'my God will supply all your needs' (4:19).

and talents to the empowering presence of the Holy Spirit. Again, the overwhelming significance of the Damascus road experience for his entire world-view is brought out in Philippians, as Paul reflects on the way his discovery of Jesus as Messiah had revolutionized his own career, and invites his converts to join him in affirming that 'I count everything as loss because of the surpassing worth of knowing Christ Jesus my Lord' (Philippians 3:8).

Timothy and Titus

1 and 2 Timothy and Titus are collectively known as the 'pastoral epistles', because they are addressed to local leaders of the early church, Timothy and Titus. Both of them are mentioned elsewhere as Paul's companions, though they also worked independently of Paul, Titus in Crete, and Timothy in Ephesus. In both style and content these three letters are quite different from Paul's other writings, but they are very similar to each other, and were probably written at about the same time.

When was Paul imprisoned?

In our consideration of Paul's life and letters, we have assumed that those letters which indicate Paul was a prisoner when he produced them were written from Rome between AD60 and 62. This is the only imprisonment recorded in Acts, and it has been natural for readers of Paul's letters from the earliest times to assume that they were written at this time. It is not, however, the only possible time and place when they might have been composed, and a significant body of opinion favours the assumption that at least one or two of these four letters were written not from

Rome, but during an unrecorded imprisonment at Ephesus, which took place during Paul's three-year stay there. There is a considerable amount of evidence that makes such an imprisonment likely.

Imprisonment in Ephesus?
2 Corinthians 11:23, written towards the end of Paul's stay in Ephesus, informs us that by comparison with other Christian workers he had experienced 'far greater labours, far more imprisonments, with countless beatings, and often near death'. In 1 Corinthians 15:32 Paul wrote that he 'fought with beasts at Ephesus', a phrase which was probably not meant to be understood literally, but as a figure of speech could easily describe a trial preceding imprisonment. Again, 2 Corinthians 1:8 speaks of 'the affliction we experienced in Asia', the Roman province of which Ephesus was the capital, while in Romans 16:7, written shortly after he left Ephesus, Paul refers to two people as 'my fellow prisoners'.

Other evidence that Paul was imprisoned at Ephesus is to be found in the Latin introductions to New Testament books that were written in the second century under the influence of the Gnostic Marcion. The second-century *Acts of Paul* includes the account of an imprisonment at Ephesus, followed by an encounter with

Junius Bassus was prefect of Rome when he was baptized a Christian on his deathbed in AD359. This carving of Paul under arrest is from his sarcophagus.

They deal with four main subjects.

FALSE TEACHERS

Many of Paul's letters were written in response to threats from various opponents: Judaizers in Galatia, ascetics in Colossae, and Jewish Gnostics of a sort in Corinth. Timothy and Titus were facing similar problems, and were under pressure to abandon the gospel message as Paul had delivered it to them.

This false teaching appears to have consisted of several elements already encountered in earlier letters. The Old Testament Law was certainly involved, for some of the troublemakers are identified as 'converts from Judaism, who rebel and deceive others with their nonsense' (Titus 1:10). It seems that these people were using the Old Testament to support their own sectarian ambitions, for Timothy is reminded that 'the Law is good if it is used as it should be used' (1 Timothy 1:8). The specific

---

lions in the arena, from which Paul was delivered by supernatural intervention. While these last pieces of evidence are of variable quality, the combination of such information with the clues provided by Paul's own writings makes it quite likely that he did suffer a period of imprisonment during his three-year stay in Ephesus.

Were the letters written from Ephesus?

The fact that Paul might have been imprisoned there does not, of course, make it necessary to believe that he wrote the 'prison letters' from Ephesus. But arguments can be advanced to support this view:

● It is claimed that the friends of Paul who are mentioned as having made contact with him during this imprisonment would be more likely to have been in Ephesus than in Rome, which was a long way from their homes. Against this must be set the fact that little or nothing of a specific nature is known about most of these associates of Paul, and the one whose activities are best documented, Luke, was certainly with Paul in Rome though, according to Acts, not in Ephesus.

● It is argued that Philemon's slave, Onesimus, would have been more likely to run away to Ephesus, which was only about eighty miles from his home in Colossae, than to Rome, which was almost 800 miles away.

This, again, is not a convincing argument, for at that time all roads literally did lead to Rome. Arguably a runaway slave would be more likely to try to disappear in the capital of the empire than in a provincial town the size of Ephesus.

● Philippians gives the impression that there was much travelling to and from Paul's prison, and Ephesus was significantly nearer to Philippi than Rome. This is often taken to be a strong argument for supposing that Philippians at least must have been written from Ephesus.

● The strongest argument for an Ephesian origin of these letters is that in them Paul was looking forward to an early release, after which he intended visiting his friends in both Philippi and Colossae. In Romans 15:28, however, he had made it plain that, after his visit to Jerusalem, his intention was not to revisit churches he had founded before, but to go west to Spain.

What, then, can we conclude from these facts? It is almost certain that Paul did have a period of imprisonment during his stay in Ephesus, and quite possible that Philippians at least, with its mention of frequent journeys between Philippi and Paul's prison, might have been written at that time. If this was the case, the letter to the Philippians would need to be dated about AD55 instead of 62.

argument seems to have been about sex and food, with some claiming that true spiritual enlightenment could only be achieved through a life of asceticism in which material bodily existence was denied as far as possible. In contradiction to this, Timothy is urged to remember that 'Everything that God has created is good; nothing is to be rejected' (1 Timothy 4:4).

These people probably had leanings towards a Jewish form of Gnosticism. There is indeed a specific mention of 'the profane talk and foolish arguments of what some people wrongly call "Knowledge" [Greek *gnosis*]' (1 Timothy 6:20). Like the Gnostics of the second century and later, they wanted to deny that this world is really God's world – and so the sooner they could escape from it, the better. Indications that Timothy's opponents were arguing about 'myths and endless genealogies which promote speculations' and had 'lost their way in foolish discussions' also

---

Did Paul write the pastoral epistles?

These three letters are very different from Paul's other letters. They were written not to churches, but to two individuals who were working among recently established Christian communities: Timothy at Ephesus and Titus at Crete. In form, subject matter and style these three letters are very similar to each other, but in all these respects they are quite distinct from Paul's other letters. The differences are so striking that a majority of scholars have concluded that, at least in their present form, they could not have been written by Paul himself.

In considering this question, four main points need to be taken into consideration.

Paul's movements

It is difficult to fit the travels of Paul, implied or described here, into the story of his movements in Acts. Three main explanations have been proposed in the effort to explain the historical references made in these letters.

● *Paul was released after the imprisonment recorded at the end of Acts.* This view supposes that, after his house imprisonment in Rome, he continued his missionary work for a period of about two years before being returned to that city and meeting his death during Nero's persecution. No such release is recorded

in Acts, of course, though in principle this is no problem since Luke's purpose was not to write a biography of Paul, but to tell how the Christian message had spread from small beginnings in Jerusalem to the centre of the empire in Rome. This view that Paul was released and carried on further work has been the traditional view since the earliest days of the church, and is still held today by some scholars. Even within its own frame of reference, however, it cannot solve all the questions, for it is still very difficult to string together all the travel references made in the pastoral epistles to produce any plausible itinerary for further missionary expeditions.

● *These letters were second-century writings.*

On this view, originally popularized in the late nineteenth century, the pastoral epistles were compiled by people who were trying to reinterpret Paul at a time when he had fallen out of favour with the church. The travel references of the pastorals were not based on actual traditions about Paul's journeys, but were created to give a touch of realism to these letters. The difficulty with this view is that some of the historical references here are hardly the kind of thing that anyone would invent. For instance, 2 Timothy 4:13 contains the instruction, 'When you come, bring the cloak that I left with Carpus at

support this identification (1 Timothy 1:4, 6). But, of course, there was more than one way to belittle bodily existence. Asceticism was only one option, and extreme permissiveness was another. At least a section of those with whom Timothy was dealing seems to have chosen this alternative: 'they will hold to the outward form of our religion, but reject its real power' (2 Timothy 3:5). For Paul, the Christian gospel had always been about changing lifestyles, not about provoking arguments.

TRUE BELIEF

In response to all this, Timothy and Titus were being encouraged to reaffirm the basic elements of true Christian faith, especially by continuing to oppose the idea that God does not care about the world we live in. The fact that Jesus himself was both truly human and truly divine clearly contradicted

---

Troas, also the books, and above all the parchments.' It is hard to imagine that a later, self-conscious imitator of Paul would invent such details, for they have no theological content or ideological purpose, nor do they recount anything essential about Paul himself. It is the kind of comment that is more likely to have originated in some real-life situation.

● *These letters were compiled from fragments of genuine Pauline letters.* Though the letters in their present form were written in the second century by someone who was trying to reassert the authority of Paul in the church, pieces of incidental information such as those just mentioned have a ring of authenticity about them. On this basis, it is suggested that five genuine scraps of Paul's writings can be discovered in 2 Timothy and Titus, and that these were incorporated into a later work by a second-century writer. Insofar as there is anything approaching a consensus on the matter, this view has a good claim, even though it has its own difficulties. For example, how or why would five such fragments have survived independently from the time of Paul, in the middle of the first century, to the time of his imitator, almost 100 years later? What kind of person would have been interested in preserving them, since they contain nothing more than scraps of personal information with no theological teaching or pastoral advice?

Church organization

Attention is often drawn to the fact that the type of church organization shown in these letters is much more developed than the structures presupposed in Paul's earlier letters. It is certainly true that the pastoral epistles reflect something much closer to the second-century church, with its ruling bishops and complicated organization, albeit in an embryonic form. Other considerations also need to be taken into account:

● Paul's earlier letters contain no examples of advice directed specifically towards church leaders, and it is therefore difficult to know what kind of advice he might have given such people, or what level of organization he might have assumed in the early Christian communities. 1 Corinthians 5:1–13 advises about church discipline, which itself implies some structure that was able to take responsibility for it, while much of the debate behind other sections of 1 and 2 Corinthians related to the claims and counter-claims of people who, in some way, were jostling for positions of control in the church.

● No functions or positions are mentioned in the pastoral epistles that are not also to be found either in Acts or in Paul's earlier letters.

● The position of Timothy and Titus was certainly not that of the later 'monarchical' or ruling bishop. They are, rather, Paul's personal representatives, and such

Paul dictated his letters to a secretary, often adding a personal greeting at the end. This wooden pen case, dating from Paul's time, contains reed pens and an inkwell half-full of black ink.

such a notion (1 Timothy 3:14–16). Not only did Jesus come into this world to share God's love, but he became personally involved with people in their humanness. The essence of salvation, therefore, is not to be found in philosophical speculation, but in humble acceptance of God's love and mercy as demonstrated in the life, death and resurrection of Jesus (1 Timothy 1:15–17). Those who have their theological priorities right will show it in the way they live, not motivated by making money or empire building, but by 'the true words of our Lord Jesus Christ' (1 Timothy 6:3–10).

CHRISTIAN BEHAVIOUR

This theme keeps arising throughout these three letters. Several passages spell out in more detail how Christians ought to behave: family relationships (Titus 2:1–5), relationships in the church (1 Timothy 5:1 – 6:2), and attitudes to secular governments (Titus 3:1–7) should all reflect

---

Did Paul write the pastoral epistles? *continued*

authority as they have stems from the fact that he was an apostle, and they had been sent by him.

● From time to time it has been suggested some sort of Gnostic heresy was in view in the pastoral epistles, which by definition would make them second-century works. But the emergence of Gnosticism and the responses of the church to it were much more complex than that. Whatever was going on in the communities where Timothy and Titus worked, it was quite different from the kind of Gnosticism found in the second century, and has many more obvious points of connection with the kind of arguments that are dealt with in 1 and 2 Corinthians and Colossians.

Doctrinal teaching

The form of teaching in the pastoral epistles is definitely distinctive. Apart from a few statements called 'faithful sayings' (for example, 1 Timothy 1:15), there is very little that connects with Paul's characteristic teaching. The doctrine of the Holy Spirit, for example, hardly features here and, when it does, it seems less related to Paul's charismatic understanding of the Spirit's role in directing the day-to-day life of the church, and more integrated with an organizational structure. These are strong reasons for locating the pastorals in a later stage of church development, though even

here things are not as clear-cut as they can be made to appear:

● Paul's 'charismatic' doctrine has often been portrayed as a free-for-all in the church, with freedom being understood as the opposite of order. But when Paul spoke of the spiritual gifts (*charismata*) in 1 Corinthians 12 – 14, he clearly meant to imply that there should be recognized ways of doing things in the church. Not every person would be equipped by the Spirit to perform the same work, and this was the basis on which some might be recognized as teachers, others as pastors, and so on. This is a different way of identifying and defining leadership, for people are not appointed to 'offices' but recognized by the things they can do well. Nevertheless, while that might be the underlying philosophy of leadership, from an external perspective it was clearly possible, in the early days, to identify those who were in such positions. Philippians 1:1 and 1 Thessalonians 5:12 show that Paul recognized such people and, according to Acts 14:23, he himself appointed some of them. The fact that they were to be Spirit-directed and empowered did not mean there was no formal or visible order about the way in which they operated.

● It is not true to say that the Holy Spirit has no part to play in the pastoral epistles. We find here the same emphasis as elsewhere on the working of the Holy

the best aspirations of the ancient world, 'so that no one will speak evil of the message that comes from God' (Titus 2:5).

CHRISTIAN LEADERSHIP

Given the nature and purpose of these letters, there is much personal advice here for Titus and Timothy about their own conduct. They are to be examples of good behaviour to all whom they serve (1 Timothy 6:11–21; Titus 1:5–9), but they must also have courage to stand firm for the truth (2 Timothy 2:1–26), recognizing that the gospel depends not on personal opinions, but on God's own purposes (2 Timothy 3:10 – 4:8). They must also ensure that those whom they appoint to serve in leadership capacities in their churches have the same qualities, and are the sort of people whom others can admire (1 Timothy 3:1–13; 4:6–16).

Spirit in the lives of believers (2 Timothy 1:14), while Timothy himself is said to have been appointed as God's servant by means of prophecy, which was one of the most characteristic ways of the Spirit's working (1 Timothy 1:18).

Style and vocabulary

The real strength of the suggestion that the pastoral epistles were not written by Paul lies in the style and vocabulary of the letters. There are about 175 words here which are not found in Paul's other letters, many of which would be more characteristic of Christian writers in the second century than the first. In addition to these words, there is a difference of style in what might be called the 'connecting tissue' of these letters, that is the arrangement of conjunctions, participles and similar grammatical features. This is rather different from Paul's other letters, and 112 of his favourite prepositions and particles are missing.

These facts are impressive, and should not be set aside lightly, though again they are open to more than one interpretation. Some linguistic experts think that the pastoral epistles are too short to provide enough material for a reliable literary analysis of this kind. In addition, both style and vocabulary are very often affected by the subject matter that is being discussed, and even the argument from the use of typical connecting particles is not entirely persuasive, as Colossians and 2 Thessalonians both have considerably fewer of these than Paul's other letters.

What has emerged from all these debates is that there are differences between the language of the pastorals and Paul's earlier letters. These differences could perhaps be explained by reference to the different subject matter, to the fact that Paul was now an older man, that the differences derive from the incorporation of traditional statements or quotations from other sources – even to the fact that he was using a different secretary. It is also possible that a letter written by Paul himself might have been revised later to improve its literary style.

Current opinion is finely balanced. All the evidence of the early church fathers supports the view that Paul had some connection with these letters, and certainly they do not reflect life in the church at a period much later than his lifetime. Some have drawn attention to many similarities between the pastoral epistles and Luke–Acts, and have suggested that Paul's friend and companion Luke could have written them in their present form after the apostle's death, using rough drafts of genuinely Pauline material as a starting point.

29 The Church and Its Jewish Origins

It is impossible to understand fully the story of the early church without appreciating that the Christian movement was deeply rooted in the Jewish faith. Jesus was a Jew, as were all his original disciples, and so were most if not all of the converts on the Day of Pentecost. But, even in the earliest days, people like Stephen were asking whether Christianity was just another sect within Judaism, or whether it needed to become something distinctive and new. These questions became more pressing once Paul and others had moved out into the wider world to take the message about Jesus to Gentile people with no previous Jewish connections. Paul clearly regarded himself as the 'apostle to the Gentiles' (Romans 11:13), yet wherever he travelled he always took his message first to the local Jewish synagogue (Acts 13:14; 14:1; 17:1–2). As a result, many of the issues dealt with in his letters have a distinctively Jewish flavour – questions about the Old Testament Law, and the nature of Christian belief and behaviour over against Jewish traditions.

These issues were to become increasingly important for every aspect of life in the early church, as Christians took over the Jewish scriptures and the Hebrew Bible (usually in its Greek version) became the Old Testament. They naturally needed to know what relationships there might be between the inherited faith of Israel and their own new experience of Jesus and the Holy Spirit. Paul's epistles deal repeatedly with this question. But there are other writings in the New Testament which show how other Christians were tackling these issues. These 'general epistles' are mostly shorter than Paul's letters, and they are also for the most part considerably less complex. But they are no less valuable for that, for they give us direct access to areas of the church's life and thinking that are mentioned nowhere else in the New Testament.

Four books in particular shed light on different aspects of the Jewish dimension in the life of the earliest churches: James, Hebrews, 1 Peter and Revelation. They all have a clear orientation towards Jewish interests, but their concerns are not identical. Indeed, their very diversity makes them all the more useful, for they provide an insight into at least four different aspects of Jewish spirituality that were adopted and further developed among the first Christians.

Christians and Jewish morality

Judaism had always been deeply concerned with behaviour. In the Roman world, Jewish people were often distinguished not so much by what they thought as by what they did. They circumcised their male children, kept the sabbath day apart and observed distinctive laws about the preparation and consumption of food. These were the things that announced to the Romans that the Jews were different. But they were not the only things. For the Jewish people also had a comprehensive code of moral behaviour. Many of the things that were taken for granted in a regular Hellenistic lifestyle were avoided by Jews – not just because they were un-Jewish, but because they seemed to be against the Law of God. As Jewish people in different parts of the Roman empire explained their ancestral faith to other people, they found that Gentiles were often attracted by their moral standards. After the self-indulgence of much Greek and Roman culture, many Gentiles found the Jewish way refreshingly simple and disciplined. Not a few Gentiles actually converted to the Jewish religion, becoming full proselytes, while many more were like Cornelius (Acts 10:1–2), adopting the beliefs and lifestyle of Judaism without necessarily taking upon themselves the requirement of full obedience to the Torah.

The foundation of Jewish morality had been laid many centuries before in the Old Testament. Besides its concern with matters of religious ritual, the Torah has a strong moral core, in the ten commandments (Exodus 20:1–17) and elsewhere (especially the book of Deuteronomy). It was concerned to ensure that worshippers in ancient Israel should carry their religious beliefs over into the affairs of everyday life. The notion that there could be a division between the sacred and the secular was quite foreign to Judaism, for all of life was lived in the presence of God. As Amos and other Old Testament prophets never tired of pointing out, it was a waste of time to make high-sounding religious affirmations in the temple if they made no difference to the way people behaved at home and in the market place.

James

Jesus' himself had made the same emphasis, and the letter of James continues this theme: it emphasizes that religious belief is worthless if it does not affect the way people live. Devotion to God does not end at the door of the church. It only begins there: 'What God considers to be pure and genuine religion is this: to take care of orphans and widows in their suffering and to keep oneself from being corrupted by the world' (1:27). The heart of real devotion to God is to love one's neighbour as oneself (2:1–13) – and without deeds that will put such sentiments into action, religious faith is worthless (2:14–26).

Like Jesus, James uses many illustrations to deliver his message. In one passage he draws a vivid verbal picture of the apparent splendour of a rich person. Like the flowers whose beauty they try to copy, such people will last for only a short time: 'The sun rises with its blazing heat and burns the plant; its flowers fall off, and its beauty is destroyed. In the same way the rich will be destroyed...' (1:10–11; 5:1–6; cf. Matthew 6:28–30). James also turns his attention to the dangers of thoughtless talk. Just as a small rudder can steer a ship many times larger than itself, so the tongue has an influence that is out of all proportion to its size – and if we are not careful it can make trouble for ourselves and for other people. Once a person loses control of their tongue, it can create conditions like a forest fire, which is started by just one small spark but is very difficult to put out (3:1–12).

James takes many illustrations from the familiar world of Palestinian agriculture. He condemns the selfishness of the employer who refuses to pay workers a proper wage for a day's work (5:1–6). Jesus had used a similar story to make a rather different point. He told of an employer who hired workers for the vineyard. They started work at different times of the day, so that when the time came for them to receive their wages some of them had only worked for an hour, while others had worked the whole day. But they all received the same pay! Jesus' hearers must have rubbed their eyes with amazement when they heard that, for in their experience employers were more likely to treat them in the way James describes. But, of course, Jesus was speaking of a different kind of employer – God – who can always be trusted to deal with people in a way that is overwhelmingly generous.

The book of James has no coherent 'argument' as such, any more than Jesus' Sermon on the Mount has a consistently argued theme (Matthew 5–7). But its message would not be lost on its readers. These people were suffering the kind of discrimination that James mentions, and they are urged to be patient and to trust in God for deliverance. What God has promised will come true, and God's people will be vindicated in the end (James 5:7–20).

A CHRISTIAN BOOK?

There are several unsolved questions about the letter of James. But two things are quite clear: it is an intensely Jewish writing, and it is concerned above everything else with correct behaviour. Some have thought it so Jewish that they have doubted whether it could really be Christian. Martin Luther had no time for it, and dismissed it as 'a right strawy epistle, for it has no evangelical manner about it' – though in assessing his opinion, Luther's narrow comprehension of Judaism and his tendency to equate it with the failings of his own medieval church need to be taken into account. Others, however, have pointed out that James mentions the name of Jesus in only two places (1:1; 2:1), and that when he gives examples for his readers to follow, he chooses Old Testament figures like Abraham (2:21–24), Job (5:11), Elijah (5:17) and even the prostitute Rahab rather than Jesus (2:25). Moreover, no

significant facts about Jesus are mentioned anywhere in the book –
not even his death and resurrection. Indeed, if we were to look for
other books of a similar kind, we would most easily find them in
writings such as Proverbs in the Old Testament and other so-called
'Wisdom' books that were popular with Jewish readers in the time of
Jesus.

Some have therefore suggested that James was not written by a
Christian at all, and that the two references to Jesus were inserted at
some later date when Christians became embarrassed by the existence
of this apparently Jewish book in their scriptures. But there is no
evidence to support this idea. A later Christian editor who set out to
change what was supposed to be a Jewish book into a Christian one
would surely have inserted far more references to specifically Christian
ideas than just two mentions of the name of Jesus.

Similarities between the teaching of Jesus and James

God is the source and giver of all good gifts	Matthew 7:7–11 James 1:17
Christians must pay attention to God's word but also be prepared to put it into practice	Matthew 7:24–27 James 1:22
Christians should share God's mercy with others	Matthew 5:7 James 2:13
Christians should endeavour to make peace in the world	Matthew 5:9 James 3:18
'Love your neighbour as you love yourself'	Matthew 22:39 James 2:8
If this teaching is followed, the true nature of the Christian will be impossible to hide	Matthew 7:16–18 James 3:12
Followers of Jesus can pray to God confident their prayers will be answered	Matthew 11:22–24 James 1:6
God is the only judge, and the one to whom Christians are responsible	Matthew 7:1–2 James 4:11–12
Christians should make promises that others can accept and trust, because they intend to keep them, instead of trying to emphasize their sincerity by using unnecessary oaths	Matthew 5:33–37 James 5:12

JAMES AND JESUS

Far from suggesting that there is something deficient about the book
of James, its similarities to Jewish ways of thinking ought to challenge
the perception of those contemporary readers who have seen a sharp
dichotomy between the early church and its Jewish origins. For the
message of James is actually very much in harmony with the teaching
of Jesus. This is more than just a superficial similarity, for there are

many detailed points at which James' advice corresponds closely to specific aspects of Jesus' teaching as we know it from the synoptic gospels.

The words of James and the words of Jesus are not *identical* in any of these passages. But the language used and the sentiments expressed are so similar that it seems obvious there must be some connection.

The letter of James

Who wrote the letter of James? And who were its first readers? Most New Testament books contain some clues that enable us to answer such questions. But in the case of James, there is virtually nothing at all that provides specific indications about either the author or the recipients of this epistle. Indeed, it is not even certain that it was really an epistle, in the sense of a letter sent from one person to a group of others.

Who was James?

Apart from the mention of a person called James in the opening sentence, the book makes no further specific reference to its writer, readers or any other event or person. There is no hint as to where James and his readers lived, nor are we told who James actually was. This was a very common name among Jewish people, and a James who is described as 'a servant of God and of the Lord Jesus Christ' could have been any Christian of that name. Similarly, the way the book describes people and their behaviour could apply to many different situations not only in the ancient world, but in most social contexts, for it deals with basic traits of human nature that are the same the world over. It is as pointless to look for the identity of the rich people of whom James complains (James 2:1–4) as it would be to try to find out who the Good Samaritan was (Luke 10:25–37).

Early church traditions give no more real help. There is no trace of this letter of James in other Christian literature until the end of the second century. Eusebius listed it as one of the New Testament books whose value was disputed (*Ecclesiastical History* III.25.3). But he also added that the same disputed books 'have been produced publicly with the rest in most churches', and then linked this one with James, the brother of Jesus and leader of the church in Jerusalem (*Ecclesiastical History* II.23.25). Though this statement in Eusebius is obviously from a much later date than any possible time when the epistle of James might have been written, many scholars are prepared to believe it, if only because it is the only hard evidence we have, and so they regard the book as the work of James of Jerusalem.

If it is necessary to link this epistle with a person by the name of James who is mentioned elsewhere in the New Testament, then undoubtedly there are only two possible candidates: James the disciple and brother of John, and James the brother of Jesus. Faced with a choice between these two, most scholars would choose the second, on the ground that James the apostle was martyred in AD44 (Acts 12:1–3), and it is assumed that this date would be too early for the writing of any of the New Testament books. In addition, that particular James does not figure prominently in any of the stories of the early church contained in the book of Acts, whereas James the brother of Jesus became well known: he features as a central figure in Acts, and is also mentioned in Paul's writings. He would certainly seem to be the kind of person who could write to other Christians with no more introduction than his name.

But a number of arguments have been put forward against this idea that James of Jerusalem wrote the letter of James:

The most likely explanation is that the writer of James knew these sayings of Jesus in a slightly different form than they now have in the New Testament gospels. The gospel materials circulated by word of mouth for some time before they were written down, and the fact that some of this teaching has a more primitive form in James than it does in Matthew might imply that James had access to it at an earlier stage than the writers of the gospels.

The letter of James
continued

● It is written in very good Greek, in an elegant style that seems to imply some acquaintance with Greek literary arts. But would this be likely if it was the work of someone from rural Galilee? This argument was often given considerable weight by scholars of previous generations, who drew a sharp distinction between the culture of Palestine (which they believed was largely insulated from Greek influence) and the culture of the wider Hellenistic world. But this is now known to have been an over-simplification of a complex set of cultural interactions between the various regions of the Roman empire. Certainly, in an area such as Galilee with a large non-Jewish population a person like James could easily have learned a good deal about the Greek language. Moreover, at a number of places in the book, the distinctive idiom and style of the Semitic languages Hebrew and Aramaic seem to have influenced its style of writing (2:7; 3:12; 4:13–15; 5:17), which in turn suggests that the writer also knew one or both of these languages.

● If this book had been written by James the brother of Jesus, would he not have made more specific mentions of his famous brother? Indeed, since James was not a disciple during Jesus' own lifetime, would it not have been natural for him to have included some account of his conversion (alluded to by Paul in 1 Corinthians 15:7)? As it is, the writer seems to go out of his way to avoid mentioning Jesus directly: surely, therefore, he cannot have been this particular James. There is some weight in this argument, but it is an argument from silence, which really depends on guesswork. If we are unsure of the identity

of an ancient author, then making judgments about what he or she might or might not have been expected to write is, at best, a very subjective business.

● In James 2:14–26 there is a passage which contrasts faith and actions as the basis of true commitment. Paul also draws the same contrast, especially in his letters to the Galatians and to the Romans, and what James writes has often been regarded as a deliberate reply to and correction of Paul's opinions. If that is the case, then James must have been written after Paul's time, probably after his views had become a source of controversy – and on any account, this must therefore have been long after any possible date for the death of James of Jerusalem. But there is no reason to suppose either that James knew Paul's writings, or, as some have suggested, that Paul knew of James. Certainly they use the same terminology, but their concerns are different – and in any case, the differences between them are nothing like as far-reaching as Protestant (especially Lutheran) interpreters have generally supposed.

● The strongest reason of all for doubting that James of Jerusalem could have written this book is its conviction that true belief should be described in purely ethical terms. James had faced this question over the admission of the Gentile converts to the church: were they to obey the whole of the Old Testament Law or not? While James did not go along with those extremists who insisted that Gentile Christians should become Jews by being circumcised, he did agree that they should observe not only the moral laws of the Old Testament, but also some of the ritual and food laws as well

ORIGINS

Two main conclusions seem justified. On the one hand, the evidence for associating this book with James of Jerusalem is not especially convincing; but on the other, there are strong reasons for placing it in a very early period of the church's life. So where did it come from, and what was its purpose?

We must recognize that we do not have enough information to give a

---

(Acts 15:13–21). Is it therefore likely that he would have written that the 'law of the kingdom' could be kept by loving one's neighbour (2:8)? There is here a significant difference between what we know of James from Acts and Galatians (and what we learn from Josephus and other historians) and what we read in the book that bears the same name. In the view of many, this difference is so crucial that it alone must cast doubt on the alleged connection between the two.

The date

Though this book might well have no connection with James of Jerusalem, a number of facts suggest very strongly that it belongs to an early period of the church's life rather than a later one.

● In its opening sentence, it addresses itself to 'the twelve tribes in the Dispersion' (1:1). Taken literally, of course, that could mean the whole of the Jewish people scattered throughout the world. But it is probably to be understood in the same way as the similar address in 1 Peter 1:1 or Paul's designation of his Galatian readers as 'the Israel of God' (Galatians 6:16). From an early time, Christians understood themselves as being part of the people of God whose story is encapsulated in the Old Testament, and for that reason they found it was natural to apply to themselves language that had previously been used of Israel. Of course, the only period in the church's history when anyone could write to the whole of God's people in this way (as contrasted with 1 Peter, which was addressed only to certain areas) was at the very beginning of its history, when the church was still visibly

Jewish and centred on Jerusalem. This implies a time after the death of Stephen, but before Paul's travels had begun.

● This is further supported by the fact that there is no sign anywhere in James of a break between Judaism and Christianity. The well-to-do oppressors of the poor (2:6–7) were almost certainly Jewish people, but they are not condemned because of that, as they might have been at a later period. They are condemned for their selfishness, not their religion or ethnicity. Moreover, the gathering so vividly described in James 2:1–4 is said to be in 'the synagogue' (2:2). This situation is very similar to that described in Acts 4–5, when Jewish aristocrats were oppressing a lower-class proletarian Christian movement.

● The background to much of the imagery of James is clearly Palestinian. The mention of 'autumn and spring rains' (5:7) would have meant nothing at all in other parts of the Roman empire, while the agricultural practices mentioned in the preceding verses are of a type that disappeared for good in Palestine after AD70, but which were widespread in the days of Jesus.

● There is no evidence anywhere in James of the later practices and problems of the church. Not only is the Jewish/Gentile controversy unknown, but there is no mention of heresy, and no reference to the organization of the church or to doctrinal arguments of any sort. In addition, the moral teaching of James makes no mention of later ethical concerns over the adoption of unacceptable Hellenistic standards in the church. Instead, it is almost exclusively directed to the kind of problems that would occur in a Jewish environment.

full answer to that question. But the kind of teaching found in James is so similar to that of Jesus himself, and uses so much of the same rural imagery, that it is not unreasonable to suppose it has a similar background. It is not inconceivable that it had its origins among those followers of Jesus who remained in Galilee after the main centre of the church moved to Jerusalem. It is impossible to prove this, of course, for we know next to

---

'Faith' and 'works' in Paul and James

When Martin Luther called James 'an epistle of straw', his main reason for doing so was that he believed James' theology was fundamentally different from Paul's – and, since Paul was his hero, he was forced to relegate James to a secondary position. A comparison of James 2:24 with Romans 3:28 will readily demonstrate what led him to this conclusion:

● James 2:24: 'You see that a person is justified by works and not by faith alone.'
● Romans 3:28: 'For we hold that a person is justified by faith apart from works of the law.'

These two statements have every appearance of being mutually contradictory. Not only do they seem to be saying opposite things to each other: they also use exactly the same Greek words to do so! But when we examine them more carefully, and especially when we place them in their proper contexts, this alleged contradiction becomes much less obvious.

● Though they both speak of 'faith', James and Paul seem to mean rather different things by this word. For Paul, it has almost a technical sense, referring specifically to that belief in and commitment to Jesus that characterize the Christian life. In James, however, 'faith' has a much broader meaning, almost being something like 'faith' as belief in God, as opposed to atheism. For James, the term 'faith' is more akin to the intellectual acceptance of theological propositions, whereas Paul's concern was more focused on faith as personal commitment.

● A similar distinction may be drawn in the way they each use the term 'works'.

When James mentions 'works', he refers to the kind of behaviour that naturally stems from commitment to Christ (1:25; 2:8). But the 'works' that Paul writes about are attitudes of self-sufficiency, the kind of acts that religious people might do in order to commend themselves to God, or to gain God's approval. James refers to the things a person will do because he or she already has a living relationship with God through Christ.

● Paul and James were addressing themselves to different practical problems, and this inevitably affected the way they expressed themselves. In Galatians and Romans, Paul appears to have been contending against the self-righteousness of people who thought that by external religious observance they could commend themselves to God. So he condemns such things – and in doing so, he echoes the teaching of Jesus (Luke 18:9–14). James, on the other hand, was fighting against the temptation to suppose that right belief of an abstract, propositional kind is all that matters – and he accordingly emphasizes that doctrines with no practical effect are worthless. Again, he also echoes the teaching of Jesus (Matthew 7:21–23).

● This entire debate depends on the mistaken understanding of Judaism as a religion of legalism, propounded by Luther and repeated by most generations of Protestant scholars until relatively recent times. But once Judaism is seen in its own terms as a faith combining both personal commitment and loving actions, the alleged dichotomy between Paul and James can be seen for what it is: the imposition of an alien modern, Western agenda on an ancient text.

nothing about such Galilean believers. But the message of James would certainly be especially appropriate to those who were worshipping in the Jewish synagogues of rural Palestine, and at the same time were trying to put into practice what Jesus had taught them. Such people might easily have been tempted to substitute religious formality for the spiritual realities of which Jesus had spoken – and, as a relative minority, they would also be open to the kind of persecution that James mentions.

If the book originated in such a context, this might also explain why its value was unrecognized in the wider church for so long. Its eventual association with an important person like James of Jerusalem would then have been a means of justifying its inclusion in the canon of the New Testament. It could also reflect the possibility that the church in Jerusalem was included in 'God's people in the Dispersion', to whom James was originally dispatched at an early stage in the history of the church.

Christians and Jewish ritual

For generations, the temple in Jerusalem had occupied a special place in the life and thinking of Jewish people. In the stories of the nation, the construction of the first temple was associated with the reign of King Solomon, who was highly esteemed as the one king (along with his father David) who had really put ancient Israel on the political map of the day (1 Kings 8:20–21). Though this empire collapsed almost overnight on Solomon's death, the temple stood as a monument to his achievements, and was to be the lasting symbol of the royal dynasty of David. It could on occasion be invested with an almost mystical significance, and even in the dark days just before its destruction by Nebuchadnezzar, king of Babylon, the people of Jerusalem managed to convince themselves that, against all the odds, the physical presence of the temple in their city would somehow save them from invasion. They were wrong, of course, as the prophet Jeremiah was quick to remind them, pointing out that they were pinning their hope on a purely outward form of religious activity instead of taking seriously the moral and spiritual demands placed upon them by their relationship with God (Jeremiah 21:1 – 23:32).

Almost 150 years after Nebuchadnezzar had plundered Solomon's temple, it was eventually patched up and brought back into regular use under the influence of Ezra and Nehemiah, whose period is documented in the Old Testament books named after them. But by the New Testament period it was in the process of being replaced with a structure even more splendid than the original had been. In 20BC, Herod the Great decided to build a new temple that would be as grand as any monument in the Roman world. But he did not live to see it finished. The work was so ambitious and costly that it went on for something like eighty years. By the time this new temple was completed, the Jews were in revolt against the Romans, and soon afterwards it was destroyed by the Roman general Titus in AD70, and was never rebuilt.

This was the temple that Jesus and the first Christians knew, and it was a centre of devotion for Jewish believers from all over the Roman empire. By New Testament times synagogues had been established in every town or city where there was a Jewish population of any size. But worship in the synagogue was not the same as worship in the temple. The synagogue had originated as a social convenience for Jews living in lands far removed from Palestine. But it was at the temple in Jerusalem that Israel's religious past could be seen in true focus. The worship of the synagogue could incorporate some of the ancient rituals such as circumcision and the old food laws, but most of the rites prescribed in the Old Testament could only be carried out in their entirety in the temple at Jerusalem. Here, the priests still offered sacrifices as their predecessors had done for generations past, and all the great religious festivals had special significance when celebrated at the temple. Pilgrims travelled from all over the empire to worship in its holy places, and it was an ambition for every pious Jew to visit the temple at least once in a lifetime. The crowds who gathered to hear Peter on the Day of Pentecost were not unusually large, and at the times of special festivals the population of Jerusalem regularly increased tenfold, or even more.

How did all this relate to Christian faith? For Gentile believers, with no previous connection with the Jewish faith, this question seemed trivial: the Jerusalem temple had never featured in their spirituality before, so why should it do so now? But for those with a Jewish heritage,

this was a matter of more fundamental importance. Moreover, it highlighted a real problem for the early Gentile mission. For the early church everywhere seems to have adopted Jewish moral standards, as laid out in the Torah. But in reality, the Torah was far more than a collection of ethical teachings. It also contained detailed regulations for the proper conduct of worship. So how should Christians relate to the ritual practices of the Jewish religion? And why adopt the morality of the Torah as normative, and not take seriously those passages that were more specifically related to formal worship?

Putting the question that way merely serves to highlight its complexity, for ultimately the role of the temple in Jerusalem could not be dealt with independently from matters like circumcision that proved to be such a problem in the churches associated with Paul. In the event, as the church became more and more Gentile, that question was ultimately solved in favour of those who, like Paul, believed that the Old Testament Law was not directly relevant to the Christian life. But in the first century there were many Jewish Christians who not only continued with practices like circumcision but also felt a special affection for the priesthood and ritual of the Old Testament. The first followers of Jesus in Jerusalem had participated freely in the services at the temple: it never occurred to them not to do so, and in any case that was where they would find others willing to listen to their new message about Jesus as Messiah (Acts 2:46; 3:1). But as time passed, things soon changed. Many

The temple in Jerusalem occupied a site with a long-established tradition of sacrifice. Temple worship came to an end in AD70 when the Romans sacked the city. The Dome of the Rock mosque was built in AD691–92 on the same site.

Hellenist Christians shared the opinion of Stephen, that the day of the temple and its rituals was finished altogether. The death of Jesus was often interpreted using the language of sacrifice familiar from the Hebrew Bible, which made it easy to conclude that Jesus' death on the cross had in some way superseded the repeated sacrifices of the Jerusalem temple. At the same time, the church in Jerusalem seems to have continued to worship in the temple, and was allowed to do so because of its relatively conservative stance on the issue of Gentile Christians. There were many others who wished to join them. After all, the first generation of Hellenist Christians had all been born Jews, and there was never any suggestion that they should deny their Jewishness in order to follow Jesus. In addition, their non-Christian compatriots were naturally eager to know where they stood. Did they support and approve of the Jewish way of doing things – or did they, like Stephen, believe that even the temple was now redundant?

Hebrews: author, readers and date

The author

According to Eusebius, the third-century church leader Origen wrote of this book, 'only God knows the truth as to who actually wrote this epistle' (*Ecclesiastical History* VI.25.14). Some translations and ancient versions of the Bible give it the title, 'The epistle of Paul to the Hebrews'. But these words are not original, and it is highly unlikely that this book has anything to do with Paul.

● For one thing, it is not really an epistle at all. When Paul wrote letters he always followed the normal practice of Greek letter-writers (see chapter 16). He also leaves us in no doubt as to who his readers were and what has caused him to write to them. But Hebrews is not addressed directly to anyone, and the only possible reason for supposing it to be a letter of some sort is the inclusion of what appears to be a personal greeting after the benediction with which the book closes (13:22–25). Some have suggested that this section was added later, to make Hebrews look more like one of Paul's letters. It has even been suggested that Paul himself added the news of Timothy

given in 13:23 to a book that Timothy had originally written. But there is nothing to support either of these conjectures.

● The language and style of Hebrews is in any case totally different from that of Paul's writings. Hebrews has just about the best Greek style of any New Testament book, and reaches a far higher literary standard than Paul could ever aspire to. Origen noticed this: 'The character of the diction of the epistle entitled "To the Hebrews" has not the apostle's rudeness in speech... that is, in style. But that the epistle is better Greek in the framing of its diction, will be admitted by everyone who is able to discern differences of style' (quoted by Eusebius, *Ecclesiastical History* VI.25.11–12).

● The concerns of Hebrews are also quite different from Paul's interests. If, as many believe, it was written primarily for the benefit of Jewish Christians, then Paul is unlikely to have written it in any case as his ministry was almost entirely among Gentiles. But even if it was written for Gentiles, its interest in the Torah is quite different from Paul's. Though Paul's attitude to the Law raises many questions, there is no doubt that his approach to it was primarily concerned with its *moral* demands. The ritual of tabernacle, priests and sacrifices which is so important in

Hebrews

This is the kind of question that inspired the New Testament book of Hebrews. The sort of encouragement and advice its author gives seems to imply that its readers were being persecuted – perhaps because of their resistance to accepting Jewish practices. This might explain why the question of Jewish worship had become so important to them: if they were prepared to conform to the traditional practices, life could be a lot easier. The stories of Acts show how religious fanatics could make life really difficult for Christian believers (Acts 13:50; 14:5, 19), and some scholars believe a similar situation is envisaged here. On the other hand, Christians throughout the Roman empire must always have been tempted to try to link themselves to Judaism, especially in times of persecution – for Judaism was a permitted religion under Roman law, whereas at this stage Christianity was not.

The writer of Hebrews argued that it was both pointless and

Hebrews simply never features anywhere in the writings of Paul.

We can therefore be quite sure that Paul did not write Hebrews. But it is not easy to decide who did. There is so little specific reference to people and events that the most diverse characters have been suggested, all with more or less equal plausibility: Barnabas, Apollos, Timothy, Aquila and Priscilla, and Luke have all been put forward as possible candidates. In reality, we are no nearer to a solution than Origen was. But it is possible to deduce some key facts about the unknown author from a close reading of the text of the book.

● The author of Hebrews did not belong to the same group as the apostles. Explaining how the Christian message had reached him, the writer comments: 'The Lord himself first announced this salvation, and those who heard him proved to us that it is true' (2:3). Some scholars have drawn inferences from this about the possible date of the book. But this statement does not necessarily imply that the writer belonged to a different generation from the apostles – only that he was not among their number. A person like Stephen would fit this description just as easily as someone from a later period.

● The author was clearly well educated. He knew how to write Greek, and was also well versed in the literary and rhetorical conventions of the Hellenistic age. Hebrews also reveals a person with some acquaintance with ideas that were common among Greek thinkers. The way the heavenly world, where Christ dwells, is contrasted with the material world in which traditional ritual worship operates, is not all that different from Plato's notion about the world of forms, or ideas, that gives meaning to the world we know through our senses.

● At the same time, the author's real background seems to be in Judaism. It has been argued that his knowledge of Plato's system came not through direct acquaintance with Greek thinking, but through knowledge of the work of a Hellenistic Jewish philosopher like Philo, who flourished in the early years of the Christian era at Alexandria in Egypt. But he also seems to have been familiar with the way Jewish teachers in Palestine interpreted the Old Testament, and some of his most distinctive imagery was very popular in various groups on the fringes of Judaism. The people from Qumran, who wrote the Dead Sea Scrolls, were expecting a Messiah who, like Jesus in Hebrews, would also be a high priest. They too had

unnecessary for Christians to keep the ritual requirements of the Old Testament Law. For this author, the message of Jesus was God's final word (1:1–3). Previous prophets in ancient Israel had spoken in God's name to the people of their own time, but they were now all summed-up and replaced by Jesus. Jesus is compared not only to the angels whom Jewish tradition identified with the giving of the Torah (1:4 – 2:18), but also to Aaron, the archetype of every Jewish priest, and other Jewish heroes like Moses and Joshua (3:1 – 4:13). But none of them was able to match Jesus. They were mere mortals, but Jesus was 'Son of God' and therefore greater than them all. Yet because of his human experience, he understood how people felt when faced with the power of evil (2:17–18; 4:14–15). He was the fulfilment of all Judaism's aspirations, 'a great high priest' who both summed up and superseded all that had gone before (4:14 – 5:10).

Continuing to write of Jesus under the imagery of the Jewish

Hebrews: author, readers and date *continued*

considerable interest in the Old Testament figure of Melchizedek and, like the writer of Hebrews, had a particular fascination with the rituals of the Day of Atonement. This has led some scholars to suggest that Hebrews was written to Christians who had come under the influence of the community at Qumran. But some of these ideas are also to be found in other Jewish documents such as the *Testaments of the Twelve Patriarchs*, while purification ceremonies like those mentioned in Hebrews 6:2 were observed by many groups in the Jewish community.

The readers

Since it is impossible to make a clear identification of the author of Hebrews, it is unrealistic to imagine that we can be certain who its first readers might have been. But there are a number of indications in the book itself that can give some impression of the kind of people they probably were.

● In recent times, it has generally been supposed that they would be Jewish Christians. This seems to be implied in the title, 'To the Hebrews'. But the ancient author did not give the book this title: like all the titles appended to the New Testament books, it was added for convenience in later centuries. It could

therefore be misleading, and some prefer to think of Gentile Christians as its recipients. Against that, it is not easy to see why non-Jewish Christians should have had such a detailed interest in the sacrificial system of ancient Israel, whereas for Jewish Christians the Old Testament and its rituals had been given by God, so it is obvious that they would have some significant questions. What was its status now? Had God's mind somehow changed with the coming of Jesus? These questions would certainly have more point for Jewish Christians than for Gentiles. They would be of greatest interest for people living in Jerusalem itself, where the temple was a feature of everyday life, and some have suggested that this must be where Hebrews originated. But a number of facts speak against this.

The church at Jerusalem was always a poor church, whereas the readers of Hebrews seem to have been reasonably well off (6:10; 10:34).

Surprisingly, in view of its subject matter, the temple itself is not actually mentioned in Hebrews. Instead, the author describes in great detail the worship associated with the tent of worship (tabernacle) used by Moses and the Israelites in their desert journey from Egypt to Canaan. This might suggest that the

priesthood, Hebrews goes on to suggest that a more suitable Old Testament image to illustrate what Jesus had done may be found in the figure of Melchizedek (5:11 – 7:28). In the original stories of the Hebrew Bible, this Melchizedek is a shadowy figure of whom we know next to nothing. In one of the psalms, the king in Jerusalem is called 'a priest for ever in the line of succession to Melchizedek' (Psalm 110:4), and later generations of Christians have applied this description to Jesus. He also appears briefly in a story about Abraham (Genesis 14:17–20), where again very little is said about him. But the writer of Hebrews uses the obscurity of these Old Testament references to argue that since 'there is no record of Melchizedek's father or mother or of any of his ancestors; no record of his birth or of his death', he must be 'like the Son of God', who is similarly timeless (7:3). He also draws attention to the fact that Abraham had recognized the greatness of this priestly figure (treating him with reverence, and giving him gifts) long before Aaron was even

---

readers did not have first-hand experience of the temple, and their only direct access to rituals like sacrifice and priesthood was through what they could read for themselves in the books of Leviticus and Numbers. This would obviously suit the situation of Hellenist Jewish Christians living elsewhere in the Roman empire.

● The readers of Hebrews also seem to have been suffering some kind of persecution. Not long after they became Christians, they had 'suffered many things, yet were not defeated by the struggle… at times publicly insulted and ill-treated, and at other times… ready to join those who were being treated in this way. You shared the sufferings of prisoners, and when all your belongings were seized, you endured your loss gladly' (10:32–34). But the author then goes on to encourage them not to evade further persecution. At the time of writing, unlike some of the early Jerusalem Christians, they had 'not yet had to resist to the point of being killed' (12:4), but that seemed as if it might be a distinct possibility.

● The book of Hebrews gives the impression that it is not addressed to an entire church, but to a group within a church. In 5:12–14 the readers are criticized because they have not yet realized their God-given potential to be

teachers – a function that not every Christian would expect to have. Then 10:25 could be taken to suggest that they were reluctant to meet with other Christians – while 13:24 asks them to convey 'greetings to all your leaders and to all God's people'. It has been suggested that Hebrews might have been addressed to some sectarian group mentioned elsewhere in the New Testament – perhaps the Colossian heretics, who were opposed in the letter to the church at Colossae. These people were certainly interested in the role of angels, and in some aspects of Jewish ritual practices. But their underlying world-view shows that they were not understanding them from the perspective of normative Judaism. For them, the Old Testament rules were a useful way to achieve quite different objectives, and that would seem to distinguish them from the concerns of Hebrews.

● The recipients of Hebrews lived in Italy, perhaps in Rome. This is made clear in 13:24: 'The believers from Italy send you their greetings'. The author was in the company of a group of Italian Christians who wished to be remembered by their friends at home. If this was in fact in Rome, then certainly the circumstances of the church there do have some interesting

born. If the great ancestor of the Jewish nation had himself paid homage to Melchizedek, then that in itself was enough to demonstrate the superiority of his position over the later priestly line descended from Aaron; more than that, for as one of a generation yet to come, Aaron was at least potentially present in Abraham's body when he met Melchizedek, and therefore in a sense he too had shared in Abraham's reverence for this person. If more proof of Jesus' supremacy was needed, then the writer of Hebrews reminded his readers of the further fact that the Old Testament priests died and were succeeded by others, while Jesus, like Melchizedek apparently, lived for ever.

Most of today's readers will struggle to comprehend exactly what Hebrews is claiming. The actual form of the author's argument depends on a way of reasoning that is simply alien to most of us. The idea that all future generations are somehow contained within the reproductive organs of their original parents might easily be dismissed as nonsensical.

Hebrews: author, readers and date *continued*

similarities to the situation envisaged in Hebrews. The last chapter of Romans shows that in the late fifties the Roman church was not one unified congregation, but a collection of separate, though not unrelated 'house churches' (Romans 16:3–15). Other evidence from the Jewish community in Rome suggests that as the Christian gospel was proclaimed in different synagogues, they made different responses to it and formed Christian congregations distinguished by their various viewpoints on questions connected with traditional Jewish observances. We also know that the Jews of Rome had a close interest in the kind of ideas that Hebrews shares with some fringe sects within Judaism.

The date

So when was Hebrews written? Various dates have been suggested, ranging from the early sixties to the end of the first century. On no account can it have been written later than about AD90, for it is referred to in *1 Clement* which was written in Rome no later than AD96. A number of arguments are involved in fixing a more precise date:

● Some have pointed to the statement in 2:3 that, 'The Lord himself first announced this salvation, and those who heard him proved to us that it is true.' They argue that this shows the author was a second- or third-generation Christian, in which case an appropriate date might be between AD80 and 90. But we have already seen that this is not a necessary inference from that verse.

● It has also been pointed out that the book seems to emphasize the human character of Jesus. It is natural to suppose that this might have been a subject of controversy at the time, which in turn would most obviously take us to the arguments about Jesus' humanity and divinity ('Docetism') that emerged towards the end of the first century. But when we examine such references closely, many of them are seen to be based on the outline of Jesus' life contained in the gospels, and they are used in Hebrews to provoke a specific recollection of Jesus' behaviour and actions as an example and encouragement (2:14; 4:15; 5:7–9; 13:12). If we compare this with the way 1 John opposes heresy (see chapter 24 below), there are undoubtedly significant differences.

● In fact there are few signs of the interests of the institutional church in Hebrews. The tension between present experience (1:2; 6:5) and future hope (9:28; 10:34–38) that was so characteristic

But this is the kind of logic that would make perfect sense in the context of the prevailing physiology of the first-century world. The more important thing to notice is the conclusion reached by the author on the basis of this discussion, which is remarkably simple considering the convoluted route taken to arrive at it: 'we have such a High Priest, who sits at the right side of the throne of the Divine Majesty in heaven. This one serves as High Priest in the Most Holy Place, that is, in the real tent which was put up by the Lord, not by humans' (8:1–2). Everything that had been achieved through the rituals of Old Testament worship – first in the 'tent' (or tabernacle), then in the temple – was only a temporary alleviation of the human condition, and those things to which the temple had looked forward had now been achieved permanently by Jesus. The sacrifices offered by the priesthood had to be repeated, because they could only account for past wrongdoing. But the sacrifice of Jesus (himself, on the cross) had more far-reaching consequences. Not

---

of the age of the apostles is still found – and there is no more church hierarchy in view than might be suggested by the vague title 'leaders' (13:24).

● The writer of Hebrews seems to suppose that the kind of worship described in the Old Testament was still in existence. 'The same sacrifices are offered for ever, year after year... the sacrifices serve year after year to remind people of their sins...' (10:1–3). These, and other similar statements, suggest that the temple in Jerusalem was still standing, and if that is the case then the book can be dated before AD70. It may be objected that Hebrews refers not to the temple, but to the tent of worship in the desert. But the Old Testament regulations were the same in each case, and might indeed have been of the same origin if the findings of much Old Testament scholarship are to be believed. In the present form of the Old Testament, there are no temple regulations as such. Solomon's temple is just assumed to have taken over the pattern of tabernacle worship laid down in the Torah. If the temple had ceased to function when Hebrews was written, it is impossible to believe that the author would not have mentioned the fact, for the literal destruction of the Old Testament ritual in AD70 would have been the final

confirmation of the whole argument of his book.

● If Hebrews was directed to readers in Rome, then the statement that they had not yet given their lives for the gospel would seem to point to a time before Nero's persecution reached its climax in AD64. The earlier persecution that they had suffered could then have been connected with the disturbances that led Claudius to expel the Jewish people from Rome for a time in AD48.

We may tentatively conclude that Hebrews was written by an unknown author in the period leading up to Nero's persecution. Its first readers were a group of Hellenist Jewish Christians in Rome who were trying to escape the political consequences of being known as Christians by observing the rituals of traditional Judaism. They wanted the protection that the empire gave to Jews, but they also wished to enjoy the privileges of being Christians. The author of Hebrews deplored this attitude: in his opinion, not only were they betraying their fellow-Christians, but their acquiescence in Jewish rituals was also in effect a denial of their faith in Christ. If they truly wished to serve him, they must be prepared to stand up and be counted as his followers, whatever the cost might be.

only was it the basis on which humanity could be accepted and put right by God, but the divine power released by it could also set them free from 'useless rituals, so that we may serve the living God' (9:14).

Now, 'God does away with all the old sacrifices and puts the sacrifice of Christ in their place' (10:9). Because of that, those who are tempted to turn back and perpetuate the old rituals of Judaism are actually denying the effectiveness of what God has done in Jesus. They are 'despising the

---

Hebrews and the Old Testament

The most distinctive feature of the book of Hebrews is the way that it uses the Old Testament to back up its arguments. Taking up Old Testament figures like Aaron or Melchizedek, and rituals like the Day of Atonement, the author suggests that these things were a kind of symbolic preview of the work of Jesus. Just as Aaron was a high priest, so was Jesus – though with significantly greater effect. His position was more directly comparable to that of Melchizedek, and the sacrifice that Jesus offered had more lasting benefits than the traditional ritual of the Day of Atonement.

If we ever think about the Old Testament at all today, this is not the way we generally approach it. We may ask questions about its morality or its picture of God, but we would not expect to find detailed descriptions of the person of Jesus (who was born at least two centuries after its latest events) hidden within its pages. Yet the underlying question that puzzled the author of Hebrews is still a relevant one: namely, in what sense is the Old Testament a 'Christian' book? Obviously, it was not written by Christians, but the author of Hebrews shared the conviction of the early church (and of later Christians) that the God of whom the ancient scriptures speak is the same God as Jesus revealed. Since God is unchangeable, it is therefore legitimate to look for some sort of unity between the Old Testament and the New Testament.

The author of Hebrews found this unity by supposing that, since the same God is involved in both parts of the Christian Bible, God's activities in the earlier stages of its story can be taken as a pattern or visual aid for what God does in the later stages. It is in this light that we can understand the way the writer of Hebrews uses the Old Testament. He is not suggesting that the people of Old Testament times understood their history and priestly rituals as a psychic glimpse into the unknown future. To them, these things were the facts of everyday life and faith. But, Hebrews argues, when Christians looked back with the benefit of hindsight, they could see how the life, death and resurrection of Jesus might appropriately be described as the 'fulfilment' of all that had gone before. Peter, for example, described Jesus as 'the servant of God' (Acts 3:13, 26; 4:25–30), no doubt referring to those passages in the book of Isaiah that have come to be known as 'the Servant Songs' (Isaiah 42:1–4; 49:1–6; 50:4–9; 52:13 – 53:12). For Isaiah and his contemporaries, the Servant was a real person or persons – the whole nation of Israel, or perhaps the prophet himself. But as Peter looked back, he found that these passages provided the imagery with which he could most authentically sum up Jesus' ministry. Hebrews is doing the same thing with other Old Testament people (Moses, Joshua, Aaron, Melchizedek), events (the Day of Atonement) and artifacts (the tent of worship in the desert).

This way of interpreting the Hebrew Bible was not unknown in Judaism. Philo of Alexandria had elevated it to an art, arguing that the apparently 'historical' events of the Old Testament could be understood as symbols of the insights of

Son of God', and insulting the Holy Spirit (10:29). They have effectively joined with those who reject Jesus, and God has no time for such people. To turn back to the old ways is to be lost, but those who trust in God and accept what Jesus has accomplished will find true and lasting salvation (10:39).

All this is strong stuff, capable of being interpreted as a sternly anti-Semitic polemic. But our author insists that it was nothing new, but the

---

Greek philosophy, at least as he understood them from his own Jewish background. Many of the church fathers later read not only the Old Testament but also the New Testament in this way, ignoring the reality of its stories and regarding them instead as complex allegories of theological truths. The fourth-century writer Hilary of Poitiers described the reasoning behind this: 'Every work contained in the sacred volume announces by word, explains by facts, and corroborates by examples the coming of our Lord Jesus Christ... From the beginning of the world, Christ, by authentic and absolute prefigurations in the person of the Patriarchs, gives birth to the church, washes it clean, sanctifies it, chooses it, places it apart and redeems it: by the sleep of Adam, by the deluge in the days of Noah, by the blessing of Melchizedek, by Abraham's justification, by the birth of Isaac, by the captivity of Jacob... The purpose of this work, is to show that in each personage, in every age, and in every act, the image of his coming, of his teaching, of his resurrection, and of our church is reflected as in a mirror.'

For people with that mindset, it mattered very little whether any of these people or events had ever truly existed. The important thing was the underlying truth that they were held to symbolize. Hebrews, however, pays some attention to historical reality, and does not treat the Old Testament as a story with no meaning apart from what later generations might choose to read into it. On the contrary, it regards all that it reports as being the actions of God in real history, and when Hebrews compares Old and New Testaments, its view of God is central, emphasizing that God is the one who gives continuity and coherence to the grand sweep of history, for what God has revealed through Jesus is the next and final stage of the revelation in the Old Testament.

This method of interpretation has often been labelled 'typology'. But to be useful this term needs to be applied quite precisely, to indicate a way of interpreting past events that treats them with integrity in their own context, while seeing within them a pattern running through history that reveals some greater underlying cause or purpose. Used in this way, 'typology' can be set over against the kind of 'allegory' found in the work of Philo and the Church Fathers, as well as books like John Bunyan's *Pilgrim's Progress*, in which their own message is the most important thing, and history is at best a subsidiary aid in the presentation of their own insights. The message of Hebrews draws attention to correspondences between Old and New Testaments, claiming to show how God's work in one period of time was fulfilled by God's work in Jesus.

This method of expounding the Christian message is not found in any comprehensive form anywhere else in the New Testament. Its main appeal would obviously be to Christians with Jewish connections. It is far removed from the questions that modern Christians ask about the Old Testament, but its essential message is not irrelevant, for it is a reminder of the faithfulness and consistency of God's dealings with people at all times and in all places (13:8).

Hilary of Poitiers (AD315–368).

natural outworking of the Jewish faith. Far from being redundant, Judaism was an essential prerequisite for the full articulation of Christian faith – and so Hebrews goes on to list a 'large crowd of witnesses' taken from the Old Testament and Jewish history, whose experience of God is part of the ongoing narrative that culminated with the coming of Jesus (11:1–38). These people will receive the same reward as faithful Christians (11:39–40), and their story should be a lasting encouragement to Christians to get their priorities right and to keep their eyes firmly fixed on Jesus alone as their example and inspiration (12:1–11). To do this, they must live at peace with others and show love for other Christians, as well as members of their own families (12:14; 13:1–21). By doing so, they will please God, who in turn will 'provide you with every good thing you need in order to do God's will' (13:21).

Christians and the covenant with Israel

The debates in the early church about Jewish morality and ritual were symptomatic of more fundamental underlying issues in the self-understanding of the earliest Christian communities. In Old Testament times, to be a member of the people of God had not been simply a matter of behaving in the same way as other like-minded people. It also involved inclusion in the covenant relationship that God had established with Israel's ancestor Abraham (Genesis 12:1–3; 15:1–21; 17:1–14; 22:16–18) and with Moses at Mount Sinai (Exodus 19:5–8; 20:1 – 24:18). The relationship had started with God's concern and care for this people. Abraham was called from Mesopotamia and found a new homeland not because of any moral or spiritual superiority that he might have possessed, but simply because God's affection was centred on him. His descendants later emerged from the shattering experience of the exodus not because of their own moral perfection but simply through the care of a loving God.

On the basis of these undeserved acts of kindness, God had made certain demands of the people. Abraham and his family were promised a great and prosperous future (Genesis 15:1–6). In response to God's goodness, Abraham had accepted that both he and his descendants should give tangible and lasting expression to this new covenant relationship that existed between them and God: 'You and your descendants must all agree to circumcise every male among you... Any male who has not been circumcised will no longer be considered one of my people, because he has not kept the covenant with me' (Genesis 17:9–14).

The same elements recur in the covenant relationship established between God and Israel through Moses at Mount Sinai. God had rescued the people from slavery in Egypt, and they were to respond with obedience to God's laws, which included moral precepts such as are found in the ten commandments (Exodus 19:4–8; 20:1–17), as well as the ritual regulations that are contained in the books of Leviticus and Numbers.

When Christians claimed that Jesus had come to fulfil what God had promised in the Old Testament, these were the promises the Jewish people would inevitably recall. Moreover, the Christians themselves believed that what they were experiencing through the presence of Jesus and the power of the Holy Spirit made them the heirs of Abraham himself. This is why questions about keeping the Law and carrying out rituals like circumcision became such important issues in the life of the church; for, on a plain reading of the Old Testament, this was the only way that any person (whether born as a Jew or a Gentile) could ever be a full member of God's covenant people. To begin with, this was not an issue, for all the first Christians were Jewish believers, and naturally followed the expectations of their faith community in such matters. But when Paul and others accepted into the church Gentiles who had not been circumcised and who saw no reason at all for keeping the Old Testament Law, what might previously have been an interesting theological discussion between Jews who were Christians and those who were not, suddenly became the focus of a burning practical issue. Traditional Jewish thinking suggested that people who would not obey the Torah could not expect God to work in their lives. But the activity of the Holy Spirit among these Gentile believers seemed to be no less remarkable than what was going on in the lives of those Christians who were also faithful Jews (Acts 10:44–48).

Paul was one of the first Christian preachers to be faced with this problem. On a pragmatic level, he was quite sure that circumcision and keeping the Law should not be required of Gentile Christians. At the same time, however, the Old Testament had made it perfectly clear that to share in the blessings promised by God a person must become a member of Abraham's family. Paul did not wish to deny that the

Mount Sinai, the traditional place where Moses received the ten commandments, and other laws for the Israelites.

scriptures were the word of God, and his opponents were not slow to remind him that being a member of Abraham's family meant circumcision and obedience to the Law.

When Paul tackled this problem in his letter to the Galatians, he argued that the blessings promised by God to Abraham did not come to fruition because he kept the Law (Galatians 3:17). That did not even exist in his day. Instead, Paul argued, the relationship that Abraham enjoyed with God was a matter of faith: 'Abraham believed and was blessed; so all who believe are blessed as he was' (Galatians 3:9). Circumcision was an external sign to indicate that a person was trying to keep the Old Testament Law. But if the Law was now redundant, then circumcision had

---

Who wrote 1 Peter?

1 Peter was well known and widely read in the church from quite early times. *1 Clement* refers to it (AD96), as also does Polycarp (AD70–155), while Irenaeus stated towards the end of the second century that it was written by the apostle Peter himself. There are good reasons for accepting this view of its authorship:

● Much of its teaching is exactly what might be expected from a disciple of Jesus. Many aspects echo the teaching of Jesus himself, sometimes following it quite closely.

The author contrasts the readers' knowledge of Jesus, which was second-hand, with his own first-hand knowledge, and he seems to have witnessed both the trials (2:21–24) and the crucifixion of Jesus (5:1). Some scholars also believe that certain passages contain allusions to gospel stories in which Peter was particularly involved. Others, however, have claimed that if this letter was the work of Peter, then we would expect to read much more about Jesus. But this argument depends on the mistaken assumption that authors will write everything they know in everything they write. We should also remember that Peter's reminiscences of the life and teaching of Jesus might well have been recorded in a comprehensive way already, in Mark's Gospel.

● There are also a number of connections between 1 Peter and the speeches of Peter in the book of Acts. Jesus' cross is called 'the tree' in Peter's speech to the Jewish rulers (Acts 5:30) and in his sermon to Cornelius (10:39), and the same unusual terminology occurs here in 1 Peter 2:24. In 1 Peter 2:22–24 Jesus is referred to in the language of the 'Servant Songs' of the book of Isaiah, and according to Acts, Peter consistently called Jesus 'the servant of God' in his earliest preaching (Acts 3:13, 26; 4:25–30). Jesus is also linked with the stone mentioned in Psalm 118:22 by Peter in his defence before the religious authorities, and again in 1 Peter 2:4, while the emphasis on the fulfilment of Old Testament promises in Acts 3:18–24 is very similar to 1 Peter 1:10–12.

● There is no sign in 1 Peter of the concerns and interests of the later institutional church. There is still a tension between the present experience of God working in the lives of Christian believers (1:8–9, 23) and what God will accomplish in the future with the return of Jesus himself (1:3–5, 7, 13; 4:13; 5:4). Nor is there any evidence of a developed hierarchy in church organization, with the consistent emphasis on all Christians being 'priests', and the leaders of the church simply referred to as 'elders' or 'shepherds' (5:1–4).

There are, therefore, several good reasons for accepting the ancient view that Peter was the author of this letter. There are, however, some other facts which might point in a different direction:

also lost its value (Galatians 5:2–12). What should matter to the Christian is 'faith that works through love' (Galatians 5:6). We have already dealt with Paul's argument, but the question is important in this context because the same issues also surface in Peter's first letter.

1 Peter

Though many of the same themes are found here, they appear in a distinctive form. Abraham is mentioned only in passing, and in a different context altogether (3:6), while there is no sign of the complex theological arguments that Paul puts forward in Galatians and Romans. The conclusion, however, is the same, for 1 Peter conveys the clear conviction

---

● Like Hebrews, 1 Peter is written in an exceptionally fine Greek literary style. Not surprisingly, it might reasonably be asked whether a Galilean fisherman would be capable of writing like this, especially one who is specifically described as 'uneducated and common' (Acts 4:13). We have already seen that the Galilean origins

of Peter, far from disqualifying him from knowing Greek, would actually point in the opposite direction, while the statement about Peter's educational achievements in Acts can hardly be taken literally. It certainly does not indicate that Peter was illiterate. Quite the reverse, for the comment is made by religious leaders who

Similarities between the teaching of Jesus and Peter

Christians should have an alert and watchful attitude	Luke 12:35 1 Peter 1:13
Christians have the privilege of calling God 'Father'	Luke 11:2 1 Peter 1:17
Christian conduct should cause non-believers to praise God	Matthew 5:16 1 Peter 2:12
Christians should not pay back evil for evil	Luke 6:28 1 Peter 3:9
There is joy to be had when the Christian is being persecuted for doing what God wants	Matthew 5:10 1 Peter 3:14
We will all have to give an account of ourselves to God on judgment day	Matthew 12:36 1 Peter 4:5
If Christians are insulted because they are followers of Jesus, they should be glad	Matthew 5:11 1 Peter 4:14
Christians should be characterized by humility, and God will make them great	Luke 14:11 1 Peter 5:6
Because God is caring for them, Christians should not be worried or anxious	Matthew 6:25–27 1 Peter 5:7

A 4th-century sculpture depicting Jesus and Peter.

that Gentile Christians have been incorporated as full members into 'the people of God' whose history began with the covenants of the Old Testament (2:9–10). It also asserts that they have achieved this position as a result of their response in faith to what God has done for them. Like the ethnic family of Abraham, Gentile Christians owe their knowledge of God not to their own piety or insight, but to God's undeserved love shown towards them. In the case of Israel, this had been demonstrated particularly in the exodus. For Christians, 'it was the costly sacrifice of Christ, who was like a lamb without defect or flaw' (1:1–19).

1 Peter was not written in the same controversial context as Paul's letter to the Galatians. But that only makes more striking its insistence

---

Who wrote 1 Peter?
continued

were expressing their amazement at the *unexpected eloquence* of people who had come from the remote hillsides of Galilee, and who (like Jesus) had not been trained in formal styles of religious speech or teaching. In order to take account of the high literary quality of this epistle, though, some take the view that Peter is to be associated with the actual content of the letter, but not with its written form. On this view, the fine Greek style would not be Peter's own, but that of Silas who is specifically identified as Peter's secretary (5:12). That of course would be true of most, if not all, Greek letters, which were generally dictated to a scribe who would then write them up in their own style.

● Why would Peter have written a letter to Gentile Christians living in Asia Minor when according to Galatians 2:8 he was 'an apostle to the Jews'? This question is often raised, but it is scarcely relevant to the matter of authorship. For one thing, in the context of Galatians Paul's statement was not intended as a hard and fast rule. He never even kept it himself as an inflexible dictum, for he preached the gospel to many Jews even though he described himself as 'apostle to the Gentiles'. In addition, we know that Peter moved about in the Gentile world from a relatively early period. Paul mentions Peter's extensive travels (1 Corinthians 9:5), and there is no good reason to suppose he could not have visited some of the places to which this letter was sent. According to Acts 16:6–10, Paul was

'forbidden' to go to this very area, and some commentators suggest that was because Peter was already working there. On the other hand, 1 Peter 1:12 seems to draw a distinction between the writer of the epistle and 'the messengers who announced the Good News' to its readers, implying that he had not been the one who first took the Christian message to this area.

● It has also been argued that 1 Peter is too similar to Paul's letters to have been written by Peter. But this is hardly convincing evidence against Petrine authorship. It presupposes that Paul was unique in the early church, saying entirely different things from anyone else. We have already argued that this is an unrealistic way to look at Paul, and we also noted good reasons for believing that he and Peter saw eye to eye on most issues. So why should 1 Peter be entirely different from Paul's writings? In any case, the two are not identical. It is significant that though the conclusions emerging out of Peter's teaching on the church and the Old Testament covenants is very similar to Paul's, in arguing for it 1 Peter uses altogether different language and imagery. The closest parallels between them are all in the ethical instructions. But these can be found in a similar form not only in Paul's writings, but elsewhere in the New Testament, which suggests that a more plausible explanation is that both Paul and Peter were passing on moral advice that was widely accepted throughout many sections of the early church.

that Christians – even Gentiles – are now the true 'family of Abraham' without compulsory obedience to the Law, for it shows how this issue was soon settled in the church along the lines that Paul had argued.

THE CHRISTIAN'S STATUS (1:1–12)

These themes appear in the very first verse of the epistle, with the greeting 'To God's chosen people in the Dispersion throughout the provinces of Pontus, Galatia, Cappadocia, Asia, and Bithynia'. This opening is similar to that of the book of James. We noticed there that 'God's people in the Dispersion' could indicate only Jewish people, though in the context it was more likely to be referring to the church. In the case of

---

Date and origin

If Peter did indeed write this letter, then obviously we must date it before his death, which took place in the persecution of Christians begun by Nero in AD64. But dating it more precisely than that depends on our interpretation of the various references to persecution that occur throughout the letter. A number of observations may be made about this:

● In all the organized persecutions of Christians that took place towards the end of the first century, obedience to the emperor – even worship of him – was a crucial test of Christian allegiance. But this was clearly not the case in the persecutions envisaged in 1 Peter. Christians are encouraged to 'respect the Emperor', and to accept his authority – even though it must come second to the authority of God (2:13–17).

● The readers of 1 Peter seem to have been surprised to be persecuted (4:12); after the persecutions of Nero, we might have expected them to accept suffering as the norm.

● The descriptions of persecution in 5:8 ('Your enemy, the Devil, roams round like a roaring lion, looking for someone to devour') and 1:7 (testing by fire) could well refer to the events of Nero's persecution itself. According to the Roman historian Tacitus, the hated Christians 'were covered with wild beasts' skins and torn to death by dogs; or they were fastened on crosses, and, when daylight failed, were burned to serve as lamps by night' (*Annals* 15.44).

Putting all these indications together, it seems reasonable to conclude that perhaps 1 Peter was written as Nero's persecution was in its early stages. We have no certain evidence that it eventually spread to Asia Minor. But even if it did not, the official persecution in Rome would certainly have encouraged people elsewhere to despise the Christians in their own cities. We do know that Peter was in Rome at the time. The term 'Babylon', used by this letter, was a favourite code word for Rome among the early Christians. As Peter saw what was happening there, he felt it would only be a matter of time before such a great evil spread to other parts of the empire. He wanted Christians to know that when their time of trial came, they were not alone in their suffering. Others were suffering too. But most important of all, God would not fail to care for them, for they were the covenant people.

The Colosseum, Rome, built by Vespasian between AD69 and 79 as a place of entertainment. Many Christians died here, in contests with gladiators or wild animals.

1 Peter, there can be no doubt at all that Christians are being addressed, and that they are for the most part, if not exclusively, Gentile Christians.

This initial greeting is followed by a thanksgiving to God, after which the letter turns to exhortation. Peter's readers are encouraged to celebrate God's goodness to them, 'even though for a little while you may have to suffer various trials' (1:6). The writer tells them that such trials are insignificant when set against God's power. Christians already know something of this power in the new life that they enjoy through Jesus. They can also look forward to 'the Day when Jesus Christ is revealed', when they will meet him face to face (1:7). Simple Gentile believers might find this difficult to understand – even the angels cannot fully do so – but what is happening to them now, and the destiny that is waiting for them in the future, is all part of God's plan that was first revealed in the Old Testament.

CHRISTIAN DEVELOPMENT (1:13 – 2:10)

The writer then goes on to remind his readers that acceptance of the good news about Jesus imposes responsibilities as well as bestowing privileges. Faith in Christ is not merely a private experience, but

---

The theme of baptism in 1 Peter

On the surface, 1 Peter appears to be an ordinary letter, written to encourage Christians who were being persecuted. But it has been suggested that there is more to it than this, and that the central part of 1 Peter (1:3 – 4:11) is not a letter at all, but consists of material originating in the worship liturgies of the early church, specifically in the context of a service of baptism. A number of features are claimed to support such an understanding of 1 Peter:

● This passage seems to be a self-contained section of the letter. The words of 4:11 would certainly make a suitable conclusion, for they contain a fuller benediction than actually occurs at the end of chapter five. Peter also says in 5:12 that he is writing a 'brief letter', and since the whole of 1 Peter is hardly 'brief', the actual letter that he wrote might only run from 4:12 to 5:14, while the rest of the book is an account of the church's worship.

● Baptism is mentioned only in one obscure passage (3:18–22). This may be

thought a good reason for doubting its importance, but in this passage Noah's deliverance from a great flood in the Old Testament is said to be 'a symbol pointing to baptism, which now saves you'. The emphasis on 'now' suggests to some that those addressed had only just been baptized. Others have claimed to be able to discern subtle changes in the language towards the end of the first chapter, and they argue that the act of baptism had actually taken place between 1:21 and 1:22. On this understanding, this part of 1 Peter is regarded as a litany for a service of baptism, complete with hymns, responses, prayers, a sermon and a benediction. Other evidence for this is drawn from the exhortation to 'Be like new-born babies, always thirsty for the pure spiritual milk' (2:2). Evidence from the *Apostolic Tradition* ascribed to Hippolytus describes how towards the end of the second century a cup of milk and honey was given to Christians who had just been baptized, to remind them of the land promised to Israel ('a land flowing with milk and honey', Exodus 3:8). But 1 Peter mentions neither the honey nor the land,

something to be shared with others, in deed as well as word. Christ's death and resurrection has 'set you free from the worthless manner of life handed down by your ancestors' (1:18), and the recollection of that should lead Christians to obey God, and share God's love with other people.

They should also grow and develop in their Christian experience, being as eager for spiritual nourishment as babies are for their mothers' milk. As they grow as Christians, so they can 'come as living stones, and let yourselves be used in building the spiritual temple, where you will serve as holy priests to offer spiritual and acceptable sacrifices to God through Jesus Christ' (2:5–9). As Christians mature in this way, they will demonstrate how they are 'the chosen race, the King's priests, the holy nation, God's own people'.

Orthodox Jews still worship at the Western Wall, the only remaining part of the platform on which the temple was built. Peter uses the term 'living stones' to describe how Christians are being built together into the fabric of a 'living temple' which rests on the foundation of the work of Jesus Christ.

---

and the milk is described as 'pure and spiritual' which also suggests it could just as easily be understood metaphorically rather than literally. Another link with the *Apostolic Tradition* has been found in 1 Peter 3:3. Here Christian women are reminded that a person's character has nothing to do with 'the way you do your hair, or the jewellery you put on, or the dresses you wear'. In later customs, women removed jewellery and clothing and rearranged their hair before being baptized. But the emphasis in 1 Peter is not so much on this, as on the positive moral virtues that should be found in the Christian.

● There are a number of places where Peter uses language and imagery taken from the Passover story in the Old Testament. He says, for example, that Christ is 'a lamb without defect or flaw' (1:19), just as the Passover lambs had been (Exodus 12:5). Christians are told to 'gird up your minds' (1:13), in the same way as the Israelites fastened up their clothing on Passover night (Exodus 12:11). And 2:1–10 has many connections with the Old Testament books of Exodus,

Leviticus and Numbers. The relevance of this Passover connection is found in the fact that Tertullian, writing at the beginning of the third century, commented that the ideal time for Christians to be baptized was at Easter (Passover).

This way of looking at the content of 1 Peter has drawn attention to some significant aspects of the theme of the epistle, but they are not convincing when used to suggest that the document itself originated as a baptismal litany. There is no compelling reason for accepting that:

● There is no way of recognizing a first-century baptismal service, for we have no real idea how baptism was carried out in the earliest churches. Where the New Testament mentions it, baptism seems to have taken place at the same time as a person's initial commitment to Christianity. There is certainly no indication that baptism was an important event in formally organized worship, as it was later. No doubt Christians soon developed their own preferred ways of worshipping, but it is highly unlikely that these were as stereotyped in the New Testament period

There is not another passage of comparable length in the whole New Testament where more Old Testament imagery that was originally applied to Abraham and his descendants is taken over and applied to the Christian church as in some way being the 'new Israel'. But there are also some interesting connections here with Paul's thinking. The picture of the church as a building constructed out of living stones (one of which, the 'cornerstone', is Jesus himself) is not dissimilar to Paul's description of the church as a living body made up of many parts, 'Christ's body' (1 Corinthians 12:12–31). Indeed, Paul might well have been familiar with the same imagery himself, for in Romans he writes of Christians offering 'a living sacrifice' that will bring glory to God (Romans 12:1–2). When Peter describes all Christians as 'priests', he is saying the same thing as Paul did when he declared that all Christians had a God-given ability that they must share with the church at large. The fact that they use entirely different language from each other only serves to emphasize how important this concept of shared ministry was to the first Christian communities.

The theme of baptism in 1 Peter *continued*

as they became in the days of Hippolytus and Tertullian.

● It is also difficult to reconcile this view with the plain evidence of 1 Peter. There is no indication at all that the section 1:3 – 4:11 has originated in a different context from the rest. It is written in exactly the same style, and the same arguments seem to carry over from one section to the other.

● This baptismal theory has no way of explaining how a baptismal liturgy for the church at Rome could have got mixed up with a letter to Christians in Asia Minor. On the face of it, 1 Peter is a letter to persecuted Christians, and we must make sense of it in that light.

The evidence that has been claimed in support of this theory could no doubt carry some weight if there were other reasons to connect 1 Peter with Christian baptism, but by themselves these considerations are hardly sufficient to establish such a connection. In addition, there are some important differences between the accounts of Hippolytus and what is contained in 1 Peter. Later, the service of baptism included exorcism, anointing and the laying-on of hands, none of which are even hinted at in 1 Peter.

The occurrence of themes that seem relevant to newly baptized Christians is probably due to the fact that Peter, like Paul, wanted to remind his readers of what was involved in being a Christian. To do this, it would have been natural to recall the commitment they had made when they first came to faith in Christ. Quite possibly he would repeat the sort of things that he was in the habit of saying to new converts, but that does not lead to the conclusion that he was giving an eyewitness report of an actual church service. Someone who has worked out effective ways of expressing things will always tend to repeat the same ideas in different contexts, and a better assumption is to suppose that the author of this book had regularly used themes found in these pages to encourage Christians in their faith. Perhaps they had been carefully crafted in the course of communication, and they were not being expressed this way for the first time here, but it is a big leap from that to the conclusion that the whole book is some kind of worship manual for the services of the church.

Peter and the church in Rome

St Peter's, Rome, beneath which is the tomb of Peter, and probably also of Paul.

After the stories of the early chapters of Acts, the course of the rest of Peter's life is unknown to us. Apart from Paul's reference to his missionary activity (1 Corinthians 9:5), and what is perhaps a cryptic mention of his death in John 21:18–19, the New Testament tells us nothing more about him. 1 Peter, of course, is evidence that he was at one time in Rome, but it gives us no further personal details.

It was not long, however, before Christians began to enquire about Peter more specifically. Just as they wanted to know about Andrew, Matthew, Philip and other disciples of Jesus, so they wanted to know what had become of the disciple whom Jesus had once called 'the Rock', on whose foundation he said the church would be built (Matthew 16:17–19).

The second-century Acts of Peter purport to tell of how Peter came at an early stage to the city of Rome and there established a large and thriving Christian community. Like Jesus, he performed many miracles, though his progress was continuously hindered by a hostile magician called Simon who, among other things, had the power to fly. According to this document, Peter's mission to Rome was cut short by the events of Nero's persecution. His Christian friends advised him to leave the city and escape martyrdom, thereby freeing himself for yet greater exploits in proclaiming the Christian message. But as he was leaving the city in disguise, Peter saw Jesus himself entering Rome, and asked Jesus where he was going. 'And the Lord said to him, "I am coming to Rome to be crucified"... And Peter came to himself... he returned to Rome rejoicing and giving praise to the Lord.' As a result of his return, Peter himself was crucified, insisting that he should be hung upside down on the cross.

Like the stories about the other disciples, all this is mostly fiction. But, like them, it probably reflects some facts, for there is no reason to doubt either that

Peter visited Rome and played an important part in the work of the church there, or that he was put to death in the persecution started by Nero. 1 Clement 5 connects the deaths of both Peter and Paul with this period, and before the end of the second century the graves of these apostles had become a place of pilgrimage (Eusebius, Ecclesiastical History II.25.5–7). At a later date, when the emperor Constantine became a Christian, he constructed a more elaborate shrine at the spot (probably in about AD333), and today the Basilica of St Peter stands on the same site. Archaeological investigation has confirmed this general account, for not only has Constantine's monument been discovered, but traces of the second-century edifice have also been found. Further remains of bones and early graves, some going back to the first century, have also been unearthed, though there is no agreement among archaeologists about their significance, with some claiming that the actual grave of Peter himself has been laid bare, while others argue that these graves are not even Christian.

Whatever the outcome of such ongoing investigations, we may be sure that Peter did die as a martyr in Rome during the persecution of Nero, and that his grave lies somewhere on the site of St Peter's Basilica. There is, however, no evidence to show that he was the founder of the Roman church, though (along with Paul) he had some connections with it from an early stage, and it is therefore not surprising that he soon became its patron saint.

CHRISTIAN BEHAVIOUR (2:11 – 4:19)

Peter goes on to remind his readers that, as God's people, they have different standards from non-Christians. They are as much at home in the prevailing cultural value-systems of the Hellenistic world as 'strangers and refugees' (2:11). Their only true allegiance is to God and so everything they do should be intended to glorify God alone. Even when they have to 'endure the pain of undeserved suffering' (2:19), they can look to the example of Jesus. For 'when he was insulted, he did not answer back with an insult; when he suffered, he did not threaten, but placed his hopes in God, the righteous Judge' (2:23).

Exactly the same principles should determine how Christians behave at home. Christian wives should be ready to share the love of Christ with their husbands – and men for their part must treat their wives with respect and affirmation. In a word, every believer should follow the advice of Jesus: 'Love one another... and be kind and humble with one another. Do not pay back evil with evil or cursing with cursing; instead, pay back with a blessing' (3:8–9).

Peter knew that it is never easy to behave like this, especially when suffering from unjust persecution. For the Christian, it involves putting God first so that lifestyles are not controlled by personal whims and fancies, but by God's standards and values (4:7). Putting God first will always be worthwhile in the end. Suffering is just a temporary thing, and Christians must look beyond it to the judgment of God, when all things will be put right. 1 Peter assures its readers that they can trust themselves to God's care, for God's promises never fail (4:19).

SERVING CHRIST (5:1–14)

Finally, Peter gives advice to those who are, like himself, 'elders' or 'shepherds' in the church. Instead of being domineering, they should be 'examples to the flock' (5:3), recognizing that the church will flourish only when all its members have 'put on the apron of humility' to serve one another (5:5). In doing so, they are following the example of Jesus, who himself had worn the apron of a slave to wash his disciples' feet (John 13:1–17). But above all, they must not lose their trust in God in the midst of persecution. Even this hardship can be transformed in the light of God's intentions for the people of the covenant: 'After you have suffered for a little while, the God of all grace, who calls you to share in eternal glory in union with Christ, will personally perfect you and give you firmness, strength, and a sure foundation' (5:10).

Hope for the future

Peter was not the first writer to face the problem of unjust suffering. It was a question that became increasingly important in the centuries just before the birth of Jesus, as is evidenced by the many apocalyptic writings produced between about 100BC and AD100. We have already explored the distinctive features of this kind of writing in looking at the religious background to the life of Jesus in chapter 1. They were generally pessimistic works, despairing of God ever being able to put things right in this world, and therefore laying more emphasis on the heavenly world instead, and containing reports of visions and dreams in which God's plans were revealed to those who needed to know. On the face of it, the kind of escapism typified by these writings seems quite foreign to the outlook of the New Testament. But there is one New Testament book that has clearly been profoundly influenced by the style, if not the thinking, of the Jewish apocalyptists.

Revelation

Probably no book in the entire New Testament is less read and less understood than this one. All the great interpreters of the past had difficulty with it. Among the Protestant Reformers, Martin Luther found it an offensive piece of work, with very little to say about Christ, and John Calvin also had considerable doubts about its value. Many modern readers feel the same way. It is not surprising that Revelation should seem a difficult and complicated book, for people today do not generally think in the same terms as Jewish apocalyptists, and find their secret language and visions to be both meaningless and bizarre. Christians in particular are uneasy with the apocalyptist's conviction that God has no relevance to the world in which we live, and they find it difficult to imagine that God's sole intention could be to destroy human society and set up some sort of other-worldly kingdom instead. At the same time, there are others for whom the book of Revelation assumes far greater importance than any other book of the New Testament. It has been claimed that it gives an insight into God's ultimate plans for humankind, even down to detailed predictions of how the world will come to an end. So what can we make of it? Does it have any lasting significance, or is it to be dismissed as an unfortunate mistake by the early church, which should never have been included in the New Testament canon?

A CHRISTIAN BOOK?

There can be no doubt that despair and pessimism about human history is fundamentally at odds with the outlook not only of the New Testament, but of the Old Testament as well. The biblical writers faced up to the tragic realities of human experience, but they had no doubt that God can and does meet men and women in the everyday events of normal life. This is at the very centre of the gospel, with the belief that through Jesus God personally shared in human existence, thereby affirming the value of life in this world as something to be embraced and celebrated.

When we look at the book of Revelation in detail, it is clear that its author shares this positive Christian emphasis on God's involvement in human affairs. Though the language and imagery in which the book is written is apocalyptic in form, its message has this distinctively Christian world-affirming emphasis.

■ Unlike every other apocalyptic book, Revelation names both its author and its first readers. It was written by a person called John, and was sent 'From John to the seven churches in the province of Asia', in the towns of Ephesus, Smyrna, Pergamum, Thyatira, Sardis, Philadelphia and Laodicea (Revelation 1:4). These churches are addressed in quite specific terms, and incidents and individuals are mentioned by name. This kind of self-confidence was never shared by other apocalyptic writers. On the contrary, they were generally so afraid of their persecutors that to have identified themselves in this way would have led to certain death. Of course, that was also the outcome for some members of these churches, but that was evidently not a good enough reason for disguising the true nature of their Christian faith.

■ Even in those parts of the book which are most similar to Jewish writings, John's visions are always closely linked to his experience of life in the church. His vision came to him 'on the Lord's day', perhaps in the course of Christian worship, and the contents of the visions have many references to the worship of the church, its confessions of faith, prayers and hymns. For examples, see Revelation 1:5–6; 4:8, 11; 5:9–10; 7:10, 12; 11:15, 17–18; 12:10–12; 15:3–4; 19:1–2, 5–8; 22:13.

The seven churches mentioned in the book of Revelation.

■ Revelation looks forward to a future intervention of God in the affairs of this world. But its understanding of this is different from that of other apocalyptists, who without exception regarded this world and all its affairs as irretrievably evil. To them, history was a meaningless enigma, and the sooner its course was stopped, the better. This had not been the view of the Old Testament writers. Though some of the prophets had looked forward to the coming of a 'Day of the Lord' when God would intervene in a final and decisive way in the affairs of the world, they believed that this would be the continuation of what God was already doing in the present order of things (Isaiah 2:6–22; Hosea 2:14–23; Joel 2:28 – 3:21). For them, the God who would inaugurate a new world order in the future was also the God who could be known here and now in the events of human life.

The apocalyptic writers rejected this view, because they could make no sense of their own present experience. But like the Old Testament, the book of Revelation makes a clear link between what God is doing in history now, and what God will do in the future. Indeed, the entire meaning of God's plan for the future of humanity is to be found in a historical event, the life, death and resurrection of Jesus himself, 'the Lamb of God' (Revelation 5). Far from the sufferings of Christians being a meaningless interlude, John declares it to be one of the most powerful responses against all forms of evil (Revelation 12:10–12).

Revelation therefore does not follow slavishly the pattern of the Jewish apocalyptic books. It presents a distinctive and positive Christian explanation of the presence of evil in the affairs of human life. Its message is expressed through conventional language and vivid Old Testament imagery, but its content goes beyond the literary form of apocalyptic writing.

THE BOOK AND ITS MESSAGE

The first three chapters of Revelation are similar to many other New Testament writings: they contain seven letters to seven churches in the Roman province of Asia. They are not real letters like those written by Paul, for they purport to come from the risen Jesus himself, and John says that their content was given to him in a vision, just like the rest of the book. But they deal with very down-to-earth matters, and show a detailed knowledge of these people and their environment. Their churches were involved in disputes over Christian beliefs, their commitment to Christ was wavering, and as a result they were in no position to face up to the challenge of sustained persecution. To do that, they needed to be wholeheartedly committed. This is a message that we find many times in the New Testament, and it is not significantly different from that of 1 Peter.

But the second part of the book (4 – 22) is quite different. Here we come face to face with the language and imagery of apocalyptic writings. No longer do the visions seem to relate to real events and people, but instead they introduce monsters and dragons in a quick succession of terrifying events. The whole section is introduced in chapters 4 and 5 by a vision of heaven which sets the scene for what follows. Here the author lays out the underlying assumptions of the way in which he understands God's workings in history. God is the one who is 'high and exalted' in absolute majesty and holiness (4:2), and men and women (represented by the twenty-four elders in the divine court) find their true significance as they worship and serve God. But they are quite incapable of reflecting every aspect of God's personality, and when a sealed scroll containing God's revelation to the world is produced, the elders are unable to open it to reveal its contents. After an angel has searched unsuccessfully in heaven, on earth and in the underworld, God's own heavenly deliverer appears on the scene in the person of the Lamb of God, Jesus Christ (5:1–8).

This is a powerful and impressive presentation of the central importance of the life, death and resurrection of Jesus in the Christian understanding of life and its meaning. It is significant that at the very beginning of his visions, John links the future destiny of the world and its inhabitants with God's self-revelation in the historical events of the life of Jesus.

The chapters that follow then present a series of visions describing how justice will be served on all those forces that are implacably opposed to God's will. Many of the descriptions here are quite horrific, and much of the language in which God's judgment is described comes from the story of the plagues in Egypt in the Old Testament book of Exodus (Exodus 6:28 – 12:36). This gives a clue to the point that John is making, for in the exodus story God's main purpose had not been the plagues: they were merely a prelude to the salvation that God had planned for the people of Israel, and through them for the whole world. So too in Revelation, the main point of the book is not to be found in God's judgment upon evil, but in the conviction that God is now in the process of making a new world from which evil will be completely banished. In this new world, people will enjoy a fresh and unfettered freedom to know God in a direct way: 'God will be with them in person... God will wipe away all tears from their eyes. There will be no more death, no more grief or crying or pain. The old things have disappeared...' (21:3–4).

There have been many attempts to arrange the visions of Revelation according to some sort of schematic pattern. One popular suggestion is that, with the exception of chapters 4 and 5, and the description of the new heavens and earth, the whole book is arranged in a pattern of seven sections of sevens:

Seven seals (6:1 – 8:1)

Seven trumpets (8:2 – 11:19)

Seven visions of the dragon and his kingdom (12:1 – 13:18)

Seven visions of the coming of the Lamb of God (14:1–20)

Seven bowls of God's anger against evil (15:1 – 16:21)

Seven visions of the fall of 'Babylon' (17:1 – 19:10)

Seven visions of the end (19:11 – 21:4).

However they might be arranged, these visions present a kaleidoscopic picture of how God will finally overcome the powers of evil. It is the work not of a self-conscious theologian but of a great artist, and like a good artist John depicts the same subject from a number of different perspectives in order to reinforce the overall impression that he wants to create.

MAKING SENSE OF THE MESSAGE

Because of the many allusions to specific events and people known to the writer and his readers, it is difficult today to appreciate fully every detail of these visions. But their impact on the original readers of the book of Revelation is not difficult to imagine. John assured his Christian readers that their present suffering was only temporary (2:10; 3:10), for their great enemy 'Babylon' (a term which John, like Peter, used to refer to Rome) would ultimately come under the judgment of God (Revelation 18). God alone is the Lord of history, with a personal interest in the destiny not only of nations but of ordinary people as well: injustice and evil would not be allowed to win the day.

This view of Revelation is consistent with the way we have tried to appreciate the other New Testament books, by setting it in its context and attempting to understand what it might have meant for those who first received it. This approach to understanding Revelation is sometimes called the 'preterist' view (from the Latin word *praeteritum*, meaning 'referring to the past'), and it seems the most obvious approach to take. Over the centuries, however, the seemingly mysterious character of Revelation's message has encouraged people to seek out other hidden meanings within its pages. During the early centuries of the Christian era, it was frequently regarded as a symbolic presentation of some of the great truths of the Christian faith. Origen and Augustine regarded its imagery as a picturesque account of the principles of God's working throughout history, and saw its weird descriptions of persons, battles and beasts not as real events, but as a dramatic presentation of the age-long opposition between God and the forces of evil. This way of reading the book can be helpful: not only does it make sense of many of the most difficult passages, but it also succeeds in relating it to the needs of its first readers, who needed to be assured of the successful outcome of the struggle in which they were engaged.

But during the late nineteenth and early twentieth centuries, a significant body of popular opinion came to look at Revelation in a different way. These so-called 'futurists' argued that its real meaning is connected with events that are still in the future even now, and its full significance will become plain only to that generation which finds itself living in 'the last days'. Some even suggested that the seven letters with

The apocalyptic writings were full of strange and intricate symbolism, mysterious creatures and messages from angels. The German artist Albrecht Dürer captured the mood of these prophetic visions in his woodcut *The Four Horsemen of the Apocalypse.*

which the book opens are not real letters at all, but part of a detailed clairvoyant insight given to John consisting of descriptions of seven successive ages of church history, reaching from the first century up to the end of time. This 'Dispensationalist' view was popularized in Christian circles particularly through the *Scofield Reference Bible* published in 1909, which argued that the present generation had reached the stage of the seventh and final letter (to Laodicea), and was therefore the one that was living at the very end of world history. Throughout the twentieth century this view exercised considerable influence, though it presents many difficulties:

■ There is of course the plain fact that several generations have believed themselves to be living in the last days, some even putting a date on the end of the world – but they have all been wrong.

■ More significant is the fact that Jesus himself explicitly warned his disciples not to indulge in this kind of speculation: 'No one knows... when that day and hour will come – neither the angels in heaven, nor the Son...' (Matthew 24:36). It is therefore hardly likely that God would have given the information only to a select band of modern readers of the book of Revelation!

■ Another serious objection is that according to this view, the book of Revelation must have been totally meaningless and irrelevant to the people for whom it was ostensibly written. If the letters to the churches of Asia were not real letters, related to the concerns of real people, that would make Revelation quite different from every other book in the whole of the Bible. It also shares the general pessimism about existence in this world that was common in apocalyptic literature, but was quite foreign to New Testament thinking.

There is no justification for regarding either Revelation or any other book of the Bible as a blueprint for the future course of world events. That is not to suggest that the Christian faith has no expectation of a better world at some future date, for the whole New Testament presents the clear conviction that there will be a point at which God must deal decisively with the forces of evil, at which time the kingdom of peace and justice announced by Jesus will become a lasting and tangible reality.

The book of Revelation confirms that conviction by assuring its readers that this world belongs to God and not to the forces of evil. Through the use of vivid and powerful imagery it emphasizes that God will act to put things right, no matter how long such action may seem to be delayed. At that time, people will not simply be able to make a new start, but will have a part in the new world, where sin, misery and evil have no further place. Those who reject the values of this new world will have no part in it (Revelation 21:27), though it is not God's intention that any should be excluded, but rather that all should respond to the offer of a new way of being: 'Come, whoever is thirsty: accept the water of life as a gift, whoever wants it' (Revelation 22:17).

The author and date of Revelation

Revelation is the only New Testament book that was explicitly dated by any writers in the early centuries. Irenaeus stated that John saw his vision 'not long ago, but almost in our own generation, towards the end of Domitian's reign' (*Against Heresies* V.30.3), and this opinion was quoted with approval by Eusebius (*Ecclesiastical History* III.18–20; V.8.6).

This corresponds quite closely with what can be discerned from the concerns of the book itself. Though there is some doubt regarding the extent to which Domitian (AD81–96) demanded that he be worshipped as divine, there is no doubt that emperor-worship in general was especially deeply entrenched in the area of Roman Asia to which Revelation was addressed. From the time of Augustus onwards, honouring the emperor was a convenient test of political allegiance. Christians did not want to be disloyal citizens, but neither were they prepared to offer worship to the emperor, and as a result many of them were persecuted and hounded to death as enemies of the state.

A significant minority opinion, however, argues that the book of Revelation was written earlier, in the days just after the persecution of Christians by Nero. Reasons for this include the fact that there is no explicit reference to the destruction of Jerusalem in AD70, and if Revelation 11:1–2 is understood literally it could imply that it was written as the final assault on the temple was underway. There is also the fact that 13:3 mentions one of the heads of the 'beast', or antichrist, having been fatally wounded but coming to life again to rule the empire – and there was a widespread expectation that Nero was likely to return in this way. In addition, depending on how the list of seven emperors in 17:9–11 is analysed, it is possible to place the seventh and final one either in the time of Nero or his successor Galba (AD68–69). Such speculations however assume that John had

actual historical figures in mind at this point, whereas in the light of his predilection for the number seven, it is just as likely that these seven emperors were never intended to be real people, but were a way of referring to the sum total of all the evil that is opposed to God. On balance, there seems no compelling reason to reject the traditional date for Revelation of about AD95.

The author of Revelation was a person called John, whom Justin Martyr identified with 'one of the apostles of Christ' (*Dialogue with Trypho the Jew* 91). The idea that he was this particular John seems unlikely, for the writer of Revelation mentions 'the twelve apostles of the Lamb' with no suggestion that he might have been one of them (21:14), while the way he introduces himself as 'your brother... a follower of Jesus... your partner' (1:9) hardly suggests he was a person of great authority in the church. But he was clearly steeped in the imagery of traditional apocalyptic writings, and we may therefore suppose he was a Jew.

At the same time, there are a number of unusual connections between Revelation and John's Gospel, which we argued in an earlier chapter had some indeterminate connection with Jesus' disciple of that name. Both John and Revelation refer to Jesus as 'the word (*logos*) of God' (John 1:1–14; 1 John 1:1–4; Revelation 19:11–16). Both of them also call Jesus 'the Lamb of God', though they use different Greek words to do so (John 1:29; Revelation 5:6–14). Furthermore, both the gospel and the letters of John seem to have had some connection with the city of Ephesus, which was also one of the churches addressed in Revelation.

One of the more plausible explanations of all this is that there was at Ephesus a 'school' of Christian thinkers established and inspired by John the apostle, and perhaps different members of this group, including John himself, were responsible for the final form of the various books which now go under his name.

30 The Enemies Within

One of the most influential factors in the changing pattern of life in the early church was the development of arguments about the nature of Christian belief, and in particular the emergence of various groups of people who, at a later period, came to be regarded as 'heretics' by the majority of Christian believers. In one sense, of course, those who were labelled 'heretics' were those who eventually lost the arguments, while the mainstream were those who won. But it would be a mistake to depict these disputes as little more than power struggles for control of the growing church. There were significant moral and theological issues involved, the origins of which can be traced back to currents of thought we have already encountered in discussing the letters of Paul. As early as the writing of Galatians, Paul mentioned people whom he believed to be proclaiming 'another gospel' (Galatians 1:6), while in Corinth he was opposed by some who clearly had a fundamentally different understanding of the Christian message (2 Corinthians 11:1–4). Probably none of these people were 'heretics' in the later, technical sense, and Paul certainly never went as far as the second-century church leaders by suggesting that they should be excluded from the church. Rather than being the local representatives of any sort of organized group within the church at large, most of them seem to have been personal opponents of Paul, who sprang up spontaneously in different places.

It is clear that Paul was not wholly successful in dealing with these matters, and some of the later New Testament books reveal how people with similar ideas to those opposed by Paul were beginning to organize themselves into distinctive movements within the church. By the middle of the second century, Montanists, Gnostics, and others had become clearly identifiable groups. But in the first century, the tensions that led to the eventual formation of separate sects were only just beginning to surface in church life, and the tendencies that can be traced towards the end of the first century were much more loosely defined.

The book of Revelation

We have already looked at the message of much of the book of Revelation. But in its first three chapters, this book reflects the conditions of the seven churches in Asia Minor to which it was addressed. The advice given by the risen Jesus to three of these churches (at Ephesus, Pergamum and Thyatira) is about their attitude to various false teachers (Revelation 2:1–7, 12–17, 18–29).

The church at Ephesus is commended because it has 'tested those who say they are apostles but are not, and have found out that they are liars' (2:2). In addition, its members are said to 'hate what the Nicolaitans do' (2:6). In Pergamum, some church members had actually followed the teaching of these 'Nicolaitans', while others are described as following

The ruins of ancient Pergamum rise high above the modern Turkish town of Bergama. Pergamum was, according to Revelation, 'where Satan has his throne', possibly referring to the Altar of Zeus which was situated between the two trees overlooking the town. Pergamum also became a centre of the official cult of emperor-worship.

'the teaching of Balaam' (2:14). The church at Thyatira had also come under the influence of false teaching, in this case from 'that woman Jezebel, who calls herself a messenger of God' (2:20).

Given the somewhat cryptic nature of these references, there is room for debate as to the precise identity of these various groups, though it is likely that they were all connected with each other, rather than being separate groups in the different cities. The Nicolaitans are certainly mentioned in both Ephesus and Pergamum, and in the message to Pergamum the followers of Balaam appear to be the same people. Though neither of these names is applied to the heretics in Thyatira, the activities of the Nicolaitans/Balaamites in Pergamum are the same as those practised by 'Jezebel' and her devotees there: they all eat food offered to idols and indulge in practices which were regarded as immoral.

Paul had dealt with both these issues at an earlier period, though he never suggested that those involved in such activities were 'heretics' in the strict sense. He had declared that eating food offered to idols was a matter of indifference to Christian believers (1 Corinthians 8) and, though he typically had less patience with instances of immorality, he generally dealt with them in a tactful and generous way, seeking to persuade rather than to dictate. Things must have changed in the interim. In Paul's time, these concerns were mainly practical issues, arising naturally as Gentile converts struggled to understand how their new faith might affect their lifestyle. But they had now become theological and doctrinal issues and, though the book of Revelation gives no real indication of the kind of beliefs that led to such activities, a number of considerations suggest that these sects were an early form of what was later known as Gnosticism:

Beliefs that later came to be associated with Gnosticism feature in several New Testament writings. Shown here is an amulet engraved with Gnostic symbols.

■ Members of one of the prominent Gnostic groups of the second century actually called themselves 'Nicolaitans'. They traced their origins back to a man called Nicolaus who, according to Acts 6:5, was one of Stephen's Hellenist colleagues in the early Jerusalem church. It is unlikely that they had any real connection with this person, but some of their practices were not dissimilar from what we read about in the book of Revelation.

■ Though the heretics opposed in Revelation were undoubtedly less sophisticated and less well organized than these later groups, there are some signs of Gnostic terminology and ideas here. For instance, Jezebel's teaching in Thyatira is referred to by John as 'the deep secrets of Satan' (Revelation 2:24), and this phrase is found among later Gnostic groups as a description of their own beliefs. The very fact that a woman should have been so prominent in this movement is also consistent with some kind of Gnostic connection, for in the Gnostic movements of the second-century, women often enjoyed a significant and conspicuous role. Indeed, this was one reason why the church after the New Testament period officially excluded women from any form of public service.

■ The evidence of other New Testament books points in the same direction. The letters of John, as well as the letters of Jude and 2 Peter, all seem to have originated in the same geographical area as that referred to in Revelation, and in all of them there are mentions of wandering teachers who operated in the same way as those who are dealt with in Revelation. 1 John explains their theology in considerable detail, and we can see from this how close these people were moving towards classical Gnosticism.

The letters of John

Like John's Gospel, 1 John spells out its author's intentions quite clearly: 'I am writing this to you so that you may know that you have eternal life – you that believe in the Son of God' (5:13). John's Gospel was written to demonstrate that Jesus was Messiah and Son of God, and to win people to faith in him (John 20:31). By contrast, 1 John was written to people who were already Christian believers, but who needed to be reassured of the truth of what they believed.

'False prophets'

It is not difficult to see why these people needed such reassurance for, like the churches mentioned in Revelation, the Christian community to which they belonged was suffering from the activities of 'false prophets' (1 John 4:1). These people had originally been members of the community, but they had left and were now trying to subvert it from the outside (2:19). Of course, that was not how the false teachers saw things. They believed they had received special revelations that were not entrusted to more ordinary Christians, and spoke of 'knowing' God in an intimate way through some secret spiritual empowerment that allegedly enabled them to live on a different plane from the others (2:4; 4:1; 4:8). They were already spiritually 'perfect' (1:6, 8, 10), living in full appreciation of the 'light' which was God (1:5; 2:9) – and so the normal, earthbound rules of Christian morality no longer applied to them (3:7–12; 4:20).

All this sounds remarkably similar to the claims of Paul's opponents in Corinth. They, too, were claiming that, because of their personal mystical experiences, they were no longer bound by the normal constraints of bodily existence (1 Corinthians 10:1–13), but that through these experiences they had already been raised to a new spiritual level, far above that enjoyed by ordinary mortals (1 Corinthians 4:7–8). It was, they said, just as if the resurrection had already come: they might seem to be living in this world, but really they had been totally liberated from it, and so they no longer shared its concerns (1 Corinthians 15:12–19).

People with similar views are also mentioned in 2 Timothy 2:17–18. 1 John does not actually say that these 'false prophets' also believed that the resurrection had already taken place through their own mystical experiences, but it is likely that they held this view too.

Docetism

There is, however, a new element in 1 John. For the 'false prophets' mentioned here had a distinctive understanding of the person and significance of Jesus himself, and it is clear from what is said about them that John's opponents were denying that Jesus was the Messiah and the Son of God (2:22–23; 4:2, 15; 5:1–5, 10–12). It was not that they denied that Jesus had revealed the power of God – but they found it difficult to comprehend how an ordinary human person could reveal the character of the eternal God. So they asserted that Jesus was not truly human at all (4:1–3).

In Greek thinking there had always been a strong conviction that this world in which we live is quite separate from the heavenly world. The Old Testament prophets had always believed that God's activity could be seen in the affairs of human experience, but Greek thinkers more typically regarded life in this world as a miserable existence, and understood the true destiny of men and women to be not here, but in the spiritual world inhabited by God. On this view of things, true salvation could only consist of the escape of a person from the 'prison' of this world into the life of the supernatural world. There were many explanations as to precisely how this might be accomplished, and it is obvious that the desire for such liberation was what motivated both Paul's opponents in Corinth, and those whose teaching the author of 1 John was opposing.

At the beginning, Christians were interested in such ideas mainly because they were attracted by the promise of exciting mystical experiences. But, as these mystics began to think through the theological implications of their experience, they inevitably found it hard to cope with the church's belief that Jesus himself – as Jesus of Nazareth – could have come from God. For if God was a part of this mystical, supernatural world, then there was no way in which God could also be thought of as a real human person. For the all-powerful, transcendent God to be imprisoned in the life of a human being would be a contradiction in terms.

One way out of the dilemma was to suggest that Jesus had only *seemed* to be the Messiah or Son of God. This view is called 'Docetism' (from the Greek word *dokeo*, meaning 'to seem'), and it is something of this sort that is opposed in 1 John. A story told by Irenaeus recounts how the apostle John once went to a public bathhouse in Ephesus, but when he got there and recognized Cerinthus – a prominent Docetist – he refused to share the same water (*Against Heresies* III.3.4). Because of this, some have suggested that 1 John was a direct reply to Cerinthus himself. He certainly argued that the 'divine essence', or 'cosmic Christ', entered the human Jesus of Nazareth at his baptism, and left him before the crucifixion, and 1 John 5:6 might be interpreted as a direct and specific reply to this: 'Jesus Christ is the one who came with the water of his baptism and the blood of his death. He came not only with the water, but with both the water and the blood.' Cerinthus, however, had many other ideas that feature nowhere at all in 1 John, and overall the problems dealt with in this letter seem to be less complex and sophisticated than the theology of Cerinthus and his followers. Indeed, with the exception of their speculation about the person of Christ, the heretics of 1 John have much more in common with Paul's opponents in Corinth, and it is probably more accurate to regard them as an intermediate stage between the Corinthian heretics and the fully developed Gnostic systems of the second century.

1 John

The author of 1 John clearly had no time for these people, for he denounced their beliefs and opposed their practices in every section

---

The books by John

We cannot consider 1 John independently from the other letters of John, and John's Gospel. 2 and 3 John are related very closely to 1 John, though they are quite a different type of literature. Unlike 1 John, they are short, personal letters, one addressed to a church and the other to an individual called Gaius. Their author calls himself 'the Elder', and in 2 John he warns his readers against wandering teachers 'who do not acknowledge that Jesus Christ came as a human being' (2 John 7–11). He was concerned that these people should not be welcomed into the Christian community, and because of this many scholars think that 2 John must have been written before 1 John, as 1 John envisages a situation in which the heretics had already been excluded from the church (1 John 2:19).

3 John advises Gaius about a man by the name of Diotrephes, who was engaged in a power struggle for control of the church, in relation to which 'the Elder' says that he intends to pay a short visit to correct 'the terrible things he says about us and the lies he tells' (3 John 9–10).

The situation envisaged in 3 John seems to reflect a stage when new patterns of church government were beginning to emerge. As the apostles and their representatives died, the corporate leadership of the earliest churches began to disappear, and new leaders were trying to assert themselves in a process which eventually led to the formal appointment of just one authoritative leader in each local church. Perhaps 'the Elder' represented the older form of church organization, and that might explain his concern about the emergence of just one person claiming to be the church's leader. In the second century, anyone with the title of 'Elder' would himself have been a part of the organized hierarchy of the church, though the writer of these letters clearly does not belong in that context. He was obviously highly respected by his readers, but he does not seem to have had absolute authority over them as he can only appeal to them to do what he believed to be right.

The majority of scholars believe that 'the Elder' who wrote 2 and 3 John also wrote 1 John, for there are many connections between the three letters in vocabulary and style, and certain statements in 2 and 3 John seem to presuppose some knowledge of the issues dealt with in the first letter. If it was possible to decide the identity of 'the Elder', we could presumably, therefore, identify the writer of all three letters.

But this is easier said than done. Guidance has often been sought in a statement attributed to Papias, who is quoted by Eusebius as having written in his *Interpretation of the Oracles of the Lord*, 'If ever anyone came who had followed the elders, I inquired into the

of his letter. He realized all too well the strong pressure that they were placing on the members of the community, and he went out of his way to assure them that they, and not the 'false prophets', were the ones who had the truth.

Beyond that, it is not at all easy to define exactly what 1 John is about. It certainly has no linear argument running through it, which has encouraged some to rearrange the letter so its various sections can fit together in what they regard as a more logical and sequential fashion, while others have explained what they believe to be inconsistencies by supposing that the letter went through more than one edition and is, therefore, the work of different writers. But neither of these suggestions

---

The books by John continued

words of the elders, what Andrew or Peter or Philip or Thomas or James or John or Matthew, or any other of the Lord's disciples, had said, and what Aristion and the elder John, the Lord's disciples, were saying.' Eusebius goes on to observe that 'It is here worth noting that he twice counts the name of John, and reckons the first John with... the other Apostles... but places the second with the others outside the number of the apostles... This confirms the truth of the story of those who have said that there were two of the same name in Asia, and that there are two tombs at Ephesus both still called John's' (Eusebius, *Ecclesiastical History* III.39.4–6).

If the 'elder John' to whom Eusebius refers was the same person as 'the Elder' who wrote 2 and 3 John, then presumably this second-generation Christian was also the author of 1 John (and perhaps had some connection with the writing of John's Gospel). But Papias' statement is itself too ambiguous to provide much guidance, for he also appears to call the disciples themselves 'elders', and Eusebius might therefore have been wrong to infer that Papias was actually referring to two different people called John. In addition, this whole argument assumes that Papias had access to reliable information. But we must treat these statements with caution, especially when we only have second-hand knowledge of what Papias actually wrote. As far as the writings of John are

concerned, it is more helpful to begin with the documents themselves.

There is a certain amount of debate about the precise relationship between 1, 2 and 3 John, and John's Gospel. There are considerable and close similarities between the gospel and 1 John. Both use the same language in the same way, and distinctive expressions such as the contrasts between light and darkness, life and death, truth and error, and the emphasis on love (not to mention the description of Jesus as the Word or *Logos*) are all found in both gospel and letter. Both of them also use the same techniques for conveying their message, initially stating an idea in a simple and easily remembered way, and then examining its implications from a number of different angles.

But there are also a number of differences. 1 John has a more restricted vocabulary than the gospel, and its emphasis is also slightly different at some points. For instance, while the gospel lays most emphasis on the present experience of the Christian (so-called 'realized eschatology'), the letter has much more emphasis on the future hope. The letter also has a stronger emphasis on the church and its sacraments, though of course these things are not entirely absent from the gospel.

It has been proposed that the gospel was edited by the writer of the letter, to bring it into line with his own thinking on

is particularly convincing. The book contains not just the author's response to those who were opposing him, but also his own theological reflections on the situation he faced. His thinking seems to be expressed in a cyclical way, with themes being identified and then visited and revisited from different angles in order to tease out their significance and meaning. From a compositional perspective, it is more a work of art than of philosophy, and can usefully be compared to a musical composition in which the main theme is first expounded, and then taken up, developed and elaborated, as the composer moves on to other themes and ideas, yet always returns to the first thought.

Whatever the form of the argument, the message of 1 John is crystal

---

these points. There is certainly some evidence that the gospel contains the work of more than one person, but it is unlikely that the original form of the gospel has been revised by someone who found it theologically unacceptable. An attractive explanation of the complex connections between the various books connected with the name of John is to be found in the suggestion that there was in Ephesus a 'school' of Christian thinking associated with and growing out of the work of John, the disciple of Jesus. He served as the theological mentor of a whole group of Christians, and was the source of the information contained in the fourth gospel (see John 21:24), but the literature as we know it now was the product of this 'school' rather than of just one individual.

In dealing with John's Gospel it was suggested that it could have been first written in what might be called a 'Palestinian edition' and, if so, then the gospel would possibly be the first of these books to have been edited and reissued from the school in Ephesus. Perhaps its message was subsequently misunderstood and misapplied by its new readers. In a Jewish context, the contrasts between darkness and light, truth and error, life and death were all ethical contrasts, whereas the same terms had always been used by Greek thinkers to describe the cosmological distinction between the divine world of spirit, in which God lives, and the evil world of matter, where we live. Some

Greek readers of the gospel could easily have been misled by these terms, and that misunderstanding ultimately led them to the position adopted by the Docetists. The way the gospel emphasizes the present reality of the resurrection in the life of Christian believers would also lend colour to such speculations.

In response to this growing threat, 'the Elder' (presumably a prominent member of the Johannine school, if not John himself) wrote 2 John to warn against such false teaching. But things went from bad to worse, the false teachers broke away from the church to form their own sect, and 1 John was written as a more theological response to the problem. Not only was the Docetic view of Jesus challenged, but it was now emphasized that the resurrection hope was very much something tangible and future, and not just a part of the present spiritual experience of Christians.

If anything like this reconstruction is correct, the date we give to these letters will depend on the date assigned to the gospel. The kind of teaching opposed in 1 John is certainly more advanced than that encountered by Paul in Corinth. There is a clear idea of 'heresy' in 1 John, but it is not as complex or as well developed as we find in the second century. Since the heretics opposed in 1 John seem to have a number of features in common with those mentioned in Revelation, a date sometime towards the end of the first century is perhaps the nearest guess we can make.

clear. Like every other New Testament writer, John was convinced that mystical experiences, however elevated, would only have meaning if they could be integrated into Christian belief on the one hand, and expressed in appropriate lifestyles and behaviour on the other. It would be of no value talking about being liberated into the world of light, unless God's light truly informed and inspired behaviour, and to say that mystical experiences actually release men and women from the power of evil is dismissed as unrealistic and untrue, for human experience more commonly demonstrates that it is not possible for a person to make themselves totally perfect and free from the influence of sin (1 John 1).

True Christians must 'live just as Jesus Christ did', but they must also face up to the reality of their moral poverty, and accept the forgiveness which only Jesus can give (2:1–6). Living like Jesus is a practical affair: it is a matter of loving other people, and this in turn means that anyone who despises others (as did the Docetists) can hardly claim to be doing God's will (2:7–14). In reality, they are just indulging their own selfishness (2:15–17).

The fact that such people could ever have been a part of the church should serve to emphasize that the day of judgment is not far off (2:18–19). The others must not be intimidated by them, for whatever the sectarians might claim, those left in the church are the true recipients of the Holy Spirit, and they are the ones who have been accepted by God (2:20–29). Not that they have done anything to deserve that love, but having now been adopted as God's children, they should ensure that they continue to do God's will (3:1–10). Taking their example from Christ's love for them, they must love one another (3:11–18), and then

---

Authors and dates

Neither Jude nor 2 Peter contains any information at all that might link them to specific events or people in the early church. The only way their background can be understood is by trying to fit them into what is known about the development of the early churches in general. Several indications seem to suggest that both these books belong to the end of the New Testament period, rather than the time of the apostles themselves:

● Unlike Paul (and 1 John), Jude does not set out to argue with his opponents. He simply denounces them, and asserts that the answer to their problems is a return to 'the faith which once and for all God has given' (Jude 3). We have seen, in a previous chapter, that the development of

a standard form of belief like this was one of the things that characterized the emerging institutional church at the end of the first century.

● Jude 17 also indicates a date later than the age of the apostles, when the writer refers to 'what you were told in the past by the apostles of our Lord Jesus Christ'. Of course, that might refer to some occasion on which the readers had actually met the apostles themselves, but the same cannot be said of the reference to Paul in 2 Peter 3:14–16, where Paul's letters are mentioned as a recognized and well-known collection of writings, and are also classified as 'scripture'. Paul's letters were probably not gathered together in a collection until after his death, and it is reasonably certain that it would have taken longer still for them to

they can be sure that they are truly living in harmony with the Holy Spirit, and in personal union with God (3:19–24).

The author keeps returning to the theme that telling the true from the false is not just a matter of human judgment, but is a test of belief that can distinguish false prophets from true believers: 'Anyone who acknowledges that Jesus Christ came as a human being has the Spirit who comes from God. But anyone who denies this about Jesus does not have the Spirit from God' (4:2–3). Having God's Spirit naturally leads to love, just as God's own being is love (4:7–21). It also leads to obedience to God's commands, and to final victory over all that is opposed to God's ways of doing things (5:1–5). With this assurance, true Christians can be certain that they will know and understand God in a way that the Docetists never could (5:6–21).

Jude and 2 Peter

The influence of false teachers is also the subject of two of the most obscure books of the New Testament: Jude and 2 Peter. These books clearly belong together, for almost the whole of Jude (in a slightly modified form) is contained in 2 Peter. But otherwise, neither book contains any information to help us identify their original readers.

The way in which Jude and 2 Peter oppose false teachers suggests that they originated in a situation quite similar to that dealt with in the opening chapters of the book of Revelation. The term *gnosis* ('knowledge') is not actually mentioned, but these teachers are described in Jude 19 as 'psychics' ('controlled by their natural desires'), and we know that this was

---

be regarded as 'scripture' in any authoritative sense.

These facts are often taken to indicate that both books must be dated sometime in the second century, even perhaps as late as AD150, though there are difficulties about quite such a late date:
● It seems likely that 2 Peter was used (along with other New Testament books) by the unknown author of a work called *The Apocalypse of Peter*. But this is commonly dated sometime in the period between AD100 and AD135, and so 2 Peter can hardly be later than that.
● There is also the fact that the description of the false teachers in Jude and 2 Peter is quite different from any known second-century heresy. There is no hint even of a Docetic view of Jesus, let

alone of the more complex theories of the classical Gnostic systems.
● There is also no trace of much of the apparatus of the second-century church. There is a consciousness of a fixed body of Christian doctrine, but no indication of an organized ministry in the church. Both Jude and 2 Peter appeal to their readers on a moral basis rather than on the basis of their authors holding any position of authority.

A minority of scholars, therefore, have tried to explain the origin of these books by understanding them in the context of a much earlier age. Certainly, they both seem to be claiming to be the work of people who flourished in the age of the apostles themselves. 'Jude, servant of Jesus Christ, and brother of James' (Jude 1) is a

a technical term used by later Gnostics. These people certainly laid a great emphasis on their own spiritual experience (Jude 8), and they argued that because they themselves had been 'raised' to a new level of spiritual life, they had also been released from the normal constraints of Christian morality (Jude 12–13, 16, 18, 23). But all this was unacceptable to those in the mainstream of the church. Jude reminds his readers that, even in Old Testament times, people had suffered divine punishment for the same kind of wrongdoing and, unless they were prepared to repent, they could expect to share the same fate (Jude 8–16).

2 Peter also suggests that these people were denying the reality of the future coming of Jesus (3:1–18). No doubt they argued that, since they themselves had already been spiritually 'raised' to heaven, there would be no further need for the kind of literal resurrection hope held by the majority of the early Christians. In any case, they said, nothing had happened, even though the church had fervently expected Jesus to return in glory. This argument had first been put forward by Paul's opponents in Corinth, but 2 Peter 3:8 introduces a new answer to it, by asserting that God's timescale is not the same as a human calendar: 'There is no difference in the Lord's sight between one day and a thousand years.' The fact that the end has not yet arrived does not mean that God's promises have failed to be fulfilled. On the contrary, the delay in the coming of Jesus is itself to be seen as an expression of God's patience in allowing people more time to change their ways.

Jude does not describe the beliefs of these heretics so precisely. He simply asserts that they 'reject Jesus Christ, our only Master and Lord' (Jude 4). It seems likely that these false teachers had not gone quite as

---

Authors and dates
continued

description that invites readers to imagine it must be that Jude, who is named in the gospels as a brother of Jesus and of James in Mark 6:3, while 'Simon Peter' is clearly intended to identify the author of 2 Peter as the apostle himself (2 Peter 1:1). But there are other matters to be taken into account:

● The early church had a number of doubts about both these books. Jude is mentioned occasionally by early Christian writers, but 2 Peter is mentioned nowhere before the works of Origen (AD185–254), and as late as the fourth century both of them were regarded either as spurious or of doubtful value. This at the very least must suggest that they were not generally supposed to be the writings of leaders of the first generation of Christians.

● Coupled with this, there is general agreement among scholars of all opinions that if 1 Peter is the work of Peter, the disciple of Jesus, then 2 Peter is not. Many writers in the early church were perplexed by the differences between the two, for in style of writing, theological emphasis and general outlook they are so different that it is impossible to think the same person wrote them both. If we are correct to connect 1 Peter with Peter himself, then we must look elsewhere for an explanation of 2 Peter.

One possible solution might be indicated by the statement of Jude 3, where the writer of Jude reports that he was in the process of writing a letter to his readers, when he suddenly realized a more urgent need to communicate with them

far as those in 1 John. They had not challenged the church's beliefs on a theological level, by declaring that Jesus was not the Son of God come as a human person, but instead (like the heretics mentioned in Revelation 2:14), they had 'given themselves over to the error that Balaam committed' (Jude 11; Numbers 22:1–35). As we have already seen, that was more of a moral and practical problem.

As the years passed, the church had to change and adapt itself to deal with new threats, and take advantage of new opportunities. But it never forgot that its thinking and behaviour must always be firmly anchored in the experiences and outlook of those first followers who had actually known Jesus. Had it not been for the continuing commitment of a small group of Palestinian peasants, the wider world would never have heard this life changing message. It was not easy for them, for their courage and boldness were regularly rewarded with persecution, and even death. But their own experience of Jesus was such that they had no thought of turning back. They knew that Jesus was not dead, but alive, and working in power in their own lives through the presence of the Spirit. Not only did this inspire them to great exploits, but it also strengthened them in the face of trials. Perhaps it is appropriate that one of the most striking ascriptions of praise to Christ in the entire New Testament should be found at the end of this most cryptic of New Testament writings: 'To the one who is able to keep you from falling, and to bring you faultless and joyful before God's glorious presence – to the only God our Saviour, through Jesus Christ our Lord, be glory, majesty, might and authority, from all ages past, and now, and for ever and ever!' (Jude 24–25).

---

immediately, in response to which he wrote the letter of Jude itself. What, then, was the original letter that he was busy writing? In view of the close connections between them, could it have been 2 Peter – and further, could it be that the earlier letter referred to in 2 Peter 3:1 was not 1 Peter, as has generally been supposed, but Jude? Jude could have been writing as Peter's representative, for Acts 15:14 mentions the habit of leaders of the Jewish church of referring to Peter as 'Simon', which might then also explain the unusual use of that name in the opening sentence of 2 Peter.

Part of the difficulty with such a precise account of the origins of 2 Peter and Jude is that virtually nothing at all is known about the activities of the Jude who was the brother of James and of Jesus. But it might be possible to imagine that Jude and 2 Peter both originate from a group of Peter's disciples, in much the same way as the Johannine letters appear to have originated from a 'school' of John's disciples. This could account for both the similarities and the differences between 1 and 2 Peter. It could also explain why certain sections of 2 Peter (like the description of the transfiguration of Jesus in 1:16–18) have struck many readers as authentic reminiscences of Peter himself. Perhaps what we have in both these short letters is a fresh application of the teaching of Peter to the concerns and interests of a Hellenistic Jewish Christian congregation somewhere in Asia Minor towards the end of the first century.

31 Reading and Understanding the New Testament.

The New Testament can be a frustrating book as well as a source of enlightenment. As we have seen, it is not one book at all, but a collection of twenty-seven writings compiled by different people at diverse times and places during the course of the first Christian century. In addition, the books themselves all have their own distinctive characteristics. Some of them, such as the gospels and Acts, contain narrative, while others are letters – either real letters like those written by Paul, or literary epistles like Hebrews, with few or no allusions to actual people. Even within individual books, there can be various literary styles. The gospels, for example, contain parables and stories, as well as teaching and the personal reflections of the evangelists on the lasting significance of what they report. Moreover, the question of how the New Testament should be understood is not only concerned with matters related to the different genres or literary styles to be found in its pages, but also relates to important considerations of ideological perspective and cultural change.

Beginning where we are

This book has been written from a Christian perspective. Though the preceding chapters have considered historical and literary questions related to the compilation of the New Testament, this has been accompanied by an exploration of the message of these books, which is motivated by a conviction that this message still has relevance for life at the beginning of the twenty-first century. Within this frame of reference, three underlying assumptions have been important:

■ For Christians, the New Testament is not just a collection of writings documenting the rise of the Christian church, it is also 'scripture', that is, it is in some way authoritative for the ongoing life of the Christian community. To a greater or lesser extent, therefore, this assumption implies that, as the New Testament is read and understood, it will serve as some sort of paradigmatic guideline or model for Christian belief today. If this is one of the purposes for which we read these books, we cannot limit ourselves to exploring them only in their literary and historical contexts. We must also explore their sociological, cultural and relational contexts, as they pertain to the spiritual search of real people in the real world, whether ancient or modern.

■ This principle leads to another, namely that modern Christians need somehow to be continuous with their roots and their heritage. To treat the New Testament as scripture means that there should be some demonstrable connection between what the church is today, and the message of Jesus and the life of the early church, together with whatever other spiritual streams have fed into these over the centuries. It is this connection with its history that allows today's church to claim with integrity that it is still, in some meaningful sense, 'Christian'.

■ The New Testament cannot and should not be separated from its total spiritual context, as if its authority and meaning were somehow insulated from other aspects of Christian faith and practice. These books form an important part of the Christian world-view, but they do not stand alone. They are part of a bigger picture and, in the context of Christian belief, their message integrates with a recognition that, because this is God's world, God is at work in circumstances and situations that can be far removed from overtly Christian influences, as well as taking account of the spirituality of those who struggle still to follow Jesus. In other words, in arriving at a fully comprehensive expression of Christian faith, the New Testament stories have to be related to a creation-centred spirituality which recognizes God's universal presence, as well as interacting with the continuing experiences of Christian people. The diagram illustrates this.

Starting points

In approaching the New Testament from this standpoint, it is important to be honest about our own presuppositions. There are many ways to read and interpret the New Testament, and Christians have no monopoly on it. Though so-called presuppositionless exegesis has often been flaunted as the only way to understand the text, the whole notion of a totally detached interpreter has deep flaws. It is neither desirable nor possible to have no starting points, and to pretend that 'objectivity' in understanding means starting with no convictions or opinions is pointless and unconvincing. No one can divorce themselves from who they actually are, and who they are becoming. Understanding any text begins with understanding ourselves, and in this context being honest about our prior faith – or lack of it – is going to be central to the enterprise of interpretation. We all have filters built into our lives, which serve to divert and process information reaching us – things like our basic values and beliefs about life, our own experiences and learning, the store of all those things we

Reading the New Testament is not primarily an exercise in ancient history, but is intrinsically connected to God's activity in the world, and the perceptions of the reader.

believe to be 'true', together with our feelings about those beliefs. The combination of these is what makes each individual's personality unique. Knowing and recognizing our own particular filters – their weaknesses as well as their strengths – is basic to all good interpretation. When scholars deny that they have such presuppositions, they lack credibility, and generally end up reaching untenable conclusions.

Reading and understanding the New Testament is, therefore, a two-way process. We bring something to the task (ourselves), and we hope to receive something from it. We speak to these books, and we expect them to speak to us. On this view, interpretation is a dynamic process, not a static one, and it is a holistic process, because it connects with other aspects of the reader's life and experience. This is quite different from the model that has been inherited from the Enlightenment, with its self-confident assumption that 'objectivity', in the sense of total detachment from the text, was both possible and desirable. That approach led to a way of looking at the text, which (like much within the world-view of recent Western culture) was mechanical and distant from human experience, because it was based on a linear view of reality that allowed the interpreter to think he or she stood completely outside the interpretive process, as the diagram shows.

The historical-critical method encouraged the mistaken idea that it is possible to interpret the text without personally engaging with its message.

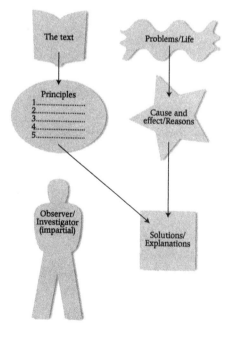

This approach has its strengths, not least of which is its ability to highlight the concerns of the ancient world in which the New Testament books originated. But, by emphasizing interpretation as a window onto the ancient world, it can make it correspondingly more difficult to understand how the text can speak to the human condition in a time and place far removed from the first-century Roman empire. A more sustainable method of reading will take account of the contemporary setting right from the outset, and will view the text as a two-way mirror. It will certainly be possible to look through the text and back into its own world, but there will also be a conscious acceptance of the possibility that the reality of our own world can be reflected there, and the encounter of the two can then be used as a starting point for asking new questions of the text, which will go beyond only historical matters. This approach owes a good deal to the insights of non-Western Christians, wrestling with the reality of social deprivation and economic challenge, and seeking to use those experiences as hermeneutical tools with which to read the New Testament text. Robert McAffee Brown has described the process succinctly: 'We bring our experience *to* the Bible, we draw new insights *from* the Bible, we go back to our own situation *with* the Bible, and see it all in a new way.' A different kind of diagram can illustrate this.

Influences

What does 'objectivity' mean in this context? A great deal of postmodern philosophy now claims that there is no such thing as objectivity, and therefore there is no point in trying to achieve it. But most ordinary people still think it is important to try to understand things 'as they truly are', with as little interference as possible from our presuppositions (which can also be prejudices). Maybe the nearest we can come to that sense of standing back from the subject-matter of study, and being as detached as possible in order to see what the text is about, is to recognize our own starting points, and then make due allowance for them – perhaps asking tougher questions, being more provocative in the way we deal with the evidence, when we find ourselves arriving at conclusions that seem to match our preconceived notions too closely. If that is the case, then we need to have some idea what kind of personal factors might be operating to influence the way we read a text from the New Testament. There are several obvious ones:

Readers might begin their reading of the Bible at different places, but a holistic understanding will always integrate its message with the rest of life.

■ Our social context has more power than we often realize. As people throughout the non-Western world have turned to the Bible in ever increasing numbers, it has become clear how our own cultural context can influence our understanding. Rich, white Western people tend to see things differently from economically deprived people in other parts of the world – or, indeed, from poor people in Western society. The story of the good Samaritan (Luke 10:29–37) has a different meaning for Westerners – who generally read it and aspire to be like the Samaritan – than for others, who are more likely to identify with the person left for dead by the roadside. Western people take it for granted that, if they are anyone in that story, they must be in a position of power and control and so, even if they might be reluctant to claim identification with the Samaritan, they are more likely to debate whether they are like the priest or the Levite than to imagine they could be the person who is beaten up. The connection of that with the recent history of Western imperialism and colonialism is too obvious to require further explanation.

■ Who we are in terms of gender and age also makes a difference. A man will read the story of Jesus' encounter with a woman caught in the act of adultery (John 7:53 – 8:11) in a different way from a woman – though both of them might struggle with the way Jesus handled the situation, with many men still thinking that the woman got off too lightly, while women might wonder why, in the face of a female in danger of immediate execution, Jesus played games by drawing pictures and words in the sand. A child would perhaps see something different again – maybe not appreciating what the issue was, but recognizing that, by doing something inherently childlike, Jesus had got the woman out of a very sticky situation.

■ Our own state of mind can also affect how we read the New Testament. In previous chapters we have noted more than once how Martin Luther's chronic depression led him to imagine that Paul suffered from the same ailment, and so he portrayed him as a defeated, broken man, oppressed by a narrow-minded Judaism in much the same way as Luther believed himself to have been treated by the medieval church. Those who bring a sense of their own lack of value to the New Testament can easily exaggerate some of its teaching on sin, while those who are uncomfortable with their own feelings will be inclined to play down the sense of human interaction that was found in the early Christian communities, and others might be tempted to emphasize the futuristic aspect of eschatology over and against the realized aspect, because they find life in a material world burdensome and challenging.

■ The same thing can be said about mental attitudes. For generations, the more obviously supernatural dimensions of the New Testament have been marginalized by Western interpreters. Christians have looked at the prominence of charismatic endowments in the writings of Paul, felt this was not to their taste, and therefore sought for ways to justify their disappearance from the life of the church. Others regularly did the same with the miracles of Jesus, while no one ever quite knew what to make of Paul's claim to out-of-body experiences as part of his spirituality (2 Corinthians 12:1–10). In the light of the rise of the New Age, and increasing awareness of such things from cultures all over the world, few people would want to adopt either of those positions today. It is obvious that the scholars of a previous generation were too much influenced by the prevailing rationalism of the time – and, of course, it might turn out to be the case that some today are too willing to embrace such things more because of cultural pressures than anything else.

■ The influence of a rationalist-materialist world-view has been especially powerful during the last two or three centuries. Reality has been understood in such a way that the only things that really mattered were 'facts', defined in a particular way that could be scientifically verified. In the hands of sceptics, this often became a tool which could be used to place a historical or literary question mark against just about anything in the New Testament, as we saw in dealing with the question of the historical Jesus. But in the hands of Christians, this same world-view regularly led to the conclusion that 'truth' is something that can somehow be proved by logic and argument and, therefore, by definition any literary analysis of the New Testament, which might suggest some of it is in a different genre from narrative history, is to be rejected. There have even been those who have insisted that, since on this view

René Descartes (1596–1650), whose ideas encouraged the notion that autonomous, rational individuals should be able to escape their presuppositions and view things objectively.

fictional material could not be a vehicle for truth, all the heroes of Jesus' parables must have been real people who did what is recorded of them in the stories he told.

A major weakness of recent methods of interpretation has been their uncritical acceptance of a reductionist approach to knowledge, which has assumed that things can be understood best by taking them to pieces. This had its origins in the scientific methods of people like René Descartes (1596–1650) and Sir Francis Bacon (1561–1626), and the further assumption that the best place for such dismantling to take place is in a laboratory, a place from which all external influences have been excluded. That scientific paradigm has now been discarded, and it is widely recognized that, even in a laboratory, the presence of the investigator makes a difference to what can happen. But it lives on in much New Testament interpretation, and even those who are Christian believers frequently think it is important to lay aside all religious beliefs or presuppositions in order to unearth what is true. Study of literary texts more broadly (not only religious ones) has demonstrated that reading and understanding is a more holistic business. Since the texts arose out of human experience in the first place, the reader's own experience of life is going to be a key factor in understanding them. That in turn means that readers interact with the text, in much the same way as Bell's theorem describes how scientists interact with the materials with which they experiment. The way a person feels about a text is of fundamental importance, and their own emerging world-view (whether that be Christian or some other) will play a part in the act of interpretation. Faith (or doubt) is not something to be hidden, but to be acknowledged as a significant element in the process of reading and understanding. The idea that a Christian and an atheist could – if both were being totally objective – reach the same conclusions on the meaning of a New Testament passage is nonsense.

The key questions to be asked of any passage in the New Testament are, therefore:

■ What is the text saying? That is, what are the actual words, as contained in the most reliable ancient manuscripts?
■ What is the text's context? That is, what are the historical circumstances and literary style?
■ What is my context? That is, who am I as a person? What expectations, presuppositions and prejudices am I bringing to it?
■ What is our context? What is the wider social group within which I belong, and which is affecting my own perceptions?

Sir Francis Bacon (1561–1626).

The text's own context

The writers of all these books lived in a very different world from the one we know, and in order to have a full appreciation of the

New Testament, we need to take account of the specific cultural circumstances in which it originated. In reality, there are several different aspects of the text's own context, which should be considered.

The sociological context

This collection of writings as a whole was brought together as the literary heritage of a religious group, as a testimony to the faith of the early church. While it might be possible to extrapolate historical data from the various books, it is always important to remember that they were not primarily written to provide such information. Moreover, the church was certainly not in the mainstream of Roman culture and, in some situations, might even have had to operate in a clandestine way. Never fully accepted by the empire, these Christian communities were also struggling to define their identity over and against the social context of their origins in Judaism, and therefore the question of identity, and defining the boundaries of the church – both theological and cultural – was a major concern throughout the first century. In addition, the different churches consisted of people drawn from diverse socio-economic circumstances, though with a clear preponderance of middle and upper-class people, especially in the urban centres of Asia Minor and the western empire. Some leaders straddled these various spheres of influence. For example, Peter began in the culture of rural Galilee, then interacted with a different style of Jewish society in Jerusalem and Judea, before involvement with the multiracial church in Antioch, and then moving on to the great urban centres elsewhere in the Roman world. To understand how these people perceived and experienced God, we need to have some degree of familiarity with an extensive span of historical and cultural circumstances – while recognizing that we are ourselves bringing our own cultural baggage to the enterprise.

World-view

The first Christians lived long before the emergence of modern science and technology, and held the typical ancient understanding of human life as being at the centre of a three tier universe. The flat disc of the earth was sandwiched between the murky underworld beneath and the dome of the heavens above, beyond which was a dark and unknowable chaos. This was a magical world, inhabited by deities and demons of many different kinds. Petronius once wrote that, on the streets of Rome, it was easier to meet a god than a person! (*Satyricon* 17). In this context, religion and everyday life were intertwined, and everything had a spiritual aspect to it. In ancient farming, for example, the sowing of seeds was a religious act, requiring honour to be paid to the gods in an appropriate way in order to ensure the success of the crops. Building a house, going on a journey, forming a relationship – all these things had intrinsically religious dimensions built into them. Though at a philosophical level the prevailing world-view imagined a great separation between the material and the spiritual, in everyday life these two stood alongside each other, as just different sides of the same coin. It takes considerable effort for people who live in a more fragmented culture to understand how people in the ancient world might have reflected on and reacted to matters of life, death and meaning.

Personal perceptions

The expectations of the average person hardly changed from the start to the finish of the Bible story. In the gospels, the concerns of a peasant economy predominate, and this naturally affects the imagery used to illustrate the message of Jesus. The imagery changed as Paul and others took their message into larger centres of population, but there is still a strong influence of rural ways of thinking running throughout the New Testament. For many Christians, the city was a place of danger – a place where Jesus had been crucified, and where persecution was often at its most violent. The book of Revelation highlights this better than most, with its cryptic references to Rome as 'Babylon' – something that had featured as a symbol of destructive urban influences as far back as the story of the Tower of Babel in Genesis 11. Eventually, Revelation 21:9 – 22:5 depicts the life of the city being redeemed, but the idea that a rural life is to be preferred over an urban one has been surprisingly persistent through much of Christian history. All this was reinforced by the expectations and horizons that were available to most people. Few people were regular travellers – Jesus himself would have been typical, for he hardly moved at all from his home area – and, in reflecting on the extensive travels of Paul, it is hard to believe that he would not have been familiar with so unsophisticated a mode of transportation as a bicycle. Perhaps as part of this heritage, home and family life were always at the centre of things, and the home was a major focus for spirituality in both the Jewish and the Roman context. Indeed, in the cities of the empire, many churches were, in effect, just one part of the typical Roman household, and several New Testament passages describe the heads of households deciding that their entire community would convert to Christianity. As well as profoundly influencing the way the Christian communities operated, this feature probably also had an impact on the way that at least some parts of the New Testament evolved. In the context of home based groups, the oral traditions of storytelling would thrive very easily, and doubtless this was how many New Testament narratives, especially the gospels, were shaped and handed on in the early years.

A missionary of the Middle Ages tells how he found the place where the Earth touches Heaven.

Discovering the message

It might seem as if interpreting the New Testament is too daunting a business to be tackled at all by ordinary people. In some ways this is true, for there is a certain body of historical knowledge with which we need to be familiar in order to begin to understand these writings fully in their context. That is why this book has laid so much emphasis on the presentation and explanation of such information. But when we think of these books as part of Christian scripture, things start to look more hopeful. Three considerations can help to guide creative reflection on the message of the New Testament writings:

■ We need to read these books with some sense of empathy towards those who wrote them. It is impossible to divorce the New Testament from the processes of thought, experience, faith and interpretation that produced it in the first place. The writers and their own perceptions and expectations of life, along with their own personal stories, are all an intrinsic part of the mixture. When Christians read the New Testament, they do regard its books in a different way than others might, because they are themselves part of the same community of faith which created them. Many things have changed in the intervening centuries, of course, not least our world-view. But insofar as they are able to, today's readers

---

The historical-critical method

In dealing with the gospels, reference has been made to various interpretive tools that have commonly been used in analysing their message: source criticism, form criticism, and redaction criticism among them, together with the kind of historical criticism implied by the long story of the quest for the historical Jesus. All these methods are relatively recent developments in New Testament study, and owe their origin and rationale to the philosophical ideas of the European Enlightenment. Starting with the growing awareness among European people of the existence of other continents and cultures, and continuing through the next four or five centuries with the development of science and technology, Western people managed to convince themselves that their new ways of doing things would deliver the human race from, what they came to regard as, its previous captivity to mythology and superstition. Whereas previously, people had tended to look to religion to help explain the meaning of things, now it seemed as if the unaided power of human reason would be able not only to discover new things about the world, but also to enable people to live in a different way, reliant only on themselves. In this new world, for the first time in history, things would be understood as they actually were, rather than as they might be explained by religious teachers who in turn could only justify their opinions by reference to God as their source. As purely rational principles were applied to the study of the human condition, it was only a matter of time before even religion itself would be subjected to the same kind of rigorous scrutiny. This was the context in which the quest for the historical Jesus had its origins, and the historical-critical method of interpreting the Bible was to flourish.

By adopting the scientific optimism of the day, based on the assumption that everything can be traced back to some relationship of cause and effect, and therefore everything can be resolved by the

need to be open to hearing what the New Testament writers were saying within their own cultural context, while recognizing that all world-view perceptions (including our own) are tentative.

■ Theologically, the message of the New Testament needs to be set within a larger frame of reference. These writings themselves bear witness to the possibility of God being known in other places, most notably through what later generations have called 'natural theology' or 'creation centred spirituality'. The stories of Jesus' birth in Matthew 2:1–12 tell of eastern astrologers travelling in search of the Christ child, on the basis of their understanding of the star which led them. In his parables, Jesus uses imagery from the natural world in a way that makes it obvious he regarded the life of plants and animals as somehow reflecting aspects of the nature of God. In a previous chapter, we noted Paul's starting points for sharing his faith with others, and his policy of accepting other people's spirituality as pegs on which he might hang the gospel. The story told in Acts 17:16–31, of his mission to Athens, is a classic example in which he had no hesitation in identifying Jesus with the 'unknown god' on the assumption that, if this is God's world, presumably God could be expected to work in the most unlikely of places. In Romans 1:18 – 2:16 he explains the thinking behind this, and

---

application of human reason and logic, scholars of the New Testament devised their own procedures for reading texts which, it was imagined, would give unhindered access to the early church as it actually was, rather than as later generations of Christians might have imagined it to be. A key part of this process would involve setting the various New Testament books in their original historical and literary context, asking how they were written, why they were written, to whom and by whom, and for what purpose. Questions like this have featured prominently in our study of the New Testament here, and there can be no doubt that, by comparison with some of the methods of interpretation that went before, this led to significant advances in understanding. Previous generations had often ignored the historical setting of the New Testament altogether, which left the books open to subjective perceptions of their meaning being imposed on them by interpreters. Now, almost for the first time, there would be some sense of boundaries

within which it would be legitimate to operate, boundaries concerned firstly with the historical setting and secondly with critical (in the sense of detached and analytical) reflection on the meaning of these writings – hence the emerging description of this way of proceeding as the 'historical-critical method'.

Great advances have taken place as a result of a process which stressed objective detachment, and historical and literary context, and we have not only noted some of them, but we have also taken advantage of them throughout this book. But the historical-critical method was not quite what its exponents claimed it to be. In particular, it was not value-free, but was actually part of a struggle within European culture to break away from any sense of knowledge coming from anywhere other than the human spirit. E.B. Pusey (1800–82) described it at the time as 'a child of disbelief', and regarded it as an effort not to build up faith, but to destroy it. More recently, Helmut Koester has confirmed the ideological bias of this

places the knowledge of God gained through nature and conscience alongside the Old Testament Law as an equally valid revelation of the divine will. In reading the New Testament, it is a mistake to exclude this bigger picture of God's activity in the world. Ultimately, the New Testament needs to be set in a context of God's work that is much broader than itself.

■ The New Testament books cannot be divorced from their human origins. Many efforts to define the inspired and inspirational character of these writings have sought to reduce them to a collection of rational propositions, which can stand alongside other similar propositional notions of truth, emanating from the philosophical nostrums of the European Enlightenment. It is perfectly natural for Christians to want Bible interpretation to be as rational as possible but, in the understandable effort of doing so, it is easy to undermine two convictions that are central to Christian faith:

Paradoxical though it might seem, weakness and vulnerability are central aspects of the New Testament's message. At the heart of all it says is the incarnation, with its amazing claim that God was best known in this world not through a rich and powerful figure, but through one who came as a child and lived a life of relative obscurity. From the

---

The historical-critical method *continued*

method of interpretation, 'designed as a hermeneutical tool for the liberation from conservative prejudice and from the power of ecclesiastical and political institutions'.

This need not surprise anyone, for we all bring our own personal, philosophical baggage to every enterprise in which we engage. Stunningly obvious though that might be, it is only in relatively recent times that the implications of this for scholarly analysis have become clear. The optimistic atmosphere of the nineteenth and early twentieth centuries encouraged previous generations to imagine that they could indeed stand outside of themselves and see things 'as they really are'. That is why the procedures of the historical-critical method were so universally adopted, and why it was taken for granted that they could be used to question so many matters that previously had seemed settled. As the twentieth century progressed, it became increasingly obvious that human reason could not solve all mysteries, nor was it necessarily going to make the world a better place. Now, the rational approach

is itself being questioned, and the whole nature of New Testament study is far less stable than it once was – so much so that it is difficult to predict where it might go in the future. One thing is certain: that we should not now make a similar mistake to those who in the past have imagined that everything that went before them was to be rejected. No doubt the historical-critical method has many flaws – some of which have repeatedly been spelled out here – but it is important not to lose sight of its benefits. By anchoring study of the New Testament in the historical and social context in which it was compiled, great advances have taken place, and these should not be jettisoned just because we can now see that previous scholars were not as dispassionate as they thought they were. What is now required is a recognition of what they got right, an honesty about what they got wrong – and an openness which will not imagine that the exercise of rationality by itself is going to provide the answer to every human question.

A synagogue in Galilee.

perspective of Western images of power, control and rationality, this is a very weak message. But if the medium is indeed the message, then we need not be surprised if the Bible also seems to share this quality of strength within weakness.

This fluid, person-centred aspect of the New Testament is also one of its great strengths. The epistles in particular give a first-hand glimpse into the faith, doubt and struggles of those who wrote them, and those to whom they were addressed. They show real people working through a process of spiritual and personal development, discovering what it could mean for them to follow Jesus in many different situations. Readers of all generations have been able to make connections with them, for people of faith in all times and places wrestle with the same questions. If the New Testament had been couched in the propositional concepts of philosophical discourse, it would have ceased to engage with the human condition long ago, for there has always been a limited number of people who search for the meaning of life in strictly abstract, analytical terms. But, as a book of stories, the Christian canon speaks as powerfully to people today as it ever did. The stories of Jesus, together with the stories of his early followers, provide a bridge across the centuries to the human stories of today, rooted in the underlying conviction that, since this is God's world, God may be discovered in the most unexpected of places.

The text of the New Testament

None of the original documents of the New Testament books still exist. Modern translations are all based on copies of copies, which date back to the earliest centuries of the Christian era. To a generation accustomed to instant access to printed books and digital information, this can seem a distinct disadvantage, for how can we be sure that what the authors originally wrote has not been tampered with or somehow distorted in the process of transmission? Questions like this have to be put in perspective, and set in the context of other ancient literature. For example, Julius Caesar wrote in the first century BC, and less than a dozen manuscripts of his work now survive – the oldest of which was produced around AD800–900, almost 1,000 years after his time. Tacitus was a Latin author living towards the end of the first century AD, most of whose work is completely lost, and only two manuscripts survive – copies made in the ninth and eleventh centuries AD! The work of the Greek historian Thucydides (460–400BC) is contained in fewer than ten ancient manuscripts, the oldest of which dates from about AD900. Yet the accounts of these three authors are vital for our understanding of Graeco-Roman history and culture. By comparison, the New Testament is remarkably well served. There are many manuscripts dating from the period between AD200 and AD300, together with scraps of manuscripts which can be dated even earlier, one of them – the Rylands Papyrus of John's Gospel – originating in about AD130, which must have been less than fifty years after that gospel was written. In addition, there are many quotations from the New Testament included in the writings of early Christian authors.

The Rylands papyrus.

Ancient documents

Ancient books were commonly written on three different kinds of material:

Leather documents, made from the skins of animals, were used in Egypt from as early as 2800BC. According to the Talmud, all copies of the Jewish Law used in public worship were written on leather made from the skins of animals designated as 'clean', and stitched together into long rolls. There are no known leather New Testament documents.

Papyrus documents were made from the papyrus plant, which grew in the rivers and marshes of Egypt. The pith was cut into strips, which were laid in two layers, at right angles to one another, so that the fibres lay horizontally on one side and vertically on the other. The two layers were then fastened together by pressure and glue, so as to make sheets which could be attached side by side to form a long strip and rolled up. The height of the roll was limited to the usual length of the strips of pith, normally about ten inches, though a typical roll could be as long as thirty-five feet – large enough to contain the longest of the gospels. At a very early period (certainly by the second century), Christians had invented a new form of book, using papyrus sheets folded down the middle and stitched together like a modern book – the codex.

Vellum documents were written on animal skins, but were different from leather by not being tanned. Vellum was originally the skin of a calf, but skins of other young animals were also used. It proved to be a very durable medium, and by the fourth century it had replaced papyrus as the material most often used for significant books, including copies of the New Testament. The majority of early copies of the complete New Testament are on vellum, written in what is called uncial writing. This was a literary style of writing, which continued in use until the tenth century AD, when it was replaced by a cursive, or flowing script (technically known as minuscule writing), with smaller letters continuous with one another. This then continued to be used for copies of the Bible until the invention of printing in about 1450. The earliest New Testament manuscripts were all written without any punctuation, and often with no spaces at all between words, which creates its own problems of interpretation. Punctuation was added in due course and, though there were earlier divisions into sections, the present divisions into chapters dates only from the thirteenth century, while subdivision into verses was introduced in the sixteenth century.

New Testament texts

In textual studies of the New Testament, five types of source material are available.

Papyrus documents

Being a vegetable material, papyrus easily decomposed in damp climates, and most papyrus documents have, therefore, come from Egypt, where the dry, warm sand helped to preserve them. Almost seventy papyrus documents containing parts of the New Testament have been found there, varying from mere scraps like the Rylands Papyrus, which contains only five verses of John 16, to the Chester Beatty Papyrus II, which has eighty-six nearly perfect leaves of what was originally a codex of 104 pages, probably containing all the epistles of Paul. These papyrus documents were written between about the first half of the second century and the fourth century, or even later. The largest papyrus documents are:

● Chester Beatty Papyrus II, containing Paul's letters and dating from the beginning of the third century, more than a century earlier than the date of the great vellum codices.

● Chester Beatty Papyrus I, containing portions of the gospels and Acts, of similar date, and belonging to the collection of eleven codices of Christian writings dating from the second to the fourth centuries, acquired by Chester Beatty in about 1930 – hence the name.

● The Bodmer Papyrus has 108 pages which contain (with one missing section) the first fourteen chapters of John's Gospel,

and dates probably from the late second century.

Vellum codices

More than 250 of these are known, with the following being the most important of them:

● Codex Sinaiticus, which is always designated by the Hebrew letter aleph (א). This dates from the middle of the fourth century and contains the complete New Testament, as well as portions of the Old Testament, along with the Epistle of Barnabas and the Shepherd of Hermas. This is a large document, with pages 15 inches by 13 inches, and four columns of writing on each page. It came to light in 1844, when Constantin von Tischendorf was visiting the ancient monastery of St Catherine in the foothills of Mount Sinai and noticed some leaves of the Old Testament part of the codex in a basket about to be burned in the monastery furnace. After complex negotiations he managed to obtain the entire codex and, eventually, it was purchased by the British Museum in London, where it is still kept.

A page from Codex Sinaiticus, which contains the entire New Testament in Greek. It is written on vellum and dates from the 4th century.

The text of the
New Testament
continued

Codex Alexandrinus (referred to as A) dates from the first half of the fourth century, and also originally contained the complete Bible, along with two epistles of Clement of Rome and the *Psalms of Solomon*. Most of the latter, along with small sections of the New Testament, are now lost. It might have been written in Alexandria, Egypt, but it was from Constantinople that it was presented to Charles I of England, and it has been in the British Museum since its foundation. The text is generally regarded as less useful than what is contained in Codices Sinaiticus and Vaticanus.

● Codex Vaticanus (known as B) dates from the fourth century, and was also originally a complete Bible, from which most of Genesis, some of the Psalms, part of Hebrews, the pastoral epistles and Revelation have disappeared. It has been in the Vatican Library at Rome since 1431, and along with Codex Sinaiticus, is highly prized as the most authoritative ancient source for the text of the New Testament.

● Codex Bezae (known as D) probably dates from the fifth century. Its pages are smaller than the others, only 10 inches by 8 inches, and it has Greek and Latin text on opposite pages, though it only contains the gospels and Acts, with a few verses from the general epistles. Its early history is unknown, but it was bought at Lyons in France in 1562 by Theodore Beza, who presented it to the University of Cambridge in England. It is of great interest to textual scholars as it contains, particularly in Acts, a very different type of text from what is found in the other great codices.

● Codex Ephraemi (known as C) dates from the fifth century. It originally contained the whole Bible, but of 238 New Testament leaves only 145 remain, though these represent all the New Testament books, with the exception of 2 Thessalonians and 2 John. This codex is a palimpsest; vellum writing material was very valuable in the ancient world, and it was a common practice to erase the original writing and use it again for a new book. In this case, what had originally been a Bible was used for the works of St Ephraim of Syria – hence its name.

Minuscule manuscripts

There are almost 3,000 of these, mostly of later date. Scripture passages are also contained in many ancient lectionaries (selections for reading in church worship). One group of these manuscripts has special interest for scholars because it contains a distinctive form of text which might have been connected with the traditions of the church in Caesarea, but many of them are of a later date and are obviously copies of inferior manuscripts.

Early versions

Versions were translations of the New Testament from the original Greek into other languages. The most important ones are in Syriac, Coptic and Latin. A particularly interesting text is the *Diatessaron* of Tatian, which is a harmony of the four gospels compiled in the second century. For a long time, this work was known only through references made to it by early Christian authors and an Armenian commentary of the fourth century, which included lengthy quotations from it. Arabic and Coptic versions of this work have been found, and there is also a fragment of the text in Greek, which might suggest it was originally written in Greek, though Tatian himself was a Syrian, and Syria is certainly where it first circulated.

Quotations in early Christian writings

Many early Christian writers are witnesses to the text of the New Testament, through the quotations from it that they included in their own writings. Unfortunately, accurate quotation was not as much appreciated in the ancient world as it is today, which makes most of these examples of limited usefulness. The most important of these writers in relation to understanding the development of the textual traditions is Origen, who seems to have used one kind of text while he was living in Alexandria and then adopted a different one when he moved to Caesarea.

Scribes and copyists

Considering that all these documents were copied by hand, it is surprising how few and relatively unimportant are the differences between them. Substantial differences occur in well under 1 per cent of the entire text, and most of them are predictable errors that copyists might easily make. These include spelling mistakes, sometimes caused by a scribe writing down a word that was more familiar than the one that had actually been dictated. Sometimes a word, or even a whole line, was left out – an easy mistake to make when two consecutive lines began with the same word. The same word might be written twice over, or a sentence unconsciously altered to make it agree with the words of a similar sentence elsewhere.

This could happen very easily when the same story or saying occurred in slightly different words in one gospel than in the others. A note made by a reader in the margin could also be included in the main body of the text as if it were a part of it. This is probably what happened in the case of 1 John 5:7, which contains a clear statement of the later doctrine of the Trinity. This verse was included in the Latin Vulgate, and some other manuscripts used by the translators of the 1611 King James Version, but it does not appear in any of the oldest codices, which is why it is no longer included in more recent translations. Very occasionally, scholars suspect that a text has been changed a little to suit the copyist's theology. For instance, in some Latin versions of John 1:13 the plural 'were born' appears as the singular 'was born', in what looks like an effort to suggest a reference to Jesus' birth of a virgin.

Classifying texts

By comparing the actual words of different documents it has been possible to develop a system for classifying them into groups, on the assumption that if one particular ancient manuscript had an unusual reading, then all those that were copied from this one would be likely to have the same unusual reading. The definitive classification of texts was first set out in 1870 by Brooke Foss Westcott and F.J.A. Hort and, though some refinements have since been made, their description of four textual types remains the standard.

Syrian texts

These texts contain many readings not found in the oldest manuscripts or versions, but seem to have been used extensively from the fourth century onwards, particularly by writers living in the neighbourhood of Antioch. Westcott and Hort proposed that a revised text of the New Testament had been issued at Antioch towards the end of the third century, from which a great many of the minuscules now known were copied. These Syrian texts are of little value in helping to identify the original text of the various books, as their variant readings are presumably the work of the revisers at Antioch.

Western texts

These are best represented by the Codex Bezae and two others, and they are also found in the Old Latin and Syrian versions. These texts tend to include considerable additions not found in other texts. As this kind of textual tradition was the first to be translated into Latin, it is considered likely that it was used by churches in the western part of the Roman empire. Its additions typically take the form of circumstantial detail. So, for example, in Acts 12:10 it includes the information that when Peter escaped from prison he went down seven steps, while in Acts 19:9 it states that Paul taught in the lecture hall of Tyrannus from the fifth to the tenth hour, and in Acts 19:28 Demetrius is described as running out 'into the street' during the riot at Ephesus. These additions have generally not been taken seriously as part of the original text, though when this Western text omits something (for instance, the mention of a second cup at the last supper in Luke 22:20), its value is likely to be taken more seriously, for its

The text of the
New Testament
continued

general tendency is towards addition rather than omission.

Alexandrian texts

This type of text is found in the Codex Alexandrinus, and Codex Ephraemi, as well as in the writings of many Christian leaders who were resident in Egypt. Its distinctive characteristics are more related to style than subject matter, perhaps originating in the understandable concern of Christian scribes in the scholarly context of Alexandria to ensure that the text of their New Testament would be available in high quality Greek. If that was the reason for its production, then the Alexandrian texts obviously add little or nothing to our knowledge of the original text written by the New Testament authors.

Neutral texts

These are the ones which have most in common with other texts. Whenever a particular manuscript diverges from others in the same group, it generally reverts to this neutral text, which is the text represented by the two oldest and largest codices, Vaticanus and Sinaiticus. When these two agree (as they almost invariably do), they are likely to be as near to the original text of the New Testament as it is possible to be.

Textual study is ongoing, and two particular developments are worth commenting on:
● As well as the four classical text types listed above, it seems possible to identify another group, which shares some of the characteristics of both Neutral and Western texts. This is the so-called Caesarean text type. Some of the minuscule manuscripts have common peculiarities, such as the placing of the story of the woman taken in adultery, which in the received text (the basis for the King James Version) was at John 7:53 – 8:11, but which could also be placed after Luke 21:38, or even left out altogether. Luke 21:38 seems a more likely place for the story, as it is more in the style of Luke than of John. The Chester Beatty Papyrus I has a Caesarean text in Mark's Gospel, and one with some Caesarean characteristics in Luke

and John, although its text of Acts is Neutral. The precise characteristics of this textual style are still less clearly defined than the others, but when Origen left Alexandria and moved to Caesarea in AD231, his quotations from New Testament writings seem to show that he gave up using the Alexandrian text and used a different form of text similar to this – hence the reason why it has been called the Caesarean text, though it is not impossible that Origen might actually have taken it with him from Alexandria to Caesarea.
● The Western text has generally been accorded more value, the more it has been studied. Many early Christian writers seem to have used this Western text in quoting from the New Testament, and this suggests it must have been reasonably early in date. Moreover, much of the additional material found in it seems quite pointless unless it belonged to an original source; there is no obvious reason why anyone would wish to invent such details as the number of steps Peter took from prison, for example. Could it be that Luke wrote different drafts of Acts, and this textual tradition reflects one of them? The presence of a number of Aramaic turns of expression in the Western text also adds to the impression that it might be of early date.

For all that, the Neutral text is still regarded as the most authoritative, though textual experts are generally prepared to consider variations from it on good grounds. Textual criticism is a painstaking business and the value of each particular variant in the text must be decided on its own merits, by asking such questions as:
– Which reading gives the better sense?
– Which reading is least likely to have been made through a mistake in copying?
– Which reading is most likely to be due to later theological influences, such as Gnosticism?
– Which reading is supported by the oldest and most reliable manuscripts, even although it might not occur in the best examples of the Neutral text?

Other Books on the New Testament

General

Aune, D.E., *The New Testament in Its Literary Environment*, Philadelphia: Westminster, 1987.

Brown, Schuyler, *The Origins of Christianity*, New York: Oxford University Press, 1993.

Carson, D.A., Moo, D.J. and Morris, L., *An Introduction to the New Testament*, Grand Rapids: Zondervan, 1992.

Reumann, John, *Variety and Unity in New Testament Thought*, New York: Oxford University Press, 1991.

Schnelle, Udo, *The History and Theology of the New Testament Writings*, London: SCM, 1998.

Wright, N.T., *The New Testament and the People of God*, London: SPCK, 1992.

The World of the First Christians

GENERAL

Barrett, C.K., *The New Testament Background: Selected Documents*, London: SPCK, 1987.

Ferguson, Everett, *Backgrounds of Early Christianity*, Grand Rapids: Eerdmans, 1993.

Kee, Howard C., *Christian Origins in Sociological Perspective*, Philadelphia: Westminster Press; London: SCM Press, 1980.

Malina, Bruce J., *The New Testament World: Insights from Cultural Anthropology*, Louisville KY: Westminster John Knox Press, 1993.

Roetzel, C.J., *The World that Shaped the New Testament*, Atlanta: John Knox, 1985.

Stambaugh, J.E. and Balch, D., *The New Testament in Its Social Environment*, Philadelphia: Westminster, 1986.

JUDAISM

Chilton, Bruce and Neusner, Jacob, *Judaism in the New Testament*, New York: Routledge, 1995.

Dunn, J.D.G., *The Partings of the Ways: Between Christianity and Judaism and Their Significance for the Character of Christianity*, Philadelphia: Trinity Press International, 1991.

Hengel, Martin, *Judaism and Hellenism*, vols 1 and 2, Philadelphia: Fortress, 1974.

Maccoby, H., *Judaism in the First Century*, London: Sheldon, 1989.

Neusner, J., *Judaism in the Beginning of Christianity*, Philadelphia: Fortress, 1984.

GNOSTICISM AND HELLENISTIC SPIRITUALITY

Couliano, I.P., *The Tree of Gnosis*, San Francisco: Harper, 1992.

Filoramo, G., *A History of Gnosticism*, Cambridge MA: Blackwells, 1990.

Goehring, J.E., ed., *Gnosticism and the Early Christian World*, vols 1 and 2, Sonoma: Polebridge, 1990.

Hedrick, C.W. and Hodgson, Jr, R., eds, *Nag Hammadi, Gnosticism and Early Christianity*, Peabody MA: Hendrickson, 1986.

Layton, B., *The Gnostic Scriptures*, Garden City: Doubleday, 1987.

Nash, Ronald H., *Christianity and the Hellenistic World*, Grand Rapids: Zondervan, 1984.

Perkins, P., *Gnosticism and the New Testament*, Minneapolis: Fortress, 1993.

Robinson, J.M., *The Nag Hammadi Library in English*, San Francisco: Harper and Row, 1977.

Walbank, F.W., *The Hellenistic World*, London: Fontana, 1981.

The Life and Teaching of Jesus

BIRTH AND EARLY YEARS

Brown, R.E., *The Birth of the Messiah*, New York: Macmillan, 1977.

Hendrickx, H., *Infancy Narratives*, Minneapolis: Winston Press, 1984.

Scobie, C.H.H., *John the Baptist*, London: SCM Press, 1964.

CHRISTOLOGY

Cullmann, O., *The Christology of the New Testament*, Philadelphia: Westminster Press, 1964.

Dunn, J.D.G., *Christology in the Making*, Philadelphia: Westminster Press, 1980.

Hengel, M., *The Son of God*, Philadelphia: Fortress Press, 1976.

Hooker, M.D., *Jesus and the Servant*, London: SPCK, 1959.

Marshall, I.H., *The Origins of New Testament Christology*, Nottingham: IVP, 1977.

Moule, C.F.D., *The Origin of Christology*, Cambridge: Cambridge University Press, 1977.

O'Collins, G., *Interpreting Jesus*, Mahwah NJ: Paulist, 1983.

Tuckett, C., *The Messianic Secret*, Philadelphia: Fortress Press, 1983.

THE KINGDOM OF GOD

Chilton, B.D., *The Kingdom of God*, Philadelphia: Fortress Press, 1984.

Dodd, C.H., *The Parables of the Kingdom*, London: Nisbet, 1935.

Kümmel, W.G., *Promise and Fulfilment*, New York: Oxford University Press, 1961.

Ladd, G.E., *The Presence of the Future*, Grand Rapids: Eerdmans, 1980.

Perrin, N., *The Kingdom of God in the Teaching of Jesus*, Philadelphia: Westminster Press, 1963.

Riches, J., *Jesus and the Transformation of Judaism*, London: Darton Longman and Todd, 1980.

PARABLES

Jeremias, J., *The Parables of Jesus*, London: SCM Press, 1972.

Kissinger, W.S., *The Parables of Jesus*, New York: Scarecrow, 1979.

Perkins, Pheme, *Jesus as Teacher*, Cambridge: Cambridge University Press, 1990.

Shillington, V.G., ed., *Jesus and his Parables*, Edinburgh: T and T Clark, 1997.

Stein, R.H., *The Method and Message of Jesus' Teachings*, Philadelphia: Westminster Press, 1978.

Wenham, David, *The Parables of Jesus*, London: Hodder and Stoughton, 1989.

MIRACLES

Fuller, R.H., *Interpreting the Miracles*, London: SCM Press, 1963.

Meier, J.P., *A Marginal Jew: Rethinking the Historical Jesus*, vol. 2, *Mentor, Message, and Miracles*, New York: Doubleday, 1994.

Remus, Harold, *Jesus as Healer*, Cambridge: Cambridge University Press, 1997.

ETHICS

Chilton, B.D. and McDonald, J.I.H., *Jesus and the Ethics of the Kingdom*, London: SPCK, 1987.

Hendrickx, H., *The Sermon on the Mount*, Minneapolis: Winston Press, 1984.

Lohse, E., *Theological Ethics of the New Testament*, Minneapolis: Fortress Press, 1991.

THE DEATH OF JESUS

Carroll, J.T. and Green, J.B., eds, *The Death of Jesus in Early Christianity*, Peabody MA: Hendrickson, 1995.

Crossan, J.D., *Who Killed Jesus?*, San Francisco: HarperSanFrancisco, 1995.

Hendrickx, H., *Passion Narratives*, Minneapolis: Winston Press, 1984.

Hengel, M., *The Atonement*, Philadelphia: Fortress Press, 1981.

Hengel, M., *Crucifixion*, Philadelphia: Fortress Press, 1977.

Jeremias, J., *The Eucharistic Words of Jesus*, London: SCM Press, 1955.

Marshall, I.H., *Last Supper and Lord's Supper*, Grand Rapids: Eerdmans, 1981.

Sherwin-White, A.N., *Roman Society and Roman Law in the New Testament*, Oxford: Oxford University Press, 1963.

RESURRECTION AND ASCENSION

Donne, Brian, *Christ Ascended*, Exeter: Paternoster, 1983.

Hendrickx, H., *Resurrection Narratives*, Minneapolis: Winston Press, 1984.

Lapide, P., *The Resurrection of Jesus: A Jewish Perspective*, London: SPCK, 1984.

Lüdemann, G., *The Resurrection of Jesus: History, Experience, Theology*, London: SCM Press, 1994.

O'Collins, G., *The Easter Jesus*, Valley Forge: Judson Press, 1973.

Perkins, Pheme, *Resurrection*, New York: Doubleday, 1984; London: Geoffrey Chapman, 1985.

Torrance, T.F., *Space, Time and Resurrection*, Grand Rapids: Eerdmans, 1976.

The Gospels

GENERAL, INCLUDING LITERARY-CRITICAL ISSUES

Barton, Stephen C., *The Spirituality of the Gospels*, London: SPCK, 1992.

Bauckham, Richard, ed., *The Gospels for All Christians*, Grand Rapids: Eerdmans, 1998.

Bellinzoni, Arthur J., *The Two Source Hypothesis: A Critical Appraisal*, Macon GA: Mercer University Press, 1985.

Blomberg, Craig L., *Jesus and the Gospels: An Introduction and Survey*, Leicester: Apollos, 1997.

Bultmann, Rudolf, *The History of the Synoptic Tradition*, Oxford: Blackwell, 1968.

Burridge, Richard A., *What Are the Gospels?*, Cambridge: Cambridge University Press, 1995.

Dibelius, Martin, *From Tradition to Gospel*, Cambridge: Cambridge University Press, 1971. Originally in German, 1919.

Dungan, David L., *The Interrelations of the Gospels: A Symposium*, Macon GA: Mercer University Press, 1990.

Evans, C.A. and Porter, S.E., *The Synoptic Gospels: A Sheffield Reader*, Sheffield: Sheffield Academic Press, 1995.

Farmer, W.R., *The Synoptic Problem*, Dillsboro: Western North Carolina Press, 1976.

Farmer, W.R., *Jesus and the Gospel*, Philadelphia: Fortress Press, 1982.

Gerhardsson, B., *The Origins of the Gospel Traditions*, London: SCM, 1979.

Green, J.B., McKnight, S. and Marshall, I.H., *Dictionary of Jesus and the Gospels*, Downers Grove IL: InterVarsity, 1992.

Hagner, Donald A., *The Jewish Reclamation of Jesus*, Grand Rapids: Academie, 1984.

Hilton, M., *The Gospels and Rabbinic Judaism*, London: SCM, 1988.

Hooker, Morna D., *Beginnings: Keys that Open the Gospels*, London: SCM, 1997.

Jacobsen, Arland D., *The First Gospel: An Introduction to Q*, Sonoma CA: Polebridge Press, 1992.

Perrin, Norman, *What is Redaction Criticism?*, London: SPCK, 1970.

Sanders, E.P. and Davies, Margaret, *Studying the Synoptic Gospels*, Philadelphia: Trinity Press International, 1989.

Stanton, G.N., *The Gospels and Jesus*, New York: Oxford University Press, 1989.

Stanton, G.N., *Gospel Truth? New Light on Jesus and the Gospels*, Valley Forge PA: Trinity Press International, 1995.

Stein, R.H., *The Synoptic Problem: An Introduction*, Grand Rapids: Baker, 1987.

Streeter, B.H., *The Four Gospels*, London: Macmillan, 1924.

Stuhlmacher, Peter, *The Gospel and the Gospels*, Grand Rapids: Eerdmans, 1991.

Talbert, C.H., *What is a Gospel?*, Philadelphia: Fortress, 1977.

Taylor, Vincent, *Formation of the Gospel Tradition*, London: Epworth, 1935.

MATTHEW

Balch, D.L., ed., *Social History of the Matthean Community: Cross-Disciplinary Approaches*, Minneapolis: Fortress, 1991.

Beare, F.W., *The Gospel According to Matthew: Translation, Introduction and Commentary*, Peabody MA: Hendrickson, 1987.

Hagner, D.A., *Matthew 1–13*, Dallas: Word, 1993.; *Matthew 14–28*, Dallas: Word, 1995.

Luz, U., *The Theology of the Gospel of Matthew*, Cambridge: Cambridge University Press, 1995.

Overman, J.A., *Matthew's Gospel and Formative Judaism: The Social World of the Matthean Community*, Minneapolis: Fortress, 1990.

Riches, John, *Matthew*, Sheffield: Sheffield Academic Press, 1996.

Schweizer, E., *The Good News According to Matthew*, Atlanta: John Knox, 1975.

Shuler, Philip L., *A Genre for the Gospels: The Biographical Character of Matthew*, Philadelphia: Fortress, 1982.

Stanton, G.N., ed., *The Interpretation of Matthew*, Philadelphia: Fortress, 1983.

Stanton, G.N., *A Gospel for a New People: Studies in Matthew*, Edinburgh: T and T Clark, 1992.

MARK

Gundry, R.H., *Mark: A Commentary on His Apology for the Cross*, Grand Rapids: Eerdmans, 1993.

Hooker, M.D., *The Gospel According to Saint Mark*, Peabody MA: Hendrickson, 1991.

Lane, W.L., *The Gospel According to Mark*, Grand Rapids: Eerdmans, 1974.

Schweizer, E., *The Good News According to Mark*, Richmond VA: John Knox Press, 1970.

Telford, W.R., *Mark*, Sheffield: Sheffield Academic Press, 1995.

LUKE

Bock, D.L., *Luke*, vol. 1, *1:1 – 9:50*, Grand Rapids: Baker, 1994.

Bock, D.L., *Luke*, vol. 2, *9:51 – 24:53*, Grand Rapids: Baker, 1996.

Danker, F.W., *Jesus and the New Age: A Commentary on St Luke's Gospel*, Philadelphia: Fortress, 1988.

Evans, C.F., *Saint Luke*, Philadelphia: Trinity Press International, 1990.

Green, Joel B., *The Theology of the Gospel of Luke*, Cambridge: Cambridge University Press, 1995.

Nolland, J., *Luke 1 – 9:20*, Dallas: Word, 1989.

Nolland, J., *Luke 9:21 – 18:34*, Dallas: Word, 1993.

Nolland, J., *Luke 18:35 – 24:53*, Dallas: Word, 1993.

Schweizer, E., *The Good News According to Luke*, Atlanta: John Knox Press, 1984.

Talbert, C.H., *Reading Luke: A Literary and Theological Commentary on the Third Gospel*, New York: Crossroad, 1982.

Talbert, C.H., *Reading Luke: A New Commentary for Preachers*, London: SPCK, 1990.

Tiede, D.L., *Luke*, Minneapolis: Augsburg, 1988.

Tuckett, C.M., *Luke*, Sheffield: Sheffield Academic Press, 1996.

JOHN

Beasley-Murray, G.R., *John*, Waco: Word, 1987.

Brown, R.E., *The Community of the Beloved Disciple*, New York: Paulist, 1979.

Cullmann, O., *The Johannine Circle*, Philadelphia: Westminster, 1975.

Ellis, E.E., *The World of St John*, Grand Rapids: Eerdmans, 1984.

Hengel, M., *The Johannine Question*, Philadelphia: Trinity Press International, 1989.

Lindars, B., *John*, Sheffield: Sheffield Academic Press, 1990.

Morris, L., *Commentary on the Gospel of John*, Grand Rapids: Eerdmans, 1971.

Porter, S.E. and Evans, C.A., *The Johannine Writings: A Sheffield Reader*, Sheffield: Sheffield Academic Press, 1995.

Smalley, S.S., *John: Evangelist and Interpreter*, Carlisle: Paternoster, 1997.

Smith, D.M., *The Theology of the Gospel of John*, Cambridge: Cambridge University Press, 1995.

Stibbe, M.W.G., *John as Storyteller: Narrative Criticism and the Fourth Gospel*, Cambridge: Cambridge University Press, 1992.

OTHER TRADITIONS ABOUT JESUS

General

Bruce, F.F., *Jesus and Christian Origins Outside the New Testament*, London: Hodder and Stoughton, 1974.

Ehrman, Bart D., *The New Testament and Other Early Christian Writings: A Reader*, New York: Oxford University Press, 1998.

Evans, C.A., *Noncanonical Writings and New Testament Interpretation*, Peabody MA: Hendrickson, 1992.

Jeremias, J., *Unknown Sayings of Jesus*, London: SCM, 1964.

Morrice, William, *Hidden Sayings of Jesus*, London SPCK, 1997.

Wenham, D., ed., *Gospel Perspectives 5: The Jesus Tradition Outside the Gospels*, Sheffield: JSOT Press, 1984.

Gnostic gospels

Crossan, J.D., *Four Other Gospels*, Sonoma CA: Polebridge, 1992.

Funk, R.W. and Hoover, R.W., eds, *The Five Gospels*, New York: Macmillan, 1993.

Koester, H., *Ancient Christian Gospels: Their History and Development*, Philadelphia: Trinity Press International, 1990.

Pagels, E.H., *The Gnostic Gospels*, New York: Random House, 1979.

Patterson, S.J., *The Gospel of Thomas and Jesus*, Sonoma CA: Polebridge, 1993.

THE QUEST FOR THE HISTORICAL JESUS

Chilton, B.D. and Evans, C.A., *Studying the Historical Jesus: Evaluations of the State of Current Research*, Leiden: Brill, 1994.

Evans, Craig A. and Porter, Stanley E., *The Historical Jesus*, Sheffield: Sheffield Academic Press, 1995.

Kee, Howard Clark, *What Can We Know About Jesus?*, Cambridge: Cambridge University Press, 1990.

Powell, Mark Allan, *Jesus as a Figure in History*, Louisville: Westminster John Knox Press, 1998.

Tatum, W. Barnes, *In Quest of Jesus: A Guidebook*, Atlanta: John Knox Press, 1982.

Theissen, Gerd and Merz, Annette *The Historical Jesus: A Comprehensive Guide*, London: SCM, 1998.

Wright, N.T., *Jesus and the Victory of God*, London: SPCK, 1996.

The Early Church

THE BOOK OF ACTS

Dibelius, M., *Studies in the Acts of the Apostles*, London: SCM Press, 1956.

Gasque, W.W., *A History of the Criticism of the Acts of the Apostles*, Grand Rapids: Eerdmans, 1975.

Hengel, M., *Acts and the History of Earliest Christianity*, Philadelphia: Fortress, 1979.

Marshall, I.H., *The Acts of the Apostles*, Sheffield: JSOT Press, 1992.

CHURCH ORDER

Bauer, W., *Orthodoxy and Heresy in Earliest Christianity*, Philadelphia: Fortress, 1971.

Dunn, James D.G., *Unity and Diversity in the New Testament*, Philadelphia: Westminster, 1977.

Judge, E.A., *The Social Pattern of Christian Groups in the First Century*, London: Tyndale Press, 1960.

Malherbe, A.J., *Social Aspects of Early Christianity*, Philadelphia: Fortress, 1983.

Meeks, W., *The First Urban Christians*, New Haven: Yale University Press, 1983.

Robinson, Thomas A., *The Bauer Thesis Examined*, Lewiston: Edwin Mellen Press, 1988.

Schweizer, E., *Church Order in the New Testament*, London: SCM, 1961.

Theissen, G., *The Social Setting of Pauline Christianity*, Edinburgh: T and T Clark, 1982.

Tidball, D.J., *An Introduction to the Sociology of the New Testament*, Exeter: Paternoster, 1983.

WORSHIP AND MISSION

Bartlett, David L., *Ministry in the New Testament*, Minneapolis: Fortress, 1993.

Cullman, O., *Early Christian Worship*, London: SCM, 1953.

Dunn, J.D.G., *Unity and Diversity in the New Testament*, Philadelphia: Westminster, 1977.

Hahn, F., *The Worship of the Early Church*, Philadelphia: Fortress, 1973.

Larkin Jr, William J. and Williams, Joel F., eds, *Mission in the New Testament*, Maryknoll NY: Orbis, 1998.

Martin, R.P., *The Worship of God*, Grand Rapids: Eerdmans, 1982.

Paul

GENERAL

Cousar, C.B., *The Letters of Paul*, Nashville: Abingdon Press, 1996.

Dunn, J.D.G., *The Theology of Paul the Apostle*, Grand Rapids: Eerdmans, 1998.

Elliott, Neil, *Liberating Paul: The Justice of God and the Politics of the Apostle*, Maryknoll NY: Orbis, 1994.

Fitzmyer, J.A., *Paul and his Theology*, Englewood Cliffs: Prentice Hall, 1989.

Jewett, R., *A Chronology of Paul's Life*, Philadelphia: Fortress, 1979.

Knox, J., *Chapters in a Life of Paul*, Macon: Mercer University Press, 1987.

Marrow, S.B., *Paul – His Letters and His Theology*, New York: Paulist, 1986.

Murphy-O'Connor, J., *Paul the Letter-Writer: His World, His Options, His Skills*, Collegeville: Liturgical Press, 1995.

Roetzel, Calvin J., *The Letters of Paul: Conversations in Context*, Louisville: Westminster John Knox Press, 1998.

Sumney, J.L., *Identifying Paul's Opponents*, Sheffield: JSOT Press, 1990.

Witherington III, Ben, *The Paul Quest*, Downers Grove IL: InterVarsity, 1998.

PAUL THE PHARISEE

Sanders, E.P., *Paul and Palestinian Judaism*, Philadelphia: Fortress, 1977.

Stendahl, K., *Paul Among Jews and Gentiles*, Philadelphia: Fortress, 1976.

Thielman, Frank, *Paul and the Law*, Downers Grove: InterVarsity, 1994.

Watson, F., *Paul, Judaism and the Gentiles*, Cambridge: Cambridge University Press, 1986.

Westerholm, S., *Israel's Law and the Church's Faith*, Grand Rapids: Eerdmans, 1988.

Ziesler, J.A., *Pauline Christianity*, New York: Oxford University Press, 1990.

CONVERSION

Kim, S., *The Origin of Paul's Gospel*, Grand Rapids: Eerdmans, 1981.

Longenecker, R.N., ed., *The Road from Damascus*, Grand Rapids: Eerdmans, 1997.

PAUL AND JESUS

Bruce, F.F., *Paul and Jesus*, Grand Rapids: Baker, 1974.

Wedderburn, A.J.M., ed., *Paul and Jesus: Collected Essays*, Sheffield: JSOT, 1989.

PAUL THE EVANGELIST

Allan, R., *Missionary Methods: St Paul's or Ours*, Grand Rapids: Eerdmans, 1989, orig., 1912.

Hock, R.F., *The Social Context of Paul's Ministry*, Philadelphia: Fortress, 1980.

O'Brien, P.T., *Gospel and Mission in the Writings of Paul*, Carlisle: Paternoster Press, 1995.

ETHICS

Furnish, Victor Paul, *Theology and Ethics in Paul*, Nashville: Abingdon, 1968.

Furnish, Victor Paul, *The Moral Teaching of Paul*, Nashville: Abingdon, 1985.

Meeks, W., *The Moral World of the First Christians*, Philadelphia: Westminster, 1986.

PAUL AS PASTOR

Best, E., *Paul and His Converts*, Edinburgh: T and T Clark, 1988.

Zuck, Roy B., *Teaching as Paul Taught*, Grand Rapids: Baker, 1998.

Colossians, Ephesians and Philemon

Barclay, J.M.G., *Colossians and Philemon*, Sheffield: Sheffield Academic Press, 1997.

Best, E., *Ephesians*, Sheffield: JSOT Press, 1993.

Bruce, F.F., *The Epistles to the Colossians, to Philemon, and to the Ephesians*, Grand Rapids: Eerdmans, 1984.

Donfried, K.P. and Marshall, I.H., *The Theology of the Shorter Pauline Letters*, Cambridge: Cambridge University Press, 1993.

Knox, J., *Philemon Among the Letters of Paul*, London: Collins, 1960.

Lincoln, A.T. and Wedderburn, A.J.M., *The Theology of the Later Pauline Letters*, Cambridge: Cambridge University Press, 1993.

Corinthians

Dunn, J.D.G., *1 Corinthians*, Sheffield: Sheffield Academic Press, 1995.

Fee, G.D., *1 Corinthians*, Eerdmans: Grand Rapids, 1987.

Hay, David M., ed., *Pauline Theology*, vol. 2, *1 and 2 Corinthians*, Minneapolis: Fortress Press, 1993.

Kreitzer, Larry J., *2 Corinthians*, Sheffield: Sheffield Academic Press, 1996.

Murphy-O'Connor, J., *St Paul's Corinth*, Wilmington: Glazier, 1983.

Galatians

Donfried, K.P. and Marshall, I.H., *The Theology of the Shorter Pauline Letters*, Cambridge: Cambridge University Press, 1993.

Dunn, J.D.G., *The Theology of Paul's Letter to the Galatians*, Cambridge: Cambridge University Press, 1993.

Romans

Donfried, Karl P., ed., *The Romans Debate*, Peabody MA: Hendrickson, 1991.

Donfried, Karl P. and Richardson, Peter, *Judaism and Christianity in First-Century Rome*, Eerdmans, 1998.

Hay, D.M. and Johnson, E.E., *Pauline Theology*, Vol. III, *Romans*, Minneapolis: Fortress, 1995.

Hultgren, A.J., *Paul's Gospel and Mission: The Outlook from His Letter to the Romans*, Philadelphia: Fortress Press, 1985.

Morgan, Robert, *Romans*, Sheffield: Sheffield Academic Press, 1995.

Sanders, E.P., *Paul, the Law and the Jewish People*, Philadelphia: Fortress Press, 1983; London: SCM Press, 1985.

Ziesler, J.A., *Paul's Letter to the Romans*, Philadelphia: TPI, 1989.

Pastoral epistles

Davies, M., *The Pastoral Epistles*, Sheffield: Sheffield Academic Press, 1996.

Houlden, J.L., *The Pastoral Epistles*, Philadelphia: TPI, 1989.

Young, F., *The Theology of the Pastoral Letters*, Cambridge: Cambridge University Press, 1994.

Philippians

Bruce, F.F., *Philippians*, San Francisco: Harper and Row, 1983.

Fee, G.D., *Paul's Letter to the Philippians*, Grand Rapids: Eerdmans, 1995.

Thessalonians

Marshall, I.H., *1 and 2 Thessalonians*, Grand Rapids: Eerdmans, 1983.

Williams, D.J., *1 and 2 Thessalonians*, Peabody MA: Hendrickson, 1992.

PAUL THE THEOLOGIAN

General

Barrett, C.K., *Paul: An Introduction to His Thought*, London: Geoffrey Chapman, 1994.

Brauch, M., *Hard Sayings of Paul*, Downers Grove: InterVarsity, 1989.

Fitzmyer, J.A., *Paul and His Theology*, Englewood Cliffs: Prentice Hall, 1989.

Ridderbos, H., *Paul: An Outline of His Theology*, Grand Rapids: Eerdmans, 1975.

Ziesler, J.A., *Pauline Christianity*, New York: Oxford University Press, 1990.

The church

Banks, R., *Going to Church in the First Century*, Beaumont: Christian Books, 1990.

Banks, R., *Paul's Idea of Community*, Eerdmans: Grand Rapids, 1980.

Ellis, E.E., *Pauline Theology: Ministry and Society*, Grand Rapids: Eerdmans, 1989.

Käsemann, E., *Essays on New Testament Themes*, London: SCM, 1964.

Käsemann, E., *Perspectives on Paul*, London: SCM, 1971.

Schatzmann, S., *A Pauline Theology of Charismata*, Peabody: Hendrickson, 1989.

The Church and Its Jewish Roots

Dunn, J.D.G., *The Partings of the Ways*, Philadelphia: TPI, 1991.

HEBREWS AND HELLENISTS

Bruce, F.F., *Peter, Stephen, James and John*, Grand Rapids: Eerdmans, 1980.

Hengel, M., *Between Jesus and Paul*, Philadelphia: Fortress, 1983.

PETER

Brown, R.E., Donfried, K.P. and Reumann, J., *Peter in the New Testament*, Minneapolis: Augsburg, 1973.

Brown, R.E. and Maier, J.P., *Antioch and Rome*, New York: Paulist, 1983.

Cullmann, O., *Peter: Disciple, Apostle, Martyr*, Philadelphia: Westminster, 1962.

1 PETER

Cross, F.L., *1 Peter, a Paschal Liturgy*, London: Mowbrays, 1954.

NABPR Special Studies, *Perspectives on First Peter*, Macon: Mercer University Press, 1986.

JAMES

Davids, P., *The Epistle of James*, Grand Rapids: Eerdmans, 1982.

Dunn, J.D.G., *Unity and Diversity in the New Testament*, Philadelphia: Westminster, 1977.

Hartin, P.J., *James and the Q Sayings of Jesus*, Sheffield: Sheffield Academic Press, 1991.

Mitton, C.L., *The Epistle of James*, Grand Rapids: Eerdmans, 1966.

THE EPISTLE TO THE HEBREWS

Casey, Juliana, *Hebrews*, Wilmington: Glazier, 1980.

Thompson, J.W., *The Beginnings of Christian Philosophy*, Washington DC: Catholic Biblical Association, 1981.

1, 2 AND 3 JOHN

Brown, R.E., *The Community of the Beloved Disciple*, New York: Paulist, 1979.

Edwards, R.B., *The Johannine Epistles*, Sheffield: Sheffield Academic Press, 1996.

Ellis, E.E., *The World of St John*, Grand Rapids: Eerdmans, 1984.

Hengel, M., *The Johannine Question*, Philadelphia: TPI, 1989.

Marshall, I.H., *The Epistles of John*, Grand Rapids: Eerdmans, 1978.

REVELATION

Bauckham, R., *The Theology of the Book of Revelation*, Cambridge: Cambridge University Press, 1993.

Collins, Adela Yarbro, *The Apocalypse*, Wilmington: Glazier, 1979.

Mounce, R.H., *The Book of Revelation*, Grand Rapids: Eerdmans, 1980.

Interpretation

Beasley-Murray, G.R., *Preaching the Gospel from the Gospels*, Peabody MA: Hendrickson, 1997.

Boers, H., *What is New Testament Theology?*, Philadelphia: Fortress, 1979.

Charpentier, E., *How to Read the New Testament*, London: SCM, 1982.

Coggins, R.J. and Houlden, J.L., *A Dictionary of Biblical Interpretation*, London: SCM, 1990.

Court, John M., *Reading the New Testament*, New York: Routledge, 1997.

Farmer, William R., *The Gospel of Jesus: The Pastoral Relevance of the Synoptic Problem*, Louisville KY: Westminster John Knox Press, 1994.

Fish, S.E., *Is There a Text in This Class? The Authority of Interpretive Communities*, Cambridge MA: Harvard University Press, 1980.

Green, J.B., ed., *Hearing the New Testament: Strategies for Interpretation*, Grand Rapids: Eerdmans, 1995.

Klein, W.W., Blomberg, C.L. and Hubbard, R.L., *Introduction to Biblical Interpretation*, Dallas: Word, 1993.

Krentz, E., *The Historical-Critical Method*, Philadelphia: Fortress, 1975.

Lührmann, D., *An Itinerary for New Testament Study*, Philadelphia: Trinity Press International, 1989.

McKnight, E.V., *Post-Modern Use of the Bible*, Nashville: Abingdon Press, 1988.

McKnight, Scott, ed., *Introducing New Testament Interpretation*, Grand Rapids: Baker, 1989.

Neill, Stephen and Wright, Tom, *The Interpretation of the New Testament 1861–1986*, New York: Oxford University Press, 1988.

Osborne, G.R., *The Hermeneutical Spiral: A Comprehensive Introduction to Biblical Hermeneutics*, Downers Grove IL: InterVarsity, 1991.